# DRAMA
## *for Students*

# National Advisory Board

# DRAMA
# *for Students*

**Presenting Analysis, Context, and Criticism on
Commonly Studied Dramas**

## Volume 21

*Anne Marie Hacht, Project Editor*

*Foreword by Carole L. Hamilton*

THOMSON
GALE
™

Detroit • New York • San Francisco • San Diego • New Haven, Conn. • Waterville, Maine • London • Munich

## THOMSON

™

## GALE

## Drama for Students, Volume 21

**Project Editor**
Anne Marie Hacht

**Editorial**
Michelle Kazensky, Ira Mark Milne, Timothy Sisler

**Rights Acquisition and Management**
Margaret Abendroth, Edna Hedblad, Jacqueline Key, Mari Masalin-Cooper

**Manufacturing**
Rhonda Williams

**Imaging**
Lezlie Light, Mike Logusz, Kelly A. Quin

**Product Design**
Pamela A. E. Galbreath

**Product Manager**
Meggin Condino

ISBN 0-7876-6818-4
ISSN 1094-9232

Printed in the United States of America
10  9  8  7  6  5  4  3

# Table of Contents

# The Study of Drama

We study drama in order to learn what meaning others have made of life, to comprehend what it takes to produce a work of art, and to glean some understanding of ourselves. Drama produces in a separate, aesthetic world, a moment of being for the audience to experience, while maintaining the detachment of a reflective observer.

Drama is a representational art, a visible and audible narrative presenting virtual, fictional characters within a virtual, fictional universe. Dramatic realizations may pretend to approximate reality or else stubbornly defy, distort, and deform reality into an artistic statement. From this separate universe that is obviously not "real life" we expect a valid reflection upon reality, yet drama never is mistaken for reality—the methods of theater are integral to its form and meaning. Theater is art, and art's appeal lies in its ability both to approximate life and to depart from it. For in intruding its distorted version of life into our consciousness, art gives us a new perspective and appreciation of life and reality. Although all aesthetic experiences perform this service, theater does it most effectively by creating a separate, cohesive universe that freely acknowledges its status as an art form.

And what is the purpose of the aesthetic universe of drama? The potential answers to such a question are nearly as many and varied as there are plays written, performed, and enjoyed. Dramatic texts can be problems posed, answers asserted, or moments portrayed. Dramas (tragedies as well as comedies) may serve strictly "to ease the anguish of a torturing hour" (as stated in William Shakespeare's *A Midsummer Night's Dream*)—to divert and entertain–or aspire to move the viewer to action with social issues. Whether to entertain or to instruct, affirm or influence, pacify or shock, dramatic art wraps us in the spell of its imaginary world for the length of the work and then dispenses us back to the real world, entertained, purged, as Aristotle said, of pity and fear, and edified—or at least weary enough to sleep peacefully.

It is commonly thought that theater, being an art of performance, must be experienced—seen—in order to be appreciated fully. However, to view a production of a dramatic text is to be limited to a single interpretation of that text—all other interpretations are for the moment closed off, inaccessible. In the process of producing a play, the director, stage designer, and performers interpret and transform the script into a work of art that always departs in some measure from the author's original conception. Novelist and critic Umberto Eco, in his *The Role of the Reader: Explorations in the Semiotics of Texts* (Indiana University Press, 1979), explained, "In short, we can say that every performance offers us a complete and satisfying version of the work, but at the same time makes it incomplete for us, because it cannot simultaneously give all the other artistic solutions which the work may admit."

Thus Laurence Olivier's coldly formal and neurotic film presentation of Shakespeare's *Hamlet* (in which he played the title character as well as directed) shows marked differences from subsequent adaptations. While Olivier's Hamlet is clearly entangled in a Freudian relationship with his mother Gertrude, he would be incapable of shushing her with the impassioned kiss that Mel Gibson's mercurial Hamlet (in director Franco Zeffirelli's 1990 film) does. Although each of performances rings true to Shakespeare's text, each is also a mutually exclusive work of art. Also important to consider are the time periods in which each of these films was produced: Olivier made his film in 1948, a time in which overt references to sexuality (especially incest) were frowned upon. Gibson and Zeffirelli made their film in a culture more relaxed and comfortable with these issues. Just as actors and directors can influence the presentation of drama, so too can the time period of the production affect what the audience will see.

A play script is an open text from which an infinity of specific realizations may be derived. Dramatic scripts that are more open to interpretive creativity (such as those of Ntozake Shange and Tomson Highway) actually require the creative improvisation of the production troupe in order to complete the text. Even the most prescriptive scripts (those of Neil Simon, Lillian Hellman, and Robert Bolt, for example), can never fully control the actualization of live performance, and circumstantial events, including the attitude and receptivity of the audience, make every performance a unique event. Thus, while it is important to view a production of a dramatic piece, if one wants to understand a drama fully it is equally important to read the original dramatic text.

The reader of a dramatic text or script is not limited by either the specific interpretation of a given production or by the unstoppable action of a moving spectacle. The reader of a dramatic text may discover the nuances of the play's language, structure, and events at their own pace. Yet studied alone, the author's blueprint for artistic production does not tell the whole story of a play's life and significance. One also needs to assess the play's critical reviews to discover how it resonated to cultural themes at the time of its debut and how the shifting tides of cultural interest have revised its interpretation and impact on audiences. And to do this, one needs to know a little about the culture of the times which produced the play as well as the author who penned it.

*Drama for Students* supplies this material in a useful compendium for the student of dramatic theater. Covering a range of dramatic works that span from 442 BC to the 1990s, this book focuses on significant theatrical works whose themes and form transcend the uncertainty of dramatic fads. These are plays that have proven to be both memorable and teachable. *Drama for Students* seeks to enhance appreciation of these dramatic texts by providing scholarly materials written with the secondary and college/university student in mind. It provides for each play a concise summary of the plot and characters as well as a detailed explanation of its themes. In addition, background material on the historical context of the play, its critical reception, and the author's life help the student to understand the work's position in the chronicle of dramatic history. For each play entry a new work of scholarly criticism is also included, as well as segments of other significant critical works for handy reference. A thorough bibliography provides a starting point for further research.

This series offers comprehensive educational resources for students of drama. *Drama for Students* is a vital book for dramatic interpretation and a valuable addition to any reference library.

**Source:** Eco, Umberto, *The Role of the Reader: Explorations in the Semiotics of Texts,* Indiana University Press, 1979.

*Carole L. Hamilton*
*Author and Instructor of English*
*Cary Academy*
*Cary, North Carolina*

# Introduction

## Purpose of the Book

The purpose of *Drama for Students* (*DfS*) is to provide readers with a guide to understanding, enjoying, and studying dramas by giving them easy access to information about the work. Part of Gale's "For Students" literature line, *DfS* is specifically designed to meet the curricular needs of high school and undergraduate college students and their teachers, as well as the interests of general readers and researchers considering specific plays. While each volume contains entries on "classic" dramas frequently studied in classrooms, there are also entries containing hard-to-find information on contemporary plays, including works by multicultural, international, and women playwrights.

The information covered in each entry includes an introduction to the play and the work's author; a plot summary, to help readers unravel and understand the events in a drama; descriptions of important characters, including explanation of a given character's role in the drama as well as discussion about that character's relationship to other characters in the play; analysis of important themes in the drama; and an explanation of important literary techniques and movements as they are demonstrated in the play.

In addition to this material, which helps the readers analyze the play itself, students are also provided with important information on the literary and historical background informing each work. This includes a historical context essay, a box

comparing the time or place the drama was written to modern Western culture, a critical essay, and excerpts from critical essays on the play. A unique feature of *DfS* is a specially commissioned critical essay on each drama, targeted toward the student reader.

To further aid the student in studying and enjoying each play, information on media adaptations is provided (if available), as well as reading suggestions for works of fiction and nonfiction on similar themes and topics. Classroom aids include ideas for research papers and lists of critical sources that provide additional material on each drama.

## Selection Criteria

The titles for each volume of *DfS* were selected by surveying numerous sources on teaching literature and analyzing course curricula for various school districts. Some of the sources surveyed included: literature anthologies; *Reading Lists for College-Bound Students: The Books Most Recommended by America's Top Colleges*; textbooks on teaching dramas; a College Board survey of plays commonly studied in high schools; a National Council of Teachers of English (NCTE) survey of plays commonly studied in high schools; St. James Press's *International Dictionary of Theatre*; and Arthur Applebee's 1993 study *Literature in the Secondary School: Studies of Curriculum and Instruction in the United States*.

Input was also solicited from our advisory board, as well as from educators from various areas. From these discussions, it was determined that each volume should have a mix of "classic" dramas (those works commonly taught in literature classes) and contemporary dramas for which information is often hard to find. Because of the interest in expanding the canon of literature, an emphasis was also placed on including works by international, multicultural, and women playwrights. Our advisory board members—educational professionals—helped pare down the list for each volume. If a work was not selected for the present volume, it was often noted as a possibility for a future volume. As always, the editor welcomes suggestions for titles to be included in future volumes.

### How Each Entry Is Organized

Each entry, or chapter, in *DfS* focuses on one play. Each entry heading lists the full name of the play, the author's name, and the date of the play's publication. The following elements are contained in each entry:

- **Introduction:** a brief overview of the drama which provides information about its first appearance, its literary standing, any controversies surrounding the work, and major conflicts or themes within the work.

- **Author Biography:** this section includes basic facts about the author's life, and focuses on events and times in the author's life that inspired the drama in question.

- **Plot Summary:** a description of the major events in the play. Subheads demarcate the play's various acts or scenes.

- **Characters:** an alphabetical listing of major characters in the play. Each character name is followed by a brief to an extensive description of the character's role in the play, as well as discussion of the character's actions, relationships, and possible motivation.

  Characters are listed alphabetically by last name. If a character is unnamed—for instance, the Stage Manager in *Our Town*—the character is listed as "The Stage Manager" and alphabetized as "Stage Manager." If a character's first name is the only one given, the name will appear alphabetically by the name. Variant names are also included for each character. Thus, the nickname "Babe" would head the listing for a character in *Crimes of the Heart,* but below that listing would

be her less-mentioned married name "Rebecca Botrelle."

- **Themes:** a thorough overview of how the major topics, themes, and issues are addressed within the play. Each theme discussed appears in a separate subhead, and is easily accessed through the boldface entries in the Subject/Theme Index.

- **Style:** this section addresses important style elements of the drama, such as setting, point of view, and narration; important literary devices used, such as imagery, foreshadowing, symbolism; and, if applicable, genres to which the work might have belonged, such as Gothicism or Romanticism. Literary terms are explained within the entry, but can also be found in the Glossary.

- **Historical Context:** this section outlines the social, political, and cultural climate *in which the author lived and the play was created.* This section may include descriptions of related historical events, pertinent aspects of daily life in the culture, and the artistic and literary sensibilities of the time in which the work was written. If the play is a historical work, information regarding the time in which the play is set is also included. Each section is broken down with helpful subheads.

- **Critical Overview:** this section provides background on the critical reputation of the play, including bannings or any other public controversies surrounding the work. For older plays, this section includes a history of how the drama was first received and how perceptions of it may have changed over the years; for more recent plays, direct quotes from early reviews may also be included.

- **Criticism:** an essay commissioned by *DfS* which specifically deals with the play and is written specifically for the student audience, as well as excerpts from previously published criticism on the work (if available).

- **Sources:** an alphabetical list of critical material used in compiling the entry, with full bibliographical information.

- **Further Reading:** an alphabetical list of other critical sources which may prove useful for the student. It includes full bibliographical information and a brief annotation.

In addition, each entry contains the following highlighted sections, set apart from the main text as sidebars:

- **Media Adaptations:** if available, a list of important film and television adaptations of the play, including source information. The list may also include such variations on the work as audio recordings, musical adaptations, and other stage interpretations.

- **Topics for Further Study:** a list of potential study questions or research topics dealing with the play. This section includes questions related to other disciplines the student may be studying, such as American history, world history, science, math, government, business, geography, economics, psychology, etc.

- **Compare and Contrast:** an "at-a-glance" comparison of the cultural and historical differences between the author's time and culture and late twentieth century or early twenty-first century Western culture. This box includes pertinent parallels between the major scientific, political, and cultural movements of the time or place the drama was written, the time or place the play was set (if a historical work), and modern Western culture. Works written after 1990 may not have this box.

- **What Do I Read Next?:** a list of works that might complement the featured play or serve as a contrast to it. This includes works by the same author and others, works of fiction and nonfiction, and works from various genres, cultures, and eras.

## *Other Features*

*DfS* includes "The Study of Drama," a foreword by Carole Hamilton, an educator and author who specializes in dramatic works. This essay examines the basis for drama in societies and what drives people to study such work. The essay also discusses how *Drama for Students* can help teachers show students how to enrich their own reading/viewing experiences.

A Cumulative Author/Title Index lists the authors and titles covered in each volume of the *DfS* series.

A Cumulative Nationality/Ethnicity Index breaks down the authors and titles covered in each volume of the *DfS* series by nationality and ethnicity.

A Subject/Theme Index, specific to each volume, provides easy reference for users who may be studying a particular subject or theme rather than a single work. Significant subjects from events to broad themes are included, and the entries pointing to the specific theme discussions in each entry are indicated in **boldface**.

Each entry may include illustrations, including photo of the author, stills from stage productions, and stills from film adaptations, if available.

## *Citing* Drama for Students

When writing papers, students who quote directly from any volume of *Drama for Students* may use the following general forms. These examples are based on MLA style; teachers may request that students adhere to a different style, so the following examples may be adapted as needed.

When citing text from *DfS* that is not attributed to a particular author (i.e., the Themes, Style, Historical Context sections, etc.), the following format should be used in the bibliography section:

> "*Our Town.*" *Drama for Students.* Eds. David Galens and Lynn Spampinato. Vol. 1. Detroit: Gale, 1998. 227–30.

When quoting the specially commissioned essay from *DfS* (usually the first piece under the "Criticism" subhead), the following format should be used:

> Fiero, John. Critical Essay on *Twilight: Los Angeles, 1992. Drama for Students.* Eds. David Galens and Lynn Spampinato. Vol. 2. Detroit: Gale, 1998. 247–49.

When quoting a journal or newspaper essay that is reprinted in a volume of *DfS*, the following form may be used:

> Rich, Frank. "Theatre: A Mamet Play, *Glengarry Glen Ross.*" *New York Theatre Critics' Review* Vol. 45, No. 4 (March 5, 1984), 5–7; excerpted and reprinted in *Drama for Students*, Vol. 2, eds. David Galens and Lynn Spampinato (Detroit: Gale, 1998), pp. 51–53.

When quoting material reprinted from a book that appears in a volume of *DfS*, the following form may be used:

> Kerr, Walter. "*The Miracle Worker,*" in *The Theatre in Spite of Itself.* Simon & Schuster, 1963. 255–57; excerpted and reprinted in *Drama for Students*, Vol. 2, eds. David Galens and Lynn Spampinato (Detroit: Gale, 1998), pp. 123–24.

## *We Welcome Your Suggestions*

The editor of *Drama for Students* welcomes your comments and ideas. Readers who wish to suggest dramas to appear in future volumes, or who have other suggestions, are cordially invited to contact the editor. You may contact the editor via E-mail at: **ForStudentsEditors@thomson.com.** Or write to the editor at:

Editor, *Drama for Students*
Thomson Gale
27500 Drake Rd.
Farmington Hills, MI 48331–3535

# Literary Chronology

**1558:** Thomas Kyd's exact birth date is unknown, but he was baptized on November 6 in London, England.

**1564:** Christopher Marlowe is born on February 6 in Canterbury, England.

**1564:** William Shakespeare is born on April 23 in Stratford-on-Avon, in Warwickshire, England.

**1590:** Christopher Marlowe's *Tamburlaine the Great* is published.

**1593:** Christopher Marlowe is killed during an alleged argument over a bar bill.

**1594:** William Shakespeare's *Romeo and Juliet* is published.

**1594:** Thomas Kyd dies.

**1606:** Pierre Corneille is born on June 6 in Rouen, France.

**1616:** William Shakespeare dies on April 23, his fifty-second birthday, in Stratford-on-Avon, Warwickshire, England.

**1636:** Pierre Corneille's *Le Cid* is published.

**1684:** Pierre Corneille dies on October 1 in Paris, France.

**1854:** Oscar Wilde (Oscar Fingal O'Flahertie Wills Wilde) is born on October 16 in Dublin, Ireland.

**1895:** Oscar Wilde's *An Ideal Husband* is published.

**1900:** Oscar Wilde dies on November 30 in Paris, France. He was buried in the French National Cemetery of Père Lachaise.

**1914:** Marguerite Duras (Marguerite Donnadieu) is born on April 14 in French Indochina, a region that is now part of South Vietnam.

**1926:** Mel Brooks (Melvyn Kaminsky) is born on June 28 in Brooklyn, New York.

**1940:** Gao Xingjian (pronounced *gow shing-yan*) is born on January 4 in Ganzhou of Jiangxi province in eastern China.

**1952:** Beth Henley (Elizabeth Becker Henley) is born on May 8 in Jackson, Mississippi.

**1961:** Nilo Cruz is born in Matanzas, Cuba.

**1965:** Naomi Iizuka is born in Japan.

**1969:** David Auburn is born in Chicago, IL.

**1980:** Beth Henley's *The Miss Firecracker Contest* is published.

**1988:** Barbara Wiechmann's *Feeding the Moonfish* is published.

**1990:** Gao Xingjian's *The Other Shore* is published.

**1993:** Marguerite Duras's *India Song* is published.

**1996:** Marguerite Duras dies on March 3 in Paris, France.

**1997:** Douglas Carter Beane's *As Bees in Honey Drown* is published.

**2000:** Gao Xingjian is awarded the Nobel Prize for Literature.

**2001:** Naomi Iizuka's *36 Views* is published.

**2001:** David Auburn's *Proof* is published.

**2001:** Mel Brooks's *The Producers* is published.

**2001:** David Auburn is awarded the Pulitzer Prize for Drama for *Proof.*

**2002:** Nilo Cruz's *Anna in the Tropics* is published.

**2002:** Nilo Cruz is awarded the Pulitzer Prize for Drama for *Anna in the Tropics.*

# Acknowledgments

The editors wish to thank the copyright holders of the excerpted criticism included in this volume and the permissions managers of many book and magazine publishing companies for assisting us in securing reproduction rights. We are also grateful to the staffs of the Detroit Public Library, the Library of Congress, the University of Detroit Mercy Library, Wayne State University Purdy/Kresge Library Complex, and the University of Michigan Libraries for making their resources available to us. Following is a list of the copyright holders who have granted us permission to reproduce material in this volume of *Drama for Students (DfS)*. Every effort has been made to trace copyright, but if omissions have been made, please let us know.

## COPYRIGHTED MATERIALS IN *DfS*, VOLUME 21, WERE REPRODUCED FROM THE FOLLOWING PERIODICALS:

*American Theatre*, v. 15, September, 1998; v. 19, February, 2002. Copyright © 1998, 2002 by the Theatre Communications Group. All rights reserved. Both reproduced by permission.—*CLA Journal*, v. 36, December, 1992. Copyright © 1992 by The College Language Association. reproduced by permission of The College Language Association.—*French Review*, v. 72, December, 1998. Copyright © 1998 by the American Association of Teachers of French. Reproduced by permission.—*Modern Chinese Literature and Culture*, v. 14, fall, 2002. Copyright © 2002 Modern Chinese Literature and Culture. Reproduced by permission.—*Modern Drama*, v. 36, March, 1993. Copyright © 1993 by the University of Toronto, Graduate Centre for Study of Drama. Reproduced by permission.—*New Republic*, September 13, 2000; May 28, 2001. Copyright © 2000, 2001 by The New Republic, Inc. Both reproduced by permission of The New Republic.—*New York*, June 5, 2000. Copyright © 2000 PRIMEDIA Magazine Corporation. All rights reserved. Reproduced with the permission of New York Magazine.—*Orbis Literarum: International Review of Literary Studies*, v. 52, 1997. Copyright © 1997 Munksgaard. Reproduced by permission of Blackwell Publishers.—*Papers on Language & Literature*, v. 33, spring, 1997. Copyright © 1997 by The Board of Trustees, Southern Illinois University at Edwardsville. Reproduced by permission.—*Renaissance Papers*, 2000 for "'Divine Zenocrate,' 'Wretched Zenocrate': Female Speech and Disempowerment in *Tamburlaine I*," by Pam Whitfield. Reproduced by permission.—*Romance Studies*, v. 17, December, 1999. Copyright © 1999 by University of Wales Swansea. Reproduced by permission.—*Southern Quarterly*, v. 37, winter, 1999. Copyright © 1999 by the University of Southern Mississippi. Reproduced by permission.—*Theatre Research International*, v. 23, autumn, 1998 for "Sound Tracks: The Soundscapes of *India Song*, by Lib Taylor; "The Spatialization of Loss in the Theatre of Marguerite Duras," by Mary Noonan. Oxford University Press 1998. Copyright © International Federation for Theatre Research. Both reproduced with the permission of Cambridge University Press and the respective authors.—*Variety*, September 10–16, 2001. Copyright © 2001. Reproduced by permission.

**COPYRIGHTED MATERIALS IN *DfS*, VOLUME 21, WERE REPRODUCED FROM THE FOLLOWING BOOKS:**

Ardolino, Frank. From ***Thomas Kyd's Mystery Play: Myth and Ritual in "The Spanish Tragedy."*** Peter Lang Publishing, 1985. Copyright © Peter Lang Publishing, Inc., New York, 1985. Reproduced by permission.—Edwards, Philip. From an introduction to ***The Spanish Tragedy***. Edited and translated by Philip Edwards. Methuen & Co., Ltd., 1959. Introduction, Apparatus Criticus, etc. Copyright © 1959 by Philip Edwards. Reproduced by permission of the author.—Ericksen, Donald. From ***Oscar Wilde***. Twayne Publishers, 1977. Copyright © 1977 by G. K. Hall & Co. All rights reserved. Reproduced by permission of the Gale Group.—Miller, Robert Keith. From "Commercial Success: *Lady Windermere's Fan, A Woman of No Importance*, and *An Ideal Husband*," in ***Oscar Wilde***. Frederick Ungar Publishing, 1982. Copyright © 1982 by Frederick Ungar Publishing Co., Inc. Reproduced by permission of The Continuum International Publishing Group.—Paige, Linda Rohrer. From "Southern Firecrackers and 'Real Bad Days': Film Adaptations of Beth Henley's *Crimes of the Heart* and *The Miss Firecracker Contest*," in ***Beth Henley: A Casebook***. Edited by Julia A. Fesmire. Routledge, 2002. Copyright © 2002 by Julia A. Fesmire. Reproduced by permission of Taylor & Francis Books, Ltd., and the author.—San Juan, Epifanio Jr. From "The Action of the Comedies," in ***Oscar Wilde***. Edited by Harold Bloom. Chelsea House Publishers, 1985. Reproduced by permission the author.

**PHOTOGRAPHS AND ILLUSTRATIONS APPEARING IN *DfS*, VOLUME 21, WERE RECEIVED FROM THE FOLLOWING SOURCES:**

Ashley, Christopher, Director, actress Cynthia Nixon, and playwright Douglas Carter Beane arrive at the opening night of the play *Mondo Drama* on May 18, 2003 at the Greenwich House Theater in New York City. Photo by Lawrence Lucier/Getty Images.—Auburn, David, at his home in Williamstown, Massachusetts, shortly after being informed he had won the Pulitzer Prize for Drama for his play *Proof*, photograph by Alan Solomon. AP/Wide World. Reproduced by permission.—Bombay Street scene, photograph. Sheldan Collins/

Corbis. Reproduced by permission.—Brooks, Mel, addresses the audience at New York's St. James Theatre as Nathan Lane, second left, and Matthew Broderick look on after their last performance in *The Producers*, Sunday, March 17, 2002. AP/Wide World Photos.—Brooks, Mel, New York City, 1966, photograph. AP/Wide World Photos. Reproduced by permission.—"Buddha in Nirvana," painting, Tibet, 18th Century. The Art Archive/Musee Guimet Paris/Dagli Orti (A). Reproduced by permission.—Cigar makers in a Cuban factory being read to by a hired reader, photograph. © Hulton-Deutsch Collection/Corbis. Reproduced by permission.—Corneille, Pierre, illustration. New York Public Library Picture Collection. Reproduced by permission.—Cruz, Nilo, photograph. Jemal Countess/WireImage.com. Reproduced by permission.—Downtown Manhattan Skyline in 1998 taken from Liberty Park in New Jersey, photograph. © Joseph Sohm; ChromoSohm Inc./Corbis.—Drawing of a geometric calculation using a semicircle, by Leonardo da Vinci, photograph. © Alinari Archives/Corbis.—Duras, Marguerite, photograph. AP/Wide World Photos. Reproduced by permission.—El Cid (Diaz de Vivar, Rodrigo), illustration. New York Public Library Picture Collection.—Engraving of Christopher Marlowe, photograph. Getty Images. Reproduced by permission.—Great Mosque of Cordoba, photograph by Ruggero Vanni. © Vanni Archive/Corbis.—Harold, Erika, Miss America, walking down aisle on September 21, 2002. AP/Wide World Photos. Reproduced by permission.—Henley, Beth, 1984, photograph. AP/Wide World Photos. Reproduced by permission.—Hindu serving tea to a Colonial woman in an undated photograph, photograph. © Underwood and Underwood/Corbis.—Hussey, Olivia, and Leonard Whiting during the death scene of Franco Zeffirelli's movie of *Romeo and Juliet*, photograph. Paramount/The Kobal Collection. Reproduced by permission.—"Looking at a Painting of Mt. Fuji," by Suzuki Harunobu, photograph. © Burstein Collection/Corbis. Reproduced by permission.—Northam, Jeremy Philip, as Sir Robert Chiltern, sitting on bed with Cate Blanchett, as Lady Gertrude Chiltern, scene from *An Ideal Husband*, photograph. The Kobal Collection. Reproduced by permission.—Panama Canal. Panama. Photograph. Bettmann/Corbis. Reproduced by permission.—Parker, Mary-Louise, with her Tony award for Best Performance by a Leading Actress in a Play for *Proof*, photograph. © Steve Sands/New York Newswire/Corbis.—Playbill cover of *As Bees in Honey Drown* from the Lucille Lortel Theatre, 1997, directed by Mark Brokaw, photograph. Performing Arts Books, NYC. Playbill ® is a registered trademark of Playbill Incorporated, N. Y. C. All rights reserved. Reproduced by permission.—Seyrig, Delphine, and Didier Flamand, in the film *India Song*, photograph. The Kobal Collection. Reproduced by permission.—Shakespeare, William, illustration. AP/Wide World Photos. Reproduced by permission.—Silhouette of a couple on a pier at sunset, Captain Dons Habitat, Bonaire, Netherlands Antilles, November 2002. Photograph by Kelly A. Quin. Copyright © Kelly A. Quin.—Stage production of *Romeo and Juliet* during the death scene, with Ralph Fiennes as Romeo and Sarah Woodward as Juliet at the Open Air Theatre, Regents Park, London, photograph. © Donald Cooper/ Photostage.—Stage production still of *Tamburlaine* with Claire Benedict as Zenocrate and Antony Sher as Tamburlaine in a production directed by Terry Hands, photograph. © Donald Cooper/Photostage.—Still of Claire Danes and Leonardo Di Caprio from the 1996 movie *Romeo and Juliet*, directed by Baz Luhrman. 20th Century Fox/The Kobal Collection/ Morton, Merrick.—Still of Greta Garbo and Fredric March from the 1935 movie *Anna Karenina*, photo-graph. © Bettmann/Corbis.—Still of Holly Hunter and Alfre Woodard from the 1989 movie *Miss Firecracker*, directed by Thomas Schlamme. Corsair Pictures/The Kobal Collection.—Still of Zero Mostel and Gene Wilder from the 1967 movie of *The Producers*, directed by Mel Brooks. Embassy Pictures/The Kobal Collection.—"Under the Wave off Kanagawa," by Katsushika Hokusai from the series *Thirty-Six Views of Mount Fuji*, photograph. © Burstein Collection/Corbis.—Watercolour depicting the "Allegory of Justice," photograph. The Art Archive/Castello Sforzesco Milan/Dagli Orti (A).—White sand beach on Paradise Island, Bahamas, February 1996. Photograph by Kelly A. Quin. Copyright © Kelly A. Quin.—Wolfit, Donald, in a scene from *Tamburlaine the Great*, by Christopher Marlowe, photograph by Maurice Ambler. Hulton-Deutsch Collection/Corbis. Reproduced by permission.—Xingjian, Gao, author photo. © Fougere Eric/Corbis KIPA. Reproduced by permission.— Young men and women dancing and smoking at the Groove Jet, Miami Beach, Florida, September 24, 1999, photograph. AP/Wide World Photos. Reproduced by permission.

# Contributors

**Bryan Aubrey:** Aubrey holds a Ph.D. in English and has published many articles on modern drama. Entries on *Proof* and *The Spanish Tragedy*. Original essays on *Proof, Romeo and Juliet*, and *The Spanish Tragedy*.

**Liz Brent:** Brent has a Ph.D. in American Culture from the University of Michigan. She works as a freelance writer and editor. Entry on *India Song*. Original essay on *India Song*.

**Laura Carter:** Carter is currently employed as a freelance writer. Entry on *Feeding the Moonfish*. Original essay on *Feeding the Moonfish*.

**Carol Dell'Amico:** Dell'Amico is an instructor of English literature and composition. Entry on *An Ideal Husband*. Original essay on *An Ideal Husband*.

**Douglas Dupler:** Dupler is a writer and has taught college English courses. Original essay on *Romeo and Juliet*.

**Sheldon Goldfarb:** Goldfarb has a Ph.D. in English and has published two books on the Victorian author William Makepeace Thackeray. Original essay on *The Spanish Tragedy*.

**Curt Guyette:** Guyette, a longtime journalist, received a bachelor's degree in English writing from the University of Pittsburgh. Original essays on *An Ideal Husband* and *Proof*.

**Joyce Hart:** Hart is a freelance writer and author of several books. Entries on *As Bees in Honey Drown* and *Le Cid*. Original essays on *As Bees in Honey Drown* and *Le Cid*.

**Catherine Dybiec Holm:** Holm is a fiction and nonfiction writer and editor. Original essays on *As Bees in Honey Drown* and *The Miss Firecracker Contest*.

**David Kelly:** Kelly is an instructor of literature and creative writing. Entry on *The Producers*. Original essay on *The Producers*.

**Lois Kerschen:** Kerschen is a freelance writer and adjunct college English instructor. Entries on *The Miss Firecracker Contest* and *Romeo and Juliet*. Original essays on *The Miss Firecracker Contest* and *Romeo and Juliet*.

**Anthony Martinelli:** Martinelli is a Seattle-based freelance writer and editor. Entry on *36 Views*. Original essay on *36 Views*.

**David Remy:** Remy is a freelance writer in Warrington, Florida. Entry on *Anna in the Tropics*. Original essay on *Anna in the Tropics*.

**Scott Trudell:** Trudell is an independent scholar with a bachelor's degree in English literature.

Entry on *Tamburlaine the Great*. Original essay on *Tamburlaine the Great*.

**Mark White:** White is the publisher of the Seattle-based Scala House Press. Entry on *The Other Shore*. Original essay on *The Other Shore*.

# 36 Views

## NAOMI IIZUKA

## 2001

Naomi Iizuka finished writing *36 Views* in the fall of 1999. It was published in book form in 2003 by The Overlook Press in Woodstock, NY. The complete text of the play was also published in the February 2002 issue of *American Theatre.* Originally, the play was commissioned and developed by A.S.K. Theater Projects in 1998. Upon completion, it was read as part of the A.S.K. Reading Series in the fall of 1999. Later, in June of 2000, the A.S.K. Common Ground Festival presented *36 Views* as a workshop. The play gained recognition from this workshop and was subsequently developed at both The Sundance Theatre Laboratory in July 2000 and Breadloaf Writer's Conference in August 2000. Following this development, *36 Views* had its world premiere at the Berkeley Repertory Theatre in September 2001, under the direction of Mark Wing-Davey. The play had its New York premiere in March 2002 at the Joseph Papp Public Theater/New York Shakespeare Festival.

Iizuka is known for her artistic blending of the ancient and the contemporary. In her plays, she has mixed Ovid's *Metamorphoses* with the darkly intriguing and deeply upsetting subculture of homeless youth. She has transported Virgil's tragic characters Dido and Aeneas to the tough, uncompromising realism of modern Los Angeles. In *36 Views*, she has successfully and creatively melded elements of traditional Kabuki theater with a modern vision of Western forms.

The play raises questions about authenticity. The play, which garners its name from a series of woodblock prints called *36 Views of Mount Fuji* by nineteenth-century artist Hokusai, constantly presents the question of what is true and what is real. The characters struggle with the authenticity of precious, ancient art objects and artifacts. They question the truthfulness of their relationships with one another. Last, and most important, the characters question the authenticity of their own decisions, their lives, and themselves.

# AUTHOR BIOGRAPHY

Naomi Iizuka, a contemporary Japanese American playwright, is one of the freshest voices in modern theater. A prolific writer, Iizuka has written a host of controversial plays in her young career that have won her acclaim and recognition.

Given that Iizuka is such a new voice, very little has been written about her life. Most everything that has been printed about Iizuka has focused on her plays and their performances. However, it is known that she was born in 1965 in Japan to an American mother of Spanish descent and a Japanese banker father. She lived in Holland as a child, and later in Chevy Chase, Maryland. In Maryland, Iizuka attended the National Cathedral School, a private Catholic institution catering to the children of diplomats.

Iizuka grew up with an incredible love of literature. However, she did not discover theater until she began studying classics and literature at Yale University. After graduating from Yale, Iizuka spent a year at Yale Law School. Iizuka worked for several years and then enrolled in the master's of fine arts program in playwriting at the University of California-San Diego, where she studied closely with playwright Adele Edling Shank. Iizuka finished her master's of fine arts in 1992.

In the ten years following the completion of her master's of fine arts, Iizuka has written many plays, including *36 Views*, *Polaroid Stories*, *Language of the Angels*, and *Skin*. She is a member of the New Dramatists. She is also a recipient of the Whiting Award, the Gerbode Foundation Fellowship, the NEA/TCG Theatre Artist Residency Program for Playwrights, the McKnight Fellowship, the PEN Center USA West Award for Drama, Princeton University's Hodder Fellowship, and the Jerome Playwriting Fellowship. She and her works have been mentioned several times on National Public Radio, and she has taught masters classes at the Kennedy Center. Needless to say, Iizuka is both a prolific and widely celebrated American playwright.

# PLOT SUMMARY

## *Act 1, Scenes 1–10*

The play opens with a crisp image that exemplifies an important theme of the play: orientalism, i.e., the style or manner associated with or characteristics of Asia or Asians. It opens with complete darkness, all except for an ancient, hanging scroll painted with a Japanese woman in a formal pose. Darius Wheeler, an Asian art and antiquities dealer, utters the first words of the play, and his story is one of danger, luck, and intrigue.

With the tone set, Iizuka begins to construct the plot of her story. A party is being held in Wheeler's loft space. This is the first place our main characters, Wheeler and Setsuko Hearn, meet. Hearn is an assistant professor of East Asian literature. The characters have an outwardly innocent conversation revolving around Wheeler's collection of art and artifacts. During the discussion, Wheeler cuts his hand on a glass and starts bleeding. Through word choice and subtle action, it is apparent that both characters find each other stimulating and intriguing.

Also at the party is Wheeler's assistant, John Bell. Although there are festivities occurring outside of the office, Bell is working. The party is being held for a famous artist, Utagawa, who has not yet arrived. Bell is frantically looking for a piece of paper when Claire Tsong, a restorer of Asian artifacts, approaches him. After a short exchange about a transcript on the desk, Bell returns to the party. Elizabeth Newman-Orr, a free agent, then enters the office. Tsong and Newman-Orr have a lofty exchange about what is an authentic artifact and what is a fake.

Outside the office, the party continues. Owen Matthiassen, the chairman of the East Asian Studies Department, approaches Wheeler and Hearn. Matthiassen informs Wheeler of Hearn's expertise and brilliance in "writing from the eleventh century, diaries, memoirs, pillow books written by women of the Heian era.'' The two scholars, Hearn and Matthiassen, and the dealer, Wheeler, have an intellectual exchange about the relationship of art and beauty to ideas and abstractions.

It is clear from this series of conversations, that the crowd at the party is highbrow, well-educated and cosmopolitan. Although not explicitly stated, the party must be located in a city that is a mecca for art, culture and capitalism. Bell interrupts the discussion to inform Mr. Wheeler that the long-awaited guest of honor will, in fact, not be arriving. With that news, the party begins to dissolve. As the guests exit, Bell introduces Newman-Orr to Wheeler. Newman-Orr is extremely interested in Wheeler; her persistence lands her a meeting with him the following night. Although she intrigues him, her intentions are unknown.

Later in the evening, after most of the partygoers have left, Wheeler approaches Matthiassen with the hopes of finding Hearn. To Wheeler's disappointment, Hearn has already left. Wheeler presents Matthiassen with a Hokusai print of Mount Fuji (the namesake of Iizuka's play). Matthiassen is insurmountably impressed. To Matthiassen's dismay, Wheeler reveals that the print, although beautiful, is fake. The party thus ends.

The transition from the party to the next day is precipitated by Tsong reading the fine print disclaimer associated with the sale of an artifact: The vendor is not responsible for its authenticity, defects, and correctness of description. As though alluding to future troubles, Tsong declares, ''Always read the fine print. There is always fine print.'' After Tsong's interlude, Hearn follows with a reading from the transcript Bell had on his desk during the party. These lulls in the dialogue are essential for developing tension between the characters and arousing interest in the transcript, which has yet to be explained.

## Act 2, Scenes 11–20

The day after the party, Bell and Tsong are in Wheeler's loft space having a conversation about art and artifacts. Tsong has dropped off an Edo period screen she recently restored for Wheeler. Tsong claims that all the pieces are ''bric-a-brac for the leisure class'' and that ''it's all just capital.'' Bell not only disagrees, he also claims that Tsong does not truly believe what she is saying. To prove her point, Tsong is willing to spray paint the screen

she has just restored. As she starts to spray, Bell darts in front of the screen, blocking the paint with his body. After ruining Bell's shirt, their conversation strays from art to Bell, who is described as an under-appreciated intellectual with low self-esteem.

As the scene ends, Wheeler and Newman-Orr enter the loft space. Bell and Tsong have left. Newman-Orr wants to know if Wheeler is capable of smuggling a recently purchased painting out of Hong Kong into the United States. The reason it must be smuggled is that the painting is considered a national treasure and, if it is discovered leaving the country, it will be seized and returned to the country of origin as an invaluable cultural artifact. The two agree that Wheeler, if successful in smuggling it out, will receive twenty percent of the purchase price, which will be placed in an offshore account, half up-front and half upon the object's delivery. Newman-Orr leaves the loft.

Wheeler is again at his desk examining the earlier transcript. Hearn's voice is heard reading the transcript as Wheeler looks at it. Bell enters and Wheeler questions him about the transcript. Bell answers with a sizeable monologue about the translation from what he believes may be an eleventh-century Heian era memoir or ''pillow book.'' Bell also gives a lengthy and surprisingly precise account of who has owned the piece through the centuries. Wheeler exits the scene with the transcript.

Later that afternoon, Tsong and Bell are again alone in Wheeler's loft. Bell is confessing to Tsong that he completely fabricated the story about the eleventh-century pillow book. He is distraught because he is dumbfounded as to why he lied and, even more astonishing, that Wheeler believed every word. Tsong is ecstatic and decides that she must create the artifact out of thin air. She plans to construct Bell's fictitious ancient pillow book so that no one knows it is a fraud.

In a corridor of the university, Wheeler presents Hearn with a copy of Bell's transcript. Hearn is mystified by the quality of the voice, even through the translation. She is enthralled and is desperate to examine the original. Also, in this exchange, Hearn accepts Wheeler's invitation to dinner.

The scene switches to Newman-Orr. She is removing a hidden recording device that was taped to her body. She rewinds the device, and her exchange with Wheeler, about the transportation of the artifact, is played back through her recorder.

### Act 2, Scenes 21–36

The second act opens with Tsong working with archaic paper—burning edges, fabricating wear and age—to create a piece of ''ancient'' art.

It is apparent that the dean and other professors at the university are very interested in the forthcoming artifact. Matthiassen and Hearn are both eager to get their hands on the original pillow book. In a conversation that takes place in a park, Wheeler and Hearn discuss the pillow book while looking at Tsong's Polaroid photographs. They are discussing the beauty of the book and the inner feelings that are expressed through the author's writings. As the conversation turns to the subject of desire and love, Hearn and Wheeler kiss. Hearn is apprehensive about continuing, but Wheeler is smitten.

In Tsong's workspace, Bell is examining her creation. He is astonished. Her work is flawless. She tells Bell that if he creates an airtight paper trail, their creation will be finished and ''authentic.'' Bell and Tsong's argument delves into the crux of Iizuka's question about authenticity. Tsong tells Bell to present the ''original'' to Wheeler and also to give him an asking price. She reminds him that the price must be exorbitant because a pillow book of this quality and age is extremely rare. They both leave Tsong's workspace.

Hearn and Wheeler are presented getting dressed together, discussing what they know about the author of the pillow book. Wheeler is tremendously drawn to Hearn and begs her to accept his invitation to drinks and a nightcap later. She is still apprehensive, but Wheeler's determination persuades her.

Later in the day, at Wheeler's loft space, Newman-Orr and Wheeler are discussing the successful, but illegal, transportation of her artifact. Bell pries open the crate containing Newman-Orr's artifact. The painting is revealed, and it is clear that it is an exact match to a painting hanging in Wheeler's loft. Newman-Orr is confused as to why there are twins. By some sort of instinct, Wheeler discovered that Newman-Orr was trying to frame him, to catch him in the throws of the illegal activity of transporting a national treasure out of the country of origin. Wheeler explains that he knew her piece was a fake and that any real dealer would know the same thing. Thus, he suspected she was working for someone else in an attempt to frame him. Wheeler asks her to leave his loft, and she complies. After she leaves, Bell tells Wheeler that the owner of the pillow book is asking one million pounds sterling for the piece.

Wheeler thinks the asking price is low. He tells Bell that he will have a check ready for the purchase by the end of the business day.

An hour later, Tsong is in Wheeler's loft space with her creation, the ''original'' pillow book manuscript. Newman-Orr arrives looking for Bell. Since he is unavailable, Tsong invites Newman-Orr out for a drink. Newman-Orr tells Tsong that she is a journalist. The two leave Wheeler's loft together.

In Matthiassen's office, Hearn and Matthiassen are discussing the fake pillow book. Matthiassen tells Hearn that it would have never occurred to him, except that he had received a call from the journalist who had interviewed the forger and seen the forgery. Matthiassen explains that after a close inspection, the anomalies of the writing, although originally overlooked, were quite dramatic. It became apparent that the piece was not an original eleventh-century Heian era pillow book.

In the early evening of the same day, Hearn and Wheeler are in his loft discussing their past, their first loves, and their families. Hearn informs Wheeler that she has resigned from her position at the university. She believes that Wheeler was using her to authenticate the fake pillow book so it could be resold for a fortune. Wheeler, however, claims he was not taking advantage of her and their relationship. He purports that his feelings for her were genuine, that they were authentic. Crushed by sadness, Hearn leaves Wheeler's loft.

In a gallery, Tsong and Newman-Orr are having a drink amidst the thirty-six Utagawa paintings hanging on the walls. They discuss how Wheeler got started in the art dealing business. It is revealed, through a kiss, that Tsong and Newman-Orr have become lovers. In the same gallery, Bell and Matthiassen discuss Bell's recent book. His book is written from the point of view of an eleventh-century, Heian-era Japanese woman—a point of view that matches that of the fabricated author of Tsong's forged pillow book.

In the final scene, Wheeler and Hearn stand apart from each other on a stage that contains only the thirty-six paintings. Through their words, it is revealed that although the fabricated pillow book was indeed a fake, it was created by a contemporary and very popular artist: Utagawa. It is exposed that Utagawa is, in fact, Claire Tsong, Wheeler's favorite art restorer and, apparently, a reclusive painter. Lastly and tragically, it is also divulged that Wheeler and Hearn never resolved their misunderstanding and never rekindled their love or their friendship. The thirty-six paintings shift their alignment, creating one large mosaic of a woman, part contemporary and part ancient. The play ends.

## CHARACTERS

### *John Bell*

John Bell is Darius Wheeler's assistant. Bell is an intellectual who proclaims to love his job and his boss. He is driven and intelligent. Bell speaks most Asian languages and is very capable of identifying and working with ancient works of priceless art. His boss, a dealer of Asian arts and antiquities, relies heavily on Bell's expertise. Despite this, Bell is driven by a story he has fabricated about an eleventh-century woman from Heian era Japan. He concocts an ancient pillow book, supposedly written by her. For a reason he cannot pinpoint, Bell is compelled to tell Wheeler that he has stumbled upon this ancient manuscript that is both beautiful and invaluable. As if coerced by an outside force, Bell enters into cahoots with Claire Tsong, a restorer of Asian artifacts, to create the ''original'' pillow book. Bell is ravaged with guilt, but cannot stop himself from playing out the scenario. He is assisted greatly by Tsong's constant prodding. Eventually, after the forgery is discovered, Bell writes a piece of fiction from the point of view of an eleventh-century Heian era Japanese woman. His book is a smash success, but he still cannot seem to understand where the muse came from to motivate him to create such an elaborate tale. He even considers the possibility of a past life.

### *Setsuko Hearn*

Setsuko Hearn is an assistant professor of Asian arts and antiquities. Hearn is well-educated and intelligent. She is highly regarded by her colleagues, including Owen Matthiassen. Hearn is an attractive woman of Asian descent. It is apparent from the earliest scenes of the play that Darius Wheeler is romantically interested in her. Hearn is also a skeptical woman, thus she is apprehensive of Wheeler's advances. Eventually, the two begin a relationship. Oddly enough, Hearn's skepticism gets the best of her in the end as she is convinced that Wheeler planned to seduce her only to get her to authenticate a fabricated pillow book created by Claire Tsong

# MEDIA ADAPTATIONS

- AsiaSource, a resource of the Asia Society, maintains a web page at http://www.asiasource.org/arts/36views.cfm containing an interview with Naomi Iizuka.

and John Bell. Unfortunately for their budding romance, the rift caused by Hearn's conclusion that Wheeler has used her for his own gain, renders a permanent end to their relationship. The couple parts ways. Although she is drawn to ancient Japanese culture (her expertise is in writing from the eleventh century Heian era), Hearn is actually a Chinese orphan. Her parents adopted her from an orphanage in Hangzhou. Her mother is Japanese and her father is of mixed European descent. Hearn was raised in Fairfield, Iowa, as an only child. She was married once when she was young, but it did not last because she was more interested in her work than her spouse.

### *Owen Matthiassen*

Owen Matthiassen is the chairman of the East Asian Studies Department. He is well-educated, respected, and intelligent. Although Darius Wheeler and Setsuko Hearn are already acquainted, Matthiassen boasts to Wheeler about Hearn's talents and expertise. Matthiassen relishes the fact that his school is incredibly lucky to have Hearn, as they almost lost her to Stanford. Matthiassen is an inquisitive man who enjoys rousing conversations, especially with Wheeler. Matthiassen is well aware that Wheeler often calls himself a materialist and a philistine, but Matthiassen believes Wheeler is lying to himself or, at the very least, discrediting his self-made qualifications. Matthiassen is full of compliments and optimism; he seems to have a true lust for life, art and conversation. Even in the end, when Hearn feels compelled to resign after authenticating a forgery, Matthiassen is inclined to tell her that the fake was very convincing. Even in moments of great shame, Matthiassen struggles to make light of uncomfortable situations.

### *Elizabeth Newman-Orr*

Elizabeth Newman-Orr is a free agent. She is a journalist attempting to pin Darius Wheeler in a sticky situation by having him transport a piece of art that is considered a national treasure. Transporting objects that are deemed national treasures is against international law. However, as Wheeler is well aware, when there is money at stake, there is always a way around the law. Armed with a concealed recording device, Newman-Orr records Wheeler accepting her proposition to transport a national treasure. Unbeknownst to Newman-Orr, Wheeler somehow sniffs her out and confronts her in a situation that is incredibly uncomfortable. Feeling devastated and without a story, Newman-Orr meets Claire Tsong. Hearn reveals that Newman-Orr is a journalist and a failing one at that. Tsong, who becomes instantly smitten with Newman-Orr upon their first encounter, decides to tell Newman-Orr about her fabricated "ancient" pillow-book forgery, giving Newman-Orr the inside scoop on an incredible story.

### *Claire Tsong*

Claire Tsong is a restorer of Asian artifacts that frequently works with Darius Wheeler. Of all the characters, Tsong is the most mysterious and confrontational. She constantly questions the authenticity of her work and how it applies to art and artifacts. Tsong's analysis of what is true is the most insightful and disturbing. It comes into being with her decision to force John Bell forward in their creation of the forged ancient pillow book. If they can create an artifact with a clear paper trail, perfect replication of style, and use the correct archaic resources, then, Tsong believes, the pillow book is as good as if it were actually created in the eleventh century. If they are successful in their creation, then, in Tsong's mind, the piece becomes authentic. For Tsong, reality is nothing but perception. Psychologically and philosophically, Tsong is an abundantly interesting character. By the end of the play, even more mysteries are uncovered, as it is revealed that Tsong lives a dual life, as a restorer of Asian artifacts and also as a reclusive painter who goes by the name of Utagawa.

### *Darius Wheeler*

Darius Wheeler is a dealer of Asian arts and antiquities. He is an adventurous soul dedicated to finding art and artifacts that will turn a hefty profit. He has turned his own business from a fledgling entrepreneurship into a respected enterprise. Wheeler's name precedes him. He is often viewed as insensitive and manipulative, yet Wheeler has little remorse about these descriptions because he believes that his actions are necessary to be successful in his business. Wheeler is also often seen as a womanizer. He enjoys beautiful things but believes that all beauty is impermanent. Hence, Wheeler rarely becomes attached to art or women, no matter how attracted he is to them. His aloof demeanor does not win him many friends, but his keen business sense and his remarkable eye for artistic gems makes him the envy of colleagues. Wheeler was raised in Bellingham, Washington. He has one sister who lives on Mercer Island in Washington State.

## THEMES

### *Authenticity*

Authenticity is the most prominent underlying theme of the play. It appears in relation to things, such as artwork and artifacts. Claire Tsong questions the authenticity of an ancient pillow book by creating a keen replica of a non-existent artifact. She believes that perception is reality—i.e., if the book is perceived as an artifact, then it *is* an artifact. Interestingly, this theme continues into the characters' relationships to one another. Setsuko Hearn and Darius Wheeler's relationship was rooted and disrupted by its authenticity. Wheeler truly loved Hearn. However, Hearn did not see his love as authentic. She believed that his feelings were untrue and he was manipulating her feelings to use her credibility to authenticate Tsong's fake "ancient" pillow book. Lastly, the fabric of authenticity is at the individual crux of nearly every main character. Each character has multiple appearances or identities. From this standpoint, it is difficult to identify which of their characteristics are truly authentic to them. For example, Darius Wheeler is an art dealer, a *wheeler-dealer* of Asian arts and antiquities. Outwardly, Wheeler seems to only appreciate Asian culture and art as a form of capital to be bought and sold. The bulk of his comments make it seem as though he has no love for the culture itself. Yet, Wheeler's very being is created by his quests to retrieve these artifacts. Without Asian arts and antiquities, Wheeler is devoid of identity. This duality carries itself through the other characters as well: Tsong, the art restorer, doubles as the recluse painter, Utagawa; John Bell, Wheeler's assistant, through

# TOPICS FOR
# FURTHER
# STUDY

- The blending of Western and non-Western styles is important in *36 Views*. One example of this blend is the use of wooden clappers throughout the play. Research non-Western styles of drama, such as Kabuki, a traditional Japanese popular drama performed with highly stylized singing and dancing, and try to find and explain other examples of non-Western elements in *36 Views*.

- Darius Wheeler believes that art should be about beauty, not ideas. Wheeler's understanding of art shares much with David Hume's philosophy in *The Enquiry Concerning Human Understanding*. Read ''Section II—Of the Origin of Ideas'' and use Hume's definitions of *ideas* and *impressions* to determine whether Wheeler's understanding of art makes sense, or if his dependence

on beauty leaves him devoid of something crucial to human understanding.

- The question of authenticity is rampant in *36 Views*. Whether it is from degradation and restoration or simply from pure fabrication, the truth of objects is constantly under question in the play. What other things change with time? Think of how things age and break down, whether wine or carbon molecules, for example, and try to examine the concept of aging and how it correlates to value.

- The play's namesake, *36 Views of Mount Fuji* by the artist Hokusai, actually consists of forty-six different prints of Mount Fuji. Research Hokusai and try to discover his motivations and influences. Is there any reason for titling the forty-six prints the *36 Views of Mount Fuji*?

---

his writing is an eleventh-century Heian-era Japanese woman; and Setsuko Hearn, assistant professor of East Asian literature, is not a worldly, metropolitan, Japanese American. Instead, she has lived a sheltered, studious young life. She is Chinese by birth, adopted from an orphanage in Hangzhou and raised by a Japanese American woman and a European American missionary in Iowa. The question of authenticity is even found in the title of the play: *36 Views* comes from a series of woodblock prints by Hokusai entitled *36 Views of Mount Fuji;* however, despite its name, this series actually consists of forty-six images.

### *Art and Value*

In the play there are two divergent understandings of art—aesthetic value and monetary value. From the perspective of Hearn and Bell, pieces of art are things of mystery and beauty. Hearn and Bell have a strong philosophic understanding of the creation and the existence of the pieces as true art. The art and artifacts possess a moral and social value. Art, for Hearn and Bell, can carry meaning,

intention, representation and illusion; art is meant to be contemplated and analyzed for all the richness it contains. The other understanding of art is one of monetary value. For Wheeler and Tsong, art and artifacts are simply physical things that, given time and others' perceptions, have earned a dollar value. Oddly enough, Tsong herself is, in fact, a creator of fine art as well as a restorer of artifacts. Yet, she is skeptical of the worth of art beyond its cash value. Speaking of art and artifacts, Tsong tells John Bell, ''it's all just capital.'' Throughout the play, art is constantly valued, both fiscally and philosophically.

### *Beauty as Impermanence*

Beauty is an important theme throughout the course of the play. In particular, how beauty relates to Darius Wheeler and Claire Tsong. Almost everyone agrees Wheeler has a keen eye for beautiful things and, as a result, a wildly successful company. Wheeler is also known for having relationships with beautiful women. Yet, like his art collecting and his changing relationships, none of the beauty is for Wheeler to keep. It is impermanent in that it moves into and out of his grasp. Also, from Tsong's perspective, the beauty in an object is in constant flux; it is never truly permanent. As she restores a piece of art, Tsong makes it beautiful. It has no permanent beauty without being tended to, which requires a level of creation. Thus Tsong concludes that beauty is impermanent.

## STYLE

### Melding Styles for the Audience

Iizuka's *36 Views* is written in such a way that the people who come to see the production will have an experience which melds Western and non-Western forms. She has successfully created a contemporary play set in a modern, metropolitan city that has strong elements of traditional Japanese Kabuki theatre.

### Monologues as Interludes and as Effective Foreshadowing

Repeatedly, Iizuka enlists her characters to do the voice-over as another character reads from the transcript of the fabricated pillow book. Throughout the play, the monologues break up the characters' dialogue. The discussions frequently revolve around arguments of authenticity and how it relates to art and the state of being. The monologues are delicately written, beautiful and poetic. The dialogue is frequently intellectual, focused, and sometimes derisive. The interplay between monologue from the pillow book and the dialogue of the characters creates a cadence that ensnares and makes the audience wonder about the significance of the pillow book. In a play heavy with questions about what is real, Iizuka effectively builds tension and highlights the importance of the pillow book by interrupting the dialogue with the readings from it.

### The Manipulation of Verisimilitude

Verisimilitude, in literature and drama, refers to aspects of a work that are perceived as true to a reader or audience. In *36 Views*, Iizuka creates a wealth of characters that are constantly questioning the truth and authenticity in physical things, in relationships to one another, and in themselves. Characters are committed to absolutes, such as Wheeler's claim that "Beautiful means beautiful." Abstractions and emotions are overlooked as petty

and meaningless. Yet, in reality, absolutes are ineffective. Concrete absolutes, unshaken by actions or perceptions, are incredibly rare, if not non-existent. Iizuka's characters are rooted in absolutes, which helps her manipulate what is true. It appears that an absolute may be the keenest, truest sense of perception; however, this idea disintegrates upon inspection. Essentially, Wheeler backs himself into a corner when he says, "Beautiful means beautiful" because his statement holds no weight. There is no meaning in his absolute statement because it has no relation to anything. If nothing but the beautiful is beautiful, then there are no beautiful things in the world because not every beautiful thing can be Wheeler's absolute "beautiful." From the perspectives of distorted perceptions of her characters, Iizuka constantly manipulates the truth in her characters. Whether it is the discovery that Claire Tsong is Utagawa or that Setsuko Hearn is an adopted Chinese orphan from Iowa, Iizuka's characters are never quite what they seem. Even the very title of the play, *36 Views*, comes from a series of forty-six, not thirty-six, woodblock prints of Mount Fuji by nineteenth-century Japanese artist Hokusai—but then again, does it? Iizuka weaves a web of fact and fiction that perpetuates a constant questioning of truth, reality and authenticity.

## HISTORICAL CONTEXT

Although not explicitly stated, it is easy to deduce that *36 Views* is set in the modern era and, most likely, in a large, culturally rich area. The last half of the twentieth century up to the present has been a tumultuous time in art. Art movements, as they were typically understood, began to recess. It was as though the artists who created movements were being replaced by the decisions of dealers and critics. In response to the current conundrum of modern art, Robert Hughes states in his book *The Shock of the New*, "The year 1900 seemed to promise a renewed world, but there can be few who watch the approach of the year 2000 with anything but scepticism and dread. Our ancestors saw expanding cultural horizons, we see shrinking ones." Iizuka must share a similar reproach. The play *36 Views* constantly and diligently questions the fabric of the contemporary art world.

From the early 1900s up to the 1970s, art was hinged to the aesthetic. Artists believed in progress and the future. They worked to deny the past in order to create new movements and a renewal of a world rich with art. Art, as it progressed, was seen to convey spirituality and transcendence. It was rich with response to social and political events. Modern artists worked to separate art from craft. Art, as history, was presented as a single narrative. The modernists saw art as a progressive change that could be viewed historically. The modernists promoted a pure appreciation of art and saw art as a great asset to society. It was reasonable and justifiable to be trained in the universals of art, in terms of a pure sense of style and technique, just as a doctor is trained in the universals of medicine. The appreciation and understanding of contemporary art soared during these years.

However, modern art began to change, both in its definition and understanding. The modern construct of art was replaced with a postmodern understanding of art during the 1970s. The change that occurred has lead many artists and historians to believe that art is dying or in recess. Postmodernism has abandoned many of the mantras that made modern art so enduring and progressive. Postmodernism has its foundations in the loss of faith in progress, thus it is seemingly damned from its inception to do nothing but appropriate the past and stew over the social constructs already created. Art is no longer dissected with philosophical rumination; it is viewed purely as a commodity. Pure appreciation of art and its essential nature is replaced with a lack of artistic hierarchy and contextual justification; the line between art and craft is virtually removed in postmodernism. Postmodernism has brought us to the precipice of the bleak disintegration of the modern concept of art. The current vision of art has, as Hughes states, left us with only shrinking horizons.

With this brief understanding of the world of modern and postmodern art, it is easy to see Iizuka's play as a means for presenting and discussing the changing elements of art. Her play is a response to art as a commodity and to the authenticity of all contemporary understandings of art. Darius Wheeler is disinterested in Utagawa's paintings because they are ''just a series of abstractions tarted up to look like art.'' For Wheeler, art is beautiful, and he believes that the contemporary concept of art—i.e., postmodernism—is more about craft and ideas than it is about beauty and transcendence. However, Iizuka does not let Wheeler be a martyr for disappearing art. Wheeler is himself a postmodernist because all the things he covets as beautiful, such as art and artifacts, are also pure commodity. They are dollars in his pocket.

It makes sense that Iizuka would try to undermine the contemporary understanding of art. As a playwright, Iizuka faces an uphill battle against the throws of postmodernism. This current, popular school of thought moves into virtually every facet of creativity—whether it is art, literature or drama. If anything is at stake, it is theater. Live drama is the oldest form of entertainment, but with the acceptance of creative works as commodity, pluralism is taking root and people are more willing to be entertained by drivel. Television and Hollywood blockbuster films threaten the very soul of contemporary theater. As a young, modern dramatist, Iizuka owes it to her art to help keep it afloat in the contemporary vision of postmodernism.

## CRITICAL OVERVIEW

Iizuka's recent play, *36 Views*, was first performed in 2001. Although there is not a great deal written about the play (it was first published in book form in 2003), the performances of it have received some divided reviews. Bruce Weber states in the *New York Times* that ''The play itself is far more crafty than moving, but a sound, probing intelligence and a niftily conceived and well-paced plot make the narrative irresistible.'' There are moments when the language feels like two symbols are conversing, as opposed to two human beings. Yet, Weber concludes in his the *New York Times* article that ''Ms. Iizuka's real achievement here is in fulfilling the demands of her ambitious premise. Revelations that conflict with or flat-out contradict our previous assumptions continue right through the final scene. Not even the context of the plot is what it seems to be.''

Iizuka is well known for crafting spectacular plots. Another of her plays, *Polaroid Stories*, is also renowned for its plot which melds Ovid's ancient work *Metamorphoses* with a grim, sad portrait of homeless youths. This play also received divided reviews from national critics, but was well received by audience members.

Iizuka's playwriting holds great potential. Although she is not a veteran playwright in years, her style holds such promise that it is hard to imagine that through her years she won't become anything but a timeless playwright. It is especially refreshing, given the contemporary state of entertainment and creativity, to see young, intellectual

*"Under the Wave off Kanagawa" by Katsushika Hokusai, from the series* Thirty-Six Views of Mount Fuji

women writing powerful social and political plays that address current issues in a startling, interesting fashion.

## CRITICISM

### *Anthony Martinelli*

*Martinelli is a Seattle-based freelance writer and editor. In this essay, Martinelli examines the perception of authenticity in the context of art and the individual.*

Naomi Iizuka's play *36 Views* takes its name from a series of woodblock prints by nineteenth-century Japanese artist Hokusai. The series is entitled *36 Views of Mount Fuji.* Despite its title, the series consists of forty-six prints. Even before a character casts a single word, Iizuka, with her creative title, has foreshadowed that her play will be rich with questions concerning what is real and authentic.

The first half of act 1 is set at a party for a renowned, reclusive contemporary artist named Utagawa. The party is being held at Darius Wheeler's loft space. Although the artist has yet to arrive,

many people are mingling in Wheeler's loft. Wheeler approaches Setsuko Hearn and their conversation quickly becomes philosophical. They are discussing beauty when Wheeler presents Hearn with a nine-hundred-year-old jade figure. Wheeler holds the jade figure and states, "human touch, it alters the stone, there's a kind of chemical reaction, it actually changes the color of the stone. With each touch it changes over time, almost imperceptible, impossible to replicate. Very old jade like this, it comes in these translucent colors I can't describe, beautiful, unimaginably beautiful." With subtlety, Wheeler has revealed that he views beauty as something in flux, something changing and, thus, impermanent. The jade is beautiful, and yet it is dynamic. Even though it is different with each touch, it is always beautiful. Wheeler is enamored and repulsed by this because he wants to be perceived as a philistine. Outwardly, he projects the image that he sees nothing but monetary value in the art that he deals. However, deep inside his soul, as shown in his love of his jade figure, Wheeler is truly drawn to the philosophical aesthetic in a thing.

Iizuka raises interesting questions as the characters in the play have conversations about the authenticity of art at Wheeler's party. For example,

# WHAT DO I READ NEXT?

- *Out of the Fringe* (1999) is a collection of eclectic plays that contains Iizuka's play *Skin.* Iizuka, as a Japanese American of Spanish descent, is included in this collection of contemporary Latina/Latino Theatre and Performance.

- Iizuka's *Polaroid Stories* (1999) is a play that melds Ovid's *Metamorphoses* with the subculture of homeless youth.

- *The Laramie Project* (2001), by Moises Kaufman, is a play documenting the aftermath of the savage murder of Matthew Shepard, a young gay man. It is an innovative theatrical composition in that the play has no scenes, only ''moments.''

- *How I Learned to Drive* (1999), a play by Paula Vogel, examines the destructive and incestuous relationship between Li'l Bit and her uncle. It is written with frank language and straightforward honesty that create a remarkably candid view of a dysfunctional family.

- *The Waverly Gallery* (2000), written by Kenneth Lonergan, is an impressive and frequently hilarious story about the last years of a fiery, talkative grandmother's battle with Alzheimer's disease.

- *History of Modern Art* (2003, 5th ed.), by H. H. Arnason, is an authoritative and brilliant examination of art from the mid-nineteenth century to today's diverse artistic movements.

- *Art in Theory 1900–2000* (2002, 2d ed.), by Charles Harrison and Paul Wood, provides an insightful overview of all the major art movements of the past century.

- *Kabuki Theater* (1974), by E. Ernst, gives an excellent yet basic history of Kabuki, the traditional Japanese theater style. It is an authoritative guide explaining the background, facts, and nuances of this ancient performance art.

---

Claire Tsong and Elizabeth Newman-Orr are having a conversation over several pieces in Wheeler's loft space. As the two characters view an art object, Iizuka writes:

ELIZABETH NEWMAN-ORR: . . . . Real? CLAIRE TSONG: Iffy. ELIZABETH NEWMAN-ORR: It looks real. CLAIRE TSONG: Lots of things look real. . . . ELIZABETH NEWMAN-ORR: You sound like an expert. CLAIRE TSONG: It's not about expertise. It's all about the eye. ELIZABETH NEWMAN-ORR: The eye? That sounds so hoodoo. CLAIRE TSONG: It's like it's physical, you know. I'm talking about a physical sensation, an instinct. It is like there's an invisible thread between you and this thing.

In this exchange, Iizuka builds into the fabric of the play a philosophical concept of human understanding: the relation between objects and perception as a construct of reality. Tsong's ''invisible thread'' is an example of eighteenth-century philosopher David Hume's theory of ideas and impressions. For Hume, impressions are ''all our more lively perceptions, when we hear, or see, or feel, or love, or hate, or desire, or will.'' Ideas, on the other hand, derive from impressions that occur in the mind. Hume states, ''All ideas, especially abstract ones, are naturally faint and obscure: the mind has but a slender hold of them.'' The ''invisible thread'' is the relation between an impression and an idea. Even though Newman-Orr thinks that Tsong's ''eye'' sounds like hoodoo, it is actually quite reasonable. Tsong is able, through training and through paying special attention to her impressions, to organize her ideas to create a keen knowledge of authentic art objects.

What is more interesting, though, is what Tsong does with her understanding of authentic art. In the last half of the act 1, David Bell, compelled by some unseen force, lies to his boss, Wheeler, and fabricates a story about an ancient but recently discovered, eleventh-century pillow book. Amazingly, Wheeler believes Bell's story. Suddenly, Bell is

> ALTHOUGH IT IS ABHORRENT TO THINK OF FABRICATING A PIECE OF ANCIENT ART, TSONG'S ACTIONS ARE AT THE VERY HEART OF IIZUKA'S QUESTIONS: WHAT IS REAL? WHAT IS AUTHENTIC?"

thrust into a conspiracy with Tsong. The two, with Tsong's constant prodding, decide to construct the fake pillow book. For Bell, the fake artifact is a vessel for a story he has welling up inside his very being. As Bell tells Owen Matthiassen at the end of the play, "I don't remember writing what I wrote. It's like it was written by another person. . . . Maybe in a past life." However for Tsong, the fake artifact is a way to actualize her feelings of contempt for the authentic.

Tsong is repeatedly frustrated by her work as a restorer. She struggles with her role in the restoration of artifacts because she sees them as "bric-a-brac for the leisure class" and "just capital." She cannot find true meaning in her craft as a restorer. She knows that she is changing an art object by restoring it and, thus, increasing its value. Yet she contemplates where this manipulation should end. While holding a can of spray paint up to a recently restored screen, Tsong states, "Would I be destroying it. . . . Or restoring it? How would I be affecting its market value? But now here's the thing: what if I happened to make it a better painting? Or better yet, what if you couldn't tell the difference?" Tsong is at the forefront of the main question of Iizuka's play. Tsong has the keenest insight into what constitutes truth and authenticity. Although it is abhorrent to think of fabricating a piece of ancient art, Tsong's actions are at the very heart of Iizuka's questions: What is real? What is authentic?

After Tsong completes the pillow book, Bell is amazed at the craftsmanship of the piece. It looks remarkable. Iizuka writes:

JOHN BELL: But it's not real. CLAIRE TSONG: Isn't it? It looks pretty real to me. JOHN BELL: It's not about what it looks like. It's about what it is. Eventually somebody's going to figure out the difference. CLAIRE TSONG: And what if they don't?

(The sound of wooden clappers) CLAIRE TSONG: Provenance.

This is the final and most direct affirmation of Tsong's understanding of authenticity. In her mind, the fake artifact becomes a real artifact if others perceive it as authentic. However, David Hume would not agree with her argument. For Hume, the idea of an object as a real artifact, as it is perceived by the mind, does not change the impression of the object as a fake artifact. Essentially, Hume would argue that if the connection of ideas that occurs in the mind of an observer leads the observer to believe that a fake artifact is real, then that observer has simply made errors in their understanding. So Tsong's attempt to create a "real" fake artifact is impossible; the fake artifact, no matter how it is perceived by an observer's mind, will never become a real, ancient artifact. Tsong has done nothing but confuse the observer. Her attempt to undermine authenticity is nothing more than an elaborate trick of smoke and mirrors.

Iizuka continues her barrage on authenticity through Wheeler and Setsuko Hearn's relationship. Although Wheeler does not want to be seen as an intellectual, it is apparent that he, like Tsong, is interested in the "invisible thread" that connects him to Hearn. He is truly smitten with her. His feelings of love for her are authentic. Of course, this is contradictory to the image that he desperately tries to project. At the party for Utagawa he says to Matthiassen, "Sad, but true. I'm a philistine," and he calls himself a "lazy bum." Wheeler defines himself as a womanizer and a hollow man only concerned with money. Yet his actions refute his self-definition. In the scene when Hearn and Wheeler first kiss, Wheeler reveals his true self to her. Iizuka writes:

SETSUKO HEARN: It's that I look at you and I don't know what I'm seeing. What am I seeing? DARIUS WHEELER: A deeply [f——]ed-up individual. SETSUKO HEARN: Is that right? DARIUS WHEELER: The worst. And the funny thing is—this is the funny thing—he's fallen for this woman who happens to see through all his [b——sh——t], this beautiful, brilliant woman, and he can barely talk when he's around her, which I know is kinda hard to believe, but it's true, and I know, I know right now he sounds like an idiot and a jerk, probably because he is an idiot and a jerk, and she should probably tell him to just get lost, but I really—I hope she doesn't, I really hope she doesn't.

Although a lengthy passage, it carries Wheeler's true feeling. He is making an honest attempt to express to Hearn the "invisible thread" that he recognizes between them. Wheeler loves her. Unfortunately, in a tragic moment of misunderstanding, Hearn does not see Wheeler's words and actions as authentic. By the end of the play, she concludes that Wheeler seduced her simply to use her and her expertise to prove the authenticity of Tsong and Bell's ''ancient'' pillow book. From her own impressions of Wheeler, Hearn concludes that his feelings for her were fabricated, tragically tricking herself and laying ruin to their budding relationship. With this, Iizuka continues to question authenticity, not only in relation to objects but also in the arena of human relationships.

The riveting plot, full of twists and turns about what is real and what is not, reaches a crescendo in the final moments of the play. Through her writing, Iizuka presents several questions about authenticity to her audience. Yet, each one occurs before the audiences' eyes. Nothing is hidden from view; namely, it is apparent to the audience that the pillow book is a fake, that Wheeler knew nothing of its fabrication, and, in turn, that his love for Hearn is real. As the play comes to a close, Iizuka plays the final trick on her audience. It is revealed, as it was foreshadowed by the play's title, that none of the main characters are what they seem. Claire Tsong, a restorer of Asian artifacts, is actually the renowned, reclusive painter Utagawa. John Bell, Darius Wheeler's assistant, is transformed, through the publication of his book, into a female, eleventh-century Japanese pillow book author. Darius Wheeler, a dealer of Asian arts and antiquities, is not an insensitive philistine and womanizer concerned with nothing but capital gains and temporary beauty but is a true admirer of Asian culture and a man capable of expressing true, endless love to another. And, lastly, Setsuko Hearn, an assistant professor of East Asian literature, is not a worldly, driven, metropolitan Japanese American as she is perceived but a lonely, brilliant skeptic; she is a Chinese orphan, adopted as a baby from Hangzhou, raised as a sheltered only child by a Japanese mother and a mixed-European father in Fairfield, Iowa. With this, at the close of the play, the audience is left with a whole new set of impressions and ideas of the characters.

Iizuka's conclusion is a perfect end to a play dedicated to questioning authenticity. It is important, both to Hume and Iizuka, that individuals realize they are in a constant struggle with their ideas and impressions. Individuals cannot rely completely on the absolutism of impressions to create understanding. Constructing a reality through the connection of ideas is the only way to achieve an understanding of the world. Yet, as Iizuka makes clear in her play, these connections do not always lead us to what is authentic.

**Source:** Anthony Martinelli, Critical Essay on *36 Views,* in *Drama for Students,* Thomson Gale, 2005.

### Naomi Iizuka and Celia Wren

*In the following interview, Iizuka comments on her inspiration for* 36 Views, *including Kabuki theatre, and discusses the origin of the idea for the pillow book in the play.*

[*American Theatre*]: *What inspired* 36 Views?

[*Iizuka*]: I became transfixed by the series of woodblock prints ''36 Views of Mount Fuji'' by [the 19th-century artist] Hokusai. It's an intriguing work. Each print is a representation of the mountain from a different perspective, in different seasons. You see the mountain and the world around it, but in some of the prints the mountain is actually very difficult to make out. As I was writing the play, the question of authenticity—What is authentic? What is true or real?—became as mysterious and somehow omnipresent as the mountain in Hokusai's study. That question, in some sense, became the mountain.

*Why the wooden clappers?*

The play has a lot of conventions from Kabuki theatre—like the wooden clappers. When I saw Kabuki for the first time, I thought it was one of the most exciting theatre-going experiences I'd ever had. It was so completely theatrical. When I began to do research, one of the things I found is that, unlike Noh, Kabuki—which is a newer and more secular tradition—has changed over time and has even seemed to welcome innovation. There was a kind of pliability and playfulness in Kabuki that seemed appropriate to the world of this play. I was really interested in figuring out how to take these structures that were non-Western and finding ways to synthesize them with Western forms.

*The Kabuki allusions seem parallel to your use of literary sources in past plays, like* Polaroid Stories, *which drew on Ovid.*

I think that with both Ovid and Kabuki theatre, I'm working with cultures that are, in different ways, foreign to me. Even though I am part Japanese, Kabuki is still remote to me, in the same way that, even though I grew up for the most part in a Western culture, Ovid is foreign to me. It's ancient. It's in a different language. It's an alien life-form, in a way. I think the question becomes: How do you take these artifacts and find a connection to them. How do you create a new life for them?

*How did the pillow book become part of the plot?*

I came across Sei Shonagon's *Pillow Book* a few years ago. I was struck by it because it was ancient, and at the same time it seemed so contemporary. I was familiar with *The Tale of Genji*, but the genre of the pillow book is very different. It includes lists and poetry, musings and opinions, anecdotes and recollections—a lot of different elements all in one work. It was many things all at once, and that appealed to me. Also, the consciousness of the writer came through in a way that was tantalizing. I try to convey in the play that excitement you feel when you've found a kindred consciousness across centuries.

*There've been a number of recent plays about art forgery and the economic value of art: Jon Robin Baitz's* Ten Unknowns, *for example. Any insights on this trend?*

I didn't set out to write a play about art forgery. For me, *36 Views* is more about how we navigate a different culture. All the characters in the play are experts in a field, and yet despite their expertise, they're struggling with something that's foreign to them. Having to make sense of alien worlds interests me a great deal, as does the related question: How do you make sense of another human being, of a consciousness very different from your own?

*The idea of orientalism, and its dangers, is another important theme.*

Absolutely. I wanted very much to write a play that in some way confronted questions about orientalism—questions about rendering objects, as well as cultures and human beings, exotic. The play looks at how impressions and assumptions get made and how far away those assumptions and impressions are from the truth. But it's complicated. I hope it's clear, for example, that Owen's love for Asian culture is a very real thing, that it's not easy to dismiss and pigeonhole. He's adopted this other culture that speaks to him in a very deep way. And the two Asian characters—Setsuko and Claire—also struggle to navigate their relationship with their cultural heritage. It's not a seamless, effortless relationship. And it's not fixed. It changes.

*In the play, Darius Wheeler criticizes one artist for being too much "about ideas." But* 36 Views *is itself packed with ideas, about culture, the nature of beauty, the value of art.*

The play is in conversation with certain ideas. I think of Darius and Claire, in particular—although they're very different, and antagonists in some ways—both as essentialists. They believe a thing is what it is, that there's this essential, definitive, unchanging truth. And the play really challenges that notion. Whether it's your relationship to a cultural tradition or to an art object, or to another person, I don't know that you can speak in absolutes. And that may be difficult or confusing or painful. I think ultimately it's a more truthful way of moving through the world.

**Source:** Naomi Iizuka and Celia Wren , ''Navigating Alien Worlds: An Interview with the Playwright,'' in *American Theatre,* Vol. 19, No. 2, February 2002, p. 32.

### Misha Berson

*In the following essay, Berson traces Iizuka's background and career.*

There aren't many young playwrights who name the Roman poet Catullus as one of their literary inspirations, along with Maria Irene Fornes and Adele Edling Shank. But for rising dramatist Naomi Iizuka, who avidly studied classical literature at Yale University, some ancient authors retain a bristling contemporary immediacy. And without any musty pretensions, she has enmeshed their archetypal visions into her own very singular, very up-to-date aesthetic.

Iizuka's *Polaroid Stories,* a combustible portrait of homeless youth that premiered at the 1997 Humana Festival at Actors Theatre of Louisville, draws deeply on Ovid's *Metamorphoses.* An earlier work, *Carthage,* presented by San Diego's Theatre E in 1993, relocates Virgil's tragic romance of Dido and Aeneas to the gritty modern underbelly of Los Angeles. In the often-produced *Skin,* Iizuka grafts Georg Büchner's expressionist fable *Woyzeck* onto the lives of aimless Californians. And even though there are no direct literary antecedents to spot in 1994's *Tattoo Girl,* this magical quest by a trumpet-playing seeker named Perpetua fashions its own brand of playfully hip mythos.

''I like theatre that startles me, and that makes me reappraise my relationship to the real,'' explains Iizuka, who is spending the current academic year in residence at Princeton University on a Hodder literary fellowship. "I think that's probably more readily accessed by going towards myth, or going toward something that's not, strictly speaking, realistic."

Since finishing her master's of fine arts in playwriting at the University of California-San Diego in 1992, Iizuka's thickly textured, impossible-to-pigeonhole aesthetic has been translated to the stage by such well-known directors as Robert Woodruff, Jon Jory and Moisés Kaufman. And while the 33-year-old writer has happily seen her plays developed and staged at such smaller, edgier spaces as Sledgehammer Theatre in San Diego, the Annex Theatre in Seattle and Tampa's Hillsborough Moving Company, her work is also provoking strong reaction in larger venues.

When Actors Theatre premiered *Polaroid Stories* at the 1997 Humana Festival, national critics were sharply divided in their response to the play's bleak and boisterous, profane and myth-inflected portraits of street kids tagged with the lofty names (and legendary fates) of Narcissus, Euridyce, Zeus and Persephone. Though the ATL production often felt like a relentless frontal assault of words and attitude, embedded in the monologic text and slamming physicality were shards of gleaming poetry, and a uniquely unsentimental empathy for a largely ignored, desperately inventive and frighteningly self-destructive subculture. Louisville audiences responded enthusiastically, notes ATL literary manager Michael Dixon.

"I thought in *Polaroid Stories* Naomi had the zapline to the Greeks through a kind of passion and obsession and desire that also applies to today's fringe culture of outcasts, runaways and drug addicts," reflects Dixon. "Their sense of need and fear seemed a perfect match for the emotions of the Greek myths, but the contemporary settings and characters gave you a new understanding of those myths that was emotional and visceral, not academic."

Iizuka describes her writing projects as "synchronistic," and *Polaroid Stories* is a case in point. She researched the play during 18 months spent in Minneapolis on a Jerome Foundation fellowship and a McKnight advancement grant, but came to its subject matter unexpectedly. "In Minneapolis I lived near an area where a lot of street kids congregated, kids who hopped freight trains and traveled a lot," Iizuka recalls. "I fell in with some of them and got to know them, and at about the same time En Garde Arts [of New York City] commissioned me to write a piece."

*"Looking at a Painting of Mt. Fuji" by Suzuki Harunobu*

Some of her new young friends "were very generous and told me a lot of things—it was like opening up this floodgate. Later they would actually sit with me while I was writing and look at my stuff and even correct me. I found them to be very smart—a lot of them write and draw and lead rich, creative inner lives. It would be a mistake just to call them victims. They don't think of themselves that way, and neither did I."

Using *Metamorphoses* as a framing device to dramatize their stories "was sort of an intuitive connection. There's something about it that really fits, because the world of Ovid's piece is so mythic, and so terrifying, and also at times really beautiful. There's something about the way these kids talk about stuff that's happened to them that seemed larger than life."

Fascinated by the subterranean worlds of renegades (the homeless kids in *Polaroid Stories*), outcasts (Jones, the lostsoul Woyzeck surrogate in *Skin*) and vagabonds (the runaway wife and mother in *Tattoo Girl*), Iizuka herself has led a more orderly existence—albeit one that has crossed many geographic and cultural borders. Born in Japan to an American mother of Spanish descent and a Japanese banker father, she lived in Holland as a child and later in Chevy Chase, Md. There she attended the National Cathedral School, a tony private Catholic institution catering ''to the children of diplomats.''

Iizuka loved literature but didn't discover theatre until she began studying the classics in earnest at Yale. About the same time she was reading Catullus and the Roman philosopher Lucretious in the original Latin, she was also seeing her drama-major friends perform freewheeling new plays and experimental versions of Eugene O'Neill and Tennessee Williams dramas.

A desultory year of law school at Yale led Iizuka to throw caution to the winds and enter the U.C.S.D. playwriting program, where she studied closely with dramatist Adele Edling Shank. ''Her work is hyperrealism, and I think what I took from that is a sense of creating an event that happens in real time, a theatre event that sort of washes over and hits the audience as it struggles for a certain kind of honesty.''

As Iizuka's own creative floodgates opened, a stream of freeform plays flowed out. Working at U.C.S.D. with teacher-directors Anne Bogart and Robert Woodruff also helped to shape her writing style, which matches a furious emotional intensity with a floating lyricism, vivid grunginess and acerbic humor.

Certainly Iizuka's ambitious, often dark oeuvre (which some critics have castigated for its avant-grimness) resonates with her peers in alternative spaces. But like many pragmatic artists of her generation, she tries to seize opportunity wherever it pops up instead of dividing the theatre world into Radical Us vs. Staid Them. ''I do feel very much at home in the experimental places, where doing theatre isn't at all about careerism or money,'' she confirms. ''I think playwrights need to find people of like mind to work with. But I'm finding that they're everywhere—at larger theatres and smaller ones. Ultimately, it's about finding people who'll take risks with you.''

If artists take those risks, will audiences? Living in movie-mad Southern California, Iizuka confronted head on the cultural marginalization of live theatre, and the seductions of the faster-paced, more popular gratifications of film and video. ''But theatre's interesting in part because it's *not* the main course in American entertainment. That can be frustrating, but also very liberating. There's this pocket where something can happen—live—and it can take much greater risks than *Godzilla* can. And

in a city like San Diego or Seattle, a lot of young people will come see it. You just have to make a theatre that speaks to them.''

**Source:** Misha Berson, ''Naomi Iizuka: Raising the Stakes: A Young Playwright Mixes the Lofty with the Lowly,'' in *American Theatre,* Vol. 15, No. 7, September 1998, pp. 56–57.

## SOURCES

Hughes, Robert, *The Shock of the New,* Alfred A. Knopf, 1991, p. 425.

Hume, David, ''Selections from *Enquiry Concerning Human Understanding,*'' in *Eighteenth-Century Philosophy,* edited by Lewis White Beck, Free Press, 1966, pp. 94–96.

Iizuka, Naomi, *36 Views,* Overlook Press, 2003.

Weber, Bruce, ''When Things Aren't What They Seem (Are They?),'' in the *New York Times,* March 29, 2002, p. E3.

## FURTHER READING

Japan Playwrights Association Staff, *Half a Century of Japanese Theater,* Kinokuniya Shoten Shuppanbu, 2000.
    This book contains a series of contemporary Japanese plays that have been translated into English. It is an excellent collection representing the skills and achievements of modern Japanese playwrights.

Ortolani, Benito, and Leiter, Samuel, *Japanese Theater in the World,* Japanese Foundation, 1997.
    This book traces the history of Japanese theater with over 700 objects, covering a vast range of theater traditions, ranging from the ancient to the avant-garde.

Shikibu, Murasaki, *The Tale of Genji,* translated by Royall Tyler, Penguin, 2002.
    Widely recognized as the world's first novel, *The Tale of Genji* is the eleventh-century tale of Genji, the son of an emperor, The book follows Genji's political fortunes and adventures.

Shonagon, Sei, *The Pillow Book of Sei Shonagon,* edited and translated by Ivan Morris, Columbia University Press, 1991.
    From the pen of Ivan Morris, one of the most gifted and accomplished translators of Japanese, comes Sei Shonagon, a contemporary and rival of Lady Murasaki. Shonagon spins tales fictionalizing court life during the Heian period.

# Anna in the Tropics

NILO CRUZ

2002

Nilo Cruz first intended to set his play *Anna in the Tropics* in the 1800s, a time when lectors (readers) played an important role in cigar factories. Cruz, however, reconsidered and decided that a historical account would be ''too complicated'' to render dramatically, so he chose instead to focus on the role the lector played in the factories during a time when personal and financial independence were inextricably linked. Speaking in an article by Jennifer Kiger for the South Coast Repertory Playgoers Guide, Cruz states that ''I decided to write about possibly the last lector in Tampa. The lectors were the first to be fired when the Depression began, so I set the play in 1929.'' Lectors read novels and news to the workers, who paid the lector directly from their own wages. Cruz also wanted to tell the story of Cubans who fled to the United States prior to the 1959 revolution. ''These were not immigrants. They were exiles who wanted Cuba's independence, and they would have been killed if they stayed there. I thought it was important to document this part of our culture,'' says Cruz (also quoted in Kiger). *Anna in the Tropics* was written while Cruz was playwright-in-residence at the New Theatre in Coral Gables, Florida, which first staged a production of the play in 2002.

*Anna in the Tropics* portrays the lives of cigar factory workers in Ybor City, Tampa, Florida, when a new lector, perhaps the last to ply his trade, is hired. The men and women remain divided in their loyalties as economic hardship and the pressure to

abandon old traditions force the owners of the cigar factory to adopt new, progressive manufacturing methods if they wish to stay in business. As the lector reads from *Anna Karenina*, a novel of adultery set in nineteenth-century Russia, he casts a spell over the workers, transforming their passions and desires through the affirming power of art. That the love they seek may result in a tragic end is ordained as much by the story of the Russian noblewoman as it is by the actions of the workers themselves.

## AUTHOR BIOGRAPHY

Cruz, the son of Tina and Nilo Cruz, was born in Matanzas, Cuba, in 1961. A staunch opponent of the new communist government, Cruz's father, a shoe salesman, was incarcerated in 1962 for opposing the increased militarization that resulted from Cuba's ties with the Soviet Union. After his release from prison, the elder Cruz was subsequently caught onboard a ship in an attempt to flee to the United States, where he would prepare for his family's arrival at a later date. Cruz's parents remained steadfast in their opposition to the Castro regime; they bought food on the black market and withheld their son from a highly organized system of physical education classes by having a physician friend declare that Nilo had contracted hepatitis. Consequently, Nilo was forced to perpetuate the lie and could not play outdoors with his friends as he had previously. In 1970, the family took a Freedom Flight to the United States, but his parents later divorced. Cruz earned a master of fine arts degree from Brown University in 1994.

In 2000, Cruz was appointed playwright-in-residence at the McCarter Theatre in Princeton, New Jersey, while receiving a similar appointment at the New Theatre in Coral Gables, Florida, which commissioned and produced *Anna in the Tropics* in 2002. Cruz has received grants from the Theatre Communications Group, the Rockefeller Foundation, and the National Endowment for the Arts. His play *Night Train to Bolina* won the W. Alton Jones Award; *Two Sisters and a Piano* received the Kennedy Center Fund for New American Plays Award. Cruz won the American Theatre Critics/Steinberg New Play Award for *Anna in the Tropics* just two days before winning the 2003 Pulitzer Prize for Drama. Upon learning that he had won the award,

Cruz had this to say (quoted in an article in the *New Theatre*): "By honoring my play *Anna in the Tropics*, the first Latino play to earn the Pulitzer Prize in Drama, the Pulitzer Prize Board is not only embracing my work as an artist, but is actually acknowledging and securing a place for Latino plays in the North American theater." Another note of interest is that *Anna in the Tropics* was selected by the Pulitzer Prize jury before the play was performed in New York City.

Cruz has taught drama at Brown University, Yale University, and the University of Iowa. Cruz's previously produced plays were set to be published in book form in 2004 by Dramatist's Play Service. His *The Beauty of the Father* was also set to premiere at the New Theatre and at the Seattle Repertory Theatre during the 2003–2004 theater season.

## PLOT SUMMARY

### *Act 1, Scene 1*

*Anna in the Tropics* begins with Santiago and Cheché betting money at a cockfight. Eliades, the bookie and promoter of the contests, calls out the names of the combatants as Santiago and Cheché make their wagers. Santiago becomes engrossed in the action, raising his bets impulsively while Cheché takes a more cautious approach. When Cheché wins the first time, Santiago tells him, "You're a lucky man."

After losing his second wager, Santiago asks Cheché for a loan of two hundred dollars so that he, Santiago, can continue betting. Here Cheché demonstrates the acumen that makes him an astute businessman, for he tells Santiago, "I don't lend any money when I'm gambling, and I don't lend any money when I'm drinking." Santiago insists, however, declaring, "With your lucky money I'll show you what I can do."

Cheché finally relents, but when neither one of them can find a piece of paper upon which Santiago may write a promissory note, Santiago carves the amount he owes on the bottom of Cheché's shoe with a knife, signing his name with an *S* below the sum. Despite this assurance, Cheché remains doubtful about whether Santiago will repay the loan. "I'll pay you back," Santiago assures him. "I'm your brother, for God's sake!'' When Santiago loses the second fight and asks Cheché to lend him two hundred dollars more, Cheché declines, saying that Santiago is ''jinxed.'' Santiago convinces Cheché to loan him the money by promising to give him part of the cigar factory if he does not pay the loan. Once Santiago has finished carving the new total, he tries to persuade Cheché to wear his shoe, but Cheché refuses, knowing that his footsteps would erase the figures, thus relieving Santiago of his obligation.

Meanwhile, Marela, Conchita, and Ofelia stand by the seaport waiting for the cigar factory's new lector to arrive. They take turns admiring his photograph, commenting upon the qualities a good lector possesses. Ofelia confesses to her daughters that she has taken some of Santiago's money to pay for the lector's trip. She does not feel guilty about taking the money because she knows that Santiago would probably lose the money gambling. ''I'll spend my money on the best lector we can get,'' Ofelia says.

The three women then provide a history of the cigar factory's previous lectors. Teodoro, an eighty-year-old man who died three months ago, should have, in Marela's opinion, given up his job years ago because his heart ''couldn't take the love stories.'' The last novel he read was *Wuthering Heights*. Conchita then remarks that Teodoro's replacement didn't last long, for reasons that are explained later in the play. Because so many ships from Europe and South America stop in Cuba, Conchita expects the lector to bring new books with him.

As the ship pulls into port, Marela confesses that she has followed the palm reader's advice and put the lector's name in a glass of water filled with brown sugar and cinnamon so that he would accept their offer of employment. Ofelia warns her daughter about playing with spells and altering another's destiny. Conchita adds that such simple spells are how witches learn their craft. She then tells a story about how one woman couldn't stop crying after she put a spell on her lover and he died. Marela admits to feeling ''awful,'' albeit more from fear that the spell will not work than from regret for having cast it.

When the women can see no sign of the lector among the many men wearing hats, Ofelia blames Marela's spell for their misfortune. Marela is nervous with anticipation at the lector's arrival, a nervousness that grows with each passing minute. Ofelia hopes that the lector will be able to detect the gardenia she wears in her hat. Marela, believing that her spell has ''ruined'' the lector's arrival, vows to

*Nilo Cruz*

return home to remove his name from the glass of water. The lector, Juan Julian, having spied Ofelia's white gardenia from afar, approaches the three women just as Marela prepares to leave. As Juan Julian introduces himself to the women, Marela, suffering from nervousness, wets herself. Rather than embarrass the young woman further with his presence, Juan Julian leaves to find the steward.

### Act 1, Scene 2

Juan Julian reports to work to perform his first reading. Cheché asks a few questions of him before figuring out that Juan Julian is a lector. ''If you're looking for a job, we're not hiring . . .,'' says Cheché. Juan Julian tries to convince Cheché that he is not looking for a job because he has already been hired. Ofelia arrives to clarify the situation.

Ofelia discusses with Juan Julian some of the other workers whom he has already met. All of these workers, who come from places such as Spain and Italy, share a desire for romance. When Juan Julian asks Marela about the man whom he has just met, she refers to Cheché by his American name, ''Chester,'' and calls him a ''clown.'' Ofelia, Marela's mother, quickly corrects her, explaining Cheché's relationship to the family and his arrival at the factory.

When Juan Julian suggests that Cheché does not like him, Ofelia dismisses this fear, saying that Cheché is intoxicated with the power her husband, Santiago, has given him. Conchita foreshadows the play's outcome when she says, ''Cheché has a knack for turning the smallest incident into a loud and tragic event.''

The women take turns explaining that Cheché's dislike of lectors is cultural: he does not understand the tradition of reading to the workers because he comes from New Jersey, so he dismisses the need for a lector completely. Furthermore, says Marela, Cheché believes that ''lectors are the ones who cause trouble.''

Marela offers that perhaps the real reason Cheché does not like lectors is because his wife, a ''southern belle from Atlanta,'' ran away with the last lector the factory hired. Ofelia believes that all lectors have been unfairly blamed as a result of Cheché's experience. She tells Juan Julian to report any trouble to her husband.

Juan Julian announces that *Anna Karenina* (pronounced Ah-nah Kar-eh-neen-ah with a Cuban accent) will be his first selection. Juan Julian offers to read from another book when Marela learns that, in Juan Julian's opinion, the book is ''Quite romantic.'' Marela believes that a love story will be good for Cheché, so she tells Juan Julian to continue.

Ofelia then engages Juan Julian in a conversation about how the landscape and climate in Tampa differs from that in Cuba. The sky seems bigger, and there is more light. ''There doesn't seem to be a place where one could hide,'' continues Juan Julian. Juan Julian and Marela flirt and philosophize with each other as they discuss the many types of light that exist in the world. Marela concludes that the light reflected off the skin is ''the most difficult one to escape.''

In a comical scene, Cheché appears holding a shoe in his hand. He is trying to collect on the debt owed to him by his brother. Ofelia tells him that she cannot honor the debt because she has no money. However, Cheché does not want money; he wants his half of the factory.

### Act 1, Scene 3

Juan Julian reads from *Anna Karenina* as he strolls among the workers, who are entranced by the sound of his voice as they handle the leaf tobacco. He reads a passage from the book, one told from the heroine's perspective, that speaks of the shame and humiliation Anna feels for betraying her husband, yet the passion she feels for her lover, a passion which is returned in kind, is worth the price she must pay. Like a good storyteller, especially one who wishes to keep his job, Juan Julian ends the story shortly thereafter to heighten the element of suspense. ''That's all for today from *Anna Karenina*,'' he says, greeted by the sound of applause.

Overcome by the passionate story Juan Julian has just read to them, Marela, Conchita, and Ofelia romanticize about the lector, referring to him as ''the Persian Canary'' because ''it's like hearing a bird sing when he reads.'' Cheché makes some insinuating comments about how the women have fallen under the spell of yet another love story, saying that ''For some reason I never hear the story the same way that you do''; but they refuse to let him spoil the enchantment and enthusiasm they feel now that a professional lector is in their midst. Palomo, Conchita's husband, enters the discussion, suggesting that perhaps the reason why he and Cheché don't interpret the story the same way is because they are men. The men and women are divided in their opinions, but Ofelia, with the support of her two daughters, defends her decision to hire a lector. ''Only a fool can fail to understand the importance of having a lector read to us while we work,'' she says.

Cheché argues that having a lector at the factory will create ''another tragic love story.'' When Palomo admits to liking love stories, Cheché stands alone. Soon everyone talks about what type of stories they like and how Juan Julian's reading has made the characters in *Anna Karenina* come alive. Marela dreams of snow and the images are so vivid that she wants to borrow a fur coat for when she travels to Russia in her imagination. ''He chose the right book,'' says Ofelia. ''There's nothing like reading a winter book in the middle of summer.''

The men exit, and the women pore over some of the more passionate lines from the book. They discuss what it must be like to be part of a lover's triangle, though the irony is not lost upon Conchita, who is thinking about her own life. The women conjecture about the characters' actions, experiencing their problems vicariously. ''When Juan Julian starts reading,'' says Marela, ''the story enters my body and I become the second skin of the characters.'' Ofelia sees that her daughter is infatuated with the lector and chides her for letting her dreams run away from her. The women then discuss dreams and whether it is foolish to have them. "We have to remember to keep our feet on the ground and stay living inside our shoes and not have lofty illusions," concludes Ofelia.

Marela and Ofelia are discussing the importance of a man's cigar when Palomo enters. He and Conchita will be working late. Marela and Ofelia bid goodbye, and soon thereafter the couple discusses Santiago's gambling habit. Conchita changes the subject by asking Palomo if he likes the novel that Juan Julian is reading to them. Conchita, eager to test her husband's reaction, asks him if hearing about Anna's affair makes him "uncomfortable." Palomo responds by saying that he does not think about the love affairs so much because "It seems like in every novel there's always a love affair." Rather, he thinks about all the money the characters have. Conchita and Palomo get into an argument over his inability to appreciate literature. Palomo thinks that "Money can buy everything," but Conchita says that money can't buy the places she occupies within her imagination.

Their conversation turns toward their marriage. "I don't know why I married you," Palomo tells Conchita. She says he married her because she gave him a cigar, one she had rolled especially for him. Conchita continues to view the beginnings of their relationship romantically, but Palomo insists that he married her because of an unnamed obligation he owed to her father. Upon hearing this, Conchita realizes that Palomo never really cared for her. Seeking an outlet for her disappointment, she once again launches an attack against him for being unable to appreciate the finer points of literature. To drive home her point, she cites an episode from *Anna Karenina* in which Anna's husband becomes suspicious of an affair; Conchita tests Palomo's ability to comprehend the example. Palomo understands her implications completely. Conchita makes a direct comparison between their lives and those of the characters in *Anna Karenina* but with a twist of irony: "Anna and her husband remind me of us. Except I'm more like the husband."

Conchita chides Palomo about his "secret love," drawing the analogy between art and life even further. She wants to know more about her husband's mistress; she wants to know what she does to make him happy. Palomo responds by asking Conchita if she wants a divorce, but Conchita would prefer to take a lover instead. Palomo blames *Anna Karenina* for putting these ideas into his wife's head, saying, "This book will be the end of us."

However, Conchita recognizes that her desires do not have to be absolute. She can learn to love her husband in a different manner than before. She quotes a line from the book: "If there are as many minds as there are heads, then there are as many kinds of love as there are hearts."

## *Act 1, Scene 4*

In this comical scene at the family house, Ofelia and Santiago, who are not on speaking terms, conduct a conversation by using their daughter Marela as an intermediary. Santiago has no money to buy cigarettes, but Ofelia refuses to give him any money, calling him "a drunk, a thief and a-good-for-nothing gambler." After a few exchanges, they speak to each other directly. Santiago threatens to pawn his wedding ring, but Ofelia, in a barbed reply loaded with double entendre that speaks volumes about the state of their marital relations, says that he might as well since "his finger got numb."

Unable to tolerate her parents' bickering anymore, Marela leaves. In an effort to mollify his wife's wounded sensibilities, Santiago comments on the new lector's performance, though he does not mention him by name. Reconciled temporarily by their interest in *Anna Karenina,* the couple discusses the qualities that make Levin "a dedicated man." Ofelia remarks that her husband was once like Levin. The topic shifts from a real estate transaction in the book to control of the cigar factory, with Santiago admitting that drink impairs his business decisions. Ofelia warns him about Cheché's attempts to mechanize production. "You need to go back to the factory," she says. Santiago agrees, saying, "To the factory I need to go back."

Ashamed of his actions, Santiago admits to having been a fool. He refuses to leave the family's house, however, until he is able to pay the debt he owes Cheché. Ofelia says that he's being silly, but Santiago insists that this is what he must do to restore his self-respect. Santiago turns the subject to Levin again, asking Ofelia about the woman whom he loves, Kitty. Ofelia explains the love triangle that prevents Levin from winning Kitty's love. Santiago, drawing inspiration from Levin's fidelity to one woman, "*swallows the gulp of love*" as he fails to tell Ofelia his true feelings for her. Thus reminded of his inadequacies, Santiago explains his poor luck at gambling as the result of his failure to perform some small ritual such as polishing his shoes or leaving the house in disarray. "Every time I lose, I feel that something has been taken from me. Something bigger than money," he says. Gambling has caused Santiago to lose self-respect, and he wonders if, perhaps, he hasn't lost Ofelia too? "If you had lost me, I wouldn't be here," she tells him. "If you had lost me, I wouldn't be by your side." What begins as a comical scene ends on a romantic note.

### Act 1, Scene 5

Juan Julian, Marela, and Conchita are at the factory. Juan Julian says that he feels "asphyxiated" when he is in a city; he prefers to be in the country instead. He philosophizes on how people allow themselves to get away from nature. He sees the "verdure of nature" as a restorative force. Conchita agrees, asking him why he chose to read Tolstoy. Juan Julian responds by saying that "Tolstoy understands humanity like no other writer does."

Conchita asks Juan Julian how he became a lector. He explains that he discovered books one summer while he and his family were forced to remain inside their house in order to maintain the appearance that they had gone away on a trip. His mother would read to him and his siblings while his father worked abroad to earn money to repay his many creditors. That's when, says Juan Julian, "I became a listener and I learned to appreciate stories and the sound of words."

Juan Julian and Conchita discuss how people from the North, like Cheché, are different from others. Conchita tells a story of how she gave a braid to a boy from New London and told him to bury it under a tree in honor of the feast of Saint Candelaria, which celebrates fertility and the growth of the soil. The boy said that he would be too embarrassed to dig a hole in front of everyone in the park, so Conchita took her braid back from him and buried it herself. The two never spoke to each other again. That, she says, is the only person she ever met who was from New England.

Juan Julian asks Conchita if she still observes the ritual of cutting her hair on the second day of February, to which Conchita replies, "Yes. My father does me the honor of burying it." Juan Julian asks why her husband does not perform the ritual, for that would be "an honor for any man." Juan Julian continues making his overture, saying that he would find "an old, wise banyan tree" and bury Conchita's hair by the tree's roots, but she says that she will cut her hair short like the film star Clara Bow, thus ending the ritual. Juan Julian says that he will find a "strong-looking tree," although he reminds her that the ritual will not count if it is not performed on the appropriate date. "I believe that everything counts if you have faith," she replies, adding that he, as a lector, should believe in "rescuing things from oblivion." Juan Julian asks if there is a story in her hair. "There will be the day I cut it," she explains, "and that story will come to an end." If one may read the story of her hair as one reads a face or a book, then Juan Julian believes that Conchita's hair should be placed inside a book instead of beneath a tree. He chooses a passage from *Anna Karenina* in which Anna realizes that she is deceiving herself. Conchita hands Juan Julian a pair of scissors with which to cut her hair, but soon they are locked in a tender embrace.

### Act 2, Scene 1

The second act begins with Juan Julian's recorded voice reciting a passage from *Anna Karenina* in which the narrator explores the "complexity" of Anna's feelings as she reflects upon "all that was in her soul." Meanwhile, Conchita and Juan Julian make love on one of the factory tables. Once they've finished and start to dress, Juan Julian tells Conchita that he would like to meet her someplace else, perhaps in a hotel. In an exchange in which both characters use strong metaphorical language to describe the other's condition, Juan Julian notes a sadness in Conchita's eyes after they make love; he recommends that she listen to a canary sing for five minutes a day to ease her sorrow. If she cannot find a canary, then he suggests that she listen to him sing while he's in the shower. Their banter is interrupted when they hear the sound of Cheché arguing.

Cigar workers gather around Cheché as he tries to explain to Ofelia a piece of machinery he has ordered. Cheché insists that he be heard because he owns shares in the factory. Ofelia has someone fetch Santiago, with the hope that he will be able to put the matter to rest. Cheché persists, however, saying that all the other cigar companies have automated production. A debate ensues about the aesthetics of a hand-rolled cigar as compared to one rolled by machine. Cheché argues that progress is not only inevitable but a necessity, for the cigar factory is operating in the same manner it was decades ago. When Ofelia asks about the workers that machines have displaced, Cheché points out that machines need workers to operate them; therefore, very few jobs are lost. Palomo enters the discussion, but Cheché interrupts him when Palomo mentions a lector at a competing factory. "Ah, Leonardo is a lector!" says Cheché. "What does he know about machines?"

Palomo defends Leonardo, saying that his friend upholds many fine traditions that machines would otherwise destroy. Cheché observes that lectors are the first to be fired from the factories because no one can hear them recite above the noise of the machinery. Cheché adds insult to injury by saying that he can see no reason why someone would want to contribute part of his or her wages to someone who reads romantic novels.

Marela defends the need for a lector, insisting that "the words he reads are like a breeze that breaks the monotony of this factory." Juan Julian joins the discussion, citing the tradition of having a lector as going back to an ancient Taino custom, for the Taino Indians believed that tobacco leaves "whisper the language of the sky." As a descendent of the cacique, or chief Indian, the lector interprets the words of the gods and brings them to the "oidores," or listeners. Juan Julian concludes by suggesting that Cheché, whom he addresses as "Señor Chester," spend more money on advertising rather than machines. "Or are you working for the machine industry?" he asks.

Ofelia supports the lector's argument by saying that more advertising will help them sell more cigars. Juan Julian tells "Chester" that cigars have fallen out of favor with the public because people wish to emulate the many film stars who smoke cigarettes onscreen. "You can go to Hollywood and offer our cigars to producers," Juan Julian tells him. He continues, saying that machines now dictate the pace of life to such an extent that no one has time for leisurely pursuits, much less nature. "So you see, Chester," says the lector, "you want modernity, and modernity is actually destroying our very own industry. The very act of smoking a cigar." All of the workers, except for Cheché and Palomo, applaud the lector's comments. Juan Julian offers to leave the room so that the workers may vote, but Ofelia tells him that it's obvious that they want him to stay. Juan Julian insists, however, upon deciding things "the democratic way."

Santiago arrives and is quickly apprised of the situation. He does not see the point of taking a vote if, in the minds of the workers, the matter has been settled. Ofelia says that taking a vote is "the American way," but Santiago fails to comprehend her logic. He introduces himself to the lector, and shortly thereafter Santiago asks for a show of hands from those workers who wish to dispense with the lector's services. Palomo and Cheché are the only ones who raise their hands. Santiago declares that

Juan Julian shall stay. He then announces that the factory will begin producing a new brand of cigar and that Marela will pose as Anna Karenina for the cigar's label. Santiago brings some clothes for her to wear, and she leaves to try them on.

Santiago demonstrates beyond question that he is in charge of the factory when he delivers a short speech telling the workers that much work and a brighter future lie ahead. The workers applaud and leave the factory. Santiago then hands Cheché an envelope filled with money, thereby settling his debt. Even though he no longer owns a share of the factory, Cheché objects to the production of a new cigar line, citing the exorbitant price of tobacco in Cuba. Santiago refuses to hear Cheché's arguments, ordering him to return the machine to the manufacturer. He asks his brother to fetch him a calendar, for Santiago must now calculate a schedule of payments for a loan that he needs to launch this new line of cigars. "This time I'm betting my money on the factory," he says.

Santiago does not understand Cheché's habit of crossing out days on the calendar before they have expired. He sees this as a sign of "apprehension, anxiety and even despair." Cheché confesses that he can no longer tolerate working at the factory because every attempt he makes at modernizing production is turned away. Santiago does not believe that this is the sole reason for his brother's discomfort, and Cheché responds by saying that he still thinks of his Mildred, his wife who ran away with the previous lector. He admits to Santiago that Juan Julian's presence reminds him of how he was cuckolded.

Marela enters, modeling the clothes her father gave her. "You'll make a great Anna," he tells her, and then he leaves to find a flower for her hair. Marela's beauty arouses Cheché's ardor. "You look beautiful," he tells her just before Juan Julian joins them. He also comments on her appearance, but he has forgotten his book and leaves to retrieve it, leaving Marela and Cheché alone.

Cheché, noticing that Marela seems to have been daydreaming more than ever lately, comments on the quality of her work. As always, Cheché blames the lector for problems at the factory. "You have to pay less attention to the reader and more attention to what you're doing," he says. Marela refuses to let Juan Julian become a scapegoat by pointing out that he reminds Cheché of his wife every time he reads from *Anna Karenina*. Cheché stands his ground, however. He accuses Marela of taking shortcuts, and he shows Marela some of the faulty cigars she has wrapped. Marela attempts to dismiss Cheché's accusations with laughter, but she stops short when she sees him looking at her with longing in his eyes. He caresses her hair, but she moves away from him. After admitting that the lector reminds him of his wife, Cheché tries to kiss Marela, but she pushes him away, warning him to never touch her again.

### Act 2, Scene 2

While isolated from the scene's action, Juan Julian recites a passage from *Anna Karenina* that describes Anna's husband's naïveté. Meanwhile, Conchita is rolling cigars at her table when Palomo enters and asks her what time she meets her lover. Conchita does not deny the accusation. Palomo wants to know if her lover reads to her, and Conchita says that he does when she looks sad. She tells her husband that, in order for her to get used to her lover's body, she must make love to him repeatedly; her lover insists upon it. "He says things a woman likes to hear," she adds without malice. Palomo wants to know more about his wife's sex life, and she complies by providing him with salacious details that he seems to enjoy vicariously. Palomo attributes his curiosity to a change he's noticed in Conchita, and he begins his questioning again by asking if the lector ever asks about him. "Yes," replies Conchita. "He wanted to know why you stopped loving me."

Despite having taken a lover, Conchita still loves her husband. She describes what it was like making love to the lector as though he were her husband. "It was terrifying," she says, because "everything seemed so recognizable, as if he had known me all along." Palomo then asks Conchita to show him how the lector made love to her, and she responds by saying, "You would have to do as actors do"; that is to say, he would have to surrender. "You would have to let go of yourself and enter the life of another human being, and in this case it would be me," she tells her husband. Juan Julian closes the book as Conchita leads her husband to her trysting place within the factory.

### Act 2, Scene 3

Santiago and Ofelia preside over the new cigar brand's inauguration as workers dressed in their finest clothes arrive at the factory. Bottles of rum and glasses are passed around. The couple shares a toast with Juan Julian, and then the three of them exit.

Palomo tells Cheché, another man whose wife has had an affair, that he can't stop thinking about Conchita and her lover. Cheché recommends that Palomo move to North Trenton to start a new life and work at one of the cigar factories there. "And there are no lectors and no good-for-nothing love stories," he adds.

Juan Julian asks Palomo to help him with the lanterns, and the two men soon engage in a conversation about love stories. Juan Julian accuses Palomo of trying to have him fired, but Palomo says that he's curious to know how the novel ends, so Juan Julian shouldn't take his actions personally. Cheché, knowing that Juan Julian is having an affair with Conchita, asks the lector if Anna's husband ever thought of killing his wife's lover. Juan Julian says that Anna's husband, being a man of power and influence, would rather avoid a scandal than resort to such desperate measures. When Palomo asks the lector which character in the novel he identifies with most, Juan Julian replies, "I like them all. I learn things from all of them." Palomo wants to know more about Anna's lover, especially about what made Vronsky become interested in her. Juan Julian is well aware of Palomo's insinuations, and he explains that Anna came to Vronsky because "she thought that he could help her." Juan Julian adds that Vronsky could help her find love and to "recognize herself as a woman all over again." Through Vronsky, Anna learns "a new way of loving . . . that makes her go back to the lover over and over again."

Santiago and Ofelia enter, and they are joined by Conchita, who accepts their invitation to have a drink. The women have a playful argument about Conchita's paisley dress which, Ofelia says, makes her daughter look like an old woman. Palomo disagrees, saying that the dress makes Conchita look more "bohemian." When Juan Julian comments on Conchita's dress, Palomo becomes more possessive of his wife and puts his arm around her waist, pulling her closer to him.

Juan Julian wants to know why alcohol is prohibited in America. In an unintentional play on words, Santiago says it is because Americans "are not socialists when they drink." Palomo then compares alcohol to literature because "Literature brings out the best and the worst part of ourselves. If you're angry it brings out your anger. If you are sad, it brings out your sadness." Ofelia, slightly tipsy from the rum, says that alcohol is prohibited because "most Americans don't know how to dance."

Santiago proudly removes the new cigar from his shirt pocket and makes a short speech telling everyone about the product's specifications. Marela enters dressed in a long black gown like the one Anna wears on the night of the ball, and everyone comments on how beautiful Marela looks. Ofelia performs the honor of lighting the first cigar, and then a ritual is observed whereby the cigar is passed from one person to another through an intermediary so as to facilitate communication with the gods. Everyone gives the cigar high praise. When his turn to pass the cigar arrives, however, Palomo disregards the ritual by handing the cigar directly to Juan Julian—an obvious slight. Juan Julian, rising above the insult, smiles and makes a gesture of supplication to the gods before taking a puff.

"We do have a cigar, señores! We have a champion!" announces Santiago. Marela proposes that they hand out free cigars in the street, but, rather than go bankrupt, Santiago offers that they fire a gunshot instead because, according to him, "No inauguration is complete without the breaking of a bottle or a gunshot." They settle on three gunshots as the proper number, and soon everyone leaves to go outside." Palomo grabs Conchita by the arm before she can leave and, in a pique of jealousy, accuses his wife of falling in love with the lector. "Maybe just as much as you are," Conchita replies, for why else would Palomo want to know so much about him? "I don't like men," Palomo answers as the sound of a gunshot and laughter reverberate. Palomo explains his interest by saying that it stems from the "old habit" of listening, but Conchita does not accept this explanation. "You're right there's something else," admits Palomo. "And it's terrible sometimes." Conchita, aware that her suspicion about her husband's sexual orientation may indeed be correct, says, "Then nothing makes sense to me anymore." The couple hears another gunshot and more laughter as Palomo insists that his wife tell her lover that she wants to "make love like a knife." Conchita wants to know why Palomo would choose a knife for a symbol, and he says it is because "everything has to be killed." Another gunshot goes off before Juan Julian and the rest of Conchita's family reenter the factory.

Ofelia, who has had much to drink, then tells a story of how when she was seventeen she was forced to model for a guava marmalade label rather than offend her mother by posing for a cigar label and causing a scandal. Everyone has a good laugh at Ofelia's expense, herself included.

Ofelia and Santiago exit, as do Conchita and Palomo, but Marela remains behind to speak to Juan Julian. Marela, full of joy, confesses that she does not want the night to end. At first Juan Julian believes that she has had too much to drink, but then he realizes that Marela is truly happy. Meanwhile, Cheché watches them from afar. Marela and Juan Julian flirt with each other, using poetical, metaphorical language. Alluding to the affection she feels for Juan Julian, Marela tells him, "But we are all blind in the eyes of those who can't see." The two share nothing more than a caress before they say goodnight. As she is preparing to leave, Marela asks Juan Julian to lend her the book. He has forgotten that he is carrying the book in his hand and does not hand it over until she promises not to read ahead.

As Marela reads a passage out loud, Cheché emerges from his hiding place, full of lust and desire for Marela. She closes the book before he grabs her by the arm. The lights fade, leaving what happens next to speculation.

### Act 2, Scene 4

Conchita and Palomo are at the factory the day after the celebration. Cheché is nowhere to be found, and a delivery boy is waiting to be paid. Palomo is about to take inventory, but Conchita says that she must first clean up the mess from the party before she can help him. Ofelia and Santiago arrive, and Santiago too wonders where his brother is. Santiago thinks that Cheché is late for work because he suffers from a hangover, as Santiago does. Marela arrives for work wearing a coat, her pockets "full of December, January and February." Ofelia worries that something is wrong with her daughter, but Marela assures her that she is fine.

Marela returns Juan Julian's copy of *Anna Karenina* to him when he arrives. Juan Julian notices her coat but does not comment on it. Palomo wonders if Cheché has come in, but still there is no sign of him. Juan Julian begins by reading a passage about a duel. As the lector reads to the workers, Cheché enters without a sound, his head "heavy with dark thoughts." The passage the lector is reading explores the thoughts of Anna Karenina's husband as he prepares himself for a duel. Meanwhile, Cheché, lurking in the background, pulls out a gun. Cheché shoots Juan Julian, firing twice, the gunshots echoing throughout the factory. The lector falls to the floor as the shocked workers look to see where the shots came from. Marela touches Juan Julian as he lies dying.

### Act 2, Scene 5

Three days after the shooting, the workers are back at their tables rolling cigars. As a gesture of mourning, Marela still wears her coat. Ofelia cannot bear the silence that has resulted from the lector's absence. "It's as if a metal blanket has fallen on us," she says. Palomo compares the silence to the one that followed the death of Teodoro, but Ofelia says that this silence is louder "because Juan Julian died before his time, and the shadows of the young are heavier and they linger over the earth like a cloud." Marela suggests that she once again write his name on a piece of paper and put it in a glass of sugar water so that Juan Julian's spirit will know that it is welcome at the factory. Tears falling from her eyes, Marela insists that this would not be a wrong thing for her to do. She awaits a response from her mother, but Ofelia remains silent. Marela insists that it is the responsibility of the living to look after the dead "so they can feel part of the world. So they don't forget us and we could count on them when we cross to the other side."

Conchita suggests that they should continue reading, but she does not know if she has the courage to do so herself. Ofelia extends an invitation for someone to read, and Palomo accepts. Ofelia wishes to get rid of "this silence and this heat." Santiago, however, suggests that they read something other than *Anna Karenina,* but Marela insists that the book should be finished. Conchita adds, "Stories should be finished or they suffer the same fate as those who die before their time."

Palomo opens the book and looks at Conchita as he prepares to read a passage about Anna Karenina's husband and an important decision he has reached. Palomo looks up from the book and stares at Conchita as he reads the following line: "In his letter he was going to write everything he'd been meaning to tell her."

### CHARACTERS

### Anna's Husband

Anna's husband, whose name is Karenin, is a man of wealth, influence, and good social standing who is at first naïve about the true nature of his wife's relationship with Vronsky. When he finally realizes that his wife is having an affair, he struggles

with how he should comport himself, for he wishes to avoid a scandal at all costs. He decides to write Anna a letter.

### Boy from New London

The boy from New London is the only person from New England whom Conchita has met. According to her, he was so shy that "when he expressed any sort of feeling, he would excuse himself." One year, on the second day of February, she gave him a braid of her hair to bury under a tree, as is the custom performed on the feast of Saint Candelaria. However, the boy was too embarrassed to dig a hole in the park where everyone could see, so Conchita took her braid back from him, dug a hole to shame him, and buried the braid herself. The boy from New London never spoke to her again.

### Carmela

Carmela is the palm reader who tells Marela that Juan Julian, a professional lector from Cuba, will come to their factory to read for them if she sweetens his name with sugar water.

### Cheché

Cheché is Santiago's half brother from "up North" who claims partial ownership in the factory as the result of winning a wager. Ever since Cheché's wife Mildred left him for a lector, he has expressed nothing but disdain for the love stories the lector reads because he believes that these tales of romance influenced his wife's decision. Despite strong opposition from his family and the rest of the factory workers, Cheché wants to modernize the cigar factory's operations with machinery that will perform production tasks more efficiently.

### Chester

*See* Cheché

### Conchita

Conchita is Ofelia and Santiago's oldest daughter. She, like her sister Marela and husband Palomo, rolls cigars at the factory. Conchita has an affair with Juan Julian shortly after he arrives; however, she makes no effort to hide the affair from her husband. Conchita takes delight in telling her husband details of her love affair because she believes that Palomo still has a mistress. Conchita defends the need for a lector at the factory because, in her opinion, money can't buy the places and things that occupy her dreams. Furthermore, she understands that ''anybody who dedicates his life to reading books believes in rescuing things from oblivion''; that is to say, without a lector, the factory would be a lifeless place to work. For her, literature offers a way of learning about the world.

### Eliades

Eliades is a gamester who takes wagers on the local cockfights he runs.

### Juan Julian

Juan Julian, ''the best lector west of Havana,'' arrives at the cigar factory at Ofelia's behest. Known to Ofelia and her daughters as the ''Persian Canary'' because ''it's like hearing a bird sing when he reads,'' Juan Julian is a man who believes in the restorative power of nature. He warns of how machines are destroying the stillness and quiet that people need to contemplate their lives to such an extent that machines, and the so-called ''modernity'' they introduce, are destroying ''[t]he very act of smoking a cigar.'' As a lector, Juan Julian sees himself as a descendent of the cacique, a Taino Indian chief, who translated the ''sacred words of the deities.'' He is a man who believes in the eternal verities. For this reason he chooses to read *Anna Karenina* because ''Tolstoy understands humanity like no other writer does.'' Juan Julian becomes involved in an adulterous affair with Conchita even though he knows that Palomo is aware of his wife's infidelity.

### Anna Karenina

Anna Karenina is the eponymous heroine of a novel by Leo Tolstoy. She forms one of two love triangles in the novel, for she is married to Karenin but has an affair with Vronsky.

### Kitty

Kitty forms part of the second love triangle in *Anna Karenina*. She is the object of Levin's desire.

### Levin

Levin is a character in *Anna Karenina* who owns a farm in the countryside. He is Santiago's favorite character because Levin is a ''dedicated man'' who reminds Santiago of himself when he was young and took over control of the cigar factory

# MEDIA
# ADAPTATIONS

- Still photographs of the cast that performed *Anna in the Tropics* at the Royal Theatre in New York may be downloaded by opening a Web browser to http://www.playbill.com/multimedia/ search/3239.html and clicking on the thumbnail images.

- *Anna Karenina* was first made into a film in 1915, though the 1935 version, starring Greta Garbo as Anna and Fredric March as Vronsky, is perhaps the most well known. Many versions of the Tolstoy classic have appeared on both the silver screen and television in the years since, with a miniseries directed by Sergei Solovyov scheduled for broadcast in 2005.

from his father. Levin is a wise and judicious man who makes sound business decisions. He is in love with Kitty.

### Manola

Manola does the stuffing at the cigar factory. A true romantic, she keeps a picture of Rudolph Valentino on her work table. Ironically, she is exactly the type of person whom Juan Julian refers to when he says that people are switching from cigars to cigarettes to emulate the stars they see on screen. Manola takes such delight in hearing romantic tales that sometimes she becomes ''a sea of tears'' when listening to them.

### Marela

Marela is Ofelia and Santiago's youngest daughter. She casts a spell to bring the lector to the factory, but then wets herself when she discovers that the spell has worked all too well. Like the other women in her family, she believes that Juan Julian should continue reading at the factory because ''the words he reads are like a breeze that breaks the monotony of [the] factory.'' Marela is so entranced by the story of Anna Karenina and her lover Vronsky that she begins to dream of snow. When her father announces the production of a new cigar inspired by the pages of *Anna Karenina,* Marela models for the label that bears the Russian heroine's name. She is the victim of Cheché's violent advances, though Cruz doesn't mention rape specifically. Dazed from the attack, Marela is further devastated when she learns of Juan Julian's death. She appears for work three days after Juan Julian's death wearing a heavy fur coat, as if to perpetuate the dream of Russia, snow, and romance.

## Peppino Mellini

Peppino Mellini is the "best buncher" at the cigar factory. According to Ofelia, he has a "soft spot for love stories." A native of Napoli, Italy, Peppino sings Neapolitan songs at the end of the workday.

## Mildred

A "southern belle from Atlanta," Mildred is Cheché's wife who ran away with the cigar factory's previous lector.

## Ofelia

Ofelia is Santiago's wife and Marela and Conchita's mother. She plays Kitty to Santiago's Levin, telling him, "If you had lost me, I wouldn't be here. If you had lost me, I wouldn't be by your side." Ofelia is responsible for bringing Juan Julian to Ybor City from Cuba, having paid for his fare with money she took from her husband. She believes that having a lector at the factory is an absolute necessity and thus strongly opposes Cheché's efforts to modernize the factory. Because Ofelia once had the opportunity to model for a cigar label but had to settle for a marmalade label instead to avoid causing a scandal for her mother, Ofelia consents to Marela posing for the new Anna Karenina label.

## Palomo

Palomo, a cigar roller, is Conchita's husband. His sexual orientation remains ambiguous, yet he seems possessive of Conchita whenever they are among other workers, especially Juan Julian. Palomo sides with Cheché when he tries to have the lector fired even though he, Palomo, enjoys the story of *Anna Karenina.* Palomo is angry when he discovers his wife's affair with the lector, but, rather than insist that she end it, he asks her probing questions about her lover, living vicariously through his wife's sexual exploits.

## Persian Canary

*See* Juan Julian

## Previous Lector

The previous lector succeeded Teodoro as lector upon the latter's death. He is from Guanabacoa, Cuba, and is described as having skin "the color of saffron." He seduces Cheché's wife Mildred with love stories and runs away with her.

## Rosario

Rosario is a woman who put a spell on her lover, who died as a result. "And not only did she lose her man," warns Conchita, "she's gone to hell herself." She cried so much after her lover's death that her face became "an ocean of tears." Rosario was so distraught that her father had to take her back to Cuba. At night a fever would overtake her, and she would run to the sea naked to meet her dead lover. Conchita tells the story of Rosario's spell to warn Marela from practicing witchcraft.

## Cookie Salazar

Cookie Salazar is the friend who lends Marela a fur coat which she wears in imitation of Anna Karenina.

## Santiago

Santiago is the owner of the cigar factory and the half brother of Cheché, to whom he owes a large debt. The debt causes Santiago so much shame that he refuses to return to the factory until the debt is paid. His marriage to Ofelia remains playful and loving despite the couple's frequent squabbles about money. Though Santiago has been secluded in the family home, he can see the positive effect the lector's reading has had on the workers. Therefore, he demands that Cheché return the machinery he wants to introduce. Inspired by Juan Julian's reading of *Anna Karenina,* Santiago launches a new line of cigars at the factory.

## Teodoro

Teodoro was the factory's lector until he died three months ago at age eighty. Marela complains that Teodoro would spit when he read, as though "sprinkles of rain were coming out of his mouth."

In Marela's opinion, Teodoro didn't have the emotional fortitude to be a lector, for he "couldn't take the love stories . . . the poetry and tragedy in the novels." Often he would have to sit down and collect himself after reading a profoundly moving passage. Furthermore, Marela says that he took too long to finish reading *Wuthering Heights*. This, says Conchita, is because he read to them "with his heart."

### Pascual Torino

Pascual Torino wears a handkerchief around his neck as he wraps cigars at the factory. He is a native of Spain, which once colonized and governed Cuba. According to Ofelia, Pascual is "A nostalgic at heart . . . [who] wants to go back to his country and die in Grenada."

### Vronsky

Vronsky is the dashing officer with whom Anna Karenina has an affair.

## THEMES

### Violence versus Reason

The opening scene of the play contrasts two approaches toward life, one violent and the other reasoned. Violence, as depicted by the savage game of cockfighting, suggests that skill, cunning, and might will always win. Although Cheché is a cautious man when it comes to gambling, he embodies the idea that physical power will triumph if reason should fail to persuade. For example, Cheché takes Marela by force when she ignores his lurid glances and innuendo. In the end, the young woman is rendered senseless from the shock of Cheché's assault. Moreover, when Cheché's attempts to mechanize the factory prove unsuccessful, he takes his revenge by killing the lector, whom he blames for upholding a tradition that, in Cheché's view, has no practical application in a modern age.

On the other hand, Santiago and Ofelia do not want to automate the factory because the machines would displace workers. They employ reason and sound judgment when making their decisions even though they know that their decision goes against the current trend. Rather than spend money on

# TOPICS FOR FURTHER STUDY

- Read the passages of *Anna Karenina* that are mentioned or read in the play. How do the events and characters described in *Anna Karenina* parallel those in the play?

- Describe the role ritual plays in the daily life of the cigar factory workers. How much of this ritual is based on superstition, and how much is associated with organized religion?

- Who were the Taino Indians, and how was their influence felt on the island of Cuba during the early part of the last century? Is their influence felt today? If so, describe how.

- What does it mean to be an *oidore,* or listener, while working at the cigar factory? How does Cruz impart symbolic value to what might otherwise be called a passive role?

- Who was José Martí? Trace the tradition of poets and novelists becoming statesmen in Latin America. Is this tradition restricted solely to Latin America? Cite examples.

- Research the history of several cigar brands, identifying any literary associations that may exist.

machinery, they decide to produce a new line of cigars, which they intend to advertise widely. Furthermore, both Ofelia and Juan Julian insist upon taking a vote to decide whether Cheché's machine will be installed at the factory. They choose a democratic process to decide an argument, and they would certainly have abided by the decision if the outcome had been different.

### Culture

Ofelia and her daughters (and, later, Santiago) understand that the best way to improve the work environment at the factory is to hire a lector who will educate and inform them as he maintains a tradition rich with cultural history. Though many of the workers cannot read or write, they can quote lines from classics such as *Don Quixote* or *Jane*

*Eyre*. Some know Shakespeare by heart. As Ofelia says, "Only a fool can fail to understand the importance of having a lector read to us while we work," for the workers are educated as a result. In an interview, Cruz explains the redemptive power of culture in *Anna in the Tropics* when he says that the play is about "the need for culture, the need for literature. Art should be dangerous."

One of Conchita's complaints about Palomo is that she cannot conduct a "civilized conversation" with him because he is unable to comprehend the lessons that may be learned from great works of literature. Instead of contemplating the actions of Anna's husband from an emotional, psychological point of view, as Conchita does, Palomo focuses on the man's wealth. Here Cruz sends up the idea that relations between the sexes would be vastly improved if they thought alike, but the point is that Palomo does not see how much his marriage resembles that of Anna and her husband. This exchange also emphasizes the transformative power of art, for Conchita now sees everything through "new eyes." As a result, Conchita experiences Anna's confusion and suffering. The broader the range of cultural knowledge, Cruz suggests, the more profound becomes the experience of human emotion.

### Nature versus Machines

One of the first observations Juan Julian makes upon arriving at the factory is that there are no hills or mountains near Ybor City; the landscape is flat, creating a sky that "seems so much bigger . . . and infinite" than the one he knew in Cuba. Juan Julian is a man who appreciates the revitalizing power of nature, and he contemplates it at every opportunity. "I don't really like cities," he says. "In the country one has freedom." He says that he feels "asphyxiated" when he is in the city, where buildings rob him of precious oxygen. He prefers to live in the country, where he can celebrate the "verdure of nature." Juan Julian lives his life in accord with the environment surrounding him, as evidenced in a discussion with Marela, in which Juan Julian acknowledges that there are many different types of light that bring the world into focus. Later in the play, when Juan Julian enters the discussion about whether machines should be introduced at the factory, he warns against them because, he says, "The truth is that machines, cars, are keeping us from taking walks and sitting on park benches"; that is to say, machines—and the fast pace of living they promote—prevent people from relaxing so that they

may better understand their place in Nature. Ironically, machines may, in the lector's words, prevent "[t]he very act of smoking a cigar."

### Tradition

Traditions maintain a way of life that is beneficial for those who practice them and this is especially true of an expatriate community such as the one depicted in the play. Ofelia and her daughters do everything within their power to hire a lector for the factory because they know that the workers depend upon the lector as a source of information about the world. "When I lived in Havana I don't remember ever seeing a tobacco factory without a lector," says Ofelia. Therefore, hearing a lector read while the workers toil has become for her a way of connecting the present to the past. She understands the importance of having a lector preserve a way of life that is threatened in the midst of a foreign culture.

Another tradition described in the play is the one observed when an inaugural cigar is lit and shared among smokers. This ritual involves passing the cigar through an intermediary, who facilitates communication with the gods, instead of directly to the person who is supposed to smoke. Palomo, however, deliberately insults Juan Julian by passing the cigar directly to him. The lector, as a descendent of the cacique, or chief Indian of the Tainos, performs a similar intermediary function when he reads aloud to the workers, for, explains Juan Julian, the cacique would "translate the sacred words of the deities." The workers, for their part, listen quietly, receiving information.

## STYLE

### Language

Though the language Cruz uses in *Anna in the Tropics* is more like common speech compared to that of his other works, it is nevertheless charged with poetry that creates what Randy Gener calls "a living image of the exile's experience." The rhythms of speech remain strong from beginning to end as Cruz occasionally presents his characters' beliefs and interior states of mind through vivid metaphorical passages, such as the one in which Marela describes her dream of snow or when Marela and

Juan Julian discuss the many different shades of light that exist and how, according to Marela, ''There's always a hiding place to be found, and if not, one can always hide behind light.'' The exchange between Conchita and Juan Julian in which they refer to their need for sanctuary is yet another example of metaphorical language in the play, for the characters alternately describe their trysting place as being ''cold and impersonal'' like a hotel or a hospital, neither place offering ''temporary relief from the world or a temporary rest from life.'' Furthermore, Juan Julian alludes to the restorative power of nature, of which sex plays a vital part, when he tells Conchita, ''I detect sad trees in your eyes after we make love.''

### Triangle Structure

The playwright, using the relationship of Anna Karenina, her husband, and Vronsky as a model for developing character relationships within *Anna in the Tropics*, presents his characters in triangular relationships to one another so as to better underscore the shifts in power and control that exist between them. For example, when Santiago loses a bet to Cheché and stays away from the factory out of shame, Ofelia must then intercede and defend the family's interests—and the tradition of the lector—against Cheché's proposed automation of the factory. Because Palomo is torn between wanting to hear the lector read from *Anna Karenina* and wanting to be rid of him for conducting an affair with his wife, Palomo alternately supports and undermines Cheché's proposal, thus forming one side of a triangle in the battle for control of the factory. Another, more comical example of how a triangular structure develops character relationships occurs when Marela intervenes in an argument between her mother and father, serving as an interpreter, or intermediary, until they are able to speak to each other directly. Finally, Palomo's passing of the inaugural cigar directly to Juan Julian breaks a triangular relationship that is intended to maintain communication with the gods.

Cruz employs the love triangle to great dramatic effect within the play. The first and most provocative example exists in the relationship between Cheché, his wife Mildred, and the previous lector, a triangle that is broken when Mildred and the lector run off together. This triangle is supplanted by yet another one involving Cheché, for he soon becomes attracted to Marela, who, in turn, yearns for Juan Julian's affectionate embrace. Per-

haps the play's most romantic example of a triangular character relationship, and the one that re-creates Tolstoy's example faithfully, both in terms of its ardor and tragic outcome, is that of the love triangle between Conchita, her husband Palomo, and Juan Julian.

### Foreshadowing

The foreshadowing used in the play heightens an element of suspense that is not fully realized until after the denouement. Early in the play, after Ofelia and Conchita have provided Juan Julian with the backgrounds of some of the workers whom he has met, they explain Cheché's opposition to having a lector at the factory, saying that this opposition stems in part from Cheché being from the North and having lived outside their culture. They go on to say that Cheché holds something of a grudge against all lectors because his wife ran away with the last one the factory hired because she became so enamored with the romantic tales he told. Conchita dismisses Cheché's cynical view as yet another one of his idiosyncrasies, for she says that ''Cheché has a knack for turning the smallest incident into a loud and tragic event.'' Little does she know how portentous these words are. Later, Cheché, unaware of the growing capacity for violence within himself, complains once more about the need for a lector at the factory, saying rather matter-of-factly that hiring Juan Julian will create ''another tragic love story.'' In retrospect, the audience comprehends the full weight of these words after the three celebratory gunshots are followed by two fired in revenge and Juan Julian lies dying on the factory floor.

Cruz also uses foreshadowing to add an element of mystery to the play. In the opening act, when Ofelia and her daughters stand at the docks waiting for the lector to arrive, Marela informs her mother that she has written the lector's name on a piece of paper and placed it in a glass of sugar water to increase the chances that he will accept Ofelia's offer of employment. Conchita then warns her sister against casting spells. She relates the story of Rosario and how her lover died as a result of her casting a spell on him. Rosario was so distraught that her father had to take her home to Cuba, where she would wander naked by the shore at night in hope of meeting her dead lover. Rosario remains alive in body but not in spirit. Marela, wearing a heavy fur coat in the heat of the Florida summer, experiences a similar fate after she is attacked by Cheché and Juan Julian has been murdered. Wearing the coat seems inexplicable to those who assemble for the final reading, yet to Marela's devastated mind and spirit this act makes perfect sense.

# HISTORICAL CONTEXT

## *Taino Indians*

When Christopher Columbus first arrived on the island of Cuba he and his men were met by the indigenous Taino Indians. The word *Taino* meant ''men of the good,'' for the Taino were a gentle race of people whose lives where inextricably linked with their natural surroundings. The Tainos were a seafaring people who lived on the verge of dense jungle, but they also developed sophisticated agricultural practices that produced cassava, corn, squash, and peanuts. The Tainos wandered about naked, their bodies decorated with colorful dyes made from earth, and they lived in homes constructed of thatch and Royal Palm. They greeted Columbus and his men with the kindness and generosity that were honored Taino values. However, the Taino population decreased rapidly as a result of exposure to disease brought by the Europeans and forced labor.

## *Ybor City*

Ybor City, a district within metropolitan Tampa, Florida, was once known as ''the cigar capital of the world'' because so many cigar factories were located there in the period from 1885 to 1940. The city was named after Vicente Martinez Ybor, a Spaniard who, like his business partners Gavino Gutierrez and Ignacio Haya, immigrated to Cuba in the nineteenth century. Ybor operated a cigar factory in Havana in 1853, but soon labor disputes, a high tariff levied on cigars by the Cuban government, and the beginning of the Cuban revolution against Spain in 1868 forced Ybor to relocate his factory to Key West, Florida. However, lack of a fresh water supply and an adequate distribution system for his cigars cemented Ybor's decision to move his base of operations to the Tampa, Florida, area, which had an established rail network and a recently improved port facility.

Ybor began developing a small community around the factory ''with the hope of providing a good living and working environment so that cigar workers would have fewer grievances against owners.'' The community grew in size until, by 1890, it had reached a population of 5,500 and was incorporated into the municipality of Tampa as Ybor City.

The community consisted of workers from all ethnic backgrounds, though Cuban exiles comprised the largest group, with Sicilians, Germans, Romanian Jews, Spaniards, and even a few Chinese composing the remainder of the population. Spanish and Italian were the two languages most often spoken in the factory.

Eventually, Ybor City rivaled Havana as a center for cigar production. In 1895, Ybor City had ten independent cigar factories, and the city continued to grow and prosper for the next two decades until the combined effects of increased cigarette consumption, automation, and the Great Depression forced many of the factories to choose between mechanizing their operations and going out of business. Many of the displaced workers either returned to their homeland or sought employment in the Tampa bay area.

# CRITICAL OVERVIEW

Linda Winer (quoted in Anders), a drama critic at *Newsday* who chaired the committee that awarded the Pulitzer Prize for Drama to Cruz, notes that *Anna in the Tropics* is ''such a luscious play, with rich imagery and a sense of myth and labor history. It takes us to a world we don't know.'' Misha Berson (quoted in Anders), another Pulitzer juror and a theater critic for the *Seattle Times*, describes *Anna in the Tropics* as ''lovely and kind of fragile, with archetypal, universal characters.'' Kathryn Osenlund, writing for *CurtainUp* when *Anna in the Tropics* appeared at the McCarter Theatre in Princeton, New Jersey, describes the play thusly: ''Romantic, yet not hackneyed, richly infused with tradition, Cruz's play quietly glows as it speaks of longings, family, jealousy, and love.''

Elyse Sommer, writing a follow-up review for the same publication when *Anna in the Tropics* opened at the Royale Theater on Broadway, notes the play's ''predictability and tendency towards historical romance plotting,'' but, nonetheless, she believes that the play ''succeeds in conveying the sense of loss that inevitably accompanies the march of time and progress—and the ability of great literature to reach out to even the simplest readers (and listeners).'' Not all critics view the play favorably, however. Clive Barnes, writing for the *New York Post,* questions whether *Anna in the Tropics* should have won the Pulitzer Prize, observing that ''[t]here have been worse winners—and better ones.'' Jonathan Abarbanel, in a review for *Theater News,* declares that ''Cruz is not subtle. He states and repeats his themes in obvious strokes, and there is much heavy foreshadowing in the play.''

Perhaps the most constructive criticism comes from Chris Anstey, who, in an article surveying the state of contemporary American theatre, cites what he considers to be the play's most obvious flaw: Cheché is not the main character. According to Anstey, Cheché should be because he, not Juan Julian, acts as the strongest catalyst within *Anna in the Tropics.* In Anstey's view, ''Cruz keeps Cheché's story obscure, a shadowy, internal affair, perhaps because his struggle is primarily with memory—his wife's infidelity; and so Juan Julian is merely a reminder, a symbol that must be killed not for itself but for what it represents.''

# CRITICISM

## David Remy

*Remy is a freelance writer in Warrington, Florida. In this essay, Remy considers the ways in which Cruz uses a triangular structure to develop character relationships within the play.*

The play *Anna in the Tropics* harkens back to a time long since forgotten, when the cigar factories of Ybor City were bustling with activity and immigrants held hopes of a better future. As Nilo Cruz convincingly demonstrates, life in a cigar factory was hard because it was subjected to so much uncertainty and doubt, but that is not to say that it was without its pleasures. In re-creating an atmosphere of strife, conflict, and division within the factory, Cruz, borrowing a page, figuratively speaking, from Tolstoy's *Anna Karenina,* uses the relationship of Anna, her husband, and Vronsky as a model for developing character relationships within *Anna in the Tropics.* By presenting his characters in triangular relationships to one another, the playwright underscores the visceral struggle waged by those who hope to survive. He creates scenes filled with drama and suspense. Moreover, communication, power struggles, and the yearning for romantic love in the play are brought into sharper focus as a result of Cruz employing this technique.

The role of an intermediary appears in key scenes throughout the play, and it fulfills the purpose of facilitating communication between men

*Greta Garbo and Fredric March in a 1935 film version of* Anna Karenina

and women who are often too stubborn to speak directly to each other, as is the case with Santiago and Ofelia, the owners of the factory. Act 1, scene 4, opens with Marela quoting words and phrases verbatim as her parents use her to wage an escalating argument about money. The irony of the situation— one whose comic effect is not lost upon Cruz as a dramatist—is that, without Marela's presence, the couple would be at a complete stalemate. Each person would not utter a word directly to the other, and so, instead of resolving their conflict about finances, as they do once Marela leaves and silence fills the room, they might have failed to realize how beloved they really are to each other. Had Marela not intervened, Santiago and Ofelia would never have reconciled their differences and moved on to a discussion of *Anna Karenina,* realizing, by the end of the scene, how much their lives mirror those of Levin and Kitty in the novel. Forming the third side of a character triangle, Marela thus enables her parents to embark upon what is at first a heated discussion but which later evolves into a tender recognition filled with romantic yearning and a strong resolve to face the future together.

Another scene in which an intermediary facilitates communication occurs in act 2, scene 3, when

# WHAT DO I READ NEXT?

- Cruz's play *Two Sisters and a Piano* (Theatre Communications Group, 2004) is set in 1991 as the fall of the Soviet Union further isolates Cuba politically and culturally. The two sisters of the play's title—one is a writer and the other is a musican—are placed under house arrest after spending time in prison for signing a manifesto against the current regime (though Cruz's characters never mention Castro by name). The sisters realize that, if they are to endure their sentence, they must redeem themselves through art.

- Many critics and lay readers alike consider *Anna Karenina* (first published in parts from 1875 to 1877) to be one of the best novels ever written. In describing the life of his troubled heroine, Leo Tolstoy also provides the reader with a sweeping portrait of nineteenth-century Russian society as it moves from a feudal economy to a modern state. For years, the Constance Garnett translation has been the standard English version, though a recent translation of *Anna Karenina* by Richard Pevear and Larissa Volokhonsky (Penguin, 2001) faithfully re-creates the power and grace of the Russian original.

- Gustav Flaubert's *Madame Bovary* (1857) is another classic of western literature that explores contemporary mores through the life of an adulterous woman. Married to a country physician who is devoted to her, Emma Bovary nevertheless seeks escape from boredom through an affair with a wealthy landowner, Rodolphe Boulanger, then another with Leon Dupuis, a notary clerk who eventually abandons her. Though there are romantic overtones within the novel, Flaubert takes an anti-romantic approach toward his heroine as she falls into disgrace and, eventually, ruin.

- Marguerite Duras's *The Lover* (1984) is a romantic novel that, like *Anna in the Tropics,* captures a moment in time—specifically, French Indochina (now Vietnam) in the 1930s. As Duras follows her fifteen-year-old protagonist through a passionate affair with a rich Chinese gentleman, she combines themes of erotic initiation with death to create a work of sensuous beauty. Partly autobiographical, *The Lover* eschews most of the narrative conventions of the traditional novel, thus allowing characters to reveal themselves by their words and actions, much as they would in a theatrical performance.

- *Tampa Cigar Workers: A Pictorial History* (2003), by Robert P. Ingalls and Louis A. Perez Jr., tells the story of how cigar workers came from Italy, Spain, and Cuba to make a life in Tampa while maintaining their ideals and culture in the face of economic hardship. Illustrated with over 200 photographs, the book documents the multiethnic communities that developed in the Ybor City area from the late 1800s through the years following World War II when Tampa became home to a large Latin population. Through oral histories and archived documents, *Tampa Cigar Workers: A Pictorial History* records the social customs and leisurely pursuits that preserved a former way of life as these immigrants adapted to a new one in the United States.

---

a cigar is lit and passed around to inaugurate the new line of Anna Karenina cigars Santiago has decided to produce. According to custom, the cigar must not be passed directly to the smoker but through an intermediary, so as to *"facilitate communication with the gods"* (Cruz's italics). Different characters take turns forming a triad as the new cigar is passed around and met with enthusiastic praise; that is, until Palomo receives the cigar and hands it directly to Juan Julian. This single gesture not only disrupts the triangular relationship among characters but forces the two men to confront each other as rivals.

*A hired reader and cigar makers in Cuba circa 1910*

The lector responds quickly to the insult—one made against him *and* the gods—by making an act of supplication. A scene that begins as a celebration ends in yet another standoff as Palomo and Juan Julian vie once more for Conchita's affection.

Perhaps the most important role of intermediary is performed by the lector. As a descendent of the cacique, or chief Indian, who "used to translate the words of the deities," the lector reads these words aloud from literary classics such as *Anna Karenina,* educating and informing the *oidores,* or listeners," who toil in the factory. Without him, many of the workers would have no knowledge of the outside world. Dramatically speaking, Cruz realizes the importance of the lector as a catalyst for change within the cigar factory. Juan Julian's readings permit Marela and Conchita greater freedom of imagination with which to lead their lives and fulfill their dreams, and Ofelia, among others, feels a strong connection to the past as she moves forward into the future.

In describing the struggle for control of the cigar factory, Cruz employs a triangular structure to delineate the shifting relationships between characters as they wield power and influence. With Santiago absent, Ofelia must assume control of operations immediately, especially if she wants to halt Cheché's

attempts at mechanization. Thus, she forms a barrier between the two brothers though her allegiance remains quite clear. Palomo, on the other hand, shifts his loyalty as the mood suits him. He enjoys hearing Juan Julian read, paying rapt attention to the tale of Anna's illicit affair, yet he sides with Cheché when a vote is taken to determine whether the lector should stay.

The love triangle, modeled after the example of Anna and her two lovers, is employed to great effect within the play, for characters involved in such a relationship embody the romantic stereotype of tragic lovers seeking escape and eternal union. The first and most provocative example—that is to say, the one triangular relationship that acts as an underlying stimulus in the play—is that of the relationship between Cheché, his wife Mildred, and the previous lector, a triangle that dissolves when Mildred and the lector run away. Because it was a lector who cuckolded him (one, moreover, from Cuba), Cheché distrusts anyone arriving at the factory to fulfill that role, even if that someone should happen to be a professional like Juan Julian. Thus, Cheché's personal animus against lectors reveals in part his motivation for wanting to modernize the factory.

Cheché is involved in yet another love triangle that ends in an unrequited manner. Throughout the

" THE LOVE TRIANGLE, MODELED AFTER THE EXAMPLE OF ANNA AND HER TWO LOVERS, IS EMPLOYED TO GREAT EFFECT WITHIN THE PLAY, FOR CHARACTERS INVOLVED IN SUCH A RELATIONSHIP EMBODY THE ROMANTIC STEREOTYPE OF TRAGIC LOVERS SEEKING ESCAPE AND ETERNAL UNION."

play, he seems tortured by the memory of his wife until, that is, he sees Marela dressed as a Russian lady when she models for the new cigar's label. He awkwardly tries to woo Marela, though his efforts often end in a leer. Marela, however, has eyes only for Juan Julian, the man who inspired her transformation by reading from the pages of *Anna Karenina*. A lover's triangle is set in motion as Marela longs for Juan Julian, who conducts an affair with her older sister even though she is married to Palomo, another roller at the factory. Cruz links triangles within triangles as the play approaches its denouement, bringing character's motivations into bold relief. Cheché, seeking fulfillment of his sexual desire, takes Marela by force, a violent act that foreshadows his eventual murder of the lector. By placing one of his characters in opposition to two others who meet tragic fates, Cruz presents a love triangle that surpasses Tolstoy's model in terms of sheer melodrama.

The play's most idealized example of a love triangle, and the one that re-creates Tolstoy's example faithfully, both in terms of its ardor and tragic outcome, is the one between Conchita, her husband Palomo, and Juan Julian. Cruz, however, modifies Tolstoy's classic love triangle by adding an element of sexual ambiguity that creates a psychological frisson between husband and wife. Palomo, aroused by Conchita's descriptions of her encounters with the lector, wants to learn more about how Juan Julian possesses her physically, prompting Conchita to remark, "You're falling in love with this man." Palomo denies this, saying that his need for addi-

tional information is merely the result of habit after having been an *oidore* for so long. When Conchita presses him, he admits that something else is bothering him. "And it's terrible sometimes," he adds. What was a heterosexual love triangle now adds a homosexual component to it, revealing more of the characters' psychological complexities. These personal motivations take yet another dramatic turn when Palomo, wanting to seize control of his wife's affair, suggests that Conchita tell her lover "to make love like a knife" because, he says, "everything has to be killed." The love triangle becomes too painful to maintain, creating a metaphorical death for at least one of the participants.

By placing his characters in triangular relationships, Cruz achieves a dramatic tension within *Anna in the Tropics* that draws upon the struggles for power and survival that mark life in the cigar factory. His homage to the Russian master confirms once again the redeeming power of art.

**Source:** David Remy, Critical Essay on *Anna in the Tropics*, in *Drama for Students*, Thomson Gale, 2005.

## SOURCES

Abarbanel, Jonathan, Review of *Anna in the Tropics*, in *TheaterMania*, September 25, 2003.

Anders, Gigi, "Work and All Play: Nilo Cruz's Play Wins the Pulitzer Prize Despite Great Odds," in *Hispanic Magazine*, June 2003.

Anstey, Chris, "It Must Be How It Is: On the Pulitzer Prize for Drama and the State of American Theatre," in *OldTownReview*, http://www.oldtownreview.com (select "Click here for the full Culture & Comment Archive"; accessed November 8, 2004).

Barnes, Clive, "*Tropics* Smokin'," in *New York Post*, November 17, 2003.

Cruz, Nilo, *Anna in the Tropics*, Theatre Communications Group, 2003.

Gener, Randy, "Dreamer from Cuba," in *American Theatre*, Vol. 20, September 2003.

Kiger, Jennifer, "Reinventing History: Playwright Nilo Cruz Rolls History, Literature and Romance into a Pulitzer Prize–Winning Drama," in *South Coast Repertory Playgoers Guide*, http://www.scr.org/season/03–04season/playgoers/anna/nilo.html (accessed November 8, 2004).

"Leo Nikolaevich Tolstoy," in *Guardian*, http://books.guardian.co.uk/authors/author/0,5917,1279539,00.html (accessed November 8, 2004).

National Parks Service, ''Ybor City: Cigar Capital of the World,'' http://www.cr.nps.gov/nr/twhp/wwwlps/lessons/51ybor/51facts1.htm (accessed November 8, 2004).

''Nilo Cruz, Cuban-American Author of *Anna in the Tropics* Is the Recipient of This Year's Pulitzer Prize for Drama and the Steinberg Award from the American Theatre Critics Associations,'' in *New Theatre,* http://www.new-theatre.org/pulitzer.htm (accessed November 8, 2004).

Osenlund, Kathryn, Review of *Anna in the Tropics,* in *CurtainUp,* http://www.curtainup.com/annainthetropics.html (accessed November 8, 2004).

Rouse, Irving, *The Tainos: Rise and Decline of the People Who Greeted Columbus,* Yale University Press, 1992, pp. 5–25.

Slovo, Gillian, ''Love in a Cold Climate,'' in *Guardian,* March 20, 2004.

Sommer, Elyse, Review of *Anna in the Tropics,* in *CurtainUp,* http://www.curtainup.com/annainthetropics.html (accessed November 8, 2004).

# FURTHER READING

Del Todesco, Charles, *The Havana Cigar: Cuba's Finest,* translated by John O'Toole, with photography by Patrick Jantet, Abbeville Press, 1997.

The author traces the history of tobacco in Cuba from Columbus's arrival to the modern day. Richly illustrated with photographs, many taken within cigar factories, this book describes in detail the processes of tobacco cultivation, curing, and, finally, the rolling of the cigar by hand.

Sontag, Susan, Preface, in *Plays: Mud, The Danube, The Conduct of Life, Sarita,* by Maria Irene Fornes, PAJ Publications, 1986.

Nilo Cruz acknowledges Maria Irene Fornes, a native of Cuba, as an important influence on his development as a playwright. Fornes avoids ideological constructs when composing her plays, focusing instead on the needs of her characters. Fornes' avant-garde plays, stark and often lyrical, revolve around characters who search for meaning in their lives in the face of psychological tyranny.

Stout, Nancy, *Habanos: The Story of the Havana Cigar,* Rizzoli International Publications, 1997.

For years the *habano* has been considered the epitome of what a good cigar should be. Stout offers a unique perspective on Cuba's growth and development as a nation, progress that has been inextricably linked to the cultivation of this valuable export. Dozens of cigar labels and art are reproduced within the volume, recreating a historical record of a bygone era.

Stubbs, Jean, *Tobacco on the Periphery: A Case Study in Cuban Labour History, 1860–1958,* Cambridge University Press, 1985.

Stubbs provides a socio-political study of the working class that developed as a result of Cuba's tobacco industry, a class that includes peasant growers, salaried workers, and slave and indentured labor. Exploring the agricultural and industrial development of the tobacco industry from its beginnings in the nineteenth century to the advent of the Castro regime, Stubbs' book offers insights into why so many Cubans sought a more prosperous life in Tampa's cigar factories.

# As Bees in Honey Drown

DOUGLAS
CARTER BEANE

1997

*As Bees in Honey Drown* is a comedy about the pitfalls of the unquenchable hunger for fame. Eager almost-famous painters, singers, musicians, business managers, and, of course, authors—the occupation of the protagonist of this play—are displayed as easily trapped victims of con artists who promise big, but empty, dreams.

The play opened in New York City at the Drama Department (where playwright Douglas Carter Beane is the cofounder and artistic director) on June 19, 1997. But four weeks later, the play moved to the Lucille Lortel Theatre in the West Village, where it played for a year and earned Beane the prestigious Outer Critics Circle John Gassner playwriting award (1998) and a nomination for the Drama Desk Best Play. Most critics concur that *As Bees in Honey Drown* is Beane's best play to date. Audiences seem to agree, as the play continues to travel around the United States, playing in most major cities as well as on many college campuses.

According to Stefan Kanfer, for the *New Leader,* much has been written in literature about con artists. But most of the con artists previously depicted have been men. Beane, however, has concocted a female version, which Kanfer describes as a ''postmodern lady no better than she has to be, in a world considerably worse than it ought to be.'' Her name is Alexa Vere de Vere. And although Evan Wyler, an author and the alter ego of the playwright, is the protagonist of this play, Alexa is the focal point. She is pretty, intelligent, and creative. But she is also

very crooked. However, she would not be as successful as she is if so many people were not so willing to take the shortcut to fame and fortune that she offers them. And that is the hub around which this play revolves.

## AUTHOR BIOGRAPHY

Douglas Carter Beane has stated that his first and foremost passion is theatre. He has written and directed numerous plays and is the co-founder and artistic director of an avant-guard theatre group in New York called the Drama Department. But, Beane has not limited his writing experiences to live performance plays. He is also a screenwriter, having written his first movie script while he was babysitting for some friends. Beane is also working on a script for a television series.

Beane has won many awards, but his *As Bees in Honey Drown* (1997) gathered the most praise. It was an off-Broadway hit that won the 1998 Outer Critics Circle John Gassner playwriting award and garnered a nomination for the Drama Desk Best Play. Most critics refer to *As Bees in Honey Drown* as Beane's best work.

Some of Beane's other plays include *The Country Club* (1999); *Advice from a Caterpillar* (1999), which was made into a movie the same year and won an award for the best film at the Aspen Comedy Festival; *Music from a Sparkling Planet* (2001); *Mondo Drama* (2003); and the musical comedies *The Big Time* (2004) and soon to be produced *Lysistrata Jones*.

In 1995, Beane took a break from theatre and wrote the screenplay *To Wong Foo, Thanks for Everything! Julie Newmar*, which starred Patrick Swayze and Wesley Snipes, who play drag queens. In the works is another movie written by Beane called *How Life Is* and a 2005 release called *Bewitched*.

## PLOT SUMMARY

### Act 1, Life

Beane's play *As Bees in Honey Drown* opens with the main character, Evan Wyler, in a photogra-

*Douglas Carter Beane*

pher's studio, having his picture taken for a magazine promotion of his first novel. The photographer convinces Evan that the way to sell his novel is for Evan to remove his shirt. Although Evan hesitates, in the end, it is this half-nude photograph that is published. It is also this photograph that attracts the attention of Alexa Vere de Vere, who appears in the next scene, wining and dining Evan.

Alexa is not only beautiful to look at, she is also very flashy. She throws high profile names around almost as readily as she spends cash. She flatters Evan as they eat lunch and cajoles him into working with her, writing the story of her life. She also carefully choreographs an image of herself as being well endowed financially but in great need of assistance with almost every other aspect of her life. She also makes huge promises, which catches Evan, who dreams of money and fame. He is also taken in by her neediness.

Scene 3 opens inside the dressing room of a swanky department store. Evan is being assisted by a clerk named Ronald. Alexa whisks in and out of the room, bringing new accessories with her and stopping briefly to admire how good Evan looks in his new suit. As Evan is distracted, Alexa also shops for herself. When it comes time to pay, she asks Evan, as she had previously asked him in the restaurant, to pay for everything with his credit card. She will, she promises, repay him in cash, as she did in the restaurant. Only this time, in the confusion she has intentionally caused, she starts to hand Evan the money, then, while he is not looking, Alexa stuffs the money back into her own pocket. She does this, however, only after giving Ronald some of the loose bills. Ronald is part of Alexa's con. He promotes her while Evan is dressing, dropping tidbits of information about how much Alexa has helped other almost-famous personalities become bright and successful stars. Then, Alexa rushes Evan out of the department store before he has time to think or remember that he has not yet been reimbursed for the credit card charges that he just signed for.

In the next scene, Alexa tells Evan, while they drive in a limousine, that she has lived an extraordinary life that needs to be recorded. She believes that her life will make a great movie. She is too busy to write it because she is so involved in living it. So she asks Evan to write it for her. As she begins relating details, Evan struggles to make sense of it all. He even, at one point, questions the veracity of her story. She mentions events that could only have happened before she was born. Alexa slips away from this confrontation by stating that she is only adding dramatic effect.

The scene becomes very distracting again as more people enter. Swen, a male model, Skunk, a rock star, and his backup singers join the couple in the limousine as they head for a very hip nightclub. Alexa dominates the conversation and continually drops the names of famous people. She consciously builds her image until she is seen as bigger than life. As they are sitting in the nightclub, a so-called friend of Alexa's, Carla, makes a brief appearance. Carla collaborates and reinforces Alexa's make-believe role as maker of rising stars. Carla pretends to be interested in promoting Evan herself. Alexa insists that Evan is her find, and she will take care of his future.

Scene 5 takes place on the Staten Island Ferry. Alexa and Evan are alone. Alexa further enhances the fantasy of Evan's future. ''You're not the person you were born,'' Alexa tells Evan. ''Who wonderful is? You're the person you were meant to be.'' Alexa asks about Evan's background in this scene and after he tells her about it, she has him throw his old clothes into the water, as he says good-bye to his old self.

Evan and Alexa are in a bedroom at the Hotel Royalton in scene 6. Evan is unsuccessfully attempting to write the story of Alexa's life. He tells her that he is not the kind of writer who can easily see into other people's heads and understand the motivations behind their actions. He asks Alexa more probing questions to help him understand her past. Alexa gives in and tells him about how her husband committed suicide. This draws Evan even closer to her, especially when Alexa states that she is nothing and is unworthy of love. Shortly after this, Evan, a homosexual, makes love to Alexa and tells her that he loves her.

Evan gets beaten up in scene 7 by Skunk, the rock star. Skunk has discovered that Alexa is not going to pay him money she has promised him. Skunk believes that Evan is in on the swindle and punches him mercilessly. He calls Evan a grifter, which is another word for a con man. In the following scene, Evan is on the phone. He is bleeding and confused and trying to get a hold of Morris Kaden, an executive at Delta Records, where Alexa has told Evan she is a manager. When Kaden's secretary hangs up on him, stating that she has never heard of Alexa, Evan calls the hotel where he was last with her. The hotel clerk tells Evan that Alexa has checked out. The clerk also informs Evan that there is an outstanding bill that Alexa has said Evan will pay. Act 1 ends with Evan crying out: ''It isn't true. It isn't true, isn't true!''

### Act 2, Art

Scene 1 is very brief. The audience watches Alexa begin her con with yet another victim. Then scene 2 quickly takes over, in which Evan, still bleeding, enters Morris Kaden's office. When Evan mentions Alexa's name, Kaden takes Evan into his private office, where he tells Evan everything he knows about her. Morris was once a victim of Alexa's too. He tells Evan to forget about the incident, to accept it as a very serious lesson. As Morris talks, a vision of Alexa from the past seeps through. She is using the same lines on Evan that she has used on everyone else, and Evan realizes how badly he has been taken by her.

''Doesn't anyone ever get her back?'' Evan asks Morris. ''Most people have lives,'' Morris answers. But Evan wants revenge. Morris provides a few leads as Evan hopes to track down Alexa.

In scene 3, Evan is on the phone talking to a dancer named Illya Mannon, who confesses she too was conned by Alexa. Illya gives Evan a few more names of victims, including Michael Stabinsky, whom Evan contacts and makes arrangements to meet.

The next scene takes place in Michael's studio/ loft. The two men, in the course of their discussion about Alexa, discover they are both homosexual, and there is a bit of sexual tension displayed between them. As they talk, Michael fills out the true background of Alexa, including her real name, which is Brenda Gelb, and how she started her con game when she helped Michael, who is a painter, sell some of his work. The one piece that did not sell, Michael confides, is the one he calls *As Bees in Honey Drown*.

As Evan is about to leave Michael's loft, scene 5 bleeds into the present, and the audience watches a young violinist, Ginny Cameron, who is being persuaded by a photographer to pose half-naked for a shot that will be used in a magazine to promote her. Ginny is then seen talking to Alexa, who wants to meet with her. Next, Ginny is on the phone with Evan, who finds out that Ginny is scheduled to meet Alexa at the Four Seasons restaurant. Evan then plans his revenge. Evan calls Morris, Skunk, Illya, and several others, all of them Alexa's victims. He tells them to gather at the Four Seasons where he hopes Alexa will appear.

In scene 6, Evan returns to his apartment and listens to his telephone messages. He hears the voices of some of the people who plan to meet at the restaurant. The last voice he hears is that of Ginny, who tells Evan that she made a mistake and told Alexa about Evan's plan of revenge. As he turns, Evan sees that Alexa is standing in his apartment. She tells Evan that he is very much like her and he should join her in her escapades. They would make a great team. She tries to convince him that the life of a writer is really very boring. She kisses Evan. He tells her that he has talked to Michael and tells Alexa to leave. She says he is not a good writer. He tells her that he does not need her.

The revenge party at the Four Seasons went on even though Alexa was missing. In scene 7, Illya and Morris give an accounting of how great the get-together was.

Scene 8 takes place in Michael's loft. They talk about art. Evan feels lost. He has lost his muse. Michael is still very much involved in painting. Michael gives Evan the notebook Evan left at

Michael's place the last time he visited. The book is filled with notes that Evan took throughout his encounters with Alexa.

Scene 9 begins with a dialog between unnamed muses. They mimic bits of conversation that took place between Evan and Alexa. Michael appears briefly, suggesting that Evan and he have developed a relationship and are living together. Evan is writing. As he continues to write, Alexa appears in Morris's office. She is angry about having just seen Evan's new book, in which Evan has recounted their affair. Alexa wants to sue Evan. Illya appears, reading Evan's book. She reads some of the lines out loud. Then, Evan joins her and so does Morris.

## CHARACTERS

### Ginny Cameron

A young violinist, Ginny is first seen in a photographer's studio, similar to the first scene of the play in which Evan is being photographed. Ginny is naked from the waist up (also similar to Evan's scene), and the photographer convinces her that her photograph in a magazine will bring her recognition. Shortly afterwards, Alexa calls Ginny because she has seen her picture. Evan uses Ginny to help set up his revenge, but Ginny warns Alexa before the damage is done.

### Carla

Carla makes a very brief appearance in act 1, while Alexa and Evan visit a posh nightclub. Carla comes across as an old friend of Alexa's and substantiates Alexa's contrived background, making Evan believe Alexa's story more fully. Obviously, Carla is in cahoots with Alexa's scheme.

### Brenda Gelb
*See* Alexa Vere de Vere

### Morris Kaden

Alexa claims to work for Morris Kaden, an executive at Delta Records. But later, when Evan goes to Kaden to see if he can help track down Alexa, Evan learns that Morris too has been one of Alexa's victims. Morris tells Evan to let go of the experience. He suggests that Evan consider the money he has lost as tuition in the school of life.

## Illya Mannon

A dancer and also a victim of Alexa's, Illya provides Evan with yet another possible lead in how to find Alexa.

## Ronald

Ronald is a clerk in a department store. He helps Evan try on a suit, as Alexa picks out ties, shoes, and perfume for Evan. Ronald is in on Alexa's con job. He promotes her, offering an authentic-sounding background for Alexa in which he alludes to other up-and-coming stars whom she has helped.

## Skunk

Skunk is a rock singer from London. Like Evan, Skunk is duped by Alexa. Unfortunately for Evan, Skunk believes that Evan is Alexa's accomplice and beats him up.

## Michael Stabinsky

Michael is a painter and the only person in the play who knew Alexa Vere de Vere when she was still Brenda Gelb. Although Michael benefited from an artist showing that Brenda/Alexa put together for his benefit, Michael did not appreciate how she conned everyone into coming to the show and buying his paintings. When Evan hunts down Michael in order to find out about Alexa, Michael flirts with Evan and suggests that they try out a relationship between themselves. The character of Michael is used to clear up the mystery of Alexa as well as to provide the antithesis of Alexa for Evan's sake. As Evan wonders about his sexuality, he is presented with the choice of a heterosexual relationship with Alexa or a homosexual one with Michael. Michael also contrasts with Alexa in his open-faced honesty and sincerity.

## Swen

While Alexa dictates the story of her life to Evan in a limousine, they stop and pick up Swen, a male model who barely speaks English.

## Bethany Vance

Alexa refers to Bethany as an alleged actress who was also a masochist. Alexa uses the story of Bethany to suggest that love is painful. Bethany was also conned by Alexa, and she provides Evan with some background information that helps his investigation of Alexa.

## Alexa Vere de Vere

Alexa is a beautiful con artist (here real name is Brenda Gelb) and is the antagonist of this play. She appears in the beginning of the drama as a well-to-do promoter of artists. She throws a lot of money around and claims that money has no hold on her. She promises great things to people who want to believe in her vision. Unfortunately, except for her ability to inspire, Alexa is a fraud. She is like an angler who baits her hook and tempts a hungry fish with a free meal only to snatch the eager creature out of the water and leave it gasping for oxygen. Her first successful con involves her friend Michael Stabinsky, a painter. And from there, she cons several musical artists and eventually the protagonist Evan Wyler. One positive thing that can be said of Alexa is that she is good at what she does. Her visions are filled with grandeur and passion, and it is through these gifts that she inspires the people around her. She provides the dream but not the means to the dream. And the cost of her vision for her victims is fairly steep. Part of her scheme to entrance her targeted victims is that she pretends to be helpless about many things in her life, a victim herself.

## Eric Wollenstein

*See* Evan Wyler

## Evan Wyler

Evan (who changed his name from Eric Wollenstein) is a novelist who acts as the protagonist in this drama. He is looking for fame and fortune at the time he meets Alexa Vere de Vere. Evan enjoys the lavish attention and convincing hype that Alexa pours on him. Eventually, although homosexual, Evan makes love to Alexa and surprises himself when his heart opens up to her. But Alexa is not sincere, and Evan falls hard when he discovers that Alexa is a fraud. He loses a lot of money because he believes in Alexa and her dreams. But he is especially affected by his emotional connection to her. The second part of the play deals with Evan's attempts at finding the truth about Alexa, if there is any. Although it appears that Evan seeks to avenge the wrath that Alexa has caused, Evan's real motive is to fit together all the pieces of the puzzle in order to figure out not only the enigma of Alexa but also to discover the truth about himself. Is he an artist? Is he homosexual? Can he love? In the end he discovers that no matter what happens to him, he can turn it into something creative and worthwhile.

# TOPICS FOR FURTHER STUDY

- There are many movies that have been made about con artists, such as *The Flim Flan Man* (1967), *The Sting* (1973), *The Paper Moon* (1973), *The Grifters* (1991), and the *Matchstick Men* (2003). Watch two or more of these movies and then write a report on the different techniques that the con artists used. What were their goals? Did they succeed or were they caught? How did they dupe their victims?

- Research the energy company Enron. Would you call what they did a con game? Layout the details of the company's crime as vividly as you can. Then present an argument either for or against the company executives and their actions.

- Victor Lustig has been called one of the greatest con artists of all times. Research this man's history. How did he con people? Do you think he would get away with his tricks today? Why or why not?

- Highlight the few times in this play that the phrase ''as bees in honey drown'' is mentioned. Study the context in which they are stated. Then write a paper discussing your interpretation of this phrase in terms of art, culture, and entertainment in the United States.

## THEMES

### Art

The topic of art is discussed rather obliquely and on many different levels in this play. Evan mentions his need to create his art when Alexa tries to lure him into joining her in her con game. Evan also describes the challenges he faces in his specific art form when he is with Michael. Because of what Alexa has done to him, Evan says he has lost the ''arrogance'' he needs to write. This arrogance is what he needs to believe that he could write something that someone else would be interested in reading. This is a possible allusion, readers can assume, to the playwright's own challenges. Beane might be implying that unless an artist is creating only to satisfy some inner need to express himself or herself, that level of arrogance has to be rather high. It takes a lot of arrogance, or confidence, to expose the inner workings of one's mind (as represented by a book, a painting, a play, or a musical performance) to a critical audience made up of mostly strangers.

Art looked at through the eyes of the character Alexa, however, takes on a different image. Alexa sees the production of art as drudgery, with little excitement and a lot of work involved in it. The thrill lasts for but a brief time—at the very beginning of the work and at the ending. And every time artists produce new works, they put their previously earned reputation on the line. They have to prove themselves and their skills over and over again.

Art, through Evan's eyes, is difficult. He produces his art in an attempt to connect with other people. But he knows that there are people out there who want to criticize what he has written or want to take advantage of his skills, but he does it anyway. Michael, in another version of the artist, wants to be left alone to paint. He works diligently to perfect the small details of his work, e.g., his intense focus on creating an image of a human ear. These men are driven by their art. They would like to be able to make a living from it, but that is not why they do it.

And then, in contrast but also in some comparison, there is the con artist, as represented by Alexa. This is a totally different form of art. It is illegitimate and sometimes illegal. But conning takes special skills and a great deal of arrogance, as does any musical or dramatic performance. And it is a performance. The con artist is an actor whose stage is the public arena. His or her audience is the victim. One would think it was not as fulfilling as creating a work of art, but the con artist might not agree. Alexa believes that art is boring; whereas her con games are thrilling and charged with the pizzazz that every artist craves.

## Fame and Fortune

Fame like honey, according to Beane's play, can give one a rush of sweet pleasure or it can drown one. It is as alluring as a Greek siren, promising allusive treasures. But like the sirens, the voice of fame also can cause disaster. Con artists like Alexa would not exist if people were not so vulnerable to the lure of fame and fortune. How quickly Alexa is able to turn heads in her direction by floating a few loose dollar bills. How easily she is able to blind people with their own desires to be important. And how painfully her victims are burned when they are finally able to see through their own folly. Fame and fortune, Beane seems to be saying, must be earned with hard work and a honing of one's skills. There are no fairy godmothers out there with magic wands, waiting to grant wishes. One must be focused and be willing to sacrifice. The painter Michael appears to be Beane's example of the perfected artist. He allows Alexa to promote him somewhat insincerely, but he is the least affected by her claims of fame. Michael works hard at his art. He works alone. His name is not splashed all over the magazines. He is content to work out the details of his art, earn a modest wage, suffer through the disappointments, and celebrate when he is able to express his creativity fully. In contrast, Evan falls for Alexa's promise of fame. He wants it before he earns it. He pays a heavy price when he discovers how foolish he has been. The price is not just monetary. He nearly sacrifices his art in the ordeal, as he is unable to write for a long time. Beane's message seems to be that fame and fortune either should be ignored or, in the least, kept in their place. They are not the gods of the arts but rather they are the devils.

## Love

Love threads its way through Beane's play in a number of ways. There is the love of art. There is the love of money. There is the love of fame. But there is also an underlying theme of the love found in a relationship. Evan is at the center of this theme of love. He retells the story of unrequited love with a man in his youth, a love that left him feeling very vulnerable. In the aftermath of that experience, Evan decided not to love again. He had occasional affairs but would not open his heart fully to anyone. But then he falls in love with Alexa, who turns him on his head. He never thought he would love again

and surely not a woman. And yet, there he is professing love to her. He is confused by it. And so might be the audience. Does he really love Alexa or does he love what she represents? He wants to be like her in some ways, but is that love? He loves her lifestyle, albeit a phony façade. He loves the way she makes him feel important and special. But that love is short-lived. It is superficial and does not stand the test of time or reality.

In the end, Beane seems to suggest, there might still be a love for Evan. It might come in the person of Michael, a fellow artist, an honest man, someone who understands the challenges that Evan faces. Michael is someone who could be a true friend. It is from this sincere relationship, Beane implies, that true love has a chance of blooming.

## Pop Culture

Beane portrays some not-too-attractive pictures of pop culture. For instance, in the scene in Michael's apartment, Evan admires a painting. It is the painting Michael calls *As Bees in Honey Drown*. It was the only painting that did not sell when Alexa arranged Michael's first showing. It was also, according to Michael, the only painting that was finished. In other words, the other paintings he had rushed through and had not completely finished his thoughts on those pieces. They were surface sketches. And yet because of the hype that Alexa created around them, people bought them. Alexa also makes references to a similar misunderstanding of paintings by the general public. She says that there are great works of art being bought by people who live in Hollywood. But the people who buy them have no understanding of them. The inference is that pop culture is very shallow. Alexa says that people want to be entertained; and the leading artists of one moment die quickly only to be replaced by the next hot artist. People want the flash, but they do not take the time to sit down and allow a work of art to penetrate them.

## STYLE

## Flashbacks

Flashbacks are a construction that is often used in movies, novels, and short stories. It is a technique that allows the author to fill in the background of the characters, which ultimately makes the present moment more complex and more detailed. This gives the audience information they had not been previously aware of. In a play, this construction of flashbacks is a lot more difficult to pull off as the players are in the same present moment as is the audience. So how does a playwright provide background information? Often this is offered in the dialog of the characters, but supplying these details can considerably slow down the pace of the play, which can, in turn, bore the audience. So in *As Bees in Honey Drown*, Beane employs a different technique to fill in the gaps, to provide clues in order that the audience might solve the mysteries, and to make the audience privilege to some of the characters' inner thoughts. The technique he uses is flashbacks.

The first time Beane uses flashback is in act 2, scene 2, while Evan is talking to Morris, the executive from Delta Records. Morris begins exposing to Evan the way Alexa cons people, and, rather than having Morris recite these lines, Beane brings Alexa into the scene. Although all three actors are present on the stage at the same time, Evan and Morris are in Morris's office and Alexa is at the Hotel Paramount. As Morris relates his knowledge of Alexa to Evan, Alexa is playing out a scene she and Evan had previously shared. And some of the lines that Alexa voices are also being stated by Morris, simultaneously. The effect is that of Morris telling Evan about Alexa as Evan recalls those same lines being said to him by Alexa. Since the audience has already heard these lines, it would not be as dramatic if Morris reiterated them to Evan. But with Alexa reading them at the same time as Morris (but off to the side), the words have a more profound emotional impact because the audience can relate to what Evan is going through as he realizes how ignorant he was to have fallen for those lines.

The double reading of the lines not only exposes to Evan the fact that he has been duped but also how he has been conned by Alexa. As Morris and Alexa re-act the various situations that Alexa and Evan had recently shared, Evan (and thus the audience) more explicitly understands how Alexa worked her con. For instance, in flashing back to the scene in the department dressing room, the one in which Alexa is supposedly buying Evan a suit, Evan sees more clearly that the so-called accidental spraying of perfume in his face was actually a ploy to distract him from the fact that Alexa had not given him money to reimburse him for the credit card charges he had placed. The flashbacks are seen in the present, a time when Evan's mind is clearer. He hears Alexa say things that he had not heard before. Evan had been so involved in the presumed gift giving that he does not pay attention to what Alexa is buying for herself. Only through flashback does he see everything clearly.

Beane uses this technique throughout the play. Another time is in act 2, scene 3, when Evan is searching through the notes he has taken while he was with Alexa. He is looking for clues. But instead of rereading to the audience what he has written in his book, Beane has Evan on the telephone talking to people whom Alexa has mentioned. The audience knows this because there is another flashback of Alexa rereading part of the dialog that she and Evan had previously shared.

There is also an extended flashback, which occurs in act 2, scene 4, when Evan goes to Michael's loft to talk to him about Alexa. Instead of using a dialog between Michael and Evan to disclose what Michael knows about Alexa, Beane has the actress who plays Alexa play out the scene with Michael. Alexa is made to look like a younger version of herself, a woman who was then going by the name of Brenda Gelb. Michael and Brenda/Alexa act out scenes for Evan and the audience's benefit, again filling in background material so everyone understands how Brenda became Alexa.

## *Point of Attack*

The point of attack is the place in the play where the real action begins, the action surrounding the conflict. In Beane's *As Bees in Honey Drown*, this point is very visible because it occurs at the time when Evan is punched in the face by Skunk. It is, in other words, a physical point of attack, with dramatic flair. Up until the moment when Skunk delivers his punch, the audience is not fully aware that Alexa is a fraud who is duping Evan. The audience is privy to a few hints but is not told in an obvious way that she is conning Evan. When Skunk hits Evan in the face and demands his money, accusing Evan of being in cahoots with Alexa, then the audience's eyes are opened to the truth.

Most plays begin in a neutral position. In *As Bees in Honey Drown*, the audience is shown that Evan is eager to find the fame and fortune that he expected would follow the publication of his first novel. Alexa arrives on the scene to help Evan find what he is looking for, or at least that is what Evan and the audience first believe: Evan is a legitimate writer and Alexa is a legitimate maker of dreams. The play from the opening scene until Skunk's punch is fairly well balanced. Alexa appears to have more power in the realm of the financial world, but

Evan has the creative talent that Alexa needs to promote. Each character brings something to each scene in equal measure. But at the point of attack in the play, that balance changes. The tension rises as Evan hunts down Alexa, determined to find out the truth about her life, to expose her faults, to avenge himself, and to return to his art. The point of attack is the beginning of the tension; and the climax is the peak of it. Between these two elements lies the gist of the action of the play.

# HISTORICAL CONTEXT

## Off Broadway

Down the middle of the section of New York City where most of the major theatre productions are made runs the street called Broadway. This street is so filled with major theatres that the name Broadway has become synonymous with theatre productions. But Broadway is not the only street in New York where theater-goers enjoy plays and musicals.

In the first half of the twentieth century, small budget plays and musicals could not afford the high costs of these big Broadway theatres, and so the producers looked for smaller, lower-cost places that were located off Broadway. Soon, the theaters in the so-called off-Broadway sections of New York City became home for plays that were considered experimental and therefore not potential big moneymakers. In the 1950s, many avant-garde playwrights like Edward Albee and Sam Shepard had their plays produced off Broadway, as did Eugene Ionesco, Samuel Beckett, and Harold Pinter. By the 1990s, when Beane's production of *As Bees in Honey Drown* was put on stage, many producers were investing in the off-Broadway districts, and a construction boom of small theaters that held under 500 seats was the result. Today, the difference in cost can be drastic, with an off-Broadway musical costing under $500,000, while a similar musical produced on Broadway might cost more than $1.5 million. Off-Broadway productions even have their own awards. The most significant are the Obies, sponsored by the *Village Voice*. Today, with the growth and popularity of off-Broadway theater, smaller, cheaper, and more experimental plays have been pushed even further away, with productions housed in districts referred to as off-off-Broadway.

## Cultural Icons

In Beane's play *As Bees in Honey Drown*, the con artist Alexa constantly drops names of cultural icons. She does this to impress the people around her. In order to understand some of the allusions she makes, the reader needs to know what these names stand for.

David Bowie is a name that Alexa mentions often. Bowie is one of the most influential pop music writers of his time. He struggled through the 1960s with occasional hits, and then in the 1970s enjoyed success not only in his homeland of England but in the United States as well. One of his biggest hits was *Fame,* a favorite theme of Alexa's and a topic discussed throughout Beane's play. Bowie also starred in movies with some success and is presently married to Iman, a supermodel and another name that Alexa mentions.

Theodore Geisel is another name that Alexa refers to. This author of many popular books for children is better known as Dr. Seuss. Most American children from the 1960s onward grew up reading Dr. Seuss's enjoyable and silly rhymes. His fame and fortune are a dream come true for many authors. Another author that Alexa refers to is Gore Vidal, who has written novels, screenplays, and dramatic pieces for the stage. He has gained some respect in the literary world but was hurt by some scathing reviews when he wrote openly about homosexuality in the 1950s. Christopher Isherwood was also an author and homosexual. He wrote a collection of stories about life in Berlin, which was later turned into the stage production of *Cabaret* (1966); its main character, Sally Bowles, is another name that Alexa drops. Sally Bowles personified the decadence that was occurring in Berlin while Isherwood lived there. In a similar allusion, Alexa mentions Holly Golightly, the main character in Truman Capote's *Breakfast at Tiffany's,* a novel published in 1958. The novel was later turned into a movie starring Audrey Hepburn. An interesting point to note is that like Vidal and Isherwood, Capote was also homosexual.

# CRITICAL OVERVIEW

Since it was first produced, *As Bees in Honey Drown* has enjoyed almost continuous production in small theatres and on college campuses across the nation from New England to Hawaii and Las Vegas to New Orleans. Most critics believe this play is

Beane's best, and audiences tend to agree as they watch the two acts of this modern satire.

Jay Reiner, writing for the *Hollywood Reporter,* finds Beane's play only "mildly amusing," but he knows why the theme of Bean's play works. "A society," Reiner writes, "that makes a fetish of fame and celebrity is made to order for a con man to exploit." The fact that Beane uses a woman as the exploiter amuses Reiner even more. Reiner says of the fact that Beane's con artist is a woman, "so much the better."

Beane's play began in New York City in a small theatre off Broadway where it played for a little over a year. Since then, the play has been produced numerous times by different production companies all over the states. Joel Hirschhorn reviews the play for *Variety* after seeing it performed on the West Coast in Pasadena. Hirschhorn writes, "Beane's indictment of the 15-minute fame and hunger for applause has resonance, and the enterprise is worth watching."

Often, in reviewing some of Beane's more recent plays, critics refer back to Beane's *As Bees in Honey Drown,* commenting on the brilliance of this earlier work. For example, Ben Brantley of the *New York Times* in a review of Beane's *Mondo Drama* refers to *As Bees in Honey Drown* as "one of the liveliest satiric romps of the last decade." In this same article, Brantley also mentions Beane's theatrical group, the Drama Department, who first produced *As Bees in Honey Drown* as "the inventive, star-studded troupe that has become the last word in downtown theatrical savvy."

## CRITICISM

### *Joyce Hart*

*Hart is a freelance writer and author of several books. In this essay, Hart explores the complexities of protagonist Alexa Vere de Vere, finding personality traits in Alexa that mirror those of her so-called victims.*

Beane's play *As Bees in Honey Drown* has a female villain who could almost outrank Cruella DeVil from the classic *101 Dalmatians.* Although similarly coldhearted, Alexa Vere de Vere, however, is not quite as flat a character as Cruella. The *101 Dalmatians* villain is a stereotypical character who represents evil personified. She has, in other words,

no saving graces. Beane's Alexa Vere de Vere, in contrast, is more real, more complex, or to put it more simply, she is more human. And when looked at even more closely, she is not very different from her fellow characters in the play, her so-called victims.

One of the first things about Alexa that stands out is that she is hungry for money and fame. She waves cash in front of her victims' faces and drops names of the rich and famous as if she knew all of them on an intimate basis. This illusion is just that— a fantasy—but it is an image that her victims want to see. They want to believe in her because they are, after all, just as hungry for money and fame as she is. How else could they be so easily duped? They all either want to be her closest friend and best ally or they dream of being just like her. They desire the life she portrays. They want to have so much money they can be as careless as she is with it. They would like to go to ridiculously fancy department stores and buy clothes that make them look better; clothes that shout out: this person has made it to the top; this person is "in"; this person is someone everyone else wants to know. And in this way, Alexa's victims are not so different from her. Their dreams mirror one another. They are all fascinated with the same superficial image.

But then, one could counter this statement by demonstrating that Alexa's victims are not like her at all. They are imaginative artists who dig down deep into themselves in order to create something new and marvelous. They are managers of corporations who stay at the office until late at night, sorting through complex negotiations. They are hardworking business people who sweat over their books and struggle to make a decent profit. They are musicians who practice their instruments until their bodies ache. Alexa's life, on the other hand, is easy. But is it? Is it so easy to pull off the image that Alexa has created? Isn't she playing a role like any actress on stage? And isn't she doing such a good job of it that she convinces her victims that she is sweet and innocent and in need of help and protection? She is, by looking at her in a completely objective and nonjudgmental way, doing so well at her art, she should be awarded a prize. And in many ways she is. Her victims' give her money. But that is dishonest, right? That makes her a liar and a fake, which is in stark contrast to her victims, who practice complete honesty.

Honesty? What honesty? Is it honest to try to sell books by attracting readers through a photo-

*Dancers at the Groove Jet night club in Miami Beach, Florida*

graph of your half-naked body as Evan did? And in an attempt to sell her CDs, Ginny, the violinist, also bared her chest. Alexa changed her name from Brenda Gelb to the more exotic Alexa Vere de Vere. And therefore, this name, in some ways, is fraudulent, right? But Evan changed his name too. He wanted to mask his Jewish heritage by changing his last name from Wollenstein to Wyler. Then, for some whimsical linguistic reason, he changed his first name too. And in another bit of dishonesty, Michael Stabinsky, Alexa's former live-in friend, allowed Alexa to create a grand illusion around him that persuaded potential customers that he was a soon-to-be famous artist. He permitted this illusion in order to sell his paintings. One could say that Alexa duped Michael's customers. But don't forget that Michael agreed to let her to do so; and he reaped the benefits. So who is really being honest? Or, at least, who is more honest than Alexa? Does honesty come in degrees? Granted, Alexa goes overboard in her debauchery. She has no sense of remorse. And there is little social worth in the art she creates. But she is not the only dishonest character in this play.

There are other traits of Alexa's that reverberate in some of the other characters, especially Evan. Take Alexa's neediness. In act 1, scene 4, while Alexa, Evan, Skunk, and Swen are in the restaurant,

Alexa claims she is about to have a nervous breakdown. She becomes distracted and jittery. Granted, her so-called breakdown is an overstatement that is precipitated by Alexa's need to feign helplessness. Part of her ploy is to appear needy so that her victims want to come to her rescue and do whatever she asks of them—like pay for her dinners, clothes, rooms, etc. But her need is nonetheless real. She, like her victims, feels needy. She needs the people she cons in order for her work to exist; and later an even deeper need is demonstrated when she exposes her feelings to Evan. For instance, in act 2, scene 6, she confronts Evan with the statement: ''You know that I am not a mirage, I am an oasis.'' With this, Alexa faces her deepest need. She wants to claim legitimacy, weight, and meaning. She is all but crying out for it. In the midst of all her deceitfulness, she desires to be real.

In a similar way, Evan demonstrates his own sense of neediness at the end of act 1 when he shows up all bloody in Morris's office. Evan has been physically beaten up by Skunk. In this fight between the two men, the only one who throws the punches is Skunk. Evan never defends himself. After this encounter, Evan walks into Morris's office with all the marks of the fight still on his face. Without saying a word, Evan cries out for help. Just by

# WHAT
# DO I READ
# NEXT?

- One of two other Beane plays that have gained the attention of critics is his *The Country Club* (2000), a comedy about a group of partygoers in a small country town and their small-town prejudices and undying promises to cling to the status quo for as long as they possibly can. The other play is Beane's *Music from a Sparkling Planet* (2002), also a comedy. This one focuses on three men and their search for hope, which they seem to have lost as they edge toward their thirties.

- David Lindsay-Abaire's name is often linked to Beane's in that they both are contemporary playwrights who like comedy. Lindsay-Abaire has won many awards for his work, which includes *A Devil Inside* (2000), a comedy of revenge, and *Fuddy Meers* (1999), a funny but harrowing tale of an amnesia victim.

- Kenneth Lonergan is an award-winning play-

wright with such hits as *This Is Our Youth* (1999) and *The Waverly Gallery* (2000). In his play *Lobby Hero* (2002), Lonergan has written a humorous account of a young security guard who tries to hide from the world after being thrown out of the navy. The young man unfortunately discovers that the lobby of a busy hotel is the last place he should have tried. Life drags him into some very bizarre stories in which he must deal with people he never would have dreamed he would ever know.

- A Tony Award–winning playwright, Richard Greenberg has written the play *Take Me Out,* which was produced in 2002 to critical acclaim. Through humor, the play looks at the serious topic of homophobia, as portrayed in one baseball team when one of the players makes it known that he is gay and then must deal with the consequences.

---

looking at him, Morris knows this young man is in trouble. Morris comes to Evan's aid, just as Evan had previously come to Alexa's when he told her to calm down and that everything would be all right. Similarly, Morris tries to calm Evan, telling him to let go of the feelings of pain and revenge that are building up inside of him. But Evan is unwilling to do this. He needs to seek out Alexa. He craves to avenge his hurt pride. He cannot accept his experience with Alexa as a lesson, as Morris suggests. Evan has an emptiness inside of him, and he wants to fill it up. He feels that Alexa has depleted him. He cannot think. He cannot write. He cannot focus on anything but getting something either from Alexa or at Alexa's expense.

Beane brings these two characters together in another way too. At one point, Alexa asks Evan about his background, specifically whether or not he was ever in love. Evans tells her his story, a sad one, which Alexa relates to. Evan once fell in love with someone who did not return his love. Alexa, upon

hearing this story, tells Evan that she had an acquaintance who was a masochist—someone who seemed to love pain. This friend stated that the line between pleasure and pain was a thin one. Alexa takes that a step further. She tells Evan, after having heard his tale of unrequited love, that the line between love and pain is also a thin one. At the moment they share this information, the two characters discover they are commiserating with one another. This moment in the play feels especially real because Beane, in his stage directions, intensifies this exchange by having the two of them, instead of looking at one another, look away at the city skyline. They are feeling too self-conscious, the playwright suggests, to look into one another's eyes. This action promotes the idea of raw emotion, of a moment of honest feelings between Evan and Alexa. Perhaps this is meant to suggest that they have both been hurt in the past. And as tough as Alexa pretends to be, it is during this exchange between her and Evan that she is at her most vulnerable. ''But we're not like that, are we?'' she asks Evan.

"WITH THIS, ALEXA FACES HER DEEPEST NEED. SHE WANTS TO CLAIM LEGITIMACY, WEIGHT, AND MEANING. SHE IS ALL BUT CRYING OUT FOR IT. IN THE MIDST OF ALL HER DECEITFULNESS, SHE DESIRES TO BE REAL."

"We're not the ones people hurt," she continues. She is not sure, but she is hoping this is true. Or at least she is hoping that Evan will think this is true. And thus, Beane binds these two characters together through their emotions, these characters who appear, on the surface, to be so dissimilar.

Possibly even more purposefully, Beane draws other comparisons between Alexa and Evan. In scene 5 in the first act, while Alexa and Evan are on the Staten Island Ferry, Evan tells Alexa that the story of her life that she is offering him sounds fictitious. Alexa responds that she adds flair to fact for dramatic effect. Since Evan is a writer of fiction, in his art he does the same. The retelling of life's events in exactly the same way and with exactly the same timing as they occurred—spread out and unfocused as life unfolds—does not necessarily make a good novel. So Evan, like Alexa, gathers information, then sorts it according to his central theme to create a dramatic affect. The difference is that Evan portrays his art for what it is—a work of fiction—while Alexa offers it as the truths of her life. They are both gifted storytellers who see the drama in life and have a need to offer their versions of reality not as a collection of facts but as a linkage of ideas. Despite the fact that Evan's art is considered legitimate, his and Alexa's means of making a living are really not that far apart. They both try to sell fiction. "We are the creative people," Alexa tells him at the end of the play, suggesting that she and Evan are alike. The context around this statement implies this shared art of theirs will protect them from the challenges of life. It is with this buffer of fictitious lives, she believes, that she and Evan will survive life unhurt.

At the end of the play, Alexa is so convinced that she and Evan are alike that she asks him to join her in her art of swindling. "The hum, the buzz, the hype, the flash, the fame," she tells him as she tries to persuade him. "This is the only thing that matters." What she does not understand is that although they share similar personality traits, certain needs, and particular gifts of creating fiction, they travel down different roads. Alexa and Evan may both be artists, but their definitions of art are as different as night and day. It is Alexa who craves the constant buzz of excitement, the stimulation of living on the edge. Evan may have craved it, but it was a passing hunger. "What if I have the desire to express myself artistically?" Evan wants to know. Alexa responds: "Suppress it." And Evan almost does. He almost falls into her pot of honey. But Alexa lies to him one time too many. And Evan catches himself before he drowns. He and Alexa may be alike, but he has his limits. So he throws Alexa out of his life and then makes his fortune by selling his fictional interpretation of hers.

**Source:** Joyce Hart, Critical Essay on *As Bees in Honey Drown,* in *Drama for Students,* Thomson Gale, 2005.

### Catherine Dybiec Holm

*Holm is a fiction and nonfiction writer and editor. In this essay, Holm looks at how this play gives a glimpse into the dark side of being an artist.*

A person without the craving, drive, or compulsion to work in the creative arts might well have difficulty understanding the challenges that creative artists face as they try to mesh their visions into the commercial marketplace. *As Bees in Honey Drown* gives the reader an experiential taste of the ramifications of being a modern-day artist or writer in the United States. Many of the reviews of this play focus on the charisma of Alexa, the amazing con artist who robs hopeful artists of their hard-earned dollars. In a larger sense, this is the story of the artist's role in this society and the factors that can either cripple these artists or propel them to success.

Artists long to bring their unique message to the world through their media. Alexa understands this need in an artist. While convincing Wyler to get rid of his agent (thus making it easier for her to begin conning him), Alexa taps into the strange dichotomy that artists deal with when they bring their art to the marketplace.

Alexa: And agents, though I don't believe in agents, do you?

Wyler: Mine is—

Alexa: Let's not deal with them. I find that agents have no imagination. No taste for . . . possibilities.

Wyler: Actually, I agree.

Ironically, Alexa will intentionally put herself in the agent-like role, taking a far greater cut of Wyler's cash than an agent ever would. She zeros in on the thing that speaks to Wyler's heart. Agents have no imagination or taste for possibilities. How can they possibly understand the artist's creative endeavors?

The starving artist becomes more real for the reader, early in the play. Wyler talks of scrounging for subway fare. He lives in a dump while peers his age own cars and homes. He is forced to do temp work to pay the rent. He is stuck in the "little breather period between critical success and financial success." Alexa plays upon the imbalance of power that exists between the marketplace for art and the creators of art. This imbalance is one big reason why many artists give up or lead difficult lives. In view of Wyler's living conditions and this power struggle, readers can see why Wyler falls for Alexa's con. Alexa's offerings seem to Wyler like a rare gift from heaven and an unimaginable stroke of luck.

Alexa knows about that important moment in time when the artist first stands at the "brink of success." Alexa understands the psyche of an artist as if she is one herself. In an amazing back-and-forth dialog with Kaden, she defines the crucial "brink of success" moment, that time when victims such as Wyler are lured into her con.

Alexa: All of us creative people—

Kaden: Brink of success, they call it.

Alexa: Tearing about trying—

Kaden: The artist wants to be—

Alexa: To feed a nation's insatiable appetite for entertainment.

Kaden: Ready to abandon all morals and logic.

Alexa: So that we can discover something new and vivid—

Kaden: Ready to be famous and, so it would follow, fulfilled.

Alexa: All holding on for dear life as we create fresher and fresher possibilities.

Kaden: Anything not to have to be you, anymore.

Alexa: As bees in honey drown.

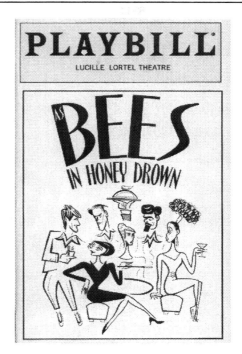

*Playbill cover of* As Bees in Honey Drown

Kaden clearly stresses the desire to do anything not to have to live in poverty and obscurity anymore. The artist may be running from himself or herself. She or he may be sick of the struggle. Alexa understands the artist though she creates nothing except the adventure of each new con. Her creativity is fed by outmaneuvering each unlucky artist who is at that brink of success. Kaden cynically admits that there may actually be some value to getting conned by Alexa. Assuming that the artist will only run into more difficulties in the future, Kaden says that Alexa's work is "the screw that toughens the skin for all the future screw attempts." It is a fatalistic statement about the world that aspiring artists face in this culture.

Kaden's dialog carries a more ominous suggestion. As artists reach for success, they may be required to lose themselves. Kaden explains why none of Alexa's victims have ever gone after her for revenge.

> We all let her go on because in an odd way, she reminds us what we were foolish enough to think of giving up. To have her life. Her sad, empty life. We all actually considered giving up ourselves.

The last sentence in Kaden's speech is crucial. If a creative artist "gives up" their self, they will be

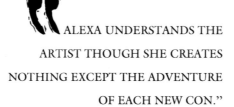

ALEXA UNDERSTANDS THE
ARTIST THOUGH SHE CREATES
NOTHING EXCEPT THE ADVENTURE
OF EACH NEW CON."

unable to create and have nothing to draw upon. Wyler reaches this point. He is no longer able to write. He gave himself to Alexa and gave her his "arrogance" too.

Mike: Why don't you go off and write something. Forget about Alexa.

Wyler: I can't write.

Mike: Yeah yeah, you can't write.

Wyler: I mean I can't write.

Mike: Are you serious?

Wyler: It isn't just the money that Alexa stole from me. She stole my arrogance. The arrogance it takes to just shamelessly write something and assume someone, anyone might read it. The gall to think I might be a success. I'm blocked. I can not write.

Undoubtedly, Alexa understands that artists have their own oddly functioning internal dichotomy. To produce powerful and compelling work, the artist must know himself or herself well, even if this means mining their unique insecurities and vision of the world. The artist must also, as Wyler points out, be able to draw on a reserve of audacity. The artist must be able to call forth enough ego to produce the work and take the risk of bringing it into the world and withstand the potential criticism and rejection that the world will offer. The artist's dichotomy is precarious, and necessary, and the artist cannot function without both extremes.

Mike's art is also affected by his relationship with Alexa. After Alexa manages to con influential people into attending Mike's art opening, Mike wonders if he has not prostituted himself.

Mike: These people, the ones coming tonight are all— they're the people I hope to one day impress with my real work. And they're here because we've . . . conned them.

Mike creates "fake art"—paintings that are meaningless compared to what he is truly capable of. His real work remains unfinished. Ironically, the paintings that mean the least to Mike—the paintings

that he creates in a hurry and without passion—are the ones that sell at the mocked up art opening. Alexa leaves Mike because she is angry, freeing him up to create art that comes to him truly, regardless of market distractions or temptations. When Wyler departs from his conversation with Mike, Mike sounds as if he has achieved real clarity about his artistic vision.

Mike: I want a place to go and paint. To be left alone for a while. And when I'm done painting, I want to get together with some friends, have a beer and talk about stuff. And we'll commiserate if my painting went poorly. And celebrate if my painting went well.

Mike goes on to create art that means something to him. This foreshadows what might be possible for Wyler.

Still, Wyler is tempted one more time during his last long encounter with Alexa. Here, the choices that the artist faces are never more obvious. The artist can remain true to his or her artistic vision and take with this choice the risks found in the precarious world of art and entertainment. Or, Wyler can opt for what Alexa offers. She states what may be Wyler's deepest fears if he falls for her persuasion. Alexa stands for "the hum, the buzz, the hype, the flash, the flame." Writers do not last long in American society, according to Alexa. The attention span of the populace will not allow for it. "Stay with me and always be popular. Fame without achievement, it is the safest bet I know."

The question of fame without achievement is a turning point for Wyler. Many creative artists face a similar crucial choice. Should one remain true to one's own internal vision even if the marketplace does not call for it? It is a difficult question and one that is at the heart of this play.

Alexa tries to convince Wyler that writing is drudgery, that the only good thing about writing a piece of work is beginning it and ending it. It is in the following dialog that Wyler's crucial choice is so apparent:

Wyler: And what if I have the desire to express myself artistically?

Alexa: Suppress it. It is every time you create that you run the risk of proving or chiseling at your reputation. Come with me. . . . Never, ever be hungry, or thirsty, or doubt yourself. Or wait in line. Or talk to bores.

Presented this way, it becomes clear just why artists need such internal fortitude to stay true to their vision. Alexa is about appearances. Wyler chooses internal truth and his own artistic vision. It is not necessarily an easy choice. Wyler still strug-

*Downtown Manhattan skyline of the late 1990s*

gles with it, even after he leaves Alexa. Wyler is "kind of lost, at sea." Wyler almost gives up writing for good.

> Wyler: It's just so incredibly difficult, you know? You try to create something. And to know there are so many people waiting to criticize or capitalize and all you want to do is make something that will connect with other people so that we all won't feel so profoundly alone. And we are all so profoundly alone. Why does it have to be so hard to try to cure that in some way. It . . . is . . . so . . . difficult.

Ultimately, Wyler makes the difficult choice, turns his back on the buzz, and returns to writing. Creative artists will recognize themselves in this play, as well as the decisions that get made about remaining true to or not remaining true to artistic vision.

**Source:** Catherine Dybiec Holm, Critical Essay on *As Bees in Honey Drown,* in *Drama for Students,* Thomson Gale, 2005.

## SOURCES

Brantley, Ben, Review of *Mondo Drama,* in *New York Times,* May 23, 2003, p. E-1.

Hirschhorn, Joel, Review of *As Bees in Honey Drown,* in *Variety,* September 8, 2003, p. 42.

Kanfer, Stefan, Review of *As Bees in Honey Drown,* in *New Leader,* September 8, 1997.

Reiner, Jay, Review of *As Bees in Honey Drown,* in *Hollywood Reporter,* August 26, 2003.

## FURTHER READING

Bigsby, Christopher, *Contemporary American Playwrights,* Cambridge University Press, 2000.
> Bigsby has put together an interesting study of some of the most controversial plays and the award-winning playwrights who have enjoyed success on the American stage.

Crespy, David A., *Off-Off-Broadway Explosion: How Provocative Playwrights of the 1960s Ignited a New American Theater,* Backstage Books, 2003.
> For an in-depth look into the history of the American theater through the production of innovative plays by beat playwrights of the 1960s, Crespy's book is the place to go. Crespy's account is filled with interviews and anecdotes about such profound thinkers and artists as Edward Albee, Sam Shephard, and Amiri Baraka, playwrights who altered the course of American theater.

Hischak, Thomas S., *American Theatre: A Chronicle of Comedy and Drama, 1969–2000,* Oxford University Press, 2000.

> This book provides a comprehensive history of the last half of twentieth-century theater in New York. *As Bees in Honey Drown* is briefly mentioned.

Maurer, David W., *The Big Con: The Story of the Confidence Man,* Anchor Books/Doubleday, 1999.

> Maurer was a professor of linguistics who became fascinated with the rash of con artists that traveled along America's highways, conning people out of their cash. Maurer has studied these people and the tricks of their trade, providing an interesting read on how the con artist's mind works.

Sinfield, Alan, *Out on Stage: Lesbian and Gay Theatre in the Twentieth Century,* Yale University Press, 1999.

> This book chronicles the history of gay and lesbian characters as portrayed on the stage from Oscar Wilde's writing to the plays produced at the end of the twentieth century. Sinfield contends that whereas gay culture was only obliquely alluded to in the past, in the last quarter of the twentieth century there has been a clearer and more honest depiction of homosexual life in theater.

# *Feeding the Moonfish*

## BARBARA WIECHMANN
## 1988

*Feeding the Moonfish* is a one-act play by Barbara Wiechmann, first performed in New York in 1988. The work is a brief study of two very unlikely companions and the powerful, life-transforming bond they form in the course of one evening. This compelling story draws on the power of natural forces, the tragedy of murder, the importance of memory, and the magical influence of the stars to shape the characters and provide a solid framework for the play. Although there are no direct references anchoring the setting in any given time period, the tone of the work reflects the social malaise of the 1980s, characterized by the advent of AIDS, Chernobyl, and the Iran Contra Affair. Despite its economy in form, *Feeding the Moonfish* has the power to illuminate a brief moment in time, demonstrating that an innocent exchange between strangers can change everything.

Much of Wiechmann's contemporary life and works are not formally chronicled; however, *Feeding the Moonfish* is included in Eric Lane's *Telling Tales: New One Act Plays*. Published in 1993, the work is a compendium of contemporary one-act plays from some of today's best playwrights in contemporary theater.

## AUTHOR BIOGRAPHY

Barbara Wiechmann grew up in Middle Haddam, Connecticut and attended Hamilton College be-

fore moving to New York where she resides as a writer and performer. She has written several plays, including *Feeding the Moonfish*, *The Holy Mother of Hadley, New York*, and *The Secret of the Steep Ravines*. Her work has been produced and workshopped at P.S. 122, the Ensemble Studio Theatre, New York Theatre Workshop, BACA Downtown, HERE, the Ohio Theatre, and the Samuel Beckett Theatre. Her work has also surfaced at the Edinburgh, New York, Philadelphia, and Seattle fringe festivals (a wide variety of unjuried and uncensored theatre). In addition to her regular appearances at the New York Theatre Workshop, Wiechmann is also a New Georges affiliated artist and has been a longstanding member of the Arden Theatre Company. She is an NYSCA grant recipient and a Jane Chambers Award finalist.

## PLOT SUMMARY

The setting for *Feeding the Moonfish* is a dock on a saltwater lake in southern Florida. The action takes place in one evening. As the play opens, the audience hears two or three long whistles and then a series of overlapping voices. "Martin, Martin, Martin," chant the voices of the moonfish as they welcome him "home." Martin responds as if he has indeed returned from a long journey. Martin asks (referring to his father): "Can I see him? I want to see him." The moonfish ignore his persistent requests, instructing him to close his eyes and "Tell us we're beautiful."

Martin tells the moonfish about a dream where he was flying in a plane. He describes it in great detail, from the moment he hits the mattress and "some stewardess is strapping me in." He takes a flight into a deep blue sky, and it's as if he were levitating or floating weightlessly "in blue heaven." He describes a flight complete with "movies, brunettes and cocktail almonds." After he shares his dream, Martin tells them that he is "home," his memories are "hot and heavy." The moonfish then ask him to put his face in the water, Martin responds and asks to see "pieces of him" floating in the coral.

Eden arrives, breaking the hypnotic trance evoked by the chanting of Martin and the moonfish. She is curious, while Martin is defensive, demanding to know how long she has been standing there. Eden admits to stowing away in the back of Martin's

car, curious to see where he goes after work. She explains her actions, saying, "you sweat to death side by side of someone . . . an they never speak a word to you, never pass the time of day, never basically even look at you, an you get curious—you know?" And, Martin concludes that waitresses are "all alike," telling Eden that she merely seeks attention.

Eden protests Martin's order that she "go home," claiming that she could be "harassed or raped or chopped up or worse." She does not understand why Martin is not flattered by her attention, nor does she understand his fascination with the rotting dock or the fish in the water. She asks what the huge fish are called and responds with skepticism when Martin tells her that the moonfish feed off the dock at night when the moon shines, explaining:

> "The moon's got a force, an it pulls an pulls at the insides of these fish and locks em into a way of behaving," he tells her. "They got no minds of their own anymore. Once the moon's got em they're hopeless beyond all control. All they got is moon minds."

Eden continues to ask questions, and Martin responds by turning the conversation back to her and her own personal history. Eden shares that her father was beaten to death and that her mother and grandmother are responsible; however, only her mother went to prison. Her grandmother is under surveillance in a nursing home. Martin suggests, "There must be some place you go home to—I'll take you home O.K.?" but Eden holds fast to her conviction that home is not a safe place.

Eden turns the conversation back to Martin, asking him "Do you think there are forces between us?" She asks him to kiss her, and he violently rejects her. Eden voices her displeasure, telling Martin he does not appreciate her, that he treats her like a "disease," some "piece of filth." But when Eden walks off, Martin is left alone, and he pleads with her to return.

The voices of the moonfish come back in chorus, and they ask Martin to picture the water. Martin shares with them his concern for Eden's safety; he fears he might harm her. The fish respond, "Nothing can happen you don't want to happen. If you make the pictures." Again, they beckon him to the water, assuring him that he will not drown and tell him that he will "see his shadow on the end of the pier," calling him to see his father and to "watch the moonfish feed."

Eden returns to the dock with an old sleeping bag and a couple of beers only to be chastised for swearing and for stealing the alcohol from the restaurant. Martin softens, and they sit and drink as Eden shares her affinity for the nighttime. Martin opens up to her and tells her the history of the docks: ''The living things were all dying,'' he says. ''But not anymore. The moonfish are making a comeback.'' When Martin shares that the fishermen who frequented the dock were responsible for the slaughter of many fish, Eden abruptly turns the conversation and asks Martin, ''do you think my mom's having an O.K. time behind bars?''

Martin responds with complete disbelief to her candor, and he asks Eden to recount the details of her father's death. The audience learns that although her mother tried to kill her father, it was her grandmother that ''dealt the actual death blow.'' When Martin asks why they did it, Eden shares that her father ''used to beat on my mom on a semi-regular basis'' and her grandmother and mother were ''merely killing him out of self-defense.'' Martin also learns that it was really Eden's stepfather, not her natural father, who was killed.

When Martin asks if the murder bothered her, Eden recalls the day she found out about it and admits that it did in fact upset her. When Eden mentions that as the police questioned her, others may have thought she was ''psycho.'' Martin assures Eden that she is not ''psycho'' then scolds her for wanting a joint. Eden responds excitedly to his lack of understanding. When Martin tells her to calm down, Eden exclaims that ''of course'' she is ''worked up,'' she has been trying to make a new friend only to be ignored. ''There's no rational way to account for the disgusting things I've seen in my life,'' says Eden.

Martin tells her she is not alone and that he in fact shares a similar past. They begin trading one shocking family secret for the next until Martin reveals that his father slit his own throat. Eden becomes quiet. Martin apologizes and offers her something to eat and then ends up chastising her for her poor behavior in front of the men that frequent the restaurant. Eden tells him that he ''shouldn't talk'' because she heard ''what you done to girls . . . to that girl.''

The two continue to argue as Martin accuses Eden of lying and Eden defiantly telling him she knows of his improprieties with a certain inebriated,

young woman whom Martin let wander around on the docks. She accuses Martin of standing by and watching the woman drown. The climax comes when Martin protests and moves to strike Eden but does not.

The tension shifts again as Eden explains the strange relationship between her mother and stepfather. Although her mother helped kill her stepfather, Eden maintains there was love between them. Despite the beatings, Eden claims that ''Forces was pulling em—just like them fish—only they could feel emotional pain in their minds too so it was worse.'' She then tells Martin that there is nothing he could do, no horrific act that could change her feelings toward him.

Martin then tells Eden he thinks she is a little sick but she assures him that he is in good company. Then Eden reveals to him that she likes him and that he has a beautiful face, and the two fantasize about their escapes. Eden wants to leave Florida while Martin's utopia is a place where he cannot see the heat, where he can ''see the lake clear down to its floor'' and the ocean floor is ''sand white,'' its creatures ''huger and wilder.''

He shares with Eden the former beauty the docks once held for him and the nights spent watching the moonfish with his father. He tells Eden that the fish talk, and she tries to hear them. Then the two settle down on the docks for a night's sleep, and, as Eden settles into Martin's arms, he tells her of his dream in which he is waiting for his father. In the dream, Martin's father comes to him, picks him up in his arms, and takes him to the docks to watch the fish feed in the stillness and complete darkness of the night without the force of the moon.

As Martin continues, his voice along with the moonfish rise in chorus recounting the activity. Martin shares a vision he has of his father cutting his own throat then falling to Martin's feet. In his dream, Martin pushes the body into the lake and the fish come to feed. Martin then reveals that his mother left his father, an event he identifies as the ultimate cause for his father's suicide.

As the scene ends, Martin tells Eden his dreams about a man and woman. Although they have nothing to do with his life, he imagines inflicting harm on the man. Eden listens, asking him to stroke her hair and to tell her she is beautiful. Martin obeys, his hand momentarily lingering on her throat as if to choke her. He then begins to stroke it and tells her, ''You're beautiful, you're so beautiful.''

# CHARACTERS

## Eden

Sixteen-year-old Eden, the play's antihero, is wise for her years. She is also a troubled teen whose fascination and free spirit lead her to stow away under a sleeping bag in the backseat of Martin's car. She is daring and defiant, insisting that she get to know Martin, despite his strong reprimands and protestations that she go home. In several instances, the not-so-typical teen demonstrates a disregard for authority. After Martin's initial objection, Eden boldly walks off, only to re-emerge with the sleeping bag and a couple beers the under-age teen has stolen from the restaurant where she and Martin work. Eden also demonstrates a surprisingly cavalier attitude about her dysfunctional family when she tells Martin about the murder of her father in matter-of-fact manner. While many people would be reluctant to share distasteful family history, Eden is forthcoming about her mother's and grandmother's incarcerations.

Eden is a multidimensional character who functions in several ways in the play. She is a foil to Martin. Both characters have experienced the loss of one parent at the hands of another. Martin responds to his tragedy by returning to the docks and by continuing to live this episode of his life in a kind of dream state. Eden appears to have accepted her father's death at the hands of her mother and grandmother. Her perceptions of the tragedy are firmly rooted in reality. Despite her mother and grandmother's crime, they remain blameless in Eden's eyes. She recognizes that the family dynamics of her mother and stepfather's relationship, while abusive, were complex, exonerating her mother and grandmother from any wrongdoing. Eden embraces her past and moves on.

Eden is also Martin's connection to the real world and a means by which he makes a psychic return to that world. She demonstrates that it is possible to make peace with the past, no matter how troubled. She is the vehicle by which Martin can finally share (for the first time) the events of his father's death and his feelings surrounding it. More importantly, Eden is there for Martin. She insists on staying with him unconditionally, and she is the one person who enables him to make peace with his past.

## Martin

Haunted by his father's suicide, a twenty-something Martin returns to the docks on a saltwater lake in southern Florida to commune with the moonfish, spiritually connect with his father, and resolve his troubled past. He is quiet and cool, absorbed by his loss. In his grief, he is prone to isolation and is withdrawn at work. When Eden comes around, he is more interested in getting rid of her than he is in getting to know her.

An unfortunate past dictates Martin's present life. He appears to lead an ethereal existence, returning to the docks often, driven to reconnect with his father and the events of his past. He often speaks to the moonfish, responding to them as if they were human, pleading with them to reunite him with his father. These imagined conversations do not necessarily suggest the workings of an insane mind but constitute a divine connection Martin has with his father. It is clear that he has not resolved the events at the dock nor his feelings surrounding his father's suicide. The events surrounding his father's death consume him and compel him to sleep at the docks night after night.

Martin's past has also shaped his perceptions of women and romantic love. He identifies his mother as the villain in his parent's relationship and holds her accountable for his father's death. Martin believes that by leaving her marriage, his mother drove his father into the loneliness that led to suicide. His anger toward his mother manifests itself in his treatment of women, and he may or may not have an abusive history with women. At one point in the play, Eden brings up Martin's reputation for cruelty and his connection to an inebriated, young woman who drowned in the water near the docks. Martin also demonstrates a dislike for women in his interactions with Eden. One moment he is protective, the next, cruelly pushing her away and criticizing her choice in clothing.

## Moonfish

The moonfish are not visible characters but appear to be imagined voices that can be considered a part of Martin's subconscious. The voices are nurturing and distinctly female, welcoming Martin to the dock: "Did you have a long day at work? Are you tired? . . . We're so happy you're home." The voices are also anxious, possessive, and all consuming. They distract Martin from his memories by demanding flattery, pleading with him to "Talk to us," "Tell us we're beautiful," in turn promising to deliver the vision of Martin's father.

The moonfish have several functions in the play. They are a connection to Martin's father, a reminder of happier times spent on the docks. Because of the memories they evoke, the moonfish appear to be a gateway to the divine. They stir in Martin the final recollections of his father and are a way to keep his father alive in his memory. The moonfish also exhibit qualities of Martin's mother, personifying, for him, all that is female. They symbolize all that his mother means to him: abandonment and the catalyst for his father's loneliness. Like his mother, the moonfish present a formidable barrier to his father by demanding his attention.

# THEMES

## *Astrology*

Elements of the astrological sign Pisces are consistent with those in the play, explaining Martin's character traits, motivations, and his relationship with Eden. The element water, the color blue and the moon tarot card all relate to Pisces. Pisces is symbolized by two fish swimming in a harmonious circle. Like the symbol, the relationship between Martin and Eden is a harmonious one. When Eden is up, Martin is down and vice versa. Key elements related to Pisces—the moon, the water, the fish, and the color blue—dot the play. This forms the basis for Wiechmann's story: the setting takes place on the docks by the water, the moonfish play a central role in Martin's subconscious and the color blue is mentioned in the "blue heaven" of Martin's dreams. Martin is prone to many Piscean traits, which is demonstrated in his deep regard for dreams and his intensely sensitive nature. Like Pisces, Martin's continual struggle to resolve his conflicting desires for isolation and companionship are played out in his relationship with Eden. The moment Eden arrives at the docks Martin rejects her and insists that she leave. When it seems that Eden has finally complied with his request to leave him alone, Martin tells her, "You don't have to leave.... Don't leave." References to the sun sign also give the work a cosmic unity from which Wiechmann implies a connection with the divine. An attraction to the moon compels the moonfish, Martin, and Eden to go to the docks. The forces of the moon govern the appearance of the moonfish, evoking memories that help Martin reconnect with his deceased father. "Natural things are moved by forces, see. The moon's got a force," he explains to Eden. Compar-

ing herself to the moonfish, Eden suggests that she and Martin "was being zapped right now by outside forces." It is in this supernatural attraction that Martin and Eden find each other and ultimately make peace with their troubled pasts.

## *Memory and Reminiscence*

It is through Martin and Eden's memories that the audience comes to understand the tragic deaths that drive both of their lives and ultimately bring them together. Martin's memories of his father also drive him, fueling his deep and desperate need to remain connected to a happier past. His desire to revisit his childhood compels him to return to the docks night after night. "I am waiting for my father. I sleep alone here," confesses Martin. Martin's memories comfort him, and his visits to the docks evoke dreams of his father: "I feel him lift me up and up and his arms rock me and his voice in my ear." Martin's dreams also haunt him. Memories ultimately lead Martin to a vision of his father's suicide. By recounting his dreams and memories of his father to Eden, Martin is set free. He unburdens himself of the suicide. In sharing his secrets, Martin is able to separate himself from his troubled past, as evidenced in his words to Eden, "You listen to me tell you this. You listen to me, and you just sit there like it was nothing. Like it was natural."

## *Murder*

Both Eden and Martin's lives are affected by tragic murders. Eden's mother and grandmother worked together to kill her stepfather, which resulted in her mother's incarceration. In recounting the moment she found out about the murder, Eden cites her reasons for being upset: "I got questioned by the police for three days.... my friends think I'm a psycho." Although his father's death is a suicide, Martin sees it as murder at the hands of his mother because she abandoned them, and Martin shares that his father "was so lonely for her." Eden accepts the murder of her stepfather as a natural consequence of a relationship with her mother while Martin lives a life of blame, acting out the anger he has toward his mother on other women. Together, Eden and Martin find a common bond in their tragedies, helping Martin to make peace with his father's death.

## *Forces of Nature*

Martin, Eden, and the moonfish are all significantly connected by forces of nature. The moonfish,

# TOPICS FOR FURTHER STUDY

- In the early nineties, Jack Kevorkian captured the nation's attention by aiding in the suicide of a Portland woman in the early stages of Alzheimer's, calling into question the legitimacy of assisted suicide. Investigate the series of events leading up to Kevorkian's second-degree murder conviction. Was he justly punished for a crime or persecuted for an act of mercy? Why or why not?

- Moonfish are said to be one of a few fish that "talk," or make sounds that closely resemble human speech. Research and write a report on these creatures. What do they look like? What physical characteristics make them attractive to Martin? How did these fish get their name?

- Some interesting parallels can be drawn between the play and the zodiac, particularly the sign Pisces. Investigate your own astrological sign. Does your behavior mirror the description? If it does not, can you account for the differences? Is

there strong evidence to suggest that sun signs can dictate character and behavior?

- In Wiechmann's play *The Secret of Steep Ravines*, a young girl revisits her memories and desires and travels beyond the realm of her imagination to unlock the secrets of a house and the people within it. How is Martin's own journey to the docks influenced by family secrets? How does the power of imagination shape Martin's perceptions?

- Investigate further the one-act play format Wiechmann uses to reach her audience. Choosing this medium poses a challenge to the playwright. Her treatment of a topic or storyline must lend itself to a simple set and a compressed amount of time. Why do you think the playwright chooses this genre? Does the form Wiechmann chooses enhance or detract from her work? Why or why not?

---

as explained by Martin, come out at night, drawn to the moon by an unseen force to feed at the edge of the docks: "The moon's got a force, an it pulls and pulls at the insides of these fish. . . . All they got is moon minds." Forces seem to be at work within Martin as he is captivated by the beauty of the fish and their ability to stir within him fond memories of his father. Eden acknowledges these forces working in humankind and declares to Martin that there are forces guiding both their lives.

Eden unknowingly draws a parallel between herself and the fish before Martin has a chance to explain their peculiar habits: "I think I come out at night—you know—like a creature." The same forces compelling the fish are at work within Eden, transforming her personality. They are also the very same forces that Eden uses to justify her parents extremely dysfunctional relationship. Ultimately, these forces draw Eden and Martin to each other and create a union with the power to transform and heal them both.

## STYLE

### Antihero

Eden is anything but a typical hero. A hero, by definition, demonstrates admirable traits such as idealism, courage, and integrity. Eden does not. She infringes on Martin's privacy without regard for his feelings by stowing away in the back of his car. The underage teen manages to steal two beers for the trip from her employer. When Eden's classmate successfully shoplifts "four bikinis, a princess phone and two Cheryl Tiegs jogging outfits," she tells Martin with admiration, "you gotta admit—she did something."

Because Eden severely lacks traditional hero values, she feels helpless in a world over which she has no control. Eden's world is an unforgiving place, providing all of the justification she needs to make her own rules. "There's no rational way to account for the disgusting things I've seen in my

life,'' she tells Martin. Despite her disregard for
authority, her inappropriate, if not excessive, candor about her dysfunctional family life and brusque
persona, Eden manages to reach Martin significantly enough to inspire a profound change in his
character in the course of one evening.

## Unities

*Feeding the Moonfish* is a one-act play following strict rules of dramatic structure. It follows
Aristotle's most important principles of drama: the
unities of action, time and place. These three principles compel a dramatist to construct a single plot
that details the causal relationships of action and
character, restricts the action to the events of a
single day, and limits the scene to a single place or
city. The action in Wiechmann's play takes place on
a dock in Florida in a single evening. The plot
begins with Martin's appearance on the docks followed by an emotional tangle he has with Eden that
eventually brings them to a mutual understanding
and peace. As the plot unfolds, the audience dis-
cerns what motivates both Martin and Eden to
behave toward each other in somewhat predictable
ways. Martin is upset about his father's suicide,
even paralyzed by it, while Eden feels free to share
with Martin the details of her stepfather's murder
without affect. This exchange provides Martin with
the outlet he needs to share his feelings with Eden
and put the past behind him. ''There's nothing I
could tell you that you'd think was crazy,'' says an
amazed Martin as he realizes Eden is there for him.
In keeping with modern drama, the work is concerned with the unity of impression. The audience is
left with the impression that Martin has for the first
time openly shared his feelings about his father's
death, with positive results, and his disturbing behavior along with Eden's troubled history hit their
emotional mark. As the mismatched pair makes a
connection, the audience is left with several problems to resolve: an inappropriate relationship between the two and the task of reconciling Martin's
abusive history with women with his apparent reha-
bilitation at the play's conclusion, which is demonstrated in his refusal to harm Eden.

## Point of View

The events of the play are presented from the
third-person point of view. The audience is left to
interpret the action without any special insight into
the characters' minds or motivations. Martin's imagined conversations with the moonfish could argu-

ably be a window into the mind of his psyche, or
they may be unexplained, supernatural events.
Whether imagined or real, at no time do they
provide the audience with sufficient insight into
Martin's motivations. The play's conclusion supports this assertion; it is defined by Martin's gentle
stroking, rather than choking, of Eden's neck. The
suspense surrounding his choice to comfort rather
than harm Eden is heightened by the audience's
uncertainty and lack of knowledge.

## Rising Action

After Eden returns with the sleeping bag and
beer, her conversation with Martin becomes increasingly complex as emotions heat up. Eden begins to share the intimate details of and her reaction
to her father's murder. In doing so, Eden expresses
her vulnerability. Martin criticizes her, Eden responds, and the two go back and forth, exchanging
insults. Martin criticizes Eden for wearing skimpy
clothing at the restaurant, while Eden provokes
Martin, questioning him about his rumored mis-
treatment of women. The tension building between
the two leads to the climax as Martin goes to strike
Eden and then stops himself.

## Resolution

At the end of the play, Martin undergoes a
dramatic shift in perception which is demonstrated
in his responses to Eden. He expresses admiration
for Eden, for her unconditional friendship, and for
her ability to truly listen to him. More importantly,
in the closing moments of the play, Martin moves
his hands from maintaining a chokehold on Eden's
neck to gently stroking it. His anger toward his
mother has resolved itself.

## HISTORICAL CONTEXT

The 1980s brought a lot of uncertainty. The economy was unstable, communism and the cold war
still loomed large, and Americans were losing confidence in the president. It is against this backdrop
that Weichmann wrote *Feeding the Moonfish*. While
there are no direct references to the time period, the
play does express an element of uncertainty as to the

# COMPARE
# &
# CONTRAST

- **1980s:** "Reaganomics," fiscal policies designed to stimulate the economy, result in a record number of corporate acquisitions, mergers, and liquidations, providing a means of greater wealth to the wealthy.

  **Today:** Despite record deficit levels, President Bush runs on a 2004 election platform of tax cuts in order to create jobs, boost spending, and lift the markets.

- **1980s:** Acquired Immune Deficiency Syndrome or AIDS is discovered by physicians and identified as an exclusively homosexual disease or "gay cancer."

  **Today:** Researchers discover the source of Human Immunodeficiency Virus (HIV) is a species of chimpanzee living in western Africa.

- **1980s:** On April 26, 1986, engineering experiments at a nuclear power plant in Chernobyl, Soviet Union, lead to a disastrous atomic chain reaction resulting in approximately twenty-five thousand premature deaths.

  **Today:** Proponents of nuclear power in the European Union fear that without reactors they will not reach their goal of reducing greenhouse gas emissions by 8 percent (from 1990 levels) by 2012.

- **1980s:** President Reagan embarks on an ambitious military program, the Strategic Defense Initiative (SDI), or "Star Wars," proposing the use of orbiting weapons systems to attack and destroy incoming intercontinental ballistic missiles.

  **Today:** The United States announces plans to abandon the Antiballistic Missile Treaty of 1972, a policy that bans certain defensive missile systems and symbolizes a major turning point in the cold war.

- **1980s:** Members of the Reagan administration make a secret arms deal with Iran in exchange for the release of American hostages held in Lebanon.

  **Today:** President Bush is accused by the popular press of lying to the American public in his arguments for taking the country to war in Iraq in 2003.

- **1980s:** The Berlin Wall, the symbolic barrier dividing East and West Berlin, the communist and the free world, is dismantled as Gorbachev, President Reagan, and East German guards look on.

  **Today:** The fall of Saddam Hussein's regime results in the looting of the Baghdad Museum and the loss of tens of thousands of objects.

---

true nature of subjects ranging from marriage to the nature of the characters themselves and, by extension, of life in the twentieth century.

## AIDS Crisis

In 1981, Acquired Immune Deficiency Syndrome (AIDS) was discovered by physicians. Human Immunodeficiency Virus (HIV), a virus that attacks white blood cells and T4 lymphocytes, causes AIDS by weakening the body's immune system, leaving it vulnerable to infection. In the early 1980s, the infection was consistently appearing in homosexu-

als or intravenous drug users. Many felt that the disease was in fact a "gay" disease, sparking misdirected moral attacks on the homosexual community. Sadly, President Reagan failed to respond to the epidemic, and the disease would take countless numbers of victims before AIDS activists raised public awareness almost a decade later.

## The Berlin Wall

The Reagan Presidency signaled the end of the cold war. Some credit the collapse of the Soviet Union to President Reagan's Strategic Defense Initiative program and his pressure tactics, while others attribute the nation's demise to financial strain. Many attribute Mikhail Gorbachev's *perestroika* (economic reform) and *glasnost* (new openness), which changed the face of Eastern Europe, for eventually contributing to the dissolve of communism in East Germany. The biggest symbol of this dark time in history was the Berlin Wall, a barrier dividing East and West Berlin, the communist and the free world. The wall, once heavily guarded, was dismantled in 1989, as Gorbachev, President Reagan, and East German guards looked on.

### Disaster at Chernobyl

The third largest city in the Soviet Union, Chernobyl, was home to a major nuclear power plant. On April 26, 1986, an experiment with the plant's nuclear reactor number 4 led to an unmanageable atomic chain reaction. The results were catastrophic. Tons of radioactive material were released causing an estimated twenty-five thousand premature deaths. The fallout was ten times that of Hiroshima and was predicted to cause eleven times the cancer deaths as those resulting from the 1945 bombings at Hiroshima and Nagasaki combined. The disaster prompted concerns regarding the safe maintenance and operation of nuclear-power facilities.

### Iran-Contra Scandal

In another grand military scheme, President Reagan made a secret arms deal with Iran in exchange for the release of American hostages being held in Lebanon. Portions of the proceeds from the deal secretly went to fund the Contras, people who were working to overthrow the Sandinista government. Congress publicly rejected such activity, making it not only illegal but unconstitutional. The scheme came under Congressional investigation, uncovering a trail that led to National Security Adviser Robert McFarlane, President Reagan, and Oliver North. In the end, President Reagan would walk away from the incident unscathed while Oliver North's initial convictions were eventually set aside. All were pardoned by President George Bush.

### Strategic Defense Initiative

Characterized by some as President Reagan's most ambitious military spending plan, the Strategic Defense Initiative (SDI), or "Star Wars" as it was referred to by critics, proposed using orbiting weapons systems to attack incoming intercontinental ballistic missiles before they had a chance to strike. Much of the technology President Reagan suggested was not in development, yet President Reagan and Bush invested $30 billion in the program. Many objectors feared that, in addition to placing a huge financial strain on the nation, the program violated the Antiballistic Missile Treaty of 1972 and made the prospect of thermonuclear war more likely.

### Reagan and Reaganomics

Known as the "Great Communicator," President Ronald Reagan based his 1980 bid for the Presidency on policies consistent with his performance as Governor of California; he would cut taxes and downsize big government to end stagflation (inflation without increase in demand or employment). President Reagan supported David Stockman's conservative economic policy called supply-side economics, a belief that government policy could stimulate production. Specifically, it was a belief that supply creates demand. Government would encourage production by reducing taxes and deregulation of industry. Out of this economic policy came the term "trickle down," a belief that by relieving the tax burdens of the wealthy money would trickle down to the American public, stimulating business investment, increasing employment opportunities, and improving the economy.

The resulting policies have been dubbed "Reaganomics." Ultimately, they did very little to stimulate the economy, neither increasing production nor consumption. Instead, President Reagan's policies provided a means for the rich to gain even more wealth. Companies chose to engage in corporate acquisitions and mergers, which meant huge profits for their investors.

## CRITICAL OVERVIEW

*Feeding the Moonfish* is one of Wiechmann's more familiar plays and perhaps the only one to make it to mainstream print. Although very little is written about the play, selected criticism on Wiechmann's *The Holy Mother of Hadley, New York* provides some insight into the playwright's critical reception. In a critical review, Matthew Murray is at times complementary, calling the "situation Wiechmann has created . . . an interesting one," characterizing the work as being "mostly touching and inspiring as a portrait of small town life and religion in the modern age." However, he is equally condemning of Wiechmann's consideration of miracles in everyday life. Referring to the characters in the play, Murray says, "Their author could stand to pay more attention to her own words." In another review, Martin Denton, while praising the production, states that "It's unfortunate that, for me at least, none of this effort provides much in the way of elucidation," yet admits, "those seeing the play after September 11 may well react differently to it than I did." It is important to remember amid this criticism that *Feeding the Moonfish*, while rarely the target of critical reception, appears in a notable collection of one-act plays along with some of the greatest playwrights of the twenty-first century.

# CRITICISM

## *Laura Carter*

*Carter is currently employed as a freelance writer. In this essay, Carter considers how the zodiac influences Wiechmann's work.*

Taken from a literal perspective, Weichmann's *Feeding the Moonfish* is a one-act human drama capturing the moving relationship between Martin and Eden, as the unlikely pair connect, forming an intensely powerful, life-changing bond that ultimately transforms them both. Examining the work from an astrological perspective, however, gives the play a harmonious depth.

Pisces is the twelfth sign of the zodiac and is symbolized by two fish positioned in harmony to one another. Pisces's element is water, its color blue, and its related tarot card the moon. Sensitive Pisces experience an intense inner life, possess a strong imagination, and are deeply influenced by the subconscious in daily life. Pisces are often pulled in opposite directions, struggling to reconcile a need for social activity and a tendency toward isolation in search of their inner selves. Their lives are strongly impacted by childhood memories and the vividness of their own dreams, so vivid that it is hard for Pisces to reconcile whether or not they are real. They often act too late in situations, leaving them to deal with feelings of regret.

Several elements of the play are consistent with Pisces. Martin and Eden's relationship mirrors the symbol of the two fish which is reminiscent of the yin and yang symbol. Like Pisces, Martin is drawn to the water. His happiest memories with his father are related to the water and time spent on the docks.

The moon also plays a crucial role in the play. Martin explains to Eden the hold moonlight has over the fish: "natural things are moved by forces see. Like the moon." These forces also tie Martin to a spot on the docks, compelling him to return night after night to make a connection with his father. Eden acknowledges these forces at work among people and asks Martin to consider the possibility of "being zapped right now by outside forces." In a dream in which Martin is in an airplane, he refers to a blue sky "so deep you could just tumble into it."

Personality traits defining Pisces resemble Martin's character. His dialogue on the docks with the moonfish demonstrates his imaginative side. Martin returns to conjure up memories of his father, sharing with Eden how he spends his evenings at the docks, "Each night I dream and in my dream I see him. Warmer, more real than life." The vividness of Martin's dreams leaves a lasting impression on him. Deeply feeling and sensitive, he remains connected to his childhood. He has been harboring feelings about his mother, causing him to act out in inappropriate or abusive ways toward women. One minute he is protective of Eden, telling her that she should not walk around in the dark alone and in the next he is accusing her of being "just a plain come-on." Martin is constantly fighting his urge to be alone with his memories and the longing for social interaction.

Like Pisces, Martin demonstrates a propensity to act when it is too late and the resulting failures are painful for him. This is best exemplified in what Eden has revealed about Martin's relationships with women. She accuses him of watching a young, inebriated woman wander off the dock and into the water then choosing to stand by and watch her drown. Martin reacts emphatically, telling Eden to "Shut up. Shut up." Earlier on, the audience is privileged to Martin's deepest fears about harming Eden. When he shares his concerns with the moonfish, they intimate that he has the power to keep her safe: "Nothing can happen you don't want to happen." Together, these events betray a great remorse in Martin and a desire to reinvent himself. He does not hide his past transgressions or fears; instead, he is eager to put them behind him.

The rhythms Martin and Eden move to can also be explained in astrological terms, providing the underlying framework for Wiechmann's play. British astrologer Richard Hills's interpretation of Pisces is very revealing in this regard. He prefaces his online description of Pisces with an explanation of how "life began in the garden of Eden, in Paradise in perfect harmony with the divine." Recalling the biblical Fall, it is the one act of disobedience that causes us to become conscious of ourselves and to lose our place in Paradise. The result, says Hills, is that we became fully human. Eventually, God restores the relationship through the advent of Christ in a more complete way than had man never left Paradise. According to Hills, Pisces straddles the divide between the human and the divine. Further, Hills states, "More than any other sign, perhaps Pisces experiences normal human life as limited, for it excludes so much that can make life more complete." Hills adds that "Some may attempt to live as if this exclusion from Paradise had never happened, and live life in a constant daydream, totally ineffective in the world as it is."

Applying Hills's theories to the play raise some interesting questions. Is Martin prone to insane muttering or does he, in truth, have a connection to the divine? If the moonfish are a means of connection with the divine, the promise to deliver Martin's father, in spirit or in flesh, becomes a reality. Certainly, examining the work from this perspective would account for the openness in which Martin approaches the docks every evening. He does not stop to question whether what he is doing is crazy or not and is not afraid to share with Eden that he does in fact have elaborate conversations with the fish.

Hills also notes that because they have a sense of otherworldliness about them, Pisces are still subject to live a life in a world of limitations. Coming to terms with a life separate from Paradise poses a problem for them. Martin struggles with his need to isolate himself on the docks every evening. He is haunted by his past and can only find pleasure in his memories of his father, memories in which he feels safe, complete, and loved. His entire objective for returning to the docks is to recapture this closeness that he feels, to "see" his father, to feel the power of that relationship in his life.

Other Pisces are able to overcome their desire to dwell among the divine. According to Hills, they successfully live in the "human arena" by infusing it with divine meaning. Eden lives in this "human arena" and looks to her reality to create her own paradise on Earth. She sees her relationship with Martin as a matter of forces working between them as Martin does with the moonfish. The difference between Eden and Martin is that Eden has come to terms with her parents' relationship, explaining its dysfunctional nature as just part of their own unique

*A couple sitting on the docks at Captain Don's Habitat, Bonaire, Netherlands Antilles*

interaction, just something they "do." She sees no victims in her stepfather's murder, only people drawn together by destiny:

> Gravity was pulling em to each other. Forces was pulling em—just like them fish—only they could feel emotional pain in their minds too so it was worse. They was real helpless. They couldn't change nothing though. They couldn't *change,* see.

Eden's view is new and different for Martin. He has lived in a tortured world up to this point, with very little forgiveness for his mother, and, on some level, perhaps even for his father for committing suicide and, therefore, abandoning him. Eden's view grounds Martin. He begins to see the situation in a different way. He begins to forgive. Martin becomes part of an open, honest exchange with Eden, indicating that he has left some of the anger toward his mother behind him. This is confirmed in the gratitude he expresses toward Eden and his ability to resist the inclination to strangle her.

By opening up to Eden, Martin has opened up a whole new realm of possibilities for himself and has gained insight into how he has perceived his life up to this point. Reaching out to Eden has healed him and made him whole in some way as demonstrated

# WHAT DO I READ NEXT?

- Tony Crisp's *Dream Dictionary: An A to Z Guide to Understanding Your Unconscious Mind* (2002) is an exploration into the unconscious mind. This dream guide discusses dream symbols and their meanings and provides a basis for engaging in dream interpretation.

- *The Virgin Suicides* (1993) is Jeffrey Eugenides' fictional account of five young men struggling to make sense of suicides committed by five sisters twenty years ago. The story is a moving account of how the tragedy of suicide impacts others.

- *The Field: The Quest for the Secret Force of the Universe* (2003) is a chronicle of scientific evi-

dence confirming the existence of a fundamental life force. Written by Lynne McTaggart, the book explains the nature of this interconnected universe and attempts to explain supernatural phenomena.

- *The Complete Prophecies of Nostradamus* (2000), by Nostradamus and translated by Edward Leoni, is a complete translation of the prophecies of Nostradamus, the sixteenth-century French astrologer. This work contains his prophecies in both English and French, historical background, commentary section, his will, and his personal letters. The stars had an enormous influence on Nostradamus and his famous predictions.

---

by his transformation at the end of the play. The sudden communion between Eden and Martin is surprising given Martin's tendencies to isolate himself at work and Eden's insinuation into his life by dishonest means. It satisfies Martin's desperate need for some sort of human connection, affirming that he has been alone with his own emotional pain for far too long. Beyond physical symbols and personal traits, the relationship between Martin and Eden has a seamless, melodious quality to it. Both characters demonstrate an astrological affinity toward one another. Eden is flighty, impulsive, intense, and unpredictable, yet Martin seems to anticipate and know how to respond to her. Despite Martin's tendency toward isolation, Eden is able to draw out his darkest personal feelings about his father's suicide and offer him solace.

In keeping with Wiechmann's other works, *Feeding the Moonfish* creates a delightful tension, challenging the audience to reach beyond conventional understanding, to see the world in divine order, a world influenced by the stars. Both Eden and Martin, while on the surface appear to be deeply disturbed individuals, are deeply interconnected. Their union, at least for the moment, serves to reconcile their misgivings about themselves and

about each other. Together, they strike a balance between the earthly and the divine. It is in this heavenly relationship that the play ultimately finds its unity.

**Source:** Laura Carter, Critical Essay on *Feeding the Moonfish*, in *Drama for Students*, Thomson Gale, 2005.

## SOURCES

Axelrod, Alan, *The Complete Idiot's Guide to 20th Century American History*, Alpha Books, 1999, pp. 395–410.

''Barbara Wiechmann,'' www.newdramatists.org/barbara_wiechmann.htm (accessed November 8, 2004).

Carney, James, and John F. Dickerson, ''Taking Aim at 2004: Can Bush Win a Second Term Running on a Platform of Tanks and Tax Cuts? An Inside Look at the Playbook for the 2004 Presidential Campaign,'' in *Time*, Vol. 161, No. 18, May 5, 2003, p. 32.

Denton, Martin, Review of *The Holy Mother of Hadley, New York*, www.nytheatre.com/nytheatre/archweb/arch_028.htm (accessed November 8, 2004).

Hills, Richard, ''Pisces Zodiac Sign in Horoscopes, Including Compatibility Issues: An Interpretation by Astrologer Richard Hills,'' www.astrology-chart.co.uk/pisces.htm (accessed November 8, 2004).

Murray, Matthew, Review of *The Holy Mother of Hadley, New York,* www.talkinbroadway.com/ob/9_10a_01.html (accessed November 8, 2004).

Pfiffner, James P., ''Did President Bush Mislead the Country in His Arguments for War with Iraq?'' in *Presidential Studies Quarterly,* Vol. 34, No. 1, March 2004, p. 25.

Sains, Ariane, ''The Uncertain Future of Nuclear Energy,'' in *Europe,* February 2001, p. 26.

Wiechmann, Barbara, *Feeding the Moonfish,* in *Telling Tales: New One-Act Plays,* edited by Eric Lane, Penguin, 1993, pp. 389–412.

> IF THE MOONFISH ARE A MEANS OF CONNECTION WITH THE DIVINE, THE PROMISE TO DELIVER MARTIN'S FATHER, IN SPIRIT OR IN FLESH, BECOMES A REALITY.''

# FURTHER READING

*Aristotle's Poetics,* translated by S. H. Butcher, Hill and Wang, 1961.

Aristotle's study of drama is a must read for those interested in literary fundamentals, including unity of plot, reversal of the situation, and character. This is the single most authoritative text used by playwrights and theorists for more than two thousand years.

Garrison, Gary, *Perfect 10: Writing and Producing the 10-Minute Play,* Heinemann Drama, 2001.

In this work, Garrison provides a simple and straight-forward approach to writing and producing the 10-minute play. An excellent pocket how-to guide for those interested in modern playwriting techniques.

Sakoian, Frances, *The Astrologer's Handbook,* reprint ed., HarperResource, 1989.

Moving beyond predictable analysis of the twelve zodiac signs, this handbook was designed to meet the demands of professional astrologers, yet is user-friendly enough for those new to the subject. A great reference tool offering explanations of all of the central concepts of astrology.

*Telling Tales: New One-Act Plays,* edited by Eric Lane, Penguin, 1993.

This collection of extraordinary plays contains Wiechmann's play and more than twenty-five one-act plays by Christopher Durang, Maria Irene Fornes, Athol Fugard, Zora Neal Hurston, Arthur Miller, John Patrick Shanely, and others. It is an excellent reference for anyone interested in contemporary theater.

# *An Ideal Husband*

## OSCAR WILDE

## 1895

*An Ideal Husband* premiered in London, England, on January 3, 1895, and was published in 1896. It was the third of Wilde's four comedic plays to be staged, and it was as big a success with audiences as the previous two. However, critics of the time were not as appreciative as audiences, which was the case for all of Wilde's social comedies. Critics thought these plays more flippant than substantive; audiences were delighted by the wonderful wit of the dramas. Numerous choice ''one-liners'' and other pithy witticisms that Wilde's dramatic characters deliver are still quoted by people today.

*An Ideal Husband* is often called a ''social comedy'' because it has both a serious (''social'') as well comedic plot line. On the one hand, the play is about a prominent politician who is in danger of losing his reputation as a paragon of integrity, owing to a youthful indiscretion that the play's villain is threatening to expose. Although the politician's transgression is not exposed, this plot line conveys the idea that there are very few people in the world who are wholly good and to pretend so is hypocritical. This is a message for Wilde's contemporaries, a late-Victorian group obsessed with purity and goodness but, of course, as imperfect as the people of any other age. On the other hand, the play is supposed to be funny, as it is, thanks to the witty bantering of the characters, especially in moments when the play is not directly concerned with the ''social'' plot.

Wilde and his play are by now firmly established in the English-language canon of literature, and most libraries hold volumes of the individual or collected plays. The Modern Library editions of Wilde's collected comedies are the most widespread.

## AUTHOR BIOGRAPHY

The writer and wit known as Oscar Wilde was born Oscar Fingal O'Flahertie Wills Wilde in Dublin, Ireland, on October 16, 1854. This lavish and romantic set of given names evokes Irish myth and heroes, conveying Wilde's parents' pride in their Irish nationality.

Wilde came from a prominent family. His father, a surgeon who operated on the monarchs of Europe, was knighted. His mother, a historian and political commentator and activist, was very prominent in the Irish freedom movements that would bring Ireland its independence from England in 1921. Both of Wilde's parents published numerous books in their lifetimes.

As a boy in school, Wilde excelled in his favorite subjects. He then spent three years at Trinity College, one of the foremost universities in Ireland. He excelled at Trinity and then made his way to Oxford University in Cambridge, England. At Oxford he distinguished himself yet again, winning prestigious prizes.

Once he had graduated and established himself in London, Wilde began publishing in various genres: poetry, drama, essays, fairy tales, and more. He was also an editor of magazines. Equally important was the fame he gained in London as a wit and a dandy (someone devoted to fashion and style). In the midst of late-Victorian England's drably coated men, Wilde went about in knee breeches, fine vests, and long hair (at least for a time). He would speak at public events and art exhibits, and people would listen, vastly amused and intrigued. The magazines that chronicled the goings on about town in London began to satirize and parody Wilde. In 1894, Wilde married; he and his wife had two sons.

*Oscar Wilde*

Wilde reached his pinnacle of fame in 1895, when *An Ideal Husband* premiered on the London stage. The Prince of Wales and many other notables were present on opening night and found the play very much to their liking. *An Ideal Husband* was the third of four highly successful plays Wilde wrote before his career was destroyed by an unfortunate and tragic turn of events.

Very shortly after the premieres of *An Ideal Husband* and Wilde's fourth comedic play, *The Importance of Being Earnest*, Wilde was found guilty of indecency and sentenced to two years in prison at hard labor. Wilde's trial followed his having charged a British aristocrat with libel for accusing him of homosexual acts—a mistake because Wilde was indeed involved with Sir Alfred Douglas at the time, and late-Victorian society was singularly intolerant of such free behavior.

After prison, his career and health ruined, Wilde lived his last days in France. He died on November 30, 1900, in Paris. In 1909, his remains were moved to the French National Cemetery of Père Lachaise. His last major works are *De Profundis* and *Ballad of Reading Goal*, both of which pertain to his terrible trial and imprisonment.

# PLOT SUMMARY

## Act 1

The action of *An Ideal Husband* takes place within about twenty four hours. Act 1 takes place at Sir Robert Chiltern's house, which is located in the fashionable part of London. The Chilterns are hosting a reception. The first two speakers of the play, two minor characters, Lady Basildon and Mrs. Marchmont, set a witty tone. They are pretty, young married women, and they speak to each other languidly and cleverly. Attention then moves to various new arrivals at the reception, such as the Earl of Caversham, who inquires after his son Lord Goring, and Mabel Chiltern, Sir Robert Chiltern's sister, who chats with the Earl of Caversham. The most important arrivals, however, are Lady Markby and Mrs. Cheveley, because the latter is the play's villain.

That something serious will be occurring in this otherwise comic play becomes clear when Lady Markby introduces Mrs. Cheveley to Lady Chiltern. Lady Chiltern realizes that she knows Mrs. Cheveley, but under a different name—the name of her first husband. Mrs. Cheveley clearly disturbs Lady Chiltern, and Lady Chiltern appears to dislike the other woman intensely.

Mrs. Cheveley has come to the party to speak to Sir Robert specifically, and, soon enough, the two find themselves alone. What she wishes to talk about is blackmail: if Sir Robert does not support what is in fact a doomed South American canal scheme in a speech to the parliament the next day, she will reveal the terrible secret of his youth, which will destroy his life and career. Shaken to his core, Sir Robert agrees to do her bidding.

At the end of act 1, Lady Chiltern succeeds in getting her husband to admit that Mrs. Cheveley has persuaded him to change his mind about the canal project. She is outraged and convinces her husband to write to Mrs. Cheveley immediately, telling her that he will not support the project in his parliamentary speech. Wondering what kind of power Mrs. Cheveley has over her husband, Lady Chiltern declares that it had better not be blackmail—that he better not be one of those men who pretend to be pillars of the community but who in fact have shameful secrets.

## Act 2

Act 2 opens the next morning, once again at the Chiltern residence. Lord Goring and Robert Chiltern

are speaking; Chiltern is telling his good friend Goring everything. At one point, Chiltern bitterly wonders why a youthful folly has the power to ruin a man's career, even when that man has spent so many years doing good works. To this Goring replies that what Chiltern did was not folly but fairly ugly and very grave: he sold a state secret for money.

Chiltern tries to explain, saying that when he was young he was poor, so that it did not matter that he came from a good family because his prospects were limited by a lack of funds. He tells how he was seduced by the teachings of Baron Arnheim, who turned his head with ''the most terrible of all philosophies, the philosophy of power.'' The baron ''preached to [him] the most marvelous of all gospel, the gospel of gold,'' he says. Chiltern says he was ferociously ambitious, and that when the chance came to make his fortune, it did not matter that it depended on a crime; he took it.

Lady Chiltern comes home while the men are conversing. She has been at a ''Woman's Liberal Association'' meeting, where, as she says, they discuss things such as ''Factory Acts, Female Inspectors, the Eight Hours Bill, the Parliamentary Franchise,'' and so on. Soon, Robert Chiltern leaves and Mabel Chiltern takes his place, asking Goring if he will meet her the next morning. Goring agrees and then leaves. Next, Lady Markby and Mrs. Cheveley are announced. Mrs. Cheveley is inquiring about a diamond broach she lost the day before, asking whether it was found by anyone at the reception. (Lord Goring found the broach and still has it.)

When Lady Markby leaves, Lady Chiltern and Mrs. Cheveley are able to speak to each other frankly. Lady Chiltern makes it clear that Mrs. Cheveley is not welcome in her house. This spurs Mrs. Cheveley to tell Lady Chiltern the truth about her husband, and she warns Lady Chiltern that she will carry out her threat. Lady Chiltern is devastated to find out that her husband is like so many other men, men who have shameful secrets. She confronts her husband and tells him that her love for him is dead.

## Act 3

Act 3 takes place in Lord Goring's house, in the library, which is connected to a number of other rooms. Lord Goring is preparing to go out for the evening when he receives a letter from Lady Chiltern. It reads, ''I want you. I trust you. I am coming to you.'' Goring rightly deduces that Lady Chiltern now knows the truth about her husband and that she needs to talk to someone.

Goring cancels his plans to go out and realizes that he must tell his servants that he is not in for anyone except Lady Chiltern; it would be disastrous for her reputation if she were found in his home without a chaperon. However, before he can do this, his father is announced. Unfortunately for Goring, his father is in the mood to lecture him. Goring tries unsuccessfully to get rid of his father and must listen to him go on about Goring's need to marry and settle down. In the meantime, Mrs. Cheveley has arrived, and a servant, thinking she is Lady Chiltern, escorts her into Goring's drawing room.

Finally able to show his father the door, Goring is put out to find Sir Robert Chiltern on his doorstep. Goring tries to get rid of Chiltern, believing all the while that Lady Chiltern is in the next room. He is concerned that Chiltern will discover his wife and misconstrue her presence in his home. Chiltern lingers and eventually overhears a sound coming from the room in which Mrs. Cheveley is waiting. He goes in, sees the woman, and returns to Goring disgusted. He believes that Mrs. Cheveley and Goring are having an affair. Goring, for his part, believes that Chiltern has just seen his own wife. Chiltern leaves and Goring sees that it is Mrs. Cheveley who is in the room.

Lord Goring has Mrs. Cheveley's diamond broach and tells her that the broach was a gift he gave to his niece, so that the only way Mrs. Cheveley could have come by it was to have stolen it, which she did. He threatens to call the police and have her prosecuted for theft unless she drops her blackmail plans. She has no choice but to concede, and Goring makes her hand over the letter Chiltern wrote all those years ago. Goring burns the letter.

### Act 4

Act 4 is the resolution of the play. It takes place in the morning room of the Chiltern residence, the same setting as act 2. Lord Goring finally realizes that Mabel Chiltern is the woman for him and proposes. Mabel is very happy, as is the visiting Earl of Caversham. Lady Chiltern has forgiven her husband but still believes he must give up public life. She thinks they should retire to the country. Lord Goring convinces her otherwise. He makes her see that her husband thrives on politics, and if she were to take that away from him, he would become bitter and disillusioned and their marriage would suffer. Lady Chiltern realizes that Goring is right and relents. Sir Robert is ecstatic.

# MEDIA ADAPTATIONS

- *An Ideal Husband* was made into a film by a British production in 1947. This film version was directed by Alexander Korda and starred Paulette Goddard as Mrs. Cheveley and Michael Wilding as Lord Goring.

- *An Ideal Husband* was adapted for television in Britain in 1969 as part of a ''Play of the Month'' series.

- Another British production made *An Ideal Husband* into a film 1998. This version was directed by William Cartlidge and starred James Wilby as Sir Robert Chiltern, Sadie Frost as Mrs. Cheveley, and Jonathan Firth as Lord Goring.

- A joint United States and Great Britain production of *An Ideal Husband* was made in 1999. This widely acclaimed version was directed by Oliver Parker and featured an all-star cast, including Cate Blanchett as Lady Gertrude Chiltern, Minnie Driver as Mabel Chiltern, Julianne Moore as Mrs. Cheveley, Jeremy Northern as Sir Robert Chiltern, and Rupert Everett as Lord Goring.

## CHARACTERS

### Lady Olivia Basildon

Lady Basildon and her close friend Mrs. Marchmont are the first speakers in Wilde's play, setting the tone with their witty banter. ''They are types,'' Wilde's stage notes say, ''of exquisite fragility,'' and they are female dandies. Lady Basildon and her friend affect a world-weary attitude, pretending to find the fashionable London parties they go to terribly boring. As Lady Basildon says of a different party the two are planning to attend: ''Horribly tedious! Never know why I go. Never know why I go anywhere.'' The duo's worldly sophistication and wit undoubtedly flattered a portion of his audience whom Wilde hoped would enjoy his play, namely fashionable society women.

### Lord Caversham

*See* Earl of Caversham

### Mrs. Cheveley

Mrs. Cheveley, the villain of Wilde's play, enters the society of the Chilterns and Lord Goring determined either to get her own way or to destroy those who will not help her achieve her ends. She comes to London from Vienna, where she has been living for some time, to blackmail Sir Robert Chiltern. She knows Chiltern's terrible, scandalous secret and has concrete evidence of his transgression (a letter he wrote). She informs Chiltern that she will expose his sinful past unless he praises a South American canal scheme instead of condemning it for the stock market swindle it is as he plans to do in a parliamentary speech. Mrs. Cheveley and her friends have invested heavily in the scheme, and if the respected Chiltern were to advise his government to support it, Mrs. Cheveley and her friends would become much richer than they already are.

Since one of Wilde's points in the play is that large fortunes often have their roots in immorality, he needed to make Mrs. Cheveley's actions thoroughly unsympathetic to draw a convincing villain. The stock market manipulation had to be something that would not only increase her wealth but also eventually entail the impoverishment of others. Further, she is a blackmailer and habitual thief and liar. Still, this said, Mrs. Cheveley delivers some of the play's choicest witticisms.

### Lady Gertrude Chiltern

Gertrude Chiltern is a sheltered, good woman who worships perfect goodness most especially in the form of her "ideal husband." The problem with her worship of perfection and of her husband is that her husband is not in fact perfect; indeed, he has an extremely disreputable secret in his past—a secret that could ruin his career.

Described as being possessed of "a grave Greek beauty," Lady Chiltern is appropriately noble in character. She is involved in all sorts of good works. For example, she is a feminist campaigning for the right of girls and women to have a higher education. She is, in short, a moneyed woman with principles: she believes that she must give something back to society by supporting charities, foundations, and other causes.

Lady Chiltern also believes that when women love men they worship them; by doing so, such women require that their men conform to their ideals of what is great. And until Lady Chiltern learns the truth about her husband's past, she is certain that he is indeed her ideal. She believes that he is a thoroughly good man committed to doing only good in the world.

Lady Chiltern must learn a stern lesson in the play: that nobody is perfect and that to wish this is naive and dangerous. Lady Chiltern, then, is not really perfectly good until she accepts the fact of, and is willing to forgive, imperfection.

### Miss Mabel Chiltern

Mabel Chiltern has her eye on Lord Goring as a husband, and the two become engaged in the play's last act. She is the sister of Robert Chiltern. She is pretty, intelligent, and pert, and she is as witty as Lady Basildon and Mrs. Marchmont are. Knowing that Lord Goring is the man for her, Mabel Chiltern is waiting gracefully and humorously, albeit somewhat impatiently, for him to realize that she is the perfect woman for him.

From Lord Goring's father's point of view, she is a clever and pleasing young woman who is far too good for the likes of his son. Mabel is a foil to Gertrude because she is a young woman who does not expect perfection from any human being. She declares that one of the reasons she likes Lord Goring is because he has faults.

### Sir Robert Chiltern

A respected parliamentarian, Robert Chiltern is confronted by his disreputable past, blackmailed, and finally saved from any public scandal. The ugly secret of his past is that his fortune rests on his having sold a state secret. As a young man, he finds out that England intends to support an extensive overseas construction project, which means that anybody who invests in the project before the announcement is made public will become rich. In other words, whoever buys stock in the companies concerned before the prices of the stocks go up, on the strength of England's interest and support of the project, will reap a fortune.

Chiltern writes a letter to alert an acquaintance who buys a great deal of stock and pays Chiltern handsomely from the vast profits. Yet, what was required of the young Chiltern and all those in the know, as he knew very well, was strict secrecy and the ethical understanding that any "insider" stock purchases were criminal actions punishable by prison time.

Chiltern is horrified to learn that Mrs. Cheveley has the letter he wrote so long ago and plans to publish it unless he concedes to her demands. Ironically, what Mrs. Cheveley wants him to do is back an overseas construction project, so that, like Chiltern before her, she and her friends can make a financial killing on the strength of their early investments. The crucial difference, however, is that the scheme in which Mrs. Cheveley has invested is a scam, but Lord Chiltern's project was not.

Despite having planned to condemn the canal scheme because he knows that it is a scam, Chiltern capitulates to Mrs. Cheveley's demands. He cannot face scandal and ruin.

Chiltern changes his mind about his speech when his wife intervenes. Lady Chiltern knows the details of her husband's political activities and convinces him to deliver the speech he knows that he should. So, he writes a letter to Cheveley communicating his change of heart.

For a time, Chiltern is able to prevent his wife from finding out why Mrs. Cheveley has so much power over him, but eventually she discovers the truth. When she does, she declares that their love is dead. Chiltern is devastated, seeing his career and entire life crumbling around him. But, luckily for Chiltern, Lord Goring, his faithful friend, is able to foil Mrs. Cheveley's plans *and* convinces Lady Chiltern that her husband still deserves her love.

### Earl of Caversham

The Earl of Caversham (Lord Caversham) is Lord Goring's father, a stock characterization of a father who is perplexed by the vagaries of a son he simply cannot understand. He spends his time chastising his son and lecturing him about what he should do with his time. Short of doing something worthwhile with his life, Lord Caversham advises Lord Goring to marry at the very least. Clearly, despite his exasperation, Lord Caversham is fond of his lazy son.

### Viscount Lord Arthur Goring

Lord Goring, a close friend of Sir Robert Chiltern, saves the day for his friend by foiling Mrs. Cheveley's blackmail attempt. He is able to prevent her from carrying out her threat because he acquires proof that she is a thief and tells her he will inform the police unless she drops her plan, which she does. Yet, Goring's involvement in the serious plot line of this play is far less entertaining than his involvement in the comedic goings-on of *An Ideal Husband*.

Lord Goring speaks the play's funniest lines, many of which are still quoted today. For example, he informs his butler Phipps that, ''To love oneself is the beginning of a life-long romance, Phipps.'' He also has a funny rejoinder for his father when Caversham says he cannot fathom how Goring can stand London society. According to Goring's father, London society has devolved into a ''lot of damned nobodies talking about nothing.'' Goring replies: ''I love talking about nothing, father. It is the only thing I know anything about.''

Lord Goring is a dandy: he is not simply *in* fashion but *trendsetting* in dress; he pretends not to take anything seriously; he values witty repartee and excels at it.

If it were not for his father urging him to realize that it is time for him to marry, Lord Goring would undoubtedly continue in his life of perfect leisure and self-absorption. However, alerted to his duty to produce heirs, Goring opens his eyes and sees that the best companion for him as wife is close at hand in the person of Mabel Chiltern.

### Mrs. Margaret Marchmont

Mrs. Marchmont is the friend of Lady Basildon. The two women are very close to each other and much the same in character.

### Lady Markby

Lady Markby is Mrs. Cheveley's immediate connection to London society, as Mrs. Cheveley is younger and has traveled to London from Vienna alone. Lady Markby introduces Mrs. Cheveley to persons whom she does not yet know and chaperones the younger woman around town. She is an established, well-liked, older member of the moneyed, aristocratic society depicted in Wilde's play.

### Phipps

Phipps is Lord Goring's ''ideal'' butler. Phipps is self-effacing and discreet. His job is not to assert himself or his own personality in any way. Yet, in conversation with Lord Goring, he is not above subtle humor—delivered quite impassively, however.

### Vicomte de Nanjac

The vicomte is a French attaché who adores all things English and at whom Lord Goring pokes fun. His purpose in the play appears to be to have given the English audiences of the time something French to snicker at. This is a very popular gesture on

Wilde's part, since the French and the English were involved in bitter political and cultural rivalries for a long time.

# THEMES

## *Scandal, Hypocrisy, and the Ideal*

Cautioning Sir Robert that she will indeed carry out her threat and ruin his career, Mrs. Cheveley declares:

> Remember to what point your Puritanism in England has brought you. In old days nobody pretended to be a bit better than his neighbors. Nowadays, with our modern mania for morality, everyone has to pose as a paragon of purity, incorruptibility, and all the other seven deadly virtues—and what is the result? You all go over like ninepins—one after the other. Not a year passes in England without somebody disappearing. Scandals used to lend charm, or at least interest, to a man—now they crush him. And yours is a very nasty scandal. You couldn't survive it.

Here, in a nutshell, is the central message of Wilde's play: the more a culture upholds stringent moral values, the more likely it is that publicly prominent people will crumble under charges of impropriety. By this Wilde does not mean that immorality or criminal behavior is acceptable. What he means is that an exaggerated attachment to moral purity leads to social ills and not social good. This might seem counterintuitive; after all, should not the respect for moral purity lead to more people being truly good? For Wilde, it just leads to more people being failures in their own eyes and others' because it is impossible for most people not to make a mistake at some point in their lives. It encourages people not to hide even their minor vices, but to proclaim loudly against any and all weakness, thereby becoming hypocrites and paving the way for their greater shame if they are ever found out for their true selves. As Mrs. Cheveley's speech makes clear, in the Victorian climate of intolerance, politicians and other social leaders were pressured to proclaim themselves paragons of purity when they were not. Consequently, when the truth of their large or small sins came to the surface, their careers and reputations were compromised or ruined.

Mrs. Cheveley's speech was not only meant for Wilde's British audiences but also for his avid American audiences. This is not simply because America was culturally close to England but also

because of pertinent American history and its continuing influence on American life. Some of the first Europeans to settle in the United States were members of Puritan sects, and what these Christian fundamentalists are most remembered for is their period of hysteria and cruelty. In their pursuit of moral purity they saw evil everywhere, declared numerous persons witches, and burned them alive (the "witch trials"). Extremism, in other words, leads only and always to tragedy, even if it is extremism in the name of good.

As far as Mrs. Cheveley is concerned, politicians who conform and project themselves as paragons of good are hypocrites. They, like Chiltern, have things they need to hide, whether in their past or in their present. Wilde's disdain for hypocrisy explains his attachment to characters who are dandies like Lord Goring. Lord Goring's dandy pose entails, essentially, the notion that he is wicked and cares about himself first of all. In other words, the values he professes are precisely the opposite of those who proclaim themselves upstanding citizens wedded to duty and the welfare of others. Yet, if the upstanding citizen cannot possibly be the paragon he or she professes to be, then he or she is akin to Goring—a person who will, at times, let his or her own interests take precedence over the public good. In short, says Wilde, it is better to be a Goring, who does not pretend to be good, than to be a hypocrite.

*An Ideal Husband*'s play on things "ideal" or pure is related to its cautionary message about the Victorian obsession with perfect goodness. Obviously, the perfect specimen of any given thing is an ideal specimen of the thing. Lady Chiltern wants an ideal husband, which is a man who fulfills his husbandly role perfectly and who is, as well, an ideal human, i.e., perfectly good. She thinks this is what she has in Sir Robert, and Sir Robert, for his part, loves his wife so much that this is what he wants her to think. In learning that she is wrong to want such a thing, Lady Chiltern's development over the course of the play is a crucial component of the play's message.

The coupling of Mabel Chiltern and Lord Goring is Wilde's antidote to the Chilterns. Mabel, notably, declares that she wants to be a "good" wife to Lord Goring, not a perfect or ideal one. Lord Goring, perhaps, is Wilde's version of a good-enough husband, as he readily admits that he has faults. The human race, Wilde seems to say, will always fall short of its ideals, but this should not be

# TOPICS FOR FURTHER STUDY

- Research the circumstances surrounding Oscar Wilde's trial and imprisonment.

- The two years Wilde spent in prison ruined his health. Late-nineteenth-century prison conditions were harsh and hard labor as a punishment was common. Research prisons and the treatment of prisoners in England from 1890, plotting the major prison reforms of the twentieth century.

- Research Wilde's mother, Lady Jane Francesca Wilde, née Elgee. What works of literature did she publish under her own name? What did she publish under the pen name "Speranza," and what was her role as a political writer in the cause of Irish independence?

- Research the major Irish uprisings against British rule in the late nineteenth and early twentieth centuries. Explore, for example, the Easter Uprising of 1916.

- Research the history of the Irish Republican Army (IRA). Are they freedom fighters, or terrorists, in your view?

- Study one or two plays by the eighteenth-century-British playwright William Congreve, a master of the comedy of manners. Compare one of the plays to Wilde's *An Ideal Husband* or *The Importance of Being Earnest*.

- Wilde's father Sir William Wilde was an aural surgeon and oculist known throughout Europe for his expertise. What was the science of ears and eyes of the time? How successful were the operations of eye and ear surgeons then compared to today? Who were some of Sir William's most well-known patients?

- Wilde's mother was an active feminist, besides being an Irish patriot. Investigate her feminist activities and the activities of feminists of the time.

---

occasion for tragedy. On the contrary, what leads to tragedy is insisting that perfection must be achieved even after the best that can be done has been tried.

### Ambition

Politicians in late-nineteenth-century England were not terribly different from politicians today. They saw themselves as public servants and entered into politics to do some good and make a difference. Yet, to go far in politics it takes ambition. Politicians who aim to reach high positions in the government have to have nerves of steel and very thick skins. They are ruthlessly attacked by members of the opposing party; even others in their own party will attempt to outmaneuver them; journalists will dig into their private lives and print anything that will sell a magazine or newspaper; and so forth. Thus, in addition to wanting to do good, a politician aiming for the top has to be very ambitious. He or she has to have some craving for glory that makes all the pain of getting to the top bearable. In the

ferociously ambitious Sir Robert Chiltern, Wilde presents just this type of politician. In doing so, he has presented his highly successful politician accurately. After all, Chiltern is only forty but he is already an under-secretary, and, at the end of the play, the prime minister offers him a cabinet position.

This depiction of the politician's hungry ambition makes sense in *An Ideal Husband*. The play is concerned with having people adopt a realistic view of the world and how it works; consequently, Wilde avoids an idealized picture of the motivations of top-ranking politicians.

## STYLE

### Wit

Wit as a type of humor is what Wilde is known for, both in his everyday life and in a number of his writings, including *An Ideal Husband*. Wit is clever humor—not bawdy, rude, silly, or visual funniness. Wit entails the delivery of an unexpected or surprising insight, or a clever reversal of expectations. For example, at one point in the play, Mrs. Cheveley says, ''a woman's first duty in life is to her dressmaker, isn't it? What the second duty is, no one has yet discovered.'' This would have provoked laughter because the popular saying she is reversing is as follows: ''A woman's first duty is to her husband.'' Victorians were known for their commitment to duty and there would have been not one person in Wilde's audience who had not heard and read the popular axiom many, many times.

### Epigram and Aphorism

Epigrammatic turns of speech are short and sweet, and they are somehow surprising or witty. Wilde's characters' wit is often epigrammatic. For example, as Mrs. Cheveley says at one point, ''Oh! I don't care about the London season! It is too matrimonial. People are either hunting for husbands, or hiding from them.'' Mrs. Cheveley's purported reason for disliking the London social season is funny. Even funnier is that what makes the season ''matrimonial'' is not simply the search for husbands.

An aphorism is a brief statement containing an opinion or general truth, which might or might not be witty. Wilde excelled in wit in the form of aphorisms. Lady Cheveley, for example, delivers quite a few aphoristic witticisms in *An Ideal Husband*. For example, ''Morality,'' she says, ''is simply the attitude we take toward people whom we personally dislike.'' Or, as she says elsewhere: ''Questions are never indiscreet. Answers sometimes are.'' There is also Lord Goring's opinion about good advice. In reply to Mabel Chiltern when she questions his having told her it's past her bedtime, Lord Goring says, ''My father told me to go to bed an hour ago. I don't see why I shouldn't give you the same advice. I always pass on good advice. It is the only thing to do with it. It is never any use to oneself.''

### Comedy of Manners

While Wilde has a serious plot and message in *An Ideal Husband*, the play is mostly comic. As such, it is close to a form of dramatic comedy known as the comedy of manners. Comedies of manners are mostly associated with eighteenth-century Europe, although they date back to the beginnings of European drama. A comedy of manners is a play whose purpose is to satirize human vagaries. They focus on a particular stratum of society and make fun of that group's pettiness, hypocrisies, vanities, failings, and so forth. In *An Ideal Husband*, for example, Wilde satirizes the hypocrisy of the English ruling classes through his portrait of Sir Robert Chiltern. Comedies of manners are also characterized by their wit, i.e., the way that the characters' dialogue is composed mostly of clever and funny bantering. This explains Wilde's attraction to the form.

### Melodrama

Melodramas tell their stories through sensational and improbable characters and turns of event. For example, villains are thoroughly villainous in melodrama, and heroes and heroines are purity itself. Rings, letters, gloves and such items are lost and found in ways that lead to all sorts of revelations and complications of plot. Heroines often end up in terrible danger, but the hero always arrives at the last moment to save the day, and so forth. Wilde employs some stock melodramatic situations and events in *An Ideal Husband*. For example, the detail of the incriminating letter from the past and the blackmail scheme on which the plot turns are melodramatic flourishes.

### Problem Play

What are called problem plays were first written in Europe in the late nineteenth century. They are called this because they tackle some pressing social development of the day. For example, the playwright credited with introducing the form in its purest, earliest form is Henrik Ibsen, whose *A Doll's House* took on the issue of feminism: the struggles of Europe's ''new'' women and their families. If critics have difficulty calling *An Ideal Husband* a comedy of manners, and some prefer the term ''social comedy,'' this is because the play has a serious element to it. This serious component reflects Wilde's respect for the problem play.

## HISTORICAL CONTEXT

### The Dandy

Dandies, of which there are many in Wilde's play, are a phenomenon of nineteenth- and early-twentieth-century Europe. Dandies were men that were known for their commitment to fashion— usually extravagant fashion—and for their love of all things beautiful in general. Nineteenth-century dandies in the new mega-cities such as, Paris, Lon-

# COMPARE & CONTRAST

- **1890s:** Dandies dress themselves in clothes reminiscent of days gone by; some carry a single flower as an accessory.

  **Today:** A wide range of distinctive clothing that indicates a particular subculture, such as punk, Goth, and hip-hop, can be seen on the street of a typical American city.

- **1890s:** Conservative Victorian ideology still rules the day, despite a new generation's sense that it is becoming ''modern.''

  **Today:** Alternative lifestyles and a general tolerance of difference coexists in the United States.

- **1890s:** Oscar Wilde's career was destroyed thanks to allegations of same-sex love affairs.

  **Today:** Same-sex marriage is legal in some countries, such as Canada; a debate over whether or not to institute state-sanctioned same-sex marriage is current in the United States.

- **1890s:** Queen Victoria, who gave the Victorian era its name, is known as the Imperial Queen; she declares herself Empress of India and Britain's world empire becomes vast.

  **Today:** The last of the British empire unravels in the mid twentieth century, and major British cities, such as London, are post-colonial, multi-ethnic metropolises.

---

don, and New York, would stroll elegantly down pedestrian boulevards and frequent fashionable places. It is said that their exquisite nature and distaste for all things rough and vulgar stemmed from their dismay over a changing world. Specifically, these city dandies were witnessing the industrialization of their environment. This involved a change from a world where rural living was dominant to a world where factories in new urban centers were being rapidly built—with all their belching, polluting coal smoke, as well as their horribly exploited and impoverished workers (ten–twelve hour or more workdays, pitifully inadequate pay, and six, sometimes seven-day work weeks). What they saw was ugliness and the worship of money no matter the environmental and human cost, so they rejected the practical and spoke for the value of the ephemeral, the delicate, and the beautiful. It was a way of insisting that the creation of wealth was evil if the quality of peoples' lives was the price.

Wilde himself was a dandy in dress for some time. After graduating from Oxford, he spent a few years dressing in what was then considered exquisite fashion when he went out in the evenings. He did not go so far as to dress unusually in the daytime, however.

Many photographs of Wilde in one of his ''exquisite'' outfits exist; and what was so outrageous then were knee breeches and a velvet waistcoat, a flowing cloak, and longish hair.

Wilde did not dress unusually for his evenings out for long; as soon as he became well known he conformed, albeit always fashionably, to the more conservative tastes of the time.

## Aestheticism

Aestheticism as a movement in the arts developed in England in the late nineteenth century, but somewhat earlier in other countries, such as France, where it had its roots. The aestheticist dictum is ''art for art's sake,'' meaning that an artwork need only be beautiful (well made) to be worthy of admiration. In other words, a work of art did not need to have any obvious social value to be great. So, for example, if an artist wished to depict the life of a criminal, as long as he or she did it well and accurately, the work of art was valuable. Also, if an artist simply wished to make a work of art, treating a subject that would not necessarily ennoble its audience, then that was fine, as long as the work was well-done. If this sounds like a reasonable formula for art, it is.

Yet, aesthetes, or followers of aestheticism, caused a stir in England at the time because during the Victorian era the English developed a taste for art with a strong social quotient. They liked their art to be obviously ennobling. They wanted art to be morally instructive, for example, in which the good was clearly distinguished from the bad, the bad was always punished, and the good was always rewarded.

A further problem with aestheticism from the point of view of traditional, more conservative Victorians was that aesthetes took their principles very seriously, some to an extreme, and flaunted them. For example, the scholar most responsible for propagating aestheticist views in England, Walter Pater, wrote works proclaiming that the enjoyment, cultivation, and experience of beauty and exquisite sensation was one of the most important human pursuits of all. He wrote these rather extravagant ideas down, most famously, in the conclusion to a book entitled *The Renaissance.* Pater's followers, aesthetes, were, of course, dandies. They dressed beautifully, spoke beautifully, and enjoyed conversations about the best of art and decoration past and present.

Pater, an Oxford don, influenced Wilde while he was a student at Oxford. Not that Wilde's interests and life can be explained solely with reference to dandyism and Aestheticism, but these formations did, nonetheless, make their mark on Wilde.

## CRITICAL OVERVIEW

Many of the more serious critics of Wilde's day either ignored or were sparing in their praise of *An Ideal Husband.* By the time the play was staged, Wilde had many enemies, both major and minor. This was the result of his years as a dandy and his entire adult life as a cutting wit. On the one hand, he was thought frivolous and immoral; on the other, his wit often had as its target the very critics who were reviewing his work.

The critics of Wilde's time who were not impressed by the play thought it like its author: frivolous and lacking substance. Printed the day after the play opened, the review in London's major newspaper, *The Times,* is a case in point. An excerpt reads as follows:

> *An Ideal Husband* was brought out last night with a similar degree of success to that which has attended

Mr. Wilde's previous productions. It is a similar degree of success due to similar causes. For *An Ideal Husband* is marked by the same characteristics as *Lady Windermere's Fan* and *A Woman of No Importance.* There is a group of well-dressed women and men on the stage, talking a strained, inverted, but rather amusing idiom, while the action, the dramatic motive, of the play springs form [sic] a conventional device of the commonest order of melodrama. Mr. Wilde's ingenuity is verbal; there is none of this quality expended upon his plot and very little upon his characters, most of whom have caught the author's trick of phrase.

Still, negative reviews were far fewer for *An Ideal Husband* than for the previous two social comedies (named above) because by now critics hesitated to fly in the face of public opinion. No matter what they wrote, Wilde's comic plays had long runs and his supporters and audiences loved them.

Once Wilde was imprisoned, theaters ceased staging his plays for a time. But, within a decade or so, *An Ideal Husband* could be seen again. Reviews of these productions concentrated less on whether the plays deserved to be staged and more on the quality of the given production: Had the play been well directed? Well acted?

What would take more time to develop is academic scholarship on Wilde. With the exception of one or two studies, Wilde and his works did not begin receiving serious scholarly attention until the last decades of the twentieth century. A number of factors contributed to this academic interest: Wilde's wise analysis of late-Victorian culture was in accord with the prevailing view of the era; an interest in how Irish writers worked with and against the rules and canon of British literature became a subject of interest; and the developing fields of gender, sexuality, and gay and lesbian studies looked with interest on writers such as Wilde.

In general, critics consider Wilde's last comedy his best. In *The Importance of Being Earnest,* Wilde finally wrote what most critics think he should have written all along, namely a pure comedy of manners. There is no "social" plot to *The Importance of Being Earnest* and no melodrama.

Even as many of Wilde's works are considered very good works of art, he is as important for *who he was* in both public and private life as for what he wrote. This is appropriate, because to the aesthete, the art of living is what matters most. Mrs. Cheveley puts it this way: "The art of living. The only really Fine Art we have produced in modern times."

*View of the Panama Canal*

# CRITICISM

## *Carol Dell'Amico*

*Dell'Amico is an instructor of English litera-
ture and composition. In this essay, Dell'Amico
considers Wilde and his play within the context of
Irish-British colonial relations.*

The country in which Oscar Wilde was born was,
for many centuries, a territory of the United Kingdom (Britain). Ireland was, then, a colony of Britain, a situation of enforced dependence that most
Irish deeply resented. Uprisings against British rule
were common until, finally, Home Rule was established in 1921. After this date, most major Irish-
British skirmishes pertained to the contested territory of Northern Ireland, a portion of the Irish island
that Britain retained owing to Northern Ireland's
large number of ethnic and religious Britons. (Northern Ireland is still British land to this day.)

Of interest to critics lately, in terms of Irish
writers such as Wilde, James Joyce, and others, is
how these authors' works might evince patterns of
anti-imperial expression. In other words, even if the
work in question has little obvious, or no evident,
political content relating to the Irish-British rela-

tions, how might the writing still be somehow
colonial? What might the writing of the colonial
writers of the world's empires have in common?

As of a few decades ago, anybody who thought
of Wilde probably thought of him as an English
author. Yet, a more accurate description of him,
perhaps, is that he is an Irish writer writing in the
language of the empire to which his country belonged. Indeed, if it were not for British imperial
ambitions, Wilde might have spoken and written in
Gaelic, the predominant Irish language that British
rulers suppressed. (School children in Ireland now
learn Gaelic, but English is still the dominant language in the country.)

While Wilde had political convictions, he did
not write much that was overtly political. Yet, he did
grow up in a household taken with the cause of
Ireland's quest for independence. His mother was
an extremely well known and influential political
organizer and writer on the side of Irish independence. She published many books on Irish history
and folklore, and, under the pen name of Speranza,
she wrote a great deal of political material for the
independence movement.

Still, even taking into account his mother's
profound patriotism and his own support of Irish

# WHAT DO I READ NEXT?

- The play *The Importance of Being Earnest* (1896) is Wilde's comedic masterpiece; it premiered a month after *An Ideal Husband* in 1895.

- *The Happy Prince and Other Tales* (1888) is Wilde's much admired first book of fairy tales.

- *Translations* (1981) is a play by the well-known Irish playwright Brian Friel. It takes place in 1833, dramatizing Britain's project of mapping Ireland and, in the process, substituting English names for the original Gaelic ones.

- The conclusion to *The Renaissance* (1873) by Walter Pater conveys the aestheticist creed that so impressed Wilde.

- Like Wilde's *The Importance of Being Earnest*, *The Way of the World* (1700) by William Congreve is said to be one of the finest and funniest comedies of manners ever written in English.

- Literary scholar Terry Eagleton's forays into fiction include a play about Oscar Wilde, *Saint Oscar* (1989). This humorous, erudite play explores the nature of Wilde's art and place in British society.

- The Norwegian Henrik Ibsen's most famous "problem play," *A Doll's House* (1889), revolutionized European theater at the end of the nineteenth century. It set a new serious standard for playwrights, moving away from the fantastical entertainments of melodrama in favor of a new social realism in which social and political problems of the day were addressed. *A Doll's House* takes on the issue of the "New Woman."

- *Patience* (1881) is a comedic operetta about aesthetes and dandies by the famed Victorian musical theater duo W. S. Gilbert and Arthur Sullivan.

---

independence, Wilde does not present himself as an obvious candidate to be studied as an Irish writer. He chose to live, after all, in London, the center of the empire; then again, this would be the likely destination of many ambitious writers of the time who were writing in English. Another interesting detail complicating Wilde's identity and status is that his family was Protestant. That is, they shared Britain's brand of Christianity, not Ireland's (Catholicism).

Nevertheless, certain critics have embraced Wilde as a colonial, Irish writer, and what might be anti-imperial about *An Ideal Husband* will now be addressed in what follows.

One of the most significant aspects of Wilde's art for colonial critics is the particular nature and focus of Wilde's wit and favorite themes. His wit, critics say, would have encouraged contemporary audiences not simply to think, but to question the notions that enabled them to construct the secure

imperial identities they presumably had. How might a populace support the vast imperial cause of Britain—the imperial project that at one point encompassed colonies stretching around the entire globe? For starters, colonial critics say, Britons had to be very sure of their cultural values and identity, and that these particular values and ways were superior to others: one did not colonize simply for financial gain; one colonized to bring to foreign peoples one's superior way of life.

How, then, to encourage British audiences to think flexibly about their identities and to question the spreading of British culture? Well, one thing would be to highlight the problem of identity as such; in this regard, Lord Goring's posing is significant (indeed, the fact that Wilde's most entertaining characters all believe in the pose is significant). To adopt a pose means to *choose* how one wishes to come off. It means that there is no real, true self (identity) that one cannot help but express; it means that one can perform and create the self one pleases, that one can create a self from scratch. This notion of making-the-self invests the individual with great critical and moral power. It substitutes the individual for the social body: each person must decide who he or she wants to be, and each person must create his or her own identity. People who believe that they have the power to choose their beliefs are likely to be people who are critical of public opinion, or at least always willing to question it, and public opinion in Wilde's time, in England, was decidedly on the side of the empire.

In *An Ideal Husband*, there are a number of instances where Wilde's wit takes as its target the notion that there is no true and inevitable self to be expressed. The best and clearest example is near the beginning of the play, in an exchange between Sir Robert Chiltern and Mrs. Cheveley. Chiltern has asked Cheveley if she is a pessimist or optimist, to which she replies that they are both just poses. Chiltern then says, "You prefer to be natural?" Cheveley replies, "Sometimes. But it is such a very difficult pose to keep up." Here, Wilde makes it clear that there is no such thing as being natural, as being oneself. In other words, one is always what one *chooses* to be.

The stage notes of *An Ideal Husband* are another place where Wilde conveys the idea that people are what they make of themselves, and, hence, that people should think carefully about what they want to believe in and who they want to be. This is conveyed in the many times that Wilde compares his characters to works of art, to reverse the maxim that "art imitates life." In other words, when thinking of art, people tend to think that artists take life as their subject: art imitates life. What so many of Wilde's stage notes humorously suggest to the contrary is that "life imitates art." Why? Because for Wilde, it would be much better for someone to read a book or see a painting and get an idea and decide to apply it to his or her own life than for an artist to observe and simply replicate what he or she has observed. In other words, Wilde wants an audience who is always willing to adopt new ideas, discard old ones, and so forth. To put this another way, Wilde insisted that people should approach themselves as "works of art," as wholly "artificial" and made-up things—as nothing but bundles of "artiface." Thus, for example, Wilde's description of the Earl of Caversham: "A fine Whig type. Rather like a portrait by Lawrence." Of Mabel Chiltern he writes, "To sane people she is not reminiscent of any work of art. But she is really like a Tanagra statuette, and would be rather annoyed if

> " HOW COULD A MAN WHO WROTE PLAYS SO SEEMINGLY HARMLESS AND DELIGHTFULLY IDIOTIC AS *AN IDEAL HUSBAND* BE CONSIDERED A DANGER TO THE BRITISH STATE? BECAUSE WILDE'S WIT BOTH ON AND OFF THE PAGE WAS AS THREATENING AND DANGEROUS AS ANY SWORD, GUN, OR ARMY."

she were told so." Of Mrs. Cheveley, the following: "A work of art, on the whole, but showing the influence of too many schools." The message is clear: art is the original thing, humans are the copy, and people should look for good art to imitate! Of course, with this Wilde knew that he was being both provocative and funny. Then as today, common wisdom has it that "artificial" persons are less admirable than persons who are somehow "just themselves."

Another aspect of *An Ideal Husband* that undoubtedly pertains to Wilde's status as a colonial is the way the play makes fun of the Victorian tendency to devote a great deal of time to doing good works. That is, throughout the play, Wilde's socialites and dandies praise the lazy and deplore the active. As a colonial, Wilde would be interested in questioning the Victorian commitment to ameliorative work because what was motivating the empire was the notion that the world outside of England needed to be saved from itself. In spreading British culture and ways, the English believed that they were doing the world a good turn (they were doing good work). For example, they thought of themselves as persons bringing Christianity to those they thought of as "heathens" (non-Christians), no matter that the "heathens" of the world had their own religions and cultures. So, Wilde asks, is your good work truly good? Do the recipients of your help truly appreciate it? Do perhaps the recipients of your help think of it as an imposition or even an unwelcome evil? Thus, for example, the following types of comments in *An Ideal Husband*: "Sir

John's temper since he has taken seriously to politics,'' says Lady Markby of her husband, ''has become quite unbearable. Really, now that the House of Commons is trying to become useful, it does a great deal of harm''; Lady Markby again: ''I assure you my life will be quite ruined unless they send John at once to the Upper House. He won't take any interest in politics then, will he?''; again, Lady Markby: ''Shall I see you at Lady Bonar's to-night? She has discovered a wonderful new genius. He does . . . nothing at all, I believe. That is a great comfort, is it not?'' There is also Mabel Chiltern's joke about where the proceeds of a theatrical event are going, another shot at Victorian high-mindedness: ''But it is for an excellent charity: in aid of the Undeserving, the only people I am really interested in.'' She also jokes in reply to the Earl of Caversham's declaration that his son Lord Goring leads an ''idle'' life: ''How can you say such a thing? Why, he rides in the Row at ten o'clock in the morning, goes to the Opera three times a week, changes his clothes at least five times a day, and dines out every night of the season.''

The eminent critic and scholar Terry Eagleton sums up the politics of Wilde's art and life as follows:

> If Wilde is not usually thought of in Britain as Irish, neither is he commonly seen as a particularly political figure. Yet Wilde is political in all kinds of ways, some of them fairly obvious and some of them not. He wrote finely about socialism, spoke up for Irish republicanism when the British sneered at it, and despite his carefully nurtured flippancy displayed throughout his life tenderness and compassion toward the dispossessed, who no doubt plucked some faint chord in himself. But he is also political in some more elusive senses of the term—political, for example, because he is very funny, a remorseless debunker of the high-toned *gravitas* of Victorian England. The Irish have often found the high . . . seriousness of the English irresistibly comic. Wilde is radical because he takes nothing seriously, cares only for form, appearance and pleasure, and is religiously devoted to his own self-gratification. In Victorian society, such a man did not need to bed the son of the Marquess of Queensberry to become an enemy of the State, though it can't be said to have helped. If he sometimes displays the irresponsibility of the aesthete, he also restores to us something of the true political depth of that term, as a rejection of mean-spirited utility, and a devotion to human self-fulfilment as an end in itself.

Wilde's affair with the son of the Marquess did lead to his trial and imprisonment and, eventually, his downfall. But, as Eagleton intimates, many already considered Wilde an ''enemy of the State'' before this; he was tried because the state knew it

had a great deal of support for its actions. How could a man who wrote plays so seemingly harmless and delightfully idiotic as *An Ideal Husband* be considered a danger to the British state? Because Wilde's wit both on and off the page was as threatening and dangerous as any sword, gun, or army. Wilde relentlessly exposed the hypocrisy of the British ruling classes, even as he flattered them and loved and admired England and the English for many good reasons. His plays suggest that the members of these ruling classes were all a bit like Sir Robert Chiltern: loud in proclaiming their goodness, but quiet about their self-interested pursuit of power and wealth—wealth that so many of them accumulated, as Wilde well knew, in the great, lucrative business that was the vast British empire.

**Source:** Carol Dell'Amico, Critical Essay on *An Ideal Husband,* in *Drama for Students,* Thomson Gale, 2005.

## Curt Guyette

*Guyette, a longtime journalist, received a bachelor's degree in English writing from the University of Pittsburgh. In this essay, Guyette discusses how Wilde uses scathing wit to create a play that, ultimately, espouses tolerance and compassion.*

In *An Ideal Husband*, Oscar Wilde stitches together multiple and varied elements to produce a seamless work that remains relevant more than a century after it was written. The playwright combines scintillating wit with both farce and melodrama, creating a piece that, over the course of its four acts, offers biting social and political commentary while espousing a philosophy that has the primacy of love and compassion as its focal point. Taken together, these elements compel Wilde's audience to consider what, exactly, makes a person truly moral.

''Deliciously absurd, morally serious, profoundly sentimental, and wickedly melodramatic, it is primarily a comedy of manners about political corruption, and love'' is the way Barbara Belford describes the breadth of this play in her book *Oscar Wilde: A Certain Genius.* And, as Mark Nichols points out in his book *The Importance of Being Oscar,* George Bernard Shaw lavished praise on *An Ideal Husband* when it first hit the stage, declaring: ''In a certain sense Mr. Wilde is to me our only thorough playwright. He plays with everything: with wit, with philosophy, with drama, with actors and audience, with the whole theatre.''

Wilde's stiletto wit is on display throughout the play. Seemingly without effort, he produces one epigram after another. These concise, pithy, often paradoxical statements are uttered by minor and major characters alike and give *An Ideal Husband* an entirely playful sheen. Nichols notes in his book that Wilde's son Vyvyan once wrote that his father viewed words as if they were ''beautiful baubles with which to play and build, as a child plays with coloured bricks.'' It is an apt analogy. Wilde's wordplay provides an iridescent foundation, each epigram indeed like a beautifully colored brick that helps form the base that *An Ideal Husband* is built upon.

The baubles are indeed splendid, providing such delight that they would make this play a memorable experience no matter what plot line is constructed around them. Nichols, in fact, spends no time analyzing the story line of *An Ideal Husband*. Instead, he is content to reel from one epigram to another, as if intoxicated by each indelible line, such as the one uttered by the character Lord Goring, who observes, ''When the gods wish to punish us, they answer our prayers.''

Among the targets skewered by Wilde is the world of high society. Take, for example, this choice remark from the character Mabel Chiltern, who says, ''Oh, I love London Society! I think it has immensely improved. It is entirely composed now of beautiful idiots and brilliant lunatics. Just what society should be.'' As rich a subject as that might have been at the end of the Victorian era, it took some nerve for Wilde to sling verbal barbs at social circles he himself was in. This play, though, is substantially more than a collection of witty one-liners and has more philosophical meat to chew on, as well. Part of the main course, so to speak, is the issue of hypocrisy, especially as it applies to the world of politics.

Wilde's gateway into the rich turf of the political arena is the character Sir Robert Chiltern, a high-ranking official who built a sterling career by constantly seeking the moral high ground. His integrity is beyond reproach, and his wife Gertrude idolizes him for his goodness, honesty, and dedication to principles. But, beneath all his respectability is a dirty secret: Chiltern's wealth, and the career in public service it afforded him, derived from Chiltern selling a state secret many years before when he was still a young man. The threat of that secret being exposed by Mrs. Cheveley forms the basis of the plot for *An Ideal Husband*.

Cheveley, in possession of a highly incriminating letter that proves Sir Robert's crime, wants

> ❝ AS SIR ROBERT SAYS HIMSELF, 'I WOULD TO GOD THAT I HAD BEEN ABLE TO TELL THE TRUTH . . . TO LIVE THE TRUTH. AH! THAT IS THE GREAT THING IN LIFE, TO LIVE THE TRUTH.' IT IS JUST SUCH A LIFE THAT GORING HAS LIVED AND IS THE HAPPIER FOR IT.''

Chiltern to lend his support, and the credibility that goes with it, to a scam that would bilk the public treasury. She attempts to blackmail him, threatening to expose his sordid actions if he does not provide assistance for her scheme, an action that would have him betray the public trust he has otherwise so rightly earned. The woman delights in taunting him. In doing so, she makes an observation regarding politics that still rings true today.

> 'Nowadays,' she chides,'with our modern mania for morality, everyone has to pose as a paragon of purity, incorruptibility, and all the other seven deadly virtues—and what is the result? You all go over like ninepins—one after the other.'

Politicians today are still expected to be without moral flaw, even though it is a recognized impossibility since they are only human. When those flaws are exposed, they are subjected to public humiliation and scorn. As the character Lord Goring observes, admitting one's weaknesses and failures does nothing to appease a public that demands the impossibility of moral perfection from its politicians. Confession would be fruitless, says Goring, explaining

> And if you did make a clean breast of the whole affair, you would never be able to talk morality again. And in England a man who can't talk morality twice a week to a large popular immoral audience is quite over as a serious politician.

Even more than the public disgrace, Chiltern fears the effect disclosure of his decades-old crime will have on his adoring wife, who, because of his perceived virtue, places him on a pedestal so high no man could ever really live up to it. Exposure of his dark secret, Sir Robert is convinced, would drive his wife away. ''It would kill her love for me,'' he tells Goring, a character largely modeled on Wilde himself. Goring, described as a "flawless dandy" by Wilde, provides an interesting and highly instructive counterpoint to Sir Robert. The latter publicly portrays himself to be a man of the highest moral scruples while concealing a shameful incident from his past; Goring, on the other hand, is, on the surface, Chiltern's polar opposite. He makes no attempt whatsoever to hide what he openly admits to be his many flaws.

As Mabel Chiltern, the sister of Sir Robert who has a romantic interest in Lord Goring, says to the self-confessed gadabout, "You are always telling me of your bad qualities, Lord Goring." To which he replies, "I have only told you half of them as yet, Miss Mabel!" Unlike Sir Robert, Lord Goring is free of guilt. He never had to bear the heavy burden of going through life concealing an act for which he is deeply ashamed. As Sir Robert says himself, "I would to God that I had been able to tell the truth . . . to live the truth. Ah! That is the great thing in life, to live the truth." It is just such a life that Goring has lived and is the happier for it.

Goring's father, the crusty and cantankerous Earl of Caversham, has not a single good word to say about his son. Caversham views his son as an idler who lives only for his own pleasure. Praising Sir Robert for his "high character, high moral tone, high principles," Caversham turns to his son and decrees, "Everything that you have not got, sir, and never will have." The irony is that when Caversham makes this observation, the audience knows just how wrong he is on both counts. Sir Robert is not quite as completely noble as the old earl believes and his son has proved himself to have a truly sterling character. He has shown himself to be a good and steadfast friend, doing all he can to help Sir Robert out of his dire predicament and asking absolutely nothing in return. Beyond that, he does his best to help Sir Robert's wife, Gertrude, see the error of her ways. First, at the point when he knows the truth of her husband's scandal and she does not, he encourages her to moderate her unrealistic view of Sir Robert as an absolute paragon of virtue, telling her that in "every nature there are elements of weakness, or worse than weakness." Goring urges Lady Chiltern to gain some degree of compassion and not expect her husband to be flawless.

'All I do know,' says Goring, 'is that life cannot be understood without much charity, cannot be lived without much charity. It is love, and not German philosophy, that is the true explanation of this world, whatever may be the explanation of the next.'

Later, after Lord Goring has saved the day by thwarting Mrs. Cheveley's attempt at blackmail, Lady Chiltern, who has indeed followed Goring's advice and forgiven her husband for his moral lapse, nonetheless pushes Sir Robert to do what she considers the honorable thing and withdraw from public life. Again, Goring steps in and provides astute counsel, saying that her urging of Sir Robert to meet an impossibly high standard by abandoning all that he has worked for is a terrible mistake. Goring says to Gertrude

'Do you want to kill his love for you? What sort of existence will he have if you rob him of the fruits of his ambition, if you take him from the splendour of a great political career, if you close the doors of public life against him, if you condemn him to sterile failure, he who was made for triumph and success. Women are not meant to judge us, but to forgive us when we need forgiveness. Pardon, not punishment is their mission.'

She again takes his advice, and all ends happily. Sir Robert's political success is assured. He and Gertrude have grown closer than ever, their love all the stronger because it is based in reality instead of some idealized fiction. As director Peter Hall wrote in a 1992 piece he penned for London's *The Guardian* newspaper, Wilde made it clear that Sir Robert's crime was clearly foolish, but along with condemnation came forgiveness. "Through the character of Lord Goring," writes Hall, "Wilde expresses his tolerance: 'Nobody's incapable of dong a foolish thing. Nobody is incapable of doing a wrong thing.'" Noting that audiences continued to respond positively to *An Ideal Husband* a century after it was first staged, Hall concludes, "The play lives not because of its wit but because of its compassion."

**Source:** Curt Guyette, Critical Essay on *An Ideal Husband,* in *Drama for Students,* Thomson Gale, 2005.

## Epifanio San Juan Jr.

*In the following excerpt, San Juan Jr. explores the themes of the past and social adaptation in* An Ideal Husband.

Wilde's least successful play on the stage and his third comedy, *An Ideal Husband,* was written between October 1893 and March 1894. It was produced at the Haymarket Theatre on January 3, 1895. When Wilde in 1899 corrected the proofs of the play for publication, he said that it "reads rather well, and some of its passages seem prophetic of tragedy to come." But Sir Robert Chiltern's predicament,

*Jeremy Northam and Cate Blanchett in a 1998 film version of* An Ideal Husband

though it bears a tenuous resemblance to Wilde's, has distinctive melodramatic overtones.

The play concerns itself primarily with Sir Robert Chiltern's past misdeed on which his fortune and eminent reputation now stand. The past, in the form of Mrs. Cheveley's immoral ends, revives in order to haunt and threaten him. Just as, in the three other plays, the past proves a force that motivates the thematic action, so here time seems to be the concept that governs the complication and resolution of the plot. The play deals with the problem of how well man, confronted with the alterable modes of his life, can adjust or adapt himself to the needs of changing situations. Where an absolute standard is obeyed despite the criticism of it by experience and actuality, there result irony, distortions, and absurdities that arouse ridicule and laughter.

Notice first how the scenes of the play shift from the "social" crowded atmosphere of the Octagon Room at Chiltern's house (Act I) to a "private" room (Act II), then to the secluded library of Lord Goring where the two letters—the fatal letter of Sir Robert Chiltern and Lady Chiltern's letter to Lord Goring—play decisive roles. The scene finally returns to the setting of Act II, where social and private interests intersect; where all the rough, disturbing edges of the misunderstanding between

husband and wife are smoothed off by obvious devices—by means of the diamond brooch that Lord Goring uses to restrain Mrs. Cheveley, and by Mrs. Cheveley's stupidity in not explaining to Chiltern the nature of the letter his wife wrote to Lord Goring. Eventually the play closes with a sense of new life for the Chilterns, while Lord Goring and Mabel Chiltern entertain the prospect of a happy marriage. The image of a stable society prevails in the end, as the conventions of marriage, family life, and public office are severally affirmed.

When Act I opens, Mrs. Marchmont and Lady Basildon, "types of exquisite fragility," display their "affectations of manner" which, however, do not make their remarks pointless:

MRS. MARCHMONT: Horribly tedious parties they give, don't they?

LADY BASILDON: Horribly tedious! Never know why I go. Never know why I go anywhere.

Mabel Chiltern states in ironic terms the combination of polished form and hollow insides that society presents: "Oh, I love London society! I think it has immensely improved. It is entirely composed now of beautiful idiots and brilliant lunatics. Just what society should be." Her indictment gains pungent venom in Lord Caversham's opinion that London

> BEHIND SIR ROBERT'S OPEN 'GOODNESS' LIES A SECRET 'TRUTH,' THE AS YET UNACKNOWLEDGED TRUTH OF HUMAN FRAILTY. HE HAS COMMITTED AN IMMORAL ACT IN ORDER TO INSURE HIS SOCIAL SUCCESS."

society "has gone to the dogs, a lot of damned nobodies talking about nothing."

Dress or fashion furnishes an index to social attitudes and values. Lord Goring pronounces: "fashion is what one wears oneself. What is unfashionable is what other people wear." When he offers to give Mrs. Cheveley "some good advice," she replies: "Oh! pray don't. One should never give a woman anything that she can't wear in the evening." The interest in appearance occupies the foreground in this exchange:

> MRS. CHEVELEY (languidly): I have never read a Blue Book, I prefer books . . . in yellow covers.
>
> LADY MARKBY (genially unconscious): Yellow is a gayer colour, is it not? I used to wear yellow a good deal in my early days, and would do so now if Sir John was not so painfully personal in his observations, and a man on the question of dress is always ridiculous, is he not?

Politics is a kind of "fashion," too, in its concern with public appearance. Lady Basildon claims to talk politics ceaselessly. Sir Robert Chiltern regards a political life as "a noble career," though our knowledge of his past belies his statement. But in the political or practical life, the criterion of success reduces moral standards to the basic level of pragmatic efficacy. As Lord Goring puts it, "in practical life there is something about success, actual success, that is a little unscrupulous, something about ambition that is unscrupulous always."

In Act IV, Lady Chiltern believes that Sir Robert's ambition has led him astray in his early days. She says that "power is nothing in itself. It is power to do good that is fine." Her husband admits to Lord Goring that he "bought success at a great price." And yet he is highly esteemed for being a respectable, selfless "public servant," a model of virtue, which is but a "front" or mask that he wears in conformity to social norms. After all, as Lord Goring remarks, almost all private fortune in society has come from dubious "speculation." On knowing her husband's guilt, Lady Chiltern hysterically complains not of his pretense but of his inability to "lie" to her for the sake of "virtues" he has been socially known for. Lady Chiltern cries out,

> Don't touch me. I feel as if you had soiled me forever. Oh! what a mask you have been wearing all these years! A horrible, painted mask! You sold yourself for money. Oh! a common thief were better. You put yourself up for sale to the highest bidder! You were bought in the market. You lied to the whole world. And yet you will not lie to me!

This exposure means a stripping of costume, an "undressing," to disclose the authentic self. One recalls Lady Markby's experience, which prefigures Sir Robert's plight, when she describes the result of immersion in the crowd:

> The fact is, we all scramble and jostle so much nowadays that I wonder we have anything at all left on us at the end of an evening. I know myself that, when I am coming back from the Drawing Room, I always feel as if I hadn't a shred on me, except a small shred of decent reputation just enough to prevent the lower classes making painful observations through the windows of the carriage.

Behind Sir Robert's open "goodness" lies a secret "truth," the as yet unacknowledged truth of human frailty. He has committed an immoral act in order to insure his social success.

Act I gives us the needed background information about the moral issue. Mrs. Cheveley remarks: "Nowadays, with our modern mania for morality, everyone has to pose as a paragon of purity, incorruptibility, and all the other seven deadly virtues." She threatens Sir Robert:

> Yours is a very nasty scandal. You couldn't survive it. If it were known that as a young man, secretary to a great and important minister, you sold a Cabinet secret for a large sum of money, and that was the origin of your wealth and career, you would be hounded out of public life. you would disappear completely. . . . You have a splendid position but it is your splendid position that makes you so vulnerable.

She elaborates on the punishment that the fallen victim is bound to receive from society:

> Suppose that when I leave this house I drive down to some newspaper office, and give them this scandal and the proofs of it! I think of their loathsome joy, of the delight they would have in dragging you down, of the mud and mire they would plunge you in. Think of

the hypocrite with his greasy smile penning his leading article, and arranging the foulness of the public placard.

Ironically Lady Chiltern thinks that her husband has no ''secrets'' from her.

Confronted with his ''shameful'' secret, Sir Robert Chiltern reflects on how most men have ''worse secrets in their own lives.'' Lord Goring himself, in planning to thwart Mrs. Cheveley's designs, believes that ''everyone has some weak point. There is some flaw in each one of us.'' Aware of human limitations, he allows for imperfections in men. Observation, if not experience, has taught him that the ''ideal husband'' is a myth. He says to Lady Chiltern in Act II:

> I have sometimes thought that . . . perhaps you are a little hard in some of your views on life. I think that . . . often you don't make sufficient allowances. In every nature there are elements of weakness, or worse than weakness.

Just as Sir Robert has a ''past,'' so does his enemy Mrs. Cheveley. She ceases to be a mystery when Lady Chiltern recalls her as a schoolmate: ''She was untruthful, dishonest, an evil influence on everyone whose trust or friendship she could win. . . . She stole things, she was a thief. She was sent away for being a thief.'' Lord Goring discovers later that she has stolen the diamond brooch he has given to a friend. Thus Mrs. Cheveley is not without her secret crime, of which Lord Goring accuses her later. Her image as an intriguing woman who ''makes great demands on one's curiosity'' is soon modified by the knowledge we get of her past life, her origin; she, who claims to possess integrity, turns out to be an embodiment of corruption.

It seems that the past, what is dead and forgotten, is always valuable for the perspective of the comic vision. The past qualifies man's pride; it gives an objective picture of any man's life. Whereas the past judges man in his finitude, the future gives him the freedom of choosing his possible, ideal selves. Mrs. Cheveley proves the most vulnerable character because, as she declares, her ''memory is under admirable control.'' The one real tragedy in a woman's life, she says, is the fact that ''her past is always her lover, and her future invariably her husband.'' Sir Robert, of course, is the ''man'' with a future, as Mabel Chiltern says; but his future rests on his past. When Mrs. Cheveley enters the scene, he starts reflecting on life:

> It is fair that the folly, the sin of one's youth, if men choose to call it a sin, should wreck a life like mine,

should place me in the pillory, should shatter all that I have worked for, all that I have built up? Is it fair, Arthur?

Lord Goring replies: ''Life is never fair, Robert. And perhaps it is a good thing for most of us that it is not.''

What is the danger that life confronts us with? It is the danger of having an open mind, an equipoise within, a balance which comes from a just calculation of the factors that affect one's life. When Lord Goring suggests that Sir Robert alter his wife's fixed views on life, Sir Robert replies: ''All such experiments are terribly dangerous.'' Lord Goring, however, counters: ''Everything is dangerous, my dear fellow. If it wasn't so, life wouldn't be worth living.'' He entertains, in short, the surprises and novelties that organic life is ever producing. In Act IV, life puts Lady Chiltern's reputation in danger. We see how Sir Robert becomes desperate, then panicked: ''I clutch at every chance. I feel like a man on a ship that is sinking.'' The disaster being still on the level of conjecture, his interjections are maudlin: ''My life seems to have crumbled about me. I am a ship without a rudder in a night without a star.'' This radically qualifies the role of Sir Robert is a man with a ''serious purpose in life,'' a ''pattern husband.'' Lady Chiltern amplifies her husband's image:

> A man's life is of more value than a woman's. It has larger issues, wider scope, greater ambitions. Our lives revolve in curves of emotions. It is upon lines of intellect that a man's life progresses.

''Lines of intellect'' versus ''curves of emotion''— this opposition involves society's failure to establish harmonious relations between men and women. It involves a milieu in which the accepted codes of behavior do not promote the sensibility of men to function integrally. Wilde's portrayal of his ''ideal husband'' sets directly the contrast between feeling and conscious thought, between perceived behavior and the groping, reckless inner self:

> The note of his manner is that of perfect distinction, with a slight touch of pride. One feels that he is conscious of the success he has made in life. A nervous temperament, with a tired look. The firmly chiselled mouth and chin contrast strikingly with the romantic expression in the deep-set eyes. The variance is suggestive of an almost complete separation of passion and intellect, as though thought and emotion were each isolated in its own sphere through some violence of will-power.

Sir Robert Chiltern speaks in character when he insists on the idea of a compartmentalized life:

"... public and private life are different things. They have different laws, and move on different lines."

Elsewhere men are called "horribly selfish" and "grossly material." Despite Sir Robert Chiltern's show of qualms and vacillation, Mrs. Cheveley is assured that he is "most susceptible to reason"— by which she means that he readily succumbs to fear of social disapproval. Women are gifted with "the moral sense." Lady Markby prefers anything other than "high intellectual pressure." To Lord Caversham, "common sense is the privilege" of men; in his view, marriage is a matter not of affection but of common sense. Mrs. Cheveley herself separates "business" from "silver twilights or rose-pink dawns." She considers being "natural" the most difficult pose of all. She holds that there is a wide gap between the rational method of science and the irrational layer of experience:

> MRS. CHEVELEY: Ah! the strength of women comes from the fact that psychology cannot explain us. Men can be analyzed, women . . . merely adored.
>
> SIR ROBERT CHILTERN: You think science cannot grapple with the problem of women?
>
> MRS. CHEVELEY: Science can never grapple with the irrational. That is why it has no future before it, in this world.
>
> SIR ROBERT CHILTERN: And women represent the irrational.
>
> MRS. CHEVELEY: Well-dressed women do.

The double aspects of life seem to be focused in Mrs. Cheveley's mysterious identity. Lord Goring describes her as "a genius in the daytime and a beauty at night." She plays with the attitudes of optimism and pessimism. What after all is the real self of a person? Lady Chiltern cannot believe her husband to be guilty of dreadful things which are "so unlike [his] real self." Her idealized image of him is that he has "brought into the political life of our time a nobler atmosphere, a finer attitude towards life, a freer air of purer aims and higher ideals." But reality is never as simple and pure as Lady Chiltern would like to imagine it. Society has become "dreadfully mixed" for Mrs. Cheveley; Lady Markby likewise, observes that "families are so mixed nowadays. Indeed, as a rule, everybody turns out to be somebody else." Just as society is complex, so truth—as Sir Robert Chiltern believes— is a very complex thing.

To the unbending, puritanical Lady Chiltern, life however appears simple and fixed. She has always been noted for her stingy exclusiveness and conservatism. She has remained unaffected by changing circumstances:

> MRS. CHEVELEY: I see that after all these years you have not changed a bit, Gertrude.
>
> LADY CHILTERN: I never change.
>
> MRS. CHEVELEY (elevating her eyebrows): Then life has taught you nothing?
>
> LADY CHILTERN: It has taught me that a person who has once been guilty of a dishonest and dishonorable action may be guilty of it a second time and should be shunned.
>
> MRS. CHEVELEY: Would you apply that rule to everyone?
>
> LADY CHILTERN: Yes, to everyone, without exception.

We know of course that Sir Robert has changed. Mrs. Cheveley, though shrewder and more worldly-wise, has not reformed her ways. With firm logic Lady Chiltern holds to her conviction that human beings are what they are, past or present; that human nature is predestined, and is permanently fixed. She accuses Mrs. Cheveley of being dishonest on the basis of her past conduct:

> SIR ROBERT CHILTERN: Gertrude what you tell me may be true, but it happened many years ago. It is best forgotten! Mrs. Cheveley may have changed since then. No one should be entirely judged by his past.
>
> LADY CHILTERN (sadly): One's past is what one is. It is the only way by which people should be judged.
>
> SIR ROBERT CHILTERN: That is a hard saying, Gertrude!
>
> LADY CHILTERN: It is a true saying, Robert. . . .

Like her counterparts in the other plays, Lady Windermere and Hester Worsley, Lady Chiltern does not believe that the sinner can make amends or work for his redemption. Addicted to histronics, she often forgets the harsh prosaic facts of experience which are necessary to obtain an adequate understanding of human nature.

In contrast with her tolerant husband, Lady Chiltern acts without regard for the variable situations of life. Sir Robert Chiltern, it must be stressed, concieves himself changed since his early indiscretion on the ground that "circumstances alter things." But his wife decrees otherwise: "Circumstances should never alter principles," Nonetheless, life's circumstances play a joke on her: when Sir Robert, in Act I, asks Mrs. Cheveley what brought her into his life in order to destroy his reputation and family honor, she answers: "Circumstances." Accident makes Robert negligent to the extent that he leaves the incriminating letter in Baron Arnheim's possession. And the accident of circumstance makes Mrs. Cheveley drop her diamond brooch, thus giving Lord Goring a weapon to prove her guilty of theft. On the whole, life offers chances to qualify, change, or confirm the truths and beliefs men hold. Sir Robert, for instance, speaks of the "wonderful chance" the Baron gave him to enrich himself unscrupulously. Later, he would bank on the "chance" that some scandal might be found involving his blackmailer Mrs. Cheveley. Desperately he exclaims: "Oh! I live on hopes now. I clutch at every chance."

We have noted previously the objective of success as a controlling force in Sir Robert's life. Early in his career he has been told that "luxury was nothing but background, a painted scene in a play"; what matters is power based on wealth. To be sure, he has never truly regretted his youthful crime. But the opportunity to acquire wealth unscrupulously he denies to others. Success, the chief social criterion of value, is parodied in the humorous puns on "triumph"; for example, Mabel Chiltern mentions a tableau in which she and Lady Chiltern are participants:

> You remember, we are having a tableaux, don't you? The triumph of something, I don't know what! I hope it will be the triumph of me. Only triumph I am really interested in at present.

Wilde describes the stage decoration in Act I: "Over the well of the staircase hangs a great chandelier with wax lights, which illumine a large eighteenth century French tapestry—representing the Triumph of Love, from a design by Boucher—that is stretched on the staircase wall." At the close of Act III, we see Mrs. Cheveley's face "illumined with evil triumph." What triumphs of course is the comic situation.

If the function of comedy is to reaffirm due proportion in life and restore "the golden mean," it is imperative that the "rules" for social existence be carefully defined. An attempt at this definition exists in Wilde's play, Sir Robert tries to expose Mrs. Cheveley's plan for a "swindle" instead of a "speculation": "let us call things by their proper names." Eventually she turns the table over him:

> SIR ROBERT CHILTERN: It is infamous, what you propose—infamous!
>
> MRS. CHEVELEY: Oh, no! This is the game of life as we all have to play it, Sir Robert, sooner or later.

When he agrees on a bargain, with his support of her speculation in exchange for the incriminating later, she says: "I intend to play quite fairly with you. One should always play fairly . . . when one has the winning cards."

Both the "game of life" and blackmail suggest commercial exchange, bargaining, profit and loss. Allusions and metaphors drawn from trade and finance are interwoven in the verbal fabric of the play. In Act I, Mrs. Cheveley appraises people according to their "price": "My dear Sir Robert, you are a man of the world, and you have your price, I suppose. Everybody has nowadays. The drawback is that most people are so dreadfully expensive," Later she exhorts him: "Years ago you did a clever, unscrupulous thing; it turned out a great success. You owe it to your fortune and position. And now you have got to pay for it. Sooner or later we all have to pay for what we do. You have to pay now." Offered a bribe, she refuses: "Even you are not rich enough, Sir Robert, to buy back your past. No man is." To Lady Chiltern, "money that comes from a tainted source is a degradation." Sir Robert confesses that while he did not sell himself for money, he "bought success at a great price." Lord Goring thinks that he "paid a great price for it." In his remorse, Sir Robert Chiltern vows that he has "paid conscience money many times" for his mistake, Mrs. Cheveley's transaction with Sir Robert, in Lord Goring's opinion, is a "loathsome commercial transaction of a loathsome commercial age." Mrs. Cheveley admits that much: "It is a commercial transaction. That is all. There is no good mixing up sentimentality in it. I offered to sell Robert Chiltern a certain thing. If he won't pay me my price, he will have to pay the world a greater price."

So in the middle of the play Sir Robert Chiltern is threatened with scandal and ruin because of what he did in the past. He declares that he has fought the century with its own weapon, wealth. He has shown the courage, cunning, and strength to yield to temptations: "To stake all one's life on a single moment, to risk everything on one throw, whether the stake be power or pleasure, I care not—there is no weakness in that. There is a horrible, terrible courage." Lord Goring's dandyism, his allowances for human vices and shortcomings, vindicate Sir Robert's resolution to defy Mrs. Cheveley. When Mrs. Cheveley boasts that she knows Sir Robert's "real character" by virtue of his letter, Lord Goring replies: "What you know about him is not his real character. It was an act of folly done in his youth, dishonourable, I admit, shameful, I admit, unworthy of him, I admit, and therefore . . . not his true character.'' Of the Chilterns' intended withdrawal from public life despite his promotion to a Cabinet post, Lord Goring remarks: ''We men and women are not made to accept such sacrifice from each other. We are not worthy of them.''

In the ''flawless dandy'' Lord Goring, we perceive the lineaments of ''the ideal husband''—at least to Mabel Chiltern, in the future. He has a humaneness absent from his literary predecessors like Lord Henry Wotton, Lord Darlington, and Lord Illingworth. The dandy, in general, enacts the cult of the self not only in thought but also in the taste for dress and material elegance. He supports ceremony and social manners in principle. If he is anarchic, that is because he feels secure within the confines of society. Gestures and dress suggest the rhythm and harmony of a mind which depends on ''the peculiar pleasure of astonishing and the proud satisfaction of never being astonished.'' Seriousness, or hypocrisy, is the ''unbecoming'' cardinal vice. As a clown armed with trivialities, the dandy exemplifies the value of external form as the emblem of what is within the self; he dissolves any disparity between the moral and the physical aspects of life. Lord Goring, in particular, abhors all romantic ideals, just as the dandies of the other comedies do. Pursuing a ''gentleman's'' routine, he exhibits ''all the delicate fopperies of Fashion.'' Compared with Phipps the ''ideal butler,'' the ''mask with a manner,'' who represents ''the dominance of form,'' Lord Goring has *élan vital:* ''He plays with life, and is on perfectly good terms with the world. . . . One sees that he stands in immediate relation to modern life, makes it indeed, and so masters it.'' Mabel Chiltern, whose good sense springs from a feeling for just proportion in matters of daily life, does not desire Lord Goring to be an ''ideal husband.'' For she feels that ''he can be what he chooses''; her only wish is to be ''a real wife to him.'' The significance of the adjective ''real'' inheres in a flexibility of attitude to life, in the knowledge of human limitations—a knowledge of which the ''ideal husband'' must have a good share.

**Source:** Epifanio San Juan Jr., ''The Action of the Comedies,'' in *Oscar Wilde,* edited by Harold Bloom, Chelsea House Publishers, 1985, pp. 45–76.

### Robert Keith Miller

*In the following excerpt, Miller gives an overview of* An Ideal Husband, *providing deeper analysis of the characters of Sir Robert and Lord Goring*

*and calling the drama much improved over Wilde's earlier ones.*

*An Ideal Husband* opened in London on January 3, 1895. Although considerably longer than either *Lady Windermere's Fan* or *A Woman of No Importance,* it proved to be an enormous success. When the Prince of Wales sent for Wilde on the opening night, the flattered playwright remarked that he would have to cut some of the scenes. ''Pray do not take out a single word,'' said the Prince, and Wilde was more than happy to leave the play as it was. While a modern audience is likely to be more critical, it cannot be denied that *An Ideal Husband* is much better crafted than either of Wilde's earlier comedies. Indeed, no less a judge than George Bernard Shaw was moved by this work to pronounce Wilde ''our only thorough playwright.''

The play centers around a group of characters who have by now grown into easily recognizable types. Once again we have a woman of high moral principle—Lady Chiltern. We have a character with a secret past (her husband, Sir Robert Chiltern), a dandy (Lord Goring), and a fashionable woman of questionable reputation, Mrs. Cheveley. But these characters show a new degree of depth. If Lady Chiltern is a good woman, she is seldom so one dimensional as Mrs. Arbuthnot. And if Lord Goring affects a dandylike pose, he is much more complex than either Lord Darlington or Lord Illingworth.

Sir Robert Chiltern is ''the ideal husband'' referred to in the title of the play. Lady Chiltern can see in him no wrong: ''He is not like other men,'' she tells Lord Goring. ''Robert is as incapable of doing a foolish thing as he is of doing a wrong thing.'' Lord Goring knows better and argues,

> I have sometimes thought that . . . perhaps you are a little too hard in some of your views on life . . . . In every nature there are elements of weakness, or worse than weakness . . . . Nobody is incapable of doing a foolish thing. Nobody is incapable of doing a wrong thing.

As the action of the play unfolds, this is precisely the lesson that Lady Chiltern—like Lady Windermere before her—must learn.

Years earlier, when he was an ambitious young man serving as private secretary to a cabinet minister, Robert Chiltern had learned that the British government was about to purchase the Suez Canal. He sold this secret to a speculator three days before the news was made public, and was paid, for this tip, over one hundred thousand pounds—easily half a million dollars in today's currency. This sum formed the basis for his subsequent career. As the play begins, he is under secretary of state for foreign affairs, widely admired as a man of moral stature, and almost certainly destined to become prime minister one day.

Unfortunately, there exists against him one piece of evidence—the original letter advising purchase of Suez Canal stock. This letter has fallen into the hands of Mrs. Cheveley, an adventuress whom Wilde describes as "a work of art, on the whole, but showing the influence of too many schools." Mrs. Cheveley has invested heavily in a scheme to promote a canal in South America, a scheme Sir Robert is preparing to denounce, in the House of Commons, as a swindle. Mrs. Cheveley is determined to keep Sir Robert from making this speech; she demands that he suppress his report and say a few words to the effect that the canal, if completed, may be of great international value. Unless he agrees to do so, Mrs. Cheveley will make public the incriminating letter that she possesses, thus effectively ruining Sir Robert's career and his marriage to a woman who will allow no compromise with deceit.

Greatly troubled, Sir Robert agrees to do as he has been told, but then he is confronted by his wife, who tells him that she had known Mrs. Cheveley when they were girls at school together:

LADY CHILTERN: She was untruthful, dishonest, an evil influence on everyone whose trust or friendship she could win. I hated her, I despised her. She stole things, she was a thief. She was sent away for being a thief. Why do you let her influence you?

SIR ROBERT: Gertrude, what you tell me may be true, but it happened many years ago. It is best forgotten! Mrs. Cheveley may have changed since then. No one should be entirely judged by his past.

LADY CHILTERN: One's past is what one is. It's the only way by which people should be judged.

The irony of this exchange is that both characters are wrong. Mrs. Cheveley is no better than she was as a girl—if anything, she is much worse, and Lady Chiltern is right to judge her by her past. But in taking such an absolute position, in arguing that everyone should be judged by the past, she has condemned her own husband, unaware that he has a past that he has kept concealed from her.

Convinced that he will lose his wife's love if he tells her the truth, Sir Robert assures her that he has never done anything dishonorable and that he will make his original speech as planned. Unfortunately,

> **"** WILDE WANTED TO BE LOVED
> AND ACCEPTED BY THE VERY
> PEOPLE HE LOVED TO TAUNT. IN
> SIMPLE TERMS, HE DID NOT KNOW
> WHAT HE WANTED. . . ."

the scandal cannot be contained. When Lady Chiltern tells Mrs. Cheveley, "Leave my house. You are unfit to enter it," Mrs. Cheveley strikes back:

Your house! A house bought with the price of dishonour. A house, everything in which has been paid for by fraud. Ask him what the origin of his fortune is! Get him to tell you how he sold to a stockbroker a Cabinet secret. Learn from him to what you owe your position.

Vowing once again to make her information public, Mrs. Cheveley leaves Sir Robert to the reproaches of his wife in a scene that reveals the essence of the play. Lady Chiltern takes refuge in theatrics:

Don't come near me. Don't touch me. I feel as if you had soiled me forever. Oh! what a mask you have been wearing all these years! A horrible, painted mask! You sold yourself for money . . . . And how I worshipped you! You were to me something apart from common life, a thing pure, noble, honest, without stain. The world seemed to me finer because you were in it, and goodness more real because you lived. And now—Oh, when I think that I made of a man like you my ideal, the ideal of my life!

Even a nineteenth-century audience would recognize that Lady Chiltern has gone too far. Because she demanded the impossible of her husband—perfection—she has catapulted from one extreme to another, from unreasoning adoration to unreasonable contempt. There is no question that Sir Robert has done a serious wrong. But our sympathies turn to him when he explains that he never wanted to be an ideal, that he would have preferred to be loved for what he is:

It is not the perfect, but the imperfect, who have need of love. It is when we are wounded by our own hands, or by the hands of others, that love should come to cure us—else what use is love at all? All sins, except a sin against itself, Love should forgive . . . . You made your false idol of me, and I had not the courage to come down, show you my wounds, tell you my weaknesses. I was afraid that I might lose your love, as I have lost it now . . . . And now what is there before me but public disgrace, ruin, terrible shame, the mockery of the world, a lonely, dishonoured death . . . . Let women make no more ideals of men! let them not put them on altars and bow before them, or they may ruin other lives as completely as you—you whom I have so wildly loved—have ruined mine!

There is, to be sure, an element of melodrama here. But the scene is nonetheless powerful and the lesson clear. Once again, we find Wilde condemning absolutes and pleading for tolerance in a world that is apt to be harsh.

At this point, the plot becomes increasingly complicated. Lord Goring had once urged Lady Chiltern to turn to him if she ever found herself in need of a friend. And now, at the beginning of Act III, he receives a note from her reading ''I want you. I trust you. I am coming to you,'' from which he rightly deduces that Lady Chiltern has learned her husband's secret. As he prepares to receive her and urge her to stand by her husband, Lord Goring is interrupted by a visit from his father. Goring instructs his butler, ''There is a lady coming to see me this evening on particular business. Show her into the drawing room when she arrives,'' and he retires offstage with his father. Mrs. Cheveley now appears, and believing that this must be the woman his employer is expecting, the butler ushers her into the drawing room. Once there, she discovers the letter Goring has just received from Lady Chiltern, which she takes as proof that they are having an affair. Sir Robert Chiltern now arrives upon the scene, anxious to have the advice of a man he respects. But when he discovers Mrs. Cheveley in Lord Goring's house, he is convinced that his best friend is in league with his worst enemy, and he leaves in disgust.

Mrs. Cheveley now makes an unexpected request. She tells Lord Goring that she will surrender Sir Robert's letter if Goring will agree to marry her. And here the already complex plot takes still another twist. We have known since Act I that Mrs. Cheveley has lost a diamond and ruby brooch. This brooch is now in Lord Goring's possession, and he shows it to her, asking if it is hers. She claims it with delight, and he fastens it to her arm, explaining that it was really designed as a bracelet with a secret spring. Once she has the bracelet on, Mrs. Cheveley cannot remove it because she does not understand how the spring works. Lord Goring knows how to work it because he had originally bought the bracelet as a gift for a cousin from whom it had been stolen ten years earlier. He threatens to expose Mrs. Cheveley as the thief unless she yields up Sir

Robert's incriminating letter. She does so, but she holds fast to Lady Chiltern's letter, finding consolation in the thought that if she cannot ruin Sir Robert's career, she can at least ruin his marriage.

All of these complications are finally resolved in the fourth and last act. When Mrs. Cheveley sends Lady Chiltern's letter to Sir Robert, Sir Robert assumes that the letter has come to him direct from his wife. Believing that his wife is prepared to forgive him, he seeks her out and discovers that this is indeed the case. Determined to make the play end happily, Wilde omits any further mention of the wicked Mrs. Cheveley. Lord Goring proposes marriage to Sir Robert's younger sister and ward, and we are told that Sir Robert has been asked to join the Cabinet in recognition of his brilliant speech denouncing the South American canal scheme. Lady Chiltern kisses her husband and promises, ''For both of us a new life is beginning.'' And on that happy note, the curtain falls.

If Lady Chiltern is able to forgive her husband, it is because she learns that she was wrong to expect him to be perfect. The notion of ''an ideal husband'' is introduced comically at first—a minor character complains: ''My Reginald is hopelessly faultless. He is really unendurably so, at times! There is not the smallest excitement in knowing him.'' But we know that Wilde is serious in encouraging his audience to resist the temptation to romanticize. It is particularly dangerous to insist on ideals, if ideals mean an inability to compromise:

SIR ROBERT: Arthur, I couldn't tell my wife . . . . she would have turned from me in horror . . . .

LORD GORING: Is Lady Chiltern as perfect as all that?

SIR ROBERT: Yes; my wife is as perfect as all that.

LORD GORING: What a pity!

To be perfect is to be rigid and incapable of human feeling. Life cannot be lived according to absolutes; we must learn to be flexible and willing to change. Lady Chiltern boasts that she never changes, and even so unsympathetic a character as Mrs. Cheveley is moved to say, ''Then life has taught you nothing . . . . I am sorry for you Gertrude, very sorry for you.''

As late as Act IV, however, Lady Chiltern reveals an almost fatal rigidity. Although it is clear that her husband regrets his one and only sin, and although she recognizes that she loves him still, she urges him to retire from public life. Because his public life is based upon ''a lie,'' it is his ''duty'' to give it up, regardless of his power for doing good so long as he is in office. But once again Lord Goring steps forward as the voice of tolerance:

> You love Robert. Do you want to kill his love for you? What sort of existence will he have if you rob him of the fruits of his ambition . . . . Rather than lose your love, Robert would do anything, wreck his whole career, as he is on the brink of doing now. He is making for you a terrible sacrifice. Take my advice, Lady Chiltern, and do not accept a sacrifice so great. If you do, you will live to repent it bitterly. We men and women are not made to accept such sacrifices from each other.

Lady Chiltern is wise enough to accept this advice, thus ensuring a stronger and happier future for her marriage. She has learned not to demand an ''ideal husband.''

Returning to this theme on a lighter note in the final scene of the play, Wilde makes Lord Goring's father counsel the imminent bridegroom to become an ''ideal husband.'' But Goring's young fiancée has the sense to declare:

> An ideal husband! Oh, I don't think I should like that. It sounds like something in the next world. He can be what he chooses. All I want is to be . . . a real wife to him.

Feminists might well argue that women get the raw end of this deal, but it would be a mistake to see the play as urging women to forgive their husbands no matter what they do. If *An Ideal Husband* focuses upon the need to be tolerant of the shortcomings of men, it is only because Wilde had already made a similar plea for women in his two preceding plays. He urges men and women alike to accept one another as they are and not to place one another ''on monstrous pedestals,'' because ''we all have feet of clay, women as well as men.''

The two men who figure the most prominently in this play deserve careful consideration. Sir Robert Chiltern is, as we have seen, a character with a past. But he is much more complex than either Mrs. Erlynne or Mrs. Arbuthnot. Mrs. Erlynne has more or less outlived her scandal; although she expresses remorse in the memorable confrontation with her daughter, she has put her past behind her in order to devote herself to gaining an untroubled future. Mrs. Arbuthnot, on the other hand, dwells almost exclusively in the past. Her sin was the single great event in her life, and she nurses its memory, determined to live a life of constant self-abnegation. If one woman is too little troubled by her past, the other is troubled too much, and compared to Sir Robert Chiltern, both are relatively one-dimensional.

Sir Robert is recognizably human. He is capable of wallowing in self-pity:

> I sold, like a common huckster, the secret that had been intrusted to me by a man of honour. I thank heaven poor Lord Radley died without knowing that I betrayed him. I would to God I had died before I had been so terribly tempted, or fallen so low.

We know that this is insincere. Regardless of any remorse he may feel, he sees the past in proportion and is determined to fight to maintain his position in the world. When he is honest, he admits ''I felt that I had fought the century with its own weapons, and won.'' And when Lord Goring rebukes him for having been so weak, he refuses to respond with platitudes:

> Weak? Oh, I am sick of hearing that phrase. Sick of using it about others. Weak? Do you really think, Arthur, that it is weakness that yields to temptation? I tell you that it requires strength and courage, to yield to. To stake all one's life on a single moment, to risk everything on one throw, whether the stake be power or pleasure, I care not—there is no weakness in that. There is horrible, terrible courage.

But then, reflecting upon the vulnerability of his success, he concludes, ''I remember having read somewhere that when the gods wish to punish us they answer our prayers.'' This is no cardboard figure, but a real man feeling an intriguing mixture of grief and anger. He neither offends us with indifference nor bores us with hysterics, and it is satisfying to find him redeemed by the end of the play.

Because Sir Robert is basically good, there is no need for him to be publicly humiliated. But he has only narrowly escaped from a real danger, as Mrs. Cheveley reminds us. Speaking of the newspapers, she envisions what would eventually come to pass in Wilde's own life:

> Think of their loathsome joy, of the delight they would have in dragging you down, of the mud and mire they would plunge you in. Think of the hypocrite with his greasy smile penning his leading article, and arranging the foulness of the public placard.

The charge of public hypocrisy is repeated by Sir Robert, who reflects bitterly upon how he would be scorned by ''men who, each one of them, have worse secrets in their own lives.'' And we should not be misled by the lightness of Lord Goring's response: ''That is the reason they are so pleased to find out other people's secrets. It distracts public attention from their own.''

Sir Robert Chiltern's fear of public ruin might well be Wilde's own. The play was written only a year before its author found himself in court, a time when Wilde was afflicted with a strong sense of his own impending doom. Describing *An Ideal Husband* in a letter to a friend, Wilde observed: "It reads rather well, and some of its passages seem prophetic of tragedy to come." But while Wilde clearly identified with Sir Robert, it would be a mistake to see that character as the sole voice of Wilde's point of view within the play.

If as a popular public figure hovering on the brink of disgrace Sir Robert finds himself in a position that was analogous to Wilde's, Lord Goring represents the way Wilde liked to see himself. Of all Wilde's dandies, Goring is by far the most interesting. Although he chooses to show himself as shallow to those who do not interest him, he is, as we are allowed to see, both wise and kind.

Wilde says that Goring is "clever, but would not like to be thought so . . . . He is fond of being misunderstood. It gives him a post of vantage." He likes to stand apart from life in order to better understand it, but he is also capable of action when those he loves need help.

Throughout the play, we see two Lord Gorings: one is the glib young man who likes to scandalize dowagers at lengthy dinner parties; the other is the loyal friend who never fails to offer wise counsel. He can be irritatingly trivial—"To love oneself is the beginning of a life-long romance"—but this is, for the most part, a manner that he assumes in order to avoid sentimentality. He is easily embarrassed by the expression of feeling. When Sir Robert tries to thank him for his help, he retreats, characteristically, into the facile: "Ah! the truth is a thing I get rid of as soon as possible! Bad habit by the way. Makes one unpopular at the club . . . . "

In Lord Goring, Wilde created a character very much like himself. Like Wilde, Goring lies about his age, claims to worship youth, is easily bored, and appears to be selfish. But as a recent critic has shown, Goring

> is also a kind of providence who settles all troubles by quick brainwork and utter detachment. Outwardly a dandy and an idler, he is inwardly a philosopher, even a man of action and decision if need be. All Wilde's friends remarked that in spite of his frivolous attitude towards life . . . . his advice in mundane affairs was singularly shrewd, and each of these characteristics is given to Goring.

The philosopher would not be possible without the dandy. It is the seemingly idle life that leaves the dandy free to observe his fellow men, and observation is the beginning of wisdom.

Thus both Lord Goring and Sir Robert Chiltern should be seen as representing different aspects of Wilde's own character. One represents the dandified self, which sees itself as superior to social norms and entitled to complete freedom; the other, the sinner with a guilty conscience who admits that he has done wrong but argues that he should not be punished. Speaking in the person of Sir Robert, Wilde

> admits that he has sinned in rejecting the mores of society. He insists, however, that he has remained uncorrupted at heart and begs society for pardon and acceptance. Speaking as Lord Goring . . . . Wilde disdains that society and demands absolute freedom for the expression of the self. He denies the existence of evil and good and maintains that the only realities are ugliness and beauty.

Like *The Picture of Dorian Gray, An Ideal Husband* reveals the conflict of the divided self. Wilde wanted to be loved and accepted by the very people he loved to taunt. In simple terms, he did not know what he wanted—the source, perhaps, of his personal misfortune, but also the source of much that gives interest to his work.

Of the three plays discussed in this chapter, *An Ideal Husband* is unquestionably the most serious. Technically it is a comedy, because it ends happily. But there is very little humor in the play beyond an occasional epigram, and the business of the diamond bracelet is distinctly melodramatic. Nonetheless, *An Ideal Husband* shows considerable improvement over Wilde's earlier plays in both construction and characterization. If it lacks the brilliant dialogue one usually associates with Wilde, it clearly has the substance with which he is seldom credited. Wilde was to write only one more play, *The Importance of Being Earnest.* But within *An Ideal Husband*, there are moments of high drama that make one wonder what new directions Wilde might have pursued had his career not ended so precipitously. This is his best play but one.

**Source:** Robert Keith Miller, "Feasting with Panthers: The Rise and Fall of Oscar Wilde," in *Oscar Wilde,* Frederick Ungar Publishing, 1982, pp. 1–24.

### Donald H. Ericksen

*In the following excerpt, Ericksen views Lord Goring as representing "a significant development in Wilde's treatment of the dandy."*

*An Ideal Husband,* according to Frank Harris, was based on a story that he had told Wilde about

Disraeli's making money by entrusting the Rothschilds with the purchase of Suez Canal shares. Pearson discounts the significance of Harris' claim by arguing that ''Sardou must have suggested it to Harris, as it is to be found in that playwright's *Dora.*'' *An Ideal Husband* was first performed at the Theater Royal, Haymarket, on January 3, 1895, with great success. Henry James, whose own play *Guy Domville* also opened the same night, saw Wilde's play at its opening. He felt the play was ''so helpless, so crude, so bad, so clumsy, feeble, and vulgar'' that he wondered ''How *can* my piece do anything with a public with whom *that* is a success?'' James was at least partly right, for his own play closed February 2 to make room for the *The Importance of Being Earnest.*

Wilde's third comedy, *An Ideal Husband,* presents in Lady Chiltern another Puritan who cannot forgive anyone who has ever done a wicked or shameful deed. Her husband Robert, whom she idealizes, has long ago made his fortune by dishonorably selling a government secret. Mrs. Cheveley, a dishonest former school acquaintance of Lady Chiltern, attempts to blackmail Sir Robert into supporting a fraudulent Argentine canal project. Sir Robert is certain he will lose his wife if his secret is revealed, but Lord Goring, the Wildean dandy, encourages him to fight Mrs. Cheveley. When Lady Chiltern learns of her husband's past, she castigates him and rejects his pleas for forgiveness. Later, Lord Goring receives a seemingly compromising letter from Lady Chiltern. By confronting Mrs. Cheveley with a diamond brooch she had stolen, Lord Goring obtains the damaging letter Sir Robert had written long ago that revealed his guilt, but Mrs. Cheveley obtains Lady Chiltern's letter and declares her intention to send it to Sir Robert that night. The next day Sir Robert officially denounces the fraudulent canal scheme and is reunited with his wife. The letter Mrs. Cheveley had sent had been an affectionate and forgiving one that had been intended for him all along. Lord Goring wins the lovely Mabel Chiltern while Lady Chiltern discovers that ''Nobody is incapable of doing a foolish thing. Nobody is incapable of doing a wrong thing.''

Although Wilde's *An Ideal Husband,* like *Lady Windermere's Fan* and *A Woman of No Importance,* centers around a conflict caused by a wife or fiance's unyielding moral rigidity, the manner in which the dandy is related to this conflict is quite new. The dandy in Wilde's two earlier comedies was a dangerous though charming villain. Lord Darlington in *Lady Windermere's Fan* nearly suc-

ceeds in breaking up a marriage. Lord Illingworth in *A Woman of No Importance* is a betrayer of women. Both figures, however, function as spokesmen for the dandiacal way of life and, on occasion, as Wildean commentators.

When in the earlier plays these figures are discredited as the conventionally moral plots demanded, there is some question in the reader's mind about the concomitant condemnation of their dandiacal message. Such a divided reaction Wilde surely did not intend. More likely Wilde was attempting to write plays that would be appreciated and understood by both Philistine and cognoscente at two different levels. Lord Goring, however, in *An Ideal Husband* represents a significant development in Wilde's treatment of the dandy. Although he retains his role as dandy and Wildean commentator, he loses the usual role as villain. Mrs. Cheveley has assumed this function. Wilde retains the woman with the past, but in this case she sins more than she is sinned against. Another vestigial remainder of the villainous dandy can be discovered in Baron Arnheim. Although, we never meet him, we learn that he is an aesthete of exquisite tastes who early seduced Lord Chiltern to his doctrine of wealth. At the close of the play, when Sir Robert Chiltern is about to terminate his political career with his wife's misguided acquiescence, it is Lord Goring's long sermon on the roles of men and women which saves the day: ''Women are not meant to judge us, but to forgive us when we need forgiveness. Pardon, not punishment, is their mission.'' Wilde could hardly realize how unacceptable such role distinctions would be for us today, but he is clearly reflecting the views of the mass of Englishmen of his time. Thus, the dandy has lost his sting.

In *An Ideal Husband* Wilde realigns his characters in such a way that, for the first time, the villain (villainess in this case) is an antagonist of the dandy. Mrs. Cheveley, in spite of her role as heavy, is as much a dandy as Lord Goring. Mrs. Cheveley, who is "a work of art, on the whole, but showing the influence of too many schools, like Lord Goring, believes that life is a pose:

> Sir Robert Chiltern: To attempt to classify you, Mrs. Cheveley, would be an impertinence. But may I ask, at heart, are you an optimist or a pessimist? Those seem to be the only two fashionable religions left to us nowadays.
>
> Mrs. Cheveley: Oh, I'm neither. Optimism begins in a broad grin, and Pessimism ends with blue spectacles. Besides, they are both of them merely poses.
>
> Sir Robert Chiltern: You prefer to be natural?
>
> Mrs. Cheveley: Sometimes. But it is such a very difficult pose to keep up.

Mrs. Cheveley, who prefers books in "yellow covers," sees life as an art form. In a conversation with Mrs. Markby, another dandy in a play where the dandies outnumber the Philistines, she expounds Wilde's view of life as an art form:

> Mrs. Cheveley: . . . Fathers have so much to learn from their sons nowadays.
>
> Lady Markby: Really, dear? What?
>
> Mrs. Cheveley: The art of living. The only really Fine Art we have produced in modern times.

Such comments are echoed in the words of other Wildean dandies. Mrs. Cheveley serves as spokeswoman on occasion for several Wildean ideas but Wilde insures that we see her as a villainess by making her a thief, a blackmailer, and a protégé of the evil Baron Arnheim. Moreover, her status as a dandy is further undercut by her conception of human relations as commercial transactions. The benevolent dandy must be above such sordidness.

A Wildean idea given especially strong emphasis in *An Ideal Husband* is that life is as capable of artistic form and meaning as a painting or a poem. The idea of life as an art form is not so explicitly presented as it is in *Intentions* or *The Picture of Dorian Gray;* but the emphasis on art, artists, artistic form, masks, poses, and such suggests the deep importance of this idea. Some characters are compared to works of art. Mrs. Cheveley is described as "a work of art . . . but showing the influence of too many schools"; Mabel Chiltern is really "like a Tanagra statuette"; Lord Caversham is "a fine Whig type. Rather like a portrait by Laurence." Others are revealed as potential subjects. Watteau

would have loved to paint Mrs. Marchmont and Lady Basildon, those "types of exquisite fragility." Anthony Vandyke would have liked to paint Sir Robert Chiltern's head. The opening scene takes place beneath a "large eighteenth century French tapestry—representing the Triumph of Love, from a design by Boucher—that is stretched on the staircase wall." Sir Robert Chiltern is a collector of art objects and has a particularly fine collection of Corots. Each of these artists, especially Boucher and Watteau, throughout or at some stage of his career represents a commitment to artificiality, sensuousity, and escapism. Phipps, Lord Goring's butler, is described as a "mask with a manner," one who "represents the dominance of forms." These details reinforce the Wildean precept that the artistic form of one's life is all-important. This notion was central to the dandiacal creed.

The imagery of masks which so permeates this drama not only reinforces the life-as-art-form theme but buttresses the plot in several other ways. Events hinge upon reversals of conceptions of self and others. Lady Chiltern cannot conceive of committing a serious social error, nor can she imagine being married to a man of anything but impeccable character. Both conceptions prove faulty. Sir Robert presents a public mask of absolute personal integrity but has actually built his fortune and career upon a deception. Lady Chiltern condemns her husband at one point for not preserving his mask of integrity by lying to her. Sir Robert, at another point in the drama, refuses Lord Goring's advice to confess because he believes his wife "does not know what weakness or temptation is." Ironically, neither of the two principals can see beyond the mask of the other.

In this, the third of Wilde's society comedies, the moralistic plot does not jar so sharply against the anti-Philistine and dandiacal elements. This harmony is achieved primarily by making Lord Goring the ally of the principal characters in their struggle against the wicked Mrs. Cheveley. The political satire also helps to dissipate the discord that existed in the earlier comedies between the comic themes and the serious ones. The plethora of rather hackneyed theatrical devices is evident as well as the insistence upon the melodramatic. More significant than all the above, however, is the substantial movement towards dramatic unity by the uniting of the Wildean life-as-art-form, "mask," "game," and "pose" themes with his central dramatic action. Wildean dandyism can be clearly recognized as a fundamental aspect of Wilde's thought and method and not a thematic excrescence. Imperfect as the blend may be, it illustrates Wilde's substantial growth as a dramatist and presages the perfection of Wilde's comedic form in *The Importance of Being Earnest.*

**Source:** Donald H. Ericksen, "The Drama," in *Oscar Wilde,* Twayne Publishers, 1977, pp. 118–52.

# SOURCES

Belford, Barbara, "A Broken Line," in *Oscar Wilde: A Certain Genius,* Random House, 2000, p. 233.

Eagleton, Terry, Introduction, in *Saint Oscar, and Other Plays,* Blackwell Publishers, 1997.

Hall, Peter, "A Warm, Impossible Love," in the *Guardian,* November 11, 1992, Features Page, p. 4.

Nichols, Mark, "*An Ideal Husband*—The Wit and The Legend," in *The Importance of Being Oscar,* St. Martin's Press, 1983, pp. 91, 138.

Review of *An Ideal Husband,* in the *Times* (London), January 4, 1895, p. 7.

Wilde, Oscar, *An Ideal Husband,* in *The Plays of Oscar Wilde,* Random House, 1932.

# FURTHER READING

Ellmann, Richard, *Oscar Wilde,* Alfred A. Knopf, 1988.
This work is currently the most thorough and definitive biography of Wilde. In it, students of Wilde can read in minute detail about the author's life and career.

Holland, Vyvyan, *Oscar Wilde,* Thames and Hudson, 1960.
This is a brief, informative book on the life of Wilde by his son, with photographs of Wilde, family, friends, and other notables. Holland corrects what he believes are inaccuracies in the major biographies of Wilde, such as those written by Frank Harris and Richard Ellmann.

Raby, Peter, ed., *The Cambridge Companion to Oscar Wilde,* Cambridge University Press, 1997.
This collection by several authors on different aspects of Wilde's career and works contains many informative, recent essays. For example, one essay explores Wilde's four comedic plays as a group, and another compares Wilde's dramatic techniques to those of other major playwrights of the time.

Roditi, Edouard, *Oscar Wilde,* New Directions, 1986.
Most recent books on Wilde by literary scholars tend to focus on narrow, specialized subjects. Roditi's study, however, is a broad, general exploration of Wilde's art. As such, it is very useful for students looking for a general introduction to Wilde.

San Juan, Epifanio, Jr., *The Art of Oscar Wilde,* Princeton University Press, 1967.
Like Roditi's study of Wilde, this scholarly exploration of Wilde is a comprehensive, useful introduction to Wilde's work.

# India Song

## MARGUERITE DURAS

### 1993

*India Song* (1973), by Marguerite Duras, is an experimental play set in colonial India during the 1930s. Through her unique use of disembodied voices as narrators, Duras presents a composite account of the tragic love story of Anne-Marie Stretter, wife of the French ambassador to India.

In 1972, Duras was commissioned by Britain's National Theatre to write *India Song* as a play, although it was not staged at that time. *India Song* was first published in book form as a play/screenplay/novel in 1973. It was adapted to film as a motion picture released in 1975 and first performed on stage in 1993.

*India Song* is narrated by four voices, two female and two male, who recall the events of one night at a party held at the French embassy in Calcutta in 1937 and the following day at the French residence on an island in the Indian Ocean. Anne-Marie Stretter is an object of fascination for everyone. Although married to Ambassador Stretter, she has taken Michael Richardson as her lover. Two other men, a French vice-consul and a young French attaché, are also in love with her. One night, Anne-Marie commits suicide by walking into the Indian Ocean to drown herself. Her story is set within the luxurious confines of European colonial life, where the privileged white colonists take refuge from the poverty, disease, starvation, and suffering of the Indian people.

*India Song* covers many themes, including love, desire, passion, and the social inequalities of colonial domination.

## AUTHOR BIOGRAPHY

Duras was born Marguerite Donnadieu on April 14, 1914, in French Indochina, a region that is now part of South Vietnam. Her parents were schoolteachers in the French colonial service. When she was four years old, her father died, leaving the family in financial distress. Duras graduated from a high school in Saigon and, at the age of eighteen, moved to Paris, France, to attend college. She earned a degree in law from the Sorbonne. From 1935 to 1941, Duras worked as a secretary in the French Ministry of Colonies. With the advent of World War II, France was occupied by Nazi Germany, and Duras joined the French Resistance movement. Her husband, writer Robert Antelme, was arrested and sent to a concentration camp in Dachau. Antelme returned home in 1945, but Duras had developed a relationship with Dionys Mascolo in his absence. She soon divorced Antelme and eventually married Mascolo, with whom she had a son. Over the course of her life, Duras developed a reputation for her many passionate love affairs, her struggles with alcoholism, and her difficult personality.

In the post–World War II era, Duras established herself as a popular novelist. As her writing style developed, she became identified with the French *nouveau roman* (new novel), that emerged in the post-war period. In the 1950s, Duras became involved in the film industry as a screenwriter and director. Her most successful screenplay, *Hiroshima, Mon Amour* (1959), was based on a novel by Alain Resnais, who directed the film. Duras also began to write plays; her theatrical style became increasingly experimental over the years, establishing her as one of France's most important feminist playwrights.

Many of Duras's works are based on autobiographical experiences. A series referred to as the India cycle is based on her childhood in French colonial Indochina. The India cycle includes the novels *Le Ravissement de Lol V. Stein* (1964; *The Ravishing of Lol V. Stein*), *Le Vice-consul* (1965; *The Vice-Consul*), and *L'Amour* (1972; *Love*), as well as the play and screenplay *India Song* (1973). *L'Amant* (1984; *The Lover*), published when Duras was seventy years old, is her most popular novel and

*Marguerite Duras*

was adapted to film in 1992. Duras was awarded the Prix Concourt, France's most prestigious literary award, for *The Lover*. Late in life, Duras, long separated from her second husband, lived in domestic partnership with Yann Andrea Steiner, a young writer. Duras died in Paris on March 3, 1996.

## PLOT SUMMARY

### Act 1

"India Song," a blues tune is heard being played on a piano. Two disembodied female voices, voice 1 and voice 2, are heard talking to each other. The two voices indicate that Michael Richardson had been engaged to a local woman in the town of S. Thala but that he met Anne-Marie Stretter at a dance one night and fell in love with her. After meeting Anne-Marie, he abandoned his fianceé and followed Anne-Marie to Calcutta. Anne-Marie, dressed in black, lounges on a couch. Michael Richardson sits next to her, while a third man stands nearby. The voices explain that Anne-Marie died one night while in India and that Michael Richardson left the country after her death.

Anne-Marie and Michael get up from the couch and begin dancing. The two voices speak as if partially remembering a story they had heard long ago. They remember that the setting of the dancing couple is the French embassy in Calcutta, India. The street sounds of Calcutta can be heard in the distance. A beggar woman is heard, shouting and laughing. The two voices recall that the beggar woman, who is crazy, is from Burma. The voices state that the beggar woman got pregnant at the age of seventeen and was kicked out of the house by her mother. They say that she spent ten years walking across Asia, before arriving in Calcutta.

Anne-Marie enters the French embassy. She stands in the middle of the room and weeps silently. Michael Richardson enters, takes Anne-Marie in his arms, and gently lays her down on the floor. He sits down beside her and watches her sleep. The voices state that Michael's former fiancée died after he abandoned her for Anne-Marie. A second man, the Stretters' guest, enters and sits beside Anne-Marie. Both men lie down next to her.

The two voices begin to recount the ''ballad of Anne-Marie Stretter.'' They say that Anne-Marie was originally from Venice and that she married a French colonial official at the age of 18. She later met Ambassador Stretter and left her first husband to marry him. For the next seventeen years, she moved with Ambassador Stretter to various cities throughout Asia.

As the two voices talk about Anne-Marie, the vice-consul can be heard in the distance, crying in despair. The voices explain that, in the city of Lahore, the vice-consul shot a gun from his balcony at the lepers and beggars below him. The voices recall that Anne-Marie first attempted to commit suicide while in Chandernagor. In the distance, a glow emanates from the horizon, which the voices identity as fires burning the people who have starved to death.

## Act 2

The setting is a reception or party at the French embassy in Calcutta. Though fragments of conversation are overheard, none of the characters onstage throughout the play are ever seen speaking. Thus, not a single word is uttered on stage by any of the characters. The snippets of overheard conversation from the guests at the reception reveal bits and pieces of information about the main characters.

Michael Richardson, Anne-Marie's lover, is at the reception. The French vice-consul from Lahore is there, and the guests gossip about his behavior in Lahore and of his attempted suicide. A young French attaché, newly arrived in India, is also at the party. Some guests are heard saying that they find Anne-Marie intriguing and wonder what she does with her time. Others inform one another that she frequently plays tennis with her two daughters and rides her bicycle early in the morning. Some guests note that Anne-Marie is dancing with her husband though they are not seen onstage.

The vice-consul stands in the garden, and the other guests avoid him. The ambassador is heard asking the young attaché to talk to the vice-consul. The young attaché goes out into the garden and approaches the vice-consul in a friendly way. He tells the vice-consul that no one can understand why he shot his gun off the balcony in Lahore. The voice of George Crawn is heard, introducing himself to the other guests as an old friend of Anne-Marie's. In a private room away from the reception, Anne-Marie dances with Michael Richardson.

The beggar woman can be seen in the garden, hiding in the bushes. Anne-Marie comes out to the garden, sees the beggar woman, then goes back in. Some of the guests are heard saying that Anne-Marie takes vacations on an island in the Indian Ocean with Michael Richardson and other friends, while her husband goes hunting in Nepal. They claim that her husband knows she has lovers but does not mind because he is older than his wife, and their marriage has become a friendship. Other guests are heard stating that Anne-Marie was once a celebrated pianist in Venice, before she got married.

Anne-Marie dances with the young attaché. The vice-consul asks a woman to dance and, to everyone's surprise, she accepts. While they are dancing, they are heard discussing leprosy and the fear of contracting leprosy while in India. The vice-consul then tells the woman that he in fact wants to get leprosy. She stops dancing and abruptly walks away.

Later, Anne-Marie dances with the vice-consul. He tells her that he loves her, but she responds that she loves only Michael Richardson. The vice-consul begs her to let him spend the night at the embassy, but she refuses. He begins shouting that he loves her and wants to stay at the embassy with her. The other guests are horrified by the shame of his display, and he is told to leave. When he refuses to leave, he is escorted off the premises. Throughout the night, he can be heard in the distance, crying in agony and calling out Anne-Marie's name as he wanders aimlessly through the city.

## Act 3

Everyone has left the party except Anne-Marie, Michael Richardson, the young attaché, the Stretters' guest, and George Crawn, who are sitting around in the reception room. The vice-consul can still be heard crying and yelling in the distance. Voice 3 and voice 4 are heard for the first time. They say that Michael Richardson left India right after Anne-Marie died and that the vice-consul resigned his post in 1938 and was never heard from again. Voices 1 and 2 can be heard, also discussing the fate of the vice-consul. The five people in the embassy doze in their chairs, as the night turns to day. While they are sleeping, voice 3 and voice 4 describe their journey by car the next day to vacation on the islands. The voices indicate that they are staying at the Prince of Wales Hotel on an island in the Indian Ocean.

## Act 4

Anne Marie, Michael Richardson, the young attaché, the Stretters's guest, and George Crawn enter the lounge of the Prince of Wales Hotel, then go into the dining room for dinner. The vice-consul appears in the garden and enters the hotel, though the others do not see him. The voices indicate that the beggar woman has also come to the island. They explain that after dinner Anne-Marie said she wanted to walk along the beach by herself. Though she does not see him, the vice-consul follows behind her.

## Act 5

Anne-Marie, Michael Richardson, and the young attaché arrive at the French residence on the island at the same time, though they have taken different routes. The vice-consul arrives soon after, unnoticed by the others. Inside, Michael sits playing the piano. The young attaché takes Anne-Marie in his arms and gives her a passionate kiss, right in front of Michael Richardson. The vice-consul watches from the window. Michael and the young attaché both walk away from the residence, leaving Anne-Marie alone with the vice-consul. Voice 4 explains that in the morning Anne-Marie walked into the Indian Ocean, committing suicide.

# MEDIA ADAPTATIONS

- *India Song* was adapted to film and directed by Duras. It premiered at the Cannes Film Festival in 1975. Voice 4 in the film, which is indicated in the script as male, is narrated by Duras.

# CHARACTERS

### Beggar Woman

The beggar woman is a mysterious figure who hides in the bushes of the French embassy garden and occasionally peeks her head out to watch the goings-on at the reception. The voices explain that she is from Burma and that she got pregnant at the age of seventeen and left home. They state that the beggar woman walked across Asia for ten years and finally ended up in Calcutta. She has lost all her hair from malnutrition and is bald. The beggar woman can be heard singing at various points throughout the play. At the end of *India Song*, the voices indicate that the beggar woman has followed Anne-Marie and her friends to the island. While Anne-Marie represents the status of white European women in colonial Asia, the beggar woman represents the conditions of life for Asian women.

### George Crawn

George Crawn is an Englishman and an old friend of Anne-Marie's. He arrives at the embassy reception and encourages the other guests to help themselves to drinks from the bar. Toward the end of the play, he travels with Anne-Marie and several of her other friends to the islands.

### The French Ambassador

*See* Ambassador Stretter

### The Guest

The guest of the Stretters' is one of the men who attends the reception at the embassy. The next day, he travels with Anne-Marie and several other friends to the islands. There is some indication that the guest may have been one of Anne-Marie's lovers.

### Michael Richardson

Michael Richardson is Anne-Marie's lover. He first met her in S. Thala, where he had been engaged to a local girl. After he met Anne-Marie at a party and danced with her, he fell in love with her and broke off his engagement. When Anne-Marie moved with her husband to Calcutta, Michael Richardson dropped everything to follow her. He started his own shipping company in Calcutta so that he could live there and be near Anne-Marie. He frequently travels with her to the island, where they vacation together at the French residence. Toward the end of the play, he plays the piano and watches as Anne-Marie shares a passionate kiss with the young attaché. The voices explain that after Anne-Marie's suicide, Michael Richardson left India and never returned.

### Ambassador Stretter

Ambassador Stretter is the husband of Anne-Marie Stretter and is the French ambassador to India. They have been married for seventeen years, during which time they have lived in various capital cities throughout Asia. Ambassador Stretter never appears as a character on stage; however, his voice may be heard offstage at various points during the reception that is held at the French embassy in Calcutta. The voices and various gossiping guests at the party indicate that the ambassador is well aware of the fact that his wife takes lovers. The Stretters' marriage has become more of a platonic friendship than a romantic relationship, so he does not mind her infidelities. Thus, when Anne-Marie vacations on the island with Michael Richardson, her husband goes on hunting trips in Nepal. During the course of the reception, Ambassador Stretter can be heard offstage talking with the young attaché, inviting him to travel with Anne-Marie to the islands and asking him to speak with the vice-consul since no one else at the party is willing to go near him.

### Anne-Marie Stretter

Anne-Marie Stretter is the central character of *India Song*. She is originally from Venice, born of a French father and a mother of unknown origin. When she was seventeen, she got pregnant and married a French bureaucrat, with whom she traveled throughout Asia. She then met Ambassador Stretter and left her first husband to marry him. At the point when the events of the play take place, she has been married to Ambassador Stretter for seventeen years and has lived with him in various capital cities throughout Asia. She has two daughters.

It is well-known that Anne-Marie takes lovers outside of her marriage. At this point, she is in love with Michael Richardson. During the reception at the French embassy, Anne-Marie dances with her husband, with the young attaché, with Michael Richardson, and with the vice-consul. The various guests at the party find her intriguing and mysterious and gossip about her extensively. The day after the party, she and four guests drive to the island to stay at the French residence there. That night, Anne-Marie shares a passionate kiss with the young attaché, right in front of Michael Richardson. Later, she commits suicide by walking into the Indian Ocean.

### The Vice-Consul

The man referred to as the vice-consul is the former French vice-consul in Lahore, India. While in Lahore, he suffered a mental breakdown and one night fired a gun from his balcony down onto the beggars and lepers crowded below. He tried to shoot himself in the head but failed to commit suicide. After these events, the vice-consul was dismissed from his post in Lahore. He then went to Calcutta to await reassignment. Anne-Marie invites the vice-consul to the reception at the embassy. Because of his outrageous behavior in Lahore, the other guests avoid him and gossip about him. The vice-consul finally asks one woman to dance with him, but when he tells her that he wants to contract the disease of leprosy (presumably because he is suicidal), the woman stops dancing and walks away from him.

Toward the end of the party, the vice-consul and Anne-Marie dance together. He tells her that he is in love with her, but she responds that she is in love with Michael Richardson. The vice-consul then begs her to let him spend the night at the embassy, but she refuses to allow this. He begins shouting that he loves her and wants to spend the night so that all the guests can hear him. The vice-consul is then told to leave the embassy and is escorted off the premises. Throughout the rest of the night, he can be heard in the distance, crying and shouting Anne-Marie's name.

The day after the party, when Anne-Marie and her friends travel to the islands, the vice-consul secretly follows them. After supper, Anne-Marie walks back to the French residence on the island and sees the vice-consul in the garden but does not say anything. The voices state that he was the only one who saw her walk into the ocean to commit suicide but that he did not do anything to stop her. They explain that soon after her death, the vice-consul resigned from his job, and no one ever heard from him again, though he may have been seen walking among the lepers along the Ganges River in Calcutta.

## Voice 1

Voice 1 is a disembodied voice that serves as one of the four narrators of *India Song*. Voice 1 is that of a young woman and is sweet but tinged with madness. Voice 1's memory of the love story of Anne-Marie Stretter is incomplete and illogical. Yet, she is so fascinated and consumed by Anne-Marie's story that she loses herself in it.

## Voice 2

Voice 2 is one of the four disembodied voices that serve as narrators of *India Song*. Like voice 1, voice 2 is that of a young woman, tinged with madness and sweetness. Voice 2 is consumed with love and desire for voice 1 and continually tries to connect the love story of Anne-Marie back to their own love story.

## Voice 3

Voice 3 is a disembodied male voice that is one of the narrators of *India Song*. Like the other voices, voice 3 is fascinated by the love story of Anne-Marie Stretter. However, voice 3 can remember almost nothing of the story and continually asks voice 4 to remind him of the events surrounding Anne-Marie's suicide.

## Voice 4

Voice 4 is one of the disembodied voices that narrates the story of Anne-Marie Stretter in *India Song*. Unlike the other voices, voice 4, a male voice, can remember every detail of Anne-Marie's love story.

## The Young Attaché

The young French attaché, newly arrived in India, is invited to the reception at the French embassy in Calcutta. Anne-Marie dances with him, and he immediately falls in love with her. She invites him to join her and her friends on their trip to the islands the next day, and he accepts. The first night on the island, while they are at the French residence, the young attaché takes Anne-Marie in his arms and kisses her passionately, right in front of Michael Richardson, who does nothing to stop them.

# THEMES

## Obsessive Love

Duras portrays the experience of love in *India Song* as characterized by obsession. Anne-Marie Stretter is a lightning rod for the obsessive love of the men who surround her. Although she is married, she has taken many lovers, and men easily fall in love with her. Thus, Michael Richardson, the vice-consul, and the young attaché are all in love with her, while Anne-Marie loves only Michael Richardson. These characters seem to have no power or control over their obsessive feelings of love. As Anne-Marie tells the vice-consul, ''I love Michael Richardson. I am not free of that love.'' The vice-consul responds that he loves her in the same way that she loves Michael Richardson. The vice-consul thus obsessively pursues Anne-Marie, despite her clearly stated rejection of him. After she sends him away from the embassy, he wanders the streets of Calcutta all night long, pathetically crying out her name and proclaiming his love for her. The next day, he secretly follows her to the island, obsessively continuing to pursue her. Duras thus explores the experience of love as one of compulsion and obsession, a human emotion that operates outside the bounds of reason and often leads to self-destruction.

## Colonialism

The events narrated in *India Song* take place in a context of colonialism. The main characters of the play are European, mostly French and English, colonial diplomats living as the most privileged members of society in a nation where the majority of the population suffers from poverty, disease, and starvation. The death and suffering of the native Indian people under the yoke of colonial domination serves as a backdrop to the central story. Their plight is evoked through frequent mention of the suffering masses of the Indian population outside the embassy. The streets of Calcutta are filled with beggars, lepers, and starving people. The countless

# TOPICS FOR FURTHER STUDY

- *India Song* presents the experiences of women in colonial India. Research and write about the status of women in India today. What laws and customs exist with regard to marriage, education, work, and political participation of women in modern Indian culture? How have these practices changed in India since the 1930s? How have these changes improved the life of women in India, if at all?

- Among Duras's fellow contemporary French feminist playwrights are Helen Cixous, Monique Wittig, and Nathalie Sarraute. Research and write about one of these writers. What are some of the major works of this author? What elements of this author's work make her a feminist writer? What attitudes, opinions, or critiques does this author's work present, regarding the status of women in society and the representation of women on the theatrical stage? If possible, try to see a performance of one of the author's plays or read reviews of a past performance. Write a review that critiques how well the performance expressed feminist views.

- The characters in *India Song* frequently mention their fear of contracting leprosy. Research and write about leprosy as it persists today in modern society. What causes leprosy and what are its major symptoms? What cures are available for the disease? How prevalent is it, and in what parts of the world is it most prevalent? What efforts are being made to prevent and treat this disease? If possible, interview a doctor, nurse, or medical professional to explain the history and nature of this disease.

- If it is available to you, watch the 1975 motion picture adaptation of *India Song*, directed by Duras. In what ways does the visual medium of cinema enhance your understanding and appreciation of the story and characters? What changes were made to adapt the play to the screen? What parts of the story do you feel suffered or where enhanced in the film version?

---

numbers who starve to death each day are burned in large fires along the Ganges River, and the glow from these fires may be seen from the embassy.

The central events of the play, however, take place in "white India," the luxurious settings of the French embassy in Calcutta, the Prince of Wales Hotel on the island, and the French residence on the island. While the white people dance and gossip, servants may be seen on stage, silently catering to their pleasures, pouring champagne and cleaning the rooms. The beggar woman, who hides in the bushes and occasionally pokes her head into the embassy garden, serves as a reminder of the suffering masses who live just outside the confines of these privileged "white" spaces and whom the white colonialists generally choose to ignore. One of the guests at the reception comments that the white people in India talk only about themselves, ignoring the Indian population amongst whom they live. Anne-Marie, on the other hand, is at least somewhat sympathetic to the plight of the Indians, as she sets out jars of clean drinking water for them and donates all of the leftovers from her parties to the starving people. *India Song* thus offers a critique of the colonial system which creates such extreme contrasts of wealth and poverty.

## Despair and Suicide

Anne-Marie serves as a symbol for the despair that surrounds her. She has attempted to commit suicide in the past, without success. On the night after the party, she succeeds in killing herself by walking into the ocean and drowning. The play does not provide any clear-cut explanation of why Anne-Marie commits suicide. However, it seems that she is particularly sensitive to the suffering and despair of everyone around her, both the Indians and the Europeans. By the end, she seems to be overwhelmed with despair about the suffering of the Indians as well as the suffering of the men who love her.

The vice-consul expresses his sense of despair more blatantly than Anne-Marie. He is known to have suffered a mental breakdown and shot his gun off his balcony in Lahore and then tried to shoot himself. His suffering is so great that he even expresses a wish that he might contract leprosy and die. The vice-consul's mental and emotional instability seem to be an expression of the despair he witnesses all around him in India. While most of the Europeans are capable of ignoring this death and suffering, the vice-consul, like Anne-Marie, is particularly sensitive to it, and is driven to despair and attempted suicide as a result.

### The Status of Women

Duras uses the central character of Anne-Marie Stretter in *India Song* as a symbol for exploring the status of women in society. Anne-Marie serves as an object of fantasy for the other characters in the play and for the four voices who narrate her story. Duras specifically constructed *India Song* such that Anne-Marie is never heard to utter a single word throughout the play. She appears as a passive figure, a physical body and an object of obsession for others that has no opportunity to speak for herself. Duras seems to be suggesting that women's status in society is similar to that of Anne-Marie, in that women's voices are often stifled by the dominant forces of a society, and women are often subjected to the fantasies projected on them by others, particularly men. Anne-Marie's decision to commit suicide is the only way she succeeds in taking action or escaping her position in life. Anne-Marie thus sees self-destruction as her only option for protesting her status within her society. Duras suggests that women's status in society renders them almost totally powerless to take positive action toward self-empowerment or to alter the conditions of their lives.

## STYLE

### Experimental Theater

Experimental theater refers to dramatic works, usually written for the stage, that question and expand the definition of the play as a literary form. *India Song* is a work of experimental theatre in which Duras experiments with generally accepted categories of genre, traditional expectations of action and dialogue, and an unusual use of disembodied voices to narrate her play.

*India Song* was originally published in book form in 1973. Though it bore the English-language title *India Song*, it was written by Duras in French. In the original French text, *India Song* is subtitled ''theatre/film/texte,'' which indicates that the story may be interpreted as simultaneously a stage play, screenplay, and work of prose fiction. Duras thus questions and expands upon generally accepted definitions of, and distinctions between, plays, screenplays, and novels.

One of the most striking experimental elements of *India Song* is the fact that none of the characters who appear on stage are ever seen actually speaking their lines before the audience. Much of the dialogue that is heard during the play is made up of bits and pieces of fragmentary conversation of the guests at the reception, who gossip among themselves about Anne-Marie, her husband, and the various men who are in love with her. When they do appear on stage, the characters mime their actions without ever speaking. Rather, all dialogue and voices that are heard throughout the play come from offstage. In one live performance of *India Song*, for example, all of the dialogue was prerecorded, and then broadcast over a loudspeaker, while the live actors performed their silent roles.

Yet another experimental element of *India Song* is Duras's use of four separate disembodied voices to narrate the story of Anne-Marie Stretter. While these voices are never identified specifically, Duras describes some qualities of the voices and the different manner in which each voice tells the story. These voices recall the story in bits and fragments, as they slowly come to remember various details and facts about it. While stage plays often have a character who serves as narrator to the central events of the play, it is unusual to have narrators who are never actually seen onstage, embodied by an actor.

## HISTORICAL CONTEXT

### British Colonial Rule in India

From 1858 to 1948, India was a colony under the rule of the British crown. When it first came

# COMPARE & CONTRAST

- **1930s:** India is a colonial holding of the British Empire. Indian nationalist movements for independence have been gaining momentum since the nineteenth century.

  **1970s:** The former British colony of India now comprises the sovereign nations of India, Pakistan, and Bangladesh, which are set up as parliamentary democracies after the British model.

  **Today:** India, Pakistan, and Bangladesh remain independent nations.

- **1930s:** Tensions between the Indian National Assembly, a primarily Hindu organization, and the All-Indian Muslim League, an Islamic organization, divide the movement for Indian national liberation. Kashmir is a region within British-controlled India.

  **1970s:** Independent India and Pakistan engage in an ongoing dispute over the border region of Kashmir. After the India-Pakistan war of 1971, Pakistan and India sign a peace accord resolving

to settle the dispute peacefully. However, beginning in 1979, Kashmir again becomes a major source of tension between the two nations.

**Today:** Escalating tensions between India and Pakistan over the disputed territory of Kashmir raise international fears of nuclear war between the two nations, both of which now possess nuclear weapons.

- **1930s:** The French government is in the era of the Third Republic, under the Constitution of 1876. France is a parliamentary democracy with voting rights extended to all adult males. Women in France do not have the right to vote.

  **1970s:** The French government is in the era of the Fifth Republic, a parliamentary democracy under the Constitution of 1956. Voting rights are extended to all adult men and women.

  **Today:** The French government remains in the era of the Fifth Republic, a constitutional democracy with universal suffrage.

---

under the domain of the United Kingdom, Queen Victoria was in power. The highest government position in India was the viceroy, a post appointed by the British government and always held by white British politicians. Originally, the British capital of India was located in Calcutta. In 1912, the capital was relocated to Delhi.

From the beginning of colonization, many Indian citizens protested against British domination. During the twentieth century, two major political organizations devoted to the struggle for Indian national independence emerged: the Indian National Congress, primarily made up of Indians of Hindu faith, and the All-India Muslim League, primarily made up of Indians of Muslim faith. Though these organizations sometimes formed a coalition, they were often divided because of ongoing tensions between the Hindu and Muslim populations of India. Two of the major Hindu leaders of the Indian

nationalist movement were Mahatma Gandhi and Motilal Nehru. Mohammed Ali Jinnah was a major leader of the Muslim League.

### National Independence

In the wake of World War II, Great Britain was forced to cede its colonial rule over India. In the Indian Independence Act, passed by the British parliament in 1947, India was partitioned into two sovereign nations. The largest was India, in which the majority of the population was Hindu; and the smaller was Pakistan, in which the majority was Muslim.

The newly formed government of India was established on the British model of parliamentary democracy. The national languages of independent India were designated as Hindi and English, while 14 additional regional languages were also recognized. The first Prime Minister of India was Nehru, who presided from 1947 to 1964. Mahatma Gandhi, though he never served in political office, continued to be a revered and influential advocate of nonviolence, until he was assassinated in 1948.

The new nation of Pakistan included two distinct regions: East Pakistan and West Pakistan. Independent Pakistan established a parliamentary democracy based on the British system, and Jinnah served as the nation's first governor-general. Military coups, the suspension of government, and the imposition of martial law have characterized the history of Pakistan since gaining independence. The Pakistani legal system has increasingly been determined by the tenets of Islamic law.

In 1947, with the establishment of independent India and Pakistan, the region of Bengal was divided. Part went to Pakistan and became East Pakistan, while the part that went to India became the province of West Bengal. In 1971, after a civil war in which India intervened, East Pakistan was granted national independence as the new nation of Bangladesh (''Bengal land''). The majority of the Bangladesh population was Muslim, and the national language was designated as Bengali. Bangladesh was established as a parliamentary democracy, after the British model. But many military coups and institutions of martial law since independence have hampered the democratic process. In 1988, a national referendum determined that Islam would be the official state religion of Bangladesh.

When the independent nations of Pakistan and India were created in 1947, the northern region of Kashmir, like the Bengal region, was divided between the two countries. The southern and southeastern portion was incorporated into India, becoming the state of Jammu and Kashmir. The northern and western portions of Kashmir became a part of Pakistan. Ever since this time, Kashmir has been a subject of hostile border disputes between India and Pakistan. In the late 1990s and early 2000s, international concern over the escalation of tensions between the two nations increased due to the fact that both India and Pakistan possess nuclear weapons.

## CRITICAL OVERVIEW

*India Song* is hailed as an experimental feminist text that simultaneously critiques colonial culture, women's status in society, and representations of the female body. Feminist critics make much of the fact that all of the voices in the play/film are disembodied and that the characters are seen as physical bodies devoid of direct dialogue. This experimental technique is regarded as a critique of traditional representations of women. As Gabrielle H. Cody, in *Impossible Performances* remarks:

> Duras's drama consistently features female protagonists who exist in a relationship of struggle with the representational frame and who ''speak back'' to the viewing authorities of a masculine symbolic.

Critics are also impressed with Duras's complex use of ''offstage'' sounds in *India Song*. Lib Taylor in ''Sound Tracks'' observes that

> The verbal text is woven into a complex, orchestrated soundscape of instrumental music, songs, non-verbal cries and utterances, screams of pain and wretchedness, sounds of street shouting, and screeches of exotic birds and animals. These elements together become a score functioning alongside the visual text.

*India Song* is further praised as a critique of British colonial rule in India and of the subjugation of the Indian people by western imperial powers. Taylor notes that Duras intentionally focuses the action of her play on the luxurious settings of colonial white culture, while portraying the world of the Indian people through offstage sounds. Thus, Taylor argues, this dissonance between sound and image ''rents the curtain of the visual spectacle of imperial power and disrupts the refined mask of western civilization.''

Marie-Paule Ha, in ''Duras on the Margins,'' similarly argues that *India Song* puts forth a critique of colonial society by demonstrating the ways in which the white colonizers try to insulate themselves within the confines of their privileged enclave, while striving to keep the Indian population on the margins of ''white India.'' However, Ha maintains, Duras demonstrates that the disease and suffering of the Indians symbolically infects the Europeans as well. Thus, she asserts:

> One of the external signs of the fissuring of the seemingly watertight compartmentalized colonial society is the deep sense of malaise and maladjustment which is wearing out its white inhabitants. In spite of the vast paraphernalia of protective artifices . . . the Europeans find their presence in the colony quite intolerable.

Thirty years after its initial publication, *India Song* continues to be the subject of extensive analysis by critics concerned with issues of postcolonial

*Didier Flamand and Delphine Seyrig in a film version of* India Song

literature and the representation of women on the dramatic stage. As Cody notes, ''Duras is one of the most important figures in the landscape of twentieth century theatre.''

# CRITICISM

## Liz Brent

*Brent has a Ph.D. in American Culture from the University of Michigan. She works as a freelance writer and editor. In the following essay, Brent discusses the relationships between the disembodied narrative voices in Duras's play.*

Voice 1 and voice 2 serve as the principal narrators in act 1 of *India Song* and return again briefly in acts 3 and 5. Although neither is identified directly and neither appears bodily on stage, their verbal interactions subtly convey the complex and emotionally charged relationship between them. Voices 1 and 2 are both described as young and female. Both voices, though sweet, are tinged with madness,

delirium, and desire. As Duras explains in her notes that precede the play, these voices ''are linked together by a love story'':

> Sometimes they speak of this love, their own. Most of the time they speak of another love, another story. But this other story leads us back to theirs. And vice versa.

Voice 1 and voice 2 each express somewhat different feelings about the story they are telling. Voice 1 is utterly absorbed in the love story of Anne-Marie Stretter while voice 2 is passionately concerned with love for voice 1. Voice 2 expresses fear that voice 1 is so wrapped up in Anne-Marie's story that she is in danger of losing herself in it. Voice 2 is thus afraid of losing the love of voice 1.

In recalling the story of Anne-Marie Stretter, voice 2 remembers the facts more clearly than voice 1. Voice 1 often asks about the details, and when voice 2 fills her in on this information, voice 1's memory is sparked. Thus, voice 1 seems to be responding to Anne-Marie's story more emotionally, while voice 2 expresses a greater degree of emotional distance from the story she tells. On the other hand, voice 2 is very emotionally caught up in her relationship with voice 1, while voice 1 seems emotionally removed from voice 2 and unconcerned with their relationship.

As the play opens, voices 1 and 2 begin to tell the story of Anne-Marie's love affair with Michael Richardson and her act of suicide by walking into the Indian Ocean. When Anne-Marie and Michael appear on stage, voice 1 becomes fascinated with the sight of Anne-Marie. Voice 2 is so concerned with the effect of Anne-Marie's presence on voice 1 that she herself pays no attention to Anne-Marie's figure on the stage. Voice 2 comments, ''How pale you are . . . what are you frightened of?'' But voice 1 does not respond, as if so absorbed by the sight of Anne-Marie that she does not hear the words of her own lover.

As voice 1 and voice 2 watch Anne-Marie dance with Michael, voice 2 asks voice 1, ''Why are you crying?'' voice 1 does not answer. Voice 1 is so emotionally involved with Anne-Marie's love story that the sight of her dancing with Michael brings her to tears; yet, voice 1 is so emotionally removed from her own relationship with voice 2 that she does not even respond to the impassioned words of her lover. Voice 2, meanwhile, is extremely concerned with voice 1's emotional response to the unfolding of Anne-Marie's story.

# WHAT DO I READ NEXT?

- Duras's screenplay *Hiroshima, Mon Amour* (1959) was based on the novel by Alain Resnais and made into a film directed by Resnais. The story is set in Tokyo during World War II and concerns the love affair between a French actress and a Japanese architect.

- *India Song* is loosely based on Duras's novel *Le Vice-consul* (*The vice-consul*), published in 1966. The novel is focused on the stories of two central characters: a French vice-consul stationed in Calcutta and a teenaged Asian girl who is abandoned by her mother after she becomes pregnant.

- Duras's most popular novel, *L'Amant* (*The Lover*), published in 1984, is the autobiographical story of a relationship between an impoverished fifteen-year-old French girl and her wealthy middle-aged Chinese lover.

- *Collected Plays* (1980), by Nathalie Sarraute (a Russian-born, French feminist playwright con-temporary of Duras), includes *It Is There, It's Beautiful, Issum, The Lie,* and *Silence.* Sarraute was also a popular novelist who introduced new ways of writing about social behavior in her work.

- A play by Monique Wittig (another French feminist playwright contemporary of Duras), entitled *Le Voyage sans fin* (*The Constant Voyage*), published in 1985, is a feminist satire based on the Don Quixote stories of Miguel de Cervantes.

- *Selected Plays by Hélène Cixous* (2004), edited by Eric Prenowitz, is a collection of dramatic writings by another French feminist playwright contemporary of Duras. This volume includes the plays *Portrait of Dora, Black Sail White Sail, The Perjured City,* and *Drums on the Dam,* as well as an interview with Cixous.

- *Marguerite Duras: A Life* (2000), by Laure Adler, is a critical biography of Duras.

---

As the story continues, voice 2 repeatedly expresses her love for voice 1, but voice 1 is unresponsive. Voice 2 declares the depths of her love for voice 1, telling her, "I love you so much I can't see any more, can't hear . . . can't live." But voice 1 does not respond to this declaration. When Anne-Marie appears on the stage dressed in black, voice 2 is moved to express her desire for voice 1 and bursts out, "How lovely you look dressed in white," but voice 1 does not respond to this passionate outburst. Later, voice 2 tells voice 1, "I love you with a desire that is absolute," but voice 1 again does not answer.

In act 3, voices 3 and 4 pick up the threads of the story, while voices 1 and 2 are again heard to continue their discussion of the story. However, voices 1 and 2 never interact in any way with voices 3 and 4. Each pair is having completely separate conversations about the same subject.

Voices 1 and 2 describe the voice-consul aimlessly wandering the streets of Calcutta, suffering over his rejection by Anne-Marie. Voice 2 draws a parallel between the situation of the voice-consul, who has lost Anne-Marie's love, and the situation of voice 2 feeling that she has lost the love of voice 1. "How far away you are . . . from me," voice 2 laments. Later, voice 2 mournfully comments to voice 1, "How far away you are. Quite absent."

As voice 1 is increasingly caught up in Anne-Marie's story and ignores voice 2's attempts to bring the conversation around to their own love, voice 2 becomes increasingly frightened that she is losing voice 1. Toward the end of act 3, voice 2 says to voice 1, "The sound of your heart frightens me. . . . Your heart, so young, a child's." When voice 1 does not answer, voice 2 calls out, "Where are you?" but again receives no response.

The relationship between voice 1 and voice 2 is a tragic love story, in which voice 2 loses voice 1 to the madness of Anne-Marie's story. In act 5, shortly before Anne-Marie's suicide, their story is heard for the last time. Voice 2, terrified, calls out to voice 1, ''Where are you? . . . You're so far away . . . I'm frightened.'' But voice 1 is never heard again.

Voice 3 and voice 4, first heard in act 3, are both male. In contrast to the emotionally intense love relationship between voices 1 and 2, voices 3 and 4 have no emotional connection to one another, except that they share a fascination with Anne-Marie's story. While voice 3 remembers almost nothing of Anne-Marie's tragic love story, voice 4 remembers almost everything in detail.

Voices 3 and 4 express themes of memory and suffering in relation to the story of Anne-Marie Stretter. Voice 3 used to know the story very well but has chosen to forget it, while voice 4 has chosen to remember it. Voice 3 finds Anne-Marie's story to be one of such great suffering that it is intolerable to remember, and thus has rejected the fascination the story holds. Voice 4, on the other hand, tolerates the fascination of the story, and manages to tolerate the suffering it evokes. Thus, while voice 3 is keenly sensitive to this suffering, voice 4 remains emotionally distant from it in order to avoid the experience of suffering. Through the characters of voices 3 and 4, Duras explores the relationship between how we remember the past and how we tolerate the suffering of others.

**Source:** Liz Brent, Critical Essay on *India Song,* in *Drama for Students,* Thomson Gale, 2005.

### Lib Taylor

*In the following essay, Taylor examines the combination of musical phrases, voices, and noises in* India Song *and how this is rendered in and informs the written, acted, and filmed versions of Duras's work.*

In both the play and the film of Marguerite Duras's *India Song* no verbal exchange is seen to take place on stage or in camera shot and all the dialogue emanates from disembodied voices which reverberate across the filmic or theatrical imagery. The verbal text is woven into a complex, orchestrated soundscape of instrumental music, songs, non-verbal cries and utterances, screams of pain and wretchedness, sound of street shouting, and screeches of exotic birds and animals. These elements together become a score functioning alongside the visual text. In this essay, I want to focus on the composition and the 'enactment' of the sound script of *India Song* and consider the way in which it functions as a stratum of eloquent signifying systems in the per-

formance of this rich and poetic text. My concern will be with the 'composite' text of novel/play/film and the way in which sound is evoked across the spectrum of reader, spectator and auditor, though my intention is not to suggest that the written text, the film and the play performance are interchangeable. I shall refer to the published text, Duras's own 1974 film version, and Theatr Clwyd's performance directed by Annie Castledine and Anabel Arden in 1993.

Like several of Duras's plays, for example *La Musica* and *Moderato Cantabile,* the title *India Song* refers directly to music, and the written text begins with directions for music to take the spectators into the world of the play.

> Au piano, ralenti, un'air d'entre les deux guerres, nomme India Song.
>
> Il est joue tout entier et occupe ainsi le temps—toujours long—qu'il faut au spectateur, au lecteur, pour sortir de l'endroit commun ou il se trouve quand commence le spectacle, la lecture.
>
> Encore India Song.
>
> Encore.
>
> Voila, India Song se termine.
>
> Reprend. De plus «loin» que la premiere fois, comme s'il etait joue loin du lieu present.

As the play/film proceeds, music becomes one of the most significant and dynamic areas of the sound text, of the entire text. The nostalgic 'India Song' itself, composed for the film by Carlos d'Alessio, resonates throughout the performance but it is intercut by sections of 1930s dance music and 'Heure Exquise', as well as by moments from Beethoven's *Variations on a Waltz* by Diabelli. These motifs come from different traditions, but together they create a medley of western instrumental music.

This miscellany is counterpointed with singing from a different cultural tradition: the poignant song of the Savannakhet Beggar Woman which can just be heard echoing intermittently across the field of sound and which also accompanies the opening titles to the film. Set within this musical score are vocal and spoken utterances; a chorus of tentative voices struggle to present scraps of narrative which is interrupted and permeated by screams of anguish from the Vice-Consul of Lahore which, in turn, merge with the half-audible human cries of the Calcutta streets. The force of words is not in their promise of access to coherent meaning; rather the compulsion of the verbal text is in its auditory

*A Hindu man serving tea to a European colonial woman*

dimension. The human voice takes on a symphonic quality as the dialogue is orchestrated into the musical composition and apprehended as melodic sound at least as much as verbal message. Marguerite Duras states at the outset: 'Les noms des villes, des fleurs, des Etats, des mers de l'Inde ont, avant tout, ici, un sens musical.' The sounds of barking dogs, drumming rain and the whir of the ceiling fan are blended into the score.

'There is, then', as Carol Murphy suggests, 'a music of the text as well as a music in the text.' The 'song' of the title encompasses more than just the refrain of the theme tune: it composes the geographical location, it constitutes historical time, it juxtaposes cultures; it is the fragments of memory, the indulgence of nostalgia, the assertion of desire. As Duras herself said, it is 'the music of India Song, the inner music of the text which creates the meaning.'

It is not appropriate here to examine fully the intertextuality of *India Song;* other critics of Duras's work, such as Susan Cohen and Leslie Hill have focused in depth upon this issue; It is, though, worth re-stating that narratives from other Duras fictions, for example, *Le Ravissement de Lol V. Stein, Le Vice-Consul* and *La Femme du Gange,* permeate *India Song,* distorting and reforming events, histories and relationships which have appeared in them.

Just as the text is destabilized by its encounter with other fictions so Anne-Marie Stretter is the product of the displaced desires, perceptions and autobiographies of the Voices who project onto the history of the central *India Song* character, weaving their own memories in an attempt to capture her fragmented identity. My interest is in the way in which this process of reformation and reinscription is present in the aural text, and in how the dynamic interplay of fictions, narration and visual imagery is extended into the 'play' of voice, music and sound. My concern is to explore how Duras positions her spectators/listeners to inscribe the aural elements of the text with meanings, and also how the soundscape problematizes both the spectators' reading position and the meanings that might be made of the text.

It is number 14 of the *Diabelli Variations* that comprises part of the *India Song* sound track and it seems no coincidence that Roland Barthes, in his essay 'Musica Practica', refers to the *Diabelli Variations* in proposing that:

> The operations by which we can grasp . . . Beethoven . . . can no longer be either performance or hearing; but reading. This is not to say that one has to sit with a Beethoven score and get from it an inner recital . . .; it would mean that with respect to this music one must put oneself in the position of, better, in the activity of an operator, who knows how to displace, assemble,

> **THE OVERWHELMING SOUND OF THE AURAL SCORE IS NOT THE VOICES BUT THE MELANCHOLIC REFRAIN WHICH CONSTANTLY DRIFTS IN AND OUT OF THE PERFORMANCE (BOTH ON SCREEN AND STAGE)."**

combine, fit together; in a word (if it is not too worn out) to structure . . . . Just as the reading of the modern text . . . consists not in receiving, in knowing or in feeling that text, but in writing it anew, in crossing its writing with a fresh inscription, so too reading Beethoven is to operate his music, to draw it . . . into an unknown praxis.

Beethoven wrote these *Variations* in response to a request by Anton Diabelli. In 1819, Diabelli circulated a waltz, which he had written, to fifty fellow composers, inviting each of them to contribute a variation to a collective project. Having at first dismissed the proposal as a 'cobbler's patch', Beethoven responded very actively to the idea and produced not one variation but thirty-three over the next four years. William Kinderman suggests that in his *Variations,* Beethoven treats the waltz,

> as a reservoir of unrealized possibilities, out of which the variations generate an almost encyclopaedic range of contexts. The psychological complexity of the *'Diabelli' Variations* arises above all from this tension between the commonplace theme as point of departure and the almost unlimited horizon of the *Variations*.

Not only is the work rich in allusion to the original waltz, it also refers to the work of other composers, including Mozart and Bach. Kinderman suggests that one of the strongest allusions is to Don Giovanni, where he detects thematic as well as musical references:

> Beethoven's relationship to his theme, like Leporello's relationship to his master, is critical but faithful, inasmuch as he thoroughly exploits its motivic components. And like Leporello, the variations after this point gain the capacity for disguise.

Kinderman's linkage of the notions of critical faithfulness and disguise with Beethoven's relationship to Diabelli's waltz is suggestive of the relationship between the *Diabelli Variations* and the dramatic structure of *India Song*. The Voices in their insistent and repeated search for the seductive 'truth' of Anne-Marie Stretter are in effect a series of variations produced by, but never returning to, Anne-Marie Stretter herself. While the play could be seen as an investigation seeking the 'truth' of Anne-Marie Stretter, it cannot function in this way. Rather than revealing her, the Voices produce ever more layers of disguising veils. In including the *Diabelli Variations* within the sound score of *India Song*, Duras signals that her interest in the process of textual reinscription extends beyond the written text (and its realization in the spoken and visual form) to the aural text (of which, of course, the vocal dialogue is part). The interwoven sounds, musical, vocal and ambient, produce an active reader/spectator, who, in Barthes's sense, 'operates' the text, continually 'rewriting it anew', just as Beethoven 'recomposed' Diabelli's waltz. The Diabelli composition has ceased to exist and is impressed on our memories, recalled and constructed through its encounter with Beethoven, and the escalating chain of variations he produces. Just as the variations displace the absent waltz, so the elusive Anne-Marie Stretter is displaced by the circulating stories which attempt to reconstruct her.

The overwhelming sound of the aural score is not the Voices but the melancholic refrain which constantly drifts in and out of the performance (both on screen and stage). At one level, this is 'India Song' and its mournful melody haunts the spectator in much the same way as it haunts the Voices striving to recall Anne-Marie Stretter. Duras specifies that this tune is a blues, a 'bittersweet' form of music in which the notes known as the 'blue notes' (the 3rd and the 7th of the key—the notes which activate the shift from major to minor keys) are prominent. In western music, the minor key is traditionally associated with melancholy and the blues exploits the possibilities this affords. While the nostalgic rhythm of the blues recalls the interwar high society, the society of colonial France, it also refers to the black slave tradition of plantation America from where, it originated. In both the theatre and film performance, the easy charm of the melody is persuasive and its compulsion threatens to drown the sounds of the dispossessed voices of India, the lepers, the beggars, the street cries, just as the European and White American harmonic versions of the blues form have engulfed its more dissonant black counterpart. In India Song the blues connote not only nostalgia for a lost past which echoes across the fading imperialism of western culture but the pain and displacement of the colonized. The cross-cultural references are not precise or insistent but the audience is nudged towards making connections. The presence of the Savannakhet Beggar Woman whose double marginalization, both by French imperialism and by the indigenous Indian population, recalls the plight of the black slave originators of the blues, exiled from their homeland and deprived of any human rights. Her atonal and haunting singing is counterposed with the easy harmony of the blues refrain, newly recomposing it as the voicing of loss and anguish, and reclaiming it as an expression of dispossession.

It is dance which transposes music into corporeal form. The abstract lyricism of music is inscribed on the body as its rhythms, tempo, inflections and mood release the body from the circumscription of social inhibition. Dance opens up spaces for bodies to 'speak' directly, unfettered by the constraints of verbal language and unrestrained by demands for lucidity and rationality. At the same time, dance disciplines and trains the body. It is formalized and constrained, restricted by the conventions of ritualized steps and defined by the music which provokes it. In *India Song* dance is a force both for liberation and containment. It expresses the sensuality of the body while acting as a formal mechanism for sanctioned social exchange. In section two of the text, where dance is the principal mode of movement, this duality is apparent in the exchanges between Anne-Marie Stretter and the various men with whom she dances at the ambassadorial reception. She is passed from one partner to the next, objectified by colonial institutions which require that, as the Ambassador's wife, she dance with every man present. While desire compels the enactment of sensuality, protocol demands formality and restraint and only small nuances of the body, the head, the eyes, the shoulders signal the difference between the pleasure of attraction and the pain of repulsion. In the film, the image of a single dancing couple dominates the screen as Anne-Marie Stretter is fetishized by a camera that lingers on her seductive body. In the corresponding moment in the theatrical performance, performers dance across comers of the stage space, slipping in and out of the reception, to watch and consume the enthralling Anne-Marie Stretter.

Carol Murphy maintains that dance is not limited to section two of *India Song* but that social interaction and exchange throughout the whole play/film might be seen as a series of dances, accompanied by the musical score.

> The music accompanies the dance of desire, which is a major thematic concern of the text. In all five of its Chapters, couples whirl from one to another in an image which reflects textual dynamics and the theme of sustained desire.

This suggests that not only is 'India Song' the sound of India but it is the song of the body sung through the 'dances' of Anne-Marie Stretter and those who are entranced by her. Throughout the play/film different configurations of men are choreographed around Anne-Marie Stretter in formalized patterns of images and movements, drawing attention to her and positioning her centrally, almost as a prima donna. The rhythm and measured pacing of the performance both on film and stage compel an audience response to music and abstract dance, where the predominant mode of access for the audience is via emotional engagement and not through suspense or narrative.

What might traditionally be recognized as 'music' is only one strain (or set of strands) in the score. The singing and the piano are orchestrated into the melange of sound which signals realities beyond the frame of the visual text and worlds beyond the boundaries of French colonialism:

> Montee du bruit derriere la musique: le bruit de Calcutta: rumeur forte, majeure. Autour: rumeurs diverses: cris reguliers des marchands. Chiens. Appels lointains.

This cacophony of exotic sounds is also a strain of 'India Song', as are the screech of the birds and the sound of rain which cannot be seen, only heard, but which evoke the sub-continent more sharply than any visual aspect of mise en scene. The insertion of dissonant and unmelodious sound into the aural text disrupts the euphony and concord created by the evocative sweetness of the blues, the solace of dance music and the structural reassurance of Beethoven. What Barthes calls the 'authority of the fundamental code of the West, tonality' is disrupted by the discord of atonality in the Beggar Woman's song and the jarring diaphony which asserts difference and threatens the boundaries of the colonial world.

It is the aural text which composes notions of 'otherness'. The only physical, bodily representation of India in the play is in the form of the servants (men in the film and women in the play) who move unobtrusively around the space. Like all the characters on stage, they are silent but neither are they represented by the spoken voice-over text. Their contained graciousness and subservience is expressed in body posture and eye level; their disturbing presence and their lack of representation in language is eloquent of their colonized position. Mise en scene both in the film and the theatre performance deliberately marginalize India within the visual field, referring only to its exotic riches exploited by European colonialism. The entirely interior setting of the play connotes India architecturally through (in Theatr Clwyd's production) a lavish screen at one side of the stage space, through the fabrics covering the sparse furniture and through the ceiling fan which whirrs around intermittently throughout the performance. Iconic reference to India is even more elusive in the film where the Embassy and the Prince of Wales Hotel reflected European domination. By contrast, the insistent voice of India is expressed in the untimely and unpredictable eruptions of non-speech which are discharged in the forms of shouts, laughter, screams, cries and even snippets of unknown languages which are present in the aural text but which are not represented within the frame of the film or stage image. Their abrupt dissonance rents the curtain of the visual spectacle of imperial power and disrupts the refined mask of western civilization.

It is the sounds produced by the Vice-Consul which are the most harrowing and immediately disruptive of harmony and concord, and he is the only figure who is seen and heard to make a sound on stage.

Le Vice-consul apparait. Il est secoue, de sanglots.

On voit ces sanglots et on les entend.

These cries are heard throughout much of the second half of the play/film, although mostly but not entirely while he is off-stage and off-camera. As a figure of the establishment who has transgressed the boundaries of diplomacy, the Vice-Consul sits between the worlds of the colonized and the colonizer. He can no longer be a representative of France and is ostracized from high society, from the 'inside', nor can he claim an affinity to the indigenous population of India, what might be termed low society, the 'outside'; he is on the margins. His only bond perhaps is with the displaced Savannakhet Beggar Woman, but even she has found a place among the lepers. It is his utter dislocation and displacement which makes his cries so very distressing. His disturbing presence disrupts the visual coherence of the stage and his anguished screams

counterpoint the desire expressed by the speaking voices. His lament disrupts the harmonious sound of the music but rather than emanating, like the street cries, entirely from 'outside', from disregarded territory beyond the flame of the civilized world, his cries are visible (in the play) and insistent. They cannot be ignored. His allegiance both to the 'inside' and 'outside' worlds breaks the boundary between the enclosed world of imperial India and the dispossessed and silenced India. His cry is part of the 'song' which expresses psychic anguish beyond the realm of verbal utterance. Juxtaposing with the mellifluous sounds of the ambassador's reception his urgent and uncomfortable howls are brutal, wild and untamed, emitted from beyond the discipline of the body and language.

The verbal dimension to the score takes the form of voice-over, as off-stage (or off-screen) voices fade in and out of the sound composition. The narrative(s) are shared by a group of tentative and uncertain speakers whose language is inflected by the imprecise memories and distorted fictions they try to represent. Anne-Marie Stretter's barely discernible identity is mediated through this interplay of orchestrated voices which accompany the five parts of the play. The play performance follows the pattern of the printed text where Voices One and Two in the first section are of women whose 'memoire . . . de l'histoire d'amour est illogique, anarchique.' There is a constant slippage between their recollection of Anne-Marie Stretter's love story and their own desires. The Voices of the fourth and fifth section are male and fetishize Anne-Marie Stretter in their retelling of events; Voice Three questions Voice Four, who has the most coherent memories of the story. The four Voices interact in section three, each consumed by a voyeuristic desire for the absent figure of Anne-Marie Stretter. In the film version of *India Song* Duras herself takes on the role of Voice Four, a role intended as masculine according to the written text. Although no single Voice is endowed with authority, it is Voice Four which is most secure in its recall of the story and Duras's distinctive voice reinforces its authorial command. Her slightly abrasive tone penetrates the sound text bringing her voice close to the audience, endorsing her commanding aural presence.

In the second section, the voices are of those gathered at the reception, commenting upon and recalling the action they only glimpse. Duras says in the introduction to the second section:

Toutes les conversations—privilegiees ou non—qui feront ou non TAIRE la reception autour d'elles

devraient donner l'impression de n'etre bien entendues
QUE PAR LES SPECTATEURS ET NON PAR LES
INVITES DE LA RECEPTION . . .

Les voix devraient arriver au spectateur avec la meme
portee que sa voix «de lecture interieure».

Although the spectator is positioned as an eaves-
dropper at the reception working to make links from
fragments, hearsay, gossip and speculation, and her/
his view of events is deliberately very partial, s/he is
given privileged aural information, more 'complete' than any of the guests. The Voices are recalling memories, constructing narratives from distorted and half-heard fictions, prompted by desire.
The spectator, too, is required to piece together what
s/he has seen and heard in the performance, to
construct a narrative from the play's fragments, but
s/he is situated as an omnipresent guest with access
to all the snippets of conversation even if some are
more audible than others.

The sonorous dimensions of the voices are
enhanced because they are immersed in a musical
soundscape. Melodic phrasing and timbre, levels of
volume and pitch, rhythmic shape, even qualities of
vibrato have as much impact on the listener as any
meaning conveyed by the words themselves. Half
finished sentences which peter out, and disconnected phrases and questions left hanging in the air,
'tune in' with the piano music, which fades into the
distance, and with the discordant, syncopated sounds
which erupt into the score. The voices are not
separated from a backing track but are embedded
within the sound score. One film version of *India
Song* uses English and French voice-overs for section two at the reception, so that for the monolingual
listener the familiarity of one language is disrupted
by the unfamiliarity of the other; the barely discernible musicality of the native language is newly
perceived by its counterpoint with the other. Stephen Connor states that,

One can hear many sounds simultaneously . . . where
it is impossible to see different objects at the same
time without disposing them in a unified field of
vision. Auditory experience is by its nature plural.
Where auditory experience is dominant then we can
say singular perspectival space gives way to plural
permeated space.

In *India Song* it is the plural auditory text that
permeates the stage space, disrupting the unified
field of the visual text. The overlapping and inter-
secting of the Beggar Woman's singing, the Vice-
Consul's cries and piano refrain creates a disjunc-
tive polyphony or a polysemic text which is worked
upon or 'operated' by the audience in Barthes's

terms: 'To compose, at least by propensity, is to
give to do, not to give to hear but to give to write.'
Since the audience are partly positioned as spectators or onlookers at the ambassadorial reception, identified with the spectating characters who
devour Anne-Marie Stretter, the activity of the
spectating audience is significant. I would suggest
that the activity of the listening audience is also
critical since they are eavesdroppers to some degree
aligned with characters, overhearing snippets of
conversation. The audience becomes both an active
or 'writerly' presence but is also implicated in the
voyeurism, exoticism and colonialism problematized
by the text.

In contemporary theatre study the significance
of mise en scene (normally defined as the visual
dimensions of performance) and its capacity to
undermine verbal domination has been a focus of
critical attention. But in the analysis of performance
visual signification has been privileged over auditory signification, except for the spoken word. Perhaps the critical potential of the sound dimension of
theatre performance has not received the consideration it warrants. Sound can have an insistence and a
bidding that is not possible with the visual text.
Stephen Connor suggests that,

The ability to close the eyes represents the power one
has over things that are seen—the power to exclude.
Hearing, however, is always receptive whether to
sound or to silence—you can look away but you
cannot listen away. You cannot turn the ear aside the
way you can look aside. Sound and silence corse upon
one from beyond.

The sound track of India Song is compelling
and tenacious. Its omnipresence is relentless. It
must be heard. Characters and spectators alike can
look away, shut their eyes to the realities beyond the
boundary of the ambassadorial residence and the
performance frame, but they cannot close their ears
to the painful cries of India. It might be argued that
since sound functions by having a physical effect on
the body, through the impact of sound waves, its
potential for registering urgency and potency is
increased (a fact exploited by action movies). Nor is
the impact of sound vibration restricted to the mem-
brane of the ear since the physical effect can be felt
throughout the entire body. Stephen Connor observes:

You can't see something from which you are not
separated. The closer something gets to you the less
you can see it whereas you cannot hear anything
unless you are in contact—the vibrations of hearing.
You hear it inside you.

The visual texts of *India Song* are doubly distanced for the spectator. As visual representation it must be distanced to be seen, but its problematic relation to the sound track and the absence of narrative action on stage or screen distances it again from conventional meaning. The sound track, on the other hand, functions quite differently. While the complexity and multiple levels of the sound track could be construed as distancing for the auditor, the audience is also close to, is literally touched by, the sound track which is emotional, moving and reverberates through the body. In the theatre the entire sound track, including the Voices, is recorded and passed through a sound system which heightens its significance and separates it from the visual performance. It seems to be in close proximity to the audience, especially the Voices; they whisper directly to us.

So far, I have made little distinction between the film and the play of *India Song* and yet in many ways they function quite differently. Duras's transposition from play text (if that is what the written text is) to film is not motivated by the desire for a definitive realization of the text. As Susan Cohen states, 'Duras's ''rewriting'' neither corrects nor destroys. It opens and pluralizes.'

The differences in the dramatic medium have implications for the way in which the sound dimension functions. In mainstream film, sound functions to anchor action and location; the sound supports the action; it is in concert with it. The sound track of a film intensifies levels of emotion and suspense, most frequently through the use of music. Alternative film challenges these conventions with disconcerting sound tracks and the use of voice-over in mainstream and alternative film is not uncommon. Apart from the popularity of the stage musical, where sound functions to augment the emotional dimension of the performance, in contemporary theatre the use of either a supporting or a disconcerting sound track is more unusual. Voice-over also is far less common in theatre, although it has been used as a critical device in, for example, *The Singular Life of Albert Nobbs*. While a spectator of the film of *India Song* is alerted to a critical dimension in the voice-over through the unusual split narration and the relationship of voice to music, the auditory track of noise and music might still be said to function as an anchor for location and cultural reference. In the theatre space the sound track is listened to differently. It is the very unfamiliarity of the deployment of voice-over and the insertion into the theatre performance of a filmic form of sound

track which makes the spectators listen anew, positioned as Barthes's 'operators', 'combining' visual images with vocal elements but also tracking sounds and 'assembling' them or composing them with fresh meanings.

The work called *India Song* is both internally multiple and fractured, and also exists in several media, each of which highlights different aspects of its cluster of signifying resources. There is no 'original' master text. However, in the transition from page to stage performance, it is the soundscape of *India Song* which becomes the dominant textual element in a very practical sense. Because of its complexity and symphonic dimension, the sound track of the Theatr Clwyd production had to be ready nearly three weeks before rehearsals were completed. Rather than create music around a play, adjusting it according to the demands of a shifting performance, Oliver Productions created a precise recorded score to which the movement and gesture were choreographed, much like dance or opera. The score acted as a kind of pre-text or frame into which the visual elements of the performance were inserted, giving aural text a rare authority to establish the dramatic elements of pace, intensity, rhythm and tonal colour. The soundscape of *India Song* with its strains of music, noises and voices evoking period, culture and location as well as nostalgia, anguish and loss as tracks of sound integrate and dissolve, has an eerie and ephemeral quality. It is an essential element of the work's thematic, textual and performance structure, and also a concretization of the principles at work in Duras's ecriture, marked as it is by re-writing, re-inscription, re-interpretation, re-configuration.

**Source:** Lib Taylor, "Sound Tracks: The Soundscapes of *India Song*," in *Theatre Research International*, Vol. 23, No. 3, Autumn 1998.

### Mary Noonan

*In the following essay, Noonan examines how Duras uses drama to create a sensory and psychological depiction of a woman's loss of self before narrative discourse begins.*

Jouer de la mimesis, c'est donc, pour une femme, tenter de retrouver le lieu de son exploitation par le discours, sans s'y laisser simplement reduire. C'est se resoumettre—en tant que du cote du «sensible», de la «matiere»—a des «idees», notamment d'elle, elaborees dans/par une logique masculine, mais pour fake apparaitre, par un effet de repetition ludique, ce qui devait rester occulte: le recouvrement d'une possible operation du feminin dans le langage. C'est aussi devoiler le fait que, si les femmes raiment si bien, c'est qu'elles ne se resorbent pas simplement dans cette fonction. Elles restent aussi ailleurs.

Luce Irigaray, Pouvoir du discours, subordination du feminin

Marguerite Duras developed a theatrical form that both staged a severing of the woman's body/presence from discourse/subjectivity, and gave expression to the distressed source of the woman's voice beyond discourse. This form of theatre appeals to the spectator who is willing to become involved in its uncovering of possible meanings of female identity through a meticulously orchestrated, slow, rhythm-based and essentially uncomfortable sifting and dredging of the processes of memory and desire. In exploring this terrain, Duras went some way toward realizing Irigaray's feminist project of 'playing with mimesis', whereby the woman resubmits herself to ideas about her self that are elaborated in/by a masculine logic, in-order to uncover the place of her exploitation by discourse.

Le theatre commence, lointain, douloureux.—*Savannah Bay*

In the 1970s and early 1980s Marguerite Duras created plays that flooded the stage with narrative text. The plays written between 1973 and 1982—*India Song* (1973), *L'Eden Cinema* (1977), *Agatha* (1981) and *Savannah Bay* (1982)—all feature a traumatic past event at their centre, and the re-telling of that happening by two or more narrators constitutes the play's action. However, there is no action in the conventional sense—the painful dredging of fragments of past story from memory is what has brought characters into being in this place.

In *India Song,* four off-stage voices try to remember, with varying degrees of difficulty and success, the story of Anne-Marie Stretter, of her love affairs, of her eventual suicide; the silent on-stage enactment appears to emerge from the confusion of versions of the story put forward by the voices.

In *Eden Cinema,* two actors, off-stage hut visible, voice the story of the Mother's failed attempts to stop the Pacific Ocean from flooding the rice fields she had bought from the colonial authorities in the French Indo-China of the 1920s, and her subsequent descent into madness. Only a few scenes are actually played and spoken by the on-stage actors, the rest is enacted without words. The on-stage actors in *Savannah Bay* slowly tell the story of Savannah, the young girl who drowned herself in

*A street in Bombay, India*

the Gulf of Siam. However, here too the representation is distanced from the narration, as the characters are involved in a compulsive re-telling of versions of a story that they can never control and to which they must always remain external. By means of disjunction of image and sound, of narration and representation, Duras brings into play the spectator's act of narrativizing, her/his compulsion to 'fill in the gaps' in the detail of the narrative provided by the representation. As the spectator listens to the sequence of variations on a central narrative motif, s/he is forced to remember earlier details, to attempt to piece the picture together from the fragments offered—an effort that is mirrored by the on-stage narrators.

Writing of feminist theatre of the 1980s, Elin Diamond notes an increased focus on the nature of narrative in plays written by women. The narrative text from elsewhere, from beyond the scene of representation, can be used to suggest the constructed nature of gender categories: 'In juxtaposed fragments of multivocal narrative the stage space becomes a scene of desire in which women were incitements to speech, never subjects of discourse.' Duras is certainly typical of this trend, in that her later plays are centred on mute or absent women about whom other characters or voices spin narra-

> MARGUERITE DURAS DEVELOPED A THEATRICAL FORM THAT BOTH STAGED A SEVERING OF THE WOMAN'S BODY/PRESENCE FROM DISCOURSE/SUBJECTIVITY, AND GAVE EXPRESSION TO THE DISTRESSED SOURCE OF THE WOMAN'S VOICE BEYOND DISCOURSE."

tives. The spectator is inevitably made to feel the force of his/her own desire to create, to know, to see, to consume the absent woman.

In *India Song*, Anne-Marie Stretter is the object of the story told throughout the playing time by four off-stage voices. She is on stage throughout the performance, but she never speaks; desired by both the off-stage speakers and the on-stage male characters, she appears as a living statue from whom tears stream, an empty, passive form. The mother who is the subject of the story that forms the basis of the representation in *Eden Cinema* never speaks directly about herself. The opening stage directions state, 'la mere restera immobile sur sa chaise, sans expression, comme statufiee, lointaine, separee—comme la scene—de sa propre histoire.' In *Savannah Bay,* the woman at the centre of the narrative of passionate young love that ends in suicide is not physically present; her lack of presence in her own life reached its apogee before the play began. However, her absence is strongly present on the stage, as the play's two protagonists, mother and daughter of the dead girl, prowl around the well of their loss.

To the extent that Duras mythifies an inaccessible feminine, the feminine as source of the mystery of origin, as death-containing and death-conferring matrix, she replicates patriarchal images of woman, and posits a withdrawal from conflict into an ideal state of bliss in the death of the female self. The woman at the centre of the narrative is in each case associated with water, with the magnetic pull of the amnion, promising eternal loss of self in fusion with the m/other:

MADELEINE. Elle etait tres jeune. A peine sortie du college. Ella nageait loin. On ne savait jamais . . . On ne pouvait jamais tout a fait croire qu'elle consentirait a vivre encore . . . qu'elle nous donnerait a lavoir encore . . . A l'entendre encore. A attendre encore qu'elle veuille bien revenir une lois encore de la mer.—*Savannah Bay*

The final image of *India Song* presents Anne-Marie Stretter walking into the sea; her suicide is presented as her only moment of power and agency in the play. At the conclusion of *Savannah Bay,* the telling story of the young woman who drowned herself upon the birth of her child reaches its climax—she is revealed as a woman who sought her own death at the high point of her exclusive passion. The woman at the source of the narrative that occupies centre stage in these later plays is generally enthralled by death, and welcomes death as a release from passion or madness, as a means of finally losing herself completely.

These are, of course, highly marked representations of femininity. However, Duras foregrounds the constructed nature of the mysterious, alluring woman at the centre of the narrative by calling attention to her mutism, her aphasia, her absent presence. At the centre of the narrative process in which both on-stage characters and off-stage spectators share stands a woman from whom the subject has departed, who is denied the 'I' of subjectivity. On the Durassian stage, the space of representation is immersed in fragmented narrative: through disjunction of narrative and enactment, voice and movement, Duras interrupts the processes of narrative and narrativity. By this means, she highlights both the centrality of the voiceless woman to the narrative and the impossibility of telling represents the woman's full story through the narrative medium. Thus, Duras uses the stage to foreground the woman as the mute 'subject' of discourse.

Another scenic strategy is Duras's handling of theatre's specular dimension. Duras frequently the woman's body as consumed by the devouring looks of others—both on stage and off. The look is central to her theatre, but like the word on this stage, it is not reciprocal. The consuming gaze founders on the desired object of perception—usually the body of the woman—; it is rarely returned. The gaze represented on this stage is frequently aggressive, coercive. The Young Woman of *Savannah Bay* circles around the older woman, watching her, transfixing her in her gaze, wanting her to deliver the story of the death of Savannah. Anne-Marie Stretter appears mute and mostly immobile on the stage of *India*

*Song,* stared at by a cohort of young male lovers and would-be lovers, watched too by the off-stage 'voices' who describe her, comment upon her, and watched of course by the spectators in the auditorium, who are made aware of their watching, of their desire to know her, to possess her. The look in *Eden Cinema* is again menacing, rooted in a desire to possess and control the other, as the Mother and Joseph watch M. Jo watching Suzanne.

This focusing on the gaze reaches its high point in the 1981 play, *Agatha.* Here, there is very little movement on stage—the two characters are described as being in a state of petrifaction, or sleep for most of the playing time. The script is built on a scaffolding of looks exchanged and withheld. While in *India Song* Duras invested very precise, detailed work on the modulation of the four off-stage voices that tell the story of Anne-Marie Stretter, her focus in *Agatha* is on the synchronization of the look, on the movement into and out of the look, For much of the text is voiced by the two characters with eyes closed—the brother and sister who are attempting to distance themselves from their incestuous desire for each other fear the look because of its power to unleash desire. And so they close their eyes, look at the ground or turn away from each other when they recount their memories of past looks shared, of the first look of recognition of shared desire. In this particular play, 'seul le texte bouge, avance': only the text moves between the bodies on the stage.

In each of these plays, the past moment of love is described in terms of the intensity of the first look of recognition exchanged by the lovers. The gaze signifies desire for the other, but on Duras's stage, the moment of shared passion belongs to the past, it is inaccessible, irretrievable. The reciprocal look, exchanged between lovers, is also locked in the past—it cannot be repeated, represented on the stage, it can only be told of. What is represented on the stage is an orchestration of looks that seem to circle around something that is unavailable.

In creating plays based on a thwarting of the gaze and a breakdown of narrative representation, Duras pushes theatrical conventions to the limits. She also takes the risk that she will find spectators who are willing to go, with the characters, into that which cannot be seen, to move into and out of the space of non-seeing, blindly, led by the voice alone: 'Nous entrons encore dans ce qui ne peut se vow (*Agatha*). Past desire is not representable in word or image, but the state of desire, 'la ou l'on est sourd et aveugle',—is recreated in the movement into and out of the fragments of story, in the tension of looks given and withheld.

The final Durassian scenic strategy that I would like to consider is one that I believe to be her signature staging technique: her spatialization of a topography that establishes the lost, pre-verbal part of the female self in relation to the self trapped in discourse. Some initial consideration of Freudian and post-Freudian theories of femininity and melancholia may help to elucidate what Duras achieved in terms of spatializing psychic or unconscious spaces in her theatre.

Melancholia, according to Freud, is the effect of an object loss that is withdrawn from consciousness, an unconscious loss that is unsayable and unrepresentable. In the woman's case, the cultural requirement of absolute repudiation of the primary object of love, combined with identification with the repudiated object, intensifies the sense of loss and can result in incomplete separation and unfinished mourning.

Failure to give up or mourn the loss of an object of love, according to Freud, results in a withdrawal of the fantasized object into the ego, and a turning-inward of the self. In her most recent work, *The Psychic Life of Power,* Judith Buffer provides an insightful interpretation of the Freudian theory of melancholia:

> Melancholia appears to be a process of internalization, and one might well read its effects as a psychic state that has effectively substituted itself for the world in which it dwells. The effect of melancholia then appears to be the loss of the social world and the substitution of psychic parts and antagonisms for external relations among social actors.

Butler comments that melancholia produces the possibility for the representation of psychic life. The withdrawal of object into the ego, the refusal to recognize the loss, the effort to sustain the love away from external reality institutes an internal psychic topography. Melancholy spatializes, and it is this potential which is harnessed by Duras in her theatre.

In *India Song, Eden Cinema* and *Savannah Bay,* the playing area occupies a small part of the stage space. Duras writes in her stage directions for *India Song* that the set should seem accidental—'vole a un tout de nature inaccessible.' Doors open stage right, stage left and at the back of the playing area, which represents Anne-Marie Stretter's living-room, to suggest the remainder of the vast ambassadorial residence, the gardens beyond, the river Ganges beyond that again and finally the city of Calcutta. The central scene of the play, a reception in the Embassy, is not represented directly on the stage, simply relayed via the soundtrack.

The staging of *Eden Cinema* calls for a large empty space surrounding another, rectangular, space. The rectangular space represents a bungalow, the empty space around the bungalow is 'the plain of Kam, in Upper Cambodia, between Siam and the sea.' The play is built on a pattern of alternating narrated scenes, where the actors mime to the sound of their recorded voices recounting the story, and fully acted scenes; light intensifies and diminishes on the rectangular playing area throughout the play to indicate changes in the narrative status of progressive scenes. A large part of the stage remains unused as the light rises and fades on the playing area—the unused space becomes the source of light, the source of the narrative voices, and the locus of what Duras refers to as 'le decor sonore'—'les bruits du soir de la plaine . . . des cris d'enfants, des rires, des aboiements de chiens, des tam-tams.'

In *Savannah Bay,* the down-stage playing space occupies a tenth of the total stage area:

> C'est la clue va etre represente Savannah Bay. Derriere cet espace de la representation, separe de lui, se trouve le decor que Roberto Plate a fait pour Savannah Bay . . . une tres grande scene de theatre . . . des rideaux de velours rouge . . . un espace central . . . de part et d'autre de cet endroit-la, il y a les deux battants d'une porte tres haute, vert sombre . . . derriere cette porte il y a deux immenses colonnes de la hauteur du theatre . . . Derriere les colonnes, cadrees par les battants de cette porte, apres une zone de lumiere presque noire, il y a la met. Ainsi le decor de Savannah Bay est-il separe de Savannah Bay, inhabitable par les femmes de Savannah Bay, laisse a lui-meme.—*Savannah Bay.*

In this play, the stage is occupied by a set made for a play that has not yet been written, that will never in fact be written, because its material is unwritable. Characters and spectators are excluded from the space of non-representation, and yet, it is the real focus of the Durassian drama, as the writer brings the spectator perpetually back to its closed door:

MADELEINE. La piece ne sera jamais ecrite. Alors, autant mourir.

JEUNE FEMME. Autant vivre, pareil . . .

MADELEINE. Pareil . . . C'est vrai, au fond.

JEUNE FEMME. Ainsi c'est une piece qui n'a ete ni jouee ni ecrite.

MADELEINE. Rien. Pour ce qui est de cette piece-la, rien.—*Savannah Bay*

And so the two women act out their play on the perimeters of a vast set constructed for a play that has not been written, that will never be written. The outer, inaccessible space is strongly associated with the story that is re-constructed in the inner, enclosed space of representation. The space that lies beyond representation is invested with sensory impressions associated with the past events that the voiced narrative attempts to reconstruct. Water, in the form of river or sea, lies beyond the playing area in all of these plays. Smells and quality of light are also evoked in relation to this other space. The aural dimension of the Durassian universe is invariably composed of voiced text, non-verbal sounds and music—a Schubert quintet and Pings 'Les mots d'amour' in the case of *Savannah Bay,* a variation on 'Blue Moon' and Beethoven's *Fourteenth Variation on a Theme of Diabelli* in *India Song,* a Brahms waltz in *Agatha.* The inaccessible space of non-representation that is a feature of Duras's later plays appears to be the source of the plays' second—and no less significant—setting, what Duras herself referred to as 'le decor sonore.' Various sounds emanate from this space in both *India Song* and *Eden Cinema*—'the noises of the plain', in *Eden Cinema;* the laughter and singing of the mad beggar woman from Burma, the noise of the monsoon rains falling on the garden in the case of *India Song.* The sound score—music, non-verbal sounds and snatches of 'foreign' language, emanate in these plays from beyond the space of representation—'comme s'il etait joue loin du lieu present . . . ''India Song'' de nouveau, lent, loin . . . ''India Song'' revient de tres loin.'

Therefore, there are two spaces on Duras's stage: the space of representation is framed by the space of unconscious memory, of the pre-verbal, marked by sensory impressions of colour, light, sound, smell and touch. The space of representation refers constantly to the other space, lost, irretrievable. The activity of narration seeks to reconstitute the lost moment of love, the lost object, but the fragments of story that emerge from the space of loss simply serve to reinforce the teller's (and the listener's) disorientation.

The body of the woman is the threshold between these two spaces—either mute and absent, although present on the stage, such as Anne-Marie Stretter in *India Song* or the mother at the centre or the drama of *Eden Cinema,* or already lost or past, such as the young girl in *Savannah Bay,* or the teenage Agatha. It is very much the woman's body that is in question: whether it be the mother's body and its relationship to its own desire and the child it carries (*Savannah Bay*), the mother's body in relation to physical exhaustion, ageing and madness (*Eden Cinema*), the white, virginal body of incestuous desire (*Agatha*) or the sexually experienced body appearing to offer seduction and promiscuity (*India Song*). The narrative fragments of the Durassian text circle around the body, tell of the speakers' desire for it.

The Durassian mythology frequently associates the woman with house or place—Agatha is the name of the summer house, fronting onto a beach, in which Agatha and her brother discover their love for each other, and to which they return to play out their final separation. The 1981 film version of the text, directed by Duras, consists of a soundtrack of the voiced text played over lingering camera footage of an empty house fronting onto a northern beach in winter; the house was shot from both inside and out, with the focus placed heavily on the windows, doors, shutters, the movement of the camera between inside and out. Savannah is the name of the young woman who finds love in the place known as Savannah Bay, who gives birth in that place, and who finally drowns herself in the waters of the bay in which she had loved to swim. The two on-stage characters who try to retrieve her from the past are dwarfed by the vast empty set at the back of which are large doors opening onto the sea. In *India Song,* the spectator witnesses Anne-Marie Stretter suffocating in the colonial setting of the ambassadorial residence; Duras uses the soundtrack to suggest the river Ganges and the city of Calcutta stretching out beyond the walls of the ambassadorial gardens. Anne-Marie Stretter is described as 'a leper of the heart in the desert of Calcutta', she 'belongs to whoever wants her', she is 'porous', born of and suffering the horror of Calcutta: she is its prostitution, its disease, its despair, she is Calcutta. The setting for *Eden Cinema* is the Mother's bungalow, to which she is largely confined throughout the play; however, she is strongly associated with the surrounding plain which she tries to reclaim from the Pacific, a struggle which results in her madness and ultimate death. The play ends with the death of the Mother, and the opening up of her house, her space, to the children of the plain, who will flood into it as the sea flooded the Mother's rice fields.

Therefore, one might conclude that the silent woman on Duras's stage is represented as housed, encased, but opening onto, referring to, a wider external space beyond—a space that is invariably associated with water, light and non-verbal sounds. The space that is not represented directly on the stage, the space that is resistant to representation, is a space of liquidity, fluidity. The Durassian woman, trapped in the scopic gaze of narrative representation, looks out, beyond, into the distance, as one might look through a window at the sea, as a writer might peer into the past in an effort to locate lost selves.

The watched woman on Duras's stage is generally represented as being unaware of herself as an object of the other's gaze. She is represented as distanced from herself—in fact, she appears to have been disconnected from her body, she has departed to another place, while her body remains on this stage. To this extent, she appears to represent Irigaray's specularized woman, trapped in a scopic economy that is not her own, consigned to 'mutism and mimetism', enveloped in the needs, desires and fantasies of the (male) other. The exclusion of the female imaginary from the Symbolic has resulted in the woman's dereliction within culture, in her inability to experience her self other than fragmentarily, as waste or excess, as 'nothing to see' or as that which overflows discursive logic. In *Ce Sexe qui n'en est pas un,* Irigaray writes of the fluid nature of the female imaginary, which cannot find expression in the 'discursive machinery' of logocentric discourse:

> Inutile donc de pieger les femmes dans la definition exacte de ce qu'elles veulent dire, de les faire (se) repeter pour que ce soit clair, elles sont deja ailleurs que dans cette machinerie discursive ou vous pretendriez les surprendre. Elles sont retournees en elles-memes . . . cela veut dire en l'intimite de ce tact silencieux, multiple, diffus. Et si vous leur demandez avec insistance a quoi elles pensent, elles ne peuvent que repondre: a rien. A tout.

Duras, in her theatre, gives scenic expression to the pain of contact with that part of (her) psychic life that is bound up with unsayable and unrepresentable loss. The spatialization of that which can only be sensed provides scenic representation of psychic splitting in a topography that establishes the lost, pre-verbal part of the female self in relation to the self trapped in discourse.

> MADELEINE. La salle est noire . . . On lui dit comme la met etait bleue . . . Comme la pierre est blanche.
>
> JEUNE FEMME. Comme la douleur est longue. (Temps.) Comme elle change. (Temps.) Comme elle devient. (Temps.) Le second voyage. (Temps.) L'autre rive. (Temps.) Le deuxieme amour.—*Savannah Bay*

In the slow voicing of fragments of narrative, in the drifting of text and gaze between the narrow space of representation and the wider space of preverbal sensation, what is enacted is the approach, and the waiting, like a second journey, a second love, an apprehension of the old, lost love, the old pain. What lies beyond the door, in vast empty spaces of the Durassian stage, is that which cannot—or will not—be represented in narrative, what has not been represented in history: female subjectivity, lost in its nascent state as a result of culture's burial of the pre-verbal mother.

> MADELEINE. Je me souviens de quelque chose, si, si, mais c'est cache. Je ne sais plus de quoi je me souviens, ni de qui c'etait, ni quand, mais c'est la . . . (elle designe sa tete) . . . Cest curieux, de ces choses-la je suis sure, du noir de la nuit. (Temps.) De la pluie. (Temps.) Des cris. Du lever du soleil le lendemain. (Temps.) De cette couleur de la mer . . . (Temps.) Du son des voix. (Temps.) Du silence entre les voix.— *Savannah Bay*

The lost love is immutable, unchanging, forever fixed in its first intensity, an intensity that placed it outside of time, without past or future. Madeleine describes the love experienced by Savannah and her young lover as 'Un amour de tous les instants. Sans passe. Sans avenir. Fixe. Immuable.' (*Savannah Bay*) The longing to return to this moment of intense feeling, now unreachable but still intact, is the source of 'douleur' or grief on Duras's stage, and grief is the source of theatre. Theatre provides the writer with the opportunity to stage the pain of voicing the longing for what is lost, the pain of struggling to establish precisely what has been lost. To love and to write is to embrace the unknowable, to agree to wander blindly in the dark:

> Ecrire, aimer, elle, elle voit que cela se vit dans le meme inconnu, dans le meme doff de la connaissance raise au desespoir.

To engage with Duras's theatre is to accept the impossibility of knowing, of finding one's way back to the origin of the story. Unless it be by means of receptivity to sound on her stage. For Duras interrupts the processes of narrativity and specularization in order to focus the listener/spectator's attention to the play of sounds. In her stage directions she shows herself to be concerned above all with the modulation of tones of voice, with the orchestration of pace and pitch, with the reverberation of her words against silence and stillness, and with the interplay of voiced text and 'decor sonore', the music and non-verbal sounds that are such a feature of the later plays. Focus on the auditory dimension of theatre would appear to offer a way out of the trap of specularization, a way of moving away from 'Woman' as she is conventionally constructed by the gaze of the (male) other, and towards an embodiment of the female text through the medium of sound. According to Claude Regy, who directed many of her works for the stage, Duras was seeking to capture what she called 'la voix de l'ecriture', to hear what the text sounds like as it emerges from the unconscious, before it is set down on paper:

> Ce qu'elle essaie de faire, c'est de restituer sa propre lecture, cette facon d'entendre l'ecrit avant qu'il soft jete sur le papier quand il arrive directement de l'inconscient et que de cette masse d'inconscient se degage un petit groupe de mots qui est a la fois musical, rythmique, sonore.

What appears to have been important to her as a writer was the process of capturing the aural quality of words as they emerged from the unconscious, to discern the musical, rhythmical associations that particular words had for her:

> Je ne m'occupe jamais du sens, de la signification. S'il y a un sens, il se degage apres . . . le mot compte plus que la syntaxe. C'est avant tout des mots, sans articles d'ailleurs, qui viennent et qui s'imposent. Le temps grammatical suit, d'assez loin.

Duras required the spectator to receive her staged texts in the same way as she felt she received them as a writer. If she was attempting to apprehend what lies beyond/before the text in her writing, then perhaps we might say that on the stage she was endeavouring to use theatre's aural/oral dimension to engage the spectator in the experience of retrieving the aural origins of the text; thus, the experience of watching one of her later plays is one of involvement in the processes of listening, remembering and composing on the basis of heard fragments. Certainly, Duras was interested in recreating the reading experience in the mind of the spectator: Claude Regy notes that she required a minimum of intervention on the part of the actors on her stage—movement was to be kept to a minimum and stylized, the text was to be 'recited', as if it were being read. This approach establishes a distance between actor and text, and places the text centre stage. In place of representational realism and narrative coherence, Duras places the power of the voiced word to resonate in the spectator/listener's auditory imagination:

> Le texte ecrit, s'il est desensable d'une interpretation sentimentalisee par un exces de jeu venant de l'acteur, si on l'entend clairement, reprend son role d'ecrit et fait completement fonctionner la memoire et l'imagi-nation des spectateurs qui retrouvent leur liberte de lecteurs.

Duras makes her project very clear in the stage directions for *India Song:*

> L'image ou la scene, du point de vue sonore, jouera le role d'une chambre d'echo. Les voix, passant par cet espace, devraient arriver au spectateur avec la meme portee que sa voix de 'lecture interieure.'

The stage then, functions as an 'echo chamber' through which the words reverberate between the writer's unconscious and the listener's unconscious. Clearly, Duras viewed her task in writing as that of cultivating a state of attentive receptivity to auditory memory, and she used the theatre to recreate the process of activating sound associations in the minds of the spectators. Therefore, the script that Duras stages is less concerned with constructing a narrative than with communicating the origins of the writing, with sounding the auditory foundations of the text. The 'outer' space that is represented on the Durassian stage as frustratingly inaccessible figures the 'inner' space to which Duras's text unremittingly directs the spectator.

Writing of women's speech in her 1977 text, *Ce sexe qui n'en est pas un,* Luce Irigaray notes that woman's speech requires a different kind of listening, if one is to hear what it has to say about what cannot be named in the symbolic. For Irigaray, woman's speech is a flux that overflows the space of logocentric discourse, into a space that is defined, within patriarchy, as that which is exterior to the space of signification: 'En dehors de ce volume deja circonscrit par la signification articulee dans le discours (du pere) rien n'est: l'afemme. Zone de silence.' Irigaray concludes that the woman may appear mute or aphasic in the logocentric context—in any case, she is not listened to when she speaks in the public forum, where there is strong resistance to 'cette voix qui deborde le sujet.' Receptivity to this voice means openness to the space of the female imaginary. This may indeed be a space of pain, of blockage, of incomplete mourning, where the nascent subject is locked in an eternal embrace with the lost object of desire. But the woman writer who draws attention to this other space may be giving expression to the distressed source of her voice within discourse. And theatre is the ideal medium for an exploration of the relations between the voice, the space of narrative and the space of what Helene Cixous referred to as 'le chant d'avant la loi.'

Julia Kristeva has written compellingly of her view of the Durassian woman, who she sees as confiscated by the lost object, inhabiting 'la cave secrete' of narcissism, in love with love and death, but alone. However, for Kristeva, the 'malady of

grief' that finds expression in Duras's work results in a form of writing that demonstrates a crisis of meaning, where words run aground in the attempt to represent the invisible, to say the unsayable: the crisis of expression that arises when the writer is determined to confront the silence of the horror in oneself and in the world. Kristeva is critical of what she perceives to be Duras's stylistic inelegances, and of the fact that in her writing she courts the madness that may arise from an exclusive fixation on the presymbolic and oedipal moment of separation from the mother on the part of the woman writer.

Clearly, Kristeva does not consider that Duras's perpetual return to the pre-verbal relationship with the mother gives rise to the kind of 'semiotic' pleasure which she described in her earlier work as pleasure derived from texts which, through their rhythms, return the reader to the rhythms, movements and sounds of the maternal body. For Kristeva, contact with repressed preoedipal or 'semiotic', drive-ridden experience is stimulated when a writer uses language in such a way as to activate the re-emergence within discourse of 'the rhythms, intonations and echolalias of the mother-infant symbiosis.' Contact with these rhythms in the text should be a pleasurable experience for the writer, and especially for the reader. However, in Kristeva's view, return to 'the joyous serenity of incest with the mother', is a linguistic journey that is best left to male writers, and her comments on Duras's work in *Soleil noir* recall her earlier warning to women writers of the perils of re-activating the pre-oedipal phase in their writing, for 'the invasion of her speech by these unphrased, nonsensical, maternal rhythms, far from soothing her or making her laugh, destroys her symbolic armour, and makes her ecstatic, nostalgic or mad.'

While Kristeva describes the pain experienced by women as a result of attachment to a love that is outside of language, before language, as 'innommable', Luce Irigaray notes that the impossibility for the woman of representing her loss within discourse, and hence of mourning the loss of her primary object of desire, is an effect of discourse itself. Irigaray writes of the woman's 'dereliction' within culture as arising from the impossibility of her mourning the loss of the object—the original separation from the mother. The woman can neither replace the lost object with substitutes, nor can she mourn the loss of this primary symbiotic relation because she has no means of representing what has been lost within the Symbolic. She writes repeatedly that the problem for women lies in the non-symbolization within culture of the relation to the mother and to the mother's body. Lack of a primary metaphorization of her female desire, of her relation to the loss of origin, to the loss of the original symbiotic relationship with the mother upon the entry into language alienates woman from her sense of identity, from her subjectivity.

The playing area on Duras's stage presents the physical body of a woman, reduced to 'appearance', bearing all the gender markings of the feminine mystique—madness, excessive passion, maternity, death-drive—and traversed by fragments of a narrative that resist coherence or closure; the uninhabitable terrain of her stage, which is also reflected in the blanks, pauses and silences in the text, suggest the lost source of the woman's voice, lost source of her writing, lost source of her self.

> Elle est le lieu au seuil de quoi le silence commence. Ce qui s'y passe, c'est justement le silence, ce lent travail pour toute ma vie … je n'ai jamais ecrit, croyant le faire, je n'ai jamais aime, croyant aimer, je n'ai jamais rien fait qu'attendre devant la porte fermee.

In waiting long moments in seemingly deserted places, in engaging with the voiced text through the auditory memory, the Durassian spectator may begin to hear and feel the distress of a perpetual return to a part of the self that is unknowable, to a primary loss that remains unsayable in narrative discourse. Thus Duras goes some way toward realizing Irigaray's feminist project of 'playing with mimesis', working the representative machinery in order to expose its machinations. By highlighting the desubjectified (female) position upon which the narrative enterprise is founded, and by insistently sounding the perimeters of a psychic topography in her staging and in her texts, Duras leads the spectator to an apprehension of the site of the woman's loss of self at the threshold of discourse.

**Source:** Mary Noonan, "The Spatialization of Loss in the Theatre of Marguerite Duras," in *Theatre Research International,* Vol. 23, No. 3, Autumn 1998.

## SOURCES

Cody, Gabrielle H., *Impossible Performances: Duras as Dramatist,* Peter Lang, 2000, pp. 1–2.

Duras, Marguerite, *India Song,* translated by Barbara Bray, Grove Press, 1976.

Ha, Marie-Paule, "Duras on the Margins," in *Romantic Review,* Vol. 84, No. 3, May 1993, pp. 299–320.

Taylor, Lib, "Sound Tracks: The Soundscapes of *India Song,*" in *Theatre Research International,* Vol. 23, No. 3, Autumn 1998, p. 205.

## FURTHER READING

Bhatia, Nandi, *Acts of Authority, Acts of Resistance: Theatre and Politics in Colonial and Postcolonial India,* University of Michigan Press, 2004.
    Bhatia provides a critical analysis of theater and drama in nineteenth- and twentieth-century India, examined in cultural, political, and historical context.

Cody, Gabrielle H., *Impossible Performances: Duras as Dramatist,* Peter Lang, 2000.
    Cody offers a critical analysis of Duras's major dramatic works.

Dwyer, Rachel, *All You Want Is Money, All You Need Is Love: Sexuality and Romance in Modern India,* Cassell, 2000.
    Dwyer provides a critical analysis of the representation of love, sex, and romance in twentieth-century Indian fiction.

Kerkhoff, Kathinka Renata, *Save Ourselves and the Girls!: Girlhood in Calcutta under the Raj,* Extravert, 1995.
    Kerkhoff offers a critical historical account of the social conditions of girls in Calcutta, India, during the period of British colonial occupation.

Markovitz, Claude, ed., *A History of Modern India, 1480–1950,* Anthem, 2002.
    Markovitz provides an overview of the history of India from the beginning of European conquest in the fifteenth century to the achievement of national independence in the post–World War II era.

Metcalf, Thomas R., ed., *Modern India: An Interpretive Anthology,* Sterling, 1990.
    Metcalf provides a collection of essays by various authors on the history of India during the era of British occupation.

Nevile, Pran, ed., *Love Stories from the Raj,* Penguin, 1995.
    Nevile offers a collection of romantic short fiction published and set during the period of British colonial rule in India.

Pati, Bisamoy, and Mark Harrison, eds., *Health, Medicine, and Empire: Perspectives on Colonial India,* Orient Longman, 2001.
    Pati and Harrison offer a collection of essays by various authors providing critical historical analysis of health and medical care in India during the era of British colonial rule.

Read, Anthony, and David Fisher, *The Proudest Day: India's Long Road to Independence,* W. W. Norton, 1998.

Read and Fisher provide a historical account of the Indian nationalist movement and struggle for national independence during the period of British colonial rule.

# Le Cid

## PIERRE CORNEILLE

## 1636

*Le Cid*, published in 1636, is considered Pierre Corneille's first masterpiece, a tragic play that was subsequently used by later playwrights as a model and a standard to follow. With *Le Cid*, Corneille changed the form of the dramatic play, a transformation that was met with great applause not only from the audience but from the ruling monarch at the time, King Louis XIII of France.

*Le Cid* is based on the deeds and subsequent legend of a twelfth-century Spanish soldier called El Cid (arabic for the lord), a man who fought against (and, as some believe, also fought with) the Moors who were in the process of taking over much of the land that Spain occupies today. El Cid was a mighty warrior and the first notorious hero of Spain. Much had been written about him in poetry and ballad, as well as in a play by the Spanish author Guillen de Castro (1569–1631). Corneille was inspired by the story of El Cid and, taking liberty from the standard dramatic form of his day, imbued his play with great passion and complex psychological insight. The result was a production the likes of which the Parisian people had never seen before.

The play relates the events of Le Cid coming of age. Le Cid's father asks his son to restore the elder man's honor by challenging Le Cid's future father-in-law to a duel. Le Cid immediately understands that no matter what he does, he is doomed. If he does not make the challenge, both he and his father will be dishonored. If he does make the challenge, he will lose the love of his future bride. The manner in

which he solves this dilemma, and the events that unfold as he does so, takes the young man from untried warrior to triumphant hero.

# AUTHOR BIOGRAPHY

Corneille is one of France's most outstanding playwrights of the seventeenth century. Although he was considered a prolific writer for his time and is best known as a playwright, literature was not his main career.

Born on June 6, 1606, in Rouen, France, to a family that had a tradition of producing lawyers, Corneille was destined to follow in his father's footsteps. He studied law under the training of Jesuit priests and, at the early age of twenty-three, entered parliament. For the next twenty-one years, Corneille practiced law (under King Louis XIII and King Louis XIV) as the king's counselor in the department of waterways and forests. Fortunately for many Parisians, law was not the only thing that interested Corneille. No sooner was he established in parliament than he decided to try his hand at writing and soon discovered he had another fruitful talent. By the time he stopped practicing law, he had written twenty plays. But he was not finished yet. While in retirement, Corneille would go on to write some of his most influential dramatic plays.

Corneille's first six plays were comedies, beginning with *Mélite* (1625). A year later, this comedy was presented in Paris and from that point on, Corneille's reputation as a playwright took off. In the next seven years, Corneille wrote almost a play a year, eventually catching the attention of Cardinal de Richelieu (prime minister of France, 1585–1642). The cardinal, a very influential figure in the king's court, wanted to use Corneille's gift of writing to promote his own political ideas. So Corneille was sponsored by the cardinal and supplied with concepts about which to write. This did not set well with Corneille for very long. After many disagreements, Corneille and the cardinal parted company. Corneille left Paris and returned to his hometown of Rouen, where he took up a private practice in law.

Immediately following his return to Rouen, Corneille did not write. This fallow period lasted for several years, but the time was not wasted. As a matter of fact, it was during this period that Corneille decided to lay aside the genre of comedy and try his

*Pierre Corneille*

hand at writing tragedy. Today, many scholars believe it was through the writing of tragedies that Corneille reached his full potential as a playwright.

Corneille's first tragic piece was *Médée* (1634), which met with only mediocre success. Corneille next produced what many critics believe was his first masterpiece, *Le Cid* (1636). The many performances of this play were cheered by packed audiences in Paris. Even King Louis XIII sent Corneille congratulations. But not everyone was happy with Corneille's play. Cardinal de Richelieu harshly criticized *Le Cid* because it broke away from the traditional classical rules of drama. Richelieu's harsh commentary against Corneille's work so belittled Corneille's skills that the playwright did not write another play for the next three years.

But this was not the end of Corneille. During those three years he advanced his art. And when he next produced a play, it equaled, if not surpassed, the mastery demonstrated in *Le Cid*. The year 1641 was a remarkable time for Corneille. First, he married Marie de Lampérière. Next, he enjoyed back-to-back productions of two more well-received tragic plays, *Horace* (1640) and *Cinna* (1641). With these plays, there was no doubt of Corneille's talents. He would go on to write many more plays before his death and for his innovations in the writing of dramatic tragedy, he is honored, today, with the title of the Father of French Tragedy.

Corneille died in Paris on October 1, 1684.

## PLOT SUMMARY

### Act 1

In the first scene, Chimene is talking to her lady-in-waiting, Elvire. Chimene is excited because she has heard rumors that her father, Don Gomes, has accepted Don Rodrigue as a suitor for Chimene's hand in marriage. Elvire confirms that the rumors are true. When pressed to answer her, Elvire tells Chimene that she told her father that Chimene has no preference of suitors and will do only as her father commands. Chimene's father is proud to hear such devotion and states that he believes that Don Rodrigue is well suited for her. Elvire then tells Chimene that the king is to choose a tutor for his son today. Elvire is sure he will select Chimene's father. Once Don Gomes is chosen, Elvire believes, Don Rodrigue's father will also propose the match between Chimene and Don Rodrigue. Despite this news, Chimene says that her spirit is perturbed, although she does not know why.

In the next scene, Infanta appears with her lady-in-waiting, Leonor. In this scene, Infanta reveals her love of Don Rodrigue, but through her conversations with Leonor, she also acknowledges that she will never be allowed to marry Rodrigue because he is below her social status in the court. She also confesses that she has purposefully brought Chimene and Rodrigue together and encouraged their love. She has done so because if they are married all hope of her being with Rodrigue will be extinguished.

Count Don Gomes enters with Don Diegue in the next scene. These men are respectively the father of Chimene and the father of Don Rodrigue. They are discussing the fact that Don Diegue has won the title of tutor for the king's son. Don Gomes is stunned by this action of the king's, having expected that he would have been chosen. Don Diegue tries to dismiss Don Gomes haughty statements stating that the king probably chose him based on love not on merit, allowing that Don Gomes may have deserved it more. This does not satisfy Don Gomes, however, and by the end of the

scene, Don Gomes slaps Don Diegue in the face out of indignation. Don Diegue draws his sword but Don Gomes easily disarms him.

In the next scene, Don Diegue despairs by himself. He has been insulted by Don Gomes and is humiliated because he is not strong enough any more to defend his honor. He must find someone younger and stronger who can.

Rodrigue, whose courage his father questions, enters the scene. When Rodrigue asserts that he is brave enough to do whatever his father asks, Don Diegue tells him to seek out Don Gomes and avenge his honor. When his father leaves, Rodrigue must weigh this heavy matter alone. If he does as his father has requested, it means he must kill Chimene's father. If he does this, Chimene will hate him. If he does not do as his father has asked him to, his father and therefore he, himself, will remain disgraced. If he is disgraced, then Chimene will not be able to love him. Rodrigue decides that he has no choice. He must challenge Don Gomes.

### Act 2

Act 2 begins with Don Gomes discussing what has just happened between himself and Don Diegue. Don Arias is with him and suggests that Don Gomes should not expose his anger concerning the king's choice of tutor. Unfortunately, Don Gomes, having not been chosen, believes that he has lost his honor among his men. He feels disgraced, and he wants the king to know. In the following scene, Rodrigue enters and challenges Don Gomes, who thinks Rodrigue a fool to do so. Don Gomes is insulted that such a young and inexperienced warrior should dare to even think he might challenge him. But Don Gomes also realizes that Rodrigue must surely be an exceptional young man and he praises himself for having chosen Rodrigue for his daughter. Don Gomes tells Rodrigue to go away. There would be no honor in Gomes's killing of such a young man. But Rodrigue insists and the two men leave to fight.

The next scene involves Chimene and Infanta, who have heard of Don Gomes's and Rodrigue's duel. They are concerned for both men but do not yet know the outcome. Chimene leaves to find them.

Infanta is left with Leonor. Infanta hopes that Rodrigue will win because then he could not gain Chimene's love and might possibly love her instead.

The king—Don Fernand—discusses with Don Arias and Don Sanche the arrogance of Don Gomes. The king is furious that Don Gomes has defied him.

Don Sanche, a suitor of Chimene, attempts to defend Don Gomes, asking that the king be lenient with him. The subject is not fully discussed as the king is worried about a navy of Moors that has been seen sailing near the shores of their empire. They discuss which path they should follow to protect themselves. Then Don Alonse enters to bring the news that Don Gomes is dead.

In scene VI, Chimene and Don Diegue beg the king to hear them out. Chimene wants her father's death avenged. Don Diegue wants the king to spare his son's life. After each pleads their case, the king asks that Don Rodrigue be brought to him.

## Act 3

Rodrigue shows up at Chimene's house. He first runs into Elvire who tells him to run away. When she sees Chimene coming, she tells Rodrigue to hide. Chimene then enters with Don Sanche. Don Sanche promises to avenge her father's death. When Sanche leaves, Chimene admits that she is completely torn apart. She must regain her father's honor by seeking Rodrigue's death. But her heart cannot bear the thought of Rodrigue dying. Rodrigue then enters and tells Chimene to kill him. Chimene insists that she must seek his death but she cannot do it. Rodrigue says he knows that he must die and prefers that it is by her hand.

In scene 5, Don Diegue is alone. He is worried for his son. He thanks the heavens when Rodrigue enters. He tells Rodrigue to go fight the Moors and keep them from the kingdom. If Rodrigue does this, all his problems will be solved. He will be a hero, and Chimene will then be able to marry him without dishonor.

## Act 4

Scene 1 opens much as the play began with Chimene and Elvire discussing rumors about Don Rodrigue, who has defeated the Moors and saved his empire. The people are rejoicing for their champion whom they now call Le Cid. Then Infanta enters the scene. Chimene confides in her that even though Rodrigue is now proclaimed a hero, she still cannot forgive him. Infanta reminds Chimene that she should make careful considerations as this is not just a personal decision but a public one. The people need a hero.

The king meets with Le Cid in the next scene, along with Don Diegue, Don Arias, and Don Sanche. Le Cid relates the details of the battle with the Moors. When Chimene shows up, the king asks Le Cid to leave, but only after giving him the highest praises for his bravery. Chimene tells the king that she still cannot forgive Le Cid and pretends not to love him. She still wants revenge, and when Don Sanche says that he will avenge her father, Chimene agrees. Whoever wins, she says, she will marry.

## Act 5

Chimene and Le Cid face one another. He insists that nothing means anything to him but her. He is still willing to give his life if Chimene declares that she wants him dead. She says she does and so Le Cid goes to face Sanche. Sanche returns later with a bloody sword and Chimene believes that Le Cid is dead. At this Chimene openly declares her love for Le Cid upon confronting the king. The king informs her that she has been misled. Le Cid lives. Le Cid is then led onto the stage by Infanta, who tells Chimene to accept him. Chimene repeats her words of love but tells Le Cid that she cannot marry him or shame will fall upon her for accepting the murderer of her father. The king tries to solve this dilemma by sending Le Cid in pursuit of the Moors in an attempt to win back their land. In time, the king believes, Chimene will be able to accept Le Cid.

## CHARACTERS

### Don Alonse

Don Alonse is a nobleman whose role is minor but who provides a way of filling in information about the activities that are going on behind the scenes.

### Don Arias

Don Arias is also described as a nobleman. He is used in this play much as the ladies-in-waiting are used, as a way for the main male characters to expose their interior dialog.

### Chimene

Chimene is Don Gomes daughter, and she is in love with Don Rodrigue. In the beginning of the play she learns that the king has approved her union with Don Rodrigue. But shortly after this, Don Rodrigue slays her father, and Chimene begs the king to punish Don Rodrigue in the name of her father. She insists that Don Rodrigue be killed even though her heart does not agree. She is torn between her love of her father and her love of Don Rodrigue. Even after she hears that Don Rodrigue has returned home a hero and is being called Le Cid, Chimene cannot forget her duty as a daughter. How can she marry the man who has slain her father? She returns to the king and begs him to punish Don Rodrigue. She proposes that Don Sanche represent her in a duel with Don Rodrigue. Whoever is victorious in this battle, she will feel that her father's honor has been avenged and she will marry the victor. When Don Sanche returns with a bloody sword, Chimene believes that Don Rodrigue is dead and she declares her love for him. The king, having seen proof that she still loves him, sends Don Rodrigue away to fight the Moors and tells Chimene to allow time to heal her wounds before she fulfills her promise to marry Don Rodrigue.

### The Count
*See* Don Gomes

### Don Diegue
Don Diegue is the father of Don Rodrigue (Le Cid). He was once a great warrior and served the king well. Because of this, the king, Don Fernand, honors him by appointing him the tutor for his son. This action angers Don Gomes, a younger man who is also a great warrior. Don Gomes insults Don Diegue by slapping him in the face and telling him that he is not worthy of such an appointment. When Don Diegue raises his sword to defend his honor, he is too weak to challenge the younger warrior. Don Diegue therefore tells his son, Don Rodrigue, that he must defend the honor of his father. When Don Rodrigue kills Don Gomes, Don Diegue fears for his son's life. He tells his son that the Moors are

planning a surprise attack on Seville and he must go stop them. If he conquers the Moor, Don Diegue believes that his son will then be honored by this feat and threats to his life for having slain Don Gomes will have been dissipated. Later, when Chimene begs the king to punish Don Rodrigue for having taken the life of her father, Don Diegue also pleads, but he begs for Don Rodrigue's life. Don Diegue tries to prove to the king that Chimene really loves his son.

### Elvire
Elvire is lady-in-waiting to Chimene. It is through Elvire's conversations with Chimene that the audience is able to explore how deep Chimene's feelings go for Don Rodrigue and to understand the challenges that Chimene must face.

### Don Fernand
Don Fernand is the king of Castile. He is a level-headed, compassionate leader who must decide the fate of several characters in this play. In the beginning of the play, Don Fernand selects Don Diegue as tutor for his son. His choice is the catalyst for most of the action in the play. Later he must decide whether Don Rodrigue should be considered a hero to be honored or a criminal to be punished. He also forces the hand of Chimene, as he tries to decide if she truly loves Don Rodrigue. In the end, Don Fernand comes up with a solution that saves Chimene's honor and Don Rodrigue's life.

### Don Gomes
Count Don Gomes is the father of Chimene and one of the king's best warriors. When the king appoints Don Diegue as tutor of his son, Don Gomes is insulted and infuriated. Don Gomes believes that he outranks Don Diegue who once was a great warrior but now has lost his power. In his frustration, Don Gomes, a very conceited man, slaps Don Diegue across the face, dishonoring him. When Don Diegue takes out his sword to save his honor, Don Gomes quickly dismisses the older man and walks away. In order to preserve his father's honor, Don Rodrigue challenges Don Gomes to a fight. Don Gomes is killed and his last words to his daughter are to seek his revenge.

### Infanta
*See* Doña Urraque

### The King
*See* Don Fernand

# *Le Cid*

*See* Don Rodrigue

## *Leonor*

Leonor is lady-in-waiting to the Infanta. Her character allows the playwright to fill in missing information through her private conversations with Infanta. Through Leonor, the audience learns how much the Infanta loves Don Rodrigue and how she has sacrificed this love.

## *Don Rodrigue*

Don Rodrigue is Le Cid, a legendary hero. He is the son of Don Diegue, and he is in love with Chimene. In the beginning of the play, Don Rodrigue's father tells him that he must challenge Don Gomes in order to save Don Diegue's honor. Don Rodrigue is torn by this request. He knows that if he does as his father has requested, he will lose the love of Chimene. If he does not avenge his father's honor, he himself will be dishonored and therefore would lose Chimene's love also. He decides that he has no choice in this matter and challenges Don Gomes and wins. Upon killing Don Gomes, Don Rodrigue begs Chimene to kill him. Don Rodrigue believes that the only way to solve the dilemma is to die, and he would rather Chimene kill him. Chimene refuses but nonetheless continues to persuade the king to punish Don Rodrigue. His father provides a possible solution for Don Rodrigue and tells him to go save the kingdom by killing the Moors, which Don Rodrigue does. He returns a hero, with the people now calling him by the honorific title of Le Cid. But Don Rodrigue does not feel this is enough to win back the love of Chimene. He accepts her challenge of fighting Don Sanche, a rival suitor, to the death. Whoever wins this battle, wins Chimene is marriage. Don Rodrigue wins although he spares Don Sanche's life, but he still knows that this is not enough to wipe out his deed of having killed Chimene's father. He knows Chimene loves him, but this awful deed keeps the two lovers from coming together. The king suggests that Don Rodrigue rid the country of the Moors. Upon his conquest and with the passage of time, the king assures Don Rodrigue that Chimene will forgive him.

## *Don Sanche*

Don Sanche is in love with Chimene, but Chimene does not love him. When Don Sanche realizes that Chimene wants her father's death avenged, he promises her that he will do it. When the time for that challenge arrives, Don Rodrigue dishonors Don Sanche by defeating him but not killing him. Don Sanche returns to Chimene with a bloody sword after the challenge. Chimene believes that Don Sanche has killed Don Rodrigue and declares her love for Don Rodrigue. Don Sanche tries to explain that this is not true but his words do not make sense to Chimene until the king intervenes.

## *Doña Urraque*

Called Infanta throughout the play, Doña Urraque is a princess who loves Don Rodrigue. She cannot hope to marry him, however, because Don Rodrigue is below her in nobility status. In order to rid herself of any remaining hope, Infanta forces the hand of fate by introducing and promoting the development of love between Don Rodrigue and Chimene. Infanta adds an intriguing element to the play as she is torn between her heart and her social status. She longs for Don Rodrigue and at the same time pushes him closer to Chimene. Toward the end of the play, when Don Rodrigue proves to be a hero in saving the kingdom from an invasion of the Moors, Infanta's hopes rise when she realizes that his heroism exalts Don Rodrigue's station in life. If he is a hero who has brought the Moor kings to their knees, then there is a chance Don Rodrigue might properly ask for Infanta's hand. But her hopes are dashed when she realizes how much Don Rodrigue loves Chimene.

# THEMES

## *Honor*

Much of the action of this play is stimulated by honor. It is for his father's honor that Don Rodrigue challenges his future father-in-law to a duel in the very beginning of the play. Before doing so, Rodrigue contemplates honor and how it affects his life. His father was dishonored by a slap in the face and the fact that his arm was too weak to challenge Don Gomes. Rodrigue is left with little choice. Honor dictates that he must fight Don Gomes. If his father is dishonored, then he too is dishonored. And honor, in this play and during this time, was more important than love. For if Rodrigue is dishonored, then it follows that he is unworthy of the love of Chimene.

Chimene also must deal with the concept of honor. She believes that her own father was dishonored by the duel with Rodrigue during which Don

# TOPICS FOR FURTHER STUDY

- Research the role of Cardinal de Richelieu, who was chief minister of France during the production of *Le Cid*. What were Richelieu's objections or criticisms of the play? What did he do to try to stop this play? How did this affect the play and Corneille?

- Read at least two different historical representations of the Spanish hero El Cid. How do they differ in the details of this man's life and his accomplishments? Make sure you find two contrasting sources. One might lean toward a Muslim interpretation whereas the other might be influenced by a Catholic view.

- Give a presentation to your class about the political atmosphere of eleventh-century Spain. How much control of Spain did the Moors have at that

time? When and how did their power collapse? How did Spain unite all the separate cultures and divided kingdoms?

- In his introduction to the play, John C. Lapp states that the concept of worthiness represents Corneille's "belief that the great-souled, the noble-hearted . . . are different from ordinary men. Their passion is more sublime, and makes almost impossible demands upon lovers." Can you think of any other play, movie, or work of fiction in which you might find another set of lovers in a similar situation and with the same "worthiness" that Corneille describes? If so, compare those lovers and the challenges they face and the conclusions they draw with the lovers in *Le Cid*.

---

Gomes lost his life. In order to protect her father's honor (and thus her own), Chimene insists that the man she loves, Rodrigue, must be killed.

During all this discussion of honor and the reactions in defense of it, it is interesting to note that the only modern act of honor in the play is the one in which Le Cid spares the life of Don Sanche. In modern times, a slap in the face might be humiliating but it is not worthy of a duel. A duel would be considered illegal. And a father might be sentenced to a jail term if he sends his son to kill a man who has merely insulted him. But when Don Sanche agrees to save Chimene's honor by challenging Le Cid to a duel; and Le Cid, in turn, does not take the life of Don Sanche, although he easily could have, then a true sense of honor, at least in reflection of modern mores, is practiced.

## *Love*

There are many different kinds of love displayed in the play. First there is the love of Rodrigue for his father. Rodrigue is willing to sacrifice his own love for Chimene in order to avenge his father. The love between Rodrigue and his father is strong

but it is not as deep as Rodrigue's love for Chimene. And yet Rodrigue is willing to lose Chimene in order to protect his father. This is because Rodrigue realizes that he has no choice. He knows he will lose Chimene no matter what he does. If he kills her father, his honor will be restored but Chimene will not be willing to marry him. If he doesn't kill her father, his honor will not be restored and Chimene will not be willing to marry him. Although Rodrigue loves his father, it is for his father's (and his own) honor that he faces Don Gomes. But it is for his love of Chimene that Rodrigue is willing to lose his own life. He feels there is no way out of his quandary and would rather die than live without Chimene. And he would rather die by her hand than any one else's. His love for Chimene is greater than his love of his own life, in other words.

Chimene also loves Rodrigue deeply. But despite her love, she would see Rodrigue dead in order to restore her father's honor. Her love for her father and her love for Rodrigue are closely linked to one another. She cannot chose which man she loves more. These are different kinds of love but both of them run deep.

Infanta also displays a love, one that she keeps all but secret. Only her lady-in-waiting knows that she loves Rodrigue. But Infanta is torn between her love of her role as a noble woman, a woman who cares very much about the welfare and stability of her kingdom, and her love of Rodrigue. If she exposes her love of Rodrigue she would be going against the rules of nobility, which declare that she must marry according to her social stature. She must marry someone who is in line to become a king. So she inspires and encourages the love between Chimene and Rodrigue. In this way, Chimene becomes Infanta's alter ego; and Infanta can love Rodrigue through Chimene.

## *Chivalry*

Chivalry is exemplified by Rodrigue. He displays his great skills as a soldier and a leader in battle in the defense of his land and protection of his king as well as his abilities as a chivalrous gentleman in his relations with Chimene. He has the brute strength and courage of a wartime hero but is equally strong enough within himself to expose his most intimate feelings toward this woman and be willing to sacrifice his life for her. Don Sanche is also chivalrous but in a much more diminutive form. He promises to defend Chimene's honor by challenging Le Cid to a duel, a duel that Don Sanche surely must have seen as one in which the odds were stacked against him.

It is interesting to note that although chivalry is a major theme in this play, there is the undercurrent of a debate going on. Chivalry is matched with the law and order of the court, as represented by the king. In one incident, that of Don Gomes disagreeing with the king about his choice of tutor for his son, the audience of this play watches a very distinct confrontation between chivalry of old with the unfolding new power of the court. Don Gomes is chastised for believing that he is more powerful than the king. Despite his many victories in battle (without which the kingdom may not have survived), Don Gomes is warned not to let the king hear his criticism. Whereas chivalry might have been more powerful in an earlier time, this play insinuates that the court of law is now the supreme authority. This is also demonstrated when Chimene must go to the king and beseech him to use the laws of the court to punish the man who has killed her father. The king, who recognizes the chivalry of Rodrigue in having protected his father's honor by killing Don Gomes, must find some way to reconcile the old customs of chivalry and the new laws of the king's rule.

# STYLE

## *The Three Unities*

The three unities, as they were called, influenced much of seventeenth-century French drama. This concept of the three unities was taken from Aristotle's *On the Art of Poetry*. But in truth, the way Aristotle's work was interpreted by neo-classic dramatists was faulty. The three unities, as interpreted by Jean Mairet (1604–1686), a dramatist of Corneille's time, stated that a drama should take place in one location only (unity of place); that the plot of events should unfold over the period of one day (unity of time); and that the focus of the play should be narrowed to the main events with no side plots developed (unity of action). Actually Aristotle only presented the unity of action and the unity of time as suggestions. Unity of place, he never mentioned. But the three unities, in Corneille's time, were considered mandatory in the construction of a drama. These unities of Aristotle's made plays rather predictable, and they confined the imaginations of dramatists. Although Corneille used the unities as a foundation, he stretched their boundaries.

Corneille, especially in his play *Le Cid*, was considered a bit of a renegade in the way he constructed this tragedy. In order to see how Corneille's play adheres to these rules of the Unities, one has to use an expansive imagination. For instance, in reference to place, one could possibly say that all the action took place within the general area around the center of the kingdom. When looked at more closely, which is what Richelieu did when he criticized Corneille for breaking the three Unities, audiences will notice that the play's scenes move from one house to another, one court to another. Corneille also stretched the time factor. He packed as many events into a day and a half as he could; and some critics have stated that there was no way humanly possible that everything could have happened during that time. For instance, poor Rodrigue must fight his intended father-in-law, confront his lover several times, travel to the seacoast, gather his military forces, plan an attack, surprise and defeat the Moors upon their landing, return to the kingdom, fight yet another challenger, console his lover once again, and face the king. If he accomplished all that in a day and a half, it is no wonder Le Cid was regarded as a medieval superhero.

Finally, there is the action. Although the main focus of the play is on Rodrigue and his relationship with Chimene, there is also the unfolding story of

Rodrigue and his father; Chimene and her father; the Moors and their threat to the kingdom; as well as Le Cid's heroic efforts to save the kingdom. On top of this there is the character of Infanta and her love of Rodrigue and the self-sacrifice and sense of duty that she must face. There is also the jealousy between old rivals and the demonstration of the power of the courts.

In his stretching of the three unities, Corneille presented his Parisian audiences with a more complex work, adding more depth to his characterizations of the legendary hero's tale. The workings of Corneille's imagination shone through the old form, opening it up to new possibilities. And for his efforts in reducing the confinements of the three unities, Corneille changed the face of dramatic presentation in France and is often credited as being the Father of French Tragedy.

### Contrast and Juxtaposition

With the construct of contrast and juxtaposition, a play's action alternates between different elements. At one point the audience is shown a point of view from one character's vision. At another, the opposing, or at least a contrasting, vision is exposed. This emphasizes the tension that creates dramatic effect, which is the reason that the audience wants to continue to be engaged in the play and find out what the final outcome will be or how the tension will be resolved. In *Le Cid* Corneille provides several different contrasting positions. The play begins in a neutral zone, with characters providing exposition, or narrative that offers the audience a foundation upon which the story of the play will rest. In this particular work, the tension begins to rise when Infanta announces not only her love but also her willingness to sacrifice that love for the sake of her kingdom. Then the contrasts between what characters need and want escalates as Don Diegue and Don Gomes conflict. Their disagreement provides the catalyst for the highest tension of this play, which is the juxtaposition of Chimene's need to honor her father and Rodrigue's need to honor his. More subtle contrasts include the old role of chivalry and battle as opposed to the new role of court rule as represented by the king.

Without conflict, the play would fall flat and the audience would become disinterested. Contrast pulls the audience into the play as they either try to figure out ahead of the action how to solve the problems or sit on the edge of their seats and watch as the characters themselves unfold the answers to all the questions that the play presents. Conflict is often the starting point for many writers as they begin to develop a work. Many writers are stimulated by a particular conflict, and they explore many possible solutions as the story progresses. Corneille, with his experience in Louis XIII's court, might have wondered how the old world of brave soldiers and military heroes would evolve under the new world order of a powerful king. *Le Cid* may have been the result of that question.

# HISTORICAL CONTEXT

### Eleventh-century Spain

From the eighth until the eleventh century, Muslims (or Moors as they were once called) controlled most of the Iberian Peninsula, which contains the present-day Spain, Portugal, and Andorra. The first Muslim leader, Abd-al-Rahman, settled his forces in Cordoba in southern Spain, and it was from this city that he and his descendents ruled for almost three hundred years. At the turn of the eleventh century, Cordoba had become one of the largest metropolitan areas in the Mediterranean. But as the eleventh century neared, the Iberian Peninsula was in no way united. Allegiance to the rulers in Cordoba deteriorated and then completely fell apart when the last leader in Cordoba died in 1036. At this time, small kingdoms (called *taifas*) declared their independence. Among the most significant of these *taifas* were Seville, Cordoba, Granada, Toledo, Lisbon, and Valencia.

In the meantime, Christian communities in northern Spain began to fight back against the Moors. In the eleventh century, as Muslim control of the peninsula began to deteriorate, Christian armies proved more successful than they had been in the past and eventually regained control of northern and central Spain. But when Christians were victorious in the city of Toledo, which marked their largest triumph, Muslims became very concerned and asked for reinforcements. Their requests were honored, and troops from northern Africa soon arrived on Iberian shores. In 1086, Muslims again controlled many of the kingdoms on the peninsula; however, they were not able to keep control. In 1094, El Cid, Spain's first legendary hero, recaptured the prominent kingdom of Valencia. Unfortunately for the Christians, upon El Cid's death in 1099, the Muslims once again took over Valencia.

# COMPARE & CONTRAST

- **Eleventh century:** The Muslim government in Spain is in a state of collapse. Small Christian kingdoms, some won through the efforts of El Cid, divide the land.

  **Seventeenth century:** Spain is united and almost entirely Christian as, over the years, non-Christians and Muslims were either persecuted, converted to Christianity, or forced to leave the country.

  **Today:** After many decades of a Franco dictatorship, Spain has a democratic constitution and is a member of the European Union.

- **Eleventh century:** The topic of drama, the costumes, and the actors are reflective of the laws of the Roman Catholic Church. Plays are usually performed by priests, and the subject matter is based on religious topics and church law.

  **Seventeenth century:** Neoclassic tragedies (in which nobility is involved and someone dies) and comedies (which revolved around the common person and domestic affairs) are the two most successful types of drama.

  **Today:** Experimentation influences much of contemporary drama, with theatre of the absurd on one end of the spectrum and social realism and dark comedy on the other.

- **Eleventh century:** The ruling monarchs are relatives of Hugh Capet (therefore the Capetian Dynasty) and include Robert II, Henry I, and Philip I. The French kingdom at this time rarely exceeded jurisdiction beyond Paris and Orleans but through the power of the Capetian kings, the foundation of France's nation-state is laid.

  **Seventeenth century:** The Bourbon Dynasty is in power and includes Henry IV, Louis XIII, and Louis XIV. But one of the real powers is Cardinal de Richelieu who diminishes the authority of the church and increases the authority of the king.

  **Today:** A constitution adopted in 1958 created the Fifth Republic of France. Today France is ruled by an elected president, an appointed senate, and an elected national assembly.

---

El Cid (also referred to as *El Campeador,* "the champion") was born Rodrigo Diaz de Vivar in 1043 in Vivar, Castile. He was of minor noble lineage on his father's side and part of the landed aristocracy on his mother's side. Raised at the court of Ferdinand I, he was a child with many privileges. At the age of twenty-two, under the rule of Sancho II, El Cid was appointed commander of the royal troops. In 1067, he was critically involved in the fall and annexation of the Morish kingdom of Zaragoza, thus signaling both his military and political prowess.

Sancho was not happy with the way the kingdom had been divided in his father's will. He began to wage war against his brother Alfonso, who ruled the other half of the land. El Cid, although he might have done so reluctantly, supported Sancho in these endeavors. When Sancho died in 1072, El Cid lost most of his political power. Some historians believe this caused El Cid to brood. And this brooding may have been the source of El Cid's attack on the Moorish kingdom of Toledo. El Cid was victorious, but since the kingdom of Toledo was under the protection of Alfonso, El Cid was exiled from all of Alfonso's lands.

It was during his exile that El Cid decided to help the Moors; and for ten years he served the leaders of the kingdom of Saragossa. His experiences with the Moors helped him to understand the Muslim world, something that would later assist him in his most victorious battle against the Muslims in Valencia.

When the wave of Muslim reinforcements from Northern Africa reached the shores of the peninsula and enjoyed a crushing victory over some of

Alfonso's territory, the Christian king swallowed his pride and requested that El Cid return to help him defeat the Muslims. After recapturing Valencia in 1094, El Cid made himself the chief magistrate of both the Muslims and the Christians who lived there.

El Cid died in Valencia in 1099; many years later, the epic poem *El Cantar de Mio Cid* (''The Song of Cid'') helped to popularize him as a legendary hero. Because of this, it has sometimes been difficult for historians to separate fact from fiction when it comes time to understanding and relating the events that made up the life of this powerful warrior.

### Seventeenth-century France

Louis XIII (1601–1643) became King of France at the age of nine, after the assassination of his father, King Henry IV. He was raised and counseled by his mother, Marie de Médicis, and Cardinal de Richelieu. Under Richelieu's influence, Louis XIII enjoyed a very authoritative rule. The king's word was to be followed by one and all. To ensure his own power, the young king had his mother exiled in 1617.

King Louis XIII was married in 1618 at the age of fourteen to an Austrian princess, Anne. One child was born to them twenty years later despite the fact that they rarely lived together. Some suggest that their son, who was to become Louis XIV, was not fathered by the king.

Although a very religious man, King Louis XIII believed in the right to commit murder, which he did. He was also a hypochondriac, almost always claiming to be sick. This did not stop him, however, from leading his army in battle. He was also bald and started the new fashion of wearing wigs.

King Louis XIII's son was only four years old when his father died. So the actual running of the country fell to his mother, Queen Anne.

Cardinal de Richelieu (1585–1642), Armand-Jean du Plessis, was the man who most influenced King Louis XIII and is still considered to be one of France's most notable politicians. Richelieu received his education (he began college at the age of nine) both at a military institution and a college of theology. At the early age of twenty-one, he was appointed bishop to a small, poor French diocese. Because of his outstanding abilities to organize and his devout religious beliefs, he was noticed by King Louis XIII's mother and brought to court. He was soon given the title of secretary of state of war and foreign affairs. In 1617, when Marie de Médicis was exiled from the Royal Court, Richelieu acted as liaison between the king and his mother. Five years later, much owed to the influence of Richelieu, King Louis XIII allowed his mother to return. After that, Marie pushed her son to award Richelieu with more power, which King Louis XIII did, giving Richelieu the title of chief minister of the royal court.

Richelieu lifted France to become a major European power. But this came at the expense of most of France's citizens. Richelieu's view of common citizens was that their role in society was strictly one of obedience to the king. This obedience involved everyone, including French artists. Richelieu believed that the king should control not only the military, financial, and social affairs of state but also the arts. Creative works without the approval of the king suffered public criticism and censorship.

Because of his political success, Richelieu is considered the founder of French Unity. He is credited with having taken France out of medieval times and making the country a powerful leader in the seventeenth-century world.

## CRITICAL OVERVIEW

When *Le Cid* was first produced in 1936, people in France recognized the name of its author but not his ability to write tragedies. Corneille was better known at that time for his comedies, which were only moderately successful. However, with the production of *Le Cid*, Corneille's reputation took a dramatic turn. It was, according to John C. Lapp, translator and author of an introduction to this play, ''a tremendous popular hit, combining all the elements calculated to please its aristocratic audience: the pangs of youthful love, heroic derring-do, tender lyricism and violent declamation.''

Corneille was a writer of ''exuberance of invention,'' writes Lapp. The success of this play, as well as much of criticism, was due in part to Corneille's departure from the accepted form of drama that was considered unbendable at the time— the unities of time, place, and action—classical rules based on what Lapp refers to as ''an erroneous interpretation of Aristotle's *Art of Poetry*.'' Instead, Corneille emphasized the ''feeling of *admiratio* or wonder he considered an essential element of tragedy,'' Lapp writes. Corneille wanted to keep the audience ''puzzling over what will happen next, or listening to the poetry.''

Despite Corneille's later successes, in which he continued his ''love of intricate situations, or surprise, of grandiose word and deed,'' Lapp writes, Corneille never again attained ''the high lyricism, the sheer youthful exuberance, the heights of exultation and depths of melancholy,'' as he did in *Le Cid*.

Today, *Le Cid* is still considered Corneille's best play. Although it has not been performed recently, an opera written by Jules Massenet in 1885 based on *Le Cid* continues to be performed internationally. The most recent production of the opera was held at the Kennedy Center in Washington, D.C., in 1999 and starred tenor Placido Domingo in the leading role.

# CRITICISM

## *Joyce Hart*

*Hart is a freelance writer and author of several books. In this essay, Hart studies the act of sacrifice as portrayed in Corneille's* Le Cid.

Pierre Corneille's *Le Cid* focuses on a legendary hero of eleventh-century Spain and his feats of heroism, chivalry, and honor. But a more pervading element of this play, one that is acted out by not only the protagonist but many other characters is that of sacrifice. A sense of sacrifice lies beneath the surface of many of the events of this play, whether it is portrayed through a deed of love, honor, or respect.

The first sacrifice, which is not the noblest of them all but rather one that sets off the motions of Corneille's play is the willingness of Don Diegue to forfeit the life of his son, Le Cid, in order to restore honor to the family name. Of course, if Don Rodrigue were to lose his duel with Don Gomes, the pain would be great for Don Diegue, but it is one thing to sacrifice another person's life and another to offer up one's own. So although this sacrifice is great, it lacks a noble edge. Don Diegue not only is offering up his son's life, he is doing so without there being a substantial reason behind his efforts. Yes, one's honor was of immense purpose in the past, but the consequences were relative only to a limited number of family members. And cost to that family could be measured maybe in a diminished livelihood but not in serious punishment. Don Diegue might have lost his honor if he had not potentially sacrificed his son, but he still could have gone on living and probably living well. So the significance

*El Cid*

of this sacrifice was not great in itself except for the fact that because of it, the rest of the actions of the play fall into place.

Don Gomes is the next victim of sacrifice, and his sacrifice was much greater. He lost his life. The reasons for losing his life were not insignificant but they were rather trivial. Could he have refused to fight Don Rodrigue? Probably. One of the main reasons he gave in was because Don Gomes thought the whole thing was a joke. Who was this young man who dared to challenge the great warrior? Don Gomes thought he could wipe Don Rodrigue out as easily as swatting a fly. And the consequences for his actions would not have mattered much. If he killed Don Rodrigue, Don Diegue would have mourned the loss of his son, and Don Gomes's daughter, Chimene, would have mourned the loss of her lover. And that would have been it. The kingdom would have hypothetically gone on as before. But that is not how events unfolded. As it turned out, the duel was very significant because Don Gomes sacrificed (albeit unknowingly) his life and therefore greatly affected the kingdom.

Because of Don Gomes's sacrifice, Don Diegue's honor was restored, the love between Don Rodrigue and Chimene was compromised, and the whole legend of Le Cid was born. If Don Rodrigue

# WHAT DO I READ NEXT?

- If you want to read the original text of the poem of the legend of El Cid, *The Poem of the Cid* (1985), by Ian Michael, Rita Hamilton, and Janet Perry, is a good place to go. This is a bilingual publication in ancient Spanish and easy-to-read English.

- Molière was a playwright contemporary with Corneille. He wrote what was called high comedy through which he criticized the social standards of his time. In his play *La Tartuffe* (1664), Molière examines the religious hypocrisy of his society. This was a very controversial play in seventeenth-century France.

- Although Molière would later top Corneille's prowess as a writer of comedy, Corneille's comic play *Le Menteur (The Liar)*, produced in 1643, is considered his best in this genre. This comedy

also has Spanish roots. It is a comedy of manners about on an eligible bachelor who tries to lie his way out of a match his father has arranged with a woman he does not love.

- In 1640, four years after *Le Cid,* Corneille wrote what is considered another masterpiece, *Horace* (1640). This play is also a tragedy. It is about patriotism and the conflict between families during a war between the ancient Romans and their Alban neighbors.

- Jean Racine, another contemporary of Corneille, wrote a very impressive tragedy called *Phèdre* (1677). The characters of this play are taken from Greek mythology. It is about a woman who falls in love with her stepson. It is considered one of Racine's best works.

---

had not killed Don Gomes, he would not have gone off and stopped the Moors from coming ashore in the kingdom in an attempt to take over the land. He would not have been renamed Le Cid. Don Rodrigue might not have been ready for such a remarkable feat as that. He was propelled, one could argue, because of Don Gomes's death to prove that he was a fearless warrior even greater than the warrior that he defeated in the duel. As Don Rodrigue outdid the older warrior in a one-on-one fight, so too would he outshine him on the battlefield. And he did.

But in killing Don Gomes, Don Rodrigue sacrifices the chances of winning Chimene as his wife. He relinquishes his deep love for her not in fact but in theory. His love for her remains in his heart, but because of what he has done, his love may never be returned. He goes into the duel with Don Gomes knowing this but also knowing that there was no way to avoid the consequences. Because of his father's and Don Gomes's argument and brief assault, Don Rodrigue stood to lose Chimene no matter what he did. And then to underscore the breadth of the price he must pay, Don Rodrigue

offers his life—the ultimate sacrifice. What better way could Corneille have demonstrated how much Don Rodrigue loved Chimene? It is as if Don Rodrigue was saying that if he could not have Chimene there was no reason to go on living. He offered her his life so that she could find peace with her father's death.

When Chimene is not willing to kill him, Don Rodrigue volunteers to go fight the Moors. Against all odds, he is victorious in leading his men against the enemies of the kingdom. When he returns a hero, Le Cid's offer to Chimene to take his life has taken on even greater meaning because he is now not just a young man who has killed one brave soldier, he is a young champion who has saved his country. In some metaphoric way, he is not only sacrificing his life but the lives of all those whom he has saved.

Chimene, too, although not quite as chivalrous, offers an enormous sacrifice. She is a dutiful and loving daughter. Her father, a noble knight, has experienced a rather shameful death. He has not died on the battlefield, defending his king. Rather he has been killed in a common field by a young, untried nobody, the outcome of a petty argument. Chimene believes that her father's long years of battles won and the resultant honors that were bestowed on him will all be lost if his death is not avenged. And she is willing, though her heart is breaking, to sacrifice not her love but the life of the man she loves in order to protect her father's name and heritage. Chimene's sacrifice is noble because she does not, or cannot, rid herself of her love for Le Cid. That love is real and cannot be dismissed through a rational decision. She demands Le Cid's life in spite of her love for him. And that is what makes her sacrifice so momentous. She cannot measure her love for Le Cid against her love for her father. Both are weighty. But they come from different parts of her and must be dealt with in different ways. Of course, she does not really want Le Cid's death, but she feels compelled to ask for it because of her love for her father. If she does not respect her love of her father than how can Le Cid respect her love for him?

And then there is Infanta. Here is a woman who has a profound love for a man she cannot have. She cannot have him not because their love would be impossible but because their love would defame the unspoken laws of nobility. Infanta is in love with Le Cid. She was in love with him before his heroism, when he was merely a young and handsome man, the son of a once-brave warrior. But she is a princess, and the love between her and a commoner would show disrespect for her nobility. The kingdom would suffer because of it. So Infanta sacrifices her love for Le Cid by purposefully and actively making Chimene fall in love with him. If Infanta can make Chimene love Le Cid and see that the two of them are married, Infanta will lose all hope of marrying Le Cid herself. With this loss of hope, she believes that she will better be able to endure the loss of her love. Infanta makes this sacrifice of herself for the king as well as for the stability of her kingdom. She will, as all young princesses do, marry a man of high rank.

Even after Le Cid becomes a hero, meriting another look at his eligibility as the husband of a princess, Infanta resists. Not only does she resist, she goes to Chimene and asks Chimene to sacrifice her pride and her filial duty to avenge her father. Chimene must make this sacrifice, Infanta tells her, to save the country from ruin. The people need a hero, Infanta tells her, and Chimene must cease her bid to see Le Cid's death.

> " WHEN HE RETURNS A HERO, LE CID'S OFFER TO CHIMENE TO TAKE HIS LIFE HAS TAKEN ON EVEN GREATER MEANING BECAUSE HE IS NOW NOT JUST A YOUNG MAN WHO HAS KILLED ONE BRAVE SOLDIER, HE IS A YOUNG CHAMPION WHO HAS SAVED HIS COUNTRY."

There is one more sacrificial act performed in the play. It is a small one but not immeasurable. Don Sanche promises to play out Chimene's wishes of avenging her father's death. Don Sanche is in love with Chimene, and he hopes this will win her hand. He challenges Le Cid to a duel. Don Sanche is no match for Le Cid either in love or in battle. But he is willing to sacrifice his life, or to at least potentially do so, in order to raise his stature in Chimene's eyes. It is in some ways a silly gesture, but one that must be done. Le Cid easily offsets Don Sanche's advances and in doing so, demonstrates his own high status as a righteous young man. He knows he is a far better warrior than Don Sanche, but he does not have to kill him to prove it. The fact that Don Sanche was willing to sacrifice his life is enough. It is as if Le Cid is saying that there have been enough sacrifices for one day. He sends Don Sanche back to Chimene, who mistakes the outcome and declares her everlasting love for Le Cid. So Don Sanche's ordeal produces the required effects without his having to shed his blood.

It is through these various acts of sacrifice that Corneille not only sets up the tension and dramatic impressions of this play but also adds complexities to his characters. The willingness to sacrifice marks a character as a person with a greater understanding of the truly noble qualities of life.

**Source:** Joyce Hart, Critical Essay on *Le Cid,* in *Drama for Students,* Thomson Gale, 2005.

## John Trethewey

*In the following essay, Trethewey examines Corneille's reasons for changing the first scene and*

*Chimene's final speech in the post-1660 version of* Le Cid.

From Act II, scene 8 of *Le Cid* (post-1660 version), Chimène plays, to the Court and public of Castile, the role of seeker after justice or would-be avenger of her father's death, a role which ends only in Act V, scene 5 when her true feelings towards her 'enemy' Rodrigue are revealed to all in a manner which makes further attempted concealment or denial of them futile. That role is one which is imposed on her, not only by Spanish manners (as conceived by Corneille), but also, I would suggest, by the conventions of French classical theatre. I would then like to go further and side with those who see this play, in its later versions, as a true tragedy, and not one which ends with the envisaged marriage of Chimène and Rodrigue as a virtual certainty. I would argue that, this role of public enmity finished, the heroine must needs continue, not only as a result of the killing of her father, but also because of the treatment she has received in reaction to her dissembling, to resist to the end, and beyond, the marriage that the King would impose on her.

Let us start with one line, spoken by Chimène, in Act V, scene 1—line 1556 of the 1682 version of *Le Cid:*

Sors vainqueur d'un combat dont Chimène est le prix.

The immediate context is Chimène's second private interview with her lover-enemy Rodrigue, in which she finds herself obliged to persuade him to defend himself against her chosen champion, Don Sanche, instead of using the projected combat as a way of committing suicide. Her attempts at persuasion in this scene are increasingly both desperate and ingenious, since not only must she oppose his frequently expressed desire for death by her agency, but she must also persuade him by using arguments of a kind that will not shock public opinion, and will not offend the code of honour, or spoil their chances of remaining striking examples to posterity of constancy in both love and conflict.

Failing at first to shake his resolution, Chimène resorts to two linked arguments which she combines in her final speech—arguments which betray, more than anything she has said previously, what could be interpreted as personal preference. First, Rodrigue must fight in order to save her from becoming the prize of Don Sanche, 'l'objet de mon aversion' (l. 1552). Secondly, following logically from this, comes the injunction quoted above to fight to gain *her,*

since the King's decree delivered in Act IV, scene 5 has dictated that, whoever the victor, 'même prix est acquis à sa peine' (l. 1457).

The line which follows in Act V, scene 1— Chimène's last in the act—is her reaction to the line she has just spoken, a confession of her shame at having uttered it:

Adieu: ce mot lâché me fait rougir de honte
(l. 1557)

There is ambiguity here. Does 'ce mot' refer to the whole of the previous line? Or is it that line's final word *prix* which is her shame? It was the King's word in Act IV, scene 5 (l. 1457), and in now pronouncing it, she emphasizes it, giving it in effect the value of a quotation, in order to express her disgust. Her injunction is in fact a reminder to Rodrigue of the Kings decree—to which, however, Chimène herself *did not* acquiesce. And she now distances herself from a possible charge of doing so by referring to that decree, and to herself in the third person, so that there is no suggestion of her having assented to Don Fernand's callous command.

The whole utterance is a matter of shame to her. It conjures up a complex mesh of emotions. Various reasons no doubt occur to the audience as well as to Rodrigue for the shame that she admits to feeling. She is outraged at having been made a prize in a contest. She possibly fears at this moment that she may have promised too much and thus endangered her good reputation. More significantly, she sees herself as having betrayed family honour: the Comte's death will never now be avenged if her words have their intended inspirational effect. And then, finally, it is the shame of a reluctant dissembler who is deceiving her lover with a piece of casuistry, knowing that his desire for her will, at least temporarily, distort his judgment and delude him into thinking that she accepts the royal decision as final and binding on her. She is deceiving him for his own immediate good, certainly, but it *is* deception, and she has no intention of giving in for the sake of his (let alone her own) ultimate happiness, as her later eight-line speech to Elvire most vigorously confirms, including as it does the promise:

. . .quoi qu'à sa victoire un monarque ait promis
Mon honneur lui fera mille autres ennemis
(v. 4. 1683–84)

That Rodrigue has indeed been taken in by her deception is clear from his brief soliloquy at the end of Act V, scene 1: the hand of Chimène is to him 'un espoir si doux' (l. 1563) for which he will gladly fight not just Don Sanche, but all the assembled 'vaillants' of Spain. Rodrigue's reaction is virtually a reprise of that which must have followed the speech of encouragement from his father at the end of Act III, scene 6, when the actor playing him, having no words to utter, must demonstrate by gesture and facial expression the passage from despair to hope and resolve.

Admittedly, there are many commentators who would reject the allegation that Chimène is here deliberately deceiving Rodrigue. There are those, for instance, who regard this line as the beginning of the dénouement, leading inevitably to marriage in a year's time as decreed by the King. My view is that she is here using a form of words which she knows will be enough, temporarily, to motivate Rodrigue to live and to win. I propose to demonstrate moreover that, as good classical practice would dictate, the dissembling on her part, which here takes place, has been prepared for in the exposition, and has subsequently been an essential part of her behaviour.

*Le Cid,* at first a tragi-comedy, became a tragedy with the 1648 edition, but it was only from 1660 that Corneille introduced a modified first scene which, in my view, despite the lightness of its tone, is an improvement—fitting perhaps for the original genre as well as the new one. The opening scene of editions from 1637–56 treated audiences to a conversation between Chimène's father Don Gomès, Comte de Gormas, and Elvire, her *suivante.* In it the latter reported the girl's dutiful indifference towards her two rival suitors. Mitchell Greenberg has persuasively suggested that the absence of Chimène from the stage in this first scene leaves us with an impression of her as one who 'does not exist as a desiring subject' since Elvire 'presents her as an indifferent object of her suitor's demands'. But there are other problems with this scene. The Comte tells Elvire that he is pleased with Chimène's indifference, and that he himself prefers Rodrigue as his prospective son-in-law. But then (in lines which were eliminated in 1660) he orders her to return to her mistress:

Va l'en entretenir, mais dans cet entretien
Cache mon sentiment et découvre le sien.
Je veux qu'à mon retour nous en parlions ensemble.
(*ed. cit.,* III, p. 107, note 3)

Obviously, Corneille had decided by 1660 that this speech signalled to an audience experienced in classical conventions a plot development in the form of an encounter which was simply not going to take place. It was not clear with whom (Elvire or Chimène) Don Gomès proposed to have his discussion on his return, and in any case he was never

> IN CORNEILLE'S FINAL VERSION, NEITHER MEDIEVAL CUSTOM NOR ROYAL ABSOLUTISM WILL MARRY OFF THIS COUPLE. THE KING, MOST DECIDEDLY, DOES NOT HAVE CHIMÈNE IN HIS GIFT."

again to meet either of them, in this or in any later version of the play. From 1660 onwards, therefore, Elvire, now promoted to *gouvernante,* opens the exposition, reporting her conversation with the Comte to Chimène but omitting any reference to a planned future meeting.

Elvire has, she tells her charge, deliberately deceived the Comte by painting a picture of an indifferent and submissive Chimène (l. 17). She quotes *verbatim* the Comte's pleased reaction which he himself spoke directly to us in the first version. To Greenberg, 'this change, it would seem, empties it of much of its dramatic force', and he quotes Corneille himself to support his suggestion: 'ce qu'on expose à la vue touche bien plus que ce qu'on n'apprend que par un récit'. But Elvire's *récit,* and the rest of her conversation with Chimène, besides converting the girl most decidedly into a 'desiring subject', allow Corneille to add an ingredient to the scene which gives it a *new* dramatic force.

It was impossible for the 1637 Elvire to convey to the audience the fact that her words to the Comte were a deliberate deception. Now however she can tell Chimène:

j'ai *peint* votre coeur dans une indifférence. . .
(l. 17, my italics)

The latter, delighted with developments, has nothing to say against this deception, as if it should be taken for granted—by women at any rate—that fathers have, on occasion, to be treated thus by female members of their household. We also learn that Rodrigue and Don Sanche have both been courting her *in secret* (13–14). Plainly the mask of indifference (if not the secrecy) must now continue so that the Comte, flattered by Elvire's depiction of a dutiful daughter, will remain without suspicion of any wilfulness or unfeminine independence of thought on her part. Elvire concludes her *récit*

(17–52) with a line from Don Gomès which must now, quoted by her, sound sublimely condescending:

> . . .ma fille, en un mot, peut l'aimer et me plaire.
> (l. 38)

Reported mockingly by the *gouvernante,* it must have an almost comic tone which the two women must make evident to the audience, since it helps to justify the gentle deception they are practising. The hint of a possible plot development in the first version of the scene has therefore been replaced in the second by a different suggestion recalling Corneille's early comedies, involving a lighthearted conspiracy which, while it might be regarded as implicit in the earliest version, was not verbally hinted at there. It soon becomes clear, also, that Chimène and Elvire are not alone in this conspiracy, for the Infante's complicity in bringing the two young people together is revealed in the next scene. Without her, and her anguished search for a means to thwart her unworthy passion, the Comte, it would seem, would have had nobody but Don Sanche to consider for the hand of his daughter.

From that slight but necessary preparation in these two scenes the horrors of the quarrel, the insult, the duel, and the death all quickly grow. But from the lighthearted revelation of dissembling in the play's opening lines comes our recognition of Chimène's ability and readiness to deceive, a readiness which women, of whatever rank, must develop in the male-dominated, warrior society depicted in this play. There is a *necessity* to deceive too, since just as she had been ready to feign dutiful indifference regarding suitors, and unquestioning obedience towards her father, it now logically follows that she must (however reluctantly in her own mind) give the impression of a similar obedience to the dictates of honour and family duty.

Her new deception begins in earnest in Act II, scene 8 when, her father dead, she must conceal her confusion and put on a mask of indignation and intransigence in front of the King and his court. Don Fernand, as a would-be absolute monarch, must also wear a mask—in his case, of infallibility. The problems in relation to Chimène that he creates for himself as a consequence of this policy begin in this scene which involves the plea made by Rodrigue's father Don Diègue, as well as that of the bereaved daughter. Her display of rhetoric is impressive but not faultless, and it is at a moment of temporary breakdown in her speech (669–70) that the King intervenes to offer words of comfort for her loss:

> Prends courage, ma fille, et sache qu'aujourd'hui

> Ton roi te veut servir de père au lieu de lui.
> (ll. 671–72)

This protective gesture is to be expected of him as a medieval monarch, but on this occasion there is more to it than feudal custom and courtesy. He sees trouble and difficult decisions ahead of him (he has, as we know, Moorish problems as well as domestic ones), and wishes to control and thereby neutralize Chimène. Nevertheless, a judgment will eventually be expected of him, both by the girl and by Don Diègue, and so, with business elsewhere in mind, he promises his petitioners that he will have the case considered 'en plein conseil' (l. 734), and at the end of the scene makes them the rash pledge: 'Je vous ferai justice' (l. 737), a pledge which circumstances prevent him from fulfilling.

Chimène is driven in her tirades of Act II, scene 8 by an understanding of what society expects of a nobleman's daughter. It colours her rhetoric and leads her to reinforce her plea with appeals to the King's own self-interest. Her real, more complex feelings are as yet unknown to anyone present. Only the theatre audience is aware of the tensions underlying her performance, having heard in Act II, scene 3 her clearsighted résumé, delivered to the Infante, of the situation, and of the dilemma in which she and Rodrigue would find themselves if a duel took place. Chimène is undoubtedly dissembling here before the King, her performance contrasting starkly, despite the logical connection between the two, with the light-hearted game at the Comte's expense that was revealed to us in Act I, scene 1. There, hope and eager anticipation, it was suggested, had to be hidden behind a façade of demure indifference. Here, on the contrary, despair and bitter regret must be masked by a show of passionate commitment. What the two performances have (or will have) in common, however, is the understanding and approval of Rodrigue. He has played two similar roles (suitor and avenger), but in his case they have ended once the Comte is dead, whereas Chimène must go on dissembling, at least in public, almost up to the end of the play.

After the death of the Comte, among those characters who are aware of Chimène's real feelings is, as we know, the Infante who is still (as always) in the girl's confidence in Act IV, scene 2 when news of Rodrigue's victory over the Moors has come through without, for Chimène, one essential detail: the consequent state of his health. It is the Infante who, with a clearsightedness and consideration greater than her father's, points out to Chimène what the consequences of the victory (coming on top of the death of the Comte) are likely to be for her. Her plea for justice, the Infante warns, will no longer carry the same weight as on the previous day:

> Ce qui fut juste alors ne l'est plus aujourd'hui.
> Rodrigue maintenant est notre unique appui,
> L'espérance et l'amour d'un peuple qui l'adore,
> Le soutien de Castille, et la terreur du More.
> Le Roi même est d'accord de cette vérité
> Que ton père en lui seul se voit ressuscité;
> Et si tu veux enfin qu'en deux mots je m'explique,
> Tu poursuis en sa mort la ruine publique
> (ll. 1175–82)

She then adds a suggestion which, with other hints dropped here and there in the play, has caused certain commentators to see her ironically as still beguiled by secret hopes for her own possible union with Rodrigue:

> Ce n'est pas qu'après tout tu doives, épouser
> Celui qu'un père mort t'obligeait d'accuser:
> Je te voudrais moi-même en arracher l'envie;
> Ote-lui ton amour, mais laisse-nous sa vie.
> (ll. 1187–90)

Those secret thoughts could quite possibly be there below the surface, and could be betrayed to an audience while remaining concealed from Chimène. But what is openly present in this speech is a lucid appraisal ('l'objectivité de la jalousie', Jacques Maurens calls it) of the new political situation and of Rodrigue's importance to the state. He is '*notre unique appui*'; loss of him would lead to 'la ruine *publique*'. Therefore, 'laisse-*nous* sa vie'. As a diplomat, she is more astute than her father who, on learning of the death of the Comte, said 'sa perte *m*'affaiblit' (l. 646), emphasizing his own personal loss rather than the kingdom's. At the same time, one can also claim that her proposed solution to Chimène's dilemma is one of the possible outcomes of the year's grace conceded by the King in Act V, scene 7. The dénouement may ultimately be *that* compromise just as plausibly as it may be either the continued complete intransigence of Chimène or the prospect of the (happy?) couple's final union. Chimène's immediate reaction to the Infante's proposal is spirited rejection in favour of implacable pursuit (ll. 1191–96), but her attitude in the play's last scene is somewhat different, as we shall see.

First, however, we must look again at the circumstances inspiring the line quoted at the beginning of this article. The King, on hearing (in Act IV, scene 3) of the victory against the Moors, decides there and then that Rodrigue must be pardoned for killing the Comte:

> Crois que dorénavant Chimène a beau parler,
> Je ne l'écoute plus que pour la consoler.

(ll. 1255–56)

One can perhaps, under the circumstances, sympathize with this decision which unites a natural enthusiasm for the impressive new champion with consideration for national security. But one cannot feel the same about his way subsequently of handling the Chimène problem, for when, in Act IV, scene 5, she appears before him once again to demand justice, instead of satisfaction (or even the proposed consolation), she gets cruel deception of the sort other judges (and other dramatists) mete out usually as punishment, when she is told that Rodrigue is dead (l. 1340). This trick, meant to wreck her performance, to reveal her love to all the court and thereby silence her demand, is only a partial success: despite fainting, despite her state of shock and confusion, she makes no verbal confession. Inevitably, her pride is injured by such treatment, and her indignation manifests itself in a renewed, even more energetic intransigence incorporating accusations of 'la justice étouffée' and of 'le mépris des lois' (ll. 1381, 1383), words which are a defiance of this absolute monarch, who (being a character in a performance) must visibly react by showing embarrassment if not displeasure. It leads directly to her demand for vengeance by recourse to a 'combat judiciaire'—perfectly logical under the circumstances as she sees them, where 'justice' is denied her, and given the trick just played on her:

> Puisque vous refusez la justice à mes larmes,
> Sire, permettez-moi de recourir aux armes. [. . .]
> A tous vos cavaliers je demande sa tête:
> Oui, qu'un d'eux me l'apporte, et je suis sa conquête;
> Qu'ils le combattent, Sire; et le combat fini,
> J'épouse le vainqueur, si Rodrigue est puni.
> (ll. 1397–98, 1401–04)

Thus does Chimène try to make Don Fernand pay for his thoughtless, unfatherly trick. But while he is now obliged to bend his absolutist principles to sanction officially this 'abus', as he calls it (l. 1409), he has other tricks up his royal sleeve. As a form of damage-limitation, in order to reassert his authority, and also to protect Rodrigue and further the scheme of uniting the pair, he first reduces the number of her champions to one, and then—after she has chosen the eager Don Sanche—makes her the prize whoever wins. The interests of Rodrigue may seem to be advanced thereby, but hardly in the heart of Chimène, who now suffers from the accumulated effects of what amounts to two clumsy royal insults, which must strengthen even more her determination to resist her feelings in his favour. It is hard therefore to *accept* that very shortly afterwards (Act V, scene 1) she would, in the line already considered, sincerely and wholeheartedly promise herself to Rodrigue.

At the dénouement, there seems to be general agreement in the court that enough is enough, that these two lovers must now be united. Don Fernand, addressing Chimène, asserts *ex cathedra*:

Ta gloire est dégagée, et ton devoir est quitte.
(l.1766)

and commands her to marry. The Infante, with a ceremonial gesture, the secret significance of which is known only to Léonor and the audience, supports her father by 'giving' Rodrigue to Chimène (ll. 1773–74). Even Don Sanche has bravely taken part in the conspiracy:

J'aime encor ma défaite,
Qui fait le beau succès d'une amour si parfaite.
(ll. 1761–62)

Only the principals fail to fall into line. It is the first time in the play that they have met in public. One could say that the only real concession they make, under these circumstances which the court regards as changed, is to consent to speak to one another. At the risk of offending the King, a possibility of which Rodrigue is well aware, he tells Chimène that she is in no danger of being claimed by him as his 'prize':

. . .Mon amour n'emploiera point pour moi
Ni la loi du combat, ni le vouloir du Roi.
(ll. 1779–80)

And as before, he offers to submit himself to her for summary execution, or to fight the champions recruited by her, no matter how numerous they turn out to be, seemingly to the end of time:

Faut-il combattre encor mille et mille rivaux,
Aux deux bouts de la terre étendre mes travaux,
Des héros fabuleux passer la renommée?
(ll. 1783–86)

The prospect of posthumous fame, or of a mythological hero's mortality (already envisaged in Act V, scene 1), makes the identity of his imagined foes somewhat vague, since although he sees himself fighting 'rivaux', his speech implies attack more than defence. Are they her champions, or are they just undefined enemies of Castile?

Her direct address to him is brief but significant: 'Relève-toi, Rodrigue' (l. 1801). Those words are a public sign that her pursuit of him is at an end (the Infante's Act IV, scene 2 analysis had something to be said for it). The court and the (Castilian) public may also hope for a marriage and a happy ending from two lines that follow, addressed to Don Fernand:

Rodrigue a des vertus que je ne puis haïr;
Et quand un roi commande, on lui doit obéir
(ll. 1803–04)

The remainder of her speech, however, offers very little hope indeed. It is a speech meant as much for Rodrigue's ears as for Don Fernand's. To her, the King's decree is a condemnation (l. 1805), it lays her open to a 'reproche éternel' (ll. 1811). And even if she should feel compelled to obey the King and agree to marry, there is no possibility (and she knows it) that Rodrigue, hearing and understanding her objections, will insist on claiming her for his bride.

Of all the myriad commentators, Octave Nadal has been one of the most clearsighted about this play's ending. The love of Rodrigue and Chimène for each other is plain for all to see and will endure all their lives, but nothing, 'ni vaillance, ni ordre royal, ni durée, ni miracle au monde—et pas même celui de l'amour' can take away from this daughter the sense of guilt that would eternally torment her if she married her father's killer. Georges Forestier holds a similar view, and has more recently been at pains to underline that, post-1648, '*Le Cid* est aux yeux du poète une *tragédie*', and he goes on to cite Corneille's view on the proper matter of the genre: 'il y a tragédie pour peu que deux amants soient déchirés par des "passions plus nobles et plus mâles que l'amour" et qui entrent en conflit avec celui-ci'. Both Chimène and Rodrigue understand the impossibility of any foreseeable resolution, even if the King, Don Diègue and the others do not. Chimène's line addressed to Rodrigue at the end of Act V, scene 1 was her last, but undoubtedly supreme, moment of dissembling. Further deception becomes impossible—and superfluous—after fate has intervened to deceive *her* in Act V, scene 5 and bring about the compromise (and the dénouement) proposed by the Infante. But not for a moment does she ever deceive herself. Her perpetual 'sentiment obscur de culpabilité' is not a feature of the Spanish versions of the legend which are more in keeping with medieval customs and thought processes, and which can make it Rodrigue's duty to marry Chimène for having killed her previous legal protector, her father. In Corneille's final version, neither medieval custom nor royal absolutism will marry off this couple. The King, most decidedly, does not have Chimène in his gift.

That is not to say that Chimène will never marry Rodrigue. It is simply that, at the end of this play, there is no sign of Chimène bowing to the King's *diktat* of line 1815, or of the young man so betraying his ideals and his love as to accept her as his 'salaire' (Chimène's word, line 1810). A year's grace might *possibly* change matters, but it would be useless—counterproductive even—for those present to look for the slightest signs of that change after only twenty-four hours.

**Source:** John Trethewey, ''Chimene's Dissembling and Its Consequences,'' in *Romance Studies,* Vol. 17, No. 2, December 1999, pp. 105–14.

## Helen L. Harrison

*In the following essay, Harrison explores the theme of royal gratitude—a king's bestowing of rewards for services rendered—in* Le Cid *and how this theme culminates in the final scene of the play.*

When the Académie Française delivered its judgment on *Le Cid,* Don Fernand's support for the marriage of Rodrigue and Chimène met with condemnation. The Academicians ruled that a marriage between a woman and her father's killer would have been immoral. At the same time, the Académie criticized the Castillean king as an abusive tyrant who lightly gave away property—namely Chimène herself—which did not belong to him. By questioning the appropriateness of the king's gift to Rodrigue, the Académie directs our attention to the problem of royal gratitude.

For a seventeenth-century audience, a king who has received extraordinary services from a subject is in a delicate position. The monarch's own interests dictate that he reward such services. In so doing, he practices the liberality expected of all nobles. He inspires his subjects to work and to fight for him. On the other hand, service to the crown must remain a duty, not a venture motivated by self-interest alone. A king must never allow those beneath him to view his gifts merely as their due. Should reward and recognition become obvious payment, the bond between a king and his subjects would become a contractual one rather than a divinely ordained relationship. While a noble who has received a favor from a peer finds himself in the uncomfortable and inferior position of being *obligé,* no subject can gain such an advantage over a monarch. The final scene of *Le Cid* is the culmination of a series of tests having to do with royal gratitude in this play. Not only the major characters but also the members of Corneille's public reveal their attitude toward monarchy as they assess the king's gifts and his method of bestowing them.

The first discussion of royal gratitude privileges deferred rewards over immediate payment for services. As Don Diègue and the Comte leave the royal council, they disagree as to whether the king has been just in making Don Diègue tutor to the prince:

> Don Diègue
> Cette marque d'honneur qu'il met dans ma famille
> Montre à tous qu'il est juste, et fait connaître assez
> Qu'il sait récompenser les services passés.
> Le Comte
> Pour grands que soient les Rois, il sont ce que nous sommes
> Ils peuvent se tromper comme les autres hommes,
> Et ce choix sert de preuve à tous les Courtisans
> Qu'ils savent mal payer les services présents.
> (I.iv.148–54)

The two warriors share the assumption that services to the sovereign should receive compensation. The parallelism of verses 150 and 154 could be read as symptomatic of similar attitudes toward the relations between subject and monarch. On closer examination, however, these verses already reveal different stances toward the king and toward gratitude. The conflict between the two men is not simply a matter of whether or not the king has made a good decision, but a question of how all such decisions should be interpreted and of who has the right to judge the monarch.

For Diègue, the king's decision results from royal justice. Don Fernand has remembered the deeds of his old champion and has decided to reward them. The verb used by Don Diègue for the monarch's action is ''récompenser,'' which means, etymologically, to reestablish a balance, to weigh one thing with another (Wartburg, *recompensare*). Finding an appropriate recompense thus entails exercising judgment. The giver rather than the receiver decides in this context what the reward should be. In praising his monarch's decision, Don Diègue depicts the king as a unique being who displays his virtue to a global and undifferentiated audience, ''tous.''

The Comte, in contrast, places the king on the same level with his nobles by destroying this uniqueness. He speaks not of ''le roi'' but of ''les rois.'' Monarchs become one class of beings who must prove themselves to another, potentially adversarial group, ''les Courtisans.'' Rather than seeing the political structure in terms of king and subjects, the current champion of Castille posits kings who need the goodwill of their vassals. In saying that kings ''savent mal payer les services présents,'' the Comte makes his sovereign little more than the employer of mercenary troops. His complaint hints that Fernand's poor example might discourage other nobles from serving him well. Nothing in his speech glosses over

*Great Mosque of Cordoba, Spain*

the immediate exchange which Chimène's father expects between the king and those who protect his realm.

The choice between Don Diègue and the Comte has thus served to expose differing views of kings and to make plain the sovereign's determination to place himself outside the bonds of obligation which would govern him were he only the first among equals. The king eschews using the coveted appointment for the purpose of retaining the military support he currently needs. He rewards good servants, but he does so in his own time and his own way. By selecting Diègue rather than Gomès, Don Fernand shows that temporal distance does not diminish the value of works which support the monarchy. The lapse of time between the older man's service and this particular reward obfuscates any resemblance which the appointment has to mercenary payment and also makes the example of royal gratitude more striking than a favor bestowed on Chimène's father would be. If pride and interest did not blind Don Gomès, he could read in the king's decision the message that the sovereign would remember and consider distinguished military service even after a warrior had lost his strength.

The ability to transcend the present and to remain above temporal constraints is a distinguish-

ing feature of royal gratitude, and it is a feature which recalcitrant nobles such as the Comte cannot accept. As Chimène's father rages over the preference accorded past rather than present services, he reveals that his allegiance lies chiefly with the old, feudal order rather than with the absolutist regime which Don Fernand strives to create. Several critics have remarked upon the conflict between Gomès and Diègue as a tension between these two conceptions of society, but it is necessary to emphasize that the transition from feudalism to absolutism is underway before the play begins. Even Don Gomès has a foot in both camps. Hence he accepts, as does Don Diègue, a second defining feature of royal gratitude, namely that the reward for services to the crown should be an opportunity to perform more services. The two men want to teach the prince. Both the past and present champion sense that their prestige and identity depend upon the sovereign's favor.

The two great nobles want the king's *reconnaissance* in both senses of the word. Gratitude for their services constitutes recognition of their identities. The chance to serve as the prince's tutor can confirm the king's belief in a warrior's valor and merit. Such an expression of gratitude would demonstrate that the king and all his realm see Gomès as he wishes to be seen, as the incomparable champion of Castille. Hence the sharpness of the barb when Don Diègue, after a speech which at first seems conciliatory, adds ''Un Monarque entre nous met de la différence'' (I.iv.208). Gomès is enough of a modern courtier to feel that his worth has been denied if the king does not recognize him, yet not enough of a courtier to see that he must accept the sovereign's choices without murmuring. The apparent slight to his honor corrodes the Comte's allegiance to the new order, just as it saps his goodwill and admiration toward Diègue and his son.

As the initial dispute over the king's gratitude separates the adherents of a new absolutism from poorly adapted feudal lords, the scene between the fathers lays the groundwork for Don Arias's words on the king's superiority to debt: ''Quoiqu'on fasse d'illustre et de considérable / Jamais à son sujet un Roi n'est redevable'' (II.i.371–72). Despite his military service, Gomès has neither the right to expect special protection for his offenses, nor the right to demand payment for his acts of valor. No subject ever has such rights. In Don Fernand's first scene with Rodrigue, however, the monarch apparently belies Don Arias's words.

After Rodrigue defeats the invading Moors, the king finds himself in a position which offers him little hope of providing a suitable recompense to his champion. Everyone now knows that Don Fernand owes Rodrigue his kingdom. Monarch or no, Don Fernand appears as *redevable*. The challenge to him is to turn his indebtedness to his own ends, to make his expressions of gratitude enhance rather than diminish his prestige, despite the inadequacy of any tangible rewards which he can bestow on his champion.

In these circumstances, the king declares the debt openly and acknowledges his inability to repay it:

> Pour te récompenser ma force est trop petite,
> Et j'ai moins de pouvoir que tu n'as de mérite.
> Le pays délivré d'un si rude ennemi,
> Mon sceptre dans ma main par la tienne affermi,
> Et les Mores défaits avant qu'en ces alarmes
> J'eusse pu donner ordre à repousser leurs armes,
> Ne sont point des exploits qui laissent à ton Roi
> Le moyen ni l'espoir de s'acquitter vers toi.
> (IV.iii.1223–30)

This speech, while denying that the hero will receive more than words of praise from his king, already constitutes a type of reward for the young courtier. The king himself recognizes Rodrigue's prowess. At the same time, this apparent declaration

> **"THE RESPONSE TO *LE CID* AS WELL AS CORNEILLE'S REVISIONS UNDERSCORE THE DIFFICULTIES OF CREATING A CONVINCING MONARCH WHO REWARDS SERVICES NOT BECAUSE HE MUST BUT BECAUSE HE CHOOSES TO DO SO."**

of royal bankruptcy works to lessen expectations that any further reward will be forthcoming. This heightens the effect of the benefits bestowed in the second part of the king's speech:

> Mais deux Rois, tes captifs, feront ta récompense,
> Ils t'ont nommé tous deux leur Cid en ma présence,
> . . . . . . . . . . .
> Sois désormais le Cid, qu'à ce grand nom tout cède,
> Qu'il devienne l'effroi de Grenade et Tolède,
> Et qu'il marque à tous ceux qui vivent sous mes lois
> Et ce que tu me vaux et ce que je te dois.
> (IV.iii.1231–32;1235–38)

On the one hand, the king protects himself and his new champion from any accusation of entering into a contractual, mercenary exchange. The king specifically says that he is still Rodrigue's debtor and that the *récompense* comes from the Moorish kings. Yet, in contrast to the Spanish source, no Moorish king is present to give the hero his new name. The king himself makes it public and thus creates for Rodrigue a new identity. In doing so, the monarch both shows his power to transform an individual and attributes prophetic powers to himself. He promises the Cid a future.

Once again, we see in this passage the ability of the king to transcend time as he displays his gratitude. All of what Rodrigue will do and be henceforth comes to read as the king's gift. Future services to the Crown become the reward bestowed for past services. And, in what is perhaps the most surprising move of all, the king's debt becomes a sign of his generosity.

Rather than negate his debt, the king memorializes it. By coopting the word Cid and making it a mark of the value he attaches to Rodrigue and the debt he owes him, Don Fernand links himself to the young hero, Rodrigue's fame to his. The personal pronouns in line 1238—*tu, me, je, te*—reinforce this association. Rodrigue's title becomes a monument not only to the young warrior but also to his sovereign.

The king's thanks to Rodrigue serve another strategic purpose. The speech provokes Rodrigue to restate the principle of a subject's endless indebtedness and to recognize his master's freedom from a system of payment:

> Que votre Majesté, Sire, épargne ma honte,
> D'un si foible service elle fait trop de compte,
> Et me force à rougir devant un si grand Roi
> De mériter si peu l'honneur que j'en reçois.
> Je sais trop que je dois au bien de votre Empire
> Et le sang qui m'anime et l'air que je respire,
> Et quand je les perdrai pour un si digne objet,
> Je ferai seulement le devoir d'un sujet.
> (IV.iii.1239–46)

While the king's own words had at first seemed to echo the ideas of the Comte, Rodrigue's clearly recall the precepts recited by Don Arias. This exchange thus demonstrates that while Rodrigue replaces Chimène's father as military champion, he will not become Don Gomès. The modesty with which Rodrigue belittles his own heroic actions contrasts favorably with the Comte's overweening pride. Rodrigue will continue to see himself as the king's ever-obligated subject.

This second example of royal gratitude functions, as did the first, as a test. The king's gratitude toward Don Diègue tested Gomès's ability to serve the emerging order, the absolutism which the king envisions but which he cannot yet completely practice. The second example requires Rodrigue to prove his loyalty to the new regime. The scene with Rodrigue cannot disguise that the monarchy of Castille needs heroic defenders and will fall without them. Nonetheless, just as the king designates Rodrigue as a hero who will win lasting glory, Rodrigue affirms his lord's status as indisputable sovereign of the realm. Royal *reconnaissance* incites the subject's *reconnaissance*. Both men benefit from this mutual recognition, but it establishes a hierarchy in which the military hero, however glorious, remains subordinate to his monarch. In recognizing an insurmountable distance between his deserts and the monarch's generosity, Rodrigue presents an example for the spectators within Fernand's court and within the Paris theater to follow.

The third scene I have chosen presents, as we shall soon see, a test to Corneille's audience as well as to the members of Don Fernand's court. Don Fernand has allowed Chimène's champion to challenge Rodrigue to a duel, but has decreed that Chimène must accept the victor of this combat as her husband. This decree is not explicitly formulated as an expression of gratitude to Rodrigue, yet the king's words suggest that he views Chimène as an additional recompense for his new champion:

> Et le combat fini, m'amenez le vainqueur.
> Quel qu'il soit, même prix est acquis à sa peine,
> Je le veux de ma main présenter à Chimène,
> Et que pour récompense il reçoive sa foi.
> (IV.v.1466–69)

Once Rodrigue has won the duel, Chimène's usefulness as royal recompense becomes even more apparent, though not unproblematic. Chimène has undergone a series of trials which prove both her love for Rodrigue and her loyalty to her father, and she now balks at a marriage which would place one above the other. The king grants her a delay of one year and enjoins Rodrigue to spend this time fighting the Moors in their own lands. Further service to the king will win Rodrigue additional glory and, according to Don Fernand, Chimène's hand. The king will collaborate with Rodrigue's valor to obtain the desired end: "Pour vaincre un point d'honneur qui combat contre toi, / Laisse faire le temps, ta vaillance, et ton Roi" (V.vii.1865–66).

Whether or not one believes that the marriage between Rodrigue and Chimène will occur depends upon whether one accepts the claims for royal gift-giving which earlier scenes supported. The king makes explicit in this scene the superiority to time which the text has already attributed to him. He has shown that he gives the future as well as the present. His decree is law, whether fulfilled immediately or in a year: "Cet Hymen différé ne rompt pas une loi / Qui sans marquer de temps lui destine ta foi" (V.vii.1845–46). This confidence functions as a sign of the king's power. Rather than make his rewards less real or less valuable, delay can in fact make his gift more palatable to Chimène and will incite Rodrigue to perform more feats for the good of the realm. Don Fernand's past generosity and his determination to establish himself as absolute should lead the audience to conclude that the marriage, which is after all historical, will take place.

Here I seem to be in the uncomfortable position of disagreeing not only with such perspicacious critics as Mitchell Greenberg but also with Corneille himself. The 1660 *examen* answers the critics of *Le Cid* who maintained that Chimène shows herself to be *impudique* in agreeing to marry the man who killed her father by asserting that the heroine never gives her consent to the marriage. Her response to the monarch's decree is silence, and Corneille warns against interpreting silence as consent in this case:

Je sais bien que le silence passe d'ordinaire
pour une marque de consentement; mais quand
les Rois parlent, c'en est une de
contradiction: on ne manque jamais à leur
applaudir quand on entre dans leurs
sentiments; et le seul moyen de leur
contredire avec le respect qui leur est dû,
c'est de se taire. (Corneille, 1: 701)

The remarks on universal eagerness to flatter kings seem more appropriate to the post-Fronde monarchy of 1660 than to either the France of 1637 or the Castille of the play. Louis XIII still faced insubordination from the *grands* and from his own family. As to Don Fernand, he is a king establishing an absolute monarchy, not yet the unquestioned center of an adoring and submissive court. Chimène's silence indeed protects her from having to give an unequivocal answer to the king's decree, but in the heat of the Querelle du Cid, neither Corneille nor his defenders explained her silence as dissent. As Couton notes, this passage from the *examen* has more to do with answering old objections to this tragi-comedy than with how Corneille or his contemporaries read the play in 1637.

Greenberg views Chimène as a scandalous figure who clings to the old regressive order represented by her father and indefinitely defers marriage with Rodrigue. I would argue instead that the deferral of the marriage is a royal decision which places this example of royal gratitude in line with the two earlier ones. By demanding that Rodrigue place his hope in time and the king, Don Fernand reminds the audience that the Crown will not forget its servants. *Le Cid* depicts a world which has undergone radical change, and the king's increased power comes with that change. Yet, the king's insistence on his own memory and foresight makes him the conveyor of continuity. The scenes involving royal gratitude thus contain the reassurance that the new order still respects the virtues of the old one. Those who feel troubled by a world in which absolutism is conquering a feudal past should respond not by rebelling but by turning their faith and service to the monarch.

Royal gratitude does not necessarily exhaust state coffers, for it may, in concrete terms, be cheap. One can argue that Don Fernand gives nothing but promises and demands. Nonetheless, he makes his subjects and the audience believe in the worth of these promises and demands. By rewarding worthy subjects with opportunities for further service and by refusing to privilege the present over the past or the future, Don Fernand transforms his gratitude from a possible sign of weakness to a means of increasing his own glory and power.

As evidence of royal power and prerogatives, Don Fernand's gifts to his subjects and his demands upon them should have won the approval of all who wished the strength of the French crown to continue to grow. The extremely successful play had almost all theater-goers, including the *nobles d'épée,* admiring a triumph of absolutism over feudalism as they applauded the love and eventual marriage of Rodrigue and Chimène. The play both urged service to the monarchy and reaffirmed that the king, although a unique being, shared the values of his nobility. The two performances of *Le Cid* at the Palais-Cardinal, the dedication of the published text to Mme. de Combalet, Richelieu's niece, and the gift of nobility to Corneille's father all suggest that Richelieu recognized the merits, and perhaps the usefulness, of this tragicomedy when he first saw it. Yet, the Cardinal and his protégés turned against the *Cid* soon after its publication. What do the attacks launched against *Le Cid* tell us about the degree to which Corneille's treatment of gratitude conformed or failed to conform to the ideologies of his time?

First of all, the critical minority agreed that the insolent response to royal gifts exemplified by the Comte deserved censure. Scudéry and the members of the Académie viewed the Comte as a *fanfaron.* The Académie specifically related "l'insupportable audace avec laquelle il [Gomès] parle du Roy son Maistre" to the Comte's attitude toward payment for services to the Crown. Gomès, according to the Académie, fits the secondary definition of *fanfaron:* "homme de cœur, mais qui ne fait de bonnes actions que pour en tirer avantage, et qui mesprise chacun, et n'estime que soy-mesme." These words, though not intended as praise of Corneille, suggest that he had succeeded in making the Comte's expectations of immediate royal payment appear to his contemporaries as outmoded and reprehensible.

Parallels between the Comte's ambition and the attitudes of the *grands* of the 1630s may partly account for Scudéry's disapproval of this character. Georges de Scudéry prided himself on being noble and on being both a poet and a warrior. His *Observations* are replete with reminders that he knows how the nobles who defend a country speak while Corneille knows only how to "parler de la guerre en bon bourgeois qui va à la garde." Scudéry and his allies in the quarrel repeatedly remind the reader of Corneille's bourgeois origins. Especially if we remember that Scudéry had close ties with the house of Condé, it seems quite credible that he would have resented the extent to which Don Gomès made the power and presumption of the *grands* and the ostentation of the old nobility look anachronistic. Despite the Cardinal's patronage, Scudéry was not ready for complete acceptance of absolutism, as his loyalty to Condé during the Fronde showed. At least in later years, he believed that the Crown could indeed be "redevable" to its *grands.*

As for the final scene involving royal gratitude, the criticisms of the Académie suggest that Corneille, in the eyes of his judges and their patron, had gone both too far and not far enough in delineating the powers of the king. On the one hand, the Académie implicitly recognized that time could not diminish the effects of royal gratitude. Instead of reading the one-year delay as introducing the possibility that the marriage would never take place at all, the Academicians rebuked Corneille for letting his king abuse power. Don Fernand allows his gratitude to one subject to make him unjust towards another. Seen in this light, Don Fernand violates the restrictions which even absolutist theoreticians like Bodin place on sovereigns, for he confiscates property without sufficient cause or compensation. His liberality comes to resemble theft. There is so little doubt about the king's ability to keep his word to Rodrigue, whatever Chimène's intentions, that he may be viewed not merely as an absolute monarch but as a tyrant.

The remarks of the Académie also suggest that Corneille has not gone far enough in differentiating royal *récompense* from contractual exchange. As we have seen, the critique regards Chimène as the king's payment to Rodrigue. Thus, Corneille's efforts to glorify royal gratitude by showing the greatness of the gift—the Cid's future and his bride—and by using remoteness in time to decrease the resemblance between the gift and payment would appear less than wholly successful, at least according to the poet's rivals. Corneille had made his audience assume Don Fernand's power to fulfill his promises, but this success had attenuated the effect of the deferral of the marriage. Time no longer obfuscates the reward's resemblance to payment. An institution whose patron favored clearly didactic drama could still find that Don Fernand acted like Rodrigue's debtor.

The 1660 edition of the play confirms how easily the king's superiority to obligation could be undermined and reminds us how much the ideological function of the play depended on the time of its reception. In this version, Chimène herself echoes the Académie's objections to Don Fernand's use of her: "Si Rodrigue à l'Etat devient si nécessaire, / De ce qu'il fait pour vous dois-je être le salaire?" This verse appears to derive from the Académie's suggestion that the poet could have made Chimène's marriage more acceptable by positing it as necessary for the state. Yet, the change threatens the claims for royal rewards made earlier in the play. The word *salaire* underscores Chimène's commodification and makes the king's gift into a calculated payment to a powerful subject. Such calculation is at odds both with noble liberality and with the king's superiority to obligation.

The change in the final scene suggests, as do some of Corneille's critical observations in the 1660 *Œuvres,* that he no longer considered Don Fernand a worthy representative of emerging absolutism. His assumptions concerning the relative power of sovereign and nobles had changed in the course of thirty-three years, in part because the monarchical ideology of *Le Cid* had gained grounds. Shedding a favorable light on the origins of absolutism had become less pertinent. By 1660, Don Fernand had lost his potential importance as a promising precursor to modern monarchs. The differences between his Castille and modern France had grown far more evident than any similarity between his moves toward absolutism and the progress of the French state. Richelieu and Mazarin had triumphed. From the perspective of 1660, *Le Cid* could appear as a story from a distant feudal past rather than as an enactment of the demise of feudalism.

Yet, depiction of royal gratitude had not become irrelevant for Corneille. The first version of *Le Cid* had, after all, offered standards of gratitude which the Crown had never met. Disappointment in royal patronage, the strengthening of central power after the Fronde, and lingering bitterness over the treatment of *Le Cid* could have decreased the poet's faith in a monarchy that would surpass the liberality of the *noblesse* and honor past services as well as present ones. The use of royal ingratitude in *Nicomède,* first performed in 1651, suggests increasing doubt that sovereigns could be both unfettered by debt and generous toward deserving subjects. Such plays as *Othon, Agesilas,* and *Suréna* reflect Corneille's continued concern with the vicissitudes of royal gratitude.

The response to *Le Cid* as well as Corneille's revisions underscore the difficulties of creating a convincing monarch who rewards services not because he must but because he chooses to do so. Any later doubts about the generosity of kings notwithstanding, Corneille bolsters absolutist ideology in the 1637 *Cid* as he makes his public applaud royal gifts and forces his rivals to denigrate noble bravado. As the text privileges royal *récompense* over common payment, the play urges allegiance to the new order and challenges those in power to make absolutism's myths of royal gratitude a reality.

**Source:** Helen L. Harrison, "*Payer* or *Recompenser:* Royal Gratitude in *Le Cid*," in *French Review,* Vol. 72, No. 2, December 1998, pp. 238–49.

## Peter Bornedal

*In the following essay, Bornedal introduces the idea of an "imaginary recipient"—a person or group of people a writer has in mind when writing—and how this phenomenon possibly accounts for the clash between a traditional code of honor and the contemporary political situation in* Le Cid.

### I. Introduction

In an earlier work I have tried to apply theoretical discussions of rationality and limitations of rationality to literary analysis, as I tried to reconstruct plot and meaning structures of the literary text in order to locate the limitations of textual meaningfulness. This limitation of rationality was defined in two ways—not necessarily excluding each other; first, as system-inherent, as a deficiency and incompleteness constitutive for consistent systems; secondly, as produced through the cacophony of different voices with which the creative self addresses himself to a variety of imaginary recipients. These imaginary recipients, it was argued, could possibly represent a variety of different interests likely to be mutually incompatible.

The concept of an 'imaginary recipient' represents the *idea* of a recipient, which is therefore 'located' in the creative *cogito* (for example, the idea of a class, an institution, a single powerful individual, or an idea multiplying into different conflicting recipients). In the introduction of this concept one emphasizes how a literary work is concerned about observing an assumed reader-interest, for example in an attempt to comply with an ideological and political horizon shared by its assumed recipient(s). Simultaneously it becomes possible to explain inconsistencies in the work as the unsuccessful result of trying to satisfy multiple

> *"LE CID IS A PLAY ABOUT HOW TO FOLLOW A CODE, NAMELY THE CODE OF HONOUR. THE PURSUIT OF HONOUR IS UNDERSTOOD AS 'CORRECT CONDUCT' IN THE PLAY. BENEATH THIS, HOWEVER, IT IS ALSO A PLAY ABOUT HOW THIS CODE BECOMES INCREASINGLY PROBLEMATIC."*

colliding interests. As such the imaginary recipient becomes a part of the structure of the text, which is now seen as a surface beneath which layers of different messages can be uncovered. Behind coherent plot-constructions, it is possible to uncover residues of conflicts, and in the analysis reconstruct these conflicts.

It is impossible to go into details with how this approach compares to other critical schools, but it can in passing be noted that the 'imaginary recipient' is an entirely different analytical concept than Wolfgang Iser's 'implied reader'—for at least three different reasons. First, whereas Iser, and other critics from the Hermeneutical tradition, are interested in aesthetic response, and in how a text is actualized or appropriated by a reader, a concept of an 'imaginary recipient' addresses the creative process, which is now viewed as a (possibly distorted) communicative process where the author constantly communicates with assumed 'others.' Secondly, critics from the Hermeneutical tradition are typically interested in how meaning emerges in the dialectics between text and reader, whereas the notion of an 'imaginary recipient' has the reverse purpose to help explaining how and why meaning breaks down, how and why inconsistencies occur in literary texts. Thirdly, although from Gadamer to Iser there are earnest attempts to prevent 'relativization' of textural analysis, it is hard to see how it is effectively avoided when the meaning of a text is 'actualized' *in* the reader, and consequently actualized differently in different readers. Focusing on the side of 'production,' it is taken for granted that a text can be objectively read, and its plot and other structures can be reconstructed to a point where also inconsistencies show up and reveal problems in the creative process.

## II. Code and text

Corneille's *Le Cid* does not represent the relationship between 'code' and 'text' in the most fortunate manner; not, at least, if we by 'code' understand the contemporary standards for composition and decorum in dramatic poetry. Thus, Corneille's text is not the most illustrious example of how the rules of the unities are implemented in a neoclassical text.

Neither the unity of time nor the unity of place are strictly observed in the work, as Corneille's critics noticed and Corneille later admitted. Too much happens within a span of twenty-four hours and the characters move between too many different places. Later, in his *Discours des Trois Unités,* Corneille defended his use of many different places by pointing out that although the scenes are enacted at different locations, his characters remain within the same city, Seville. But in his later *Examen* of the play, Corneille admits these and other errors; errors of which he had been criticized by the French Academy. The question of the rules becomes a question of the probable, the 'vraisemblable,' and the proper, the 'bienséance.' Transgressing the rule of the unity of time has two consequences: it makes the play 'invraisemblable,' improbable, and it violates the doctrine of 'bienséance,' a notion indicating that one should not simply depict truth on the stage but beautify it according to the conduct and proprieties of polite society. When Corneille does not observe the rule of the unity of time, he ultimately offends these principles—and not only the law of probability, also the doctrines of conduct and propriety. As we shall see, he ultimately offends the preeminent recipient of the play, the king.

The problem in Corneille's play is that too much happens within twenty-four hours. For instance, Rodrigue's fight with the Moors should realistically have worn him out so much, that he would have needed two or three days of rest. Instead, after the fight the king immediately arranges the duel with Don Sanchos. Corneille recognizes that this goes too fast.

> [Regarding] the duel with Don Sanchos, which the king arranges, he could have chosen another time for the duel than two hours after the fight with the Moors. Their defeat did exhaust Rodrigue long enough to earn him two or three days of rest.

The same rule of time is violated with regard to Chimène when she twice, within twenty-four hours, seeks the king, pleading him to revenge her slain father. This is importune, pressing the king for the same request within such a short span of time. As Corneille notices, it works in the novel about Cid, where there is no time-limit and seven days pass between Chimène's requests, but on the stage it appears as if Chimène seeks the king both the evening and the following morning.

> The same rule pushes Chimène to ask the king for justice a second time. She had already done that the evening before and had no reason to come back the next day to bother the king. She had no reasons for complains, since she could not claim that he did not keep his promises. The novel would have given her seven or eight days before bothering the king again, but twenty-four hours did not allow that. This is the inconvenience of the rule.

If we assume that the unity of time is strictly observed, if the action of the play elapses within twenty-four hours, then the play is an insult to the king. In the first case, the king appears inhumane by not letting Rodrigue rest a while after his triumphant battle, because he instead arranges the duel with Chimène's defender, Don Sanchos. In the second case, the king is offended because Chimène importunately presses the king for justice both night and day, without respect for his sovereignty. In both cases the conduct towards the king is impudent. Either Corneille depicts the king as insensitive, or he lets his heroine treat him disrespectfully. If the rule of the unity of time applies, Corneille indirectly offends the king. If it does not apply, the conduct of the characters might have been justifiable.

The unity of time apparently is not observed, but it should have been so, and if it *were* observed as it ought to, the play is without 'judgment of conduct,' as Georges de Scudéry complains. When the fictive universe of *Le Cid* is condensed into one day, time becomes scarce and precious. However, it is first and foremost in relation to the king that this implausibility becomes offensive. It is the king one ought to give time, and give him considerably more time than twenty-four hours. This is the essence of Corneille's apology: he has not given the king more than twenty-four hours; he admits his disrespect, and apologizes.

The problems of time and place were, however, only one of the criticisms Corneille was exposed to by contemporaries. Corneille was criticized for neither respecting the unities nor the decorum of the stage, and furthermore for plagiarizing and 'stealing' the most beautiful verses. The problem of the 'unities' is only one point in the charges brought against Corneille. According to Scudéry, just about everything is wrong with the play. His complaints are:

> That the topic is worth nothing.
> That it opposes all the main rules of a dramatic poem.
> That it lacks judgment of conduct.
> That it is full of bad verses.
> That almost all its beautiful parts are stolen.

But one issue is particularly devastating, the role of Chimène. It is unforgivable that she accepts Rodrigue's presence in her bedroom so soon after he has killed her father, and it is 'invraisemblable et immoral' that she by the end marries her father's murderer—particularly if we assume it happens within twenty-four hours.

The French Academy was finally called upon to mediate in the polemic between Scudéry and Corneille. They maintained the criticism—although not as severely as Scudéry—and the basic charge that Chimène acts immorally and improbably marrying the man who slew her father. In his later "*Examen*" of *Le Cid,* Corneille defends these accusations by pointing out how Rodrigue's and Chimène's sensitive conversation makes the spectator either forget or forgive the error.

> The two visits Rodrigue pays to his mistress offend the propriety of the part when she is in grief. Strict duty would have required that she refused to talk to him, and that she locked herself up in her chamber instead of listening to him, but allow me to say with one of the best minds of this century, that their conversation is so full of noble feelings that mostly people have not noticed this flaw, and those who have noticed it, have forgiven it.

It is a question of whether one ought to follow the 'vraisemblable' or the 'bienséance,' whether one should remain truthful to history or beautify the facts in order to make them suitable to current opinions and conventions. In the case where Corneille is accused of the implausibility of the visit to Chimène's bedroom, he defends himself by pointing out the embellished dialogue. In the case where he is accused of imprudence by letting Chimène marry her father's murderer, he argues that he is just describing what is historically correct.

> It is true that in this matter it should have been enough to save Rodrigue from danger, without pressing him to marry Chimène. This is the historical fact and it pleased in its own time although it would not in ours; and I fail to see why Chimène accepts this in the Spanish author although he gave more than three years to the comedy. In order not to contradict history, I felt I could not dispense with the idea, notwithstand-

ing the uncertainty of its effect, and is was only so I could reconcile the theatrical rules of propriety and the reality of the events.

However, in these discussions about whether or not Corneille observes the rules of decorum and unity, something more general is at stake, something defining the neoclassical paradigm in a more profound way. First, the play and the code defining the composition of the play *can* be discussed between author and critic. This changes with the Romantic definition of poetry, but at this point poetry is still defined as something that implicates society, and as an action—a linguistic action—within the bounds of society. Poetry is still an object of (rational, pseudo-rational, or even irrational) discussion. Thus, poetry has to observe the rules defined by the society it addresses. It must, in other words, inscribe its potential recipients and internalize its own context of reception. These two aspects of the poem, conventionality and receptivity, organize and form signification on a deep-structural level of *Le Cid.*

As such, the recipient is part of the structure of *Le Cid.* A 'general' or 'imaginary' recipient in the text reveals itself as Corneille's awareness of code and decorum. This 'general' receiver is not only made up by the specific audience to which the work is composed, but by the social-political-ideological horizon in which the work is supposed to function. The 'general' recipient is as inherent in the work as the different messages it conveys. The purpose of the present interpretation is to reconstruct these interdependent layers in the text, to expose their internal logic—or lack of logic. The text therefore is like a surface beneath which layers of different messages can be uncovered. Inconsistent and conflicting, these messages echo ideological conflicts existent in the social groups which first and foremost constitute Corneille's addressees. Behind a quite coherent plot- construction, it is possible to discover these sediments of conflicts, conflicts which the author tries to resolve for the simple reason that he, at this particular historical point of time, is concerned about the audience and tries his best not to offend them. In the interpretive work we shall reconstruct these conflicting messages—hereby actually 'deconstructing' the apparent and superficial organization of the text.

*Le Cid* is a play about how to follow a code, namely the code of honour. The pursuit of honour is understood as 'correct conduct' in the play. Beneath this, however, it is also a play about how this code becomes increasingly problematic. If this does not seem obvious in a first reading of the play, this is what is at stake in the subsequent reception of *Le Cid,* and in the fervent polemic it launches. In these debates, partly introduced above, it is indisputable that Corneille (who on behalf of the characters in the play meticulously observes the code of honour) among notable critics, The French Academy, and even Richelieu, was not successful in matters of 'conduct.' But whether or not Corneille succeeds in *Le Cid,* whether or not his Chimène is an opportune sketch of a heroine, whether or not his unities are stretched beyond the probable, he writes acknowledging a conventional code and potential recipients. It is this state of affairs we shall address in the following interpretation.

### III. The code of honour

In order to understand the logic of the conflicts in the play, it is necessary to understand the prevailing and underlying value-system, what we shall term the 'code.' This is the system against which everything is measured: man, woman, love, existence, death.

The value-system is fundamental, and therefore no other systems found it. It is in itself (consequently and by all good logic) inexplicable and random. It is *The Law* of the play, a horizon taken for granted, a 'categorical imperative' of honour one might say. Kant is easily paraphrased: 'act in such a way that the maxim of your action always corresponds to the universal law of honour.' This Law is exposed in the behaviour and speech of the characters as something they have to observe, interpret, and react to in the most correct manner.

Ignoring or overlooking this Law would be worse than anything else, worse, for example, than death. Such disregard would annihilate the characters as subjects. The annihilation of their individual, corporeal, and empirical being would be insignificant, but the annihilation of their imaginary being— as the esteem they hold in the eyes of the other and as their self-esteem—would be disastrous not just to the person, but to the person's name and family.

The underlying value-system we imply here is the code of honour. A man's or woman's value is measured in honour as a value beyond life and death. The economy of honour constitutes a 'general economy' of the play. It is recognized among the characters as constituting a value-system according to which they can and should adjust their actions. It is the 'general equivalent' of human action. The play is about how one can increase one's

value within this value-system, increase one's esteem (and thus self-esteem), and consequently increase one's worth and 'price'; and, conversely, about how one avoids a decrease in one's worth.

Because individual action is ultimately measured in esteem, it is far beyond the individually comfortable and agreeable. Characters in the play are at any point ready to die if dying gives them higher esteem than living. Death is chosen over life, if death makes the subject more worthy and a higher priced subject in the eyes of the other. This is represented in numerous places in the text. Because death in the play tends to increase rather than to decrease subjective worth, the text has an implicit problem in putting a restraint on the eagerness with which the characters are ready to sacrifice themselves. It has to transform this suicidal tendency— this drive toward death and self-destruction which it suggests as an appropriate solution to a dishonourable life—into something more constructive. It has to make life an honourable alternative to death.

In this quest for the highest honour and esteem, the text is discussing, expounding, and interpreting the code. It attempts to determine 'the most honourable' action, given diverse circumstances. This is the teaching of the text. It is a lesson in how to behave honourably. The text sets forth different examples and situations. For instance, it often places a character in a dilemma, giving him or her the choice between two equally, or almost equally, honourable alternatives. The problem of the character here becomes whether he or she is able to *interpret* and *identify* which alternative would be the more honourable—giving him or her the most esteem and worth. The representation of this problem is the 'teaching' of the text, the solution is its 'pleasure.'

After Rodrigue has avenged his insulted father by killing Don Gomez, the father praises his son; he has given him satisfaction; the family honour is restored. The fact that Rodrigue has killed the father of his beloved Chimène and broken his bond to her does not occur to the old man as a major problem.

From the beginning, Rodrigue stood in a dilemma: should he carry out his duty as a son, or should he follow his feelings of love for Chimène. In this dilemma Rodrigue makes the right and only possible choice. He recognizes, after discussing and interpreting the problem by himself for the sake of the audience, that his first obligation is to his father. He must restore the honour of the family. Speaking to Don Diego: ''The honour was your due. I could no less, / Since I'm your flesh and blood, and bred by you.'' But he perceives another obligation, his obligation toward Chimène.

Don Diego recognizes his son's sacrifice, a sacrifice that brings him, as a father, in debt to his son, because although Don Diego gave his son *life,* Rodrigue has given his father back his *name,* and as the name carries all the worth of a person Rodrigue has given his father something more valuable than life. Now Don Diego is indebted to Rodrigue.

> Carry Your victory still further. Think
> *I gave you life; you gave me back my name.*
> *And, since I cherish glory more than life,*
> *My debt to you is all the heavier.*
> But from our heart remove such weaknesses.
> There's but one honour, mistresses abound!
> Love's but a pleasure; duty's a command.

Don Diego perceives only one obligation, the duty toward the family, or rather *the name.* Women are not included in the economy of his system because they are abundant and can be replaced. A name cannot. Rodrigue, however, has another, stricter, interpretation of honour. Compared to Don Diego's patriarchal attitude, it is youthful and romantic. One also has certain obligations with regard to the woman one loves, and he starts at his father's insensitivity in the matter.

> What you say, father?
> . . . . . . . . . . .
> you dare urge me to inconstancy!
> Like infamy weighs equally upon
> The craven warrior and the faithless heart.
> Do not this wrong to my fidelity.
> Let me be chivalrous but not for sworn.
> My ties are strong and are not broken thus;
> My troth still holds, even if I hope no more.
> And still I cannot win or leave my love,
> The death I seek will be the sweetest pain.

A 'faithless heart' with regard to his beloved he is not; he has an obligation towards her. Remaining faithful to Chimène is, however, less a recognition of her personal well-being than it is an acknowledgment and recognition of the integrity of her name. His fidelity consists in supervising that her name remains intact, even if that will cost him his life. In this intent he does not care about her, his, or their happiness. His final obligation would be to defend her name as he has already defended his father's. As this noble act would imply giving her the satisfaction family honour demands, it implies offering her his life, as his life is what she now must pursue as retribution for her slain father. To save her name and worth, his last display of duty is to sacrifice himself, that is his life, but certainly not his name.

On the contrary, the price of his name goes up with this recognition of duty, with this readiness to self-sacrifice.

This, at least, is how Rodrigue interprets the code of honour. This is what would give him the highest worth. His father, however, perceives him as having another obligation, the obligation towards the king. Thus Rodrigue is confronted with another dilemma. He is not just torn between his duties toward his father and his beloved. Having made the choice to fight Don Gomez, he is torn between his duty toward Chimène and his duties toward the king as his soldier. Therefore, the text places him in two different dilemmas, twice he confronts situations where he has to choose between two unpleasant alternatives. At first his obligations towards the king don't seem quite as important as his obligations towards his beloved because choosing to serve the king and forgetting Chimène might raise the suspicion that Rodrigue is trying to rescue his own life, and consequently values life above honour—a major ignominy within the horizon of the play. In this general economy, life is, compared to honour, always the lesser value.

Whereas the text dissolves Rodrigue's first dilemma with a logical argument, making it evident that he has no other choice than to fight Don Gomez, the text, strictly and logically speaking, never solves the second dilemma. To reach a solution, however, it uses another strategy: it increases Rodrigue's value to the king. It makes him invaluable for the survival of the kingdom. Into his qualms and perplexities it intersects his successful and triumphant combat with the Moors, making him a priceless subject to the king, a subject who cannot be wasted in privat matters of love and honour. As such it never 'teaches' the audience a logical solution to what one ought to select in a given choice between honour and king as it makes this choice dependent on current power-relations. It acknowledges the political circumstances of the state as more significant than a 'logical' solution of the dilemma.

## IV. The lack of choice and freedom

When the characters are placed in dilemmas, they apparently have a choice: should Rodrigue choose to revenge his father, or should he choose Chiméne? But the outcome of these choices is always predetermined. Insofar as the characters observe and understand the conventional code, the choices are pseudochoices because the characters know what is in advance required from them. The choice is always a choice in favour of the name, and against oneself. The honourable choice invariably has this structure, against oneself but for the name.

Therefore, dilemmas are typically only seeming, merely displayed in the text in order to demonstrate, to 'teach' how one chooses what one has to choose. A dilemma is a pretext for exposing the argument guiding the action of the noble individual. In Rodrigue's first 'choice' between avenging his father or cherishing his love for Chimène, he has in reality no choice. His contemplation of this situation is a display of the value-system that 'thinks' him. First Rodrigue displays a superficial and naive interpretation of his dilemma—this sounds like a choice, like a genuine *either-or*.

> If I avenge him, then I must lose *her*.
> One fires me on. The other holds me back.
> The shameful choice is to betray my love,
> Or live in infamy.

Those are seemingly the possibilities: honour or love. But soon Rodrigue realizes that he has in fact *no choice*—what makes his decision easy, although with no less devastating consequences. If he chooses 'love,' if he abstains from duelling, he only earns the contempt of his beloved. *His* choice of love would deprive him of *her* love. This path is cut off and it leaves him with only one possibility. Rodrigue discusses this more intelligent interpretation of his dilemma with himself, an interpretation with which he realizes his lack of freedom.

> Taking revenge, I earn her hate or wrath,
> And, taking no revenge, I earn contempt.
> One makes me faithless to my dearest hope,
> One unworthy of her.
> My ill increases if I seek a cure.
> Everythings swells my grief.
> Come then my soul, and, since we have to die,
> Let's die at least without offending her.

Here he presents his insight into the logic and code of honour. The choice is not a choice he can make in freedom. His first naive assessment of this dilemma, where he actually discussed his alternatives as if they were open options, is now seen as shameful— as he notices: ''let's hasten to revenge; / Deeply ashamed at having wavered so, / Let's hesitate no more.'' Whatever he does he loses her, but in one case he will not lose her respect.

Chimène also knows the code of honour. She knows that Rodrigue has in fact no choice, and Rodrigue knows that Chimène knows just that. He obviously counts on that knowledge when he chooses to defend his father instead of retreating from his duties and cherishing his amorous passions. Rodrigue

knows that he would never merit his beloved by *not* fighting her father. As soon as he disregards his immediate inclinations for Chimène, when he 'sets against her charms' this thought, he realizes this situation.

> You would certainly have tipped the scales [in the
>     choice between her and duty]
> Had I not set against your charms the thought
> That I, dishonoured, did not merit you,
> That, though I shared in your affection, yet
> Who loved me brave would hate me infamous;
> What to obey, and listen to your love,
> Would make me quite unworthy of your choice.

This dialectical insight into one another's decisions is only possible because the characters share a common code. If a common code determines humans and their logic, they are always able to infer the thinking of the other.

Chimène knows that she could ask Rodrigue not to fight her father. But she also knows that if he obeyed her, it would only make her ashamed of a man who defied the fundamental laws of honour. She knows furthermore that Rodrigue would never allow himself to be represented as a craven in the eyes of the other, and especially not in hers. She consequently knows that her choice is not free. In the choice between *imploring* or *not imploring* Rodrigue to abstain from fighting, the first possibility is not really there. The dilemmas never reflect real individual freedom.

> If he obeys me not, what grief is mine?
> If he obeys, what will they say of him?
> A man like him, to suffer such a slight!
> Whether or not he yields to love for me,
> I can be only shamefaced or distraught
> At his respectful Yes or rightful No.

And when later Rodrigue explains to her his reasons to fight, Chimène accepts his explanation: ''Rodrigue. Ah! It's true. Although your foe, I cannot blame your 'No' to infamy.''

It is the characters' fate to be caught up and trapped in their own code.

## V. *The deathdrive of the text*

With the exception of the king, all the characters seek death in their pursuit of honour. Everyone in the play is ready to die if his or her name is at stake. The infanta would rather die than succumb to her love for Rodrigue and suffer a loss of social rank: ''So mindful am I [of her social status] that I'll shed my blood / Before I stoop to sullying my rank.'' Don Gomez is prepared to die rather than to compromise his pride by apologizing to Don Diego.

Don Diego prefers death to living his life in disgrace by not revenging Don Gomez's insult. Rodrigue, in the first case, risks death rather than seeing his father's name sullied; and in the second, he prefers death to disloyalty towards his beloved. Chimène would rather take her own life (were Rodrigue to die) than giving up her demand for his death as retribution for her father's death. Her defendant, Don Sanchos, risks death rather than refusing to defend a woman of esteem and virtue.

A fundamental 'death-drive' structures the text. But it is death understood as a 'trade in' for worth, not as ultimate relief from an intolerable life, as in a romantic understanding. It is not death understood as darkness, nothingness, nirvana, or as an eternal oblivion promised a subject who wishes to abandon his or her intolerable bonds to the world. On the contrary, the 'world' is never more present than in speculations on death. Death is not the annihilation of *the subject,* but its consecration and magnification.

Although death would in fact solve conflicts and frustrations in the play, it is *never* first and foremost contemplated as such. It is considered because it would be the most honourable choice. If the infanta contemplates death, it is not *because* she is desperately in love with Rodrigue and cannot have him—which is the case. She does not contemplate death as a release from this unbearable conflict. On the contrary, she contemplates death as a possibility she would have to choose if she could no longer control herself, if she yielded and married him. If she actually got whom she loved, if she lowered her rank and worth to such an extent, *then* she would have to choose death. Death is the option in a hypothetical situation in which she marries her beloved. Death is not contemplated because of Rodrigue's *actual absence,* but because of his *hypothetical presence* as a desired subject.

Death never annihilates the characters as subjects. They continue to live *in the other;* that is to say, they continue to have worth in the eyes of the other *in* death, and *after* death. This interminable existence as a valuable subject, even after death, is internalized in the character's self-reflection upon death. According to this self-reflection, death is not the end, but the continuation and survival of *the name.* Nowhere else in the play is trust in the code and distrust in the individual given stronger expression. The subsistence of the individual is not essential, but his/her 'price,' honour, worth, and name is.

The 'death-drive' of the text is not a longing for nirvana, but a belief in 'name' before and above life,

of subject before and above the individual, of code before and above emotions. The text, however, puts a restraint on this 'death-drive'—only Don Gomez actually dies during the play. The restraint is the king. He intervenes for example in the conflict between Rodrigue and Chimène (who as individuals love each other, but as subjects pursue an honourable death) by actually decreeing them to get married to end their conflict. Against the law of honour, the king dictates his own law: the law of power, the law of the politically opportune. It is not politically opportune to have subjects pursuing death. Politicians can neither rule dead people nor those fearless of death. Against the permeating 'death-drive' of his subjects, the king introduces a 'drive' towards life, insofar as he introduces a *reason* to live; this reason is explicitly his power.

## VI. *The role of the king*

The kingdom is at stake. The king cannot do without his most brilliant subjects. He cannot allow them to kill each other in duels. As mentioned in the introductions to the French edition of Corneille's works, this was an urgent problem at the time of Corneille, a problem Corneille cannot permit himself to ignore because the greater part of his audience came from the ruling aristocracy. Furthermore, Cardinal Richelieu had tried to put a stop to the widespread practice of duelling among knights, nobility, and musketeers in France as this custom decimated his best men. In this light, the code of honour, pervading Corneille's play and defended so stubbornly by his heroes and heroines, is not in the best interest of some of the recipients of the play. Cardinal Richelieu is undoubtedly such a potential reviewer, a projected recipient in Corneille's creative self, because the play is dedicated to the niece of the cardinal, Madame de Combalet. Corneille is therefore fully aware of Richelieu as a reviewer of the play, and he is hardly ignorant of Richelieu's opinion about duelling and the code of honour that impels it. In the text, therefore, Corneille has to represent an acceptable solution to the ongoing conflicts. If these conflicts were all carried out according to the code, this would imply the demise of most of the play's important characters.

In *The Cid,* Corneille fails to please the authorities (the play got a harsh and condemning reception by Richelieu). One problem is the romantic interpretation of the code of honour, but still worse is the disobedience that characterizes the relationship between the king and his subjects. The play is poor politics. Throughout the play, the code of honour dominates the interaction between men and women. The king is the single subject who opposes this code. Because his interests and the code of honour conflict, he tries to impede his subjects' pursuit of honour.

Obedience towards the king should be a self-evident obligation. Compared with the importance of the king's interests, the subjects should readily denounce their private pursuits; but the characters do not realize this order of things. They only reluctantly submit themselves to the will of the king when honour is at stake. Don Gomez denies to abide by the king's decree when Don Diego is favoured as tutor of the king's son. Despite the king's command, Don Gomez does not retract his insult of Don Diego. The king has to explain what should have been obvious, that his law is higher than the law of honour.

> There is no dishonour in obeying me.
> Besides, the affront is mine. He has disgraced
> The man I made the tutor of my son.
> To slight my choice is to attack myself
> And seek to weaken my authority.

Placing the law of honour above the king obviously weakens the king's authority. The play *says* so, but it nevertheless *does* the opposite by accepting, at every turn, honour as prior to royal authority. The hero of the play, Rodrigue, never considers giving up his obligations to Chimène, which honour dictates. He persistently offers her his life instead of realizing that his services to the king are indefinitely more important. Neither does the heroine of the play, Chimène, renounce her demand for Rodrigue's death which honour dictates as retribution for her slain father. Even when she realizes that Rodrigue, after his triumphant battle with the Moors, is becoming invaluable to king and kingdom, she upholds her demand. The infanta's explanation of the political order of things does not move Chimène.

> Willing his death, you will the state's collapse.
> What! to avenge a father, is it right
> To hand Spain over to the enemy?
> Can your demand be justified for *us*?
> Must we share punishment without the crime?
> . . . . . . . . . . .
> Deprive him of your love, but not his life.

The prospect of the state's collapse, 'to hand Spain over to the enemy' in the case of Rodrigue's death, does not persuade Chimène, and it does not compel her to forgive him and give up her request of revenge. Her duty 'knows no bounds,' and neither does king and kingdom constitute an obligation.

> Ah! Such forgivingness is not for me.
> The duty which impels me knows no bounds.
> Whate'er my love may say on his behalf—
> Adored by all and cherished by the king,
> surrounded by his bravest warriors—
> My cypresses make his laurels fade.

The 'cypresses' as a symbol of death in Chimène's family overshadows the 'laurels' as a symbol of Rodrigue's victory.

The king is surrounded by disobedient subjects pursuing their honour rather than his rule. The name weighs heavier than the interest of state and kingdom.

But as the characters have dilemmas, the text now has a dilemma because it professes 'honour' as the major value among the characters, but still recognizes that this value-system conflicts with the political interests of the king. Consequently, the problem of the text is to mediate between two conflicting value-systems: honour and political power.

Don Gomez's insult indicates the first incidence of disobedience, the first conflict between honour and power. This conflict resolves itself, when the count is slain in the duel with Rodrigue and is as such punished for his pride. But in the second incident, when Rodrigue seeks death at the hand of Chimène, because he nobly offers her satisfaction, this conflict is not easily resolved. The text has here to explain why these two characters do not follow the imperatives of their value-system and choose death as they ought to do. In diverging from this course, the text has to justify its 'political' choice, its sudden favouritism of the law of power.

In this endeavour, it appeals both to our feelings and our reason. Under any circumstance, it would be a pity if Rodrigue and Chimène carry out their intentions and destroy themselves. From the beginning, the text strives to soften the conflict by showing not just their duties, but also the injustice in how these ironclad duties pull the two apart. The text appeals to the emotions of the recipient, but it appeals to our reason as well because it would be too much of a waste if Rodrigue were to sacrifice himself on the altar of honour, when the existence of the state depends upon him. The text increases his value; he becomes an asset who cannot die for love. Although the individual in general is less valuable than his or her name, Rodrigue, after his success against the Moors, becomes more valuable than himself. His noble self-destructive project becomes futile.

At a certain point the text now has to give in to its own persuasion. But it is prepared and constructed to give in and bend at a certain point, a point where the text legitimately can choose the pragmatic solution above the idealistic: the law of the king above the law of honour. This is also the point where the 'politics' of the text is inscribed. The play may be poor politics, but nevertheless politics is inscribed in its thematic and plot structure. It is inscribed for the simple reason that Corneille believes in the political reviewer (and in the receiver in general); for example, he believes in Richelieu. Thus, Corneille is not writing for himself, as the romantic poet; he is observing the social and political conventions of the time, not neglecting them as belonging to an inferior world, unsuitable for an artist to take part in.

At the point where Rodrigue becomes too valuable to be wasted, the text instates the law of king and state as superior. One has now to yield, not to the rules of honour, but to the rules of power. This power relation is disguised, however. Never does it become a question of the king simply issuing decrees. The king is not represented as a despotic sovereign, he is represented as just and wise. Among all his idealistic subjects, he is the only one who is capable of *seeing* when they remain *blind* to all other purposes than their own honour. The king *naturalizes* his commands. The 'politics' of the text does not simply manifest itself by a sudden emphasis on 'power' instead of 'honour.' If such a shift were represented as a royal decree forced upon his subjects, it would establish the king as a tyrant, and Corneille as either a fool or a revolutionary. The text understands in full the ideological importance of *naturalizing and humanizing* this new emphasis on power. In this undertaking it constitutes the king as the only humanist in the text—and flatters the potential aristocratic spectator of the play. It manages to 'translate' the king's political concerns into general human concerns. What is advantageous to the kingdom is beneficial to the subjects.

The text represents the king's superior wisdom by making him realize that beneath the surface, Chimène in fact loves Rodrigue and wishes to marry him. The king understands this as soon as he sees Chimène's anguish when she mistakenly believes that Rodrigue has been killed in the duel with Don Sanchos. Chimène is convinced that Don Sanschos's return from the duel with Rodrigue means that Rodrigue is defeated and dead. In her misconception of the situation she reproaches Don Sanchos for

Rodrigue's death. This reaction is interpreted and explained to the king by Don Sanchos as an indication of Chimène's true love for Rodrigue.

> Sire, she was deceived by her excess of love.
> I came to tell the outcome of the fight.
> This gallant knight of whom she is entranced,
> As he disarmed me, said to me: "fear naught.
> I'd rather have uncertain victory
> Than shed the blood Chimène hazarded.
> But, since my duty calls me to the king,
> Report the combat in my name.
> On my behalf, bear her the victor's sword."
> I went to her. This sword deceived her, Sire.
> She thought me victor, seeing me return.
> Her anger suddenly betrayed her love
> With such an outburst of impatience that
> I could not win a moment's audience.

This is the *denouement* of the play. Here we notice a certain *discovery* and *reversal* at stake, insofar as the king and his servants *discover* Chimène's real love for Rodrigue beneath her request of revenge. As this *discovery* directly causes the king to demand that Chimène abandons her plans of revenge and marries Rodrigue, it also *reverses* the fortune of hero and heroine. It turns their bad fortune into good fortune. When Don Sanchos convinces the king of Chimène's love for Rodrigue, the king, as the only person raised above the rule of honour, releases Chimène from observing her obligations.

> You must not be ashamed of what you feel
> Or seek to disavow it, as in vain
> Your modesty still urges you to do.
> Honour's redeemed and duty is discharged.
> Your father's satisfied. He is avenged
> By hazarding Rodrigue's life so oft.
> You see how heaven disposes differently.
> You did all for the Count. Do something for
> Yourself. Do not oppose my order which
> Gives you a husband you so dearly love.

Thus, the king issues a decree in the end, as he orders Chimène to marry Rodrigue. But everybody understands that this was her dearest hope, and that this decree just signifies the wisdom and humanity of the king. The text spells it out. When the king commands Chimène to marry the man she 'dearly loves,' he only 'commands' her to follow her deepest desire. This is how the text finally makes the law of the king superior to the law of honour. It is how it is ideologically defensible and justifiable to change the emphasis from honour to power. The king's power becomes the more humane and natural choice. In his interest of maintaining a strong state, the king pursues the most secret desires of his subjects.

**Source:** Peter Bornedal, "The Law of the Name: The Imaginary Recipient in Corneille's *Le Cid*," in *Orbis Literarum:*

*International Review of Literary Studies,* Vol. 52, No. 3, 1997, pp. 157–77.

# SOURCES

Clarke, John, *Pierre Corneille: Poetics and Political Drama under Louis XIII,* Cambridge University Press, 1992.

Lapp, John C., Introduction, in *Le Cid,* Harlan Davidson, 1955, pp. v–xi.

Lyons, John D., *The Tragedy of Origins: Pierre Corneille and Historical Perspective,* Stanford University Press, 1996.

# FURTHER READING

Carlin, Claire L., *Women Reading Corneille: Feminist Psychocriticisms of "Le Cid,"* Peter Lang, 2000.

Five different feminist literary critics analyze Corneille's *Le Cid* to explore why this play retains interest in contemporary times. The critics include Julia Kristeva, Carol Gilligan, Jessica Benjamin, and Jane Gallop.

Clarke, David, *Pierre Corneille: Poetics and Political Drama under Louis XIII,* Cambridge University Press, 1992.

Clarke provides an in depth study of the political times that surrounded Corneille as he tried to distin-guish his own beliefs from the pressures that were put on him to conform to Cardinal de Richelieu's demands.

Fletcher, Richard, *The Quest for El Cid,* Oxford University Press, 1991.

There are many versions of the legend of El Cid but also many stories that refute the legend. This book by Fletcher is an interesting study of what the author claims to be more reliable historical facts about El Cid. Although claimed as an eleventh-century hero in Spain, Fletcher believes El Cid was not as heroic as some people would believe.

Knight, R. C., *Corneille's Tragedies,* Rowman and Littlefield, 1991.

Corneille's tragic plays, beginning with *Le Cid,* changed the course of French drama. Many scholars have studied Corneille's works to extract the model role that they played, but their focus was on the first three or four tragedies that Corneille wrote. In Knight's work, all of Corneille's tragedies are examined, giving a fuller understanding of the playwright.

Menocal, Maria Rosa, *The Ornament of the World: How Muslims, Jews, and Christians Created a Culture of Tolerance in Medieval Spain,* Back Bay Books, 2003.

In this book, Menocal displays medieval Spain as a rich culture of literature and science with an unusual tolerance of differences in cultures. She claims that secular poetry rose from this mixing of cultures and spread throughout Europe. She focuses on the Andalusian kingdoms that thrived before Christian monarchs expelled or killed all non-Catholics in Spain.

# The Miss Firecracker Contest

BETH HENLEY

1980

*The Miss Firecracker Contest* is a two-act play that was originally produced in Los Angeles in the spring of 1980. It was the first play that Beth Henley wrote after *Crimes of the Heart*, but it was already in production before *Crimes of the Heart* won the Pulitzer Prize. Eventually, both plays were produced on Broadway and made into movies with screenplays also written by Henley. Holly Hunter played the lead role in both the Broadway and movie versions of *The Miss Firecracker Contest*. It became available in book form in 1985 from the Dramatists Play Service.

This story belongs in the group of Southern Gothic comedies for which Henley is best known. Its heroine, Carnelle, is an irrepressible young woman who thinks that winning the local beauty contest will restore her soiled reputation and make her somebody in her small Mississippi community. The family and friends who help her along the way are a dysfunctional bunch who tackle life in their own peculiar ways. There is a former beauty queen cousin, Elain, who comes to offer advice and to run away from her husband and children. Elain's brother, Delmount, has come home from the mental institution to sell the family house and provide Carnelle another way out. Wandering into the chaos as Carnelle's seamstress is sweet and strange Popeye, who falls in love with Delmount. The general conclusion the characters reach is that, even if the real

you is not the fulfillment of your hopes, you will be more at peace if you learn to define and accept your own self.

# AUTHOR BIOGRAPHY

Beth Henley's birthplace and upbringing have determined the subject and setting of many of her plays. Born in Jackson, Mississippi on May 8, 1952, Elizabeth Becker Henley is the second of four daughters of an attorney and state senator, Charles Boyce, and an actress, Elizabeth Josephine Henley. As a child, she attentively watched her mother's work in regional theatre and followed this interest to a fine arts degree at Southern Methodist University in 1974. Although she aspired to be an actress, she wrote her first play *Am I Blue* while in college. She taught at the Dallas Minority Repertory Theatre for a year after graduation, studied and taught for another year at the University of Illinois-Urbana, then moved to Los Angeles.

She soon realized that breaking into acting was a futile effort and turned to playwriting. Her second play, *Crimes of the Heart*, was first produced in 1979 and went on in 1981 to be the first play ever to win a Pulitzer Prize before it appeared on Broadway. It was also the first Pulitzer given to a female playwright in twenty-three years. Subsequently, the play won a Tony nomination for best play, as well as an Oscar nomination for best adapted screenplay when the movie version was produced in 1986. *The Miss Firecracker Contest*, another Henley play that was produced in 1980, was also made into a movie in 1989.

In addition to her continued work in playwriting, Henley has written screenplays and television scripts. In most of her work, Henley gives the lead roles to women. Most of her works can be classified as Southern literature because they are set in the South and expertly reproduce Southern dialect and colloquialisms. Further, they can be considered Southern Gothic because death and freakish disaster permeate the plots, adding to a comic style that has the audience laughing at the humor and wincing at the pathos at the same time. Her characters tend to be misfits who, like real people, are not always successful in overcoming their flaws. Nonetheless, Henley treats them with compassion and optimism.

# PLOT SUMMARY

### Act 1, Scene 1

As *The Miss Firecracker Contest* opens, Carnelle Scott is practicing her talent routine for the upcoming Fourth of July beauty pageant in Brookhaven, Mississippi. A seamstress, Popeye Jackson, arrives and Carnelle hires her to make a pageant costume. As Popeye takes measurements, she tells Carnelle that she got her sewing start making outfits for bullfrogs. Popeye comments that the house is scary, and Carnelle explains that it belonged to her recently deceased Aunt Ronelle. Carnelle adds that her aunt's cancer treatment involved a pituitary gland transplant from a monkey that resulted in Ronelle "growing long, black hairs all over her body." The dialogue continues to reveal how Carnelle was orphaned and grew up with her aunt, uncle, and the two cousins she adores. Popeye notices a picture of Carnelle's cousin Delmount and falls in love immediately. Carnelle reveals that Delmount has recently been released from a mental institution.

Then Carnelle's other cousin, Elain, arrives unexpectedly. Elain won the town beauty contest fifteen years earlier. In discussions of the pageant, it is revealed that Carnelle has a promiscuous past that might keep her from winning. Elain admits that she has left her husband and two sons. Popeye comes back to find Delmount and explains to him how she got her nickname. Delmount tells Carnelle that he has returned to sell the house but will give her half of the proceeds to help her move away from Brookhaven. Carnelle gets the idea of winning the contest as a way to leave in a "blaze of glory." Delmount also lashes into Elain for not helping him to get out of the mental hospital.

### Act 1, Scene 2

The next Saturday, Carnelle awaits the phone call that will tell her she has made it into the contest finals. While they wait, Elain takes a phone call from her husband and tells him that she is not coming home. Delmount is thrilled though he knows that Elain never follows through on her plans. They fight over memories of their mother. Popeye arrives, and since the phone call is well past due, everyone assumes that Carnelle did not make the finals. Popeye reveals to Elain and Carnelle that she is in love with Delmount. Elain tells Popeye that Delmount is unstable. Popeye tries to talk to Delmount about his poetry and his nightmares, but he leaves with a headache. Elain tries to console Carnelle and Popeye. Then the phone call finally comes announcing that Carnelle has made the pageant finals. A celebration ensues, which Delmount fails to appreciate.

### Act 2, Scene 1

At the pageant, Carnelle talks over the different contestants' chances with the pageant coordinator, Tessy. Then, Carnelle's former lover, Mac Sam, drops by her dressing room but leaves when Delmount arrives excited about the success of the auction of his mother's things. They also discuss the contestants before Carnelle reveals that Popeye is in love with Delmount. Elain arrives to announce that she has been asked to give a speech about her life as a beauty queen. Delmount and Mac Sam hunt down Popeye to repair the dress Elain has loaned to Carnelle. A wild scene ensues as Carnelle, way behind schedule, frantically tries to get dressed as everyone offers advice.

### Act 2, Scene 2

The pageant unfolds. Carnelle trips and falls on her face. The crowd laughs, calls her "Miss Hot Tamale" and throws things at her. Delmount attacks the worst tormentor but is pelted with rocks until Mac Sam rescues him. Popeye and Elain comically try to treat his wound, then discuss how Popeye lost her job. Mac Sam proceeds to do smoke ring tricks, and Delmount follows by wiggling his ears. Carnelle returns to the stage just as Elain receives flowers from her husband. She has decided to go back to him because she knows she is used to the life he can give her. Carnelle's dance routine is a hit with the crowd, and her expectations are raised again. However, she comes in last in the contest. Although the others tell her she does not have to suffer more humiliation by following the float in the parade, Carnelle insists that she must follow the rules.

### Act 2, Scene 3

Carnelle runs off to hide after she spat and screamed at rude bystanders during the parade. Elain goes off to meet Mac Sam for a once-in-her-life fling. Delmount and Popeye go to see the fireworks together. Carnelle sneaks back into the

*Beth Henley*

dressing room to retrieve her things, but Mac Sam finds her there and asks her for one more night together. She declines, planning to go home, but Delmount and Popeye talk her into joining them. As they watch the fireworks, Carnelle confesses to not knowing the point of it all, but they all agree it is a nice night out.

## CHARACTERS

### Popeye Jackson

Popeye is the seamstress who makes Carnelle's costume; she becomes involved in the pageant madness while adding further strange elements to the story. A funny character with a hard life, Popeye got her nickname from a childhood prank that caused her eyes to bulge, but left her with the ability to hear through her eyes. She is a semi-literate, naïve, and always out-of-luck young woman who learned to sew as a child by making outfits for bullfrogs because she didn't have any dolls. Popeye is sin-

# MEDIA ADAPTATIONS

- The screenplay for *The Miss Firecracker Contest* was also written by Henley. Produced as *Miss Firecracker* (1989), the movie starred Holly Hunter, Mary Steenburgen, Tim Robbins, Alfre Woodard, and Scott Glen. It was directed by Thomas Schlamme. The film was released by HBO Studios in 1997 on VHS and by First Look Pictures on DVD in 2004.

cerely kind and curious about everything. Popeye falls in love with Delmount just from seeing his picture. Popeye is rewarded with Delmount's returned affection; this theme is perhaps the heart of the play.

### Tessy Mahoney

As the beauty contestant coordinator, Tessy is supposed to keep Carnelle on schedule and cue her appearances on stage. Tessy's ugliness makes her another misfit at the beauty contest. Her past scandalous tryst with Delmount adds one more bizarre twist as she flirts with him anew.

### Elain Rutledge

Elain is Carnelle's cousin, and she is everything that Carnelle is not. Although they grew up together, Elain was the spoiled beauty and Carnelle the misfortunate orphan. Elain won the Miss Firecracker contest when she was just 17, while Carnelle is 25 and pushing the eligibility limits. Elain did everything her mother told her to do by going to junior college and parleying her beauty into marriage with a wealthy man. To Carnelle, it appears that Elain has everything: the big house in the big city, a husband and children, beauty, and class. Elain, however, feels suffocated by her life and comes back home with the intention of leaving her husband and two sons because she doesn't like them. Naturally, she is asked to give a speech at the

town's Fourth of July festivities about her life as a beauty. Delmount accuses Elain of never being able to go through with any of her threats. As predicted, she gives in to her husband's pleadings and decides to go back to him because, she says, "I need someone who adores me." Her selfishness enables her to dismiss the needs of her family, but doesn't allow her to leave the luxuries to which she has become accustomed.

### Mac Sam

One of Carnelle's former lovers, Mac Sam seems to truly care about her, even if she did give him syphilis. The carnival's balloon vendor, he cheers on Carnelle as she competes in the beauty contest. Mac Sam is tubercular, drinks heavily, and hasn't bothered to get his syphilis cured because he is tired of life—but not so tired that he doesn't ask Carnelle to spend the night with him. When she declines and says goodbye, he remarks: "I'll always remember you as the one who could take it on the chin" and then he leaves to meet Elain for a wild night.

### Carnelle Scott

The play revolves around Carnelle's attempt to win her town's annual Fourth of July beauty contest. She is 25 years old, works in a jewelry store, and is known around town as "Miss Hot Tamale" for her promiscuous past. However, Carnelle is trying to change all that. She got her syphilis cured, joined a church, volunteers for the cancer society, and invites an orphan to dinner every week. Carnelle is insecure and has low self-esteem. After Carnelle's mother died when Carnelle was an infant and her father abandoned her at age nine, she grew up with her aunt who favored Carnelle's older cousin, Elain. Her father came back after her Uncle George died, but soon her father died as well. Shortly before the time of the story, Carnelle's mean Aunt Ronelle dies. Having been surrounded by death all her life, Carnelle is trying to make sense out of life and find her own identity. Carnelle sees the Miss Firecracker contest as a way to redeem herself and to be somebody. She doesn't understand that the social system will never permit her to win, that dyeing her hair bright red will look ridiculous instead of patriotic, or that stomping her feet to music is not tap dancing. Once her cousin Delmount offers to give her enough money to start a new life elsewhere, Carnelle further imagines that being Miss Firecracker will allow her to go out in a "blaze of glory." Instead, after working really hard to prepare, she is humiliated by the crowd and finishes in last place. Although she has enough integrity to fulfill the duties of the person in last place, she spits and screams at the people who taunt her during the parade and then hides. Carnelle's tenacity evokes the loyalty of family and friends. They admire Carnelle's spunk and the indomitable spirit that enables her to spring back, even after the mortification of the pageant, to enjoy the night's fireworks.

### *Delmount Williams*

After he has spent time in a mental institution and worked at a job scraping dead animals off the road, Carnelle's cousin and Elain's brother, Delmount returns to town to sell his mother's house. He intends to use the proceeds to go to college to study philosophy, but he offers half the proceeds to Carnelle to enable her to leave town and start a new life. Although perhaps more realistic than the rest of his family, Delmount is unstable and has a history of rash actions, such as rushing out to beat up the guys who taunt Carnelle during the pageant. He also has an obsession with exotic beauty that always gets him into trouble and results in gruesome nightmares about women's dismembered bodies. Yet, Delmount has a sensible disdain for the phoniness of the beauty pageant. He doesn't respect Elain's life choices either, especially the one that left him in an asylum when she could have gotten him out. However, he always forgives her transgressions. Delmount is amazed to learn that Popeye is in love with him, having been entranced with his ability to wiggle his ears and write poetry. But he then falls for her, too, and therein might be Delmount's redemption.

## THEMES

### *Seeking Identity*

A common theme in the works of Beth Henley is that her characters are seeking their identity, particularly the female lead seeks her identity as a

## TOPICS FOR FURTHER STUDY

- Considering the characters, their situations, and the choices that they make, does this play express a feminist message? Write an opinion essay as your answer.

- Three female playwrights won Pulitzer Prizes in the 1980s: Beth Henley in 1981; Marsha Norman in 1983; and Wendy Wasserstein in 1989. Research these women and compare their prize-winning works.

- The work of Beth Henley is often described as Southern Gothic. What is Southern Gothic and what elements of *The Miss Firecracker Contest* fit into this category?

- Beth Henley is often compared to other Southern writers such as Eudora Welty, William Faulkner, Flannery O'Connor, and Tennessee Williams. Research one of these writers and discuss his or her similarities to Henley.

- Do you think that beauty contests are sexist and demeaning to women, or do you think they have value in U.S. culture? Write an essay defending your position.

woman outside of her family and her relationships with men. In *The Miss Firecracker Contest*, Carnelle is trying to find an identity other than orphaned cousin, other than "Miss Hot Tamale," and other than the ugly loser she sees herself to be. She does not find her identity in a beauty title, but she may yet find it with the help of her family and friends and her resilient nature. Elain is seeking an identity as her real and complete self as a woman rather than that of the proper wife and mother. However, Elain doesn't have the courage to leave her security for any longer than a one-night fling. Her identity is tied up with being adored; therefore, she must go back to the life that sets her on a pedestal—a miserable pedestal, but a pedestal nonetheless. Delmount is also seeking a new identity. He wants to go to college to study philosophy and try to find a new life away from the claims and labels put on him by his hometown. His new identity, though, may be a reflection of Popeye's love. It is typical of Henley that, although some of her characters succeed in their quest for identity, they usually do so only partially and with compromises.

## Beauty

True beauty, and the only kind that should count ultimately, is internal. Unfortunately, internal beauty is hard to discern, and an awful lot of fuss is made over the external kind. Consequently, Carnelle, who has worshipped her beautiful cousin since childhood, and witnessed the perfect life that beauty has supposedly brought to Elain, thinks that physical beauty is all that matters. Carnelle says, "I feel sorry for ugly people, I really do." So, she is intent on proving her beauty even though she worries that she is actually ugly herself. As a teenager, she sought affirmation from men, only to discover that they were after her "carnal" beauty. In a desperate effort to redeem her reputation, Carnelle again tries to prove that she has physical beauty as well as the other features that the community finds attractive. When that fails, Henley gives ample evidence of the beauty of friendship—through Mac Sam's tribute when he says that Carnelle can really take it on the chin and through the comradeship that Carnelle finds with Delmount and Popeye as they watch the fireworks. In the process, Henley pokes fun at the culture's vanity while simultaneously showing the insidious harm that it does. For example, Elain's speech about life as a beauty makes it seem that she doesn't have to be anything else; she has an excuse for not following other dreams. Elain has found sufficient power in being beautiful to satisfy her needs, but she is stuck with being Miss Firecracker all her life. Carnelle has escaped that label, albeit painfully, and is still free to mature as a woman.

## The Need to be Loved

Carnelle has a desperate need to be loved. She grew up without the love of parents and with the disdain of her aunt. Consequently, she looked for love in one sexual affair after another. Once she realized that promiscuity brought her only disgrace and the nickname "Miss Hot Tamale," she sought a form of love through acceptance. Carnelle wants to belong to her community, so she joins a church and does charitable work. The ultimate sign of acceptance, though, would be winning the Miss Firecracker Contest and becoming queen of Brookhaven, Mississippi.

Elain also has a need to be loved, but not in the form of admiration for her beauty or the silly infatuation of her husband. Unfortunately, Elain has only a brief exposure to this awareness before she decides that her greater need is to be adored and pampered as the icon of Southern femininity that she has set herself up to be. Delmount also has a need to be loved, but he is so frightened and confused by his sexual fantasies that he doesn't realize his need to be loved until he is confronted with the true love of Popeye. Luckily, Delmount seems to instantly succumb to the power of innocent love, indicating that there might be hope for him.

# STYLE

## The Foil

A foil is a character whose personality or physical qualities obviously contrast and thereby emphasize those of another character. Elain serves as the foil to Carnelle. Carnelle thinks that Elain has everything that a woman could want: beauty, a rich husband, a big house, pretty clothes, a place in the best social circles, and the title of Miss Firecracker. Carnelle worries that she is ugly while Elain can give a speech on her life as a beauty. Elain has done everything according to propriety, while Carnelle has made herself a social outcast because of her promiscuous past. Carnelle is single, lives in her aunt's house by the charity of her cousins, and apparently has trashy taste. In the end, however, Carnelle has achieved more personal success than Elain because Carnelle has dared to take a risk while Elain feels trapped in her life.

## Southern Literature

*The Miss Firecracker Contest* fits into the genre of Southern literature because it is about the Southern United States and is written by a playwright who was reared in the South. The play uses

Southern voice and dialect, which Henley accomplishes precisely. In addition, a characteristic of Southern literature that applies to this play is the importance of family: Carnelle lives in her aunt's house and idolizes the two cousins who are important characters in the play. Another characteristic is a sense of community: Carnelle's whole world is the town of Brookhaven, Mississippi, as well as her reputation in it, and her efforts to gain acceptance through one of the town's biggest community events, the annual beauty contest. A sense of human limitation or moral dilemma is also characteristic of Southern literature. The story of *The Miss Firecracker Contest* is built around the limitations of its characters and their search for their identities.

Critics often discuss the elements of Southern Gothic in Henley's work, i.e., stories that include grotesque, macabre, or fantastic incidents. In the case of *The Miss Firecracker Contest*, there are numerous references to incidents such as Aunt Ronelle's hairy illness, the bizarre ways Carnelle's uncle and father died, Popeye's eyes and her frog costumes, Delmount's bloody dreams, the Mahoney sisters' deformed kittens, and so on. In Henley's hands, these elements are used for comic effect, but they also serve to point out the sad and pathetic nature of the characters' lives, as well as their resilience.

# HISTORICAL CONTEXT

## The 1970s

The 1970s was a period of recovery, as well as continued turmoil, for the American people. The 1960s had been violent, troubled times that saw three major political assassinations, the Civil Rights movement, the Vietnam War, and anti-war demonstrations. The pendulum swung back towards conservatism with the election of Richard Nixon for president in 1968. However, his administration was riddled with scandal, resulting first in the resignation of the vice-president and eventually in the resignation of the president himself. The Watergate investigation led the headlines for months while Gerald Ford, the first president ever to serve without having been elected to the office, or even that of the vice-president, tried to restore normalcy. Ford was replaced by Jimmy Carter, the first Southern president since before the post-Civil War Reconstruction era. Carter was successful in negotiating peace between Egypt and Israel, but wasn't successful in

getting the American hostages freed from Iran until the day he relinquished his office to Ronald Reagan in 1981. The sexual and technological revolutions of the 1960s and 1970s, as well as integration, changed the culture of the United States. In the process, the job market developed more openings that could be filled by women just as women were demanding more opportunities.

## The Climate for Women Playwrights

In the 1970s, Beth Henley wrote her first plays, including *The Miss Firecracker Contest*, which is set in no particular time period. This play needs little adjustment, if any, as the times change. By 1980, Henley had two plays going on stage. In 1981, she won the Pulitzer Prize for best drama, but she was the first woman to do so in twenty-three years. The situation for women playwrights was paradoxical. In the 1930s to the 1950s, the only female playwright of note was Lillian Hellman. During the 1970s and 1980s, there was a noticeable proliferation of young women playwrights. Women were ''in'' to the point that plays by women of the 1960s were resurrected. However, their subjects were not necessarily about women or from a woman's perspective, as women writers tried to fit into the male-dominated mainstream. Despite the number of women writing plays, few were getting them produced on Broadway or in regional theatres. One had to look to Off- or Off-Off Broadway to see a play written by a woman. Although two more women playwrights won Pulitzers in the 1980s (Marsha Norman in 1983 and Wendy Wasserstein in 1989), by the end of the decade only 7 percent of the plays on stage nationwide were written by women. This male dominance continues into the 2000s. Another three women won the Pulitzer Prize in Drama around the turn of the century (Paula Vogel in 1998; Margaret Edson in 1999; Suzan-Lori Parks in 2002). Despite this, only 17 percent of plays in production in America in 2002 were written by female playwrights.

## The Culture of Beauty Pageants

Beauty pageants, although held across the country, are more of a Southern phenomenon, perhaps because the image of a Southern lady can be taught through these events. As anthropologist Robert H. Lavenda explained: ''Small-town pageants are about social class, achievement, community values, and femininity in a small-town context, and they are training for the social positions toward which many of the candidates aspire.'' Furthermore, and this is a

# COMPARE & CONTRAST

- **Late 1970s:** Former First Lady Betty Ford enters a treatment program for alcohol and prescription drug addiction.

  **Today:** The Betty Ford Clinic, founded by the former-First Lady and frequented by celebrities, is the nation's best known treatment center for addictive behaviors.

- **Late 1970s:** Garfield the cat cartoons make their first appearance in the nation's newspapers.

  **Today:** The enormously popular cartoon cat, having made television specials and sold millions of items of Garfield paraphernalia, branches out to his first feature-length movie in 2004.

- **Late 1970s:** The first "test-tube baby" is born in England, resulting from a successful in-vitro fertilization and embryo implantation into the mother.

  **Today:** Thousands of IVF babies are born each year as the process has become further improved and culturally accepted, despite some moral and ethical objections.

- **Late 1970s:** Statewide limitations on indoor smoking are passed in Iowa and New Jersey.

  **Today:** Indoor smoking is almost universally prohibited in public places in the United States.

- **Late 1970s:** AIDS has not yet been recognized as a new disease. The most common sexually-transmitted diseases are syphilis or gonorrhea, which can be easily cured.

  **Today:** AIDS, as an incurable disease, is the worst of the sexually-transmitted diseases and has spread in epidemic proportions around the world.

- **Late 1970s:** The Ayatollah Khomeini gains control of the country of Iran, which quickly becomes a major concern after 400 Americans are taken hostage by his followers and not released for 444 days.

  **Today:** Iran is making some progress toward a more democratic society while America is involved in a war and its aftermath with Iran's neighboring country, Iraq.

- **Late 1970s:** In 1976, NASA lands spacecraft on Mars for the first time, the Apple II computer is produced in 1977, and the first ATMs are built in 1978.

  **Today:** Personal and laptop computers are common household items in the United States, cell phones allow instant communication, and NASA goes back to Mars for further exploration.

point that Carnelle didn't realize in the play, "The pageant is not designed to select the most beautiful young woman in town, but rather a suitable representative for the community." Often, suitability is determined by the importance of the candidates' families. Carnelle kept going over the list of finalists and comparing herself to the others in terms of beauty. She thought she had a real chance to win because she was sure she was prettier than the others. Realistically, however, as Elain feared, Carnelle came in last due to the bad reputation, which made her the least representative of the values of the community. Young women enter these

contests, as Carnelle does, because they have something to prove, or because they need to be loved and think adulation will be a sufficient substitute. Fortunately for Carnelle, she realizes, albeit too late, that such a contest can be ludicrous when one has the love of friends and family.

## CRITICAL OVERVIEW

Critical reactions to *The Miss Firecracker Contest* have been mixed. Among the favorable reactions is a 1994 *English Studies* article that praises *The Miss Firecracker Contest* for the "depths in even the most objectionable characters and the enormous toughness in some of life's apparent losers." Furthermore, the article asserts that Henley "puts most faith in friendship ... Brutal conditions cannot destroy their victims as long as emotional support comes from somewhere."

In contrast, Harry Bowman, writing for the *Dallas Morning News* declared that *The Miss Firecracker Contest* has no heart and no point. The reviewer found the characters to be "strange and weird" caricatures who fail to become human. "Carnelle becomes just another simpleton. And not a very appealing one at that. She has a strident edge that keeps snagging on the viewer's sensibilities." Patrick Taggert, the reviewer for the *Austin American-Statesman,* admits that "You either love [Henley's] grotesque characters and frenzied action or you hate them," but he also said that she carves "up Southern manners and archetypes" in *The Miss Firecracker Contest.* Moreover, her characters

> seldom speak below a loud roar, never know a subtle gesture. She cartoonishly savages her characters, all the while making feeble attempts to show how innately noble these poor pieces of trash really are. How does she illuminate this nobility? With the occasionally insightful line of dialogue or a phony, late-hour epiphany, as when Carnelle realizes she doesn't have to belong to anything, least of all her crazy community.

Ironically, Carnelle's realization about the value of independence comes after she has pursued fitting into her community by conforming to its values. It is a feminist lesson, but feminists have not been certain that Henley's plays are feminist. Yes, they have strong female lead characters, but Elain's attempt at rebelling against social conventions fails, and she resigns herself to her stereotyped role. Carnelle, instead of asserting a lesson learned or a life transformed, says at the end of the play, "I don't know what the main thing is. I don't have the vaguest idea." A discussion about *The Miss Firecracker Contest* in *Realism and the American Dramatic Tradition* concludes that the play conveys "nostalgia for the traditional family" and an admiration for "a determined, if pathetic, quest for and celebration of female identity." Furthermore, Henley parodies female sexuality: "Carnelle suffers for illicit sex and finds affirmation only in family at play's and quest's end."

Paul Rosenfeldt, writing in *The Absent Father in Modern Drama,* a book that examines "the pattern of the absent father" that appears to span

*Erika Harold crowned as Miss America 2003*

"the scope of modern drama," finds this pattern in Henley's works. Certainly, in *The Miss Firecracker Contest* this absence is emphasized. Carnelle's father leaves her with relatives. After Elain and Delmount's father dies, Carnelle's father returns, but he also dies soon after. However, it should be noted that the mothers, too, are both deceased. Further, this book purports that, "Unlike the American son, the American daughter of the absent father lives in a world where there is no possibility of escape through space and distance." In *The Miss Firecracker Contest,* Henley implies that Carnelle may yet escape.

Other criticism about Henley's plays as a body of work runs the gamut from positive to negative. The *Austin American-Statesman* declared that Henley's works are "heavy-handed, offensive and alternately sickly sweet and sneering," while other critics comment on Henley's clearly delineated characters, heartwarming stories, compassionate portrayal of human failings, and optimistic endings. The *New York Times* review expresses the confusion of elements that may be the cause of the varied reactions:

> We hear about midgets, orphans, and deformed kittens—and they're the fortunate ones. Other charac-

ters, whether on stage or off, are afflicted by cancer, tuberculosis, venereal disease, and most of all, heartbreak. Even so, the evening's torrential downpour of humor—alternately Southern-Gothic absurdist, melancholy and broad—almost never subsides.

Generally, the critics talk about Henley's place in Southern literature. She has been compared to Eudora Welty, Flannery O'Connor, and William Faulkner. However, Richard Schickel, writing for *Time* speculates that

> Though [Henley's] territory looks superficially like the contemporary American South, it is really a country of the mind: one of Tennessee Williams' provinces that has surrendered to a Chekhovian raiding party, perhaps. Her strength is a wild anecdotal inventiveness, but her people, lost in the ramshackle drams and tumble-down ambitions with which she invests them, often seem to be metaphors waywardly adrift. They are blown this way and that by the gales of laughter they provoke, and they frequently fail to find a solid connection with clear and generally relevant meaning.

As a living author who continues to write steadily, Henley and her works cannot yet be fully assessed. However, William Demastes, author of a book on the new realism in American theatre, is probably right to assume that Henley will continue to "draw from and build upon her small-town world of Mississippi and use her uniquely trained eyes to perceive in that microcosm the modern absurdities of existence."

# CRITICISM

## *Lois Kerschen*

*Kerschen is a freelance writer and adjunct college English instructor. In this essay, Kerschen shows how Henley uses each character and bizarre anecdotes to create both the comedy and the message in this play.*

A constant litany of the bizarre runs through Henley's dialogue. Her plays are sometimes called tragicomedies, or black comedies, because the humor is achieved through eccentric characters who have experienced strange incidents in their lives. These incidents, often involving violence and death, are sprinkled throughout the play for their comedic effect and for what they reveal about the characters. Some critics find this technique to be too much, but others appreciate the creativity and enjoy the anecdotes that range from the merely unusual to the outright ludicrous. Nothing is anywhere near nor-

mal for Henley's characters: Carnelle has dyed her hair bright red, Delmount can wiggle his ears, Popeye has bulging eyes, Mac Sam is riddled with diseases, and perfect Elain is emotionally frigid and completely self-centered. They can't even find plain ice to put on Delmount's wound. Instead they use a purple snow cone—they were out of cherry, Popeye explains, as if that makes perfect sense.

The element of death is introduced early when Carnelle gets acquainted with Popeye and tells her matter-of-factly that "people've been dying practically all my life. I guess I should be used to it by now." Carnelle's mother died when she was barely a year old. After Carnelle came to live with the Williams family, her Uncle George fell "to his death trying to pull this bird's nest out from the chimney." Then her father "drops dead in the summer's heat while running out to the Tropical Ice Cream truck." Popeye commiserates by telling how her own brother died when he was bitten by a water moccasin.

Aunt Ronelle is an influential character in the play, even though she is also dead. Robert Andreach, in a book about creating the self in contemporary drama, explains that Aunt Ronelle reared Carnelle to feel "inferior to her two cousins. To compensate, [Carnelle] concentrated on the one area where she felt that she could excel: with the males in the town." Aunt Ronelle's importance to the characters is evident from the number of times she and her fatal illness are mentioned. Carnelle tells Popeye about Aunt Ronelle in the opening scene when Popeye observes that the house is scary. It seems that her aunt had cancer of the pituitary gland, so surgeons replaced it with one from a monkey. The transplant lengthened her life only a month or so and had the "dreadful" side effect of causing her to grow long, black hairs all over her body just like an ape. This event is a source of conflict between Elain and Delmount, who have the typical sibling argument about who Mama loved best. Delmount thinks their mother had the embarrassing transplant just to be mean to them. But Elain ennobles the experience by repeating as an adage, in various forms throughout the play that "Mama was enlightened by her affliction."

According to critic Patrick Taggert, writing for the *Austin American-Statesman,* Delmount "seems to serve no other purpose than to permit Henley to have at least one character yelling and throwing things." While that is not exactly the case, it is true that Henley tends to use her male characters to

# WHAT DO I READ NEXT?

- Robert Harling's *Steel Magnolias* (1988) is another story of strong Southern women who support and encourage each other during times of challenge. Harling's novel was made into a blockbuster movie in 1989, starring Sally Fields, Dolly Parton, Shirley MacLaine, Daryl Hannah, Olympia Dukakis, and Julia Roberts.

- Alan Ball wrote *Five Women Wearing the Same Dress* (1998), a comedy about five very distinct women who feel the same about an upcoming wedding.

- *Beth Henley, Vol. 1: Collected Plays 1980–1989* (2000) and *Beth Henley, Vol. 2: Collected Plays 1990–1999* (2000) in the Contemporary Playwrights series form a two-volume set of all of her works to date, each prefaced by anecdotes from some of her collaborators.

- *Three Famous Short Novels* (1958), by William Faulkner, contains *The Bear, Old Man,* and *Spotted Horses,* and is a good sampling of the diversity of this Southern writer.

- *The Collected Stories of Eudora Welty* (1982) illustrates the complexity of stories and characters that made Welty an icon of Southern literature.

- Tennessee Williams's classic play *The Glass Menagerie* (1944) has since become required reading in most American schools and has been produced on stage and published countless times.

- Southern writer Flannery O'Connor's stories were collected in *The Complete Stories.* This book contains thirty-one short stories of penetrating dark humor, which Flannery wrote before her death in 1964 at the age of thirty-nine.

---

catalyze the action of the female characters. In that light, Delmount has a problem with women. His confusion fits in perfectly with the women around him, who are also confused about themselves. Delmount claims that he has "a weakness for the classical, exotic beauty in a woman. I've been a fool for it. It's my romantic nature." Yet he has dreams about dismembered women. Linda Rohrer Paige in *Feminist Writers* speculates that "Delmount's imagination can envision women only from a limited, warped, or distorted perspective." Delmount is conflicted by the patriarchal image of women; this is the image he has been taught to use as a standard of beauty. This is at odds with his intuitive understanding that there is more to beauty than the cultural stereotype. Consequently, when a woman doesn't fit into his preconceived mold, in his dreams she becomes, as Paige surmises, "violently fragmented, disembodied, a portrait of beauty aborted."

Delmount's problem may be cured by Popeye. She isn't a classic beauty, or even a beauty, and it could hardly be said that her bulging eyes are "exotic." However, Popeye's love for Delmount may be just what he needs to get over his unrealistic expectations about women. It is poetic justice that he should fall in love with someone so outside his image of a beautiful woman. Perhaps by breaking away from the confines of his rigid expectations, he will break free from a number of his neuroses. One thing that Delmount and Popeye have in common is that they are both social outcasts who cannot imagine what is so important about the Miss Firecracker contest.

Popeye may be a calmer, more down-to-earth person than the others in the play, but her anecdotes reveal her off-kilter perspective. First we learn that she practiced sewing as a child by making clothes for bullfrogs because she didn't have any dolls. At one time she had a boyfriend who wanted her to meow and purr and liked to pet her as if she were a cat. Fortunately, Popeye recognized that behavior as weird. The reason for her name is a tragic tale in itself. Her brother threw some gravel into her eyes and then treated the stinging pain with ear drops instead of eye drops. From that point on her eyes bulged out, so people started calling her Popeye.

ONE THING THAT DELMOUNT AND POPEYE HAVE IN COMMON IS THAT THEY ARE BOTH SOCIAL OUTCASTS WHO CANNOT IMAGINE WHAT IS SO IMPORTANT ABOUT THE MISS FIRECRACKER CONTEST."

She may have to use a magnifying glass to see up close, but she can now hear voices through her eyes, a unique talent indeed.

The character of Delmount further deals with the problem of beauty in his relationship with his sister. In large measure, Delmount gets his image of beauty from Elain. But he sees how messed-up beauty has made Elain and that adds to his confusion about beauty. Delmount loves his sister, but she left him in a mental institution when she had the power to get him out. He hates her for that, but as he says, he always forgives her for everything she does. "You'd think," he complains, "after you left me in that lunatic asylum, I'd know better than to trust you." Does he forgive her because she is his sister, or because beautiful people always get away with the harm they cause? Delmount, like the rest of society, may give latitude to some people just because they are beautiful. But he is left wondering how far anyone can trust beauty. Perhaps that is why Delmount falls for Popeye—her trustworthiness is ultimately more attractive than physical beauty.

The part of Mac Sam is a small one; he doesn't even appear until the second act. Nonetheless, he, too, is a male character who is useful to the plot. His most important purpose is to deliver the line to Carnelle, "I'll always remember you as the one who could take it on the chin." He also catalyzes the action by bringing the frog to Carnelle, thus letting her know that Popeye is somewhere nearby. Mac Sam provides a sympathetic male ear for Delmount, serves as Carnelle's biggest cheerleader, but he is also a link to her promiscuous past. Mac Sam also provides Elain with her one reckless night under the wisteria trees.

The story that Popeye tells about the midgets is a perfect example of Henley's style. It starts out as a cute story about two midgets, Sweet Pea and Willas, who marry and move into a darling little house made for their size. Then the story turns tragic: their child is born "regular size" like all their relatives and soon outgrows their "mite sized furniture." Consequently, they have to relinquish their child to Sweet Pea's mother to rear, and their hearts are broken. With this anecdote, the audience is moved from sweetly funny to sadly painful. Perhaps this anecdote is a mini-lesson in the midst of the running message that Henley wants the audience to understand: that being different, ugly, odd, or quirky can be difficult at best and excruciatingly demoralizing at worst. Henley may exaggerate the strangeness of her characters, but the point is that we all have our odd traits, yet we are still lovable, worthwhile people.

This technique is used in reverse in Carnelle's story. She was an unwanted child abandoned by her father with nothing but a pillow case full of dirty rags. She had ringworms all over her head, so Aunt Ronelle shaved off her hair to treat the sores. Carnelle went around wearing a yellow wool knit cap pulled down over her head. Delmount said she was an ugly sight and never did attain any self-esteem. He says she had to "sleep with every worthless soul in Brookhaven trying to prove she was attractive." With the beauty contest, Carnelle has once again chosen the wrong way to prove herself and winds up with just more humiliation. Instead of a yellow wool cap, she wears a faded red dress that doesn't fit and then she trips on the hoop skirt and falls flat on her face. Nonetheless, her natural resilience is already bringing her back to hopefulness within a few hours after the pageant. On one of the worst days of her life, Carnelle looks up at the fireworks and says, "Gosh, it's a nice night." She still has no idea what it all means, but the audience is left with the impression that she will keep trying to find out.

Henley's signature is not only her weird humor but also her optimism. The anecdotes may often be sickening and sad, but they make a point while also somehow being funny and upbeat. Some of her characters may fail temporarily in their attempts to solve their problems, but in *The Miss Firecracker Contest*, the band of strange underdogs has taken steps forward together that may get them there someday.

**Source:** Lois Kerschen, Critical Essay on *The Miss Firecracker Contest,* in *Drama for Students,* Thomson Gale, 2005.

## Catherine Dybiec Holm

*Holm is a fiction and nonfiction writer and editor. In this essay, Holm looks at how Henley treats the theme of appearance in this play.*

*The Miss Firecracker Contest* is a play about appearances. Appearances, literal and figurative, drive the lives and the motivations of these characters. Appearances make or break these people. The effects of appearances in these characters' pasts continue to haunt them and direct their choices and thoughts. It is no doubt intentional that the title of the play, and the event that the title refers to, is a beauty and talent contest. Even more interesting is the fact that this could easily have been a play about one main character's struggle with her own appearance. But in this play Henley gives her reader lots to think about. Even the secondary characters in this play change as a result of the Miss Firecracker contest and its consequences.

Carnelle starts out as a terribly insecure character who is utterly convinced that the Miss Firecracker contest is the one and only way to erase her "hot tamale" past. Her insecurities are apparent in the first few pages of the play. Carnelle badly wants Popeye to know how special and important the upcoming Miss Firecracker contest is. When Popeye hesitates in her responses or does not respond the way Carnelle expects, Carnelle gets uncomfortable. Carnelle is interrupted in the middle of her routine by Popeye's arrival, and it almost seems as if Carnelle wants, or hopes, for glowing accolades from Popeye. Popeye, on the other hand, seems unconcerned with appearances or affectations; her answers and her dialog throughout the play are usually direct and to the point.

> Carnelle: Wheew! Oh, and please excuse the way I look, but I've been practicing my routine. It's coming right along.
>
> Popeye: Good.
>
> Carnelle (after an awkward moment): Well, I guess what I should do is show you some sketches.

Carnelle seems to overreact with exaggerated disappointment when Popeye admits that she has never heard of the contest. However, Carnelle is almost ridiculously relieved when Popeye admits that she has only been in town for a few weeks and probably would not have known about the contest.

Carnelle is so insecure that she cannot bear the thought that her world and her efforts might actually be small and inconsequential. Based on her hopes for her looks, Carnelle hopes to put her past behind

> " PERHAPS HENLEY IS TRYING TO SAY THAT UNMARRED BY OUTER BEAUTY, A CHARACTER'S INNER BEAUTY MAY MORE EASILY SHINE THROUGH TO THE SURFACE."

her, win the contest, and leave the town and her old life behind in a "blaze of glory." The power of firecrackers and the power that Carnelle might achieve if she is indeed able to leave in a "blaze of glory" is alluded to in several different ways. The color red indicates fire, or a blaze. Carnelle is referred to as "Carnation." Carnelle wears a red dress of Elain's during part of the contest. Carnelle spits and hisses like a firecracker when she is heckled cruelly by the crowd. Carnelle does leave "in a blaze," though it is not the blaze she originally imagined.

Carnelle is also not confident about her looks and seems to take comfort in talking about how other people think she could have been a model. She is so lost in her own reverie that she is startled when Popeye tries to get her to relax.

> Carnelle: They say, "You should be up in Memphis working as a model. You really should."
>
> Popeye: (Trying to get Carnelle to relax her tightly tucked in stomach) You can just relax.
>
> Carnelle: What? Oh, I'm fine. Just fine.

When Popeye tells of sewing clothing for bullfrogs, Carnelle tries to make a joke of it, but her insecurity about her appearance leaks through again. Popeye, who is unfettered by any worries about her own appearance, completely misses the fine line that Carnelle walks between attempted humor and sad insecurity.

> Carnelle: Well, I certainly hope you don't think of me as any bullfrog.
>
> Popeye: Huh?
>
> Carnelle: I mean, think I'm ugly like one of those dumb bullfrogs of yours.
>
> Popeye: Oh, I don't.
>
> Carnelle: Well, of course you don't. I was just joking.
>
> Popeye: Oh.

Carnelle (suddenly very sad and uncomfortable): Are you about done?

Brought face to face with her insecurities about her appearance and her life, Carnelle throws in a spontaneous kick, knowing it is one thing she can do better than others can do. Throughout the play, Carnelle continually compares herself to the other contestants. Missy is ugly but can play the piano. Another girl is pretty but has yellow teeth. The reader gets the sense that Carnelle is hanging onto what little esteem she can carve out for herself. Carnelle achieves her esteem at the end of the play through the catharsis of her own anger and the realization that ''I was trying so hard t'belong all my life.''

It is interesting that the two least outwardly attractive characters in this play seem completely unconcerned about their appearances. Popeye wears thick-rimmed glasses and eccentric and non-stylish clothes but seems to move through the world innocently and removed from society's judgement about appearances. Mac Sam unselfconsciously coughs up clots of blood in all kinds of company and jokes about taking bets on which of his body organs will disintegrate first. Both of these characters have a compelling inner quality, however, that Carnelle and Elaine and Delmount do not realize within themselves until the end of the play.

Popeye is described as a ''small glowing person.'' There is a compelling quality to Popeye that makes the reader take notice of her, even though she is plainer than Carnelle and Carnelle's extended family. Popeye hears voices in her eyes, and she is aware enough to be scared by the feeling inside Carnelle's house, even though Popeye knows nothing of the tumultuous history in that home. Popeye looks at a picture of Delmount and knows instantly that she is in love. Popeye seems to be guided by an inner clarity that the better looking characters in the play lack.

Mac Sam, for his stooped appearance, constant cough, and emaciation, still has eyes that are ''magnetic and bloodshot at the same time.'' Mac Sam is ''extraordinarily sensual,'' which makes him interesting in this play. He manages to be attractive in spite of his looks.

Delmount is so obsessed with appearance that he will not make advances toward any woman who does not possess ''at least one classically beautiful characteristic.'' He alternately dreams of beautiful women and ugly women and, in a moment of confusion, seduces the town's ugly twins, Tessy and Missy. Delmount is also obsessed with repressing his own insanity, symbolically represented by his attempts to straighten his wild and curly hair. Elain calls him on his own internal struggle, when both Delmount and Elain are close to making important realizations about themselves.

Elain: So why do you straighten your wild hair? Why do you have horrible, sickening dreams about pieces of women's bodies? Some all beautiful, some all mutilated and bloody. I hate those dreams. They scare me.

In the end, Delmount dreams a magnificent dream of Popeye, a woman who he would have formerly not given a second look. Delmount falls in love with Popeye, somehow managing to bypass his former obsession with perfection in appearance. Popeye, with her own unerring inner voice, seems as if she knew that eventually her love for Delmount would be returned.

Elain's dialog takes a leap into a more honest realm as she finally leaves the superficial level that she had inhabited for so long and makes plans for a tryst with Mac Sam. ''I'm gonna be a reckless girl at least once in my dreary, dreary life,'' she says. Elain has taken her own journey from her original role as a beauty queen. In the beginning of the play, Elain feels burdened by her pretty face and her own good looks. Even so, she is thrilled to be chosen to speak about beauty at the contest. After the fiasco at the Miss Firecracker contest, Elain ruefully admits that Carnelle probably will not have much reason to admire her anymore.

Mac Sam is less concerned with appearance than Delmount, Elain, and Carnelle start out. All Mac Sam likes is a woman who can ''take it right slap on the chin.'' This foreshadows Carnelle's experience in the Miss Firecracker contest, when she is taunted, heckled, and pelted with peanuts. She reacts by fighting back and spitting like a firecracker, giving a double meaning to the title, and an allusion to a new strength that Carnelle has found inside herself.

Carnelle: I'd never been so mad as I was. And I spit out at everyone. I just spit at them. Oh! That's so awful it's almost funny!

Later, Mac Sam refers to her with real affection and alludes to his original mention of what he prefers in a woman, over appearances. He says to Carnelle, who has just departed, ''Goodbye, Baby. I'll always remember you as the one who could take it on the chin.''

The dichotomy that runs throughout this play is a theme of inner versus outer beauty. Surprisingly, Elain sums this up in reference to her own deceased mother, recalling that "Mama was at her most noblest when she was least attractive." The reader never meets this character but can easily picture the abusive mother who, for some reason, turned saint-like after an operation that left her with freakish side effects. Perhaps Henley is trying to say that unmarred by outer beauty, a character's inner beauty may more easily shine through to the surface. *The Miss Firecracker Contest* uses the themes of outer and inner appearances to guide these characters' journeys toward a realization of true beauty.

**Source:** Catherine Dybiec Holm, Critical Essay on *The Miss Firecracker Contest,* in *Drama for Students,* Thomson Gale, 2005.

### Linda Rohrer Paige

*In the following excerpt, Paige examines how the film version of* The Miss Firecracker Contest *focuses primarily on Carnelle and how the story is changed and cleaned up.*

*Miss Firecracker,* Henley's next film after *Crimes of the Heart,* again captivated audiences. As with *Crimes,* the screenwriter adds and subtracts, shifts and rearranges, thus telling new stories to old audiences. Yet, Henley remains true to her original vision. With her second film, Henley again foregrounds themes of transformation and autonomy, endeavoring to capture the spirit of the original play, *The Miss Firecracker Contest.*

In *Miss Firecracker,* the screenwriter transposed the title from its original emphasis upon the beauty contest to one almost exclusively concentrating on a single, heroic figure, Carnelle Scott. With a new title, *Miss Firecracker,* Henley further delved into Carnelle's complex relationship Elain, the beautiful cousin whose rivalry with Carnelle complicates her love. *Miss Firecracker* parades passions across the screen, and what more talented and passionate actor than Holly Hunter could Henley bring to the starring role of her heroine, Carnelle? A natural progression to follow the playwright from the stage to screen, Hunter, who starred in the Manhatten Theatre Club's premiere production of the play, seemed a logical choice for the role: "'Holly has a strange ability to be passionate and vulnerable, but extremely tough and rageful,' Henley says of her longtime collaborator. 'Also, she knows how to walk the edge between truth and humor. Holly hears the music of what I write.'" Given the

new, concentrated focus on Carnelle, the screenplay produces a rather different sort of story than that of the original play. Rather than a carnival of funny, bizarre, and touching characters, the film develops and displays a certain faintheartedness about her character as well. Whereas *The Miss Firecracker Contest* makes clear that Carnelle has been a bad girl, actually contracting syphilis and transmitting it, most notably, to her friend and previous lover, Mac Sam, the film slashes all references to Carnelle's association with disease, acknowledging nothing coarser than the protagonist's nickname of "Miss Hot Tamale." In the original play version, Carnelle sheepishly apologizes to Mac Sam for giving him syphilis. Not only does the film forfeit this apology but also it deletes Mac Sam's easy dismissal of it. Instead, the pair appears like reunited lovers, with no major hint, at first, that for Carnelle, the flame has died. Despite Mac Sam's tubercular coughing attacks, evidence of at least one of his diseases, the couple has a hearty spin on the tilt-a-whirl, smooching and cuddling, whirling to the carnival music. Indeed, this romantic scene, obviously designed for a Hollywood sell, deletes grotesque elements that frequent the play. Note the contrast between film and play when Mac Sam treats Carnelle to a glimpse of one of his blood:

> MAC SAM: Yeah. (*Cough, cough.*) Yeah, (*Cough, cough, cough, cough, cough.*) He spits up blood.
>
> CARNELLE: Mac Sam, what's wrong? Are you choking?
>
> MAC SAM: Nah. I'm just spitting up clots of blood.
>
> CARNELLE: What?
>
> MAC SAM: It's nothing. Happens all the time. Look at that clot there; it's a nice pinkish-reddish sorta color.
>
> CARNELLE: You're making me sick, here. Sick

Though still likeable, the film versions of Carnelle and Mac Sam lack the complexity that Henley incorporates into her play's characters. Thus, the film loses something distinctive in the relationship, becoming a simpler version of the stereotypical dying-but-sexy-man-supports-idealistic-girl.

Perhaps the key to unlocking the strengths of *Miss Firecracker,* and surprisingly overlooked by critics of both the play and the film, is by exploiting the fairy tale motif which inspires Henley's characters and themes. Fairy tale threads, intertwined with codes of southern chivalry, portraits of family disintegration and transformation, and searches for identity stitch Henley's characters tightly to her audiences. On some level, we already know these characters from their fairy tale counterparts, and

*Holly Hunter and Alfre Woodard in a 1989 film version of* The Miss Firecracker Contest

here Henley makes us care about them all over again. This film is not simply a retelling of the familiar tale, with handsome princes (Tim Robbins as Delmount in the film), would-be princesses (the Miss Firecracker contestants), and dark, sinister stepmothers and wicked stepsisters (Ronelle and Elain) intent on beguiling or belittling a traditional heroine. Henley's psychologically complex fairy tale inverts the traditional stories, adding a contradictory quality to them. When asked if her work allowed her to write about repression buried ''in [her] own life,'' Henley quipped,

> I don't know. I write about things I'm concerned with, that are troubling me; and I suppose some of what you write is unconscious and subliminal. That's sort of where the magic comes from: it's not plotted logically like ''This is something I want to explore.'' But it does come from inside you.

As evidenced in *Crimes of the Heart*, Henley's fragmented, and even dysfunctional characters—what one movie reviewer characterizes as ''half crazy people''—sometimes exhibit exquisite powers for making others whole, functional human beings.

In both play and film, Henley subverts traditional fairy tale plots by a series of inversion and appropriations. Thomas Schlamme directs Hunter as the exuberant, orphaned misfit, Carnelle Scott, a young woman craving acceptance, worrying about being ugly, and aspiring to the coveted title of Miss Firecracker, the fairy tale equivalent of attending the ball. Mary Steenburgen, cast as Carnelle's cousin Elain, encapsulates the idea of the southern belle, graced with beauty and charm, but is similar to the queen of ''Snow White'' fame, who fears displacement and time's passage. References to Elain's ownership of beautiful clocks indicate a figurative attempts to control time and the ''mirror on the wall.''

The film begins and ends with a flashback of a young Carnelle, a wooly hat atop her head in July to conceal head lice, gazing into the sun, awe-stricken by her cousin Elain's beauty: ''Anyway, it was way back that first year when I came to live with them. She was a vision of beauty riding on that float with a crown on her head waving to everyone. I thought I'd drop dead when she passed by me,'' exclaims Carnelle. These lines, typically Henley, link beauty with death, a theme upon which Henley elaborates in her film. Carnelle admits being ready to ''drop dead'' at the sight of beauty.

Unrealized by Carnelle, a beautiful swan lies dormant beneath her ugly duckling exterior, but she needs visible proof of her value. As Robert L. McDonald submits in ''A blaze of glory'': Image and Self-Promotion in Henley's *The Miss Firecracker Contest,''* only public affirmation will satiate Carnelle's thirst for respectability:

> For Henley's characters, the public arena is a place of magic, to be exploited rather than avoided for its potential to reveal what might otherwise remain hidden and silent in their private lives. In fact, Carnelle's admiration for the way Aunt Ronelle handled herself during the trial of her illness, even emerging as something of a local celebrity, points to her own basic motivation for wanting to enter The Miss Firecracker Contest: to provide for a similar kind of public metamorphosis, replacing her well-worn (and admittedly well-earned) vernacular title of ''Miss Hot Tamale'' with something more appropriate to her newly uplifted self.

Elain's problem duplicates the one from which the evil queen of ''Snow White'' suffers. How does one maintain value in a patriarchal world which recognizes a woman only for her beauty? Elain combats this dilemma by preoccupying herself with beauty, by becoming narcissistic. In *The Culture of Narcissism,* Christopher Lasch observes that the ''narcissist depends on others to validate h[er] self-esteem. [S]he cannot live without an admiring audience (10). Now married and with children, Elain, nevertheless, fears replacement. Her story, not unlike the wicked queen's in ''Snow White,'' appears equally tragic:

> The real story begins when the Queen, having become a mother, metamorphoses also into a witch—that is, into a wicked ''step'' mother: ''. . . when the child was born, the Queen died,'' and ''After a year had passed the King took to himself another wife.''

> When we first encounter this ''new'' wife, she is framed in a magic looking glass, just as her predecessor—that is, her earlier self—had been framed in a window. To be caught and trapped in a mirror rather than a window, however, is to be driven inward, obsessively studying self-images, as if seeking a viable self. (Gilbert and Gubar 37)

On another level, Elain seems the perfect ''Cinderella,'' replete with ceremonial carriage and escort. Her charming ''prince'' of a husband, Franklin, however, turns out to be a self-absorbed, although rich, toad. In the play *The Miss Firecracker Contest,* he remains an absent character, which works effectively, powerful despite his absence (like Old Granddaddy's in *Crimes*), but, in the film, we glimpse a somewhat ordinary looking man as he exits the house, golf bag in tow. The aura of power dissipates considerably.

> *THOUGH STILL LIKEABLE, THE FILM VERSIONS OF CARNELLE AND MAC SAM LACK THE COMPLEXITY THAT HENLEY INCORPORATES INTO HER PLAY'S CHARACTERS. THUS, THE FILM LOSES SOMETHING DISTINCTIVE IN THE RELATIONSHIP, BECOMING A SIMPLER VERSION OF THE STEREOTYPICAL DYING-BUT-SEXY-MAN-SUPPORTS-IDEALISTIC-GIRL.''*

More in the play than in the film *Miss Firecracker,* audiences recognize in Elain one who has repressed the life force, and longs, Rapunzel-like, to ''let down her hair.'' The play leaves the audience not knowing if Elain will return to her rich spouse, where she, assuredly, must settle for appearances, her beautiful home, and her clocks. Still, *The Miss Firecracker Contest* engages audiences in a fantasy that this Rapunzel likely will realize. Will she keep her rendezvous with another prince, the blood-coughing Mac Sam, her new romantic interest who still carries a venereal disease? Elain of the *Firecracker* film would never contemplate, much less agree, to such an assignation. This difference makes her an altogether different kind of character from the one in the play, less ambiguous and less thought provoking. In his review of *Miss Firecracker,* Randy Parker castigates the film's Elain, labeling Steenburgen's ''performance as Elain . . . adequate,'' but argues that ''her character is so nauseating that you don't feel the least bit of sympathy for her.'' The play does contain ambiguity as concerns Elain's future, however, revealed in a phone conversation with Franklin:

> . . . I—I don't want to come home . . . I mean not ever, or for awhile, or for not ever . . . I feel like I'm missing my life . . . I don't know about the children. They'll manage . . . Oh, for God's sake, Franklin, no one's going to bake them into a pie! . . . Oh, please! I don't want to discuss it anymore. I'm tired of it all, I'm through with it all. Good-bye! (*She hangs up the phone. She is stunned and shaken by what she has done*).

The play indulges in multiple layers of ambiguity, unlike the film, thus pointing to Elain's complexity as well as her fairy tale antecedents: she wants excitement and yearns to step down from the pedestal, just once to engage in reckless behavior, but already her future has always been prescribed, determined, for her. In one of the play's heated confrontations with her brother, Delmount Williams, Elain screams, "Mama always loved you ten times better than me . . . I had to win contests and be in pageants before she'd give me any notice at all." Indeed, audiences wonder why Elain's mother, Ronelle, dispossesses her only daughter, leaving the house and furnishings to her son. When Delmount, in the film, threatens to "give away" the family house if he "can't sell it," Elain angrily accuses him of having "everything" to her "nothing" even though she has tried outrageously hard to please their mother. Perhaps a believer in fairy tales, Ronelle assumed that young ladies marry wealth and success when they get a husband.

In the play as well as the film, Carnelle recounts that her Aunt Ronelle once proclaimed that Elain "had it all" up there, "just like a queen in a castle." Figuratively trapped, however, Elain has moved merely from one type of prison to another (the fairy tale-like Atlanta estate). Thus, Aunt Ronelle leaves her touch not only on the house, but also on her children, and by extension, on her niece. Elain reminds Carnelle that Ronelle always said, "Pretty is as pretty does." Though not literally making Elain spin gold, Ronelle teaches her daughter to value winning, getting the gold crown. The beautiful Elain learns well this lesson. As Lasch's examination of American culture suggests, "The narcissist admires and identifies [her]self with "winners" out of h[er] fear of being labeled a loser." The play, but not the film, of *Miss Firecracker* indicates that Ronelle equates winning with sustenance, food, for she preaches that beauty pageants are the "gravy" of life, a necessary prerequisite for winning a rich husband. Indeed, Ronelle shares some of the tendencies of Old Granddaddy in *Crimes of the Heart,* who wishes marriage for Babe to a rich husband. Both Elain and Carnelle digest the perverted message that beauty signals acceptance, and that, without it, woman will be denied a seat at the table of success, left to a bland diet of potatoes—with no "gravy"!

To Elain, Carnelle's obsession with winning the coveted crown of "Miss Firecracker" threatens her reality of the world, all that she accepts in life as truth. Now invited back to Yazoo City, Mississippi, *Miss Firecracker*'s replacement for the original locale of Brookhaven, Elain mounts a pedestal, quite literally, to deliver her speech, "My Life as a Beauty." In the play, cousin Elain does bring the famous red dress that Carnelle insists upon wearing for the pageant, but, in the film, she hides it from Carnelle. This dress, that once gained Elain a metaphorical invitation to the ball, the winning of the Miss Firecracker title, must not be relinquished. Indeed, the dress in the play, *The Miss Firecracker Contest,* does not appear even to be the one that Elain wore to the Miss Firecracker contest. It has been worn by Elain instead to the Natchez Pilgrimage. Making this dress the one worn to capture the beauty title, Henley paints a portrait of *Miss Firecracker*'s Elain as a Cinderella turned into a wicked queen. In their analysis of "Snow White," Sandra Sandra Gilbert and Susan Gubar point out that queens and Snow Whites (or Cinderellas) are, in a sense, one. Angels and monsters are often combined in the same character. Appearing more complex, and worthy of our interest, the Elain of the play deserves the audiences' care, even sympathy, despite her having swallowed patriarchal prescriptions divvied out by her mother.

Also intent upon succeeding as a beauty, Carnelle hires her own seamstress, although she has just lost her job. Winning the Miss Firecracker Contest becomes her sole goal in life. In both the play and the film, Carnelle guides her new seamstress friend, Popeye, through the living room, praising along the way her Aunt Ronelle's "special touch," the antique spinning wheel that her celebrated aunt had "fixed . . . up." Henley conjures in audiences' minds another fairy tale figure who pricked her finger on an old artifact like this, a spinning wheel owned by Rumpelstiltskin, the dwarfish villain who demanded that another beauty spin gold. Like Rumpelstiltskin and Old Granddaddy in *Crimes,* Ronelle, though an absent character in both the play and film, spawns resentment in her children: Delmount refers to his mother, in storybook fashion, as "mean," a spiteful monster, an "ape." The film alludes to Ronelle's famous medical case, in which doctors had operated on her cancer, replacing her pituitary gland with a monkey's, thus causing her to "grow long, black hairs all over her body . . . just like an ape," but only the play delves deeply into the sick relationship this monster-mother maintained with her children prior to her death. Certainly, the film humorously capitalizes on this supernatural description of Delmount and Elain's ''ape'' mother, but sadly, it ignores her significance to Henley's over all theme of transformation, one which the playwright threads into her main plot. Omitting in the film *Miss Firecracker* Delmount's claim that his mother ''turned herself into a monkey to get at us—just to be mean,'' Henley inspires her audiences to be less prepared to attach a negative motive to Aunt Ronelle's unusual metamorphosis.

In *Firecracker,* the play, Carnelle and Delmount undergo positive change, and so too does Elain to some extent, but Aunt Ronelle's metamorphosis proves faulty. This transformation does not heal or integrate, but is monstrous, dismembering. Her transformation, unlike her son's in which his dreams of fragmented women become whole, may have been stimulated by malice, or so Delmount charges. Again, Gregor Samsa's metamorphosis comes to mind. In transferring this play from the stage to the screen, Henley's Aunt Ronelle's story may echo Gregor's, for both of them metamorphose toward death, not life. Transformation through love remains one of Henley's dominant themes, but in Ronelle, the playwright and screenwriter reverses the order of positive metamorphoses. Indeed, the scenes in the film *Miss Firecracker* that introduce Ronelle's exploits seem superfluous, unengaging, and not noticeably or understandably connected to Henley's theme of transformation. The film refuses to challenge audiences, though the play does, to contemplate Aunt Ronelle or her motives. Thus, the bizarre details of the absent antagonist's metamorphosis instigate rollicking laughter, but not thoughtfulness.

With Delmount, however, a positive transformation occurs due to the influence of Popeye, who swears that her heart gets ''hot'' at the sight of him and who appears unaffected by his reputation, his ''checkered past,'' which Carnelle details for her. To her, Delmount is Prince Charming, this southern gentleman who fights for woman's honor, no matter the consequence, even if it costs his freedom. Indeed, one such bout already landed him in an insane asylum:

> DELMOUNT: . . . I challenged that man to a duel! A duel! I can't help it if the weapons he chose were broken bottles! It was an honorable act in defense of a woman with beautiful, warm, bronze skin. I do not regret it.

Cutting a ''romantic figure'' with his Byronic poetry, his wild eyes and hair, Delmount, in both *The Miss Firecracker Contest* and *Miss Firecracker* is described as having a ''strange, obsessive eye for beauty.'' In the film we see him fight for the cause of beauty and woman by thrashing Ronnie Wayne for throwing popcorn and ice at Carnelle during one of her numbers at the beauty pageant.

Functioning as a defender as well as healer, Popeye becomes a helpmeet for several characters. Most noticeably she heals Delmount Williams. In both the play and the film, Henley endows her seamstress, Popeye, with magical powers. Hearing voices through her eyes, Popeye has abilities not unlike Meg's in *Crimes of the Heart.* Whereas society may consider Delmount a misfit, dysfunctional, insane, or just a vile ''toad,'' as Elain calls him at one point, Popeye sees in him beauty. Under her positive influence, he is transformed, an action as miraculous as changing bullfrogs into doctors and nurses or frog queens donned with leaf capes. Indeed, this frog motif figures significantly in the film, but not to the complicated degree that it pervades the play. In the play, every major character carries with him or her ''frog'' connotations or associations. With Popeye, Delmount feels whole, as symbolically suggested by Delmount's dreams, which lose their terror as his visions of Popeye replace nightmares of fragmented women. In the play, and echoed in the film, Delmount announces his transformation:

> DELMOUNT: Oh, Popeye! (*He grabs her and kisses her full on the mouth.*) I've been dreaming about you at night. I see you riding across the sea with a host of green whales. Popeye, I love you.

Though the play complicates Delmount's character by romantically involving him with Popeye, Henley's *Miss Firecracker* the film adds an element of surprise by casting Alfre Woodard in the role of Popeye. Amazingly, and not very realistically, the film suggests no racial tension occurs as a result of this coupling. Ironically, and unbelievably, the film's characters ignore the possibility of miscegenation. Yazoo City appears blind to racism, but only with this one relationship. This oddity seems ironic, considering the film's periodic allusions to issues of race: Carnelle just knows that she will defeat black or Asian contestants, and Elain laments the quality of the pageant's ''going down, down, down'' once blacks enter as contestants. Racism as a theme in *Miss Firecracker,* however, remains relegated to the fringes of the film, treated somewhat similarly as wife battering in *Crimes,* yet audiences remain uncomfortably aware of its presence, thinking that at any moment an embarrassing incident will occur. Perhaps Ronnie Wayne may turn his attentions from throwing items at Carnelle to harassing Popeye.

Film audiences are made to feel uncomfortable also with the theme of incest, which Henley insinuates subtly into the plot of Miss Firecracker. This idea, more radical than Delmount's romantic interest in a black woman and more bizarre than Popeye's being an outfitter of bullfrogs, remains in audiences' minds. Though the play contain some intimations of incest between Delmount and his sister, Elain, the film exacerbates the problem by inserting a bedside scene in which Elain crawls onto her brother's bed to comfort him after one of his ghastly nightmares. What soothes Delmount, however, causes the audience anxiety and discomfort. Even the scene in which the pair dances may contribute to this angst. Delmount Williams appears to be a modern-day equivalent of Faulkner's Quentin Compson. Obsessively concerned with his sister's behavior and her supposed betrayal of him, especially as regards Elain's marriage, which she refuses to end, Delmount strikes an awkward chord with theater audiences. Why should a brother devote so much of his energy and thought to convincing his sister to end her marriage? Why then does Delmount repeatedly label Elain as unreliable, her "trademark," when he rants about her marriage?

Unlike the beauty, Elain, Popeye earns "Cinderella" status in her own right, finding her Prince Charming in the character of Delmount. Their courtship, one of the funniest and most appealing in the film, retells other legends as well. When explaining to Carnelle that she learned to sew by making costumes for bullfrogs, Popeye presents herself as a kind-hearted princess, one not repelled by the frog-prince, Delmount, made ugly by his checkered past. In some ways, the casting of a black woman in this role complements Henley's vision that worth cannot be measured by one's face. Black skin is but another symbolic "dress" of the humanity within a person.

Intricately interweaving images and associations, Henley fashions "Cinderellas" from unusual angles and perspectives. Elain, as described above, seems to epitomize the fairy tale princess the morning (or decade) after the ball. In both the play and the film, she is the only character who really does get to go to the ball (having captured the Miss Firecracker title), but, now trapped with her prince, she remains disappointed. The Elain of the film will return to the castle and the clocks, stuck in time. The Elain of *The Miss Firecracker Contest,* however, may free herself, at least momentarily, by meeting her new but diseased prince, Mac Sam, underneath a mimosa tree. Mac Sam's disintegration parallels Gregor's, perhaps, for throughout the play, he noticeably loses his health and his body. Yet he is also the character to offer Carnelle "eternal grace." With the play's audience privy to information of which Elain remains unaware, we realize that she may be inheriting something after all, a venereal disease, but at least, she may "have some real fun before [she] drop[s] dead off this planet."

Carnelle, aided by her very own fairy godmother, Popeye, rises to the film's platform to present her routine, dressed in her red star-spangled costume and twirling a patriotic red, white, and blue wooden rifle. Carnelle, both an ugly duckling and a sort of frog prince herself, having lived metaphorically in rags, her soiled reputation finds redemption, ironically, in not winning the "Miss Firecracker" Contest. Only then do her inner strength and beauty emerge—interior beauty rather than a surface beauty. In the play, *The Miss Firecracker Contest,* Carnelle gets her chance to wear Elain's antebellum red dress, a metaphorical glass slipper, but it does not fit any more than Cinderella's stepsisters' feet can fit into the glass slipper. Other contestants also attempt to make their bodies fit into their own glass slippers, maiming themselves in the process. For instance, one contestant becomes permanently hunchbacked from incessant piano practice. In her resolve "to follow that float," Henley's protagonist gains respect for herself, realizing that no dress should be worn for a lifetime. In the film, *Miss Firecracker,* Carnelle, wearing both the red dress that she found hidden in Elain's suitcase and her old yellowed cap from childhood, confronts a petrified Elain at the bottom of a staircase. When Carnelle asks for an explanation, Elain responds, "it just wouldn't do . . . because it's mine." Discarding from her head the yellowed, wooly cap, Carnelle adds, "And I guess this is mine . . . but I'm not gonna wear it forever." Thus, Carnelle requires no Cinderella masks, and certainly not the Mardi Gras mask that Elain presented to her earlier as a gift. "I just thought of you when I saw it. You'll have to wear it to a mask ball," Elain had joked. The scene indicates that Elain's Cinderella mask of beauty cakes her face, forever locking her in a beauty pose, a position that brittles over time.

The fairy tales discussed here as background to *Miss Firecracker* evince dark and menacing threads. In particular, these stories contain ideas of family cruelty and betrayal, as does *Crimes of the Heart.* Elain, the adored cousin, portrays something close to the "Snow White" queen, bringing the dress with her, but lying, and refusing to relinquish it. Sharing even the possibility of beauty with another woman threatens Carnelle's cousin. The play, however, takes a more generous, more focused view of its characters. In *The Miss Firecracker Contest,* Elain, more subtly, first forgets to bring the dress, self-centered creature that she is, but then has it sent. Unfortunately, or perhaps fortunately, Carnelle looks terrible in it. Thus, the fault lies not directly with Elain that Carnelle will fail to emerge a fairy tale "Miss Firecracker," for she does deliver the dress. In the play, Henley's protagonist does get her chance with the glass slipper—the red dress—but cannot wear it successfully. Thus, Henley's depiction of Carnelle symbolically suggests elements of both the ugly stepsister as well as the beautiful Cinderella. Though older and less appealing as a character, Elain remains in both the play and the film, ironically, the true story princess after all, the only woman audiences meet who wins the Miss Firecracker contest. Her fate in the film, however, Henley seals with no storybook romance. Finally, by examining these characters in light of their fairy tale counterparts, one appreciates the mythic depth with which Henley crafts her Miss Firecrackers. Both play and film audiences delight in recognizing a familiar story pattern, as they do here. These tales, which appear and reappear in *Miss Firecracker,* have been altered, blended in a way that casts new light on the original tales, marked by their rigidity and pervasive cruelty. They tell stories of regeneration, rebirth, and autonomy.

Being a heroine *may* mean marrying the man of one's dreams; or, it *may* not. Henley's world has room for both kinds of endings, and for the prince charming, who is also a frog prince, and the princess who thinks herself a frog. *Crimes of the Heart* and *Miss Firecracker* prove transformation possible. Whereas the metamorphosis of Kafka's Gregor Samsa leads to death—only a hollow shell evidence that a life existed—Henley's stories predominantly reveal positive changes: new ways of seeing, hearing, becoming whole. Other types of transformations, those from the stage to the screen, open up new avenues for Henley's audiences to explore. Her films teach us the value of the human spirit and inspire us to get through those "real bad days."

**Source:** Linda Rohrer Paige, "Southern Firecrackers and 'Real Bad Days': Film Adaptations of Beth Henley's *Crimes of the Heart* and *The Miss Firecracker Contest,*" in *Beth Henley: A Casebook,* edited by Julia A. Fesmire, Routledge, 2002, pp. 128–53.

## Robert L. McDonald

*In the following essay, McDonald explores the impetus behind characters seeking public attention in* The Miss Firecracker Contest.

Tennessee Williams, perhaps as sensitively as any writer we have had, expressed the conflicts arising from the public tidiness, the emphasis on image, that southern culture has traditionally demanded of its gentlemen and women. Williams himself felt the scrutiny of the public eye immediately with the success of *The Glass Menagerie,* and succumbed to what he later called "the catastrophe of Success," a life founded more on image than substance. It took a while for him to discover and admit the hard lesson about self-abnegation, about the falseness of "the public Somebody you are when you 'have a name,'" as he put it. Many of his characters, particularly the women, seem controlled by the need to keep "the public Somebody" intact, even as the real self— what Williams called "the solitary and unseen you that existed from your first breath"—begins to atrophy. Amanda Wingfield, Blanche DuBois, and even Maggie the Cat: these women seem tragically obligated to the mythology of the Southern Lady, ever conscious of the preeminence of the unruffled public persona.

In the world of Williams's spiritual heir, fellow Mississippian Beth Henley, we are offered a different understanding of the importance of image. In plays such as *The Glass Menagerie* and *A Streetcar Named Desire,* Williams treats the disintegration of the southern aristocracy and the consequent socioeconomic and moral decline of the family. Henley's characters inhabit the spaces—exemplified by the abandoned, dilapidated ancestral homes we see in *Crimes of the Heart* and *The Miss Firecracker Contest*—where Williams left his fallen, broken gentility. Her primary characters are the next generation, the less pretentious blue-collar sons and daughters of the New South. They are rougher around the edges in speech, action, and appearance, without the kinds of masks worn by Williams's characters, because they are farther away, in both time and spirit, from the ideals that required them. Henley's characters live in a more contemporary South that is, for better or worse, a less self-conscious South, one less inhibited by social forms and thus less restrictive of individualism.

In Henley's world, all the seams show, at times almost defiantly so. Impulse, if not instinct, seems often to govern a character's actions. We see this in the Pulitzer Prize–winning *Crimes of the Heart*

> IN FACT, PERHAPS WHAT *THE MISS FIRECRAKER CONTEST* FINALLY, MOST PROFOUNDLY REVEALS IS A MESSAGE THAT THE FLAMBOYANT OR 'THE LUDICIOUS,' TO USE HARBIN'S TERM, CAN BE READ AS A SIGN OF LIFE, AS EVIDENCE THAT A CHARACTER IS BIG ENOUGH TO DREAM BEYOND THE CONFINES OF WHAT PASSES FOR REASON AND ACCEPTABILITY."

when Babe explains her reasons for shooting her husband, Zackery. Really, she has grown weary of their relationship and acts out of fear of Zackery's increasingly violent attitude toward her—which has included physical abuse—and his threats concerning her young black lover, Willie Jay. For the first half of the play, however, Babe is allowed to explain her actions by saying she shot her husband "'Cause I didn't like his looks. I just didn't like his looks," as she tells an unnerved but accepting Lenny. Here, propriety registers as unconventional and individually determined, with an implicit assumption that *what people will say,* or what reason might dictate, is less important than how legitimate the action feels to the actor. Henley once remarked, in fact, that her South was a place where the individual was permitted not just to exist but to insist upon expression:

Individuality or independence is applauded in the South much more so than in other places. . . . There's a wildness in us [humans generally] that we are always trying to subdue. It's important to have the ability to tell stories and do outrageous things like throw steaks out your plate-glass window.

Expressing that "wildness" or "outrageousness" has become Henley's trademark, particularly in her creation of young female characters who, in another generation, might have been demure southern ladies but who are now unapologetic for their tendency to draw attention to themselves with the unpredictable things they say and do. In Henly's world gaining attention is not only permissible, it

can be admirable as evidence of a character's right to assert her individuality, her specialness. Again in *Crimes of the Heart,* for example, the MaGrath sisters' cousin Chick is alarmed that "today's paper" detailing Babe's shooting of Zackery is going to cause "some mighty negative publicity around this town," something she has called Babe's attention to in order to exact an acknowledgment of the humiliation the whole affair is sure to bring. But because Babe compares her predicament to the fabulous saga of her mother, who years earlier had mysteriously hanged herself and her old yellow cat in the basement, and had gotten "national coverage" for it, there is something closer to envy than to remorse in her reply to Chick: "I told her, 'Mama got national coverage! National!' And if Zackery wasn't a senator from Copiah County, I probably wouldn't even be getting statewide." Like her Mama, Babe had "had a bad day. A real bad day," and she had expressed it in a spectacle that would, in an oddly satisfying way, affirm her ability to act and not simply conform to a life that was unsatisfactory. If the community will be scandalized, the people who matter most to Babe, her sisters, are both just amazed (albeit in different ways):

Meg: . . . So, Babe shot Zackery Botrelle, the riches and most powerful man in all of Hazelhurst, slap in the gut. It's hard to believe.

Lenny: It certainly is. Little Babe—shooting off a gun.

Meg: Little Babe.

If the mantra of polite women in the South of Tennessee Williams was "to keep hold of myself," in Blanche's "faint" words to herself at the beginning of *Streetcar,* and to avoid at all costs any public attention other than platonic appreciations of beauty and grace, Beth Henley's characters operate in another South altogether. For there, participating in spectacle, even beckoning the spotlight by some flamboyance, is presented as a very natural means of developing and articulating self-worth, a means of transforming a character like "Little Babe" into a force to be reckoned with. One of the most artfully conceived sources of Henley's darkly offbeat humor is her characters' often desperate contrivances to draw attention to themselves, to whoop up some notice, a bit of publicity, in the name of confirmation and self-advertisement.

The very best example of this in Henley's corpus is *The Miss Firecracker Contest,* a play brimming with people demanding that we pay attention to them: from Popeye's weird life stories about how she got her name to Elain's generally supreme presence as a beauty, "the most beautiful thing in the whole wide world," Tessy Mahone exclaims. There is even the asserted and oddly revered memory of Elain and Delmount's deceased mother, Carnelle's Aunt Ronelle, who is remembered not so much as a person—because she was, at best, an unpleasant one if you listen to her children—but as "a famous medical case." As Carnelle explains to Popeye, her aunt had experienced "dreadful side effects" when doctors tried to treat her cancer of the pituitary gland by replacing it with the gland of a monkey. It was a verifiable "tragedy," Carnelle says, definitely qualifying Aunt Ronelle as "A saint or an angel; one or the other," because she bore the burden publicly—a world away from the inviolable rule of keeping-up-appearances that hides Amanda Wingfield's desperation, keeps Miss DuBois's disintegration in the shadows, and installs the face of connubial bliss on the very frustrated Maggie Pollitt.

For Henley's characters, the public arena is a place of magic, to be exploited rather than avoided for its potential to reveal what might otherwise remain hidden and silent in their private lives. In fact, Carnelle's admiration for the way Aunt Ronelle handled herself during the trial of her illness, even emerging as something of a local celebrity, points to her own basic motivation for wanting to enter The Miss Firecraker Contest: to provide for a similar kind of public metamorphosis, replacing her well-worn (and admittedly well-earned) vernacular title of "Miss Hot Tamale" with something more appropriate to her newly uplifted self. When the legendary Elain insinuates that her cousin should not get her hopes up about the pageant, Carnelle responds bluntly:

> I know why you're worried. You think I've ruined my chances, cause—'cause of my reputation. . . . Well, everyone knew I used to go out with lots of men and all that. Different ones. It's been a constant thing with me since I was young and—. . . . I just mention it because it's different now, since Aunt Ronelle died and since—I got that disease. . . . Anyway, I go to church now and I'm signed up to where I take an orphan home to dinner once a week or to a movie; and—and I work on the cancer drive here just like you do in Natchez. . . . My life has meaning. . . . Everything's changed. And being in that contest—it would be such an honor to me.

In preparation, Carnelle has dyed her hair an intense bright red and has been earnestly putting together her talent, which she describes as a "kind of a tap-dance-march-type-a-thing" choreographed to "The Star Spangled Banner." When the curtain rises, we see her practicing the routine, using a wooden spoon and stainless steel knives instead of the actual roman candle and sparklers she will ignite for the real performance. As she goes through the motions, she shouts, "'Pow,' each time she imagines [the roman candle] goes off."

Carnelle looks absurd—the dependably honest Delmount offers that her hair makes her "look like a bareback rider in the Shooley Traveling Carnival Show"—and her character might immediately dissolve into caricature if Henley had not endowed her so persuasively with a dream. From the first time we see her, even in the mania of the play's opening moments, there is something in Carnelle's earnestness that makes her come alive as one of those people who has drawn a line in her life between a desperate past and a gloriously imagined future. She stomps and parades and tries very hard to master the dancing and twirling of her talent routine. And she fairly twinkles when she tries to explain to Popeye, a seamstress who has just moved to town, exactly what the Miss Firecracker Contest is. Popeye thinks Carnelle must want such a flashy costume, made of red, silver, and blue silky material, for a dance contest, but the ebullient aspiring queen corrects her: "Well, no; . . . it's for the Miss Firecracker Contest. . . . It's the beauty contest. They have it in Brookhaven every Fourth of July. It's a tradition. It's a big event. It's famous." Carnelle wants the kind of costume that her imagination conjures for an occasion of this magnitude, "something really patriotic. Kinda traditional. You know, noble, in a sense." She is unimpressed by Elain's dismissal of the whole affair as "trashy," especially since Elain herself won the contest fifteen years before, forever impressing little Carnelle, then a recently abandoned sickly nine-year-old, as "a vision of beauty riding on that float with a crown on her head waving to everyone." "I thought I'd drop dead whe she passed by me," Carnelle recalls.

Elain maintains that "there's nothing to" the contest, possibly because she knows that Carnelle does not stand much of a chance of winning and wants to head off the heartbreak, but also, certainly, because she understands that there is in fact not much to the kind of confirmation that winning a beauty pageant brings. By all accounts, Elain has a lush life in Natchez, with a nice house, a decent husband named Franklin, and two children, but she has decided to leave all of this in pursuit of something more fulfilling, we presume. In the end, she chooses to go back home—to that life of "beautiful clocks," as she summarizes her world in an off-handed comment to Carnelle—but she nevertheless seems to understand what her ''life as a beauty'' has done to her. A commentator on the film version of the play characterized Elain as someone who might be only ''passably beautiful, but [who] radiates her right to rule in life as Astonishingly Beautiful as she ruled on the parade float. She's mastered Inner Float.'' With echoes of Amanda Wingfield and Blanche DuBois, that is exactly Elain: beaming the image of a life of utter composure—lovely but very, very exhausting. Even though Elain wishes for a more honest way of life, and even samples a grotesque version of it with the emaciated Mac Sam in a last-night rendezvous under the wisteria, she has grown accustomed to ''the limitations [being beautiful] brings.'' And in the end, confirming what she has always known about herself, Elain discovers that the superficial pleasures afforded by life as Mrs. Franklin Rutlege of Natchez are just too much to give up. As she tells Delmount, sounding pitiful but certain, ''I need someone who adores me.''

If only in theory or appearance, however, Elain at least has a choice: she can go, she can stay, she can leave again if and when she wants. She has status, class, complete mobility, and any ''limitations'' of that life seem negligible, even laughable, when compared to those of being plain, damaged-goods Carnelle Scott. That is Carnelle's perception of Elain's situation, at least, and it is the reason she is uninterested in any lessons that might emerge from a more careful examination of her cousin's life. Carnelle wants the feeling as well as the reality of a similar choice, and this means more than simply the opportunity to leave Brookhaven in pursuit of a new life to match her new self-image of respectability. She wants to leave, as she says over and over, with stars in her eyes, ''in a blaze of glory . . . in a crimson blaze of glory!'' She wants the citizens of Brookhaven to see her up on the stage and then maybe even riding on the float—crown, sash, and scepter—as irrefutable evidence that Miss Hot Tamale has remade herself. She wants a sparkler-and-roman-candle display of publicity for the new Carnelle Scott, on her way out of town and up in the world. She wants nothing less than a spectacle for her departure and is not at all dampened by Delmount's description of the pageant as ''a garish display of painted up prancing pigs.'' Ignoring him and any other effort to deter her, Carnelle remains firm in her belief that the opportunity to participate in the contest will mean nothing less than the chance to create ''visible proof'' of her new self.

Delmount speculates, no doubt correctly, that behind Carnelle's all-consuming desire to enter The Miss Firecracker Contest is the fact that the circumstances of her childhood prevented her from ''attain[ing] any self-esteem.'' ''Had to sleep with every worthless soul in Brookhaven trying to prove she was attractive,'' he comments to Elain. Some of the hilarity and all of the poignancy in this play derive from the fact that we can see so clearly what Carnelle cannot about the mechanism she has selected for unveiling the worth she has at last discovered within herself, indeed, from the fact that she feels she must be so public about it at all. She must ultimately be disappointed—as she is when she comes in not first, not third, but fifth out of five contestants—because she hopes to change her image in a peculiar, insular world where images take hold as virtual absolutes. Carnelle thinks change is just a matter of publicly registering an image of difference. She does not recognize what all the others—Elain, Delmount, and even Mac Sam—seem to understand: that what we often have is only the illusion of the opportunity for change. (Again, witness Elain's ultimate ''decision'' to return to Franklin and her life of face cream and ''beautiful clocks.'') This is a truth that does not change in the transition from the South of Williams's characters to that of Beth Henley's: identities remain very much socially constructed, and in the static categories of small-town southern life, that means that the power to remake a public image lies beyond individual motivation. What is different is that Henley makes her central character so willfully public in her determination to ignore this fact. By subjecting herself to the pageant as a community-sanctioned agency of confirmation, thereby asking for the community worse, further humiliation. After all, her judges, representing their constituency, are a notoriously unforgiving lot. When Carnelle allows some consideration for the odds-on favorite Caroline Jeffers's discolored teeth—''I hear she took medicine for seizures that she had as a child and it scraped off most of her tooth enamel''—Tessy Mahoney, the pageant coordinator, replies curtly: ''I heard that too, but it doesn't matter. . . . I really don't think the judges are interested in sentimentality—just the teeth themselves.''

Funny, yes, but also painfully true, aud another moment of potential insight that floats past Carnelle because she is not interested in it. Entering the contest, the new Carnelle Scott is the ultimate unflappable optimist. Minutes before she has to be on stage for ''the opening Parade of Firecrackers''—when she is running late, she is sweaty, her ''makeup is running right down [her] face,'' and her dress does not fit—she is still ready to go on, because despite it all, she says, ''my head is ready.'' The fact that Henley creates her as such a wonderfully sympathetic character suggests that she admires Carnelle for the effort she is willing to make, for her boldness in trying to launch herself in that ''blaze of glory.'' She prefers Carnelle's loud and obvious failure to Elain's resignation and retreat, and so, probably, would most of us.

In a compelling resolution, Henley transforms Carnelle and grounds her as a realist during the play's last act. The transformation begins with Carnelle's sense that things are not exactly going well when she fails down in her pageant dress, which inspires a rowdy crowd to begin chanting ''Miss Hot Tamale,'' bringing her as close as ever to tears: ''It's awful! It's so awful! They never forget! They never do!'' It is Henley's realization of the possibility of exposure that looms for so many of William's characters, with a crowd of Stanley Kowalskiesque figures in possession of the ''truth'' and quite enthusiastic about revealing the charade. But rather than shrink from it, Carnelle takes the blow and builds it into a resolve, a firm assertion that since she lost she will do what the losers do, tote an American flag while following the winner's float on foot: ''Look,'' she tells Delmount, ''if you come in last, you follow that float. I took a chance and I came in last; so, by God, I'm gonna follow that float!'' By the very last scene, Carnelle has calmed down and realizes that losing the contest ''doesn't matter,'' because ''the main thing is—well, the main thing is . . . Gosh; I don't know what the main thing is. I haven't the vaguest idea.'' The truth that she thought she understood about what it would mean to live life as a verified ''beauty'' has vanished; it has been replaced by what sounds less like stoic acceptance than it does a comfortable acceptance of life as spontaneous, with human agency tuned to the moment. Carnelle's last line is a simple expression of a simple appreciation, signaling a refreshing kind of personal growth: ''Gosh, it's a nice night,'' she is able to say, watching the fireworks show at the end of the frightful contest day. Such a resolution would have been unthinkable for most of Williams's women, trapped as they were in a life that required a predictable, visible sameness of both action and response.

Carnelle's transformation from dreamer to realist can be read as evidence of what Billy J. Harbin calls Henley's ''grave vision masked by and realized through a depiction of the ludicrous.'' But this in not a pessimistic play—and neither should it be trivialized by dismissing Carnelle as a ''desperate southern-sexpot figure'' and the whole play as one which, like too much of Henley's writing, in the opinion of one critic, ''regrettably does not break through masculinist/modernist assumptions'' about female sexuality and autonomy. What happens in this play concerns a woman's constructive reimagining of what is possible in her life. Indeed, the entire action revolves around a theme of liberation—with the main event occurring, not incidentally, on the Fourth of July—and the possibility for one person to claim significance by her own deliberate action. She may look silly in the process, and she may fail with great pain and even embarrassment. But again, we must admire her for the effort—the noisy, dazzling spectacle of her failure, as well as the maturity of her acceptance that she will have to try another time, another way. There is a certain satisfaction in witnessing Carnelle's effort, collapse, and then small signs of recovery that is not available in the interior tragedies of Tennessee Williams's women. Those lives often merely wither, or implode. Henley's heroines—Carnelle, the MaGrath sisters in *Crimes of the Heart,* and Marshael in *The Wake of Jamey Foster* all qualify— show no obligation to the old social requirement that surfaces remain pleasant even when the inside is dissatisfied or sick. Instead, they play the messiness of life out publicly, on the stage of the world. In fact, perhaps what *The Miss Firecraker Contest* finally, most profoundly reveals is a message that the flamboyant or ''the ludicious,'' to use Harbin's term, can be read as a sign of life, as evidence that a character is big enough to dream beyond the confines of what passes for reason and acceptability.

**Source:** Robert L. McDonald, '''A Blaze of Glory': Image and Self-Promotion in Henley's *The Miss Firecracker Contest,*'' in *Southern Quarterly,* Vol. 37, No. 2, Winter 1999, pp. 151–57.

## Alan Clarke Shepard

*In the following essay, Shepard explores the effects of the feminist movement on the female protagonists of Henley's plays, in particular examining the recurring images of homicide and suicide.*

Beth Henley's tragicomedies study the effects of the feminist movement upon a few, mostly proletarian women in rural Mississippi, who are more likely to read *Glamour* than Cixous and Clement's *The Newly Born Woman.* We are invited to sympathize with isolated heroines whose fantasies demonstrate the difficulty of conceiving female subjectivity while entrenched in patriarchal epistemes, whose resilience is expressed in their canny, survivalist compromises with the codes of passive southern womanhood. Their compromises may be precisely located in the recurring imagery of homicide and suicide that pervades Henley's scripts. Take Elain in *The Miss Firecracker Contest* (1979), for example, an aging beauty queen in flight from a suffocating marriage and motherhood. When her estranged husband worries that she may kill their children in a fit of fury, Elain answers him by quashing the idea of her repressed rage spiraling murderously out of control: ''Oh, for God's sake, Franklin, no one's going to bake them into a pie!'' Franklin, borrowing from classical tragedy, baits Elain to circumscribe, even to annul her anger and her flight. One subtext of his inflammatory trope of filicide is that Elain's bid for greater autonomy threatens to incite a domestic ''tragedy.'' Yet the word ''tragedy'' is Elain's own assessment of impending doom. Though Franklin makes her ''ill,'' without him she is ''feeling nothing but terror and fear and loneliness!'' And so, after a few minutes of ''reckless'' infamy under the wisteria bushes with an alcoholic carnival hand, she expects to return to her ''dreary, dreary life.'' No Medea she, Elain occupies the periphery of *Miss Firecracker,* but the arc of her brief rebellion illuminates a paradigm of female surrender running through Henley's plays. The southern heroines populating her tragicomedies frequently erupt in anger toward those (including themselves) who engineer or sustain the emotionally impoverishing circumstances of their private lives; and just as often, they retreat from the schemes of violence bred by that anger. They relish murderous and suicidal fantasies, they repudiate them. The problematics of their rage is my subject.

The shadow of violent death is diffused across Henley's landscapes At times it is treated with the *sprezzatura* of black comedy. Accidents of nature abound, wacky in their studied randomness: Carnelle's father has died chasing ''the Tropical Ice Cream truck,'' her Uncle George fell ''to his death trying to pull this bird's nest out from the chimney''; Popeye's brother has been fatally bitten ''by a water moccasin down by the Pearl River''; Lenny's horse Billy Boy has been ''struck dead'' by lightning; Jamey Foster has been fatally ''kicked in the head by a cow''; an orphanage has burnt, blood vessels burst, cars and pigs exploded. Katty observes that ''life is so full of unknown horror.''

But at other times the half-baked threats of homicide and suicide swerve toward the rant of revenge tragedies. Unlike accidents of nature, these threats have knowable if not justifiable causes, reactions to betrayals and injustices made visible as the plays unfold. Yet the fantasies of murder entertained by these heroines signify no commitment to the principle that drives revenge tragedies, namely that revenge is an heroic prerogative of the wronged party, for traditionally revenge has been a masculine mode, from which these heroines mostly draw back. The fantasies secreted in Henley's texts are indeed not so much retributive as palliative. They are strategies of coping with the residual scars of emotional abandonment, or with a fresh crisis of the same, a recurring motif in Henley's art. Consider those of the widow Marshael in *The Wake of Jamey Foster* (1982). Estranged from her husband Jamey, who eventually dies from being filliped in the head—by a cow—during a pastoral tryst with his mistress Esmerelda, Marshael is abandoned a second time in a thunderstorm by family friend Brocker Slade, to whom she has turned in her grief, as they are travelling home from the hospital bed of her then-critically-ill husband. Slade later surfaces at Marshael's house to launch a half-hearted campaign to cajole her into forgiveness, cooing, ''God, M., honey, [. . .] I'm about ready to run jump into the Big Black River.'' To his self-pity she replies coolly, ''Well, don't forget to hang a heavy stone around your scrawny old neck'' (47–48). But recommending his suicide is as far as Marshael's rage goes. It rapidly devolves into despair, with Marshael vesting herself in the role of invalid. The particular stresses of earlier days, inscribed in the ''purple and swollen'' ulcers on her gums, the rash on her knuckles, have now become general and overwhelming: she is, she says, ''sick of betrayal! Sick!'', echoing Elain's sentiment in *Miss Firecracker* that her husband Franklin makes her ''ill.'' Yet as in *Firecracker,* again it is a man who is both the source and the cure of a heroine's disease. *The Wake of Jamey Foster* ends in a tableau of Slade soothing Marshael to sleep with the lullaby ''This Old Man Comes Rolling Home,'' in whose refrain (of the same words) Marshael takes comfort from its implicit promise of Slade's enduring paternal presence. He is redeemed, no longer a ''scrawny old neck,'' but an ''old *man*'' (my emphasis). As the cure suggests, then, Marshael's rage against betrayal is not a liberating or even die-breaking action signalling her escape from heterosexist oppression, but a conservative, paradigmatic strategy for recuperating an emotionally dysfunctional man.

The embryo of this pattern of repudiated rage appears in *Am I Blue* (1972), the first of Henley's plays to be staged. *Am I Blue* investigates the pressures of gender relations, specifically of sexual initiation, felt by two adolescents, Ashbe and John Polk (or J.P.). They meet in a seedy New Orleans bar, return to the apartment Ashbe shares with her always absent father, and, compromising, agree to dance until dawn. Against our gendered expectations that men are always the sexual aggressor, it is the younger Ashbe who presses J.P. to have intercourse. When he refuses fearing that Ashbe would ''get neurotic, or pregnant, or some damn thing,'' she retaliates—she feigns having poisoned his drink dyed a suspicious blue: impulsively she hypothesizes his murder, only to recant the fiction immediately, then internalizes her anger, which, though tied to J.P.'s refusal, speaks of larger rejections and wounds.

Yet more striking than Ashbe's threat of the mickeyed highball are the fantasies of murder entertained by both teenagers. Enroute to the apartment, Ashbe, scooping up a stray hat from the street, wonders aloud whether it might not have been ''a butcher's who slaughtered his wife or a silver pirate with a black bird on his throat''; J.P. fears that she ''probably [has] got some gang of muggers waiting to kill me.'' While he registers the practical risks of picking up a stranger in a bar, she romanticizes murder; the pirate Blackbeard roams the interstices of her imagination. In Ashbe's terms, a pirate's violence both creates and signifies his autarkic self; and Ashbe, virtually alone in the world, vicariously produces one, too, through her well-developed fantasy life, which privileges the swashbuckler mode, where violence is glamorous, sovereign, and artificial. But other fragments of her fantasy life belie her pose of nonchalance toward violence. They show Ashbe grappling with feelings of inexplicable rage, inexplicable to her because she possesses only an adolescent, even nascent, sense of herself as an autonomous being. For example, she describes visiting a grocery to smash bags of marshmallows, an act of rage comically diverted from its true object; she claims to have stolen ashtrays from the Screw Inn (it discriminates against the helpless, she says pointedly), and to have practiced the passive-aggressive art of voodoo against a clique of schoolmates. From all this, J.P. avers that Ashbe is ''probably one of those people that live in a fantasy world.'' In the most bizarre flight of fancy, she holds out hope of having sex with J.P. so that she might conceive, then travel to Tokyo for an abortion, explaining that she is ''so sick of school I could smash every marshmallow in sight.'' Mary Field

''M ELAIN OCCUPIES THE PERIPHERY OF *MISS FIRECRACKER,* BUT THE ARC OF HER BRIEF REBELLION ILLUMINATES A PARADIGM OF FEMALE SURRENDER RUNNING THROUGH HENLEY'S PLAYS.''

Belenky and others have observed that oppressed women who are reconstituting themselves as autonomous subjects sometimes use ''the imagery of birth, rebirth and childhood to describe their experience of a nascent self.'' But Ashbe's struggle to develop as a subject results only in the cross-eyed impulses to smash marshmallows and to conceive only to abort. The latter mirrors the pattern of repudiated rage: she imagines internalizing, then expelling not only a fetus, but also the pressures of conventional commitments imposed upon young women to reproduce; to please and serve men, whatever the cost (recall Ashbe's imaginary butcher who slashes his wife's throat); to disavow the aggression typically associated with the masculine sphere. In the end, however, like Marshael, Ashbe abandons her resistance and, encircled by J.P.'s arms, dances to Billie Holiday. Relinquishing the murderous power of a blue mickey for ''the blues'' as soon as a man's company is even provisionally secured, Ashbe goes passive toward her own pain. Even the play's interrogative title serves notice of her surrender to the external regulation of her own feelings: *Am I Blue?*

Henley's heroines who have passed beyond adolescence do not similarly romanticize the murder and mutilation of women in later texts, where the playwright explores relationships between men's abuse of women and women's surprising, apparent diffidence or even absence of rage in return. Breaking the conspiracy of silence that surrounds domestic abuse, a conspiracy once silently tolerated, then contested, by Babe in *Crimes of the Heart* (1981), for example, whose medical history narrates the injuries inflicted by her husband Zackery, these texts map out the cycle of emotional and physical battering. The abuse comes first; and though bids for greater subjectivity sometimes follow a sudden escalation of the abuse, enduring, transformative rage seldom does, for that is largely a privilege of "autarkic selfhood," about which Henley's women, like Ashbe, seldom more than fantasize. If it is true, as George Mariscal has said, "that all forms of subjectivity are conceived in a bitter struggle for power and hegemony," then the absence of rage or its diffident expression by Henley's abused women invites us to study the strategies by which the men organize, control, even amputate the heroines' "bitter struggle."

Key moments expose the violence against women inscribed in the institutions of marriage and motherhood in Henley's plays. Two marriages near the brink of collapse—one peripheral, one central to a plot—illustrate their strategies. In *The Wake of Jamey Foster* Katty and Wayne Foster arrive to mourn Jamey's sudden death. The wake itself Henley depicts humorously; it is the spectacle of Wayne's treatment of Katty that transforms comedy into tragicomedy. Like Delmount in *Miss Firecraker,* who dreams at night of women's bodies dismembered, Katty and Wayne live in a violently phallic universe. Wayne, who calls Katty a "twat," sexually harrasses his sister-in-law Collard, confident that men are entitled to control women's bodies: calling her "Charlotte," imposing his preference for her "proper name," he lifts her chin, marking her as his sexual property. Collard protests: "Lifting my chin up like that—you're making me feel like some sort of goddamn horse—[. . .] Oh, so you do like your women dirty?" Katty witnesses this exchange, and immediately moves to protect her own claim to Wayne's twisted affections: "Just because I lose those babies is no reason to treat me viciously—no reason at all! You know I can't help it!"—as if it might be possible ever to justify such abuse. Falsely blaming herself, Katty fails to see, as Collard does, how he is titillated by dehumanizing women into chattel. Yet what Katty has seen precipitates a household crisis. She barricades herself in shame in an upstairs bath, emerging much later to announce, in sorrow and frustration,

I hate the me I have to be with him. If only I could have the baby it would give me someone to love and make someone who'd love me. There'd be a reason for having the fine house and the lovely yard.

Of course the same impulse that has driven Katty to mold herself to Wayne's desire for a submissive wife keeps her from reconfiguring her life. She remains committed to their marriage, answering Marshael's inquiry into her next move with numb resignation: "Why, nothing. That's all I can do. I don't have children or a career like you do. Anyway I don't like changes." Katty takes refuge behind the "incompetency 'demands' of the conventional feminine role."

What makes Katty interesting as a specimen of rage repudiated is not her response to Wayne's cruelty but a childhood experience she confides during an intimate talk with the other women, who have congregated in Marshael's bedroom to comfort and cheer her as she mourns. The lights go up on them in the midst of their trading stories of the cruellest thing they have ever done. The segue to Katty's story suggests its dramaturgic importance:

KATTY (*Pulling at her hair with glee.*) Oh, it's so awful! It's too horrible! You won't think I'm sweet anymore!

COLLARD We don't care! We don't care!

PIXROSE No, we don't care! Tell us!

Collard and Pixrose function as a Greek chorus. They deliver the judgment of a community of women—"We don't care! We don't care!"—that sharply contrasts with the conventional commitment to sentimentality imposed upon women by the male characters in these texts. Moreover, it is possible to hear in Pixrose's "Tell us" a resemblance of a similar moment in *Portrait of the Artist* in which Joyce may be punning on the Greek noun *telos.* Like Stephen Dedalus, who is engaged in challenging the authority of the Roman Catholic Church to establish the ultimate purpose of life, Katty challenges with her story of girlhood violence the authority of men to establish the *telos* of women:

KATTY One Easter Sunday I was walking to church with my maid, Lizzie Pearl. Well, I was all dressed to kill for in my white ruffled dress and my white Easter bonnet and carrying my white parasol. Well, we had to pass by the Dooleys' house, and the Dooleys were always known as white trash, and that bunch really despised me. Well, Harry and Virginia Dooley came up and shoved me down into a huge mudhole. [. . .] [Later that day] [. . .] Lizzie Pearl and I sneaked back over to their back yard and yanked the chirping heads off of every one of their colored Easter chicks—We murdered them *all* with our bare hands!

It is difficult to reconcile this portrait of Katty with the other that prevails. In Wayne's absence, she paints herself "with glee" as fully capable of retaliating violently against indignities she has suffered. In Wayne's presence, however, she regresses to the role of a child, even using baby-talk to soothe him as he pretends to grieve the loss of his brother: "Why we're all gonna do every little bitty thing we can do to unburden poor, old Papa Sweet Potato."

Katty's regression is intriguingly linked to her apparent inability to carry a fetus to term. Because Wayne reduces Katty to a "twat," he continuously snuffs out her adult interiority, where interiority signifies not simply an emotional and physical readiness to bear children but also a mature knowledge of the terrain of one's own imagination, memory, and will. This link between male sexuality and the death of female interiority is reiterated elsewhere in *The Wake* when Collard abruptly propositions Slade: "Brocker, honey . . . you gonna leave me forever unravished?" With his eye on Marshael instead, Brocker Slade refuses, and Collard, affronted, strikes back: "Oh, Marshael. Right, Marshael. Well, that's all right then. 'Course she's nothing like me. She doesn't caress death and danger with open legs." Here Collard represents heterosexual intercourse as an act of heroic bravado, a potentially fatal sacrifice on the woman's part. (The metaphor also evokes the literal risk of death that women face during childbirth.) Later, her observation that sex with men threatens the death of the female subject is explicitly linked to Katty's instinctive regression. As Slade serenades Marshael from outside her window, Collard, protecting her sister as well as herself, throws a nest of bird's eggs at him, then assigns him responsibility: "Look! Now you've made me murder these baby eggs! I've done murder!" Just as Collard sacrifices the embryonic lives of birds in a feeble attempt to ward off the dangers of Slade's predatory and at this time unwanted sexual advances toward Marshael, so Katty has killed Easter chicks to signify her resistance to the conventions of feminine obsequiousness, perhaps even to the expectation of motherhood. It is no accident of the text that Katty remains childless, her body expelling the embryonic fruits of her sexual relations with Wayne to preserve what little interiority is left her by their marriage. She controls her uterus if nothing else.

Although these narratives of "murder" intuitively link Katty and Collard, Collard is distinguished by openly resisting the imposition of patriarchal conventions. As we have seen, she furiously rejects sexual harassment from her brother-in-law Wayne, and in another memorable scene, as he insists that Marshael attend Jamey's wake, like it or not, Collard mocks him: "Look, just because you'll always have the taste of leather in your mouth, doesn't mean the rest of us have to." Turning upon Wayne the equestrian metaphor previously applied to herself, Collard scorns him for having accepted the patriarchal bridle. Reversing the sign, she emphasizes the double standard by which men profit, and women suffer, from submitting to patriarchy— we know that Wayne has become a powerful small-town banker, Katty his slave. Yet it is also Collard who most articulates the toll of women's resistance against patriarchy. Ambivalent toward Slade, whom she once invited to "ravish" her, Collard is even more ambivalent toward her own reproductive freedom. In a magnetic scene, she recounts for the other women the aftermath of her abortion, which she imagines to be a violent act:

> I went out and ate fried chicken. Got a ten-piece bucket filled with mashed potatoes and gravy, coleslaw, and a roll. First it tasted good and greasy and gooey. Then I felt like I was eating my baby's skin and flesh and veins and all. I got so sick—

In contrast to Ashbe's flippant scheme to parlay an abortion into a Tokyo vacation in *Am I Blue*, this painful memory illustrates the anguishing material consequences of Collard's resolve not to be bridled. It leaves her not simply "sick," but nightmarishly guilty. Again Henley records the cost of women's liberation in graphic images of animal dismemberment. Associating the fetus and the fried chicken, which is the third appearance in *The Wake of Jamey Foster* of the trope of fowl destroyed (Easter chicks/bird eggs/fried chicken) as a sign of challenge to the conventions of gender, especially of the obligation to nurture, Collard imagines herself feeding off her own interior: "I felt like I was eating my baby's skin and flesh and veins." From another point of view, though, Collard is not a cannibal but a survivor. In this instance, to reject the fetus is to preserve her nascent claim to self-determination. Perhaps it is that claim that produces as much guilt as the abortion itself.

If Henley's plays collectively forecast the high price yet to be paid by virtually everyone for the manifold inequities long borne by women, the most expansive treatment of this idea is in *Crimes of the Heart*. Not the fairy tale of female bonding that Lorimar made it out to be in its 1986 production, *Crimes of the Heart* studies the origins and effects of domestic abuse, tracing the rise and fall of its principal heroine's rage, fingering the female conspirators of culturally sanctioned violence against women, exposing the link between sexism and racism, suggesting the often grave costs of women's coming to know themselves as wholly volitional beings.

Hovering over the MaGrath family in *Crimes of the Heart* is a curse as particular as any in Ibsen, Tennessee Williams, or Sam Shepard, and as general as post-classical Western culture itself: long ago, the matriarch of the MaGrath clan, in fury and despair, hanged herself and her cat in the fruit cellar of the family home. Her suicide affirmed for her daughters the ideological link between women's exercise of self-determination and Death, a link dating at least from early Christian constructions of Eve's primal disobedience. *Crimes of the Heart* dramatizes its continuing damage to the next generation, especially through the fallout from Babe and Zackery Botrelle's exploded marriage. Long physically abused by "the richest and most powerful man in all of Hazlehurst," Babe has denied the significance of her own fractures and bruises, breaking free only after watching Zack maul Willie Jay, her fifteen-year-old African-American lover. Although Babe is enraged by Zack's racism and his consequent physical abuse of Willie Jay, Babe's first response is to think of suicide, as her mother had done, then epiphanically to reject suicide as a viable response to explosive anger:

> Why, I was gonna shoot off my own head! [. . .] I thought about Mama . . . how she'd hung herself. Then I realized—that's right, I realized how I didn't want to kill myself! And she—she probably didn't want to kill herself.

Instead, fittingly, she shoots Zack in the belly, inflicting *quid pro quo* an ironic even if uncalculated revenge on a "bully" who had threatened to cut out Willie's "gizzard." Though Babe is no avenger, her shooting Zackery might seem to presage a heroine's decisive new commitment to self-determination. But near the end of *Crimes of the Heart* Henley dashes that hope, having Babe comically regress toward suicide. Without success she tries to hang, then to asphyxiate herself in a gas oven. Babe suffers the by-now-familiar arc: once vented, her rage boomerangs. In effect she mentally implodes, just as her compatriot Marshael does in *The Wake* Recall that Marshael, though liberated by her husband's sudden death from one cycle of emotional neglect, is still furiously angry at him, confessing that she feels as if "a hole's been shot through me, and all my insides have been blown out somewhere else."

In earlier plays, heroines abort their rage or, what amounts to the same thing, turn it inward, for obliquely palpable reasons that spectators must infer. In *Crimes,* however, the playwright delivers a direct cause of Babe's reversal, namely Zackery's

intention to commit her to the Whitfield psychiatric hospital. His plan disorients but also catalyzes Babe, who *"slams the phone down and stares wildly ahead:* He's not. He's not. [. . .] I'll do it. I will. And he won't.*"* The indicative verbs here signify that Babe again turns to suicide as the only gesture of self-determination available in a universe otherwise controlled by those such as her estranged lawyer-husband, who is ominously confident that psychiatric clinics stand ready to isolate, punish, and perhaps reprogram women who, in their rage, repudiate the hegemony of men. Zackery is obviously a "total criminal," as Babe's defense lawyer claims. Yet Henley insists we not dismiss him as an aberrant loner, but see him as an integral member of a community that permits, even expects, men to abuse women, and that expects women to cope with it by clinging to the theorem of female martyrdom. That theorem is best expressed in a colloquial commonplace by Elain, the ex-beauty queen, who counsels Camelle on her loss of the Miss Firecracker title: "Just try to remember how Mama was enlightened by her affliction." Though none of the women in *Crimes of the Heart* has in so many words similarly advised Babe to tough out Zackery's abuse, Babe has nevertheless learned well not to expect others to validate her supposedly unfeminine rage, neither before nor after she shoots Zackery. Thus when her sister Lenny and cousin Chick question Babe as to motive, she is virtually mute, offering only that she "didn't like [Zackery's] looks." Obviously ridiculous, this red herring intensifies her silence. Elizabeth Stanko observes that abused women's silence "is linked to an understanding of [their] powerlessness; it is a recognition of the contradictory expectations of femaleness and probable judgments others commonly render about any woman's involvement in male violence." Henley sharpens her critique of women who collude with oppressive forces by depicting Babe's attorney Barnette Lloyd as steadfastly supportive of his accused client, suggesting how little one's gender necessarily dictates one's politics.

Indeed, in small ways and large, Lenny and especially Chick reproduce the inequities of gender that have been insinuated into every social discourse. Lenny, for example, anticipates Zack's psychiatric prescription, telling Meg, "I believe Babe is ill. I mean in-her-head ill." Lenny fails to see how her diagnosis reinforces a double standard of provocation, in which men's "retaliatory behavior is acceptable," and women's is not. But it is cousin Chick, who works the system well enough to have been accepted to membership in the Hazlehurst Ladies' Social League, who is Zackery's far more malignant if still unwitting conspirator. Deploying the concept of ''shame'' to police other women, Chick consistently attacks what she takes to be the MaGraths' lack of obedience to a code of woman-hood that emphasizes decorum, not subjectivity; submission, not independence. She is not simply a watchdog, but a burlesque obsessed by ''the skele-tons in the MaGraths' closet,'' her anger rising as the sisters' violations mount. After spying Meg returning from a night with Doc, for example, Chick bashes Meg in order to recruit Lenny into conscious alliance with the model of suffocating female sub-jectivity endorsed by the Ladies' Social League. Chick pities not Meg but Lenny:

> You must be so ashamed! You must just want to die! Why, I always said that girl was nothing but cheap Christmas trash! [. . .] Meg's a low-class tramp and you need not have one more blessed thing to do with her and her disgusting behavior.

When Lenny refuses to concede Meg's deprav-ity, Chick explodes, inadvertently revealing the root of her anger:

> I've just about had my fill of you trashy MaGraths and your trashy ways: hanging yourselves in cellars; car-rying on with married men; shooting your own hus-bands! [. . .] [*Turning toward Babe*] And don't you think she's not gonna end up at the state prison farm or in some mental institution. Why, it's a clear-cut case of manslaughter with intent to kill! [. . .] That's what everyone's saying, deliberate intent to kill! And you'll pay for that! Do you hear me? You'll pay!

''Manslaughter,'' from the lexicon of law, aptly describes Chick's judgment of the MaGraths' viola-tions, their budding refusals to ''pay'' into a patriar-chal discourse that brands women ''cheap Christ-mas trash,'' that blames the victim for spouse abuse, that again insinuates death as the inevitable conse-quence of women's self-determination (''you must just want to die!''). In Chick's eyes, resistance is indeed man/slaughter.

Against Chick's slavish dependence upon per-nicious communal values, Henley juxtaposes Meg's apparently fierce independence. Faced with the artifacts of her sister's medical history, for example, which records the consequences of Zack's spousal violence, Meg rants, ''This is madness! Did he do this to her? I'll kill him; I will—I'll fry his blood!''; in the Senecan image Meg boldly claims the pre-rogative of revenge abdicated by most of Henley's other heroines. And later, she quells Babe's self-recriminations by erasing the privileged line be-tween sanity and madness, declaring, ''Why, you're just as perfectly sane as anyone walking the streets of Hazlehurst, Mississippi''; in Meg's circuitous compliment we may hear an indictment of the citizenry for continuing to tolerate domestic violence.

In these moments of bravado Meg seems stronger than Babe for openly resisting the forces under which Babe has long suffered, but elsewhere Henley suggests that Meg likewise suffers from deep am-bivalence about the scope and strength of her own freedom. Feigning heroic indifference toward the dangers of smoking, for example, she reiterates the link between women's self-determination and death that led her mother to hang herself in the fruit cellar: ''That's what I like about [smoking], Chick—taking a drag off of death. [. . .] Mmm! Gives me a sense of controlling my own destiny. What power! What exhilaration! Want a drag?'' Unlike Lenny and Babe, who seem glued to Hazlehurst, Meg has attempted to wrest her destiny away from the Ladies' Social League by exiling herself to Los Angeles, a move that demonstrates autonomy and mobility. In L.A., though, she has met failure. Once an aspiring singer, she has succumbed to clerking for a dog food company, and in her words has recently gone ''in-sane,'' winding up in the psychiatric ward of L.A. County Hospital. The cause, as we gradually come to see, is the residual effects of her mother's suicide. Much like Carnelle in *Miss Firecraker,* who la-ments that ''people've been dying practically all my life,'' and ''I guess I should be used to it by now,'' Meg has stoically attempted to block out the pain of having been the one to discover her mother's body. Yet Babe recalls that during girlhood outings to the public library and the Dixieland Drugstore,

> Meg would spend all her time reading and looking through this old black book called *Diseases of the Skin.* It was full of the most sickening pictures you've ever seen. Things like rotting-away noses and eye-balls drooping off down the sides of people's faces, and scabs and sores and eaten-away places. [At Dixie-land Drugs, examining a crippled-children poster, Meg would say] ''See, I can stand it. I can stand it. Just look how I'm gonna be able to stand it.''

The memory illustrates Meg's resolve to steel herself against loss, an early decision that continues to sabotage her life as an adult. Reversing the usual pattern in Henley's plays, it has been Meg who abandoned her sometime lover Doc, rather than vice versa, during Hurricane Camille: returned from L.A., she confesses to him, ''It was my fault to leave you. I was crazy, I thought I was choking. I felt choked!'' Meg's fear of ''choking'' not only recalls her mother's suicide by hanging, but also illuminates what is for her virtually a synaptic link between romantic alliances with men and the potential snuffing out of her own life. But, she tells Doc, ''I was crazy.'' Apologizing, labelling her earlier perceptions of risk as signs of mental illness, Meg now repudiates her own intuition and thus repatriates herself into the Hazlehurst community. À la Elain in *Miss Firecracker,* she too ''comes home.''

Meg's maneuver is consonant with the pattern of surrender that is woven through Henley's scripts. We may conclude that these heroines engage in quasi-feminist rebellion, if they engage in it at all, for psychological rather than political motives. Babe makes the point best when she refutes what is to her the alarming possibility that she intended her interracial liaison with Willie Jay to be a political statement: ''I'm not a liberal! I'm a democratic! I was just lonely! I was so lonely. And he was so good.'' Babe's verbal slip—an adjective for a noun—reveals an inarticulate command of the political, at least disqualifying her from playing the conscious iconoclast. As in this instance, Henley's heroines seem not to recognize as such the feminist awakenings that bubble to the surfaces of their consciousnesses, as they seek to repair and preserve their lives within the system they have inherited. Yet they come to life inside Henley's crucible of populist tragicomedy, in which regressive comic fantasies and tragic aspirations collide; osmotically the heroines have absorbed some of the energies of the feminist movement, and in their own ways, they grope toward liberty.

**Source:** Alan Clarke Shepard, ''Aborted Rage in Beth Henley's Women,'' in *Modern Drama,* Vol. 36, No. 1, March 1993, pp. 96–108.

# SOURCES

Andreach, Robert J., *Creating the Self in the Contemporary American Theatre,* Southern Illinois University Press, 1998, p. 129.

Bowman, Harry, ''*Firecracker* Pops, Sputters at Stage No. 1,'' in the *Dallas Morning News,* September 20, 1985, p. 1c.

Demastes, William W., *Beyond Naturalism: A New Realism in American Theatre,* Greenwood Press, 1988, p. 144.

———, ed., *Realism and the American Dramatic Tradition,* University of Alabama Press, 1996, p. 208.

Lavenda, Robert H., ''Minnesota Queen Pageants: Play, Fun, and Dead Seriousness in a Festive Mode,'' in the *Journal of American Folklore,* Vol. 101, 1888, p. 175.

Paige, Linda Rohrer, ''Henley, Beth,'' in *Feminist Writers,* edited by Pamela Kester-Shelton, St. James Press, 1996.

''A Review of *Four Plays,''* in *English Studies,* Vol. 75, No. 3, May 1994, pp. 259–61.

Rich, Frank, ''*Firecracker,* A Beth Henley Comedy,'' in the *New York Times,* May 28, 1984, p. 11.

Rosenfeldt, Paul, *The Absent Father in Modern Drama,* Peter Lang, 1996, p. 11.

Schickel, Richard, ''The Miss Firecracker Contest,'' in *Time,* Vol. 123, June 11, 1984, p. 80.

Taggert, Patrick, ''Grotesque Characters Dampen *Miss Firecracker,''* in *Austin American-Statesman,* May 12, 1989, p. E1.

# FURTHER READING

Betsko, Kathleen, and Rachel Koenig, ''Beth Henley,'' in *Interviews with Contemporary Women Playwrights,* William Morrow, 1987, pp. 211–22.

This interview covers Henley's creative process, her involvement in the production of her works, her family, themes, and literary goals.

Bryer, Jackson R., ed., ''Beth Henley,'' in *The Playwright's Art: Conversations with Contemporary American Dramatists,* Rutgers University Press, 1995, pp. 102–22.

This interview was conducted in October of 1991 and examines Henley's techniques as a playwright, the influences on her work, her interaction with the theatre, and her challenges as a writer.

Evans, Everett, ''Beth Henley's Play at Alley: *Miss Firecracker* Author Gets a Bang out of Being a Southern Writer,'' in *Houston Chronicle,* January 12, 1986, Zest, p. 8.

This article is a summary of Henley's career as well as an interview with her about the creation of *The Miss Firecracker Contest.*

Murphy, Brenda, ed., *The Cambridge Companion to American Women Playwrights,* Cambridge University Press, 1999.

This volume is a history of American women playwrights up to the end of the twentieth century. Each chapter covers one or more playwrights in a topical context such as comedy, melodrama, or feminism.

Neimark, Jill, ''Why We Need Miss America,'' in *Psychology Today,* Vol. 31, September–October 1998, p. 40.

The cultural ideals and conflicts that are reflected in the Miss American pageant are examined in this article.

Renner, Pamela, ''The Mellowing of *Miss Firecracker:* Beth Henley—and Her Impetuous Characters—Are Undergoing Transformations,'' in *American Theatre,* Vol. 15, Issue 9, 1998, p. 18.

This article discusses the recent changes in perspective in Henley's works, such as softer tones and more mature characters.

Son, Diana, ''Girls Just Want to Write Plays: Reflections on the Theatre's Double–x Chromosome History,'' in *American Theatre,* Vol. 20, May–June 2003, p. 52.

This history of female playwrights briefly covers the 1600s to the early 2000s and offers solutions to the problem of women's obscurity in the theatre.

# The Other Shore

## GAO XINGJIAN

## 1990

*The Other Shore* by Gao Xingjian was written in 1986. It was originally scheduled to be produced by the Beijing People's Art Theater but, for political reasons, it was banned and never staged in mainland China. That the play was never allowed to be produced in China is somewhat ironic given the fact that Xingjian originally wrote *The Other Shore* as a ''pure drama'' and as an exercise for actors, and he has steadfastly stated his belief that literature should remain independent and free of political considerations. But the work nevertheless raised the ire of authorities, and it proved to be a turning point in Xingjian's life: although it was not the first of Xingjian's works to be banned, the state's decision on *The Other Shore* convinced the playwright that if he was to continue to write unhindered by state controls, it would not be inside mainland China. In 1987, Xingjian left his native land for France, where he lives in exile. Eventually *The Other Shore* was performed, under Xingjian's direction, in Taiwan in 1990 and in Hong Kong in 1995, and later in Europe and the United States.

The play's title refers to the concept of ''paramita'' or ''nirvana,'' the land of enlightenment in Buddhism. According to Buddhist belief, humans experience an actual visible life full of suffering, but by living according to the virtues of ''paramita''—morality, patience, meditation and wisdom—they can cross the ''river of life'' to the other shore and experience enlightenment.

*The Other Shore* reveals many themes and traits characteristic of Xingjian's writing. Thematically, the play addresses issues of collectivism and individualism—themes that Xingjian has addressed throughout his career, and ones that are considered to be highly political in the Communist Chinese context. *The Other Shore* also addresses the more personal theme of salvation: the actors cross the river of life to reach nirvana, only to find that nirvana does not exist.

Stylistically Xingjian is considered avant-garde; his works seldom follow conventional narrative modes, and *The Other Shore* is no exception. The play comprises a series of seemingly disconnected scenes with no discernible plot or character development. The play clearly shows the influences of Jerzy Grotowski, the Polish dramatist who devised the concept of "poor theatre," in which the "non essentials" of theater such as costumes, sound effects, makeup, sets, and lighting are eliminated as a way to emphasize and redefine relationships between actors and the audience. In *The Other Shore*, the actors take on multiple roles and must quickly change personas several times in the course of the play. In conventional theory of acting, best represented by Constantin Stanislavski's theory of "total immersion," an actor fully takes on the persona of the fictional character. In *The Other Shore*, the actors never fully leave their role as actors. The purpose of the play is not to reproduce life realistically, but rather to provide a hypothetical world that allows the actors to continually reinterpret their roles.

While the play itself has not garnered any awards, Xingjian has been widely acclaimed as a writer. Prior to his being awarded the Nobel Prize for Literature in 2000, he was the recipient in France of Chevalier de l'Ordre des Arts et des Lettres in 1992; Prix Communauté française de Belgique in 1994; and Prix du Nouvel An chinois in 1997.

## AUTHOR BIOGRAPHY

Gao Xingjian (pronounced *gow shing-yan*) was born January 4, 1940 in Ganzhou of Jiangxi province in eastern China. The son of a bank official and amateur actress, Xingjian grew up in a creative environment and became an avid reader, painter, and writer at an early age. He was schooled at the Beijing Foreign Languages Institute from 1957 to

*Gao Xingjian*

1962 where he studied French literature. His mother was relocated to the countryside by the government in the early 1960s—as he was later—where she died in a drowning accident. The details surrounding her death are largely unknown. During the Cultural Revolution (1966–1976), Xingjian was sent to a reeducation camp and was not able to publish any of his work until 1979. It was during this time that he also destroyed several of his manuscripts out of fear of recrimination by the authorities.

During a seven-year period beginning in 1980, Xingjian wrote prolifically for Chinese literary magazines and published his first four books: *A Preliminary Discussion of the Art of Modern Fiction* (1981); *A Pigeon Called Red Beak* (1985); *Collected Plays* (1985) and *In Search of a Modern Form of Dramatic Representation* (1987). Although several of his plays during this period were produced at the Theatre of Popular Art in Beijing—including *Alarm Signal* (1982) and *Bus Stop* (1983)—his work began raising the ire of Communist Party members. In 1986, *The Other Shore* was banned, and between then and the early 2000s China has prohibited the publication and production of all of Xingjian's plays.

In 1982, Xingjian was mistakenly diagnosed with lung cancer, the disease that killed his father, and the following year the Communist Party criticized his works as "spiritual pollution." In response to these events, he set out on a ten-month-long walking tour along the Yangtze River that ultimately resulted in his most famous work, *Soul Mountain* (1989). In 1987, Xingjian became a political exile and settled down in Paris. In 1998, he became a citizen of France and continued to live there. After he voiced his opposition to the Tiananmen Square massacre in 1989, he was kicked out of the Chinese Communist Party for good, and in 1999 his autobiographical account of the Cultural Revolution, *One Man's Bible* was published. In 2000 Xingjian became the first Chinese Nobel Laureate.

In addition to his writing, Xingjian has exhibited his art widely and has translated many European dramatists into Chinese, including Samuel Beckett, Eugene Ionesco, Antonin Artaud, and Bertolt Brecht. In addition to the Nobel Award for Literature, he has been the recipient of Chevalier de l'Ordre des Arts et des Lettres by the French Government in 1992, Prix Communauté Française de Belgique 1994, and Prix du Nouvel An chinois 1997.

# PLOT SUMMARY

According to Xingjian, *The Other Shore* was originally written as an exercise for actors, and indeed, the play opens up with a troupe of actors, acting as themselves, playing a game with ropes. The Lead Actor instructs the troupe how to handle the ropes, providing possible ways to interpret the meaning of the game. The game the actors are playing is a serious one, but as serious as a game played by children: there is playfulness in the game as well as profound concentration.

After a time, the Lead Actor beckons the group to follow him across the water to the other shore. It is dark, and the actors turn into the Crowd as they reach the other shore. Upon their arrival, they have all lost their memories and their speech, and they have come to realize that their destination is not the nirvana or the shore of enlightenment that they had expected: it is a dead shore, with only oblivion surrounding them.

Woman emerges from the oblivion and walks through the crowd, teaching them words, and helping them to learn how to differentiate themselves from one another. Man soon appears and addresses Woman, but as the Crowd grows confident in its use of language, it turns against Woman and threatens her. To no avail, Man tries to protect Woman, but the Crowd presses in and kills her.

Man has become the de facto, albeit reluctant leader of the Crowd. He lectures the Crowd on the murder of Woman and then proceeds to meet Young Girl, whom he recognizes from his childhood, and Mother, with whom he has a brief argument concerning his future. Man leaves Mother and meets Card Player, sitting beneath a lamp drinking and playing cards. All the while, Crowd is following behind Man.

After some basic instructions, Card Player convinces Man and Crowd to join him in his game. Winners will receive a taste of wine, while losers must stick a slip of paper against their faces, marking themselves as losers of the game. Man soon discovers that the game is rigged, and that there is no way for him or the Crowd to win. But the Crowd wants nothing to do with Man's assertions; they side with Card Player and turn against Man, trying to convince him that he is wrong. Man becomes confused and begins to second guess himself.

A Zen Master briefly appears, chanting, and Young Man is then seen trying to convince Young Girl—who has been meditating—to allow him to touch her. She refuses, and Father enters the scene, scolding Young Man on several accounts. Young Man walks away and notices a wall of people. Old Woman is standing in front of a "crack" in the wall, and he talks her into allowing him through to see the goings-on behind the wall. Young Man enters and observes what seems to be a side-show of sorts, in which a man is trying to sell the Crowd Dogskin Plasters. Mad Woman appears, taunting the Crowd. The men in the Crowd want her taken away. Mad Woman claims they have all slept with her and do not want the secret revealed. Soon the Crowd has had enough of Mad Woman, and she is tied up and gagged.

Meanwhile, Young Man disappears, and Man, who has until now been meditating off to the side, reappears with Shadow. As they walk, Shadow echoes Man's inner thoughts and words. They soon encounter several individuals, each of whom is looking for something specific. Some of these individuals ask Man about his own search, but Man does not know what he is seeking. Soon he is badgered by the individuals and by Stable Keeper, who all insist that he must be looking for something, or if he is not, perhaps he has already found it, or perhaps he is nothing more than a troublemaker. But Man simply wants to be left alone.

When Stable Keeper finally confronts Man, Man crawls through Stable Keeper's crotch and finds a key on the ground which opens a door that's never been opened. Inside Man finds pieces of mannequins, which he begins to rearrange and which, in turn, begin to take shape as female figures. The figures take on a life and begin to move around Man, gyrating and eventually taking control of their own bodies. Man becomes exhausted, crawls away from the figures like a worm, and the figures disappear.

Shadow speaks to Man, narrating Man's lonely journey. After accusing Man of vanity, Shadow disappears and is replaced with the Crowd who surround man, badgering him and criticizing him and laughing at him in cold and sinister voices. When Shadow returns to take Man away, claiming that he is Man's heart, the Crowd retreats and everyone exits the stage.

One by one, each of the actors reappear on stage, as actors, and talk idly about the play and about this and that. The sound of a baby crying is presumed to come from the baby of one of the actors, and the sound of a car starting is heard in the background as the actors talk of the play and of how they will be getting home now.

## CHARACTERS

### Actors

Actors playing themselves open and close the play, helping to give the drama its circular movement: the play ends as it begins. When the play opens, a single actor leads the troupe in an exercise with ropes and, as the play ends, the actors reflect upon the play they have just acted in as they leave for their non-theatrical lives. Xingjian originally conceived of *The Other Shore* as a training piece for actors.

### Card Player

The Card Player offers the Crowd and Man a chance to win a drink of wine with a deceptively

# MEDIA ADAPTATIONS

- The Nobel Prize committee maintains a Xingjian web page at http://www.nobel.se/literature/laureates/2000/index.html with links to other interesting sites.

---

simple card game, but Man discovers that the game is rigged, and it is impossible for him or the Crowd to win. When Man tries to point this out to the Crowd, the Crowd doesn't believe him and jeers Man. The Card Player manipulates the Crowd and convinces its members and Man that Man is wrong. One possible interpretation is that the Card Player represents the manipulative and coercive state, able to play the masses against dissenting individuals.

### Crowd

As the actors make their way across the river, they exhaust themselves and awaken on the other shore without their memories or language. In the process they have been transformed from actors on a stage into a Crowd, made up of countless nameless individuals. This Crowd will be present throughout the play, acting as a counterpoint to individuals such as Man and Woman who attempt to realize their own identities within the drama, but unable to do so because of the Crowd. Upon being taught language by Woman, members of the Crowd learn to distinguish themselves as individuals within the collective force, and soon the Crowd turns against Woman and kills her. Later the Crowd also turns against Mad Woman and Man, and in turn is cheated by Card Player. Several times throughout the play it is clear that the Crowd is in need of a leader, but it is as equally clear that it will turn against anyone who stands up to take on that role.

### Father

Father approaches Young Man when Young Man touches Young Woman against her will. As a cautious man, Father has prepared for rain by carrying an umbrella despite the dry weather. Father tries to advise Young Man, but to no avail, and when they argue with one another, Father denies that Young Man is his son. The argument is portrayed as a classic generational disagreement between father and son.

### Lead Actor

As the play opens, an actor leads the troupe in an exercise with ropes. The game is a simple one, with each participant holding an end of a rope, and moving according to the rules established by the Lead Actor. Although the Lead Actor compares the game to a children's game, it is nevertheless a serious one, and the leader makes it clear that the rope held by each actor represents the forces that push and pull at relationships, from the simple to the complex, whether they be that of husband and wife, for instance, or each individual's relationship to God. When the Lead Actor takes hold of one end of each of the ropes, with each member of the troupe holding on to the other ends, the relationship becomes, in effect, between that of the individual and society. The rope holds and binds the actors together, with the Lead Actor acting as the social force, able to manipulate both individual actors as well as the entire troupe. Through these series of games, the Lead Actor and the troupe establish the themes that will be developed over the course of the play.

### Mad Woman

After Young Man enters through a ''crack'' in a wall of people to view a side-show lead by a Plaster Seller, Mad Woman approaches him. She is clearly a scapegoat for the Crowd. She claims that the men are afraid of her because they have all secretly slept with her and don't want to be revealed. The men's wives, she claims, are afraid of becoming like her: nothing more than a mere prostitute for their men who will dump them when the sex has ended. The Crowd wants her taken away but she continues to taunt the Crowd until the Crowd takes action by tying her up and gagging her.

### Man

Man establishes himself early in the play as the first individual character to stand apart from the Crowd. Originally a part of the Crowd, once he leaves the Crowd to stand on his own he is looked upon by the Crowd as a potential leader; however,

Man is reluctant in this leadership role. He is indecisive, largely in part because of his inquisitiveness; he has a stronger desire to learn the truth than he does to be a leader. He also does not want to raise a family, as Mother wants of him; he has ambitions he wants to pursue first. As a result, he pleases no one. The Crowd continually taunts him and keeps him from completing his search. Man pleads with the Crowd to leave him alone. Only in the end is he finally able to escape the pressures of the Crowd by following his heart.

### Mother

Mother plays a small role in *The Other Shore*. She meets Man after the Crowd has killed Woman and tries to talk him into settling down to raise a family, but to no avail.

### Shadow

Shadow acts as an alter ego to Man, following him at first in synchronous steps, echoing his voice and his thoughts. After a time, Shadow addresses Man directly, giving Man advice. Shadow eventually stands apart from Man, narrating Man's movements and thoughts in the second person. In the end, after Man has found the key he has been looking for, Shadow reappears as Man's heart and slowly drags Man offstage.

### Woman

Woman emerges on the shore across the river and is the first person the members of the Crowd meet when they awaken from their sleep. Woman offers them the gifts of language and wisdom, which they then use in return to kill her. She pleads with the Crowd before her death, but to no avail.

### Young Girl

Young Girl makes her first appearance when Man sees her and recognizes her as a girl he had always longed for years earlier. Young Girl wordlessly listens to Man then disappears into the Crowd. Later, Young Man tries to touch Young Girl while she is meditating, but she refuses him.

### Young Man

Young Man appears in three separate but linked scenes. First, he appears with Young Girl, unsuccessfully trying to convince her to let him touch her.

He then enters into an argument with Father, who disowns him as result, and in his final scene he talks Old Woman into letting him in to a side-show in exchange for his Mother's gold pen.

# THEMES

## *Collectivism*

The theme of the collective is introduced in the first scene of the play when the Lead Actor instructs the other actors to hold one end of their rope while he holds the other. Thus, the entire group is bound together through the ropes and through the Lead Actor, giving him the ability to manipulate the entire group. Bound together collectively, the action of any individual will now affect the entire group; thus it becomes essential for the individual actors to consider the collective when they act. And throughout the play, the Crowd acts as an organic unit, collectively expressing its feelings. Its first actions result in the death of Woman, and throughout the play it works against the desires of Man to express himself individually. This theme, in the context of Communist China where the rights of the collective have historically been given precedence over the rights of the individual, is a highly political issue.

## *Conformity*

Related to the collectivism theme, the theme of conformity stresses the need of individuals to conform to the needs and desires of the larger collective. This is cogently expressed toward the end of the play with Man in his indeterminate search. The Stable Keeper and the Crowd taunt him, claiming he's "looking for trouble" and that he should admit his wrongs and repent. Man simply wants to be left alone and the Crowd is unable to accept this. In the context of Communist China, with its priority on the needs of the collective, one's ability to conform is an essential attribute for success.

## *Control*

Control is a necessary component not only of any totalitarian government, but also of any human relationship. Issues of control arise in friendships, work relationships, marriages, and communities. The game with the rope elucidates the various ways men and women, individually and collectively, exert control over one another, through language, body movements, and physical force. The Crowd is irrepressible in trying to control Man. Father, Mother, and Stable Keeper also try to exert their forms of control over Man, but in the end, once Man is able to follow his heart, he is able to finally act on his own, apart from external controlling factors.

## *Freedom*

Man's ultimate goal is to liberate himself from the controlling forces weighing him down. The actors' early attempt at reaching the other shore, or nirvana, falls short once they realize that there is no nirvana. Man then sets out in a life-long search that will, if he is successful, ultimately liberate him. While it is clear that Man is not at all certain of what he is in search of, it becomes equally as clear as the play progresses that his ultimate goal is to be able to continue his search unimpeded by external pressures. Man is essentially searching for the freedom that will allow him to continue his search.

## *Individualism*

Man and the Mad Woman are two individuals in *The Other Shore* who stand apart from the Crowd and who are continually pressured by the Crowd to conform. Mad Woman has become the Crowd's scapegoat; she is accepted by the Crowd as long as she keeps silent with her rants, but when she refuses to bend to the Crowd's wishes, the Crowd ties her up and gags her. The Crowd cannot kill Mad Woman for it needs her as a scapegoat. Man, on the other hand, is able to survive the pressures of the crowd with his individualism intact; he is able to follow his heart and continue his search despite the Crowd's best efforts.

## *Language*

During the game with the ropes, the Lead Actor discusses how people can "pull" and "be pulled" by language. Simple phrases such as "Good Morning" and "How are you!" can act as invisible ropes between people. The stage directions during the game also call for the actors to express several emotions and states of beings, such as intimacy, abandonment, and repulsion, in "all kinds of sighs and screams but without resorting to the use of language." Language here is both expressed with and without words, but in both cases it has immediate effects on relationships. Right after the rope

# TOPICS FOR FURTHER STUDY

- In his Nobel Prize acceptance speech (which can be found at http://www.nobel.se/literature/laureates/2000/index.html), Xingjian wrote, ''In order that literature safeguard the reason for its own existence and not become the tool of politics it must return to the voice of the individual.'' What does Xingjian mean by this statement? Does this mean that literature should never be ''political'' and that it should only concern itself with the concerns of the individual?

- Xingjian has been deeply influenced by the writings of Jerzy Grotowski, the Polish dramatist who devised the concept of ''poor theatre.'' Research Grotowski and his theory of ''poor theatre'' and explain its influence on *The Other Shore*.

- Research the existentialist movement in France during the 1940s. What were the primary beliefs? Did they share political goals? Do you consider Xingjian an existentialist? Why or why not?

- While *The Other Shore* can be read in the context of the controlling forces Chinese Communism has upon the individual, can the play be read in the context of democratic countries such as the United States? Are there social forces at work in the United States that one can apply Xingjian's play to?

- Research the Buddhist concept of ''the other shore,'' or ''*bi'an.*'' How does one reach the other shore? Where does the phrase come from? Are there Judeo-Christian parallels to the other shore? Muslim parallels? Do you think Xingjian is criticizing Buddhism in *The Other Shore*?

game, the actors journey across the water to the other shore where, when they awaken, they find they have lost all language and must be taught anew. Without language, the individuals have no way of differentiating themselves from one another; they have lost the concept of self. It is only through the teachings of Woman that they are able to regain their language; however, in this case, once they have fully acquired language, they turn on Woman collectively and kill her. Language, in its many forms, has the ability to bring people together, pull them apart, and even destroy them.

## Power

At the heart of all the relationships in *The Other Shore* is power. Whether it is the Lead Actor expressing his power by controlling the rope game, the Card Player expressing his power by manipulating the Crowd, or the Crowd expressing its power by killing Woman. Power is an intrinsic component of every relationship. Under a collective system, the power of the individual is far less than that of the collective; individuals are thus in a constant state of vulnerability vis-à-vis the collective. However, as *The Other Shore* seems to show, the individual can attain a certain amount of power over the Crowd by following his or her own heart.

## Relationships

*The Other Shore* is a play of relationships. The play opens with actors defining and redefining their own relationships with one another. Soon the relationship of the individual, as expressed primarily in the character of Man, to the collective, as expressed by the Crowd, becomes the play's focus. Other relationships include the archetypal parent-child and boy-girl relationships. None of the relationships in *The Other Shore* exists free of the constraints imposed by the social constraints in which they exist. The pressures of the Crowd have a continual effect on all relationships in the play.

## Salvation

There is no salvation in the classic sense of the word in *The Other Shore*. The actors' journey across the river to the other shore where they hope to achieve nirvana is for naught: not only do they not attain enlightenment, but the journey causes them to lose their language, and they must be taught to speak as children are taught. Ultimately, there is no escape from the suffering of this world; humans will never realize the ultimate truth that is known only in nirvana. The only hope for humans is to continue their search without fear of reprisal, for it is in the search itself that, quite possibly, salvation may be found.

# STYLE

## Improvisation

While Xingjian provides some stage directions, the actors are expected to improvise throughout their performance. Xingjian provides little direction for the actors, telling them only to communicate "without resorting to language" or to play with "imaginary ropes." This allows the actors to explore their characters more fully, without the impediment of direction. This also fits into his criticism of what he calls the "spoken drama" of contemporary theater in which literal words and their meaning become the driving force of drama. Xingjian is interested in the ways humans communicate, control, coerce, love, and live with one another non-verbally, without words and their various constructs. Improvisation allows the actors to offer a multitude of possibilities of how humans interact with one another.

## Minimalist Setting

Following the theories of Jerzy Grotowski, Xingjian has removed all but the most essential props. With the exception of the necessary lighting and some ropes, the stage is barren. This allows the director to emphasize the relationships between the actors themselves, and between the actors and the audience.

## Shifting Points of View

In the Chinese language, because there are no verb conjugations, the subject of the sentence can be omitted, leaving the reader with several possible interpretations of meaning. Often the context can help one determine whether the narrator is speaking in the first, second, or third person point of view, but with Xingjian, who is most interested in exploring the many facets of the self, this linguistic shift offers him a multitude of ways to explore the characters.

Although this effect is largely lost in translation, the idea of exploring the multitude of dimensions that each character inhabits is vital to understanding Xingjian's drama.

## Suppositional Theater

A term coined by critic Sy Ren Quah, "suppositional theater" refers to the hypothetical setting created by the playwright. Although the play clearly has cultural and political overtones relevant to contemporary Chinese society, the setting itself gives off no particular time frame or setting. The stage directions indicate that the time "cannot be defined or stated precisely," and that the location is "[f]rom the real world to the nonexistent other shore." Furthermore, the directions state that the play can be performed in virtually "any empty space as long as the necessary lighting and sound equipment can be properly installed."

## Theater of the Absurd

The Theater of the Absurd refers to the dramatic movements of the 1940s and 1950s and was portrayed in the plays of writers such as Samuel Beckett, Jean Genet, and Eugene Ionesco. The term was used by existentialist French philosophers Albert Camus and Jean-Paul Sartre. Xingjian was profoundly influenced in his writing by French existential thought and much of *The Other Shore* is directly influenced by French absurdist drama.

## Tripartite Actor

The term "tripartite actor" is Xingjian's and refers to the three states of existence the actor experiences at the time of a performance. While traditional acting theories, such as Constantin Stanislavski's theory of "total immersion" call for the actor to completely enter into the state of the character, Xingjian attempts, in his drama, to have his actors employ three separate states of existence: their own "non-acting" state, the "neutral" state they enter as they are preparing to become the character, and the state they must embody to become the character. The "neutral" state interests Xingjian the most, and in *The Other Shore* he explores this state by having the actors play both themselves as actors, and quickly move into the roles assigned to them by the play. By embodying all three states simultaneously, the actor can sympathize, empathize, pity, admire, and even criticize his or her own character.

# HISTORICAL CONTEXT

*The Other Shore* is not set in any particular time or place. Xingjian's original intention with the play was to create what he called "pure drama" and to use the play as an exercise for actors. To that end, the actors who participate in *The Other Shore* must change roles throughout the performance quickly and dramatically, moving in and out of multiple personas and using improvisational techniques throughout.

However, none of this is to say that the play does not have an historical or political context. The play's themes of collectivism and individualism recur throughout Xingjian's writing, and one need look no further than his native China and its political structures to see the reasons for Xingjian's preoccupation with those themes.

In 1949, nine years after Xingjian was born, Mao Zedong, as the leader of the Communist Party and the Red Army in China, helped found China as a united country, quickly reversing the years of humiliation the country suffered at the hands of occupying forces dating back to the British in 1842. Under Chairman Mao, as the masses referred to him, China grew to be a world power but not without horrible human consequences. One of Mao's many goals was to create a "New Socialist Man" through a widespread program of cultural purification. Many of the various political and economic programs Mao initiated to that end—including various five-year plans and the "Great Leap Forward" of 1958—proved disastrous and resulted in massive famine and widespread unrest. Over time the Communist Party would amass greater and greater political and social power, to the point that it would effectively become a totalitarian party that, for the stated good of the masses, would dictate where individuals worked and what they could read and write.

Mao's rule eventually led to the Cultural Revolution, also known as the Great Proletarian Cultural Revolution, a decade-long movement that would have a profound impact on all arts and intellectual development in China for years. From 1966 to 1976, this social experiment, led by Mao and designed to "purify" the Communist Party ranks, saw Mao's Red Guard attack intellectuals and remove all vestiges of "bourgeois" influences from society. Millions of people were forced into manual labor, tens of thousands were executed, and countless others de-nounced by the state and imprisoned or sent into forced labor, never to be seen again. In short, the Cultural Revolution exhorted individuals to sacrifice themselves for the good of the larger masses. Over the course of the nearly three decades that he ruled China, Mao was directly or indirectly responsible for the deaths of an estimated thirty to forty million people, primarily through starvation, putting him in league with Joseph Stalin and Adolph Hitler as one of the twentieth-century's most brutal political leaders.

Xingjian's mother was one of the many victims of Mao's social policies. In the early 1960s, as Xingjian started coming into his own as a young writer, she was sent by the government to the countryside to work, and later drowned there. The details of his mother's relocation and death are obscure and largely unknown. Although theater became the vehicle of choice for the Communist Party to extol their propaganda throughout the countryside during the Cultural Revolution, Xingjian was not in a position to benefit. The drama that was used by the state was written and performed under strict ideological guidelines, and Xingjian himself was sent to a reeducation camp in the countryside. It was during this period that he destroyed several of his manuscripts out of fear of recrimination by the authorities.

Following Mao's death in 1976, party moderates took control of China and many of the policies initiated by Mao were abandoned. In 1980, Deng Xiaoping became the leader of the Chinese Communist Party, and he proceeded to open China to outside investments and initiated a movement referred to by some as "Market Socialism." While ordinary people could not theoretically open up new businesses, outside investors could take stakes in Chinese companies. While there seemed to be a general opening up of society the government continued to crack down on political and intellectual dissent. It was during Xiaoping's reign that Xingjian saw several of his works banned. Shortly after *The Other Shore* was banned in 1986, Xingjian left China for Paris where he could live and write without restriction.

Although *The Other Shore* is not an overtly political work, its focus on the individual and the stifling pressures of the collective run counter to the precepts of China's Communist Party. While it is possible to appreciate Xingjian's play outside of his native land's political context, the play can only be fully understood in light of the historical and political forces under which Xingjian was raised and grew as a writer and artist.

## CRITICAL OVERVIEW

When news spread in 2000 of Xingjian being awarded the Nobel Prize for Literature, China quickly responded negatively. "This shows that the Nobel Prize for Literature has virtually been used for political purposes and thus has lost its authority," the then director of the Chinese Writers' Association declared in the online edition of the *People's Daily*. He further commented that "China boasts many world-famous literary works and writers, about which the Nobel Committee knows little." China's Foreign Ministry also called the award a political maneuver the nation took no pride in.

While most other commentators around the world praised Xingjian for his brave dissident status, the fact was that most Westerners—and most Chinese—had never heard of Gao Xingjian. True, he had received several awards in France, where Xingjian had been living in exile since 1987, and most of his major works had been translated into English and the major European languages, but the esoteric worlds of his plays and prose works had never appealed to a broad audience. In fact, prior to the Nobel committee's decision, several United States publishers rejected *Soul Mountain*, the novel that he has become best known for.

*The Other Shore* was written for the Beijing People's Art Theater in 1986 but not produced until 1990 in Taiwan and again in Hong Kong in 1995. After the Nobel Prize Award in 2000, Xingjian's dramatic work finally began receiving more widespread attention in the United States.

In a 2000 review of *The Other Shore*, the Chinese University Press edition of the anthology in which the English translation of the play was included, Howard Goldblatt, writing in *World Literature Today*, does not refer to the play itself, but calls Xingjian a "major figure in world drama, and the most innovative, if not the most famous, playwright China has produced in this century." He goes on to call the translations by Gilbert C. F. Fong "smooth, idiomatic, and lively." "Elegant when called for, colloquial when demanded," he adds, "the lan-

guage retains the illusion that the characters are speaking in English, and contemporary English at that."

In a 2002 *Journal of Asian Studies* review, Deirdre Sabina Knight calls "the wretched loneliness of the characters" that inhabit Xingjian's plays the one element that unites the plays collected in the anthology. As for *The Other Shore* itself, she writes that as Man's "beleaguered search for direction lays bare the dangers of collectivism for any sort of moral rectitude, he ends so bereft of counsel that he resorts to compulsively rearranging mannequins." Knight calls the translation successful "in conveying much of the effect of Gao's inventiveness, particularly the repetitive chanting timbre of the dialogues," but concludes by saying that the "plays are above all performances, and their power comes forth when they are acted aloud by multiple overlapping voices."

In 2003, Sons of Beckett's West Coast in Los Angeles premiered *The Other Shore*. In a *Los Angeles Times* review of the play, Rob Kendt called the play

> essentially a series of individuation psychodramas: The group discovers the communion of language, then turns it against one another; the group, under the sway of a demagogue, gangs up on an honest man; a young man finds himself spurned by mother, father, girl and society.

Kendt writes that the performance itself was "nothing so much as an experimental theater class in which very green actors rehearse/emote/create a purportedly avant-garde show."

## CRITICISM

### Mark White

*White is the publisher of the Seattle-based Scala House Press. In this essay, White argues that* The Other Shore *can be read both as a critique of China's collectivist system and as an example of absurdist drama.*

A casual reader of Gao Xingjian's *The Other Shore* might conclude that the play is little more than a plotless, disjointed work made up of a series of

*An eighteenth-century Tibetan painting titled "Buddha in Nirvana"*

seemingly unrelated scenes. That such a reading is possible should not be surprising, given Xingjian's original intention that the play be a training exercise for actors.

In defense of such a reading, the play can be viewed as an exercise for actors, designed to test their versatility by forcing them to take on multiple and quickly changing roles. And in further defense, not only does the play lack a coherent plot with the dramatic complications and resolutions that most dramatic works embody but there is also little, if any, perceivable character development in the course of the play's single act.

Nevertheless, limiting oneself to such a reading is ultimately shortsighted, for *The Other Shore* can also be read as a structurally sound and coherent dramatic work, written in the vein of the Theater of the Absurd, that explores the impact the collective has on individual consciousness. While not overtly political, *The Other Shore* addresses profound psychological, social, and political issues that have been, literally, matters of life and death for millions of men and women in Xingjian's native China.

One of the characteristics of Xingjian's works—and one that has kept Xingjian from being published in China and ultimately led him to settle in exile in

France—is his decidedly western, existentialist, individualistic, and, ultimately, apolitical worldview. Xingjian's earliest influences were the European existentialist philosphers and absurd dramatists of the 1940s and 1950s—writers such as Eugene Ionesco, Samuel Becket, Jean Genet, and Jean-Paul Sartre. China, under the intellectual stranglehold of Mao Zedong, was narrowing its definition of what it considered to be acceptable, and therefore publishable: literature that the government believed could further the country's authoritarian and collectivist ends. Xingjian, meanwhile, was expanding his influences to include writers who were decidedly anti-authoritarian and individualistic in their orientation.

As China's many reform movements under Mao—notably the Cultural Revolution of 1966–1976—led to the deaths of tens of millions of Chinese and the banishment and imprisonment of tens of thousands of intellectuals and artists, Xingjian's commitment to maintain the purity of his artistic vision deepened. The brief publication and attempted production of *The Other Shore* in 1986 offers an example of this commitment and marked a dramatic turning point in the writer's life. When the authorities banned the play, rather than remain in his native country to continue to write under

# WHAT DO I READ NEXT?

- *The August Sleepwalker* (1990), by Bei Dao, one of China's premier poets, collects Dao's poems written between 1970 and 1986. Like Xingjian, Dao reaches beyond Chinese tradition to create his art and has come to be known for his highly experimental and subjective style. And like Xingjian, Bao's commitment to artistic freedom has forced him to live outside of his native China, in exile.

- *One Man's Bible* (1999) is Xingjian's fictionalized account of his life during the Cultural Revolution. Told from the third person point of view, the book draws on the narrator's life as an aspiring writer, surrounded by colleagues, neighbors, friends, and even family members he cannot trust out of fear of investigation by the authorities.

- Although best known for his writing, Xingjian has become internationally recognized as a painter as well. His paintings, in fact, have been used as the designs for many of his book covers. *Return to Painting* (2002) collects more than one hundred of Xingjian's paintings that span a forty-year period beginning in the 1960s, along with an essay on art by Xingjian.

- Famous for his novella *Raise the Red Lantern* (1993), which was made into a popular movie,

Chinese writer Su Tong has created a raw, unflinching portrait of societal and familial life in 1930s China in his novel *Rice* (2004). Tong is considered one of China's leading avant-garde literary figures. Although his novels and stories take on themes familiar to mainstream Chinese writers, his work is characterized by a style uniquely his own that relies on dream-like imagery and narrative gaps that leave room for interpretation.

- *Soul Mountain* (1999) is Gao Xingjian's fictional account of his ten-month journey along the Yangtze River after he was misdiagnosed with lung cancer. A wandering, almost plotless novel with a narration that moves between the first, second, and third points of view, *Soul Mountain* touches upon themes of mortality, environmental catastrophe, and sexuality and is considered by many to be Xingjian's masterpiece.

- *To Live* (2003) is Yu Hua's often brutal novel recounting the horrors that have beset China. Influenced by the Cultural Revolution, Hua's work is noted for its violence and stark imagery. After Fugui gambles his family's fortune away, he is eventually conscripted into the army, and upon his release, has to deal with the country's land reform and the famine it creates, while members of his family die bitter deaths.

---

the constant shadow of governmental and self-censorship, Xingjian decided to leave China so that he could continue his art unhindered.

*The Other Shore* is not an explicitly political work. Xingjian, in fact, has clearly stated his position on the relationship of politics to art numerous times. ''In order that literature safeguard the reason for its own existence and not become the tool of politics,'' Xingjian writes in his Nobel Prize acceptance speech, ''it must return to the voice of the individual, for literature is primarily derived from

the feelings of the individual and is the result of feelings.'' In the Chinese context, in which the needs of the collective are rendered far more important than those of the individual, any work that explores the relationship of the individual to the larger society can have profound political reverberations. On one level, *The Other Shore* is just that: an exploration of the impact the collective, as represented by the Crowd, has on the individual, as represented first by Woman, and then by Man. This theme is introduced in the opening scene in which the actors are playing a game with ropes.

---

**" MAN'S NEED TO CONTROL HIS OWN DESTINY IN *THE OTHER SHORE*, HIS YEARNING TO SIMPLY GO HIS OWN WAY WITHOUT BEING BADGERED BY THE CROWD, IS XINGJIAN'S REPRESENTATION OF THE INDIVIDUAL'S PLIGHT WITHIN THIS COLLECTIVE STRUCTURE."**

As the game begins, each actor is holding onto an end of a rope, with another actor holding on to the other. In this way numerous relationships are created, with the Lead Actor existing autonomously of the larger group and offering only verbal instructions. But when the Lead Actor instructs each of them to give one end of their rope to him, each actor then becomes directly connected to him. "This way you'll be able to establish all kinds of relationships with me," he tells the group, "some tense, some lax, some distant, and some close, and soon your individual attitudes will have a strong impact on me. Society is complex and ever-changing, we're constantly pulling and being pulled."

A representation of a collective organism, with a single leader—not unlike that of the structure of the Chinese state—has now been created. Each individual can only act now with the knowledge that his or her actions will be felt by the leader and will also impact the whole, and the leader can act unilaterally on any number of the ropes at any given time. Although there is no authorial intrusion by Xingjian that renders judgment on this model, it is obvious that the structure will severely curtail the actions of the individual. Not only will the individual be unable to act autonomously of the larger organism, but when he or she eventually does act, the collective leader will know immediately. Anonymity has been made impossible here; the leader will know the precise actions of each of the individuals at all times.

As the play continues, the actors arrive to the other shore, having left their roles as actors and subsumed the roles of members of the Crowd. On the shore, they discover that they have lost their language and their memories. Woman emerges from the mist and helps them to speak again, but the Crowd soon uses their language against Woman. Man emerges to intervene, but to no avail: the Crowd accuses Woman of ulterior motives and threatens her. The Crowd, having been seduced by the power of its "own increasingly venomous language," drags Woman away from Man and strangles her to death.

From this point on, the relationship of the individual to the Crowd will be the theme that ties the subsequent scenes together and provides the work with much of its structural unity. Crowd wants Man to lead them, but Man refuses. When Man meets Card Player, he quickly realizes that the game that Card Player is inviting him and the Crowd to play is impossible to win. Man tries to help Crowd see the truth of this manipulation, but the Crowd sides with Card Player and taunts Man, at one point even trying to pull his pants down in an act of both humiliation and comic relief. Does Card Player represent the state in this scene, continually manipulating the Crowd, the masses, for its own ends, and convincing them to work against their own self-interests by isolating dissenters? This interpretation is certainly possible, but regardless, Man, like Woman before him, has become the Crowd's object of scorn.

Man continues on his journey, briefly transforming into himself as a Young Man meeting his young girlfriend, his Father, and taking in a sideshow. He then returns as a Man to continue indeterminate search, taunted relentlessly by the Crowd and others until Shadow, acting as Man's heart, takes him away.

In Man's search, it becomes clear that he is uncertain of exactly what he is looking for, but it becomes equally clear that the search itself is what continues to drive Man; he simply wants to be left alone to do as he pleases. "I'm going my way!" Man is finally able to say. "I'm not bothering anybody, and nobody's bothering me, okay?" But the Crowd, along with Stable Keeper, continues to taunt him and even accuses him of being a trouble maker.

The ability of the Chinese political system to survive for so long has in part been the result of the success its had in rigidly controlled the intellectual lives of its citizens by controlling what books and magazines can be published, what plays and movies can be produced, and what art work can be exhibited. As much for the purpose of controlling the public intellectual life of the country, these acts effectively control the very thoughts of the individual. At various times in its history, particularly during the Cultural Revolution, average citizens have been afraid to speak their minds even to their closest friends and family members, from fear of being turned in to the authorities. Man's need to control his own destiny in *The Other Shore*, his yearning to simply go his own way without being badgered by the crowd, is Xingjian's representation of the individual's plight within this collective structure. Man can not pull his own rope as he sees fit; his rope is tethered to the Crowd and as a result he must suffer extensive restrictions.

Is there a way out? Yes and no. The system is so relentless in its pursuit of Man that even when Man is finally able to follow his own heart and leave the Crowd, he does not experience the ecstasy, or even the slight happiness, one would expect. His heart is described as "extremely old," and he can only weakly follow, as if not only the long struggles he has endured has worn him down, but the uncertainty of what lies ahead also weighs on him. This exhaustion may also be the result of Man realizing what an absurd situation he is in. A reading of *The Other Shore* in the context of its lineage as an absurdist drama can help speak to this interpretation.

By the time *The Other Shore* was written in 1986, Xingjian had long established himself as a playwright in the vein of the existentialists and absurdist writers of Europe, especially the French. The Theater of the Absurd, a dramatic movement that originated in Paris in the 1940s, had its philosophical roots in the existential thought of philosophers such as Sartre and Camus, who maintained that the idea that man can grasp the true meaning of life is a false one and that the ultimate truth, if it exists at all, is unattainable. Life, therefore, is absurd. Perhaps the most famous of plays in this school is Samuel Beckett's *Waiting for Godot* in which two men sit on a park bench throughout the entire performance awaiting the arrival of a man who never comes.

In Buddhist belief, the "other shore" refers to the state of enlightenment, or nirvana, that humans who have lived a righteous life can reach once they cross the river of life. Once the actors have crossed the river in the opening scenes, they quickly realize that there is only "oblivion." There is no nirvana, no state of enlightenment. Perhaps this is why Man, in the play's final scene, is exhausted, and his heart is portrayed in such lifeless terms. Perhaps he has

come to the realization, that after a life of struggling, to be left alone, ultimately makes no difference and that his search has been a fruitless one.

This fruitless search for the truth, and the characters' inner turmoil and sense of confusion and anxiety, is not only portrayed in absurdist drama through explication, it is also conveyed through seemingly absurd images and dialog. Absurdist plays do not attempt to render the world realistically; instead, they tend to bring out the inner life of the characters caught in this absurd life through dream-like and nightmarish imagery. There is also a tendency of plays to end, more or less, where they have begun, thereby adding to the absurdity.

So what may appear to be disjointed, seemingly unrelated scenes that give *The Other Shore* its structure are, in fact, Xingjian's renderings of the inner life of Man as he vainly tries to find meaning in the absurd world into which he's been born. There is no logic to his turmoil, just as there seems to be non logic to the movement of the play. Man has been given an absurd situation to try to understand, but comprehension is impossible. And the play coming full circle at the end, with the actors once again on stage no longer in character, but as themselves, only adds to the absurdity, and enhances the tragedy of the individual trying to make sense, and free himself, of it all.

**Source:** Mark White, Critical Essay on *The Other Shore*, in *Drama for Students*, Thomson Gale, 2005.

## *Sy Ren Quah*

*In the following excerpt, Sy Ren focuses on Gao's "unique mode of narrative . . . and his experimentation with language."*

"I am," says the Stanislavskian actor as he prepares to take up his role. The ideal relation between the actor and the character for Russian/Soviet director Konstantin Stanislavsky is for the two to become completely merged, suggesting a "condensed and almost absolute truth on the stage." When actors transform themselves into their characters, there exists on stage one and only one truth—the truth of the character's world—while the actors disappear and lose their own identities.

Many dramatists, Western and Chinese alike, have worked within the artistic paradigm established in Stanislavsky's method of performance. The Stanislavskian paradigm is not only concerned with representing reality on stage; it constitutes an entire system, both technical and ideological, of

THE SPONTANEOUS CHANGES
BETWEEN SEVERAL DRAMATIC
ROLES BY THE ACTORS IN *THE
OTHER SHORE* . . . INDICATE THAT
GAO IS MORE INTERESTED IN
EXPERIMENTING WITH THE
DIFFERENT CAPACITIES AN ACTOR
CAN ASSUME IN HIS PERFORMANCE
THAN SIMPLY ADOPTING IT AS A
NOVEL TECHNIQUE.''

how this reality is to be represented. Although the system's primary concern is performance, it has also greatly influenced playwriting in the twentieth century. To break away from this paradigm, some dramatists, such as Bertolt Brecht, Samuel Beckett, and Jerzy Grotowski, have constructed different theatrical sign systems. In the case of contemporary Chinese dramatists, Gao Xingjian is the rare exception to the rule of the Stanislavskian paradigm. Gao joins the ranks of Brecht and others who have consciously attempted to search for a new relationship between the actor and the character and to experiment with unique forms of dramatic narrative. It should be noted that, although Gao is renowned as a playwright, he stands out from other contemporary Chinese playwrights in being an experienced theater director. Since his first production in 1982, he has been a *de facto* codirector of all three of his plays staged in China. Since moving to France in 1987, he has also been invited on many occasions to direct his own plays. A discussion of how performance theories inform his playwriting might provide us with some interesting perspectives otherwise unnoticeable. In this article, I focus on Gao's unique mode of narrative (expressed through the characters' voices) and his experimentation with language, part of his creative effort to establish a dramaturgy different from that of his contemporaries.

## The Neutral Actor

In his search for a more comprehensive and flexible identity of the actor, Gao begins, in *Alarm Signal* (Juedui xinhao; 1982)—his first play, which expresses the grievance and disillusionment of Chinese youth in the early 1980s—to allow his characters to speak in three different spatial modes: reality, memory, and imagination. In the memory and imagination modes, characters are able to express their sentiments more freely than in the reality mode. While they shift swiftly between each mode, the actors always maintain their identities as characters in the dramatic context. It is quite different in *Bus Stop* (Chezhan; 1983), Gao's famous absurdist play about a group of suburbanites waiting for a bus that never arrives. Toward the end of the play, the actors detach themselves from their dramatis personae and resume their identities as actors, commenting on the issues and characters presented earlier in the play. In *Bus Stop,* actors take on two identities: that of the actor and that of the character. *Wild Man* (Yeren; 1985), Gao's third and final play produced in China, is a much more ambitious production that experiments with new forms integrating Eastern and Western theatrical arts and explores issues beyond immediate social concerns, such as nature conservation and the marginalization of alternative cultures. In addition to his dramatic role as the Ecologist, the lead actor also assumes the capacities of a narrator and an observer.

The use of the narrator in *Wild Man* clearly suggests Brecht's influence on Gao's exploration of the actor's capacity. The play begins with an actor (who later plays the Ecologist) explaining the dramatic situation to the audience. As the drama unfolds, the same actor, on several occasions, detaches himself from the character he plays to provide observations and comments on dramatic incidents. Gao's Ecologist reminds one of the Brechtian character Shen Teh in *The Good Person of Szechwan,* who directly addresses the audience in two separate modes: in prose, when she acts in the role of the narrator; and verse, in the role of the observer. Brecht's intention is to present his theatre with various points of view beyond that of the conventional single perspective of the central figure.

In addition to acknowledging the political connotations of Brechtian theater, Raymond Williams examines its formal significance and observes that Brecht's conventions of exposition and commentary offer an ''open sequence of scenes'' in which ''a movement corresponding to a flow of action'' is presented not as a product but as a process. The use of such conventions creates an open structure of representation. The audience is deliberately and consistently invited to exercise its reflection on the events and on the actors' self-reflection. Although

Brecht does not require the audience's physical participation, unlike Augusto Boal and his Forum Theater, the intellectual and emotional involvement of its members, nevertheless, constitutes an important part of the performance process and is an essential element of the dramatist's concern.

Brecht's intention is to demonstrate the dialectic relationships that exist between individuals and the historical process. He has created a form that allows the objective examination of such relationships, and he does this by alienating the actors, and hence the audience, from the dramatic situation. His ultimate concern is, however, to focus on the sociopolitical situation in which individuals are trapped and to indicate the alternatives that are available to people within historical reality.. In Mitter's view, Stanislavsky wants the audience to believe in absolute reality, whereas Brecht wants them to believe in relative reality. Clearly, the function of the Brechtian narrator, among other things, is closely related to the revelation of different aspects of reality in a specific historical context. Gao Xingjian's use of the narrator in *Wild Man* exhibits an ideological interest in environmental issues and the dilemma of human existence that is akin to that of the modern West, but the unique narrative developed in his later plays reveals a desire to transcend any immediate social concerns.

The Brechtian narrator is not Gao's sole inspiration. Readers of Gao's dramatic texts are often reminded of traditional Chinese theater as well. For example, the actor speaking aside in a capacity alienated from his/her dramatis persona, a technique which Gao frequently adopts, is a common convention of traditional Chinese theater. The spontaneous changes between several dramatic roles by the actors in *The Other Shore* (Bi'an; 1986) indicate that Gao is more interested in experimenting with the different capacities an actor can assume in his performance than simply adopting it as a novel technique. Gao stresses the flexibility of role changing beyond the limitations of spatial and temporal conditions. A Brechtian narrator may be helpful in releasing the actor from the Stanislavskian immersion in the character, but he also restricts the actor to just another role. Gao is searching for a narrative that allows his actors flexibility in the playing of different dramatic roles.

In an attempt to free the actor from specific role(s), Gao critiques the conventional two-dimensional relationship between the actor and the character. When an actor takes up his role as a character. Gao observes, he experiences a transitional state between his own identity in real life and that of the character. The conventional duality of actor and character seems to neglect this in-between state, which is especially discernible in a *xiqu* (traditional Chinese theater, often translated as "opera" or "music-drama") actor. In discovering this identity, what he calls the "neutral actor" (*zhongxing yanyuan*), Gao proposes a "tripartite of performance" (*biaoyan de sanchongxing*) to open up a new sphere of possibilities. He observes:

> As a well-trained and experienced *xiqu* actor prepares to put on his make-up, he begins to undergo a process of self-purification. He detaches himself from his personal daily life, entering the state of a neutral actor. When he has completed his face painting and dressed in his costume, his posture, tone, and mien will be totally different from that of his usual being. As the gong and drum sound, ready in rapt attention and full energy, he goes onto the stage to perform his character. This process of transformation is more apparent when a male actor is taking up a female role, such as that of the *dan* in Peking opera or the *onnagata* in Kabuki.

This state of transition exists only for a short time, so brief that even the actor himself may not be aware of it, as he is normally intensely occupied with the task of entering his character. Gao further analyzes this process as follows:

> A man has his experience, character, mentality, behavior and expression as a man. When he plays a female role, he has first to purge himself of his own gender and character, taking up the identity of a neutral actor. He may be a youth, or a sixty-year-old man like Mei Lanfang, but with the help of physical and vocal training, he enters such a state of preparation. The costume and make-up will also cover up his male identity. Once he is on stage, he will instantly assume his role, be it a fishing girl or an imperial concubine.

In his representation, Gao reveals that he is most interested in the psychological experience of the actor in this transitional state.

In this transition, the actor has to leave his personal world to enter the character's world. The conventional concept of the duality of performance recognizes the existence of these two worlds, as well as the ways in which an actor can successfully achieve the transformation. In proposing the neutral state, Gao wishes to do more than simply accomplish such a transformation. As the objective of a conventional actor is to fully enter the character's world, the state of neutrality is only a means to an end; once the actor has achieved the transformation, the means is no longer necessary. Even for a Brechtian actor, although the way he plays the character is important, the ultimate emphasis is on the actor's perception of his own historical situation. By contrast, in prolonging the state of neutrality, Gao wants his actor to maintain the consciousness of being in such a state throughout the performance. In so doing, the actor is not only able to enter as many roles as is required but also to maintain a substantial amount of objectivity in his interpretation of characters. He thus acquires the ability to interact with both the character he is playing and the audience.

Such flexibility is clearly illustrated in *The Other Shore* and *The Nether City* (Mingcheng; 1991). *The Other Shore* was designed as a play for the training of actors. It does not have a linear plot, and there are many different roles to be taken up by members of the ensemble. As members of an ensemble, the actors begin as neutral actors who, following the lead actor's instructions, demonstrate the process of role-playing. They appear to possess no specific temperament or personality. Gradually, as they go through different dramatic situations requiring increased sophistication, they become fully developed characters. As all the dramatic settings are purely hypothetical, the play does not seek to present a world of absolute truth. Moreover, actors transform into different characters in each situation and must maintain the ability to change roles quickly. The fundamental element at work is the actors' subjective control over their imagination and performance. It is their identity as neutral actors that enables them to maintain autonomy from their dramatis personae.

**Source:** Sy Ren Quah, "Performance in Alienated Voices: Mode of Narrative in Gao Xingjian's Theater," in *Modern Chinese Literature and Culture*, Vol. 14, No. 2, Fall 2002, pp. 51–56.

# SOURCES

Fong, Gilbert C. F., Introduction, in *The Other Shore: Plays by Gao Xingjian,* translated by Gilbert C. F. Fong, Chinese University Press, 1999, pp. ix–xlii.

Goldblatt, Howard, Review of *The Other Shore: Plays by Gao Xingjian,* in *World Literature Today,* Vol. 74, No. 4, 2000, pp. 801–02.

Grotowski, Jerzy, *Towards a Poor Theatre,* edited by Eugenio Barba, Routledge, 2002.

Kendt, Rob, "*Other Shore:* A Barren Experience," in *Los Angeles Times,* October 10, 2003, Sec. E, p. 33.

Knight, Deirdre Sabina, Review of *The Other Shore: Plays by Gao Xingjian,* in the *Journal of Asian Studies,* Vol. 61, No.1, 2002, pp. 216–19.

Kong, Shuyu, and Hawes, Colin A., "View from the *Other Shore* of Gao Xingjian," University of Alberta Express News, http://www.expressnews.ualberta.ca/expressnews/ (accessed October 20, 2004).

Lee, Mabel, "Returning to Recluse Literature: Gao Xingjian," in *The Columbia Companion to Modern East Asian Literature,* Columbia University Press, 2003, pp. 610–16.

Quah, Sy Ren, "Performance in Alienated Voices: Mode of Narrative in Gao Xingjian's Theater," in *Modern Chinese Literature and Culture,* Vol. 14, No. 2, Fall 2002, pp. 51–98.

Stanislavski, Constantin, *An Actor's Handbook,* Methuen Publishing, 1990.

Tay, William, "Avant-Garde Theater in Post-Mao China: *The Bus Stop* by Gao Xingjian," in *Worlds Apart: Recent Chinese Writing and Its Audiences,* edited by Howard Goldblatt and M. E. Sharpe, 1990, pp. 111–18.

Xingjian, Gao, "Gao Xingjian—Nobel Lecture: The Case for Literature," translated by Mabel Lee, http://www.nobel.se/literature/laureates/2000/index.html.

# FURTHER READING

Brecht, Bertolt, *Brecht on Theatre,* translated by John Willett, Hill & Wang Publishers, 1964.

    Bertolt Bertolt was the most influential German dramatist and theoretician of the theater in the twentieth century and had a profound influence on Xingjian's development as a dramatist. This book includes selections of Brecht's critical writing, including his seminal essay, "A Short Organum for the Theatre."

Chen, Xiaomei, *Acting the Right Part: Political Theater and Popular Drama in Contemporary China,* University of Hawai'i Press, 2002.

    A cultural history of *huaju,* or modern Chinese drama, from 1966 to 1996, this book covers the period of the Cultural Revolution when theater was chosen as the state's primary vehicle to promote proletarian art.

Chen, Xiaomei, ed., *Reading the Right Text: An Anthology of Contemporary Chinese Drama,* University of Hawai'i Press, 2003.

    Six new plays from contemporary China, translated into English for the first time, are included in this collection. Unlike Xingjian's plays, none of these plays has been banned by Chinese authorities. As a result, this collection gives a good counter balance to Xingjian's style and subject matter.

Grotowski, Jerzy, *Towards a Poor Theatre,* edited by Eugenio Barba, Routledge, 2002.

    Grotowski, the founder of Poland's Theatre Laboratory in 1959, became known for his concept of a "poor theatre," in which "non essentials" of theater such as costumes, sound effects, makeup, sets, and lighting are eliminated, as a way to emphasize and

*A white shore on Paradise Island, Bahamas*

redefine relationships between actors and the audience. His work had a great influence on Xingjian.

Heng, Liang, and Shapiro, Judith, *Son of the Revolution,* Vintage, 1984.

Heng's account of his youth during China's Cultural Revolution was a ground-breaking and seminal treatment of that dark and tumultuous period of Chinese history.

Stanislavski, Constantin, *An Actor's Handbook,* Methuen Publishing, 1990.

Stanislavski has had perhaps the greatest influence on acting than any other individual. His theory of "total immersion," in which the actor immerses himself completely into his character, has long been the standard theory of acting and one which Xingjian rebelled against in his dramatic works.

# The Producers

## MEL BROOKS
## 2001

Mel Brooks adapted his Broadway musical *The Producers* from his own 1968 movie of the same name. The film was only a modest success, but it did win the Academy Award for best original screenplay. Over the course of more than thirty years it became a cult classic, with legions of devoted fans who knew the script line-for-line. The musical, on the other hand, was a phenomenon from its beginning. At the 2001 Antoinette Perry (''Tony'') Awards, it took twelve statues—the most ever won by any Broadway show. The show sold millions of dollars in tickets before it even opened and continued to sell tickets for dates years into the future. In the months after the destruction of the World Trade Center, when the entertainment world in New York City was devastated by huge financial losses due to audience uncertainty, the unstoppable popularity of *The Producers* is sometimes credited with saving Broadway.

The story concerns Max Bialystock, a washed-up Broadway producer, and Leo Bloom, a meek accountant who comes to do his books. When Bloom casually notes that a producer could make more money on a show that failed, because the show's investors would never have to be paid back, Bialystock thinks up a plan to gain them millions. They set about looking for the worst Broadway show imaginable, settling on *Springtime for Hitler, A Gay Romp with Adolf and Eva at Berchtesgaden.* They then enlist a flamboyant gay producer, assuming that he can make the show even more unbearable.

*The Producers* is populated with colorful characters and enlivened with witty songs filled with sly cultural references. It also relies heavily on crass and obvious stereotypes meant to offend all equally, with mincing gays, sex-object women, greedy Jews, bubble-headed Swedes, oversexed old ladies, gruff Irish cops, and kick lines of singing Nazis.

## AUTHOR BIOGRAPHY

Mel Brooks was born Melvyn Kaminsky in Brooklyn, New York, on June 28, 1926. He lived in Brooklyn until joining the army during World War II. In the army, he performed in troop revues. When he returned to the United States, he worked as a stand-up comic for a short time at resorts in the Catskill Mountains, where many New York comedians went to hone their skills. Brooks took a job writing for the legendary television program *Your Show of Shows,* with other writers that included Carl Reiner, Woody Allan, and Neil Simon. He went with the star of the show, Sid Caesar, to his follow-up program, *Caesar's Hour.* After winning an Emmy award for his writing, Brooks struck out to produce and direct his own works. He and Reiner had some success in the early 1960s with their character *The 2000 Year Old Man,* which spawned a hit comedy album and led to a series of concert engagements.

In 1964 Brooks married Anne Bancroft, a famous film and stage actress. Their marriage has lasted for over forty years. In 1965 he wrote and produced, along with Buck Henry, the situation comedy *Get Smart,* which ran on network television for five years.

Brooks's first film was a short independent work called *The Critic.* His second film, in 1968, was *The Producers,* for which he won an Oscar for best original screenplay. In 1974 he created what many consider to be his greatest comedy, *Blazing Saddles,* a spoof of westerns. That began a golden age for him, with a series of popular film parodies: *Young Frankenstein* in 1974, which played off of the Universal monster movies of the 1930s; *Silent Movie* in 1977, a tribute to the silent era of film; and *High Anxiety* in 1977, which parodies the films of director Alfred Hitchcock. Brooks's comedies in the 1980s and 1990s were considered uneven in quality and were poorly received by audiences, although 1987's *Spaceballs* was so popular that studios considered producing a sequel, but Brooks dropped the idea.

*Mel Brooks*

Brooks has also been influential as a producer in Hollywood. In addition to his own films, his production company, Brooksfilms Limited, has backed such critically acclaimed films as *84 Charring Cross Road, Frances,* and *The Elephant Man.*

Brooks has often written songs for his own films, such as the original ''Springtime for Hitler'' number for the 1968 film of *The Producers,* but he never considered writing for the stage until David Geffen, one of the founders of Dreamworks SKG studio, urged him to adapt his movie. His work has earned Antoinette Perry (''Tony'') Awards for the play's music and for co-writing the book with Thomas Meehan, a longtime collaborator who is best known for writing the book for *Annie.*

## PLOT SUMMARY

### Act 1, Scene 1

The first scene of *The Producers* takes place outside of the Schubert Theater on Broadway on a June evening in 1959, where Max Bialystock's latest show, *Funny Boy!*, has just opened. A musical version of Shakespeare's *Hamlet,* the show is closing that night, reviled by critics who could not even stay to the end. Bialystock sings a song about how famous and successful he once was.

### Act 1, Scene 2

Leo Bloom, a mild accountant, shows up at Bialystock's office to do his bookkeeping. One of Bialystock's backers, an amorous old lady, comes in, and Bloom is forced to hide. After she leaves, Bloom finds a discrepancy in the account but decides that it does not matter since the show closed early, and investors will not expect any money back. Bloom idly mentions that a producer could make more with a failure than with a hit, because he could sell unlimited shares and keep all of the money. Bialystock tries to convince him that they should become rich doing just that, but Bloom is too timid to break the law.

### Act 1, Scene 3

At Whitehall and Marks, the office where Bloom works, the accountants sing about how unhappy their lives are. Mr. Marks shouts at Bloom for coming in six minutes late, sending Bloom into a fantasy about what it would be like to be a producer, surrounded by beautiful chorus girls. At the end of his reverie, Bloom quits his job.

### Act 1, Scene 4

Bloom returns to Bialystock and explains his decision to join in his production scheme.

### Act 1, Scene 5

Bialystock and Bloom search through stacks of scripts, looking for one that is guaranteed to be a flop. The winner is *Springtime for Hitler,* a light-hearted look at the dictator who was responsible for the Holocaust. Bialystock takes out two hats and puts on one, but he refuses to let Bloom wear the other: these are ''producer'' hats, he explains, and Bloom is not a real producer until the show opens.

### Act 1, Scene 6

On the roof of the Greenwich Village building he lives in, Franz Liebkind, wearing a Nazi helmet and lederhosen, sings about how lonesome he is in America, accompanied in his song by the pigeons that he keeps in cages. Bialystock and Bloom arrive to obtain the rights for *Springtime for Hitler,* which Liebkind wrote. Liebkind is excited about their interest in his play, but refuses to let them produce it unless they take ''the Siegfried Oath,'' pledging

their allegiance to Hitler. Bloom wants to leave, but Bialystock convinces him to take the oath and to put on the swastika armband Liebkind gives them.

### Act 1, Scene 7

They are let into the apartment of Roger De Bris, a particularly untalented director, by De Bris's assistant, Carmen Ghia. De Bris enters in a gown, which he plans to wear to the Choreographers' Ball. He is hesitant about directing *Springtime for Hitler* because it is so serious, and asks for advice from his ''production team'': a group of outrageously gay stereotypes who parade through the living room. Bialystock convinces De Bris that he could win a Tony Award for doing a serious drama, and De Bris agrees to direct the show.

### Act 1, Scene 8

Ulla arrives at Bialystock's office. She is a tall, shapely Swedish blonde bombshell with a thick accent that makes her words barely intelligible. Both men are smitten with her sensuality and want to hire her, though the show is not in rehearsals yet. They end up asking her to work as a secretary until the show opens, and she agrees. Bialystock decides that he has to go to his ''investors''—a group of little old ladies who give him money for his plays as long as he has sex with them.

### Act 1, Scene 9

This scene takes place in ''Little Old Lady Land,'' populated by chorus lines of old ladies with walkers and canes, who Bialystock sweet-talks in song. When he has collected two million dollars, he goes back to Bloom and tells him that they are ready to put the play on. All of the important characters— Ulla, Roger De Bris, Carmen Ghia and Franz Liebkind—come on stage for a rousing song to end act 1.

### Act 2, Scene 1

Bialystock and Bloom return to their office to find that Ulla has cleaned it and painted it white, entirely changing its dismal look. Bialystock leaves, and Ulla and Bloom, left alone, dance and sing a duet that shows that they are in love with each other.

### Act 2, Scene 2

At the theater, auditions take place for *Springtime for Hitler,* with a succession of inappropriate actors showing up and performing unlikely material in Hitler costumes. Franz Liebkind finally interrupts to show how it should be done, and Bialystock realizes that, with his over-earnestness, he would be the perfect actor to play the part.

### *Act 2, Scene 3*

Outside of the Schubert Theatre on West 44th Street, the same setting as act 1, scene 1, people are arriving for the *Springtime for Hitler* opening. Bloom wishes everybody good luck to the horror of all. They explain to him that according to Broadway superstition wishing good luck will only bring bad luck. He asks what he should say instead, and they tell him, ''Break a leg.'' When Bloom says that, Liebkind trips walking to the stage door and breaks his leg. For a moment, it looks as if the show must be cancelled, but Bialystock asks Roger De Bris to take the role of Hitler.

### *Act 2, Scene 4*

The musical production of ''Springtime for Hitler'' is garishly inappropriate, with glamorous dancers and glorious songs celebrating the Führer.

### *Act 2, Scene 5*

Back at the office, Bialystock and Bloom realize that the show is a hit with the critics and that their plan is ruined. Bloom wants to take the two sets of accounting ledgers he kept to the police and turn himself in, and he and Bialystock fight over the account ledgers. De Bris and Carmen Ghia come in, and then Liebkind comes in, brandishing a pistol, angry because the effeminate De Bris made Hitler look foolish. He fires a few times before the police show up. While arresting Liebkind, the police notice the two sets of books and take Bialystock away to jail as well. But Bloom, hidden behind a door, escapes notice. He leaves for Rio de Janeiro with Ulla and the two million dollars.

### *Act 2, Scene 6*

In jail, Bialystock receives a post card from Rio and feels betrayed, singing a song about all that has happened.

### *Act 2, Scene 7*

Bialystock is about to be sentenced in court when Bloom and Ulla return. Bloom gives back the money, the old ladies admit they did not mind being cheated, and Bialystock and Bloom sing a song about what true friends they have found in each other.

### *Act 2, Scene 8*

In prison, Bialystock, Bloom, Liebkind, and other prisoners sing and dance through a new show, *Prisoners of Love*. A guard comes in with the news that the governor has pardoned Bialystock and Bloom because of the laughter and joy they have brought to the convicts.

### *Act 2, Scene 9*

In front of the Schubert Theatre again, the marquee says, ''Bialystock and Bloom present 'Prisoners of Love.''' A large production number takes place, with male and female chorus dancers in prison stripes.

### *Act 2, Scene 10*

Bialystock and Bloom, in tuxedos and their producer hats, come out to sing a song about their success, friendship, and ongoing partnership.

## CHARACTERS

### *Max Bialystock*

Max Bialystock is one of the two producers referred to in the play's title. As one song points out, Bialystock was once the ''King of Broadway.'' When the story opens, however, he is washed-up, having produced a string of flops so terrible that they regularly do not make it past the first performance. The theater showing his current work, *Funny Boy!*, even had a special sign made up for Bialystock's works, with ''Opening Night'' on one side and ''Closing Night'' on the other, to save time. The only way that Bialystock has been able to put shows on at all is by romancing lonesome old ladies, who invest in his shows in exchange for his companionship. He keeps a cabinet of photos of these ladies, bringing out one at a time, making each woman believe she is special to him.

Bialystock is defined by his crass immorality. When Leo Bloom points out that he can make more money with a flop than with a hit, he does not think twice before setting his scheme into motion. He is so greedy that he is willing to ignore his Jewish background and swear an oath to honor Adolf Hitler in order to secure the rights to Franz Liebkind's play, which he knows will be the worst production ever to hit Broadway.

Late in the second act, Bialystock has a song, ''Betrayed,'' that humanizes him, showing that his

# MEDIA ADAPTATIONS

- The movie that *The Producers* was based on was only a moderate success when it was released in 1968, but it has gone on to become a cult classic. It stars Zero Mostel as Bialystock and Gene Wilder as Bloom. The film is available on a special edition DVD from MGM/UA.

- The original Broadway cast album of *The Producers,* starring Nathan Lane, Matthew Broderick, Brad Oscar, and Cady Huffmann, was recorded in 2001 and is available from Sony Classical.

- *Recording ''The Producers'': A Musical Romp with Mel Brooks* is a DVD documentary that follows the in-studio recording of the Broadway cast album, featuring Brooks and all of the members of the original line-up. It was released by Sony Classical in 2001.

loss is more than money and the jail time that he faces—that in fact, he has bonded with Bloom as a friend and mentor, and feels let down. When Bloom returns to testify for him in court, however, Bialystock tells the judge that his friendship with Bloom is the first true friendship he has ever had. Bloom is the first person that he has ever trusted. By the end, Bialystock is the same spirited rake that he was at the beginning; he throws his efforts into producing the show *Prisoners of Love,* another terrible-sounding musical that is destined for Broadway success.

## *Leopold Bloom*

One of the show's two central characters, Leopold Bloom is the more complex of the two. He is a meek accountant, so frightened by Max Bialystock's natural vivacity when they first meet that he is reduced to cowering on the floor, fondling the small blue blanket that he has retained from childhood. Bloom's fear is offset, though, by his deeply-held desire to be a Broadway producer. After being exposed to the show business life during his visit to Bialystock's office, Bloom returns to his office at

Whitehall and Marks and notices how acutely unhappy he is as an accountant. He then decides to join Bialystock in his illegal scheme.

Bloom's fascination with show business is reinforced when he meets Ulla, the gorgeous blonde bombshell who comes to work for Bialystock and Bloom as a secretary before taking her place in the show *Springtime for Hitler.* Bloom is smitten with Ulla, so much so that when he and she have a duet at the beginning of act 2, he throws his security blanket into the garbage. His interest in her is sweet and romantic, as he sings about her beautiful face. This is contrasted with Max Bialystock's reaction to her, which is clearly steeped in lust.

When the plot to defraud the investors is found out, Bloom proves to have become the man that Bialystock urged him to be, running away to Rio de Janeiro with the beautiful girl and the ill-gotten loot. Bloom has a conscience, though, and returns before Bialystock is sentenced. In the song in the courtroom, Bloom acknowledges the changes that Bialystock has made in his life, taking him from a glum and borderline-tragic life to one filled with joy. The case for their close friendship is made so convincingly that the judge sends them to jail together.

The name Leopold Bloom is taken from James Joyce's novel *Ulysses,* a fact that is referred to in act 1, scene 4, when Bloom asks, ''When's it gonna be Bloom's day?''—in Joyce's novel, ''Bloom's day'' is June 16th, the date that the program gives for the events in *The Producers.*

## *Roger De Bris*

De Bris is a pretentious, flamboyantly gay director. His apartment is filled with eccentric show-business people, each a different homosexual stereotype. When Bialystock and Bloom first approach De Bris (pronounced like ''debris''), he is wearing a flowing evening gown, which he explains is his costume for the Choreographer's Ball. He is hesitant to direct *Springtime for Hitler* because he finds the subject matter too serious: as De Bris explains in a song filled with double entendres, he feels that the key to a successful Broadway hit is to ''Keep It Gay.'' This point is made again when his usual associates, such as his set designer, choreographer, and lighting director, come out, each a more outrageously gay caricature than the last.

The producers count on De Bris's natural bad taste to ensure that their musical will be a failure: as

Bilaystock explains to Bloom as they are hiring him to direct, "This guy couldn't direct you to the bathroom."

When Franz Liebkind breaks his leg and cannot perform in the show, De Bris steps in to play Hitler. The result is a truly effeminate Hitler, who seems enraptured with the public's attention.

### Carmen Ghia

Carmen Ghia is Roger De Bris's "common-law assistant" and is as openly gay as De Bris is. In the play, Carmen Ghia functions to explain De Bris's more antic notions and to give the director another gay character to argue with cattily. It is Ghia who knows De Bris well enough to suggest that he would know all of the words to the starring role in *Springtime for Hitler* and would have a secret desire to step into the part when Liebkind is incapacitated.

### Gunter

Gunter is a Nazi assistant to Franz Liebkind, who drops Franz off in front of the theater on the night of the *Springtime for Hitler* opening.

### Hold Me-Touch Me

Hold Me-Touch Me is the most obvious of the little old ladies that Bialystock romances in order to secure backing for his show. While Hold Me-Touch Me's scene with Bialystock is longer, her personality is not distinguishable from the other ladies, such as Lick Me-Bite Me, Kiss Me-Feel Me, or Clinch Me-Pinch Me.

### Franz Liebkind

Liebkind is a Nazi who lives in New York City, in Greenwich Village. He has written a play to lionize his hero, Adolf Hitler. Bialystock and Bloom determine, after reading dozens of plays, that Liebkind's must be the worst play ever; it is certain to fail.

As if the subject of his play were not enough to prove Liebkind's mental instability, the play has great fun with his delusions. For one thing, he dresses in lederhosen and wears a Nazi helmet. In addition, Liebkind is so enthusiastic about having his version of Hitler's life seen by the public that he does not recognize the contempt that Bialystock and Bloom, who have obviously Jewish names, have for him and for Hitler. Liebkind makes them put on swastika armbands and swear their devotion to Hitler. Liebkind claims to know little-recognized, highly unlikely facts about Hitler, such as the fact

that he could paint an entire apartment in an afternoon—two coats!—and that he was a good dancer, and that his middle name was "Elizabeth." Before he is approached by the producers, Liebkind is on the roof of his apartment house, singing about how much he misses Bavaria. He is alone but is backed up by a chorus of singing pigeons, indicating the extent of his separation from reality.

After an extensive audition process, Bialystock realizes that Liebkind is the perfect choice to play the starring role in *Springtime for Hitler,* ensuring that the play will be a flop. On opening night, though, after the cast has explained to Bloom that Broadway superstition requires saying "break a leg" instead of "good luck," Liebkind actually does slip and break his leg, and has to be replace in the show.

After the play, Liebkind goes to Bialystock and threatens to kill the producers. His gun goes off, summoning the police, and they all end up in jail together.

### Mister Marks

Leo Bloom's boss at the accounting office where he works, Mr. Marks is described as "a short-tempered, cigar-chomping little tyrant." His petty badgering makes Bloom decide to quit the accounting business and try his hand at being a producer.

### Ulla Inga Hansen Bensen Yonsen Tallen-Hallen Svaden-Svanson

One of the more obvious jokes in the script is that, after introducing herself with a nine-word-long string of names, Ulla announces that is just her first name. Bialystock declares that they do not have time to hear her last name, too.

Ulla is a voluptuous blonde who shows up at Bialystock and Bloom's office to audition for a part in their new play. She is cast as Eva Braun, Hitler's lover. But they also give her a position as their secretary in order to keep her around.

Much is made of Ulla's Swedish accent and her poor ability to understand or speak English. With no skill whatsoever as a secretary, her office work is limited to picking up the telephone and saying "Bialystock and Bloom" repeatedly, like a parrot.

Ulla is aware of her own sensuality; her audition for the producers is a song called "When You Got It, Flaunt It." Later, when she is singing the duet "That Face" with Leo Bloom, it becomes clear that she is sincerely attracted to him. In the end, after

Bloom has been to prison, Ulla is with him, starring in the new musical that Bilaystock and Bloom have developed.

## THEMES

### Greed

At the core of Bialystock and Bloom's scheme to defraud the backers of their production is greed. Max Bialystock is so greedy that he ends act 1, scene 2, on his knees, praying to God, "Oh, Lord, I want that money!!" When scene 4 begins, presumably some time later, he is still on his knees, still praying. Leo Bloom is not initially as motivated by greed as he is inhibited by fear, but, after returning to the pool of unhappy, browbeaten accountants at Whitehall and Marks, he becomes convinced that, deep down, he really does want to have the things that money can buy.

To Bialystock, wealth represents the kind of lifestyle that he once knew, which he sings about in "The King of Broadway": champagne, fine clothes, huge hotel suites, and the adoration of beautiful chorus girls. His greed is pushed further with the arrival of Ulla, whose beauty represents the worldly things that are unattainable for a man like him, who does not have money. Bloom's greed is a copy of Bialystock's until, at the beginning of act 2, he permits himself to open up to Ulla's charms. When Bloom takes the two million dollars and runs away to Rio with Ulla, his action is almost as much an act of fear as of greed; Bialystock would have found it a dream fulfilled to be rich in a tropical paradise with a beautiful girl, but Bloom leaves the country to run away from the police.

### Maturation

There is nothing subtle about the way that the play uses Bloom's little blue blanket as a symbol for his barely-repressed infantilism. When he first meets Bialystock, he is driven to hysterics, afraid of Max's natural overwhelming vitality. The only thing that can calm his panic is stroking his face with his blanket, like a young child would do. This returns him to the security and comfort of childhood. Bialystock openly mocks Bloom and shows his disgust, but Bloom holds fast to the behavior that has comforted him all his life.

Bloom takes a small step toward maturity when he stands up to his boss, Mr. Marks. Having been exposed to the excitement of Broadway producing and fraud, Bloom realizes that the boring routine that he once thought of as comforting is, in reality, soul-deadening.

It is love, however, that makes Bloom give up his security blanket. He realizes that his "minor compulsion," as he puts it, might hurt his chances with Ulla. Still, he does not actually throw the blanket in the garbage until he has danced with her, when he is certain that he and Ulla are in love with each other. Maturity, for Bloom, means accepting the fearful uncertainty of love, leaving the world of familiar things for a world of greater promise.

### Community

*The Producers* shows two lonely, distrustful individuals opening up to become part of the social world that surrounds them. Both Max Bialystock and Leo Bloom admit this growth in their song "Til Him," in which they each identify themselves as having lived unfulfilled lives when they tried to face the world all alone. Up to the time of that realization, Bialystock, who made a practice of taking advantage of his investors, feared that anyone he met was trying to take advantage of him. Bloom had been too timid to face up to society's disapproval until he saw how Bialystock lived without approval. Each man's negative qualities cancel out the other's over the course of the play, so that, united, they find comfort. This opening up to each other is symbolized in the way that, having been called "Bialystock and Bloom" repeatedly through the play, they refer to themselves in their final song as "Leo and Max."

This play's sense of building a community goes beyond the friendship between the two main characters, though. The coterie of odd people that they pick up in the process of trying to achieve the worst play ever becomes like a family to them. In the end, the people whom they chose because they were unlikable become indispensable to Bialystock and Bloom. Even though he is a deranged, talentless Nazi who has tried to kill them, Franz Liebkind is, almost as a matter of course, given a part in their *Prisoners of Love* show while they are incarcerated— just as Ulla, Roger De Bris, and the rest are naturally included in their success when they are freed. Bialystock and Bloom find themselves, over the course of the play, forming a theatrical troupe of misfits who are part of the theater scene but do not belong any place else.

# TOPICS FOR FURTHER STUDY

- Contact an attorney who specializes in entertainment law and find out why Bialystock and Bloom's scheme to over-sell a losing show would not work. Or why it would.

- The centerpiece of this play is the production number "Springtime for Hitler," poking fun at the dictator who terrorized Europe in the middle of the twentieth century. Write a similar song to a modern dictator, such as Sadaam Hussein, that could be used in a mock musical about him.

- Leo Bloom quits his accounting job because his boss, Mr. Marks, is such a tyrant. Interview several people about the worst employers they

have ever had, and the actions that they dreamed of taking in order to leave their unhappy situations.

- Franz Liebkind tells the producers a little-known (and probably wrong) fact, that Adolf Hitler's middle name was "Elizabeth." Find out the middle names of ten famous politicians and research why they were given those names.

- At the end of the play, Leo Bloom has earned the right to wear a "producer hat." Research various hat styles and determine which would be appropriate for various professions that usually do not have hats, such as teacher, accountant, hairdresser, etc.

## STYLE

### *Motivating Idea*

To a great extent, the plot of a show like *The Producers* derives naturally from the central idea. Once Brooks decided to work with the conceit of a producer working to become rich by mounting a losing production, there are certain events that would naturally have to take place. The story would have to establish the protagonist's previous lack of success; it would have to introduce someone who gives Bialystock his main idea; then there would have to be a succession of interesting, eccentric characters intended to comprise a truly awful play, and investors to be swindled; followed by a play-within-the-play of truly terrible proportions; then the surprising success of the play; and the unintended consequences of the play's success.

Following this basic structure, Brooks adds plot devices that make the story even more appealing to mass audiences. The subplot of a love interest between Bloom and Ulla adds a humanizing effect, for instance. Also, Brooks follows the show's emotional high point, the "Springtime for Hitler" production number, with several points that make this story of greed and embezzlement end pleasantly.

Having Bloom return from Rio at the end to save Bialystock affirms the lasting strength of friendship; having the producers go to prison affirms society's rules against swindling; and having them released against all probability and become successful producers gives audiences the satisfaction of seeing characters they have come to care about end up happy.

### *Stereotype*

Usually, the use of stereotypes indicates that the author of a piece lacks imagination or is so opposed to a group of people that he or she has not bothered to think of individual characteristics for his characters. The stereotypes that Brooks includes in *The Producers* are so numerous and so obviously offensive that they have a different effect. Instead of reflecting poorly on the author, audiences, knowing that no writer could be *that* insensitive, are invited to reflect on the stereotypes instead. Brooks's many "gay" jokes surrounding Roger De Bris, Carmen Ghia, and their friends are not so much jokes about gays as they are jokes about gay jokes. The black accountant singing like a slave is not meant to imply that black people meet the slave stereotype, but to show that the situation is like that of the slave stereotype; and the sexist imagery of Ulla as an unintelligent sex object falls apart when she sings her song ''When You've Got It, Flaunt It,'' showing that she is in fact in control of her fate, fully aware of the personality that others might find foolish. Brooks's stereotypes are acceptable because he does not use them in ignorance, but instead uses them to shock the sensibilities of audiences who are used to fewer stereotypes, which forces audiences to think for themselves.

# HISTORICAL CONTEXT

## Broadway Musicals

Brooks has chosen to set *The Producers* in 1959. The 1950s are considered to be the heyday of the Broadway musical. They were integral to American pop culture, the source of the music that dominated the top-ten lists on the radio just as rock and roll made its debut. Shows from the 1950s that still run in frequent revivals into the 2000s include *Guys and Dolls, Kiss Me Kate, My Fair Lady, The King and I,* and *West Side Story.* Composers of these musicals included such legends of the stage as Cole Porter, Leonard Bernstein, and the team of Richard Rogers and Oscar Hammerstein II. Rogers and Hammerstein are credited with defining the modern Broadway musical with their 1943 show *Oklahoma!*: while there had been stage shows with musical numbers in them, *Oklahoma!* is considered the first show to integrate lyrics into the storyline instead of stopping the action every once in a while for a vaguely relevant song. As the culture became more media savvy, though, the traditional Broadway musical increasingly came to be seen as sentimental and trite.

By the end of the twentieth century, the Broadway musical was more about spectacle than about stories or tunes. Huge, multi-million dollar productions used an increasing amount of clever and expensive moving sets, light shows, and costuming. These dazzled audiences, but their relationship to traditional musicals seemed to go no further than presenting music and action together on the stage. Audiences came to see them because they each had some new achievement, but the performances of the actors onstage became less and less important. Investors poured millions into elaborate stagings of *The Phantom of the Opera, Sunset Boulevard, Miss Saigon,* and *Kiss of the Spiderwoman.* A notable development was the interest of huge entertainment corporations; this brought needed cash to Broad-

way, which had gone through some very lean years in the 1980s. The Disney company, with investments in everything from film to theme parks to radio, started to recycle its cartoons for the stage; the first was *Beauty and the Beast* in 1994 and, when that was a success, Disney bought the New Amsterdam Theatre to mount its twelve million dollar production of *The Lion King,* which proved to be a worthwhile investment. It seemed that the future of Broadway musicals was to be bigger, brighter, louder, and more expensive.

When *The Producers* hit Broadway, it represented a throwback to earlier days of song and dance. Brooks's score is clearly patterned on the tunes and themes of 1950s musicals, and the entire production can be done with just a few sets and no exotic or expensive special effects. It rewrote the rules by proving that a musical could be a breakout success without an overly elaborate production—relying on characters, tunes and solid performances to hold audiences in their seats. The tide seems to have turned, with musicals, such as *Urinetown* and *Avenue Q* relying more on wit than spectacle to keep audiences entertained.

# CRITICAL OVERVIEW

When *The Producers* opened its trial run in Chicago, it was well-received, but was not the universally-loved, critic-proof behemoth it was to later become. *Chicago Sun-Times* theater critic Hedy Weiss was impressed by the show, but was well aware that it was a ''buoyant boisterous musical-theater time machine,'' referring to Mel Brooks's ''giddy, childlike, pseudo-naïve irreverence and intentional bad taste'' and ''the blatant silliness of his old-time jokes and attitudes.'' Weiss went on to say, ''Unapologetically politically incorrect, he has concocted what 50 years ago would have been called 'the tired businessman's show,' with sexpot and all—a pure, simple, self-confidently anachronistic entertainment.''

Two months later, the show opened in New York, taking the town by storm. In the *New York Times,* which has a long-standing tradition of setting the standards for Broadway (and, by extension, for the theater world), Ben Brantley's review from April 20, 2001, started, ''How do you single out highlights in a bonfire? Everybody who sees *The Producers*—and that should be as close to everybody as the St. James Theater allows—is going to be

*Zero Mostel and Gene Wilder in a 1968 film version of* The Producers

hard-pressed to choose one favorite bit from the sublimely ridiculous spectacle that opened last night. . . . It is, to put it simply, the real thing: a big Broadway book musical that is so ecstatically drunk on its powers to entertain that it leaves you delirious, too.''

To deal with the unprecedented popularity of the show, ticket prices were immediately hiked, from $90 to $100. Later, to foil scalpers who were monopolizing the best seats for months to come, the show's backers took the unprecedented move of raising top prices to an astronomical $480 apiece.

At the 2001 Antoinette Perry (''Tony'') Awards, *The Producers* made history by receiving 12 statuettes, breaking the record of 10 awarded to *Hello Dolly* in 1964. Among the Tonys won were best lead actor (Nathan Lane); best featured actor (Gary Beach); best featured actress (Cady Huffman); best director and best choreography (Susan Stroman); and, unexpectedly, best musical score for Brooks, who, at 74 years old, had never written music for a Broadway show before.

One area of contention about this show has always been its offensive comic portrayals of blacks, women, gays, etc. Jim Seavor, writing for a largely gay audience in the *Providence Journal-Bulletin*,

acknowledged complaints that the play made fun of homosexuals, but his response was that it was funny; that there were other venues where audiences can see more well-rounded portrayals; and that, in the context of *The Producers*, gays are ''simply part of a large group of over-the-top characters. Everyone is a target.'' He also pointed out that the characters that seem outrageous to audiences are taken as being fairly normal by other characters on the stage. He concluded, ''In a way, it's a relief to sit there and laugh at what we've been told we should no longer laugh at.''

## CRITICISM

### David Kelly

*Kelly is an instructor of literature and creative writing. In this essay, Kelly examines the way Brooks's play uses mildly shocking stereotypes to make audiences reflect on the Broadway musical tradition.*

Mel Brooks's theatrical adaptation of his 1968 film *The Producers* has been an unmitigated success from the moment it arrived on Broadway, garner-

# WHAT DO I READ NEXT?

- Brooks and co-writer Tom Meehan wrote supplemental essays and margin notes for a large, illustrated book of *The Producers* that was released by Roundtable Press in 2001.

- Another musical that opened on Broadway at the same time as *The Producers* was Mark Hollmann and Greg Kotis's *Urinetown*. More bitingly satirical, *Urinetown* is a parable about a futuristic world in which a malevolent corporation controls all of the public toilets and collects money from anyone who needs to use them. This play uses rousing music that is as reminiscent of the musical's glory days as that used in *The Producers*.

- There are any number of good books showing what is required in putting on a musical production. One good contemporary example is

- Matthew White's *Staging a Musical* (1999), which covers all of the basic requirements in a straightforward way. It was published by Theatre Arts Books.

- The year after *The Producers* opened, the big musical to open on Broadway was *Hairspray* (2002), also based on a semi-successful movie (in this case, a 1988 John Waters film). The book is by Mark O'Donnell, Marc Shaiman, Scott Wittmann, and Thomas Meehan.

- There is a long history of making fun of Adolf Hitler. Even when he was at the height of his power, political cartoonists made a point of mocking him. Zbynek Zeman's book *Heckling Hitler,* published by I. B. Tauris in 1987, examines this.

---

ing a record number of Antoinette Perry Award ("Tony") nominations and awards, and raising levels for ticket prices. There are obvious factors involved in its success, such as two big stars, solid musical performances, and terrific production values all around. What critics usually express surprise about, however, is that Brooks is able to make mass audiences warm up to the show's more offensive elements. At the heart of the story is a one-joke premise—a campy musical gala featuring Adolph Hitler. Brooks surrounds this with moth-eaten stereotypes—sex-maddened old ladies, brainless buxom blondes, swishy homosexuals, a slavish black character and Jews, belligerent and cowardly. The satire in *The Producers* runs the meager gamut from offensive to irrelevant. Brooks gives audiences much to dislike, and they have responded by lining up for tickets.

No one ever said that a musical comedy has to be thoughtful or tasteful. It might even be taken for granted that the most money is to be made in pandering to the audience's least common denominator—providing mindless entertainment that the greatest number of people can be comfortable with.

The odd thing about *The Producers* is how it can be comforting to the audience by dealing in offensive images. In part, this might just say something about who the average theatergoer is: someone who does not find offense in unflattering portrayals of blacks, Irish, Jews, Swedes, the elderly, gays, or females. Surely none of these groups can be excluded from the droves of people racing to the play. What is missing from the play's images is the actual offensiveness. Though the play is clearly centered on offensive characters, they are presented in a way that even the mainstream patron of musical theater would be hard pressed to find objectionable. In using sensitive cultural images without offending anyone's sensibilities, the end product might have been bland; instead, Brooks has absorbed the energy from poor taste while throwing out its poisonous effects.

In his notes about how he came to bring *The Producers* to the stage, Brooks said that he wanted to do an old-fashioned musical comedy, the kind that he felt they had stopped making around 1960 (quoted in Brooks): "Unhappily, as far as I'm concerned, the musical comedy was replaced by what might be called the musical tragedy, the kind of show, often from London, in which you sit in the dark all evening without laughing once. And though you stopped smoking years ago, because you know that smoking causes cancer, you long throughout the show for a Lucky Strike.'' With his reference to the somber contemporary blockbusters of writers such as Andrew Lloyd Webber, and Brooks's invocation of a past that came before people knew about cancer and smoked Lucky Strikes with abandon, Brooks has identified the mandate for *The Producers* as light-hearted nostalgia. The whole production is steeped in the past: the Third Reich of the 1930s and 1940s, the musicals of the 1940s and 1950s, and the original film of the 1960s. According to the script, the play is set in 1959, though its sense of reality is so skewed that there is nothing particularly significant about that date (other than its relationship to Brooks's quote about musical tragedies).

Nostalgia is particularly useful for musical comedy because its very nature is to show the world in a sanitized, rosier light than one sees when looking at the present. Audiences accept broader characterizations in nostalgic comedies, as if people were simpler in the past than they are in the present. The stereotype of the blonde Swedish kitten, to give one example, would be much more offensive if she were being passed off as a part of contemporary reality, as if the woman's movement had made no progress from the 1960s to the present: since the play is set before the 1960s, both in date and in spirit, the character of Ulla can, when played by a strong performer with a good sense of self, be taken as an egotist, not a victim. Gags about Irish cops, Jewish accountants, and an African American office worker singing a Negro spiritual do not linger in the air announcing their staleness, as they did when they were more common, in the 1950s and 1960s. Instead they act as nostalgic reminders of the vaudeville tradition that Brooks, if not most of his audience, might remember.

The tone of lighthearted cornball stereotyping this production attains is centered on the two leads, Max Bialystock and Leopold Bloom. Both represent traditional Jewish stock characters. Bialystock, conniving and greedy, is a schnorrer, taking advantage of others, directly descended from Shakespeare's Shylock, seen onstage four centuries earlier. If Bialystock is threateningly aggressive, though, Bloom is at least as infuriating in his neurotic insecurity. Bialystock is not threatening to the play's audience because he is introduced, in the very first song, as an abject failure. Bloom, simpering into his

> " AS THE SCRIPT SHOWS BIALYSTOCK AND BLOOM GO THROUGH THE PROCESS OF DEVISING THE WORST SHOW POSSIBLE, BROOKS, BY MAKING THE CHARACTERS IMPOSSIBLE TO TAKE SERIOUSLY, FORCES AUDIENCES TO THINK ABOUT THE SHOW THEY ARE ATTENDING."

security blanket, is drawn at least as broadly in his own way as Bialystock is. They are both character types, defining a world of even broader character types.

At the start of the second act, the play goes further toward defining what audiences should expect from its characters by creating a romance between timid Leo Bloom and Ulla, the blonde sex goddess who leaves the male characters gape-jawed. If Bloom and Ulla were at all realistic, a romance between them would not make sense: Bloom is so timid that he has a panic attack when Bialystock raises his voice, while Ulla is so self-assured that she auditions with a song called ''If You Got It, Flaunt It.'' Since they are general character types, though, their romance fits the story just fine, mostly as an indication of how producing a show has raised Bloom's confidence. More important than what it says about Bloom, though, is what their romance does for the structure of the show: it allows Brooks to introduce a romance, an element that every musical comedy is bound to have. The focus of *The Producers* is not supposed to be on characters, but on the musical comedy genre.

Such a stance might seem to cheapen the value of the play, relegating it to the category of ''mere entertainment'' instead of a serious work that deserves its many awards. But focusing on the show itself, and not the characters, is what makes *The Producers* relevant in the modern world. It is a show about show business, making its points without dwelling on them. As the script shows Bialystock and Bloom go through the process of devising the worst show possible, Brooks, by making the characters impossible to take seriously, forces audiences to think about the show they are attending.

*The Producers* reflects on itself in the way that it pays homage to the musicals of the 1940s and 1950s in its tunes, choreography, characterizations, and plot. To all of the retrospective elements of the show, Brooks has added a very modern element by consciously trying to offend prevailing sensibilities. At an earlier time—say, the time when the play is set—the offense may have come from the very presence of an integrated chorus, or of openly gay characters. The world has changed, though. For modern audiences, the element of shock, though mild, derives from the ways that minorities are treated onstage. Society has come so far beyond stereotyping that even bringing out these old characterizations of the sexpot, the schnorrer, the dirty old women, and the milquetoast makes audience stop and wonder if their mere presence is offensive. In fact, none of these comic characters makes a statement about people in general, so, no, they are not actually objectionable. But they *seem* wrong, and that makes this musical comedy seem like it is flaunting the social rules.

The most contemporary area of offensiveness is in Brooks's handling of its gay characters. Characters like Roger De Bris and his "common-law assistant" Carmen Ghia are tagged as ridiculous from the moment they are introduced, with foolish names and costumes. They have a production team of gay stereotypes clearly derived from the openly gay 1970s musical group The Village People, as well as a signature song which uses the word "gay" every few lines. It all seems as if they should be scandalous. In contemporary society, after all, there is no more question of equal rights for races or genders, but the legal battles over the rights of gay couples to marry and adopt keep this issue in the news. In fact, these gay characters are more likely to amuse than offend gay rights advocates. In a song like "Keep it Gay," *The Producers* accomplishes three things simultaneously: it taps into the backwards-looking nostalgia for 1950s and 1960s attitudes; it touches on a contemporary social issue; and it shows Brook's subtle touch, in being able to go near controversial subject matter without raising ire.

The central gag of *The Producers*—the sight of Adolf Hitler interpreted by a swishing, effeminate homosexual—is so obvious that it should have audiences enraged—not because Hitler is praised,

but because he is so universally despised that, in mocking him, Brooks sets his sights so low. The humor relies on the contemporary notion, which is the basis of shock humor, that each person will feel that they will get the joke but that the person sitting next to them might be outraged. Aside from a very few extremists, though, there really is no group that is going to object to this play ridiculing Hitler. Except for a very few audience members who might be attending a musical comedy but have absolutely no sense of humor, there is very little danger that anyone could watch Roger De Bris's mincing and not realize that Hitler is being mocked. At the core of this play is a scandal in theory, but one that never really materializes, hence, the play's commercial success.

In the 1968 movie, Brooks cut between showing the debacle of the *Springtime for Hitler* musical onstage and showing the shocked faces of the audience members as they realized what they had stumbled into (apparently, having missed the play's subtitle, *A Gay Romp with Adolf and Eva in Berchtesgaden,* when they purchased their tickets). The stage play—coming after a quarter century of what has come to be called, derisively, "political correctness"—relies on audiences to assume that someone around them is always going to be offended by something.

Brooks's *Springtime for Hitler* production number is one of the most rousing, whistle-able songs to play on a Broadway stage in years. Audiences do not have to be told that they like it. And, due to Brooks's careful use of stereotypes, they are well aware that what they like might offend others. All that is required for this play to work is that audiences believe that Bialystock and Bloom would be blind to the play's obvious charm. Their characters are shallow enough that it is not hard to believe anything of them: love, betrayal, male bonding, ignorance, principles or cowardice. All that matters for this to be a comedy is that people believe that Bialystock and Bloom are happy in the end and that the audience walks out of the theater happy.

**Source:** David Kelly, Critical Essay on *The Producers,* in *Drama for Students,* Thomson Gale, 2005.

### Robert Brustein

*In the following review, Brustein details some of the controversy surrounding* The Producers *and praises Brooks for showing that comedy can not only expose "stupidity and pretension," but "can also exorcise and nullify evil."*

The cover of a recent issue of *The New Yorker* depicts a lone spectator scowling in the midst of a theater audience rocking with laughter. The unhappy dissenter is Adolf Hitler, and the audience, of course, is watching *The Producers* (St. James Theatre), Mel Brooks's musical remake of his classic movie.

Everyone is familiar with the premise of *The Producers:* how the failed producer, Max Bialystock, gets the idea from his nerdy accountant, Leopold Bloom, that by over-subscribing a flop he can make more money than he could by producing a hit. Bialystock and Bloom finally discover the play ''that will close on page four,'' namely *Springtime for Hitler,* an epic by the neo-Nazi Franz Liebkind (Brad Oscar) designed ''to show the world the true Hitler, the Hitler with a song in his heart.'' When the play turns out to be an unexpected, if unwanted, success, Bialystock is convicted of larceny, despite his heartrending defense (''I know I'm a backstabbing, despicable crook—but I had no choice. I'm a Broadway producer''). After a few months of hesitation on a tropical isle, Bloom elects to join Bialystock in jail, though both are soon released to bring their new convict musical. *Prisoner of Love,* to Broadway. It is a hit—an intended hit.

Obviously there are some people—other than Hitler and his skinhead following—who would frown at *The Producers.* Letters to *The New York Times* are already charging Brooks with insensitivity to the Holocaust. Let us concede that insensitivity and bad taste are inseparable from the production; indeed, they are practically its organizing principles. Let us also concede that Brooks's willingness to give offense is the primary reason why this event is proving so exhilarating. And the exhilaration is palpable. Never in my long theatergoing life have I been part of such an ecstatic audience. I do not mean people desperate, at $100 a throw, to applaud their expenditure. I mean a really happy audience—wreathed in smiles before, during, and after the performance.

Despite some early misgivings, I had a pretty terrific time myself. Admittedly, Nathan Lane as Max Bialystock, while unquestionably very funny, still suffers from his compulsive eagerness to please. In his second attempt to play a role originated by Zero Mostel (Pseudolus in *A Funny Thing Happened on the Way to the Forum* was the first), Lane again shows the extent to which he lacks Mostel's subversive ferocity, his manic marginality. In his black slouch hat and red velvet jacket, he is also much more soi-disant than the seedy Zero—no

---

... HIS BOOK AND HIS LYRICS ARE ENTIRELY NONPAREIL, AND SO IS THE ANIMATING IDEA BEHIND THE SHOW.''

---

strands of hair pasted over his forehead or rolls of fat draping over his belt. And although Matthew Broderick is priceless as the nerdy Leopold Bloom, carrying his remnant of a security blanket like a lost flag, he cannot quite scale the heights of uncontrollable hysteria that made Gene Wilder such a terrified wreck in the part. The movie also had a tougher satiric edge than the show. (A younger Mel Brooks, for example, would never have tolerated the musical's courtroom climax, with its soggy reconciliations and unconvincing character reversals.)

But the musical of *The Producers* is a more lighthearted creation than the movie, almost a different species, with its own special conventions and demands, for which Lane and Broderick may be more appropriate casting. What it sacrifices in savagery it gains in form, enjoying a tighter, more coherent structure than the somewhat ungainly film. Thomas Meehan, who collaborated on the book, has managed to curb some of Brooks's excesses as a writer, and Susan Stroman, who wittily staged and brilliantly choreographed the show, has avoided some of his overkill as a director.

To be sure, excess and overkill are Brooks's trademarks, the qualities responsible for his wildest comic flights—the epic farting scene in *Blazing Saddles;* the ''morning after'' in *Young Frankenstein* when Madeline Kahn, having been shtupped by the Frankenstein monster, wakes up warbling, ''Ah, sweet mystery of life!'' (not to mention the scene in which the monster and Dr. Frankenstein appear on stage in top hat and tails, tap-dancing to ''Puttin' on the Ritz''); Brooks himself playing Louis XIV, surrounded by a bevy of beauties, in *The History of the World, Part I,* demonstrating to the movie audience why ''it's good to be the king.'' But we have occasionally suffered the defects of these virtues in such clinkers as *Life Stinks* (so did the movie) and *Robin Hood: Men in Tights* (whose only funny element was its title). Brooks's unwieldy sense of form may have been eliminated from the musicalized *Producers,* but mercifully his irrepressible good humor and his fecund imagination were preserved. The evening is virtually an *hommage* to this great comic artist, with dozens of quotations from his past movies. Indeed, his voice can be heard everywhere, even on stage, lip-synched by an actor singing the immortal lines: ''Don't be stupid, be a smarty / Come and join the Nazi Party.''

Rather than look for holes in the fabric, we ought to embrace this new old-fashioned musical comedy with gratitude. It is a refreshing tonic after all those decades of moral instruction from Rodgers and Hammerstein, and urban neurosis from Stephen Sondheim, and melodious angst from ''new wave'' musicals such as *Falsettos* and *Rent.* As John Lahr has observed in his *New Yorker* notice, *The Producers* recalls the good old days of comedian-driven musicals—comedians, we should note, who were originally schooled in vaudeville and burlesque. Lahr's father, Bert, was one of the linchpins of this movement (and his goofy, pained innocence seems to have influenced Lane's performance in the current production). So were Bobby Clark, Jimmy Savo, Ed Wynn, and Jimmy Durante—and later Milton Berle, Sid Caesar, Phil Silvers, and Zero Mostel. A number of these comics were Jews, including Lahr, though he rarely played Jews on stage. (I fondly remember him as a raffish plutocrat in *The Beauty Part,* explaining his state of undress to his wife: ''I had to give the maid a severe dressing-down.'')

It took Mel Brooks to tap the inexhaustible oil well of satiric deflation at the foundation of the Jewish experience. This mother lode he pumped to a fare-thee-well in the ''2000 Year Old Man'' series, playing an aging Yiddish kvetch who claims to have been a participant in all recorded history. (''Did you know Joan of Arc?'' ''I went with her, dummy, I went with her!'') The same ironic contrast between lowliness and loftiness characterizes *The Producers.* Take as a pictorial example the theater posters on the walls of Max Bialystock's office—*This Too Shall Pass, The Kidney Stone, The Breaking Wind, A Streetcar Named Murray, She Shtups to Conquer, Katz, High Button Jews*—which deflate some of Broadway's most sanctified commodities with outrageous Jewish humor.

Of course, Brooks was hardly the first to ridicule Hitler. In *The Great Dictator,* Chaplin satirized him as a pompous egotist (with a Jewish barber as his double) famously bouncing a globe of the world off his behind, when not vying with Mussolini over

whose barber chair could attain greater height. Brecht turned him into a narcissistic actor in *The Resistible Rise of Arturo Ui.* Even the Three Stooges did a number on him with their crude brand of thumb-in-the-eye slapstick. Still, nobody can touch Brooks when it comes to letting the air out of evil icons (he did the same to Torquemada and the Inquisition), generally by exposing how much they have in common with showbiz. Here he turns Gauleiters and storm troopers into chorus boys, while ripping the last shred of dignity from Hitler by making him a Judy Garland wanna-be whispering ''I love you'' to the audience that he is trying to seduce.

Outraged letters to the editor notwithstanding, it is a lot easier to make fun of the Nazi movement now than it was thirty-three years ago. It would be hard to replicate today that supreme moment in the film when the audience, watching the opening number of *Springtime for Hitler,* is shocked into paralyzed silence before bursting into applause. For one thing, we are half a century away from the event; for another, we are too familiar with the movie. In the musical, therefore, this ''gay romp with Adolf and Eva in Berchtesgaden'' is performed before a live audience applauding it in the St. James—not so much a play-within-a-play as a hit-within-a-hit.

So the satire on Nazism is the easy part. But like *Springtime for Hitler, The Producers* is designed ''to offend people of all races, creeds, and religions''—not a difficult task in our present age of hypersensitivity. Theatrical gays get the worst (or the best) of it. There is a rich scene in the apartment of Roger de Bris (a stage director, not a *mohel*), whom Bialystock and Bloom are trying to sign for their intended flop. It includes a staircase entrance by this flaming queen in a huge wig and sequined dress, not to mention the classic ''Walk this way'' moment in which Bialystock and Bloom start swishing behind a particularly effeminate majordomo. Piling Pelion on Ossa, it also features four or five superbly funny entrances by the director's entirely gay production team, including his ''common-law assistant'' Carmen Ghia (Roger Bart). Like other groups adept at self-satire (Jews and blacks, for example), some gays may find this kind of send-up insulting in the hands of an outsider; but it is really no different from the kind of bitchy humor gays often turn on themselves.

De Bris ends up playing Hitler after Franz Liebkind, the Nazi who wrote *Springtime for Hitler,* literally breaks a leg on opening night. (The musical wisely drops the outdated hippie character played in the movie by Dick Shawn.) Leibkind's assistant tells de Bris, "You're going out there a silly, hysterical screaming queen, and you're coming back a passing-for-straight great big Broadway star!" As camped by the incomparable Gary Beach, de Bris's first entrance as "Adolf Elizabeth Hitler" ("descended from a long line of English Queens") is enough to guarantee him his Tony. Glowering at the audience with his hands guarding his crotch, he suddenly crumples his body and lifts his arm above his head like a demented teacup, displaying a gleaming set of teeth below his Hitler moustache.

Radical feminists will not like this show much either, since it signals the return of woman as sex object—the long-legged, skimpily dressed showgirl sashaying in her traditional bent-kneed style. These dress parades are almost invariably used for comic purposes, as in the climactic Third Reich production number, when the female chorus descends the stairs in abbreviated Bavarian costumes, with a collection of sausages, pretzels, and German eagles on their heads. Stroman concludes the sequence with a Busby Berkeley-inspired extravaganza—even zanier than the one in the movie, involving goose-stepping storm trooper puppets against a mirrored back wall borrowed from *A Chorus Line*—that redefines the word, "show-stopper." (She has also choreographed a dancing chorus of homing pigeons.)

Also borrowed from a more Aristophanic, less censorial theatrical period is the buxom sidekick, often a nurse, here a secretary—a Swedish beauty with a hyphenated name so long it takes a court stenographer three minutes to record it. As played by Cady Huffman, Ulla (to use the shortened form) is a willing object of Bialystock's and Bloom's lust, especially after arousing them with a particularly lubricious song and dance ("Even though we're sitting down, we're giving you a standing ovation"). It is nice to be reminded that once upon a time in the theater men and women were allowed to feel sexual attraction.

As if enough constituencies had not been offended yet, the *Times* has also received letters from angry people in Florida retirement homes protesting that handicapped old ladies are among those mistreated in the show. Bialystock raises capital by servicing wealthy old widows, each with her own suggestive nickname ("Hold-me, Touch-me," "Lick-me, Biteme," "Kiss-me, Feel-me"). As a form of fore-play, all of them propose suggestive games, to which an exhausted Bialystock replies,

"Let's play a game where there's absolutely no sex—the Jewish princess and her husband." Among a number of rousing production numbers is one, "Little Old Lady Land," in which these aging women (some of them played by men) raucously perform on walkers. Only in America could it be considered offensive to depict aging women as capable of erotic and energized behavior.

The quality of performance and production is at a consistently high level. Matthew Broderick plays Bloom with hunched modesty and adenoidal shyness, performing (particularly in "I Wanna Be a Producer") with surprising musical comedy assurance. Despite my reservations about Nathan Lane, he has never been more disciplined than here under Stroman's watchful direction, though I dread to think what he'll be doing with the part three months hence. All of the other aforementioned actors, and the well-drilled ensemble that supports them, add energy and gaiety. William Ivy Long's costumes are witty and splashy, and Robin Wagner's sets are sumptuous recreations of a glorious Broadway past.

But the real hero of the evening is Melvin Brooks. Over the marquee of one of Bialystock's flops is the credit: "Entire production conceived, devised, thought up and supervised by Max Bialystock." Brooks, who in addition to all his other duties is one of the producers of *The Producers*, might claim the same credits. His music, though a decent enough approximation of Broadway show tunes, seems rather derivative, but his book and his lyrics are entirely nonpareil, and so is the animating idea behind the show. The Jew who finally buried Hitler, Mel Brooks demonstrates that comedy is not only capable of exposing stupidity and pretension. At times, it can also exorcise and nullify evil—not as powerfully, but sometimes more lastingly than a hundred Sherman tanks, a thousand B-42s, or a million GIs.

**Source:** Robert Brustein, "The Jew Who Buried Hitler," in *New Republic,* May 28, 2001, p. 27.

### *Lawrence Christon*

*In the following essay, Christon examines how impressions of the film version of* The Producers *has changed, especially since the reworking of the story into a musical.*

New York The latest word on *The Producers* is that ticket orders are now on sale for the Christmas season of 2002. Mel Brooks' Broadway adaptation of his own 1968 film has won a record-breaking

*Mel Brooks, Nathan Lane, and Matthew Broderick after the last performance of* The Producers *at New York's St. James Theatre, 2002*

slew of Tony Awards, and available seats are so hard to get that the voice mail of the show's press representative offers this stony injunction: "Do not leave requests for house seats. Any telephone requests for house seats will not be returned."

Question: If *The Producers* is so great now, why wasn't it so great then? Though, like *Harold and Maude,* it became an instant cult delight, it opened to generally dismal notices.

"I wasn't crazy about the original," says Andrew Sarris, ex-film critic for the *Village Voice* who now reviews films for the *New York Observer.* "I panned it. We were still too close to the real thing" (Nazi Germany and the Holocaust). "Things didn't work cinematically. It wasn't well-made. It was more like specialized cinematic vaudeville. The bad taste wasn't just about Hitler and gays, it was about women, too."

### Against the Grain

Timing may have had something to do with it as well. One of the most brutal, divisive decades in American history was drawing to a close, and with it the horrible televised spectacles of assassination, burning inner cities, campus revolt and body bags

flown home from the war in Vietnam. The feminist slogan "The personal is political" was a public mantra completely lost on cinematic down-on-his-luck producer Max Bialystock (Zero Mostel) and his timid accountant, Leopold Bloom (Gene Wilder) as they schemed to sell 25,000% of a sure-fire flop to a bunch of gullible old women "stopping off," as Bialystock says, "to get a last thrill on the way to the cemetery."

Memory doesn't serve that way anymore, despite *The Producers'* unretouched, unexpurgated presence in cable reruns and video. Notions of taste now seem either quaint or starchy edicts of a new kind of shock troop, the P.C. police. When a female moviegoer buttonholed Brooks with the charge that *The Producers* stooped to vulgarity, his memorable reply, "Madam, it rises below vulgarity," now seems the timely riposte, where earlier it would have been merely objectionable.

### Don't Ever Change

*The Producers* on Broadway has meant rediscovery of a 75-year-old figure who stands against our ideal of self-reinvention by virtue of never having changed. Not through the late '40s and early '50s era of writing for TV's *Your Show of Shows* and *The Sid Caesar Show* and the later TV hit, *Get Smart.* Not through the classic record series *The 2000 Year Old Man* nor *Blazing Saddles, Young Frankenstein, Silent Movie, High Anxiety* or *History of the World—Part I.*

''Much of Brooks humor,'' the late Kenneth Tynan observed in *Show People,* ''. . . is inspired by fear: fear of injury, illness, sex and failure; and also of unfriendly Gentiles, especially large ones, and most particularly if they are Germans or Cossacks.''

And in his stage review of *The Producers, The New Yorker*'s John Lahr celebrated comedy's defiance of death itself by quoting, from the same Tynan essay, Brooks as a PFC in war-torn Europe in WWII:

''Along the roadside, you'd see bodies wrapped up in mattress covers and stacked in a ditch, and those would be Americans, that could be me. I sang all the time . . . I never wanted to think about it . . . Death is the enemy of everyone, and even though you hate Nazis, death is more of an enemy than a German soldier.''

### Before the Rise
Before he convinced producer Joseph E. Levine that he could indeed direct *The Producers,* Brooks had fallen on hard times, which included divorce from his first wife, a Broadway flop called *All American* and a failed screenplay called *Marriage Is a Dirty Rotten Fraud.*

''He'd dropped off the screen,'' recalls Larry Gelbart, one of Brooks' Sid Caesar cohorts who'd gone on to other successes. ''He was out of it. No one thought he'd direct.'' Gelbart also recalls Brooks touting a novel called *Springtime for Hitler,* which later became *The Producers.*

''But all he had was a title. There was no novel.''

What Brooks had instead was what he's always had—a matchless talent for madcap verbal improvisation. As conceived, Leopold Bloom, one of the main characters from James Joyce's *Ulysses,* was to be a tidy, dutiful, timid Jewish accountant fully prepared ''to play it straight and trudge right to his grave.''

### 'Bite, kiss, take, grab . . .'
Then he runs into Max Bialystock the producer. ''Bite, kiss, take, grab, lavish, urinate—whatever

you can do that's physical, he will do.'' The two catalyze each other. Mild Leo hatches a fraudulent scheme and their lives are never the same.

Ten years passed between a writer-director's handshake and delivery of *The Producers* final cut, and 32 years more before it became a Broadway smash musical. A lot of people still don't think there's anything funny about fascism, and grim echoes of the Holocaust are still with us. But *The Producers* audacious energy hasn't dated.

Isn't that one definition of a classic?

**Source:** Lawrence Christon, ''*Producers* Pic Gains Stature as Time Goes By,'' in *Variety,* September 10–16, 2001, pp. A26, A30.

## SOURCES
Brantley, Ben, ''A Scam That'll Knock 'Em Dead,'' in the *New York Times,* April 20, 2001, Sec. E, Pt. 1, Col. 1, p. 1.

Brooks, Mel, and Tom Meehan, *The Producers,* Hyperion, 2001, p. 24.

Seavor, Jim, ''At Large—Tasteless Is Transformed by a True Sense of Glee,'' in *Providence Journal-Bulletin,* September 30, 2001, Arts Sec., p. J-01.

Weiss, Hedy, Review of *The Producers,* in the *Chicago Sun-Times,* February 19, 2001, Features Section, p. 37.

## FURTHER READING
Flinn, Denny Martin, *Musical! A Grand Tour,* Schirmer Books, 1997.
    Examining the history and different styles of stage musicals, Flinn ends his survey with the 1995–96 season, in despair that the era of Broadway musicals was over (a situation that *The Producers* was instrumental in changing).

Hofler, Robert, ''Broadway Tuner Has the Reich Stuff,'' in *Variety,* April 16, 2001, p. 1.
    Hofler's article, from the show-business trade paper *Variety,* examines the coming sensation of *The Producers* weeks before it even reached Broadway.

Holtzman, William, *Seesaw: A Dual Biography of Anne Bancroft and Mel Brooks,* Doubleday, 1979.
    Not much has been written at length about Brooks's life, but this book, covering his early years with his wife, gives a good sense of the private man.

Jones, John Bush, *Our Musicals, Ourselves: A Social History of the American Musical Theatre,* Brandeis University Press, 2003.

This book is exhaustive in its understanding of the ways in which musical theater reflects society.

# *Proof*

## DAVID AUBURN
## 2001

*Proof* (2001), a play by David Auburn, won the Pulitzer Prize in 2001, as well as several other major awards for drama. The play is set in Chicago, where Robert, a former genius of a mathematician who suffered from mental illness, has recently died. Robert appears in the play talking with his daughter Catherine, a depressed college drop-out who stayed at home and cared for her father over the last few years of his life. As preparations are made for the funeral and Catherine's sister Claire returns from New York, Catherine forms a tentative friendship with Hal, a mathematician who is one of her father's former students.

The plot moves into high gear when Hal discovers in one of the notebooks that Robert left behind a proof of a mathematical theorem that mathematicians had thought impossible. It is a sensational discovery, but Catherine stuns Hal by claiming she wrote the proof. But did she? The handwriting in the notebook looks very like her father's. As the mystery develops and resolves, the playwright explores issues such as what the link may be between genius and madness and whether either or both can be inherited. But *Proof* is also a story about human relationships, suggesting that developing trust and love can be as difficult, and just as uncertain, as establishing the truth of a mathematical proof.

## AUTHOR BIOGRAPHY

David Auburn was born in Chicago in 1969. Raised in Ohio and Arkansas, he attended the University of Chicago where he studied political philosophy. At the time, Auburn did not know he wanted to be a writer, but he joined a student group that performed comedy sketches. Auburn started writing some of the sketches and found he had a talent for it. He then started to write longer pieces. After Auburn graduated in 1991, he won a writing fellowship offered by Steven Spielberg's Amblin Productions, and he moved to Los Angeles to learn the craft of screenwriting. When the fellowship ended, Auburn moved to New York where he wrote plays and had some of them performed in tiny theaters. During the day, Auburn worked as a copywriter for a chemical company. In 1994, Auburn was accepted into the playwriting program at Juillard, where he also studied acting. Auburn soon gave up acting to concentrate on playwriting. His work at Juillard led to his first major play, *Skyscraper* (1997). In this play, the lives of a group of people are changed as they discover their connections with each other during the demolition of a crumbling skyscraper in Chicago.

In 1998, the Dramatists' Play Service published several of Auburn's one-act plays under the title *Fifth Planet and Other Plays*. The title play charts the friendship between two observatory workers as it waxes and wanes over the course of a year. Other plays in the collection included *Are You Ready?* in which the fates of three people drawn to the same restaurant are altered in an instant; *Damage Control*, about a politician and his aide during a crisis; *Three Monologues*, depicting a young woman's solitude; *We Had a Very Good Time*, in which a married couple travels to a dangerous foreign country, and *What Do You Believe about the Future*, in which ten characters answer the question posed by the play's title.

*Proof*, Auburn's most successful play, premiered at the Manhattan Theatre Club in May 2000 and opened at Broadway's Walter Kerr Theatre on October 24, 2000. The play won the Pulitzer Prize for Drama in 2001, the Joseph Kesselring Prize, the Drama Desk Award, and the Tony Award for Best Play of 2001. Auburn has written a screenplay based on the play, and the film was in production as of 2004.

Also in 2004, Auburn had his play *The Journals of Mihail Sebastian* debut at the Keen Company in New York on March 6. A one-man show, it is adapted from the writings of Mihail Sebastian, a Romanian novelist and playwright, whose journals recalling anti-Semitism in Romania during World War II were published in 1996. The expressionistic play covers six years in Sebastian's life, with the journal being created over the course of the evening.

## PLOT SUMMARY

### Act 1, Scene 1

*Proof* begins at one o'clock in the morning on the porch of a house in Chicago. Catherine sits in a chair, exhausted, and is startled when she realizes her father, Robert, is there. Robert gives her a bottle of champagne and wishes her happy birthday. He wants her to celebrate her birthday with friends, but she says she has none. Robert expresses concern about her, saying that she sleeps until noon, eats junk food, and does not work. He tells her to stop moping. She has potential and there is still time. It transpires that Robert did his best work by the time he was in his mid-twenties. After that, he became mentally ill. Catherine is worried that she will inherit the illness.

It then transpires that Robert died a week before, of heart failure, and the funeral is the next day.

Hal, a former student of Robert's, enters. He has been working on Robert's notebooks, but Catherine says there is nothing valuable in them. Hal invites her to hear him play in a rock band, but she is not interested. He speaks about how he admired her father, who helped him through a difficult period in his doctoral studies. This was four years ago, when Robert's illness went into remission. Catherine, fearing that Hal may be taking one of her father's notebooks from the house without permission, demands to see his backpack. She finds nothing there, but as he is about to leave, a notebook falls from his jacket pocket. She accuses him of stealing it and calls the police. He protests that in the notebook, Robert wrote something appreciative about Catherine on her birthday four years ago. Hal was going to wrap the notebook and give it to her.

### Act 1, Scene 2

The next morning, Catherine and Claire, who has arrived from New York, are drinking coffee. Claire tries to be kind, but Catherine is not receptive. Claire quizzes Catherine about Hal and about why she called the police, but Catherine resents the questioning. Hal enters unexpectedly, and there is a moment of confusion as Catherine berates her sister.

Hal quickly exits, leaving Claire saying that decisions must be made. She wants Catherine to stay with her in New York.

### Act 1, Scene 3

That night, there is a party following the funeral. Catherine is on the porch when Hal, who has been playing in the band, approaches her. He compliments her on her dress and talks about how mathematicians consider they are past their peak after the age of twenty-three. He refers to them as men, but Catherine mentions Sophie Germain, an eighteenth-century Frenchwoman who did important work on prime numbers. Catherine apologizes for her behavior the day before, and Hal confides that he thinks his work in mathematics is trivial. They talk about how elegant Robert's work was. Catherine then surprises Hal by kissing him. Hal reminds her of when they first met, four years ago, and they kiss again.

### Act 1, Scene 4

Hal and Catherine have spent the night together, and the next morning she gives him a key to the bottom drawer of her father's desk. Claire enters with a hangover. She tells Catherine that she would like her to move to New York. Catherine says she would prefer to stay in Chicago, but Claire replies that she has already sold the house. They quarrel. Catherine complains that Claire never helped to take care of their father; Claire replies that she worked fourteen-hour days so she could pay off the mortgage on the house. She says that Robert should have been sent to an institution, but Catherine disagrees. Hal returns with a notebook. Inside it, he says, is a proof of a theorem about prime numbers. If it checks out, it will show that when Robert was supposedly insane, he was doing some of the most important math work in the world. Catherine stuns him by saying that it was she who wrote it.

### Act 2, Scene 1

It is a September afternoon four years earlier. Robert and Catherine talk on the porch. Catherine says she has enrolled as a math major at Northwestern. She tells him that since he has been well for nearly seven months, he does not need her there all the time. Robert is not happy about her decision and says she should have discussed it with him. Hal enters. At this time, he is Robert's graduate student, and he brings a draft of his dissertation. Robert says he will look it over and tells Hal to come by his office in a week. Then, he realizes that it is Cathe-

*David Auburn*

rine's birthday, and he had forgotten it. He is annoyed with himself, but Catherine tells him not to worry. They agree to go out to dinner. As Catherine goes out to dress, Robert begins writing in his notebook.

### Act 2, Scene 2

Catherine, Hal, and Claire discuss the newly discovered notebook. Catherine insists that she wrote the proof, working on it for years after she dropped out of school. Hal and Claire are skeptical. Claire thinks the proof is written in her father's handwriting. She suggests that Catherine talk them through it to convince them, but Hal says that would not prove anything, since her father might have written it and explained it to Catherine later. Catherine is unhappy that they do not believe her. She says she trusted Hal and wanted him to be the first person to see the proof. He still cannot believe that she wrote it, since to do so she would have to have been as good as her father. After Catherine snaps at him, he exits. Catherine and Claire struggle over the notebook and Catherine throws it to the floor.

### Act 2, Scene 3

The next day, Claire berates Hal for taking advantage of Catherine and sleeping with her. She refuses to let Hal talk to her, but she does let him take the notebook. She tells Hal to figure out what is in there and advise the family about what to do.

### Act 2, Scene 4

It is winter, three and a half years earlier. Robert is on the porch in the cold, writing in a notebook. When Catherine, who is a student at Northwestern, arrives, he tells her that he is working again. He feels he has regained all his intellectual brilliance and is excited about what he will be able to produce. He wants her to collaborate with him and hands her his notebook, which Catherine reads slowly. It is confused, rambling nonsense. She puts her arm around him and takes him inside the house.

### Act 2, Scene 5

Back in the present, Claire and Catherine prepare to leave for New York. At first, they appear to be getting on well, but when Claire tells her how much she will love New York, Catherine gives sarcastic replies, and the two women quarrel. Claire exits, upset. Hal enters. He is excited. The proof has checked out. Catherine is not surprised and tells him to publish it. He now believes that it is her work because it uses new mathematical techniques that he thinks Robert would not have known. He wants Catherine to talk about her work so he can understand it better. Catherine is upset that he did not trust her in the first place. He hands her the book. She says that doing the proof was just a matter of connecting the dots. Her father knew nothing of her work. Hal asks her to go through it with him, and she picks up the book, finds a section, looks at him, and begins speaking.

## CHARACTERS

### Catherine

Catherine is Robert's twenty-five-year-old daughter. A college dropout, she has spent several years at home caring for her mentally ill father. A few years earlier, when his illness went into remission for almost a year, she enrolled as a sophomore at Northwestern University in Evanston, Illinois. She dropped out of that program and returned to look after her father when he again became ill. Their relationship, although sometimes antagonistic on the surface, was sustained by strong mutual affection.

Catherine is worried that she may inherit her father's illness, and the signs of mental instability are already there. Although she is a highly intelligent woman, she has no direction in life and often, according to her father, sleeps till noon. Some days she does not even get out of bed. She is obviously suffering from depression, and her attitude about life is bitter. Claire, her sister, wants her to move to New York so she can keep an eye on her and arrange for the best medical treatment, but Catherine resents her interference. Evidence of her unstable mental condition emerges in Claire's report of her aggressive behavior toward the police officers who came to the house after Catherine reported a burglary in progress (which was her extreme reaction to Hal's attempt to smuggle out one of her father's notebooks).

Hal attempts to befriend Catherine. She then takes the lead and seduces him. Wanting to show affection and trust, she allows him to discover the amazing mathematical proof that she has written in one of her father's notebooks. She is upset when Hal does not believe she wrote it and feels that her trust in him has been betrayed. Eventually, Hal is convinced that she wrote the proof, and the mathematical genius that Catherine inherited from her father is finally revealed and acknowledged. It appears that Catherine and Hal may be on their way to a rewarding relationship, both professionally and personally.

### Claire

Claire is Catherine's efficient, practical, and successful sister. Unlike Catherine, she has inherited none of her father's erratic genius. Instead, she has made a career in New York as a currency analyst. She made enough money to pay off the mortgage on the family home in Chicago, even when she was living in a studio apartment in Brooklyn, New York. Claire lives with her boyfriend, Mitch, who also has a successful career, and they plan to marry in January. Claire and Catherine have never gotten along well, and when Claire returns from New York for their father's funeral, they quarrel. Claire feels responsible for Catherine's welfare and wants her to move to New York, but Catherine resents what she sees as Claire's interference in her life. It transpires that they have quarreled in the past over how to care for their father. Claire thought he should be sent to an institution, but Catherine believed it was important for him to remain near the university. Claire has little understanding of Catherine and regards her as mentally ill, but she means well and takes her family responsibilities seriously.

## Hal

Hal, whose full name is Harold Dobbs, is a twenty-eight-year-old mathematician who teaches at the University of Chicago. He also plays drums in a rock band made up of mathematicians. Hal is a former student of Robert's, whom he admires immensely, not only for the brilliance of his achievements in mathematics but because Robert helped him through a bad patch in his doctoral studies. Hal first met Catherine briefly four years earlier, and when he meets her again, he tries to make friends with her. He seems rather shy and inexperienced with women, and it is she who seduces him rather than the other way round. After they spend the night together, he is ready to fall in love with her. Hal also confides in Catherine that he is dissatisfied with the progress of his career. His academic papers are being rejected by journals, and he feels that his work is trivial. Although he does not openly acknowledge it, this is one of the underlying reasons that he is examining Robert's notebooks. If he can discover something important, it will boost his career and perhaps make a name for himself. He is thrilled when he finds the proof in Robert's notebook and takes some convincing by Catherine that it is her work. This harms their relationship, since Catherine is annoyed that he does not believe her. When Hal is convinced, he reacts with humility rather than jealousy. He tries to repair their relationship and asks Catherine to go over the proof with him so he can ask questions and understand it better.

## Robert

Robert was a famous mathematician who has just died of a heart attack in his fifties. He is already dead when the play begins, but he appears in the first scene in Catherine's imagination and returns in two later scenes, which flash back to earlier years. Robert was a mathematical genius. When he was in his early twenties, he made major contributions to game theory, algebraic geometry, and nonlinear operator theory. According to Hal, his former graduate student, he invented the mathematical techniques for studying rational behavior. While he was still in his twenties, Robert was afflicted by a serious mental illness, which dogged the remainder of his life. He became so incapacitated that his daughter Catherine had to stay at home to care for him. Robert had a deep affection for Catherine. He realized the sacrifices she made in caring for him, and he believed that she saved his life. Robert was also worried that she appeared to be wasting her life. Four years before his death, Robert's illness went into remission, and he was able to teach again for

# MEDIA ADAPTATIONS

- *Proof* was adapted to film and set to release in the United States some time in 2005. The screenplay is written by David Auburn and Rebecca Miller. Directed by John Madden, the film stars Anthony Hopkins as Robert, Hope Davis as Claire, Jake Gyllenhaal as Hal, and Gwyneth Paltrow as Catherine. Paltrow reprises her role as Catherine, which she played on stage in London's West End.

one academic year. During that year, Robert thought he was back at his best and would once more be able to do exciting, pioneering work in mathematics. He even asked Catherine if she would collaborate with him, but she soon found out that his notebooks were full of nonsense; his mind was confused, and he was lapsing into insanity.

# THEMES

## Genius and Madness

Robert and Catherine, the two mathematical geniuses, are brilliant but mentally unstable, and they are contrasted with the other two characters, Hal and Claire, who lack the genius of the other two but are better adjusted to the world.

Robert revolutionized the field of mathematics when he was in his early twenties, but he has waged a long battle with mental illness. The implication is that the illness is somehow connected with his genius. Another implication, in addition to the fact that genius, at least in this case, appears to be inherited, is that insanity may be inherited too. Catherine worries about this possibility, and although Robert tries to reassure her that it is not the case, she too shows signs of mental instability. She is too depressed to function effectively, and her life is not moving in a positive direction. She is bitter and finds it hard to trust the good intentions of others. And yet she is as brilliant as her father.

# TOPICS FOR FURTHER STUDY

- Women have made valuable contributions to mathematics in the nineteenth and twentieth centuries. Research the work of two female mathematicians and briefly describe their achievements.

- What do you think Catherine means when she refers in the play to "proofs like music?" What might mathematics and music, which on the surface seem so different, have in common?

- What signs does Catherine show that she is suffering from depression? What is depression? How is it recognized? What are the causes of it? How is it treated?

- In the script, the playwright uses the word "beat" as a cue for the actors. "Beat" means a pause in the dialogue, a moment of silence. It can indicate a moment of confusion or awkwardness or a change of mood in the characters. Examine act 1, scene 1, after Hal enters. From there to the end of the scene there are eleven beats during Hal's conversation with Catherine. Imagine you are playing Hal or Catherine. What is each character feeling during each beat? Describe what the actors would need to convey at each beat.

---

Genius is therefore presented as a fragile thing; it can produce great intellectual achievements but may be inimical to personal happiness and stability. There is a price to pay for being an extraordinary individual.

The genius of Robert and Catherine is contrasted to the more pedestrian figures of Hal and Claire. Hal is a hard worker, a competent mathematician, and probably a good teacher, but he lacks the spark of genius. His work, as he says himself, is trivial. The big ideas elude him, and always will. This is why he combs through Robert's notebooks, hoping that some spark of genius will fly out from the pages, enabling him to bask in reflected glory. Claire too is competent and practical, "very quick with numbers," and this has enabled her to have a successful career as a currency analyst. But making money in the big city is a far cry from genius, which Claire acknowledges in her father but does not understand. She is too well adjusted to the world to have any interest in the beauty of abstractions.

Thus through the four characters the play contrasts the mundane and the ordinary, on which the day-to-day world turns, with the exceptional and the extraordinary, which is the rare stuff of genius that creates the peaks of human achievements.

### Love and Trust

The certainty of a mathematical proof, which can be followed logically and established as absolutely true beyond any doubt, is a sharp contrast to the fragility and uncertainty of human life and relationships. Unlike in mathematics, truth in life is a harder thing to understand and grasp. Much of it, the play suggests, depends on trust. Catherine and Robert trust each other, and Robert believes that his daughter's love for him saved his life. There is never any doubt of the strength of the bond between father and daughter. But the other central relationship in the play, that between Catherine and Hall, is more problematic. It develops tentatively, and issues of trust soon surface. The truth is hard to determine. Catherine is suspicious of Hal's motives in going through Robert's notebooks, thinking that he may want to publish some of her father's work under his own name. Hal vigorously denies this, but she does not believe him, and perhaps Hal may not be willing to acknowledge even to himself that his motivation may not be entirely disinterested. He knows, after all, that his career has stalled, and a major discovery such as he seeks might give it a boost.

The relationship between Hal and Catherine moves in an awkward dance of mistrust followed by attempts at trust. In act 1, scene 1, Catherine thinks he is stealing a notebook, and he is, but not for the purpose she thinks. In act 1, scene 4, she tries to show her regained trust when she gives him the key to the drawer which contains her proof. But then when she claims the proof is hers, the tables are turned; it is now Hal who mistrusts Catherine, refusing to believe that she is capable of such work of genius. In turn, she once more becomes suspicious of him, saying the reason he wants to take the proof is to show off to his colleagues: "You can't wait to show them your brilliant discovery," she says. Mistrust again fills the air, on both sides. The proof that sits harmlessly in the notebook may embody a beautiful, irrefutable truth, but for the people arguing over it, such truth is elusive, not only about who wrote the proof, but also in terms of the truthfulness of their relationship.

The uncertainty continues into the final scene. Hal has overcome his doubts about whether Catherine wrote the proof, but she is still dealing with the hurt feelings that arose because he did not trust her word at first. She now plays devil's advocate and makes a telling comment that plays on the contrast between mathematical certainty and the uncertain, ambiguous world of human activities and relations. Even though Hal has carefully elaborated his reasons for concluding that the work is hers, she says that none of the arguments he has produced prove anything. ''You should have trusted me,'' she says. It seems that trust is the only way that certainty can be established in this uncertain world; it is the only thing that can guide people through the complexity of human relationships, although the play leaves no doubt about how easy it is to undermine trust and how hard it is to maintain it. To Hal's credit, he does not try to argue with Catherine. Like a fine mathematical proof (''streamlined, no wasted moves,'' as Hal says of Robert's work), he takes the surest way to the goal, acknowledging that she is correct: he should have trusted her. It is on that basis of trust that he and Catherine can go forward together.

# STYLE

## *Exposition*

The exposition of a play is the introductory material, which creates the tone, introduces the characters, perhaps suggests the theme, and gives the background information necessary in order to understand the play. In this play, the exposition is done with great economy and skill. So much is accomplished in the first eight pages of the script, amounting to less than half of the first scene, in which Robert and Catherine talk to each other. In this short time, the audience learns that there is affection as well as frustration between father and daughter; that Robert is a mathematician and a genius who did his best work while he was in his twenties and who is now mentally ill; that Catherine is depressed, has no friends, and does not like her sister; that she has some mathematical knowledge and can banter with her father about mathematical concepts; that she is worried about inheriting his illness. All this is accomplished within a couple hundred mostly short lines of dialogue.

## *Theatrical Surprise*

The playwright shows that he is a master of the theatrical surprise, a moment when something is revealed that the audience up to that point had not known or guessed. Halfway through the first scene, for example, Robert says that the only reason he can admit that he is crazy is because he is also dead. This is a startling moment and also a surprisingly humorous one (the intensity and sadness of the play is offset many times by humor). Another aspect of this strategy of surprise is the fact that in a number of scenes, a new piece of information is produced near the end to give a twist to the interactions of the characters. This occurs for example at the end of the first scene, when Hal reveals the real reason he tried to sneak out with the notebook. It also occurs in act 1, scene 3, when Hal reveals that he and Catherine have met before. The most stunning use of this technique occurs at the end of act 1, when Catherine claims that she is the author of the proof.

# HISTORICAL CONTEXT

## *Sophie Germain*

Sophie Germain, the French mathematician so admired by Catherine in *Proof*, was born into a middle-class family in Paris in 1776. She first became interested in mathematics when she was thirteen. Confined to her home because the French Revolution had broken out, she taught herself mathematics in her father's library. Her family tried to discourage her, considering that mathematics was not an appropriate field of study for a girl. But Sophie persisted. She obtained lecture notes from the École Polytechnique, an academy founded in 1794 that trained mathematicians and scientists but refused to enroll women. Becoming interested in the work of J. L. Lagrange, she submitted a paper to him under the pseudonym Antoine-August Le Blanc, a man who was a former student at the academy. Lagrange was impressed by the paper and wanted to meet the author. Overcoming his surprise at discovering a young female mathematician, he agreed to become her mentor. This gave Germain entry into the circle of mathematicians and scientists that had up to then been closed to her.

In 1804, Germain began corresponding with the German mathematician, Carl Friedrich Gauss (as Catherine tells Hal in *Proof*), one of the most brilliant mathematicians of all time. Germain shared with him her work in number theory. It was three years before Gauss discovered that the bright young correspondent whom he had been mentoring was a woman. A dozen years later, Germain wrote to the mathematician Legendre, presenting the work in number theory that was to become her greatest contribution to mathematics. In 1816, Germain was awarded a prize by the French Academy of Sciences for her work in explaining mathematically the vibration of elastic surfaces. That Germain continued work in this area was another of her lasting contributions to mathematical theory. Germain died in 1831, before she could accept an honorary degree from the University of Göttingen that Gauss had convinced the university to award. Germain's contribution to mathematics was all the more remarkable because, like Catherine in *Proof*, she lacked formal academic training.

### Trends on Broadway

When *Proof* was first produced in 2000, it was the latest in a number of plays that took their inspiration from intellectual disciplines such as mathematics and physics. The aim of the playwrights seemed to be to give the audience some substantial food for thought as well as an evening's entertainment. The fashion began with British playwright Tom Stoppard. Stoppard's *Hapgood* (1988; revised 1994) used the intricacies and paradoxes of quantum physics as metaphors for the world of espionage during the cold war. In 1994, Stoppard wrote *Arcadia,* another play in which the audience found themselves immersed in quantum physics, as well as chaos theory. Like *Proof, Arcadia* features a young woman with an extraordinary grasp of mathematical theory. Also like *Proof*, it alludes to a nineteenth-century woman who made an impact on mathematical theory. This was not Sophie Germain but Ada Byron, Lady Lovelace, the daughter of the poet Lord Byron, who worked with mathematician Charles Babbage in developing the theory of a new calculating machine. The mathematical plan she wrote is now considered to be the first computer program.

Other plays which drew on quantum physics included Michael Frayn's *Copenhagen* (2000), a sophisticated investigation of a meeting between physicists Werner Heisenberg and Niels Bohr in 1941, and *Hypatia* by Mac Wellman, which was based on the life and death of Hypatia, a fifth-

century mathematician and philosopher. According to Bruce Weber, whose *New York Times* article, "Science Finding a Home Onstage," is about the contemporary fashion of writing plays with scientific content:

> This flowering use of science as narrative material and scientific concepts as metaphors for the stage . . . . provides evidence that science is re-entering the realm of popular culture, not just in imaginative, futuristic fiction but also in other mainstream and alternative forms: from historical reconstruction and theoretical abstraction to fluffy romance and contemporary realism.

## CRITICAL OVERVIEW

As might be expected of a Pulitzer prize-winning play, *Proof* was received enthusiastically by audiences and most reviewers. The stunning revelation at the end of act 1, when Catherine announces that it was she, not her father, who wrote the proof, was regularly greeted with gasps by the audience. Bruce Weber, in the *New York Times*, called *Proof* "an exhilarating and assured new play . . . that turns the esoteric world of higher mathematics literally into a back porch drama, one that is as accessible and compelling as a detective story." Weber admired the pacing of the play, and further noted that it "presents mathematicians as both blessed and bedeviled by the gift for abstraction that ties them achingly to one another and separates them, also achingly, from concrete-minded folks like you and me." Weber also appreciated the spirit of the play in which there was no meanness; the characters struggling to deal with the devastating effects of mental illness were all "good people."

Weber reported again on the play over a year later, noting in the *New York Times* that it was still playing to sold-out houses at the Walter Kerr Theatre. A change of cast had not diminished its appeal, but rather shown that the characters and their relationships could be given "new and distinct emotional shadings."

In *Variety,* Robert Hoffler wrote of the play's "rich, aching melancholia" and praised its ambitious structure and its sense of humor: "The mercurial nature of the mathematician's art is refracted everywhere, usually in ways that offer a humorous counterpoint to somber loss." In *Library Journal,* Robert W. Melton was equally enthusiastic, describing *Proof* as a "wonderful" play: "[its] deft dialog, its careful structure, and the humanity of the central characters are themselves proof of a major new talent in the American theater."

One dissenting voice was that of Robert Brustein, in *The New Republic,* who complained that although the playwright had a competent grasp of his material, the plot was too thin. The author "runs out of material so quickly that, by the middle of the second act, the play jerks to a halt and starts running in place."

# CRITICISM

### Bryan Aubrey

*Aubrey holds a Ph.D. in English and has published many articles on modern drama. In this essay, Aubrey discusses the parallels between the mathematicians Robert, Catherine, and Hal and the lives and creativity of real life mathematicians, especially John Forbes Nash Jr.*

In researching *Proof,* Auburn consulted with a number of mathematicians and also read the biographies of prominent mathematicians, aspects of whose lives find their way into the play. When Hal tells Catherine that some of the older mathematicians he encounters at conferences are addicted to amphetamines, which they take to make their minds feel sharp, he is amplifying the well-known story of mathematician Paul Erdös who began taking amphetamines so he could keep up the fast pace of his mathematical work. When friends persuaded him to stop taking the amphetimines for a month, Erdös complained that he had not been able to do any creative work during that time and promptly resumed taking the drugs.

Andrew Wiles is another mathematician whose story finds an echo in *Proof.* Wiles, a professor of mathematics at Princeton University, worked for many years to prove Fermat's Last Theorem when the conventional wisdom was that such a proof was impossible. In 1993, Wiles announced at a conference that he had proved the theorem. It transpired that he had been working on it in solitude, in an office in his attic, for seven years, telling no one of what he was doing. This surely inspired the picture

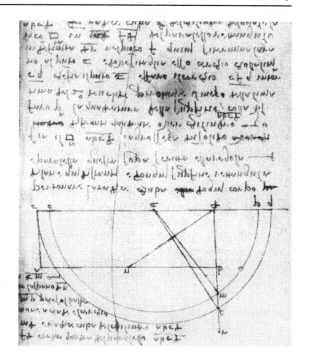

*Drawing of a geometric calculation by Leonardo da Vinci*

presented in *Proof* of Catherine, who also works in solitude and in secret, and then suddenly, out of the blue, unveils a ground-breaking mathematical proof.

But the mathematician whose life story is most closely linked to *Proof* is John Forbes Nash, Jr, who is the subject of *A Beautiful Mind* (1998), a biography by Sylvia Nasar which was made into a popular movie in 2001. Nash was a mathematical genius. In 1949, when he was twenty-one years old and a graduate student at Princeton University, he wrote a slim, twenty-seven-page doctoral thesis on game theory (a theory of how people behave when they expect their actions to influence the behavior of others) that revolutionized the field of economics. Nash became a professor at the Massachusetts Institute of Technology (MIT) when he was only twenty-three and quickly went on to solve a series of mathematical problems that other mathematicians had deemed impossible. He seemed destined to become one of the greatest mathematicians in the history of the discipline. Then, in 1959, when Nash was thirty years old, his behavior, which had always been eccentric, became bizarre and irrational. He heard strange voices and became obsessed with the idea of world government. He accused a colleague of entering his office to steal his ideas. He turned

# WHAT DO I READ NEXT?

- Auburn's *Fifth Planet and Other Plays* (2001) contains several one-act plays that Auburn wrote before *Proof*. The plays are *Fifth Planet, Are You Ready, Damage Control, Miss You, Three Monologues, What Do You Believe in the Future*, and *We Had a Very Good Time*.

- *Wit* (1999) is a Pulitzer Prize–winning play by Margaret Edson. The protagonist is a female scholar of English literature who specializes in the work of the seventeenth-century poet, John Donne. She is now dying of cancer and uses the experience to explore mortality, the value of human relationships, and how life should be lived.

- *Copenhagen* (2000) is a Tony Award–winning play by Michael Frayn about Werner Heisenberg (a physicist who was head of the Nazi's attempts to develop a nuclear bomb), Danish physicist Niels Bohr, and his wife Margrethe. Bohr and Heisenberg met in Copenhagen in 1941, and

what they discussed has been a matter of dispute ever since. By adapting to the theater principles drawn from quantum physics, Frayn cleverly shows it is impossible to reach an objective understanding of what the two men discussed that day.

- *The Mind-Body Problem* (1993), by Rebecca Goldstein, is a coming-of-age novel set in Princeton's mathematics community, about a young Jewish woman who marries a world-renowned mathematician.

- *Strange Brains and Genius: The Secret Lives of Eccentric Scientists and Madmen* (1998), by Clifford A. Pickover, examines the connection between genius and madness in a highly eclectic way. Pickover profiles many eccentric scientists, from Nikola Tesla to the Unabomber, Ted Kaczynski (who was a mathematician), as well as some writers and artists.

---

down the offer of a chair at the University of Chicago with the explanation that he was going to become Emperor of Antarctica. Nash was admitted to McLean Hospital in Belmont, Massachusetts, where he was diagnosed as a paranoid schizophrenic.

Schizophrenia is a severe mental disorder that distorts thinking and perception. It leads to a loss of contact with reality and bizarre, sometimes antisocial behavior as the sufferer withdraws into his own inner world. Schizophrenia is difficult to treat and there is no cure. Nash spent the next thirty years afflicted with the disease, which would occasionally go into temporary partial remission before returning. His career was destroyed although he made a surprise recovery during the 1990s. He resumed living a normal life and studying mathematics and was awarded the Nobel Prize in 1994.

The parallels between the real life of Nash and the fictional life of Robert in *Proof* are many, and they prompt questions of whether genius and insan-

ity are linked and whether both are inherited. Robert is clearly a Nash-like figure. Hal reminds Catherine in act 1, scene 1 that when Robert was in his early twenties he had made major contributions to three fields: game theory, algebraic geometry, and nonlinear operator theory. These are exactly the same fields, according to Nasar, in which the young Nash made his impact. Nasar also points out that in the early days of his illness, Nash seemed to have a heightened awareness of life:

> He began to believe that a great many things he saw—a telephone number, a red necktie, a dog trotting along the sidewalk, a Hebrew letter, a sentence in the *New York Times*—had a hidden significance, apparent only to him. . . . He believed he was on the brink of cosmic insights.

This is echoed by Robert, as he recalls his mental state soon after he became ill. He tells Catherine about the clarity with which he saw things, and he believed that his mind was even sharper than before:

If I wanted to look for information—secrets, complex and tantalizing messages—I could find them all around me. In the air. In a pile of fallen leaves some neighbor raked together. In box scores in the paper, written in the steam coming up off a cup of coffee. The whole world was talking to me.

Although the play does not mention the exact nature of Robert's illness, the hallucinations and delusions he suffered from make it clear that he, like the real-life Nash, was schizophrenic. Robert was no doubt mistaken when he claimed that his mind had become sharper, because during his illness his mental processes no longer bore any relation to reality. As with Nash, the insights he thought he had contained meanings known only to him and were useless for objectively verifiable mathematical knowledge. Just as Nash believed that powers from outer space, or foreign governments, were communicating with him through cryptic messages in the *New York Times* that only he could decode, so too Robert used to borrow large numbers of books from libraries because he thought that aliens were sending him messages through the Dewey decimal numbers on the books, and he was trying to work out the code.

Was Nash's insanity, or that of Robert in *Proof*, somehow related to their genius? The idea that creativity and madness are linked is an old one. Plato wrote in his dialog Ion that the poet was inspired with a kind of divine mania, and cultural history turns up many examples of exceptionally creative people who have been afflicted with mental illness of one kind or another, including the philosopher Friedrich Nietzsche, the artist Vincent van Gogh, and the writer Virginia Woolf. In more modern times, American poets Sylvia Plath and Robert Lowell suffered from mental illness. (In 1959, Lowell was a patient at McLean Hospital in Belmont when Nash was admitted.)

The most common type of mental illness amongst creative artists is manic-depression, also known as bipolar disorder. This is not the same as schizophrenia. Although manic-depression can produce delusions, it is mainly characterized by extreme mood swings, ranging from great elation to deep depression. Research suggests that creative artists, poets in particular, are two to three times more likely to suffer from manic-depression than scientists. For the poet or writer, it is possible that manic-depression can enhance creativity, since the mood swings may offer more acute insight into the peaks and troughs of human experience, which in turn can lend the artist's work a profundity that

> UNLIKE SCHIZOPHRENIA, GENIUS IS NOT TRANSMITTED THROUGH GENES, AND THERE ARE NUMEROUS EXAMPLES OF GENIUSES WHOSE OFFSPRING HAVE BEEN DISTINGUISHED ONLY BY THEIR MEDIOCRITY."

might escape those who live on a more even emotional keel. Creative people who suffer from manic depression are often able to function quite normally between episodes, which is usually not the case with schizophrenia.

It would seem that schizophrenia, far from being somehow linked with creativity, is in fact inimical to it, since the feeling of heightened awareness it may produce translates only into delusional perceptions, not deeper insights into truth. Although there does seem to be a certain unusual quality to the minds and personalities of many great scientists and philosophers, madness does not describe it. Nasar points out many examples of men of genius, including Immanuel Kant, Ludwig Wittenstein, Isaac Newton, and Albert Einstein, who had emotionally detached, eccentric, solitary, inward-looking personalities that may have been useful in promoting the kind of creativity that these disciplines require. Such people—Nash was one of them before his illness—are able to think not only more profoundly but also in different ways than less gifted individuals. Nash was used to solving problems in ways that had not occurred to others. He developed this habit of thinking ''out of the box'' at an early age. His sister reported that Nash's mother was once told that her son, then in elementary school, was having trouble with math, because he could see ways of solving mathematical problems that were different from the methods the teachers were used to.

When Nash was a mature mathematician, his mind not only worked faster than anyone else's, he continued to approach mathematical problems in unusual ways that would unlock new possibilities that astonished his colleagues. Nasar reports that Donald Newman, a mathematician who knew Nash at MIT in the 1950s, said of him that ''everyone else would climb a peak by looking for a path somewhere on the mountain. Nash would climb another mountain altogether and from that distant peak would shine a searchlight back onto the first peak.'' Sometimes when Nash presented his unexpected results to professional audiences, there would be some who said they could not possibly believe them, so novel was Nash's approach to the problem.

Auburn clearly incorporated this dimension of Nash's mind into the character of Robert in *Proof*. When Hal says to Catherine that hard work was not the secret of Robert's success, she contradicts him but immediately explains that the work went on almost unseen, and Robert's success resulted from his taking an unusual starting point:

> He'd attack a question from the side, from some weird angle, sneak up on it, grind away at it. He was slogging. He was just so much faster than anyone else that from the outside it looked magical.

Hal's immediate response, about the beauty and the elegance of Robert's work, also corresponds to what mathematicians said about Nash's work. It is quite common for mathematics to be described in this way, as if it somehow partakes in the essential beauty and order of the universe. The French mathematician Henri Poincaré wrote about the aesthetic feeling known by all mathematicians when they recognized these qualities revealed in their work, describing it as ''the feeling of mathematical beauty, of the harmony of numbers and forms, of geometric elegance.''

A final aspect of Nash's life finds its way into *Proof* in Catherine's worries that she may inherit her father's illness, even though the depression she suffers from is not related to the symptoms of schizophrenia. Catherine is right to be concerned, since expert opinion considers that although the cause of schizophrenia is unknown, there is a genetic factor in the disease. It can be inherited and, indeed, Nash's own son, John Charles Nash, was diagnosed, like his father, as a paranoid schizophrenic. Like his father also, John Charles Nash was a mathematician, brilliant but without his father's spark of genius. Unlike schizophrenia, genius is not transmitted through genes, and there are numerous examples of geniuses whose offspring have been distinguished only by their mediocrity. So for Catherine in *Proof* to inherit both Robert's genius *and* his mental illness would be a very unlikely event in real life, although of course, as *Proof* shows, it can be turned into excellent drama. Nash himself discovered this when at the age of seventy-three his biographer, Nasar, took him to see a performance of

the play. An article in the *Los Angeles Times* by John Clark contains Nasar's description of how Nash reacted:

> 'He loved it,' says Nasar, who admits she was a little nervous about his response. 'It was so much fun to see him laugh and react to *Proof* because [the father] is clearly inspired by Nash's story, and to witness John Nash seeing this on the stage in front him—it was adorable.'

**Source:** Bryan Aubrey, Critical Essay on *Proof*, in *Drama for Students*, Thomson Gale, 2005.

### Curt Guyette

*Guyette, a longtime journalist, received a bachelor's degree in English writing from the University of Pittsburgh. In this essay, Guyette discusses how Auburn highlights the uncertain nature of human existence by contrasting it with the certainty found in mathematics.*

In his Puliter Prize–winning play *Proof*, Auburn brings into high relief the uncertain nature of life by contrasting it with the world of mathematics, where the truth or falsity of an idea can be proved with absolute certainty. In the world of numbers, two plus two always equals four; there is no doubt involved. But in matters of flesh and blood, especially in the way people relate to the world around them, there is no formula for absolute knowledge.

The tenuous nature of reality as perceived through human eyes is vividly depicted in the play's very first scene. Catherine, the troubled daughter of Robert, a brilliant mathematician of world renown, is having a revealing conversation with her father early in the morning of her twenty-fifth birthday. During the conversation, it is revealed that Robert suffers from mental illness. By its very nature, mental illness radically distorts a person's perceptions of the world. It is also the nature of such an illness that the person afflicted with it is deluded into thinking that his perceptions are completely grounded in reality. As Robert tells Catherine, ''Crazy people don't sit around wondering if they're nuts.'' As their conversation continues, he reinforces the point by saying, ''Take it from me. A very good sign that you're crazy is an inability to ask the question, 'Am I crazy?'''

Robert is, in fact, an expert on the subject. After displaying mathematical genius in his early twenties, his career had been cut short by a debilitating mental illness. This is a man who, after rocking the math world with his proofs, began attempting to decipher the Dewey decimal codes of library books because he was convinced that they held hidden secret messages. Consequently, Catherine is wary of accepting the insights of a certified crazy person. It is not until midway through this first scene that the audience discovers that Richard is actually dead and that the action playing out in front of them is only a figment of Catherine's imagination, calling into question her sanity. As a result, from the outset, the audience itself is forced to ask the question: What is true and what is not—and how do you prove the conclusions arrived at?

This theme is carried throughout the play as Auburn compels the audience to keep wondering what the truth is. There is a particularly poignant scene near the end of act 2 when Robert makes another appearance, this time in a flashback. After suffering through years of mental illness, he has experienced months of clarity. His recovery has been so significant that Catherine, who had given up pursuit of her own career in mathematics in order to care for him, was able to return to school. She pays a visit to her dad and finds him sitting outside in the freezing cold, working. He tells her that his "machinery," meaning his brain, is once again firing on all cylinders. He is exhilarated to the point of being overheated and has gone out into the December day in order to cool off. Trying to describe for his incredulous daughter the incredible feeling that he is experiencing, Robert tells her that it is not as if a light has suddenly turned on in his mind, but rather the whole "power grid" that has been activated after years of dormancy. "I'm back!" he tells her. "I'm back in touch with the source—the font, the— whatever the source of my creativity was all those years ago. I'm in contact with it again." She reads what he has been scribbling in his notebook and in an instant it becomes painfully clear that what has returned is not the spark of genius but insanity.

The play's most significant questions are raised about Catherine, who is the main focus of uncertainty. Has she inherited her father's genius? Does she suffer from the same mental illness that afflicted him? Have both the incandescent brilliance and the dark demons been passed from father to daughter? Again, unlike the world of mathematics, the answers to those questions are anything but clear-cut. It is part of Auburn's genius that he constructed a play guaranteed to hold the audience's interest by inserting the compelling elements of a mystery into what is, at its heart, the story of complex human relations. In an interview with Mel Gussow of the *New York Times*, Auburn notes that the genesis of this play can be traced to two ideas. One involved

writing about two sisters "quarreling over the legacy of something left behind by their father." The other had to do with someone whose parent suffered from mental illness and began to wonder whether she, too, might be starting to succumb to madness. To pull the audience along, Auburn tells Gussow that he wanted to use what Alfred Hitchcock referred to as a "Maguffin," or plot device involving an object of mysterious origin. In this case, Auburn chose to insert the discovery of a mathematical proof into the story. That proof, whose existence is revealed at the end of act 1, provokes two essential questions: Is it indeed a brilliant breakthrough and, if so, who produced it—Robert or, as she herself claims, Catherine?

The character asking those questions is Hal, a former student of Robert's who has gone on to become a mathematics professor. He also has had a romantic eye on Catherine for many years. The question of the proof's validity is relatively easy to solve. Writing about this play in *The Chronicle of Higher Education*, David Rockmore explains that this is fundamental to the concept of a proof. "Assuming that a person knows the language and has the background," writes Rockmore, "anyone could, in theory, check all of the steps and decide on the correctness of a proof, and any two persons would make the same judgment." Determining whether Catherine is the source of this brilliant piece of work, or is instead merely suffering from the same sort of insane delusions that afflicted her father, is a much more difficult task. As Rockmore, a professor of mathematics at Dartmouth College, observes, "In statements about life, proofs of similarly absolute certainty are difficult, if not impossible, to derive."

Consequently, Auburn does not wrap his play up into a neat and tidy package. In that sense, it mirrors life. As the play approaches the final curtain, Hal comes to believe that it was indeed Catherine who produced the proof. It is Catherine herself who keeps the mystery alive, telling Hal:

> You think you've figured something out? You run over here so pleased with yourself because you changed your mind. Now you're certain. You're so . . . *sloppy*. You don't know anything. The book, the math, the dates, the writing, all that stuff you decided with your buddies, it's just evidence. It doesn't finish the job. It doesn't prove anything.

That is the way life is. Very few things are completely provable beyond a shadow of doubt. But absent proof, there is always possibility. And so, it is entirely appropriate that this play ends on an optimistic note. There is the promise that Catherine is indeed every bit as brilliant a mathematician as her father. There is also the very real possibility that she will not be overtaken by madness and will instead be able to keep a firm grasp on reality. As the curtain falls with her and Hal sitting side by side, there is no proof positive that the two will find happiness and build a life together. There is, however, hope.

**Source:** Curt Guyette, Critical Essay on *Proof,* in *Drama for Students,* Thomson Gale, 2005.

### John Simon

*In the following excerpt, Simon heaps praise on* Proof, *saying all parts of the play "spell J-O-Y."*

Manhattan theater club does it again! David Auburn's *Proof* is what *Copenhagen* ought to be: a play about scientists whose science matters less than their humanity. Here, those of us who want their dramatic characters to be real people need not feel excluded. Robert, a world-famous mathematician who went crazy; Catherine, his mathematically brilliant but too-depressed-to-work daughter; Hal, a young math teacher going through Robert's hundred-plus confused notebooks: and Claire, Robert's older daughter and a successful actuary, are above all fascinating individuals. Robert isn't any less human even for being, through most of the play, dead. All four—whether loving, hating, encouraging or impeding one another—are intensely alive, complex, funny, human.

The very first scene in *Proof* is masterly: a birthday dialogue between father and daughter, in which Catherine, alive, is barely living, and her celebrated father is sparklingly trying to rouse her into action although he is (I hate to give it away but must) dead—Catherine's fantasy. Yet this mysterious, droll, and electrifying scene is really exposition in disguise: something generally a bore, but here so splendidly reconceived as to fascinate—as indeed all of *Proof* does.

So here we have Robert, the near-genius mathematician who went mad and eventually died, and Catherine, who gave up a potentially great mathematical career to look after him and, in the process, let herself run down, perhaps irreversibly. Here, too, is Claire, the narrowly practical daughter, who wants to save Catherine from what may be incipient madness by dragging her from Chicago to New York and supervising her life—benignly as she sees it, but horribly as Catherine does. And here is Hal,

revering Robert's work and secretly in love with Catherine, bumbling and bungling everything. Out of this curious quartet, Auburn creates emotionally and intellectually enveloping music.

The performances are perfect: Larry Bryggman's lovable but exasperating Robert; Johanna Day's officious yet well-meaning Claire: Ben Shenkman's clumsy but gradually maturing Hal. As for Mary-Louise Parker, her Catherine is a performance of genius. Is there another young actress as manifold, incisive, sexy, and effortlessly overpowering? Add to this Daniel Sullivan's superb direction and the classy production values (by John Lee Beatty, Jess Goldstein, and Pat Collins), and it all spells J-O-Y. Instead of taking up more time reading, you are urged to run and get your tickets immediately.

**Source:** John Simon, "*Proof* Positive," in *New York,* June 5, 2000, p. 106.

### Robert Brustein

*In the following excerpt, Brustein places* Proof *within the company of other recent one-word title plays and says it is "not exactly the brilliant debut that some have been claiming."*

*Proof,* which recently re-opened at the Walter Kerr Theatre after a run at the Manhattan Theatre Club, is the latest in a string of plays with one-word titles that represent the theater's belated tribute to the conceptual mind. Tom Stoppard probably started the whole fashion with *Arcadia,* a period comedy that features, among other things, dialogues on English gardening and Newtonian physics. But the trend has exploded in the last few years to include Yasmina Reza's *Art,* an argument provoked by a post-modern painting, Margaret Edson's *Wit,* an infirmity play surrounded by a frame of metaphysical poetry, and Michael Frayn's *Copenhagen,* a scientific discourse on the subject of quantum theory, indeterminacy, and atomic fission. These are the major examples of a genre with terse titles and prolix personae that has now managed to occupy the middle (or the middlebrow) ground of the Western stage.

I am still trying to figure out why this development leaves me somewhat less ecstatic than it does my critical colleagues. Obviously we should encourage anything that raises the intellectual level of our benighted theater; and it is also true that some of these plays (notably *Wit*) have a lot more going for them than mental pyrotechnics. Yet the danger of this kind of Cliffs Notes approach to playwriting is that the dramatist, simply by dropping names or equations, will feel relieved of the obligation to investigate the emotional and spiritual aspects of the material, and the spectator will leave the theater feeling a lot more intelligent than he actually is. ''Tell me where is fancy bred,'' Shakespeare wrote, ''Or in the heart or in the head.'' There is no doubt that this playwright, at least, located the seat of the imagination (which he called ''fancy'') in the non-cerebral parts of the human body.

*Proof* is David Auburn's first major production; and if it is not exactly the brilliant debut that some have been claiming, it certainly represents the work of a writer with a fairly decent grasp on his not terribly fanciful material. The ''proof'' of the title is a breakthrough mathematical equation regarding prime numbers, the authorship of which is a subject of dispute. Catherine (Mary-Louise Parker) is the daughter of an intermittently psychotic and recently deceased professor at the University of Chicago (Larry Bryggman), whose ghost comes to visit her from time to time. She has a fling with one of her father's graduate students (Ben Shenkman) after she finds him rifling through her father's notebooks. She is in conflict with her rather unimaginative sister (Johanna Day), who has come to sell the family house and move Catherine to New York. And when this relatively under-educated woman claims to be the author of the theorem in question (I am ruining what is intended to be a stunning first act revelation), there is some debate as to whether she is really treading in her father's demented footsteps.

We never learn the actual nature of the discovery, or why it constitutes such a great contribution to human knowledge. By his own admission, Auburn does not know or care much about mathematical theory. But what makes this play problematic is not its author's ignorance regarding prime numbers. It is the thinness of his plot. He runs out of material so quickly that, by the middle of the second act, the play jerks to a halt and starts running in place. *Proof* sometimes looks like a rather austere stage version of *Good Will Hunting,* insofar as it features a whiz kid central character who is also an *idiot savant.* But if *Good Will Hunting* was concerned with questions of class, *Proof* focuses on questions of gender—how ''Shakespeare's sister'' could have written all his plays if she hadn't been forced to shine unappreciated on the ocean floor, and so on.

David Auburn's writing may not be terribly electric or dynamic. But Daniel Sullivan's direction muffs the few opportunities that the playwright

*Mary-Louise Parker with her Tony award for* Proof

offers to hoist the action out of the quotidian. With its spectral visitations from the heroine's father and its non-linear treatment of time, *Proof* is, after all, something of a ghost story. But the production remains mired in domesticity. It is relentlessly realistic, with John Lee Beatty contributing another in his gallery of Edward Hopper brick structures, and Neil A. Mazzela's lighting failing to distinguish between the gritty present and the ethereal past.

Where the evening does prosper is in the acting, especially in Mary-Louise Parker's Catherine. I first saw this fine actress in 1988 playing Emily to Eric Stolz's George in the Lincoln Center production of *Our Town.* Young as she was at the time, she made it instantly clear that she was born for the stage, a promise that she confirmed nine years later playing L'il Bit in *How I Learned to Drive.* Here she turns the twenty-eight-year-old Catherine into a restless, angry ragdoll of a woman with a frazzled slouch, who manages to accomplish one of the speediest costume changes in recorded history. (She goes up a whole flight of stairs, then appears seconds later on stage in a completely new set of rumpled clothes.) That she can also create such texture out of her underwritten role is an even more impressive feat of stage magic.

**Source:** Robert Brustein, "Or in the Heart or in the Head," in *New Republic,* September 13, 2000, pp. 28–29.

# SOURCES

Auburn, David, *Proof,* Faber and Faber, 2001.

Barbour, David, "*Proof* Positive" in *Entertainment Design,* Vol. 43, November 2000, p. 19.

Brustein, Robert, Review of *Proof,* in the *New Republic,* November 13, 2000, pp. 28–29.

Clark, John, "So Smart It Hurts," in *Los Angeles Times,* December 16, 2001.

Foster, John Evan, Review of *Proof,* in *Theatre Journal,* Vol. 53, No. 3, October 2001, Performance Review Sec., pp. 503–04.

Gussow, Mel, "With Math, a Playwright Explores a Family in Stress," in the *New York Times,* May 29, 2000, Sec. E, Col. 2, p. 1.

Hoffler, Robert, Review of *Proof,* in *Variety,* Vol. 380, No. 11, October 30, 2000, p. 34.

Melton, Robert W., Review of *Proof,* in *Library Journal,* April 1, 2001, p. 100.

Nasar, Sylvia, *A Beautiful Mind,* Simon & Schuster, 1998.

Poincaré, Henri, "Mathematical Creation," in *The Creative Process: A Symposium,* edited by Brewster Ghiselin, New American Library, 1960, p. 40.

Rockmore, Daniel, "Uncertainty Is Certain in Mathematics and Life," in the *Chronicle of Higher Education,* June 23, 2000, Opinion & Arts Sec., p. 89.

Weber, Bruce, Review of *Proof,* in *New York Times,* May 24, 2000, p. B3.

———, Review of *Proof,* in *New York Times,* October 27, 2001.

———, "Science Finding a Home Onstage," in *New York Times,* June 2, 2000, p. B1.

# FURTHER READING

Billington, Michael, Review of *Proof,* in *Guardian,* May 16, 2002.

This review of the British production of *Proof* at London's Donmar Warehouse censures the playwright for not explaining what the crucial mathematical theory is. Billington calls this the weak point of the play.

Feingold, Michael, Review of *Proof,* in *Village Voice,* June 6, 2000.

A review that is generous in its praise. Feingold points out that Auburn has no interest in explaining the finer points of mathematics; it is simply a given that for three of the four characters, mathematics is something they love, and the play is more of a love story than anything else—love of mathematics, love of father and daughter, and the growing love of Hal and Catherine.

Heilpern, John, Review of *Proof,* in *New York Observer,* June 19, 2000, p. 5.

A laudatory review that praises the play's evocation of love between father and daughter, the fragility of life, and the discovery of love. The only flaw Heilpern sees is that the mystery of who wrote the proof is too easily resolved.

Parker, Christian, "A Conversation with David Auburn," in *Dramatist Magazine,* December 10, 2001.

In this interview, Auburn talks about how he became interested in writing plays and how his career developed.

# *Romeo and Juliet*

## WILLIAM SHAKESPEARE

## 1594

The exact year in which William Shakespeare wrote *Romeo and Juliet* is unknown, but it is definitely one of his earlier works, and one of only two tragedies written in the period from 1590 to 1595. The other tragedy, *Titus Andronicus* followed the conventions of Seneca and Marlowe, i.e., built around a single heroic figure, but *Romeo and Juliet* was innovatively different. The plot was based on a fourteenth-century Italian short story, or novella, written by Matteo Bandello, that included elements of history, tradition, romance, and fable. This story had been put into verse form in 1562 by British poet Arthur Brooke. In Shakespeare's hands, fashionable elements of Elizabethan drama were inserted, certain characters were magnified, and sensational scenes were added. In addition, Shakespeare surrounded the innocent lovers with the mature bawdiness of other characters. In truth, the play was experimental for its time, but it was well-received by contemporary audiences and remained popular through the centuries. For a long time, critics tended to downgrade *Romeo and Juliet* in comparison to Shakespeare's later tragedies. But in the twentieth century the play gained appreciation for its unique merits and became a standard of high school study and was produced in various media.

*Romeo and Juliet* is as much about hate as love. The play opens with a scene of conflict between the two feuding families and ends with their reconciliation. Nonetheless, the play is considered one of the greatest love stories of all time, complicated by the

interplay of fate and repeated misfortune in timing. The juxtaposition of light and dark, the injection of comic moments, and the beauty of the language of love further enhance the play and make it a classic for all time.

# AUTHOR BIOGRAPHY

William Shakespeare was born to John and Mary Arden Shakespeare in Stratford-on-Avon, in Warwickshire, England, on April 23, 1564 and died there fifty-two years later on April 23, 1616. This period was remarkable in British history in that it was both the time of the Renaissance and the Elizabethan age (1558–1603). Shakespeare received a good classical education as a child, but he did not go on to university studies. In 1582, at age eighteen, he married Anne Hathaway. A daughter, Susanna, was born to them in 1583, and twins, Hamnet and Judith, in 1585. Shakespeare went to London to become an actor and playwright in 1588, the same year that the British navy defeated the Spanish Armada. From 1592 to 1598 he devoted his talents mostly to chronicle histories (tragedies) and comedies, including *Romeo and Juliet*. In 1594, he had become associated with a successful theatrical troupe called the Lord Chamberlain's Men (later, under King James I, the King's Men), and was eventually a prime shareholder and the principal playwright. In 1599, this company built the Globe Theater. However, Shakespeare also gained popularity as a poet for works such as *Venus and Adonis* and *The Rape of Lucrece,* both written about his patron, the Earl of Southampton. A collection of Shakespeare's sonnets was not published until 1609, although his friends had been reading them for years. By 1597, Shakespeare was prosperous enough to buy a large, handsome home in the center of Stratford, and he was soon recognized as England's greatest dramatist. From 1601 to 1609, he wrote his great tragedies and romantic comedies. In 1610, he retired to Stratford-on-Avon, but he continued to write and produced four more plays until his death. In the four hundred years since, his reputation has not diminished. Although there is continued debate about whether he actually wrote all the plays and verse attributed to him, nothing has ever proven otherwise. Consequently, the appreciation of his talent and genius has grown such that he is generally considered the greatest playwright of all time.

# PLOT SUMMARY

## *Prologue to Act 1*

The prologue tells the audience that this story will be about two prominent families of Verona, Italy, whose ancient feud is erupting anew and that a ''pair of star-cross'd lovers'' from these families will end the violence by ending their own lives.

## *Act 1*

In scene 1, Capulet servants, Sampson and Gregory, and Montague servants, Abraham and Balthasar, start a street fight that is joined by Benvolio, a Montague relative, and Tybalt a Capulet relative. Escalus, the Prince of Verona, learns about the fight and angrily decrees a death penalty for anyone caught in further feuding. Benvolio finds Romeo and learns that Romeo is forlorn because the girl he loves, Rosaline, will not return his affection because she has chosen to remain chaste. Benvolio advises Romeo to move on with his life and look at other girls. Romeo, however, is quite sure that he cannot forget Rosaline.

Scene 2 opens with Lord Capulet being approached by Count Paris, a relative of Prince Escalus, about marrying Capulet's daughter, Juliet. Capulet thinks Juliet is too young to marry but agrees to let the two meet at a party he is hosting that night. By accident, Romeo and Benvolio find out about the party, and Benvolio encourages Romeo to crash the party with him.

It is in scene 3 that the audience meets the garrulous nurse and learns that Juliet is only 14 years old. Lady Capulet discusses the idea of marriage to Paris with Juliet, who has not yet given marriage any thought, but she obediently agrees to consider the match.

Scene 4 finds Mercutio, another relative of the prince, joining Romeo and Benvolio and other friends on their way to the party. Mercutio teases the lovesick Romeo by scoffing at love. As they reach the party, Romeo expresses a feeling of impending doom.

Scene 5 takes place at the Capulet's party where a disguised Romeo spies Juliet and falls instantly in love. Lady Capulet's nephew Tybalt discovers Romeo's presence but is prevented from attacking Romeo by Lord Capulet who does not want such a disturbance at his party. In a brief encounter with Romeo, Juliet too falls in love. Later, they each learn separately from the nurse the family identity of the other.

### Prologue to Act 2

The chorus dramatizes the complications faced by both Romeo and Juliet in their love for one another but predicts that passion will lend them the power needed to be together.

### Act 2

In a very short scene 1, Benvolio and Mercutio try to find Romeo, who has climbed a wall to hide in the Capulet orchard. His friends give up when Romeo will not respond to their calls.

Scene 2 is the famous balcony scene in which, ignoring the danger, Romeo hopes for a glimpse of Juliet outside her window. Romeo overhears Juliet talk about her love for him. He then approaches her, and, after declaring their love, the two decide to marry. Juliet promises to send Romeo a messenger in the morning to make plans for their wedding.

In scene 3, Romeo goes to see Friar Laurence to arrange the wedding. Friar Laurence agrees to marry the two in hopes that their union will end the feud.

In scene 4, Romeo meets his friends Mercutio and Benvolio, who are discussing a challenge sent by Tybalt to Romeo. Juliet's messenger, the nurse, arrives and speaks privately to Romeo. The wedding is set for later that day.

In scene 5, the nurse returns to Juliet and, after much teasing to exasperate the eager Juliet, she reveals her news. Juliet uses the excuse of going to confession to get to Friar Laurence's cell.

A tiny scene 6 accomplishes the wedding of Romeo and Juliet.

### Act 3

In scene 1, later that day, Benvolio and Mercutio encounter Tybalt and are already sparring with words when Romeo arrives. Tybalt attempts to provoke Romeo into a fight, but Romeo will not fight because, although unknown to the others, he and Tybalt are now relatives by marriage. Instead, Mercutio challenges Tybalt and is killed by a deceitful stab from Tybalt when Romeo tries to separate

*William Shakespeare*

them. Tybalt flees and Mercutio dies. Romeo is so enraged that he tracks down Tybalt and kills him. Benvolio urges Romeo to flee. Just then, Escalus arrives and banishes Romeo from Verona.

In scene 2, the nurse tells Juliet that Romeo has killed Tybalt. Despite her intense grief over Tybalt, Juliet's love for Romeo wins out, and she asks the nurse to find Romeo.

Scene 3 finds Romeo in Friar Laurence's cell. Romeo learns of the banishment order and almost commits suicide when he realizes he may not be able to see Juliet again. However, the nurse's arrival and the friar's confidence that the crisis will blow over if Romeo will just hide out in Mantua for a while encourages Romeo to go see Juliet.

A brief scene 4 finds Capulet deciding that marrying Paris will soothe what Capulet assumes is Juliet's grief over Tybalt's death. Capulet sets the wedding for three days away and instructs his wife to tell Juliet.

Scene 5 takes place at dawn after Romeo and Juliet have spent the night together. Just after their heart-wrenching farewell, Juliet's mother arrives and tells Juliet that she is to marry Paris. Juliet refuses, and a terrible fight with her parents ensues.

The nurse counsels Juliet to forget Romeo and marry Paris. Feeling betrayed by all, Juliet makes another excuse to see Friar Laurence.

## Act 4

Scene 1 is back at Friar Laurence's, where he tells Juliet to take a potion that will cause her to appear dead until Romeo can come to rescue her and take her away with him to Mantua.

In scene 2, Juliet claims that she has repented of her disobedience and agrees to marry Paris. Lord Capulet is so pleased, he moves up the wedding to the next morning.

Scene 3 finds Juliet asking the nurse to leave her alone that night. She then worries about trusting the friar, but she takes the potion anyway.

Scene 4 shows the whole Capulet household working through the night to prepare for the wedding.

In scene 5, the nurse finds Juliet apparently dead. The wedding preparations are changed to those of a funeral.

## Act 5

Scene 1 takes place in Mantua as Romeo's servant Balthasar arrives, bringing the news of Juliet's death. Romeo decides to risk his own life by returning immediately to Verona. He buys poison from an apothecary with the intent of dying beside Juliet.

In scene 2, Friar Laurence learns that his letter to Romeo explaining Juliet's deception was not received. His messenger, Friar John, was confined by quarantine. Friar Laurence sends another letter to Mantua and heads off to the Capulet burial chamber to be there when Juliet awakens.

In the final scene, Paris goes to Juliet's tomb to mourn her but finds Romeo there and assumes that, as a Montague, Romeo is desecrating Juliet's grave. A fight ensues and Paris is killed. Romeo places him beside Juliet, then takes the poison, kisses Juliet, and dies. Friar Laurence finally arrives, but Juliet awakens and sees Romeo. Upon hearing noises, Friar Laurence runs away, but Juliet will not leave. Juliet kisses Romeo, stabs herself, and dies. The arriving guards find the bodies, send for the prince, and discover the friar in hiding. The prince, the Capulets and the Montagues all arrive, and Balthasar, Paris's page, and Friar Laurence explain everything. Escalus confronts the two families with the results of their feud and the two lords reconcile

with promises to build gold statues to each other's lost child. The play concludes with the prince's declaration:

> For never was there a story of more woe
>
> Than this of Juliet and her Romeo.

# CHARACTERS

## Abraham

A Montague servant, Abraham and Balthasar are the opponents to Sampson and Gregory in the opening fight scene.

## The Apothecary

The apothecary's appearance is brief but critical. It is his poverty that forces him to violate the law and his own morals in selling Romeo the poison that he will use in suicide.

## Balthasar

Romeo's servant Balthasar brings the mistaken news to Romeo that Juliet is dead. He also witnesses the fight between Paris and Romeo and then Romeo's suicide. It is then Balthasar who verifies Friar Laurence's explanation to the prince.

## Juliet Capulet

The daughter of Lord and Lady Capulet, Juliet is in love with Romeo. Just entering her teenage years, she is an innocent girl with a practical nature and remarkable strength who is willing to go to great lengths, even defying her parents and faking her own death, to be with Romeo. Although Juliet is willing to consider Paris's proposal, once she meets Romeo at the Capulet party, her heart is set only for him. Nonetheless, she is wary enough to suspect his intentions since he is a Montague, a family enemy. She thus requires that he marry her to prove his sincerity. Her love for Romeo is strong enough to forgive him for killing her cousin Tybalt and to chance the friar's risky plan to avoid marrying Paris. Juliet also shows a new maturity in being able to recognize the nurse's betrayal and to break their strong bond as well as that with her parents. Although suicide is always a negative choice, for Juliet it is a final demonstration of the strength and commitment of her love for Romeo.

## Lady Capulet

As Juliet's mother, Lady Capulet tries to keep peace in the family by attempting to convince Juliet to marry her father's choice of a husband for her.

# MEDIA ADAPTATIONS

- An audiocassette of *Romeo and Juliet* was made by Caedmon Audio in 1996 and features Claire Bloom and Albert Finney.

- A film version of *Romeo and Juliet* (1936) was released in black and white, starring Norma Shearer and Leslie Howard and directed by George Cukor. It is available on VHS from Warner Studios.

- A color film version of *Romeo and Juliet* (1956) starring Lawrence Harvey was made available on video in 1997 by Hallmark Entertainment. It was also released on video by MGM/UA in 2000.

- Kultur Video released a 1966 filming of Prokofiev's ballet version as performed by Rudolf Nureyev, Margot Fonteyn, and the Royal Ballet. It is available on both VHS and DVD.

- The 1968 blockbuster version directed by Franco Zeffirelli and starring Olivia Hussey and Leonard Whiting is available on video from Paramount Studios.

- A BBC and Time-Life Film production of *Romeo and Juliet* was part of a BBC series on The Shakespeare Plays in 1978. Digitally remastered for DVD in 2001, it is distributed by Ambrose Video Publishing.

- A 1996 film version, using Shakespeare's language in a modern update and starring Leonardo DiCaprio and Claire Danes, is available on video from Fox Home Entertainment.

---

We learn that she married and gave birth at Juliet's age. However, she is not close to Juliet and relies on the nurse to be a surrogate mother.

### Lord Capulet

Lord Capulet is a paradoxical character who can be the perfect genial host in public but a tyrannical father when he thinks his authority is questioned. He loves his daughter very much but makes the classic parental mistake of trying to force her to do something because he thinks it is best for her. His decision to move up the wedding of Juliet and Paris is the catalyst for the complications that result in his daughter's death.

### The Chorus

The chorus is actually a single character functioning as the narrator who reveals the plot to the audience.

### Prince Escalus

As ruler of Verona, Prince Escalus is intent on stopping the feud between the Montagues and the Capulets and bringing peace to the streets of his city. He issues a warning that the offense of fighting between members of the two houses will be punished by death, but when Romeo kills Tybalt the prince orders only banishment. When the feud results in the deaths of Romeo and Juliet, the prince tells their families that they are to blame, but he also blames himself for being unable to stop the feuding in time.

### Gregory

A servant of the house of Capulet, Gregory and fellow Capulet servant Sampson show that the Montague-Capulet feud extends to the servants when they pick a fight with the opposing family in the opening scene of the play.

### Friar John

A minor character, Friar John is the messenger who gets quarantined and thus fails to get the message to Romeo from Friar Laurence that Juliet is only asleep and not dead.

### Friar Laurence

A well-meaning priest and expert in herbal medicines, Friar Laurence is Romeo and Juliet's confidant. His role is to be the advocate of moderation and the problem-solver. He marries Romeo and Juliet in hopes of ending the feud between their families through their love. However, it is his plan to help Juliet escape to be with Romeo in exile that backfires and leads to the deaths of the young pair. He confesses his guilt to the prince at the end of the play and is forgiven for his participation in the tragedy.

### Mercutio

Another kinsman of Prince Escalus, Mercutio is Romeo's intensely witty, satirical, and imaginative friend. It is Mercutio who gives the famous speech about Queen Mab and who teases Romeo relentlessly. He is a scene-stealing character whose puns, such as "ask for me tomorrow, and you shall find me a grave man" in reference to his own death, are memorable. He is mortally wounded in a swordfight with Tybalt but does not die until he has called for a plague on the houses of Montague and Capulet. For those who see the action of this play as determined by fate, this curse is the determining factor. It is in revenge for Mercutio's death that Romeo kills Tybalt and is thus forced to leave Verona and Juliet.

### Benvolio Montague

Benvolio is Romeo's cousin and good friend. His calm, thoughtful demeanor is a foil to the character of Romeo's other good friend, Mercutio. Benvolio's role, though relatively small, has some key moments. It is Benvolio who discovers the reason for Romeo's melancholy and then encourages him to go to the Capulet party where Romeo meets Juliet. It is Benvolio who tells Romeo that Mercutio is dead and then urges Romeo to run away after Romeo has killed Tybalt.

### Lady Montague

Lady Montague appears only at the beginning of the play to express worry about Romeo's melancholy and later is reported to have died of grief when her son is banished from Verona.

### Lord Montague

Romeo's father, Lord Montague, makes only slight appearances in the play, but it is evident that he has loving concern for his only son. At the end, he and Lord Capulet end their feud and pledge to build gold statues to each other's dead child.

### Romeo Montague

Romeo's relationship with Juliet, the daughter of a rival family, is the center of the drama. The teenage son of Lord and Lady Montague, Romeo seems an overly sensitive lovesick boy at first. His behavior vacillates between extremes of joy and despair, love and hatred. The speed with which he forgets his infatuation with Rosaline and falls in love with Juliet may seem fickle, but it may also indicate a maturing from a silly crush to a commitment in true love. Romeo's soliloquy beneath Juliet's balcony is one of the most often quoted lines from a play:

> But, soft! What light through yonder window breaks?
>
> It is the east, and Juliet is the sun.

The depth and fluctuation of his feelings is evident in his resolve not to fight with Juliet's cousin Tybalt, out of love for her, and his rage that leads him to kill Tybalt, out of loyalty and affection for his friend Mercutio. Romeo marries Juliet to prove the sincerity of his love, but he must leave her when he is banished for killing Tybalt. He almost takes his life in despair over being separated from Juliet but is convinced by his good friend, Friar Laurence, to let time heal their problem. However, time is an enemy to the couple throughout the play, and when Romeo thinks Juliet is dead, he once again determines to take his own life. In trying to reach Juliet's tomb to commit this act, he encounters and is forced to kill Paris. In his rush of passion, Romeo dies before he can be told that Juliet is still alive. His death then causes Juliet to commit suicide also. Although their deaths are tragic, they have the effect of ending the feud between their families.

### Nurse

The nurse is a comic and vulgar figure in the play whose lewd remarks and long-winded speeches provide a break in the tension of the tragedy. More of a mother to Juliet than Juliet's mother, the nurse has reared Juliet and loves her to the point of being willing to do anything to make Juliet happy. Consequently, she is willing to be the go-between for Romeo and Juliet and to help them get married and have a wedding night. However, her more physical than emotional interest in love leaves her unable to understand Juliet's willingness to endanger herself for Romeo. To the nurse, it is better for Juliet to drop a relationship that is difficult to maintain and marry into a soft life with Paris. This advice seems a betrayal to Juliet and forces her to seek out a desperate plan to escape rather than confide in her closest advocate. Like everyone else at the end of the play, the nurse must face failure and grief.

### Count Paris

A kinsman of Prince Escalus, Paris is Juliet's suitor. Lord Capulet approves of and promotes the match. Paris is a true gentleman who loves Juliet and has no idea that he is in the middle of two lovers. On a visit to Juliet's tomb, he mistakes Romeo for someone who is trying to desecrate her grave. In the ensuing fight, Paris is killed by Romeo who grants Paris's last wish to be buried next to Juliet.

### Peter

Peter is the nurse's servant who carries messages and run errands.

### Rosaline

Although Rosaline does not actually appear in the play, she is the reason for Romeo's initial lovesickness. Further, it is only because he hopes to see Rosaline that Romeo agrees to go to the Capulet party where the pivotal moment occurs when he meets Juliet.

### Sampson

A Capulet servant, it is Sampson and his fellow servant Gregory who open the play by picking a fight with some servants of the Montague family.

### Tybalt

A nephew of Lady Capulet, Tybalt is Juliet's hot-tempered cousin who is the most hateful towards the Montagues. When he spies Romeo at the Capulet party, only Lord Capulet's stern restraint prevents Tybalt from attacking Romeo. Later, still feeling insulted but unable to goad Romeo into fighting, Tybalt provokes Mercutio and kills him. Then, in rage of revenge, Romeo forgets that Tybalt has become a relative by marriage and kills him. It is Juliet's grief apparently over Tybalt's death that gives her father the excuse to bring joy to the house with a wedding for Juliet and Paris. This turn of events precipitates the tragic plan of faked death that leads to the suicides of both Romeo and Juliet.

## THEMES

### *The Power and Passion of Love and Hate*

Although *Romeo and Juliet* is considered one of the world's greatest love stories, it can be argued that the love story is only a vehicle for the resolution of the story about hate, that is, the feud between the two families. After all, the story starts with a street fight between Montague and Capulet servants and ends with a peace agreement between the two lords. The power of hate is illustrated in the first scene by the exhibition of enmity between servants of the two families. The extent of the hatred has grown from the family itself to its servants. The power of love is seen, of course, in the determination of Romeo and Juliet to defy their families and be together. They love their parents, but the hate between the families causes the young couple to hate those who would keep them apart. The passion of Tybalt's hate is seen in his inability to forget about the party crashing. Even though his uncle talks him out of a fight that night, the next morning he sends a challenge to Romeo's house. Romeo's love for Juliet prevents him from quarrelling with Tybalt because he does not want to fight with his beloved's cousin, who has become his cousin by marriage. But his love for his friend Mercutio is powerful enough to turn into a rage of hateful revenge, so Romeo attacks Tybalt for killing Mercutio. For Juliet, the death of her cousin is a test of her love for Romeo. Which is stronger: her love for her family or for Romeo? As it turns out, her love for Romeo is strong enough to allow her to forgive him for his terrible deed, to choose her family by marriage, her husband, over her blood family. Juliet's love is further tested when she has to overcome her doubts about the trustworthiness of Friar Laurence and her fear of taking the potion. Again, her love is strong enough to risk everything. Romeo's love is strong enough to risk the Prince's punishment to get to Juliet's tomb. Both have love strong enough to be willing to die for the other, and they do. Thus, the whole play is a clash of passionate love and passionate hate, each strong enough to cause tragedy.

### *The Individual versus Society*

A standard type of plot conflict, the individual against society, applies in *Romeo and Juliet* because the young couple is pitted against social and public institutions that are barriers to their relationship. First, of course, is the barrier of family, not only

# TOPICS FOR FURTHER STUDY

- Romeo and Juliet is a story that ends with the suicides of the two teenage lovers. Research the extent of the problem with teenage suicide in the early 2000s and provide a list of resources for those seeking help.

- Juliet's parents try to arrange a marriage for her. What cultures in the 2000s still follow the practice of arranged marriages?

- An important element in the story of Romeo and Juliet is the sword fights. In the early 2000s, sword fighting is known as the sport of fencing and is an Olympic event. Find out more about this sport and report on its modern practice and events.

- Could the tragic ending of *Romeo and Juliet* have been prevented? Cite some instances where a different action or turn of events might have saved the young couple. What would you have done in their place?

- Compare the tragedies of ancient Greek theater to those of Shakespeare. What are the differences and similarities? Specifically, what was new about *Romeo and Juliet* for a tragedy in its time period?

- Compare *West Side Story* to *Romeo and Juliet*. Match up the characters and the story lines. Comment on how Shakespeare's story has translated into a modern setting and conflict.

---

because Romeo and Juliet are from feuding houses, but also because Juliet's father has decreed that she will marry someone else. In Juliet's society, the father, as head of the household, has absolute power. Disobeying him means not only a breach within her family, but a breach of the social fabric that guides family structure in the culture. In fear of dire consequences, Romeo and Juliet have to marry in secret. They have to keep that secret from family and friends. Except for Friar Laurence, they have no one to rely on but each other. Even Juliet's devoted nurse turns on her and leaves her to make the biggest decisions of her life on her own. Finally, after Romeo is banished by the prince, even the local government is involved in keeping the pair apart.

## *The Problem of Time*

While lousy timing fits into the theme of the action being determined by twists of fate, it is not just rotten luck that affects time in *Romeo and Juliet*. The chronology of the play is a rush of time. Romeo and Juliet are married the day after they meet. Romeo kills Juliet's cousin the same day and is banished from Verona only a day after the prince has first announced his intent to severely punish anyone caught fighting because of the Capulet/ Montague feud. The couple has only one night of honeymoon before Romeo must run away, as Friar Laurence says,

> till we can find a time
>
> to blaze your marriage, reconcile your friends,
>
> Beg pardon of the Prince, and call thee back.

When Friar Laurence devises his plan to rescue Juliet, he needs time to get a message to Romeo, but that time is taken away when Lord Capulet moves up the date for Juliet's wedding to Paris. That change might not have been ruinous if Friar John had not been delayed on his way to find Romeo. There is so little time that the Capulet household stays up all night to prepare for the wedding that turns out to be Juliet's funeral. If only Friar Laurence had made it to the tomb in time, he might have been able to prevent Romeo from killing Paris and/or himself, which would have prevented Juliet from killing herself. But time is against them.

## *Fate and Forebodings*

Elizabethans expected a tragedy to rest upon a twist of fate. Although Shakespeare made *Romeo and Juliet* more complicated than that, there are certainly numerous references to fate in the play, perhaps as a concession to the audience's expectations. The play opens with a reference to "star-crossed lovers" as if their fates are predetermined by their astrological signs. On the way to the Capulet party, Romeo has a sense that something will happen at the ball that will lead to doom. Later, with his dying breath, Mercutio calls a curse upon the feuding families: "A plague on both your houses!" Then Romeo says, after killing Tybalt, that he is "fortune's fool." When Romeo thinks that Juliet is dead, he tells the stars that he will defy them, as if he knows that fate wants to keep them apart, so he will win by joining Juliet in death. All the accidents of timing in the play seem to be fate working against the young lovers for the Elizabethan audience did not see these incidents as coincidences but rather as the hand of fate directing the action.

# STYLE

## *Light and Dark Polarity Motif*

A motif is a recurring element such as an incident, formulaic structure, or device that can help to develop and inform the text's major themes. A visual motif used in *Romeo and Juliet* is the contrast of light and dark, but in a sensory way, rather than in the sense of good and evil. For example, Romeo's balcony speech depicts Juliet as the sun that banishes the envious moon and turns night into day. In like manner, the morning after their wedding, they both try to delay Romeo's departure by pretending that it is still night, knowing that "More light and light, more dark and dark our woes." Ultimately, because the light of their love is not allowed to burn brightly, they both choose the darkness of death.

## *Shakespearean Tragedy*

A Greek tragedy has one central heroic, but flawed, figure. *Romeo and Juliet* had two central characters, and neither is presented as having the characteristics of a classical hero. Prior to Shakespeare, Elizabethans used a twist of fate as the single causative factor for the tragic ending. Shakespeare, however, devised more complicated causes stemming from character traits and motives. Another difference between the Greek and Shakespearean tragedies is the use of irony. In a Greek play, the audience is aware of the irony that the hero does not see. The chorus exists to advise the audience about what to expect. For example, the audience knows the secret of the parentage of Oedipus,

but Oedipus does not and proceeds to marry his mother. Although Shakespeare uses a chorus in *Romeo and Juliet,* only the basic plot and ending were revealed, not how the drama is to unfold. Shakespeare allows the audience to discover the irony for themselves.

## *Use of a Chorus*

Acts 1 and 2 only are introduced by the chorus, a lone actor who serves as a narrator for the play. The speech of the chorus is written in the form of a sonnet with an ending couplet. Shakespeare's prologue to *Romeo and Juliet* follows the Greek pattern of letting the audience know from the start how things are going to end. Otherwise, Shakespeare deviates from the Greek model by not revealing any of the irony or complexity of the tragedy, instead leaving that to the audience's own interpretation. The prologue of the second act assures the audience that Romeo's old feelings for Rosaline are gone and that he and Juliet now love each other. The chorus points out that although the couple has little opportunity to interact, their passion gives them the power and the ingenuity to get together. In other words, where there's a will there's a way if powered by love.

## *Blank Verse*

The normal form of speech in Shakespearean drama is blank, or unrhymed, verse. This form of verse works well for all scenes and persons whose appeal is mainly to the emotions of the spectator or reader. Each unrhymed line has five stresses; however, Shakespeare subtly varied the stresses, as well as rhythms, pauses, and tones in order to convey different moods and even the personal peculiarities of a character.

## *Rhymed Verse*

In the early plays, such as *Romeo and Juliet*, Shakespeare used quite a bit of rhymed verse in five-stress lines, usually in couplets. The prologues to Acts 1 and 2 end in a couplet, as does the play itself. Couplets also often come at the end of a scene or episode to signal changes to those behind the stage. In the process, the couplet achieves an aesthetic end to the dialogue and signals a change in action to the audience even before the actors leave the stage (e.g., act 1, scene 2, Romeo says, "I'll go along, no such sight to be shown, But to rejoice in splendour of mine own"). After a passage of blank verse or prose, rhymed verse could also have the effect of stiffening the dialogue and heightening the emotion. When Romeo and Juliet first meet, their dialogue becomes a sonnet, thus emphasizing the rise of their emotions. Shakespeare cleverly used rhymed verse for another effect—that of contrast—by having one character talk in blank verse while another uses rhymed verse.

### Prose

The use of prose in a play that is mainly in verse has the effect of lowering the emotional level and quickening the pace of the play. Prose speech works best for passages of comedy and as the speech of the lower or more comic characters (e.g., the opening dialogue between Sampson and Gregory).

## HISTORICAL CONTEXT

### The Renaissance

Both the story of *Romeo and Juliet* and Shakespeare's life take place during the Renaissance, a period that begins in the fourteenth century and extends into the seventeenth century. The term renaissance means rebirth and refers to the revival of an interest in the classical cultures of Greece and Rome. However, there are many social, political, and intellectual transformations that comprised the Renaissance. As the influence of the Roman Catholic Church and the Holy Roman Empire waned with their inability to maintain stability and unity among the Europeans, the feudal structure broke up and the power shifted to nations that were developing their own monarchies and language. Also of great importance were city-states (e.g., Florence, Italy, as controlled by the infamous Medici family and perhaps fictional Verona as ruled by Prince Escalus). Many details in *Romeo and Juliet* connect it to Italian Literature with which Shakespeare was familiar. One parallel is Pyramus and Thisbe (Ovid). More immediate, Shakespeare probably based his play on the Italian version by Luigi da Porto who sets the tale of Romeo and Juliet in Verona (1530).

During the sixteenth century, ancient Greek and Roman literature was rediscovered, translated, and then widely read. The classical writers focused on the human condition; they explored human nature and asserted some valuable insights about what causes human suffering and what works to establish social order. These ideas, along with many others, converged as a philosophy called humanism. It was

in the broadest sense a focus on human beings as opposed to a focus on the supernatural. Renaissance writers such as Shakespeare were well-read in classical literature and were influenced by it. In one sense, *Romeo and Juliet* dramatizes how an inherited feud coupled with impetuosity can disrupt the state and ruin good people's lives. The play shows that passion can be disruptive, dangerous, and destructive, and yet ironically it also expresses love and grief. Through the loss of these two young lovers, the feuding families find reconciliation, and order in the community is reestablished. This examination of the human scene is an example of humanism with clear connections to classical handling of tragedy, as in *Oedipus* by Sophocles and *Pyramus and Thisbe* by Ovid.

### Elizabethan and Jacobean Literature

By the time Shakespeare was born, Elizabeth I was already on the throne. Her long and influential reign from 1558 to 1603 defined the era. As a playwright, Shakespeare was fortunate to write in a time when the arts were supported by patrons and his English contemporaries included Ben Jonson, Sir Walter Raleigh, Christopher Marlowe, Robert Southwell, Thomas Campion, Edmund Spenser, Sir Philip Sidney, John Lyly, and Michael Drayton, all important writers, critics, and celebrities of the Elizabethan Age whose reputations have lasted into modern times. There are numerous and diverse distinguishing characteristics of Elizabethan literature. This name is strictly a time division in honor of one of England's greatest rulers. However, it is a time in which the poetry of the sonnet, the Spenserian stanza, and dramatic blank verse were very popular. It is unquestionably a golden age for drama. In the area of prose, this era produced historical chronicles, pamphlets, and literary criticism as the first novels began to appear. The tone of literature seemed more darkly questioning during the reign of James I as writers explored the problem of evil. This was the time in which Shakespeare produced his greatest tragedies. His theatre company enjoyed a cordial relationship with the court where the popularity of the masque, an extravagant courtly entertainment, returned. Also during Jacobean times (Jacobean is the name of the period in which James I reigned in England), Jonson influenced comedy with an acid satire and poetry with a lucid and graceful style that was copied by a group of writers known as the Cavalier poets. Meantime, Francis Bacon and Robert Burton were making a name in prose literature with a tougher yet more flexible style. Jacobean literature was undoubtedly an important contribu-

# COMPARE & CONTRAST

- **1300s:** Chaucer receives great acclaim in his own lifetime (1343–1400) from both the British public and the royal court for writing the *Canterbury Tales* and other poetic works.

  **1590s:** Shakespeare starts his career in the London theaters and enjoys popular success from the beginning, even garnering the favor of Queen Elizabeth I.

  **Today:** Both Chaucer and Shakespeare are still considered to be geniuses of literature by people around the world, and their works are studied as part of the standard curriculum in most schools.

- **1300s:** The papacy leaves Rome and is located in Avignon, France from 1309 to 1377 because of political pressures from the French. The first rumblings of the Reformation are heard in England from John Wycliffe.

  **1590s:** The Reformation is in full swing. The conflicts between Protestants and Catholics are often violent, and European countries align according to Protestant or Catholic affiliation.

  **Today:** The world still struggles with religious conflicts. Protestants and Catholics have reached accord in many areas, except for some tension yet in Northern Ireland. However, Muslim extremists wage a holy war in many areas of the world, and some governments forbid religion entirely.

- **1300s:** In 1346, the Black Death kills almost a third of the people of Europe and Asia.

  **1590s:** Plague closes the theaters in 1593, and other such diseases pose a deadly threat. Elizabeth I barely survives small pox, and Shakespeare later succumbs to a mysterious fever.

  **Today:** The plague and small pox are virtually eliminated around the world. Other new contagious diseases such as the ebola virus and AIDS have arisen, but where modern medicine is available, the potential for an epidemic is minimized.

- **1300s:** Important innovations are the blast furnace, the standardization of shoe sizes in England, and, at the end of the century, the Dutch use of windmills.

  **1590s:** The first knitting machine is invented as well as the first flush toilet. Coal mining begins in Germany, and scientists begin to investigate magnetism and electricity.

  **Today:** Technology and computers are universal, and technology witnesses  advances occurring so quickly that some equipment is outdated within months of installation.

tion to the arts, but perhaps the greatest achievement of the age was the production of the King James version of the Bible in 1611.

# CRITICAL OVERVIEW

Even after four hundred years, literary criticism of Shakespeare's *Romeo and Juliet* and critical reviews of its productions are still being written. Nonetheless, the critical essays written through the centuries remained valid and illustrate how interpretation is affected by various literary movements. Oddly enough, Shakespeare's contemporaries did not review the plays, and other writers barely mentioned him well into the seventeenth century. At that time, Ben Jonson (1572–1637) was held in higher regard as a playwright. Also esteemed as a critic, Jonson considered Shakespeare a talented, but undisciplined writer, according to Augustus E. Ralli in his book on Shakespearean criticism. John Dryden, a seventeenth-century writer, was the first great Shakespearan critic. In his ''An Essay of Dramatic Poesy,'' Dryden compares Shakespeare and Jonson, saying that he admires Jonson but loves Shakespeare because ''when he describes anything, you more than see it, you feel it too.'' Even though he praised Shakespeare, Dryden also found he was ''many times flat, insipid, his comic wit degenerating into clenches, his serious swelling into bombast.''

Critics into the eighteenth century continued this view that Shakespeare had more natural ability than educated refinement. They discussed his artistic faults rather than his merits, unless they were pulling out those soliloquies and other passages that they thought could stand on their own out of context. In 1775, Elizabeth Griffin commented on the ample selection of ''poetical beauties'' in *Romeo and Juliet.* However, she found little for moral evaluation except the foolishness of a young couple embarking on plans of their own without the consent of their parents. Thus, Griffin was the first critic to lay the blame for the tragedy not on fate but on Romeo and Juliet.

Even more than Shakespeare, the eighteenth-century neoclassicists believed strictly in the unities of place, action, and time, which Aristotle explained in his *Poetics.* Thus, these critics thought the story of a play should take place in one setting; have a causally connected plot, each event causing the next one in line; and that all of these events should occur within one twenty-four hour day. Samuel Johnson, a moderate neoclassicist and the prime literary figure of his time, excused Shakespeare from these three unities. He found *Romeo and Juliet* to be one of Shakespeare's most pleasing dramas and found the plot varied, believable, and touching. He also thought Shakespeare correct to mix tragedy and comedy because real life is a mixture. Still, Johnson was one of those critics who felt that Shakespeare's work lacked sufficient moral emphasis. Ralli reports that Alexander Pope, another leading eighteenth-century writer and critic, theorized that Shakespeare's genius was dragged down by his involvement with actual theater production, implying that Shakespeare wrote to please the audiences instead of according to the structures of classical rhetoric.

Meanwhile, in Germany, August von Schlegel and others were finding *Romeo and Juliet* to be nearly perfect artistically. Schlegel said of this play: ''It was reserved for Shakespeare to unite purity of heart and the glow of imagination, sweetness and dignity of manners and passionate violence, in one ideal picture.'' Back in England, Samuel Taylor Coleridge, considered a great nineteenth-century Shakespearean critic, began to share the German view. Coleridge suspected that Shakespeare's irregularities were actually evidence of psychological and philosophical genius. William Hazlitt, another Shakespearean critic of the English Romantic movement, was also an admirer of Schlegel. Hazlitt attributed more depth to the love of Romeo and Juliet than previous critics who found their love shallow and sentimental. Following Hazlitt's lead, by the end of the eighteenth century, Shakespearean scholarship began examining the playwright's techniques of characterization.

In the nineteenth century, criticism associated Shakespeare's genius with many intellectual movements and religious theories. Suddenly, Shakespeare no longer had faults but presented intriguing problems for the astute scholar to explain. In the twentieth century, New Critical scholars searched for something new to say, focusing on minute textual details in order to come up with new theories or interpretations. It is to the credit of the Romantics, however, that they returned to a discussion of the sheer enjoyment of the plays that audiences experienced. In the early 2000s, Shakespeare's works continued to be read, performed, and critiqued by scholars around the world. After all this time, criticism had become a blend of schools of thought and argued interpretations based on new information found by researchers or new approaches connected to advancing theoretical understanding. Generally speaking, though, it is safe to say that Shakespeare is considered the greatest playwright of all time.

# CRITICISM

## *Lois Kerschen*

*Kerschen is a freelance writer and adjunct college English instructor. In this essay, Kerschen considers whether fate, the personal characteristics of Romeo and Juliet, or the demands of justice determine the outcome of the story.*

Whenever a tragedy occurs, people want to know what went wrong. They look for the causes, the reasons for the end result. With *Romeo and Juliet,* the opinions have varied as literary criticism has taken different viewpoints through the years. Since William Shakespeare named the play for the two central characters, the immediate reaction is to look

*Claire Danes and Leonardo DiCaprio in a 1996 film version of* Romeo and Juliet

at them for fault. However, Shakespeare is never that simple, so a deeper analysis is warranted.

The great German Shakespearean critic, August von Schlagel, blamed fate for the tragedy, but in the sense that the cruel world is too terrible a place for a love as tender as that of Romeo and Juliet. Instruction books such as Kelley Griffith's *Writing Essays about Literature* very matter-of-factly blame fate as well by telling students that "if the plot is only part of a larger or ongoing story, then the characters are more likely to seem at the mercy of forces beyond their control." Therefore, since the plot of *Romeo and Juliet* is actually only one episode of a long feud, the young couple, according to Griffith, "cannot escape the undertow of their families' history." Even the powerful prince cannot prevent the tragedy, although he tries, because Romeo and Juliet are identified by fate as "star-crossed" and "death-marked."

It must be noted that the family feud is the reason that Romeo and Juliet's relationship is a "forbidden love." It should also be noted that the play begins with a fight scene between servants of the two families and ends with a peace agreement between Lords Montague and Capulet. The family feud could then be seen as a bookend structure around the lovers' story. Shakespeare did not create

the story—he inherited it. The feud is part of the previous versions that he draws upon, in which the the feud serves as a complicating device that keeps the lovers apart. However, placing the feud first and last in the play, that is, in the most attention-getting spots for the audience, indicates that the feud is the most important facet of the story. Although this play is considered one of the greatest love stories of all time, viewed from another angle, it may be that it is a story about hate; a story that is the final episode of a long-running saga. The love affair of Romeo and Juliet may be only a device to bring about an end to the feud and show how terrible the consequences can be of such violent and vindictive behavior. As a result, the blame according to this theory can be placed with the demands of justice.

Further support for this interpretation is the realization that violence runs throughout the story, linking each event. Romeo meets Juliet at the Capulet party but his presence there fuels Tybalt's challenge to him the next day. That challenge leads to the deaths of Mercutio and Tybalt. That violence is the reason that Romeo is banished. His banishment leads to the risky ruse of Juliet's death, which leads to Romeo coming to Juliet's family tomb. There, the family feud causes Paris to assume that Romeo has evil intent and the resultant fight costs Paris his life.

# WHAT DO I READ NEXT?

- For those wanting an affordable, unabridged edition of all 37 plays and the sonnets, a good choice is *William Shakespeare: The Complete Works,* published by the Library of Literary Classics in 1990.

- *The Essential Shakespeare* has updated language for Shakespeare's greatest plays and a narrative guide. It was published in 2001 by Xlibris Corporation as part of its Essential Library series for the modern reader.

- Christopher Marlowe, a contemporary of Shakespeare, was also an outstanding playwright and the author of *Tamburlane* and *Dr. Faustus. A Preface to Marlowe* is an examination of his

plays and poetry. Written by Stevie Simkin, it was published by Longman in 2000.

- A modern-day musical version of *Romeo and Juliet* is *West Side Story.* Norris Houghton published a book with Laure Leaf in 1965 that compares the two hugely successful versions of the story.

- Shakespeare's *Romeo and Juliet* was a reworking of the poem "Romeus and Juliet" by British poet Arthur Brooke. In February of 2005, AMS Press was expected to publish a copy of this poem in *Brooke's "Romeus and Juliet": Being the Original of Shakespeare's "Romeo and Juliet,"* thus making this work newly available for comparison.

---

The entrapment and despair that the feud has precipitated next results in the death of both Romeo and Juliet. With these events in mind, it would be easy to see this play as being about the feud, not the lovers. After all, Juliet says, "My only love sprung from my only hate!"

Many studies of the play remark on the relationship of love and hate. Could Juliet's love spring from hate because they are both intense passions? A nineteenth-century German scholar, Hermann Ulrici, said that the love of Romeo and Juliet had an ideal beauty but was condemned from the beginning because of its "overpowering and reckless" passion that disturbs "the internal harmony of the moral powers." Ulrici concluded that Shakespeare brings balance back to the situation through the deaths of the couple and the end of the feud. Following this interpretation, Denton Snider, an American scholar, later agreed that Romeo and Juliet are destroyed by their own love. He said that, just as with the passion of hate, the intensity of love's passion blots out reason and self-control and leads to destructive behavior. Snider also thought that there was a moral justice involved in that the fire of love that consumes Romeo and Juliet is the

fire of sacrifice that is rewarded with peace between their families. Snider writes, "The lovers, Romeo and Juliet, die, but their death has in it for the living a redemption."

So, the argument comes back to the idea of justice. In 1905, American scholar Stopford Brooke wrote that the feud is the central event and cause of the tragedy and that the accord reached at the end was the goal of justice. Brooke counsels that discussions of fate as a determinant in the story would be more correct if the name "Justice" were given to fate.

While Brooke and others reject the mere happenstance of fate for the more intentioned aim of justice, the conclusion is still that outside forces bring Romeo and Juliet to their doom. Another slight turn of the viewpoint sees justice as a moral lesson. In this light, there is the unsympathetic view that Romeo and Juliet are foolish children who are inevitably headed toward ruin because they do not consult or gain the approval of their parents for their marriage. Once again, the sentiment is that passion leads to head-strong, reckless behavior such as a refusal to obey constituted authority (one's parents, one's ruler). This results in a disruption of hierarchical order, and the tragedy works to reestablish that order through loss and grief. One's attention is drawn to the two central figures, and a quite natural reaction is that Romeo and Juliet are impetuous kids. In that case, this story can be interpreted as having a more universal message about young love and not just about the two young lovers in the play. Undoubtedly, it is the universality of Shakespeare's dramas that has made them classics, so perhaps Shakespeare's intent was not just to tell a story, but to give an example. If the theme were not timeless, then Leonard Bernstein might not have taken the story and transformed it into *West Side Story*. There are foolish teenagers in every generation, and there is senseless feuding in every culture.

Although it has been suggested that the love of Romeo and Juliet was too ideal to survive in this imperfect world, it would seem a shame to think of true, passionate love inevitably leading to a bad result. Perhaps the problem is not with the intensity of the emotion, but the inability to control and direct that emotion in a positive way. If that is the case, then Romeo and Juliet are doomed, not by the fates, not by the judgment of justice, but by their own character flaws. Shakespeare may have altered the classic form of the Greek tragedy, but that does not mean that he totally ignored the Greek formula for the tragically flawed hero.

It can be said that part of Romeo's character flaw is that he believes in the fates and therefore feels powerless to help himself. He has a bad feeling that going to the party may lead to eventual doom, but he goes anyway. He surrenders himself to the guidance of the gods not just out of piety but perhaps because he shirks responsibility. Killing Tybalt is a rash act that needed not have happened if Romeo had been better able to control himself. Instead, Romeo succumbs to an irrational and violent reaction and then feels sorry for himself as ''fortune's fool'' who has been pushed by fate into committing the terrible deed.

Juliet's nature is more practical and cautious, but her innocence and the intensity of her love are her downfall. Moverover, she lives in a family where her father does not know how to express his love except to make decisions for Juliet that he thinks are in her best interest. Her mother is too cold and distant to give her good advice, and her nurse, though she loves Juliet, is too crude to understand the delicacies and dangers of first love. Consequently, Juliet is not chastised by the critics as much as Romeo for being rash. As a young girl practically

> PERHAPS THE PROBLEM IS NOT WITH THE INTENSITY OF THE EMOTION, BUT THE INABILITY TO CONTROL AND DIRECT THAT EMOTION IN A POSITIVE WAY. IF THAT IS THE CASE, THEN ROMEO AND JULIET ARE DOOMED, NOT BY THE FATES, NOT BY THE JUDGMENT OF JUSTICE, BUT BY THEIR OWN CHARACTER FLAWS.''

restricted to her house by the social customs of her time, she has very little control over anything anyway. Romeo, however, is older and has slightly more autonomy.

Is it fate, a need for justice, or the characters themselves who bring a tragic end to *Romeo and Juliet*? Can it be a combination of all these factors? They seem to be inextricably mixed, despite the efforts of the critics to separate them. Ben Jonson and many others have admitted to Shakespeare's genius, even though they found other faults in his work. Scholars have commented on the depth of Shakespeare's understanding of human nature and the psychological aspects of his plays. Is it not possible, then, the Shakespeare was smart enough and sensitive enough to have picked up on all the nuances of a human situation and been able to incorporate highly complex emotions and interactions in *Romeo and Juliet*? Shakespeare was aware of the conventions of his time and the expectations of his audience for certain elements of tragedy. But he was also innovative enough to blend some of the traditional aspects of tragedy with a much more intricate and multi-faceted dramatic structure that included an amazing depth of characterization. There is a reason that Shakespeare is considered the greatest dramatist of all time, and that reason may be that he was able, better than anyone else, to fill his plays with a richness that, four hundred years later, had scholars still mining its depths.

**Source:** Lois Kerschen, Critical Essay on *Romeo and Juliet*, in *Drama for Students,* Thomson Gale, 2005.

*Olivia Hussey and Leonard Whiting in a 1968 film version of* Romeo and Juliet

### Bryan Aubrey

*Aubrey holds a Ph.D. in English and has published many articles on Shakespeare. In this essay, Aubrey discusses two film versions of the play.*

*Romeo and Juliet* has always been one of Shakespeare's most frequently performed plays. However, since the late 1960s, many more people have become familiar with the play through movie versions than through live performances in a theater. Franco Zeffirelli's lush *Romeo and Juliet* (1968) has proved enduringly popular. In 1996, Baz Luhrmann's frenetic *William Shakespeare's Romeo + Juliet* was a big box-office hit for the Australian director.

The challenges faced by a director who wants to make a film of a Shakespeare play are immense. Not too long ago, Shakespearean purists rejected the very idea of filming Shakespeare. Shakespeare appeals to the ear, they said, whereas the cinema appeals to the eye, so there is a natural antipathy between the two forms. Film favors action, whereas in a Shakespeare play characters often give long speeches. These ''talking heads'' can be effective on stage, but filmgoers, conditioned by the conventions of the medium, become impatient or bored with them. The film director must therefore cut the

original text considerably. Zeffirelli's *Romeo and Juliet,* for example, contains only a third of the original text, and Zeffirelli was roundly criticized by some Shakespeare scholars for the drastic nature of the cuts, as well as for shifting lines within scenes and occasionally adding a line or half-line of dialogue. The critics complained that Shakespeare was not a hack screenwriter whose work could be chopped up and rearranged at will. But others noted that Zeffirelli had shown himself to be a master of his craft because he was able to compensate for the omitted text by recreating it visually.

Zeffirelli's stated intention was to popularize *Romeo and Juliet* by bringing it to a mass audience. With this goal in mind he decided to cast two young and unknown actors in the title roles. This was a break with tradition since Shakespeare's lovers were usually played by more experienced actors. In a 1936 film version, Norma Shearer, who was 36 years old, played Juliet, and Leslie Howard, 46 years old, played Romeo. In the play, Juliet is barely fourteen years old, and Romeo not much older. So, Zeffirelli chose Olivia Hussey, age fifteen, to play Juliet and Leonard Whiting, age seventeen, to play Romeo. Although older, more experienced actors might have been better able to deliver the lines, they would have found it hard to convey the extreme youth and innocence of the protagonists, which is central to the play and its repeated contrasts of youth and age.

Zeffirelli's film begins with a sober off-screen reading of the prologue by Sir Laurence Olivier as the camera pans across Verona as seen from high above. (Zeffirelli was a great admirer of Olivier's work and this was a deliberate reference to the opening of Olivier's 1944 film of Shakespeare's *Henry V.*) The film then cuts to a busy, noisy, market square, and a wealth of visual detail piles up as the camera pans. It is clear from the beginning that this will be a spectacular film, one in which the setting itself becomes—as Zeffirelli believed it should—like a character in the action.

Although Zeffirelli was forced to cut much of the text, he succeeded in creating visual images that effectively convey Shakespeare's verbal images and themes. This can be seen from two examples, the first of which comes right at the beginning of the film. When the two Capulet servants enter, the camera shows only their legs, clad in tights, and their crotches, which display prominent codpieces. This image replaces the aggressive sexual talk in this scene in the play. After the initial sword fight, the sword-wearing Tybalt enters in a similar codpiece-emphasizing shot. The audience is being invited to identify male sexual energy and pride with the violence that pervades the play.

Interestingly, Zeffirelli does not present Romeo in this way. Faithful to Shakespeare's text, his Romeo is more contemplative, even dreamy, and unwilling to fight until his friend Mercutio is killed. Then, he gets dragged into the cycle of violence. Feminist readings of *Romeo and Juliet* often emphasize this point, arguing that the tragedy results not from the workings of fate, which is the traditional view of the play, but because of the rigidity of the male-dominated social order that Romeo at first resists but that eventually overwhelms him.

The second example of how visual imagery can present verbal themes occurs at the Capulet ball, as Jack Jorgens notes in his book *Shakespeare on Film.* At first, the dancers form two separate circles. After Romeo has set eyes on Juliet and joined the dance, the dancers form two concentric circles, with Romeo in the outer circle and Juliet in the inner one. This might seem on the surface to be an image of harmony, but it should be noted that the circles are moving in opposite directions—a clear allusion to the theme in the play of the inextricable linking of the opposites of love and hate, unity and separation.

LEONARDO DICAPRIO, SELECTED FOR HIS APPEAL TO TEENAGERS, IS AN ADEQUATE, EVEN CHARMING ROMEO WHO SPEAKS THE VERSE REASONABLY WELL, BUT IT IS CLAIRE DANES'S JULIET WHO LEAVES THE DEEPER IMPRESSION."

Another highlight of Zeffirelli's film, and an example of how he makes up for textual cuts with visual treats, is the long duel sequence between Mercutio and Tybalt. This not only makes gripping cinema but also gives the director a chance to further characterize Mercutio and Tybalt. Killing Mercutio seems to have been the last thing on Tybalt's mind, and Mercutio's death is made even more poignant by the fact that right up to the end, his friends think it is just one more of his jokes.

The purists may have groaned at some of Zeffirelli's methods, but he was certainly vindicated at the box-office. The film became a worldwide success. It has been called a film for the 1960s, and indeed it did succeed in capturing the *zeitgeist* of those turbulent times of "flower power," sexual freedom, and anti-Vietnam war protests. The brief shot of the lovers nude anchors the film in that uninhibited sixties era, as does the very first shot of Romeo walking toward the camera carrying not a sword but a flower. "Make love not war," one of the slogans of the sixties counter-culture, is the subtext here.

If Zeffirelli's was a film for the sixties, Luhrmann's *William Shakespeare's Romeo + Juliet* was squarely aimed at the youth culture of the 1990s. The film begins (and also ends) with a shot of a small television in the middle of the darkened screen. On the television, a female news anchor reads the prologue as if it were a news item. This is a very different world than that revealed in the stately prologue read by Olivier in Zeffirelli's film. An off-screen male voice then repeats the prologue as a montage shows the main characters, and some of the words even appear on screen as well, as headlines in newspapers. The director clearly wants to ensure that the audience understands every word of the Shakespearean verse.

The film then leaps into the hot, combustible world of Verona Beach, with its feuding families and family-loyal gangs. Both the Capulets and Montagues appear to be gangland bosses dealing in real estate or construction, and their gun-toting minions, pumped up with testosterone, drive around town in convertibles, looking for trouble. The guns bear the brand name ''Sword,'' thus neatly making sense of the Shakespearean text when the mayhem breaks out.

The opening sequence sets the pace, the camera keeps moving, and it hardly lets up throughout the film. Nor does the soundtrack, a mix of pop and classical, in which hip-hop bands such as Garbage and Radiohead rub shoulders with Mozart and Wagner.

As a director, Luhrmann is inventive and willing to take risks, which give the film an admirable freshness. He certainly has some fun with the Capulets' ball, creating it as a fancy dress extravaganza in which Mercutio is a high-stepping drag queen, Lady Capulet a comic turn, and poor Juliet a winged beauty stuck with the eager but inane suitor Paris, whose picture is shown, in a nice touch of directorial wit, on the front cover of *Time* magazine as ''Bachelor of the Year.'' When Juliet escapes for a moment, she and Romeo gaze at each other through a fish tank.

Leonardo DiCaprio, selected for his appeal to teenagers, is an adequate, even charming Romeo who speaks the verse reasonably well, but it is Claire Danes's Juliet who leaves the deeper impression. She is a more mature, expressive and articulate Juliet than Olivia Hussey in the 1968 film. Her face registers a range of emotions with impressive subtlety. Danes conveys Juliet's practical nature, and she seems older than Romeo, even though this is not the case. DiCaprio's Romeo is a romantic and a dreamer. In both cases, this is quite true to Shakespeare's play.

Luhrmann also exercises his creativity in the traditional balcony scene, in which Romeo and Juliet first pledge their love. This Romeo, like every other Romeo for four hundred years, spies a light at the window and thinks he sees Juliet, but then who should poke her head out of the window but the disapproving Nurse. Meanwhile, Juliet just happens to be taking the elevator downstairs, and when the two finally meet face to face outside, she is so surprised she falls backwards into the swimming pool, taking Romeo with her. The scene that follows has all the innocent appeal that the text demands.

Like Zeffirelli, Luhrmann manages to convey Shakespeare's themes through some startling visual effects. In this all-action, quick-cutting movie, which was aimed at the supposedly short attention spans of teens, there are nonetheless two moments of utter stillness. The first is when the lovers are shown lying asleep together, and this foreshadows the moment they lie together in death at the end. The position of their bodies, with Juliet's right arm draped over Romeo's midriff, and both heads turned to the right, is almost exactly the same in both shots. As in the Shakespearean text, love and death are intimately, tragically, linked.

In the death scene, Luhrmann makes a dramatically effective innovation. Juliet shows signs of life several times as Romeo prepares to take the poison. He is looking elsewhere and fails to see her. Then, just as he downs the fatal mixture, Juliet wakes up fully, smiles and touches him on the cheek. It is too late, but Juliet utters her last speech, beginning ''What's here?'' while Romeo still lives, and he is still alive as she kisses him, hoping that some drop of poison is left on his lips that will dispatch her too. Romeo's final line, ''Thus with a kiss I die,'' is spoken to a conscious, anguished Juliet, about a kiss initiated by her, not, as in the text, by Romeo on the lips of a Juliet he believes to be dead.

In the cutting of the text, Luhrmann makes different decisions than Zeffirelli. Luhrmann gives more insight into Romeo's state of mind at the beginning of the film. As in Shakespeare's play, Romeo is stuck in love-sick melancholy, pining for a woman named Rosaline who apparently scorns him. This is omitted in Zeffirelli's film, with the result that some of Romeo's lines after he has met Juliet are deprived of their full meaning. Luhrmann includes the scene in which Romeo buys poison from an old apothecary (omitted in the Zeffirelli film, which does not explain how Romeo acquired the poison). Both films omit the incident at the end of the play where Romeo kills Paris, presumably because neither director wanted the hero to have too much blood on his hands. Neither filmmaker fully brings out the reconciliation of the families at the end, although this is clearly announced in the prologue.

But carping over inevitable textual cuts should not obscure the fact that both Zeffirelli and Luhrmann brought a freshness of vision to a four-hundred-year-old play, translated it into a new medium, and in each case won for Shakespeare's tragic story a new generation of enthusiastic admirers.

**Source:** Bryan Aubrey, Critical Essay on *Romeo and Juliet*, in *Drama for Students,* Thomson Gale, 2005.

### Douglas Dupler

*Dupler is a writer and has taught college English courses. In this essay, Dupler examines the concept of romantic love as it appears in one of the greatest love stories of all time.*

The main characters of *Romeo and Juliet* are young ''star-crossed'' lovers who experience a love that lifts them into ecstatic extremes of emotions for a few days and then leads them to a tragic ending. The idea of love that appears in this play, that a certain type of romantic love can make people willing and able to transcend boundaries and constraints, has lived in Western literature for many centuries. The power of this idea of love has fueled the imaginations of readers and theater audiences for generations. For Romeo and Juliet, this type of love pits them against their parents and against their society, against their friends and confidants, and creates conflict with their religious leader. Their love ultimately brings them the possibility of exile and then helps to bring about their death. At the same time, their experience of love gives each of them the strength and desire to pursue their love against the odds and makes them willing to die for love. Although the play happens in the span of less than one week, both main characters undergo much change. In the end, the death of the young couple heals a long-standing rift between their families. In this play, romantic love is portrayed in a way that reveals its power and complexity; this love is at once invigorating, destructive, transformative, and redemptive.

In the beginning of the play, Romeo is heartbroken over a young lady, Rosaline, who does not return his affection. He is gloomy and withdrawn and claims that he is sinking ''under love's heavy burden.'' Romeo at first describes love as a ''madness'' and as a ''smoke raised from the fume of sighs.'' Romeo's friends, who wish to see him lifted above his melancholy, urge him to stop philosophizing about his lost love and to seek another young lady as a new object of his affections. Benvolio urges Romeo to heal himself of love's despair by ''giving liberty unto thine eyes.'' Mercutio does the

same when he tells Romeo to lessen his sensitivity and to ''be rough with love.'' When Romeo meets Juliet, his vision of love changes profoundly. Later, Friar Laurence acknowledges this change when he remarks to Romeo that his feelings about Rosaline were for ''doting, not for loving.''

At the same time Romeo is dejected about unfulfilled love, Juliet, not quite fourteen years of age, is being urged by her nurse and her mother to consider marrying Count Paris. For both of these older women in Juliet's life, what matters most is a socially advantageous marriage, and this marriage is being arranged before Juliet has even seen her suitor. Juliet, however, seems to intuit that this type of pairing will not sustain her; she promises her guardians that she will view, but may not like, her arranged suitor. Already, for both Romeo and Juliet, there is a sense that there is a type of love that goes beyond the common, that is special and worth patience and suffering.

Then comes the scene in which Romeo sees Juliet for the first time. He is instantly enamored and entranced, and his melancholy and despair are quickly transformed. Not long before, Romeo had been speaking of Rosaline's charms but upon seeing Juliet, he claims he ''ne'er saw true beauty till this night.'' From the beginning, there is also something ephemeral and impractical about this love. Romeo sees a ''beauty too rich for use, for earth too dear.'' For Juliet, this sudden love is complicated as well, and she exclaims, ''My only love, sprung from my only hate.''

The romantic love between Romeo and Juliet occurs with a glance and enters them through their eyes. This is rich symbolism. First, romantic love in this way becomes individualized and has nothing to do with cultural constraints or the advice of mentors. This love seizes the couple with a recognition that seems to go beyond them. This ''passion lends a power'' that awakens each of them and energizes them. For Romeo, this awakening increases his sense of beauty and his feelings for the world as evidenced in his poetic declarations to Juliet. Romeo's language overflows with a sudden awareness of the beauty of the world and the new importance that has been added to his life. Romeo resolves that even ''stony limits cannot hold love out.'' In addition to the enticements of the attraction, each lover feels a danger in this type of loving. Romeo later states to Juliet that ''there lies more peril in thine eye'' than twenty swords, while Juliet worries that their love is ''too rash, too unadvised, too sudden.''

*Ralph Fiennes in an Open Air Theatre production of* Romeo and Juliet, *Regent's Park, London*

For Juliet, this new feeling strengthens her against the cultural forces that would deny her love and freedom. She pledges that she would "no longer be a Capulet" if such denial would be necessary to sustain her love. Juliet's new feelings of love awaken her to the difficulties of her situation as a young woman in her culture. It is a rough and male-dominated culture. From the beginning, minor characters bicker and threaten violence, with one serving man declaring that women are the "weaker vessels" and another one bragging about "cruelty to the maids." It is a world of long-standing feuds and quick aggression. The friar, or the religious authority, at one point refers to fear as "womanish" and tells Romeo that his tears, or his emotional feelings, are "womanish," implying a disrespect for both the feminine and for Romeo's romantic feelings. Theirs is a world where Juliet's kind of strength is not honored, as when Friar Laurence tells Romeo, "women may fall when there's no strength in men."

Juliet struggles to honor her feelings of love for Romeo. Her closest friend in the play, the nurse, argues against Juliet's love for Romeo and tries to convince her to consider the arranged marriage with Paris. The nurse tells Juliet, "you know not how to

choose a man," capitulating to the demands of male authority rather than to the demands of the feminine heart. Juliet also faces tremendous pressure from her parents, who will not allow her individuality and freedom when it comes to considering marriage. Her father uses despicable and shaming language when trying to force her to marry Paris. He threatens to exile her to the streets, calling her "unworthy," "a curse," and a "disobedient wretch." In keeping with the patriarchal arrangment of power, Juliet's father treats Paris with respect and deference. Later, Capulet denigrates Juliet's freedom of choice by referring to it as a "peevish self-willed harlotry." Knowing her place in this society, Juliet's mother refuses to make a stand for her daughter's freedom, pressuring her to accept her father's demands. Juliet despairs over this outward pressure, wondering why fate was so hard on "so soft a subject" as herself. Finally, the force of love prevails within Juliet. Although outwardly she denies her truth and agrees to marry Paris, inwardly she knows that her love for Romeo has given her intense resolve, or the "power to die" if necessary.

Romeo also struggles with the harshness of the world around him. When Romeo is at his most vulnerable and emotional, his friends urge him to quickly move out of his moodiness into the world of action. For Mercutio, love is nothing more than a ''fine foot, straight leg, and quivering thigh.'' Even Romeo doubts his new feelings of peace and reconciliation that his love for Juliet has brought to him. After Romeo's failed attempt to make peace with Tybalt, Mercutio is slain, and Romeo is unable to remain in his peaceful state. Referring to Juliet, he shouts, ''Thy beauty hath made me effeminate.'' This failure to respect the ''effeminate'' feelings he experiences with Juliet is Romeo's undoing; when he slays Tybalt in an uncontrolled rage, he sets into motion the tragic ending of the story.

Romeo is not the only character who cannot fully transform or overcome the side of his nature that betrays or fails to support the noble qualities of romantic love. Several characters in the play add their parts to the tragic ending. Mercutio, despite Romeo's peaceful influence, stirs up the fight scene in which he is slain and leads to Romeo's banishment. Juliet's parents, rather than respecting her free will and her true feelings, work against her and force her into what she believes is a hopeless situation. Juliet, constrained by her society, is unable to stand up for her love of Romeo; she lies when she accepts her parents' demands to marry Paris. In a sense, society fails when the letter from the friar to Romeo is not delivered, which would inform Romeo of the ploy to save the young couple. Friar Laurence plays an integral and yet morally ambiguous role in the play. The friar respects and acknowledges the love between Romeo and Juliet when he agrees to secretly marry them. However, by doing this in secret, he subverts the established secular order. In the end, rather than mediating from his position of religious authority, the friar devises a secretive plan that goes wrong and leads to the death of the young lovers.

Love is so powerful for Romeo and Juliet because it takes on spiritual dimensions. Romeo mentions that he will be ''new baptized'' by their meeting and claims that his love for Juliet is actually ''my soul that calls upon my name.'' Juliet acknowledges the ''infinite'' qualities inherent in her feelings. Love, or the ''religion of mine eye,'' as Romeo has called it earlier, creates powerful forces in each. Juliet acknowledges that ''God joined my heart and Romeo's.'' When Romeo is banished from the city for killing Tybalt, he claims to the friar that banishment is worse than death because it would be banishment away from Juliet. Again, Romeo seems to be mixing religious feelings with

> IN THIS PLAY, ROMANTIC LOVE IS PORTRAYED IN A WAY THAT REVEALS ITS POWER AND COMPLEXITY; THIS LOVE IS AT ONCE INVIGORATING, DESTRUCTIVE, TRANSFORMATIVE, AND REDEMPTIVE.''

his feelings of love for Juliet. He states that his banishment would be ''purgatory, torture, hell itself'' and that ''Heaven is here, where Juliet lives.'' In the Biblical sense, hell is the absence of God, while for Romeo, hell now becomes the absence of love as he has mixed his spiritual longings with his romantic ones. The death of the lovers occurs in a vault, and although the lovers themselves fail to resurrect, as was the friar's plan, a new peace is brought with the reconciliation of the warring families.

**Source:** Douglas Dupler, Critical Essay on *Romeo and Juliet,* in *Drama for Students,* Thomson Gale, 2005.

### Charlotte Lennox

*In the following excerpt, Lennox argues that Shakespeare did not base* Romeo and Juliet *on Bandello's* Ninth Novel—*what she calls the original Italian story*—*but worked from an English translation or from Pierre Boaistuau's French version.*

On the Incidents in the [Ninth Novel of Bandello], Shakespear has formed the fable of his *Romeo and Juliet,* one of the most regular of all his Tragedies. . . . [Yet] I think it will not be difficult to prove, or at least to make it appear highly probable, that he never saw, and did not understand the Original, but copied from a French Translation extant in his Time; or, what is equally probable, from an English Translation of that French one, both very bad, in some Places rather paraphrased than translated; in others, the Author's Sense absolutely mistaken, many Circumstances injudiciously added, and many more altered for the worse, or wholly omitted. The Story of *Romeo and Juliet* may be found translated in a Book, entitled *Histoires Tragiques extraictes des Oeuvres de Bandel* [by Pierre Boaistuau]. . . . A literal Translation of this Story, from the French, is in the second Tome of the *Palace of Pleasure* . . . , translated into English by William Painter, from several Greek, Latin, Spanish and Italian Authors. . . . (pp. 89–90)

Had Shakespear ever seen the original Novel in Bandello, he would have been sensible that the Translation of it is extremely bad: That he did not see it, must be owing to nothing else than his not understanding Italian; for can it be supposed, that having resolved to write a Tragedy upon the Subject of an Italian Story, he would rather chuse to copy from a bad Translation of that Story, than follow the Original.

This Supposition would be as absurd as to imagine a Man would slake his Thirst with the muddy Waters of a polluted Stream, when the clear Spring, from whence it issues, is within his Reach. That Shakespear consulted the Translator, appears from his having followed him in all the Alterations he has made in the Original; some few of which I shall take notice of, and shew that in some Places he has not only taken Circumstances from the Translator, but also made Use of his Thoughts and Expressions. (p. 90)

The Translator makes Juliet, upon hearing that her Cousin is slain by Romeo, break into Complaints and Reproaches against her Husband, and after she has for some Time given a Loose to her Resentment, her returning Tenderness for Romeo forces her to repent of the injurious Words which, in the first Emotions of her Grief and Rage, she had uttered against him; she condemns herself for her too hasty Censure, and begs Pardon of the absent Romeo for her unkind Reproaches.

There is not the least Foundation for all this in the Original. Bandello every where shews Juliet so much engrossed by her extreme Passion for Romeo, that all other Affections, all Tyes of Consanguinity, all filial Duty and Obedience is swallowed up in the Immensity of her Love; and therefore when the News of Tibbald's Death and Romeo's Banishment is brought to her at the same Time, she does not weep for the Death of her Cousin, but for the Banishment of her Husband. (p. 91)

[Juliet's] superior Affecion for Romeo is also painted by Shakespear in that Speech wherein she laments his Banishment, and acknowledges it is a greater Misfortune to her than the Death of all her Relations would be; but both these Circumstances the Translator has in common with Bandello: He differs from him in making Juliet complain of her Husband's Cruelty in killing her Cousin, and Shakespear has exactly followed that Hint. (p. 92)

In Bandello, the Friar, who is sent with the Letters to Romeo, is detained at a Monastery in Mantua: The Translator makes him be stopped at his own Convent in Verona; which last is followed by Shakespear.

There is no Mention made in the Original of the Apothecary, of whom Romeo buys the Poison; there we are only told that he had mortal Drugs in his Possession, which was given him by a Spoletto Mountebank in Mantua, long before.

The Translator makes him walk through the Streets in Mantua in order to find a Person that would sell him such a Composition, and accordingly he goes into the Shop of an Apothecary, whose Poverty is observable from the miserable Furniture of it; and he for a Bribe of fifty Ducats furnishes him with a strong Poison.

Shakespear has not only copied this Circumstance from the Translator, but also borrowed some Hints from him in his celebrated Description of the miserable Shop.

These few Instances are sufficient to prove that Shakespear took the Incidents on which he has founded his Tragedy of *Romeo and Juliet* from the Translation; and consequently that he did not peruse, because he did not understand, the original Italian.

His Management of the Tomb Scene, and the Death of the two Lovers, is entirely copied from the Translator, who differs greatly from the Original in those Circumstances. The plain and simple Narration of that melancholy Event in Bandello is more natural, more pathetic, and fitter to excite the Passions of Pity and Terror, than the Catastrophe of the Tragedy, as managed by Shakespear, who has kept close by the Translator.

In Bandello, when Pietro informs his Master of Juliet's Death, Astonishment and Grief for some Moments deprive him of Speech; recovering a little, he breaks into Complaints and Self-Reproaches; then, wild with Despair, he flies to his Sword, and endeavours to kill himself, but being prevented by his Servant, he sinks into an Excess of silent Sorrow, and, while he weeps, calmly deliberates on the Means he should use to die in the Monument with Juliet.

The Translator makes Romeo, upon receiveing the fatal News, resolve immediately to poison himself; and for that Purpose Romeo dissembles his Affliction, and tells his Servant he will go and walk about the Streets of Mantua to divert himself; but his real Design is to procure some Poison, which having purchased of a poor Apothecary, he goes immediately to Verona.

Shakespear has here copied the Translator exactly, and makes Romeo in the Midst of his Affliction for the Death of his Wife, and while the horrible Design of killing himself was forming in his Mind, give a ludicrous Detail of the miserable Furniture of a poor Apothecary's Shop; a Description, however beautiful in itself, is here so ill timed, and so inconsistent with the Condition and Circumstances of the Speaker, that we cannot help being shocked at the Absurdity, though we admire the Beauty of the Imagination.

There appears so much Contrivance and Method in Romeo's Design of buying Poison, and going to Verona to drink it in the Monument of his Wife, that he might expire near her, that we can hardly suppose it to be the spontaneous Effect of a sudden and furious Transport of Grief. In the Original therefore we see him not taking this Resolution till the first violent Sallies of his Sorrow are abated; till after, in a sudden Transport of Despair, he had ineffectually endeavoured to fall upon his Sword; but while he forms that fatally regulated Design, he is dissolved in Tears, and plunged in a calm and silent Excess of Sorrow. (pp. 93–5)

Romeo, in the French and English Translations, dies before Juliet awakes, and the Friar and Peter enter the monument the same Moment that he expires; then Juliet awaking, they press her to leave the Monument, but she refusing, and they both being alarmed at the Approach of some Soldiers, cowardly run away, and Juliet, left alone, stabs herself with a Dagger.

Shakespear has copied all these Circumstances from the Translator. Romeo dies in the Play before Juliet awakes; the Friar fearing to be discovered by the Watch, as he calls it, but there is no such Establishment in any of the cities of Italy, presses her to leave the monument; she refuses; he runs away; and she stabs herself with Romeo's Dagger.

> ❝ THERE IS NOT ONE INCIDENT OF SHAKESPEAR'S INVENTION IN HIS PLAY OF *ROMEO AND JULIET,* EXCEPT THE DEATH OF PARIS BY ROMEO: THIS CHARACTER MIGHT HAVE BEEN VERY WELL SPARED IN THE DRAMA; HIS APPEARANCE IS OF LITTLE USE, AND HIS DEATH OF STILL LESS. . . . ❞

In Bandello, while the dying Husband is holding her lifeless Body, as he supposes, in his Arms, and shedding his last Tears for her Death, she awakes; she opens her Eyes, gazes on him, and entreats him to carry her out of the Monument.

Romeo is for some Moments lost in a Transport of Surprize and Joy to see her alive, but reflecting that he is poisoned, that he must shortly die and leave her, his Agonies return with double Force: How pathetically does he complain of his miserable Destiny! With what tender Extasy does he congratulate her Return to Life! With what affecting Sorrow lament his approaching Death, which must tear him from her! nor is the Astonishment, the Grief, and wild Despair of the wretched Juliet less beautifully imagined. (pp. 97–8)

Had Shakespear ever seen the Italian Author, these striking Beauties would not have escaped him; and, if by copying the Translation only, he has given us a very affecting Tragedy, what might we not have expected, had he drawn his Hints from the beautiful Original. (p. 99)

There is not one Incident of Shakespear's Invention in his Play of *Romeo and Juliet*, except the Death of Paris by Romeo: This Character might have been very well spared in the Drama; his Appearance is of little Use, and his Death of still less, except to divert our Compassion from the two principal Persons in the Play, whose Deaths make up the Catastrophe of the Tragedy.

Paris seems only introduced to fall by the Hands of Romeo; and why must our Compassion of the unfortunate Romeo be suspended by the undeserved Fate of Paris? What Necessity is there for making Romeo, who is all along represented as an amiable and virtuous Character, imbrue his Hands in the Blood of an innocent Youth, (whose Death is of no Consequence) just before he expires?

This Incident, however, is the only one of the Poet's Invention throughout the Play: The Fable and all the Characters, except Mercutio, were formed to his Hands. (pp. 99–100)

**Source:** Charlotte Lennox, ''Observations on the Use Shakespear Has Made of the Foregoing Novel in His Tragedy of *Romeo and Juliet*,'' in *Shakespear Illustrated; or, the Novels and Histories, on Which the Plays of Shakespear Are Founded, Vol. I,* AMS Press, 1973, pp. 89–100.

## Stopford A. Brooke

*In the following excerpt, Brooke argues that the feud between the families is the central event in* Romeo and Juliet, *stating that the play depicts the process by which ''Justice'' achieves harmony and reconciliation through the sacrifice of the innocent lovers.*

In the first four scenes [of *Romeo and Juliet*], so long and careful is [Shakespeare's] preparation, all the elements of a coming doom are contained and shaped—the ancient feud, deepening in hatred from generation to generation, the fiery Youth-in-arms of whom Tybalt is the concentration; the intense desire of loving in Romeo, which thinks it has found its true goal in Rosaline but has not, and which, therefore, leaps into it when it is found in Juliet; the innocence of Juliet whom Love has never touched, but who is all trembling for his coming; the states-man's anger of the Prince with the quarrel of the houses; and finally, the boredom of the people, whose quiet is disturbed, with the continual inter-ruption of their business by the rioters—

Clubs, bills, and partizans! Strike! beat them down!
Down with the Capulets, down with the Montagues!
[I. i. 73–4]

a cry which seems to ring through the whole play. It is impossible this should continue. Justice will settle it, or the common judgment of mankind will clear the way.

The quarrel of the houses is the cause of the tragedy, and Shakespeare develops it immediately. It begins with the servants in the street; it swells into a roar when the masters join in, when Tybalt adds to it his violent fury, when the citizens push in—till we see the whole street in multitudinous turmoil, and the old men as hot as the young. . . . Then, when the Prince enters, his stern blame of both parties fixes into clear form the main theme of the play. He

collects together, in his indignant reproaches, the evils of the feud and the certainty of its punish-ment. We are again forced to feel that the over-ruling Justice which develops states will intervene. (pp. 35–6)

[By the end of *Romeo and Juliet,* Justice] has done her work. She has passed through a lake of innocent blood to her end. Tybalt, Mercutio, Paris, Romeo, Juliet, Lady Montague, have all died that she might punish the hate between the houses. Men recognize at last that a Power beyond them has been at work. 'A greater power,' cries the Friar to Juliet, 'than we can contradict hath thwarted our intents' [V. iii. 153–54]. The Friar explains the work of Justice to the Prince; the Prince applies the punish-ment to the guilty—

Where be these enemies? Capulet! Montague!
See what a scourge is laid upon your hate,
That heaven finds means to kill your joys with love;
And I, for winking at your discords too,
Have lost a brace of kinsmen; all are punish'd.
[V. iii. 291–95]

The reconciliation follows. That is the aim of Justice. The long sore of the state is healed. But at what a price? We ask, was it just or needful to slay so many for this end? Could it not have been otherwise done? And Shakespeare, deeply con-vinced, even in his youth, of the irony of life, deeply affected by it as all his tragedies prove, has left us with that problem to solve, in this, the first of his tragedies; and has surrounded the problem with infinite pity and love, so that, if we are troubled, it may be angry, with the deeds of the gods, we are soothed and uplifted by our reverent admiration for humanity.

Shakespeare could not tell, nor can we, how otherwise it might have been shaped; but to be ignorant is not to be content. We are left by the problem in irritation. If the result the gods have brought about be good, the means they used seem clumsy, even cruel, and we do not understand. This is a problem which incessantly recurs in human life, and as Shakespeare represented human life, it passes like a questioning spirit through several of his plays. I do not believe that he began any play with the intention of placing it before us, much less of trying to solve it. But as he wrote on, the problem emerged under his hand, and he became aware of it. He must have thought about it and there are passages in *Romeo and Juliet* which suggest such thinking, and such passages are more frequent in the after trage-dies. But with that strange apartness of his from any personal share in human trouble, which is like that of a spirit outside humanity—all the more strange because he represented that trouble so vividly ann felt for it so deeply—he does not attempt to solve or explain the problem. He contents himself with stating the course of events which constitute it, and with representing how human nature, specialised in distinct characters, feels when entangled in it.

This is his general way of creating, and it is the way of the great artist who sets forth things as they are, but neither analyses nor moralises them. But this does not prevent any dominant idea of the artist, such as might arise in his imagination from contemplation of his subject, pervading the whole of his work, even unconsciously arranging it and knitting it into unity. Such an idea seems to rule this play. It seems from the way the events are put by Shakespeare and their results worked out, that he conceived a Power behind the master-event who caused it and meant the conclusion to which it was brought. This Power might be called Destiny or Nemesis—terms continually used by writers on Shakespeare, but which seem to me to assume in his knowledge modes of thought of which he was unaware. What he does seem to think is; That, in the affairs of men, long-continued evil, such as the hatreds of the Montagues and Capulets or the Civil Wars in England, was certain to be tragically broken up by the suffering it caused, and to be dissolved in a reconciliation which should confess the evil and establish its opposite good; and that this was the work of a divine Justice which, through the course of affairs, made known that all hatreds—as in this case and in the Civil Wars—were against the Universe. We may call this Power Fate or Destiny. It is better to call it, as the Greek did, Justice. This is the idea which Shakespeare makes preside over *Romeo and Juliet,* and over the series of plays which culminates in *Richard III.* (pp. 63–5)

[In] *Romeo and Juliet* the work of Justice is done through the sorrow and death of the innocent, and the evil Justice attacks is destroyed through the sacrifice of the guiltless. Justice as Shakespeare saw her, moving to issues which concern the whole, takes little note of the sufferings of individuals save to use them, if they are good and loving, for her great purposes, as if that were enough to make them not only acquiescent but happy. Romeo and Juliet, who are quite guiltless of the hatreds of their clans and who embody the loving-kindness which would do away with them, are condemned to mortal pain and sorrow of death. Shakespeare accepted this apparent injustice as the work of Justice; and the impression made at the end upon us, which impres-

> IN *ROMEO AND JULIET* THE WORK OF JUSTICE IS DONE THROUGH THE SORROW AND DEATH OF THE INNOCENT, AND THE EVIL JUSTICE ATTACKS IS DESTROYED THROUGH THE SACRIFICE OF THE GUILTLESS."

sion does not arise from the story itself, but steals into us from the whole work of Shakespeare on the story, is that Justice may have done right, though we do not understand her ways. The tender love of the two lovers and its beauty, seen in their suffering, awaken so much pity and love that the guilty are turned away from their evil hatreds, and the evil itself is destroyed. And with regard to the sufferers themselves, there is that—we feel with Shakespeare—in their pain and death which not only redeems and blesses the world they have left, but which also lifts them into that high region of the soul where suffering and death seem changed into joy and life. (pp. 67–8)

**Source:** Stopford A. Brooke, ''*Romeo and Juliet,*'' in *On Ten Plays of Shakespeare,* Constable, 1925, pp. 35–70.

## Richard G. Moulton

*In the following excerpt, Moulton argues that in* Romeo and Juliet *Shakespeare was not concerned with depicting the processes of moral retribution, as he had done in other plays, but was composing a tragedy of accident as well as destiny.*

I believe that no mistake has done more to distort Shakespeare criticism than the assumption on the part of so many commentators that retribution is an invariable principle. Their favourite maxims are that the deed returns upon the doer, that character determines fate. But these specious principles need careful examination. If the meaning be merely this, that the deed often returns upon the doer, that character is one of the forces determining fate, then these are profound truths. But if, as is usually the case, there is the suggestion that such maxims embody invariable laws—that the deed always returns upon the doer, that character and nothing but character determines the fate of individuals—then the principles are false; false alike to life itself and to the reflection of life in poetry. (p. 46)

[One] of the principles underlying the exceptions to the universality of retribution, one of the forces that will be found to come between individual character and individual fate, is that which is expressed by the term Accident. I know that to many of my readers this word will be a stumbling-block; those especially who are new to ethical studies are apt to consider that their philosophical reputation will be compromised if they consent to recognise the possibility of accidents. But such a feeling rests upon a confusion between physics and morals. In the physical world, which is founded upon universality and the sum of things, we make it a preliminary axiom that every event has a cause, known or yet to be discovered. But in the world of morals, where individual responsibility comes in, it is obvious that events must happen to individuals the causes of which are outside individual control. (pp. 49–50)

The moral system of Shakespeare gives full recognition to accident as well as retribution; the interest of plot at one point is the moral satisfaction of nemesis, where we watch the sinner found out by his sin; it changes at another point to the not less moral sensation of pathos, our sympathy going out to the suffering which is independent of wrong doing. A notable illustration of the latter is the tragedy of *Romeo and Juliet*. In this play Shakespeare engages our sympathies for two young and attractive lives, and proceeds to bring down upon them wave after wave of calamity, which come upon them not as the result of what Romeo and Juliet have done, but from accident and circumstances not within their control. Instead of wrong and retribution, we have in this case innocence and pathos. Here however a misconception must be avoided. To say that Romeo and Juliet are innocent is not the same thing as to say that they are perfect. No one cares to discuss whether these young souls had not their full share of original sin; nor is it relevant to inquire whether two different persons in their situation might or might not have acted differently. The essential point is that in the providential dispensations of Shakespeare's story, the tragedy overwhelming the lovers is brought about, not by error on their part, but by circumstances outside their control, by what is to them external accident. (pp. 50–1)

In the dim background of the story, for those who care to look for it, may be seen a providence of

retribution: evil has brought forth evil, where the feud of the parents has caused the death of the children. This retribution is seen balanced by its opposite, for the heroism of Juliet is a good that but brings forth evil. But in the foreground, at every turn of the movement, we see emphasised the strange work of providence by which accident mocks the best concerted schemes of man; pity, not terror, is the emotion of the poem. It is accident which has brought Romeo and Juliet together, and they have loved without sin; accident has converted Romeo's self-restraint into the entanglement of exile from his bride; the smallest of accidents has been sufficient to turn deep wisdom and devoted heroism into a tragedy that engulfs three innocent lives [Romeo, Juliet, and Paris].

There are certain passages of the play into which have been read suggestions of folly and its penalty, but which in truth are entirely in tune with the prevailing impression of irresistible circumstance. When Juliet says—

> I have no joy of this contract to-night;
> It is too rash, too unadvised, too sudden;
> Too like the lightning, which doth cease to be
> Ere one can say, 'It lightens';—
> [II. ii. 117–20]

and Romeo answers—

> I am afeard,
> Being in night, all this is but a dream,
> Too flattering-sweet to be substantial;—
> [II. ii. 139–41]

the two are not making confession of faulty rashness: it is only the common thought of new-born love, that it is too good to be true. Similarly, when the Friar says to Romeo—

> These violent delights have violent ends . . .
> Therefore love moderately;—
> [II. v. 9, 14]

he is not blaming, but fearing: his own action shows that this is the sense. The Friar justly rebukes the desperate fury of Romeo at the sentence of banishment; but this fault of Romeo does not affect the movement of events, for he does not act upon his fury, but on the contrary lays it aside, and submits to the counsel of his spiritual adviser—the counsel which eventually turns to his ruin.

On the other hand, it may be said that in this more than in any other play Shakespeare comes near to being a commentator on himself and to giving us his own authority for the true interpretation. In the prologue it is the author who speaks: this opening of the plot exhibits, not sin and its consequences, but a suggestion of entangling circumstance; when he speaks of the "fatal loins" of the parents, the "star-cross'd lovers," and their "misadventured piteous overthrows" [Prologue, 5, 6, 7], Shakespeare is using the language of destiny and pathos. For what is spoken in the scenes the speakers alone are responsible; yet a succession of striking passages has the effect of carrying on the suggestion of the prologue—dramatic foreshadowings, unconscious finger-pointings to the final tragedy, just like the shocks of omen that in ancient drama brought out the irony of fate. . . .

[In these passages] Destiny itself seems to be speaking through the lips of the dramatis persona. In their more ordinary speech the personages of the play reiterate the one idea of fortune and fate. Romeo after the fall of Tybalt feels that he is "fortune's fool" [III. i. 136]. The Friar takes the same view:

> Romeo, come forth; come forth, thou fearful man:
> Affliction is enamour'd of thy parts,
> And thou art wedded to calamity;
> [III. iii. 1–3]

he sees in the banished husband a prodigy of ill luck, misfortune has fallen in love with him. Juliet feels the same burden of hostile fate:

> Alack, alack, that heaven should practice stratagems
> Upon so soft a subject as myself!
> [III. v. 209–10]

Romeo recognises the slain Paris as "one writ with me in sour misfortune's book" [V. iii. 82]; his last fatal act is a struggle "to shake the yoke of inauspicious stars from this world-wearied flesh" [V. iii. 111–12]. The wisdom of the Friar receives the detention of the messenger as "unhappy fortune" [V. ii. 17]; in the final issue of events he tremblingly feels how "an unkind hour is guilty of this lamentable chance," how "a greater power than we can contradict hath thwarted our intents" [V. iii. 145–46, 153–54]. The note struck by the prologue rings in the final couplet of the poem: no moral lesson is read, but the word pathos is found in its simple English equivalent—

> For never was a story of more WOE
> Than this of Juliet and her Romeo.
> [V. iii. 309–10]
> (pp. 61–4)

**Source:** Richard G. Moulton, "Innocence and Pathos: The Tragedy of *Romeo and Juliet*," in *The Moral System of*

"THE ESSENTIAL POINT IS THAT IN THE PROVIDENTIAL DISPENSATIONS OF SHAKESPEARE'S STORY, THE TRAGEDY OVERWHELMING THE LOVERS IS BROUGHT ABOUT, NOT BY ERROR ON THEIR PART, BUT BY CIRCUMSTANCES OUTSIDE THEIR CONTROL, BY WHAT IS TO THEM EXTERNAL ACCIDENT."

---

*Shakespeare: A Popular Illustration of Fiction as the Experimental Side of Philosophy,* Macmillan, 1903, pp. 46–64.

### William Hazlitt

*In the following excerpt, Hazlitt claims that in its mixture of young and old, its conflicting views of love and sexual relationships,* Romeo and Juliet *"presents a beautiful coup-d'oeil of the progress of human life.*

It has been said of *Romeo and Juliet* by a great critic, that "whatever is most intoxicating in the odour of a southern spring, languishing in the song of the nightingale, or voluptuous in the first opening of the rose, is to be found in this poem." The description is true; and yet it does not answer to our idea of the play. For if it has the sweetness of the rose, it has its freshness too; if it has the languor of the nightingale's song, it has also its giddy transport; if it has the softness of a southern spring, it is as glowing and as bright. There is nothing of a sickly and sentimental cast. Romeo and Juliet are in love, but they are not love-sick. Every thing speaks the very soul of pleasure, the high and healthy pulse of the passions: the heart beats, the blood circulates and mantles throughout. Their courtship is not an insipid interchange of sentiments lip-deep, learnt at second-hand from poems and plays,—made up of beauties of the most shadowy kind . . ., of evanescent smiles, and sighs that breathe not, of delicacy that shrinks from the touch, and feebleness that scarce supports itself, an elaborate vacuity of thought, and an artificial dearth of sense, spirit, truth, and nature! It is the reverse of all this. It is Shakespear all over, and Shakespear when he was young.

We have heard it objected to *Romeo and Juliet,* that it is founded on an idle passion between a boy and a girl, who have scarcely seen and can have but little sympathy or rational esteem for one another, who have had no experience of the good or ills of life, and whose raptures or despair must be therefore equally groundless and fantastical. Whoever objects to the youth of the parties in this play as ''to unripe and crude'' to pluck the sweets of love, and wishes to see a first-love carried on into a good old age, and the passions taken at the rebound, when their force is spent, may find all this done in the *Stranger* and in other German plays, where they do things by contraries, and transpose nature to inspire sentiment and create philosophy. Shakespeare proceeded in a more straight-forward, and, we think, effectual way. He did not endeavour to extract beauty from wrinkles, or the wild throb of passion from the last expiring sigh of indifference. . . . It was not his way. But he has given a picture of human life, such as it is in the order of nature. He has founded the passion of the two lovers not on the pleasures they had experienced, but on all the pleasures they had *not* experienced. All that was to come of life was theirs. At that untried source of promised happiness they slaked their thirst, and the first eager draught made them drunk with love and joy. They were in full possession of their senses and their affections. Their hopes were of air, their desires of fire. Youth is the season of love, because the heart is then first melted in tenderness from the touch of novelty, and kindled to rapture, for it knows no end of its enjoyments or its wishes. Desire has no limit but itself. Passion, the love and expectation of pleasure, is infinite, extravagant, inexhaustible, till experience comes to check and kill it. Juliet exclaims on her first interview with Romeo—

> My bounty is as boundless as the sea,
> My love as deep.
> [II. ii. 133–34]

And why should it not? What was to hinder the thrilling tide of pleasure, which had just gushed from her heart, from flowing on without stint or measure, but experience which she was yet without? What was to abate the transport of the first sweet sense of pleasure, which her heart and her senses had just tasted, but indifference which she was yet a stranger to? What was there to check the ardour of hope, of faith, of constancy, just rising in her breast, but disappointment which she had not

yet felt? As are the desires and the hopes of youthful passion, such is the keenness of its disappointments, and their baleful effect. Such is the transition in this play from the highest bliss to the lowest despair, from the nuptial couch to an untimely grave. The only evil that even in apprehension befalls the two lovers is the loss of the greatest possible felicity; yet this loss is fatal to both, for they had rather part with life than bear the thought of surviving all that had made life dear to them. In all this, Shakespear has but followed nature, which existed in his time, as well as now. The modern philosophy, which reduces the whole theory of the mind to habitual impressions, and leaves the natural impulses of passion and imagination out of the account, had not then been discovered; or if it had, would have been little calculated for the uses of poetry. (pp. 83–5) This play presents a beautiful *coup-d'oeil* of the progress of human life. In thought it occupies years, and embraces the circle of the affections from childhood to old age. Juliet has become a great girl, a young woman since we first remember her a little thing in the idle prattle of the nurse. Lady Capulet was about her age when she became a mother, and old Capulet somewhat impatiently tells his younger visitors,

> I've seen the day,
> That I have worn a visor, and could tell
> A whispering tale in a fair lady's ear,
> Such as would please: 'tis gone, 'tis gone, 'tis gone.
> [I. v. 21–4]

Thus one period of life makes way for the following, and one generation pushes another off the stage. One of the most striking passages to shew the intense feeling of youth in this play is Capulet's invitation to Paris to visit his entertainment.

> At my poor house, look to behold this night
> Earth-treading stars that make dark heav'n light;
> Such comfort as do lusty young men feel
> When well-apparel'd April on the heel
> Of limping winter treads, even such delight
> Among fresh female-buds shall you this night
> Inherit at my house.
> [I. ii. 24–30]

The feelings of youth and of the spring are here blended together like the breath of opening flowers. Images of vernal beauty appear to have floated before the author's mind, in writing this poem, in profusion. Here is another of exquisite beauty, brought in more by accident than by necessity. Montague declares of his son smit with a hopeless passion, which he will not reveal—

> But he, his own affection's counsellor,
> Is to himself so secret and so close,

So far from sounding and discovery,
As is the bud bit with an envious worm,
Ere he can spread his sweet leaves to the air,
Or dedicate his beauty to the sun.
[I. i. 147–53]

This casual description is as full of passionate beauty as when Romeo dwells in frantic fondness on ''the white wonder of his Juliet's hand.'' The reader may, if he pleases, contrast the exquisite pastoral simplicity of the above lines with the gorgeous description of Juliet when Romeo first sees her at her father's house, surrounded by company and artificial splendour.

What lady's that which doth enrich the hand
Of yonder knight?
O she doth teach the torches to burn bright;
Her beauty hangs upon the cheek of night
Like a rich jewel in an Æthiop's ear.
[I. v. 41–6]
(pp. 86–8)

Speaking of *Romeo and Juliet*, [Schlegel] says, ''It was reserved for Shakespeare to unite purity of heart and the glow of imagination, sweetness and dignity of manners and passionate violence, in one ideal picture.'' The character [of Juliet] is indeed one of perfect truth and sweetness. It has nothing forward, nothing coy, nothing affected or coquettish about it;—it is a pure effusion of nature. It is as frank as it is modest, for it has no thought that it wishes to conceal. It reposes in conscious innocence on the strength of its affections. Its delicacy does not consist in coldness and reserve, but in combining warmth of imagination and tenderness of heart with the most voluptuous sensibility. Love is a gentle flame that rarifies and expands her whole being. (pp. 89–90)

The tragic part of this character is of a piece with the rest. It is the heroic founded on tenderness and delicacy. Of this kind are her resolution to follow the Friar's advice, and the conflict in her bosom between apprehension and love when she comes to take the sleeping poison. . . .

Romeo is Hamlet in love. There is the same rich exuberance of passion and sentiment in the one, that there is of thought and sentiment in the other. Both are absent and self-involved, both live out of themselves in a world of imagination. Hamlet is abstracted from every thing; Romeo is abstracted from every thing but his love, and lost in it. . . . He is himself only in his Juliet; she is his only reality, his heart's true home and idol. The rest of the world is to him a passing dream. (p. 90)

**❝ HE HAS FOUNDED THE PASSION OF THE TWO LOVERS NOT ON THE PLEASURES THEY HAD EXPERIENCED, BUT ON ALL THE PLEASURES THEY HAD *NOT* EXPERIENCED. ALL THAT WAS TO COME OF LIFE WAS THEIRS.''**

Romeo's passion for Juliet is not a first love: it succeeds and drives out his passion for another mistress, Rosaline, as the sun hides the stars. This is perhaps an artifice (not absolutely necessary) to give us a higher opinion of the lady, while the first absolute surrender of her heart to him enhances the richness of the prize. The commencement, progress, and ending of his second passion are however complete in themselves, not injured if they are not bettered by the first. The outline of the play is taken from an Italian novel; but the dramatic arrangement of the different scenes between the lovers, the more than dramatic interest in the progress of the story, the development of the characters with time and circumstances, just according to the degree and kind of interest excited, are not inferior to the expression of passion and nature. . . . Of the passionate scenes in this tragedy, that between the Friar and Romeo when he is told of his sentence of banishment, that between Juliet and the Nurse when she hears of it, and of the death of her cousin Tybalt (which bear no proportion in her mind, when passion after the first shock of surprise throws its weight into the scale of her affections) and the last scene at the tomb, are among the most natural and overpowering. In all of these it is not merely the force of any one passion that is given, but the slightest and most unlooked-for transitions from one to another, the mingling currents of every different feeling rising up and prevailing in turn, swayed by the mastermind of the poet, as the waives undulate beneath the gliding storm. (pp. 91–2)

The lines in [Romeo's] speech, describing the loveliness of Juliet, who is supposed to be dead [V. iii. 91–120], have been compared to those in which it is said of Cleopatra after her death, that she looked ''as she would take another Antony in her strong toil of grace'' [*Antony and Cleopatra,* V. ii. 347–48]; and a question has been stated which is the finest, that we do not pretend to decide. We can more easily decide between Shakespear and any other author, than between him and himself.—Shall we quote any more passages to shew his genius or the beauty of *Romeo and Juliet?* At that rate, we might quote the whole. (pp. 93–4)

**Source:** William Hazlitt, ''Characters of Shakespeare's Plays: *Romeo and Juliet,*'' in *Characters of Shakespeare's Plays & Lectures on the English Poets,* Macmillan, 1903, pp. 83–94.

# SOURCES

Abrams, M. H., ed., *The Norton Anthology of English Literature,* 5th ed., Vol. 1, Norton, 1986, pp. 1845–47.

Brooke, Stopford A., *On Ten Plays of Shakespeare,* Constable, 1925, pp. 35–70.

Coleridge, Samuel Taylor, *Shakespearean Criticism,* 2d ed., Vol. 1, edited by Thomas Middleton Raysor, Dutton, 1960, pp. 4–11.

Dryden, John, ''An Essay of Dramatic Poesy,'' in *The Norton Anthology of English Literature,* 5th ed., Vol. 1, edited by M. H. Abrams, W. W. Norton, 1986, pp. 1845–47.

Griffin, Elizabeth, *The Morality of Shakespeare's Drama Illustrated,* reprint, Frank Cass, 1971, pp. 495–99.

Griffith, Kelley, Jr., *Writing Essays about Literature,* Harcourt Brace Jovanovich, 1986, p. 72.

Hazlitt, William, *Characters of Shakespeare's Plays and Lectures on the English Poets,* Macmillan, 1903, pp. 83–94.

Johnson, Samuel, *Johnson on Shakespeare,* edited by Arthur Sherbo, Yale Edition of the Works of Samuel Johnson, Vol. 8, Yale University Press, 1968, pp. 939–57.

Jorgens, Jack J., *Shakespeare on Film,* Indiana University Press, 1977, p. 85.

Ralli, Augustus E., *A History of Shakespearian Criticism,* Vol. 1, Oxford University Press, 1932, pp. 21–22.

Snider, Denton J., *The Shakespearian Drama, a Commentary: The Tragedies,* Sigma Publishing, 1887, p. 78.

Ulrici, Hermann, *Shakespeare's Dramatic Art: History and Character of Shakspeare's Plays,* translated by L. Dora Schmitz, Vol. 1, George Bell and Sons, 1876, pp. 381–97.

von Schlegel, August Wilhelm, *A Course of Lectures on Dramatic Art and Literature (1809–11),* translated by John Black, Henry G. Bohn Publishers, 1846, pp. 400–01.

Witherspoon, Alexander M., and Frank J. Warnke, eds., *Seventeenth-Century Prose and Poetry,* 2d ed., Harcourt Brace Jovanovich, 1963, pp. 118–19.

# FURTHER READING

Asimov, Isaac, *Asimov's Guide to Shakespeare: A Guide to Understanding and Enjoying the Works of Shakespeare,* reissue ed., Gramercy, 2003.

　　Well-known scientist Asimov clarifies the complexities of Shakespeare with explanations, synopses, and information about the mythological, historical, and geographical backgrounds of Shakespeare's works.

Bloom, Harold, *Bloom's Notes: William Shakespeare's ''Romeo and Juliet,''* Chelsea House Publishers, 1996.

　　Harold Bloom, an authority on Shakespeare, provides very brief but excellent ''notes'' with biographical and bibliographical information, character and structural analysis, and excerpts from some of the best criticism through the years on *Romeo and Juliet.*

Dobson, Michael, and Stanley Wells, eds., *The Oxford Companion to Shakespeare,* Oxford University Press, 2001.

　　This book covers biographical information, literary criticism, historical and cultural information, and much more about Shakespeare and his works. The plays are given scene-by-scene explanations as well as other notes.

Gervinus, G. G., *Shakespeare Commentaries,* translated by F. E. Bunnett, rev. ed., 1877, reprint, AMS Press, 1971, pp. 204–29.

　　Gervinus, a well-known German Shakespearean critic of his time, looks at the poetry of *Romeo and Juliet* as well as what he considers the central theme of passion. Gervinus thinks Friar Laurence is Shakespeare's mouthpiece in the play.

Goddard, Harold Clarke, *The Meaning of Shakespeare,* University of Chicago Press, 1960.

　　Goddard writes essays about Shakespeare's plays that are insightful and opinionated and full of ideas to provoke thoughtful consideration of Shakespeare's genius.

Guizot, M., *Shakespeare and His Times,* Harper and Brothers, 1852, pp. 161–73.

　　Guizot criticizes the contrast between the innocent and ideal feelings that Shakespeare shows in *Romeo and Juliet* and the unnatural, ill-fitting language that Guizot thinks are used to express them.

Kermode, Frank, *The Age of Shakespeare,* Modern Library, 2004.

　　This book is a good overview of the life of Shakespeare, the influences of the age in which he lived, and the practices of the theater at the time.

# The Spanish Tragedy

## THOMAS KYD
## 1592

*The Spanish Tragedy* (New York: W. W. Norton, revised edition, 1989), a play by English dramatist Thomas Kyd, was written between 1582 and 1592, when the first known performance took place. Kyd was a popular dramatist in his day, although most of his plays have been lost. *The Spanish Tragedy* is one of very few extant plays that can with certainty be attributed to him. The play is important not only for its own merits but also because it is the first example of a revenge tragedy, a type of play that was to become extremely popular on the Elizabethan stage during the last decade of the sixteenth century and beyond. The most famous of all revenge tragedies is Shakespeare's *Hamlet,* and some of the plot devices in *The Spanish Tragedy*, such as the protagonist's hesitation in carrying out his revenge, are echoed in Shakespeare's play.

Kyd based *The Spanish Tragedy* on the tragedies written by the Roman playwright Seneca, whose plays focused on murder and revenge. The emphasis was on a malignant fate that led inevitably to a bloody and horrific catastrophe.

Although *The Spanish Tragedy* is not performed in the early 2000s, its intricate plot, full of intrigue and even containing comic incidents, its swift-moving and sensational action, the questions it poses about the nature of justice and retribution, and the well-developed character of the revenger, Hieronimo, make it a rewarding play to read.

## AUTHOR BIOGRAPHY

The exact date on which Thomas Kyd was born is unknown, but he was baptized on November 6, 1558, at a church in London. His father, Francis Kyd, was a successful scrivener, that is, a man who copied documents. Kyd's father was sufficiently well off to send his son to the Merchant Taylors' School, which had a reputation for high academic standards. Kyd entered the Merchant Taylors' School when he was seven years old, in 1565. The poet Edmund Spenser was also a student there at the time. Kyd may have remained at Merchant Taylors for eight to ten years, although his date of departure is unrecorded.

After leaving school, Kyd was probably apprenticed to his father, although this cannot be established beyond doubt. By 1583, he had begun writing plays for the company of actors known as the Queen's Company. Kyd wrote for this company until 1587, although none of his plays has survived. In 1587 or 1588, Kyd entered the service of a lord, possibly the earl of Sussex, as a secretary or tutor. In 1588, he published a translation of Tasso's *Padre di Famiglia,* under the title *The Householder's Philosophy. The Spanish Tragedy*, the play on which Kyd's fame rests, was written between 1582 and 1592, probably before 1587. It was the first example of an Elizabethan revenge tragedy and enjoyed great popularity during Kyd's lifetime and beyond. What other plays Kyd wrote is a matter of conjecture. He may have written *Soliman and Perseda,* and many scholars argue that he wrote an early version of *Hamlet,* although no trace of such a play exists.

In 1591, Kyd shared his lodgings with the dramatist Christopher Marlowe. In 1593, Kyd was arrested and questioned about whether he had any role in writing pamphlets that incited violence against foreigners in London, who were being blamed for outbreaks of the plague and a rise in unemployment. There is no evidence that Kyd did anything wrong; he was under suspicion only because of his association with Marlowe, who was notorious for his atheism. Marlowe was also arrested but was quickly released (and killed in a tavern brawl twelve days later). Kyd was not so fortunate in his dealings with the authorities. Heretical writings were found at his lodgings, but Kyd claimed they belonged to Marlowe. He was subjected to torture during his brief period of imprisonment, but he was not convicted of any crime.

After his release, Kyd wrote *Cornelia,* an adaptation of a play by the French playwright Robert Garnier. It was published in 1594. In his dedication, Kyd commented about the bitter times and great suffering he had endured.

Kyd died later that year, at the age of thirty-six. He was buried on August 15, 1594.

## PLOT SUMMARY

### Act 1

*The Spanish Tragedy* begins with the ghost of Andrea, a Spanish nobleman, and the personified abstraction of Revenge. Andrea explains that he was killed in battle against the Portuguese. This deprived him of his secret love, Bel-Imperia, and his ghost has now emerged from the underworld to seek revenge. Revenge promises the ghost of Andrea that he will witness his killer, Prince Balthazar, killed by Bel-Imperia. These two characters remain on stage throughout the play.

At the Spanish court, a general explains that during the battle, Balthazar was defeated in single combat by Horatio and taken prisoner. This ensured Spain's victory, and Portugal has agreed to pay Spain tribute. Balthazar is treated leniently, being merely detained in Spain as the guest of Lorenzo.

At the Portuguese court, the viceroy of Portugal is deceived by Villuppo into believing Balthazar is dead.

Back in Spain, Horatio tells Bel-Imperia of the circumstances of Andrea's death, and she transfers her affections from Andrea to Horatio, who was Andrea's friend. She also vows to have vengeance on Balthazar. Balthazar, encouraged by Lorenzo, declares his love for Bel-Imperia, but she rebuffs him.

The king of Spain holds a banquet, attended by the Portuguese ambassador, to celebrate the new alliance between the two countries. The ghost of Andrea complains to Revenge at seeing Balthazar so well received at the Spanish court. Revenge tells him that friendship will soon turn into enmity.

### Act 2

Lorenzo, trying to advance Balthazar's cause with Bel-Imperia, gets her servant Pedringano to admit that she is in love with Horatio, because he has seen letters she sent to him. Lorenzo promises Balthazar that he will get rid of Horatio, leaving Balthazar free to win Bel-Imperia's love. In scene 2, Balthazar and Lorenzo, helped by Pedringano, spy on Bel-Imperia as she and Horatio discuss their love for each other. The new lovers arrange to meet in secret at night, in a garden on Horatio's father's land, where they will not be disturbed.

After a scene in which the duke of Castile agrees to the marriage of his daughter to Balthazar, Lorenzo and Balthazar, informed by Pedringano, surprise Horatio and Bel-Imperia at their secret meeting. They hang and stab Horatio and abduct Bel-Imperia. The disturbance arouses Hieronimo from his bed, and Hieronimo cuts down Horatio and laments his murder. Isabella, his wife, joins him, and he vows revenge. Meanwhile, the ghost of Andrea is again irritated, because he has seen his friend Horatio rather than his enemy Balthazar killed. Revenge replies that he only has to wait, and he will see Balthazar brought low.

### Act 3

At the Portuguese court, Alexandro is about to be put to death when the ambassador arrives with the news that Balthazar is alive. The viceroy releases Alexandro and condemns Villuppo to death because of his false claims that Balthazar was dead.

In Spain, Hieronimo, mourning for his son, receives a letter from Bel-Imperia in which she tells him that Horatio was murdered by Lorenzo and Balthazar. She calls on him to take his revenge. Hieronimo, suspicious that the letter may be a trick, resolves to investigate before he takes action. After Hieronimo talks with Lorenzo, Lorenzo becomes suspicious that Hieronimo may know something about the murder. He fears that Balthazar's servant, Serberine, may have said something to him. Lorenzo pays Pedringano to kill Serberine, but after Pedringano shoots Serberine, he is apprehended by three constables, who take him to Hieronimo. Lorenzo then arranges for Pedringano to be executed, while falsely telling him that a pardon already enacted will be revealed at the last minute (thus buying Pedringano's silence). The scheme goes wrong when the hangman shows Hieronimo a letter he has found on the dead Pedringano's clothing that confirms that Lorenzo and Balthazar killed Horatio. Hieronimo resolves to go to the king and seek justice. In the meantime, Isabella goes mad in her grief over her dead son, and Bel-Imperia, who is being kept in seclusion by Lorenzo, bemoans the fact that Hieronimo has not yet avenged Horatio's death.

Lorenzo sends for Bel-Imperia, who rails at him for abducting her. Lorenzo explains that he killed Horatio to protect her honor, since they had met in secret. He reminds her of how her reputation suffered because of her clandestine love affair with Andrea. He also explains that he abducted her lest the king should have found her there. He kept her in seclusion because he wanted to spare her the anger of their father, who is angry at Andrea's death. Balthazar again presses his claim to her love, but Bel-Imperia remains unresponsive.

Meanwhile, the grief-stricken Hieronimo contemplates suicide but decides against it, since if he dies there will be no one to avenge Horatio. Meanwhile, the king, the duke of Castile and the Portuguese ambassador agree on the marriage of Balthazar and Bel-Imperia. Hieronimo bursts in, calling for justice, but after he is restrained and ushered away, Lorenzo tries to convince the king that Hieronimo is not only mad but also wants for himself the ransom paid by Portugal for Balthazar.

Hieronimo forms a plan for vengeance, but waits until the best time to execute it. Meanwhile, he pretends he knows nothing of the guilt of Lorenzo and Balthazar. However, the grief of a man named Bazulto for his murdered son causes Hieronimo to reproach himself for delaying his revenge.

The viceroy arrives for the wedding, and Castile reproaches his son Lorenzo for obstructing Hieronimo's access to the king. When Hieronimo enters, summoned by Castile, Hieronimo pretends to be reconciled with Lorenzo. The act concludes with the ghost of Andrea again calling for revenge. Revenge reassures him, in the process explaining to Andrea the meaning of a ''dumb show'' (mimed performance) they have just witnessed.

### Act 4

Bel-Imperia reproaches Hieronimo for failing to avenge Horatio and tells him that if he does not act, she will carry out her revenge herself. Hieronimo reassures her that he has a plan, and asks her to join with him. Lorenzo and Balthazar enter and ask Hieronimo to devise some entertainment for the Portuguese ambassador. Hieronimo produces a tragic play that he wrote when he was young. He assigns them all parts. Balthazar is to play Soliman the Turkish Emperor who pursues a woman, Perseda (played by Bel-Imperia), who kills him after one of Soliman's men (played by Hieronimo) kills her husband, Erastus (played by Lorenzo).

Isabella, believing that Hieronimo has abdicated his revenge, curses the garden where Horatio was murdered, and then kills herself.

The play is acted in front of the Spanish king, the viceroy of Portugal, and other members of the court. At the appropriate moment in the plot, Hieronimo stabs Erastus (Lorenzo). Bel-Imperia stabs Soliman (Balthazar) and then stabs herself. The on-stage audience does not realize the deaths are real, not feigned. Then Hieronimo produces the body of Horatio and explains how Horatio was murdered, and that the deaths of Balthazar and Lorenzo are real, designed by him. Bel-Imperia he had intended to spare, but she took it upon herself to commit suicide. Hieronimo then tries to hang himself. He is restrained, and the king demands that he explain himself fully. Hieronimo refuses to explain what role Bel-Imperia had in the plot, and bites out his tongue rather than speak. A pen is brought for him to write down an explanation. Hieronimo indicates he needs a knife to mend the pen, but when the knife is brought, he stabs the duke of Castile and himself.

In the final scene, the ghost of Andrea is pleased by what he has witnessed. He looks forward to welcoming Horatio, Bel-Imperia, Isabella and Hieronimo in pleasant circumstances. Revenge tells him that he can hurl his enemies to the deepest hell, and Andrea picks out the punishments for them that best please him.

## CHARACTERS

### Alexandro

Alexandro is a noble in the Portuguese court. He is falsely accused by Villuppo of accidentally causing the death of Balthazar in battle. He is condemned to death by the viceroy, but the truth eventually comes out, and Alexandro is released.

### Ambassador of Portugal

The ambassador of Portugal acts as a liaison between the courts of Spain and Portugal.

### Balthazar

Balthazar, the prince of Portugal, kills Don Andrea in battle, and thus becomes the object of the desire for revenge exhibited by Andrea's ghost. Balthazar falls in love with Bel-Imperia, angering the ghost still further, since Andrea was Bel-Imperia's lover. Balthazar is frustrated by Bel-Imperia's lack of affection for him, and he participates in the murder of Horatio, whom Bel-Imperia loves, in order to remove his rival. In the play-within-the-play, Balthazar plays the role of Soliman, the sultan of Turkey. He is stabbed to death by Bel-Imperia.

### Bel-Imperia

Bel-Imperia is the daughter of Don Ciprian, the duke of Castile, and the brother of Lorenzo. She was Don Andrea's lover before he was killed in battle by Balthazar. After Andrea's death, Bel-Imperia falls in love with Horatio. She hates Balthazar, since he was the cause of her lover's death. Bel-Imperia writes a letter to Hieronimo, informing him of who killed Horatio, and she expects him to carry out his revenge against the murderers. In the play-within-the-play, Bel-Imperia plays Perseda. She kills the character Soliman, played by Balthazar, and then stabs herself to death, even though her suicide is not called for in the role she is playing.

### Christophill

Christophill is Lorenzo's servant.

### Don Ciprian

Don Ciprian, duke of Castile, is the brother of the king of Spain, and father of Lorenzo and Bel-Imperia. He plays little part in the main action, although he does rebuke Lorenzo for thwarting Hieronimo's access to the king. Don Ciprian then effects what he believes to be a reconciliation between the two. Although the duke is innocent of any involvement in the death of Horatio, Hieronimo kills him after the play-within-the-play is over.

### Duke of Castile

*See* Don Ciprian

### Ghost of Don Andrea

Andrea was a Spanish courtier who was in love with Bel-Imperia. He was killed in battle by Balthazar, and his ghost now demands revenge against Balthazar. The ghost and the personified figure of Revenge emerge from the underworld and watch all the events of the play unfold at the Spanish court.

## Hieronimo

Hieronimo is the knight marshal of Spain and the father of Horatio. Filled with grief at Horatio's murder, Heironimo vows to take revenge on his son's killers. But before he acts, he wants to make sure he knows for certain the identities of the guilty men. He does not take Bel-Imperia's word for it when she writes him a letter telling him what happened. Hieronimo decides to watch and wait, and not to betray his suspicions to anyone. He is finally convinced of the guilt of Lorenzo and Balthazar when an incriminating letter is found on the body of the hanged Pedringano. But still Hieronimo is frustrated; he cannot understand why heaven does not hear his call for justice and vengeance. He goes almost mad with grief, and contemplates, but ultimately rejects, suicide. Hieronimo goes to the king demanding justice, but Lorenzo interrupts him before he can explain himself. Finally, Hieronimo devises a form of revenge by means of a performance of a tragic play he wrote when he was young. He ensures that the two guilty men play characters who are killed. During the course of the play, Hieronimo really kills Lorenzo and ensures that Balthazar is killed by Bel-Imperia. When the play ends, Hieronimo brings out the dead body of Horatio and explains himself to the shocked audience. He tries to hang himself, then bites out his tongue rather than divulge the full story to the king. He stabs the duke of Castile and then stabs himself.

## Don Horatio

Don Horatio is the son of Hieronimo and a friend of Andrea's. Horatio defeats Balthazar in single combat during the battle between the Spanish and Portuguese armies. He then takes the place of the dead Andrea in Bel-Imperia's affections. Horatio is killed by Lorenzo and Balthazar because he is an obstacle to the marriage between Balthazar and Bel-Imperia.

## Isabella

Isabella is Hieronimo's wife. Grief-stricken over the murder of her son Horatio, and the delay in exacting revenge against his killer, she eventually goes mad and commits suicide.

## King of Spain

The king of Spain is an honorable man. Although he celebrates the Spanish victory over Portugal, he does not behave vindictively towards the defeated foe. He treats Balthazar, the captured prince, generously, and welcomes Balthazar's proposed marriage to Bel-Imperia, since this will cement an alliance between Spain and Portugal.

## Lorenzo

Lorenzo is the son of the duke of Castile, and Bel-Imperia's brother. He is an evil, scheming character who will stop at nothing to ensure that Bel-Imperia elevates her status by marrying Balthazar. He plans and takes part in the murder of Horatio, and then arranges for two of his accomplices, Pedringano and Serberine, to be killed. Lorenzo plays the character of Erastus in the play-within-the-play. He is killed by Hieronimo.

## Pedringano

Pedringano is a servant of Bel-Imperia. Lorenzo uses him to advance his scheme against Horatio, and also persuades him to kill Serberine. Pedringano is then arrested, and Lorenzo buys his silence by promising him a pardon. But Lorenzo double-crosses him, and Pedringano is hanged.

## Don Pedro

Don Pedro is the brother of the viceroy of Portugal.

## Revenge

Revenge is the personified abstraction of the desire of Don Andrea to be revenged on Balthazar. When Don Andrea's ghost becomes frustrated at the events he witnesses, which do not seem to be leading in the direction he wants, Revenge promises him that revenge will come; all the ghost must do is wait.

## Serberine

Serberine is a servant of Balthazar who is killed by Pedringano on the instructions of Lorenzo.

## Viceroy of Portugal

The viceroy of Portugal is deceived by Villuppo into believing that his son Balthazar was killed in battle. When he finds out that he has been deceived, the viceroy condemns Villuppo to death. The viceroy mends relations with Spain by agreeing to pay tribute. He also consents to the proposed marriage between Balthazar and Bel-Imperia. The viceroy is a spectator at the play during which his son is killed.

### *Villuppo*

Villuppo is a Portuguese nobleman who gives the Viceroy false information about the fate of Balthazar. He insists that the Prince was killed in battle, even though he knows this is not true. When his lie is discovered, Villuppo is put to death.

# THEMES

### *Justice and Revenge*

The single theme of the play is revenge. The theme appears in many different aspects of the plot, with varying degrees of moral justification. It is introduced at the very beginning, when the ghost of Andrea wants revenge on Balthazar for having killed him in battle, although there is nothing the ghost can directly do to bring it about.

The next character who wants revenge is Bel-Imperia, whose desired victim is also Balthazar, since he killed her lover, Andrea. Initially, she plans to use Horatio as her means of vengeance, and when Horatio is murdered, she has a double motive for revenge.

The third example of the desire for revenge is Balthazar, who wants revenge on Horatio for taking him prisoner in battle and being an obstacle to Balthazar's attempt to win Bel-Imperia.

The last and most important example of the revenge theme is Hieronimo, who seeks revenge for the slaying of his son, Horatio. Hieronimo's wife, Isabella, shares his desire.

Even though Horatio's murder does not occur until late in the second act, Hieronimo's revenge is the main focus of the play, as it is he who has suffered the greatest wrong. It might be argued, for example, that Andrea has little cause to seek revenge on Balthazar, since they met on the battlefield in a fair fight. But Hieronimo has what anyone might regard as just cause. Also, the audience has witnessed the murder of Horatio directly—in contrast, the audience has only been told about the death of Andrea—which gives this aspect of the plot more emotional force.

Once the revenge plot is in place, the question becomes how it is to take place. Whose responsibil-

ity is it to exact revenge? Hieronimo's first thought is that he will do it himself. But Isabella introduces the idea that "the heavens are just" and that time will bring the villains to light, and, presumably, to punishment.

Not long after this, in act 3, scene 2, Hieronimo, frustrated at not knowing the identity of the murderer, severely questions the notion of cosmic justice. In lines 9–11, he appeals directly to the "sacred heavens," saying that if the murder

> Shall unrevealed and unrevengéd pass,
> How should we term your dealings to be just,
> If you unjustly deal with those that in your justice
> trust?

Immediately after this appeal, Hieronimo finds the letter from Bel-Imperia, informing him that the murderers are Balthazar and Lorenzo—which suggests that the wheels of cosmic justice are in fact responsive to his plight. However, Hieronimo is beginning to believe that he must carry out the vengeance himself. But he is very concerned about the idea of justice. He does not want to strike until he is certain of the guilt of those whom he suspects. When Hieronimo finally comes upon incontrovertible proof of the identity of the murderers, he thanks heaven because he believes it is the gods who have refused to let the murder go unpunished.

Still concerned with justice and how to execute it, Hieronimo resolves to take his case to the king and seek secular justice. It is only the intervention of Lorenzo that stops him explaining the whole story to the king. With the failure of this strategy, and after briefly considering the Christian idea that revenge should be left to God, Hieronimo decides to take vengeance into his own hands. Even then, he believes that his solution to the problem is in fact "wrought by the heavens." Most modern readers feel that Hieronimo goes too far, since he also kills the duke of Castile. The duke is innocent of any wrongdoing; he is killed simply because he is Lorenzo's father.

This excess on the part of Hieronimo makes it difficult to argue that he is merely the agent of divine justice. It appears that he has stepped over the line that divides a just avenger from a murderer and a villain. His final actions also suggest that any human attempt to enact justice is fraught with danger and prone to error. An example of the fallibility of human justice occurs in the trial and execution of Pedringano. Pedringano may deserve his fate, but the legal process he goes through fails entirely to establish the fact that he was acting on the orders of Lorenzo, who, at least in this instance, escapes punishment.

## STYLE

### Dramatic Irony

The play consistently employs dramatic irony, a situation in which one or more characters act without full knowledge of the facts, but those facts are known by the audience. For example, in act 1, scene 3, the viceroy of Portugal mourns the son he believes to be dead, but the audience knows Balthazar is alive. In act 2, scene 2, when Bel-Imperia and Horatio declare their love for each other, the audience knows that a plot is already in motion to destroy their love. Indeed, in that same scene Lorenzo and Balthazar, unseen watchers, state explicitly what awaits the two lovers. The audience is also aware that after Pedringano has murdered Serberine, the pardon Pedrigano so confidently expects, and on which he bases his words and actions, does not exist.

There is also a dramatic irony that frames the entire play, since on several occasions, the figure of Revenge tells the ghost of Andrea what the outcome will be. The audience is not allowed to forget this, since those two characters remain on stage throughout the play. The effect of this dramatic irony is to show that, even while the characters are plotting to avoid or hasten certain events, their fate is already determined, though unknown to them. The characters may think they are in control of their situation, as Lorenzo and Balthazar do, but they cannot escape the destiny that is marked out for them.

### Stichomythia

The play frequently employs a rhetorical device known as stichomythia, which Kyd derived from Seneca, the Roman writer of tragedies. Stichomythia is a quick-fire dialogue between two or more characters, in which each character gives a one-line response. The responses often echo the words of the previous line. An example occurs in act 2, scene 3, lines 24–30 in the dialogue between Bel-Imperia, Balthazar and Horatio:

> BEL-IMPERIA: Why stands Horatio speechless all this while?

# TOPICS FOR FURTHER STUDY

- Research the English attitude towards Spain in Elizabethan times. Analyze ways in which this attitude sheds light on the play.

- Does Hieronimo retain the sympathy of the audience until the end of the play, or does he become a villain too? Does his madness cloud his judgment?

- Research the work and influence of the sixteenth century political philosopher, Niccolo Machiavelli. In what sense might Lorenzo be considered a Machiavellian figure?

- What is the difference between revenge and justice? Are the two concepts sometimes merged? Can revenge ever be justified?

---

> HORATIO: The less I speak, the more I meditate.
> BEL-IMPERIA: But whereon dost thou chiefly meditate?
> HORATIO: On dangers past, and pleasures to ensue.
> BALTHAZAR: On pleasures past, and dangers to ensue.
> BEL-IMPERIA: What dangers and what pleasures dost thou mean?
> HORATIO: Dangers of war and pleasures of our love.

### Anaphora

Another frequent device is anaphora, the repetition of a word or words at the beginning of each line of verse, as in Lorenzo's speech in act 2, scene 1:

> 'In time the savage bull sustains the yoke,
> In time all haggard hawks will stoop to lure,
> In time small wedges cleave the hardest oak,
> In time the flint is pierced with softest shower—'

### Alliteration

Alliteration, the repetition of initial consonants, is another frequently used device. It occurs, for example, in Hieronimo's speech at the beginning of act 3, scene 7, where he questions where he can run to with his woes, ''woes whose weight hath wearied the earth?'' The blustering winds, he continues, have "Made mountains marsh with spring-tides of my tears, / And broken through the brazen gates of hell."

# HISTORICAL CONTEXT

### The Revenge Play

After Kyd had shown the way with *The Spanish Tragedy*, the revenge play became extremely popular on the Elizabethan stage. John Marston's *Antonio's Revenge,* Christopher Marlowe's *The Jew of Malta,* and Shakespeare's *Titus Andronicus* and *Hamlet* are some of the most outstanding plays of this type.

The revenge play was adapted from the work of the Roman playwright Seneca (4 B.C. to A.D. 65). Seneca wrote nine tragedies, based on Greek models, but his plays were meant to be recited rather than performed on a stage. They consisted mainly of long speeches, and action was described rather than presented directly. Seneca's theme was revenge and retribution, and his subject matter was lurid; his plays feature crimes such as murder, incest, and adultery, and there is much blood, mutilation, and carnage. Ghosts appear frequently, and the plays end in a horrible catastrophe. Seneca emphasized that man was helpless to avert his tragic fate, but if he could meet it with stoic resolve he would in a sense remain undefeated.

Seneca's plays held great appeal all across Renaissance Europe. In England, the first original English tragedy based on Seneca's model was *Gorboduc,* by Thomas Sackville and Thomas Norton, which was first performed in 1562. During the 1560s, many translations of Seneca's plays, and original plays based on Seneca, were written by university playwrights. Another Senecan revival occurred during the 1580s, in the work not only of Kyd but also of George Peele.

The Senecan basis of *The Spanish Tragedy* can be seen in Kyd's theme of murder and revenge, the presence of a ghost, and a bloody trail of events. At one point, Hieronimo even carries a copy of Seneca's play *Agamemnon* in his hand and quotes from it. But Kyd and his contemporaries made one important change to the Senecan tradition. In *The Spanish Tragedy,* typical Senecan horrors (the hanging and stabbing of Horatio, and Hieronimo's self-mutilation, for example) are shown directly on stage rather than being merely reported by a messenger. This appeared to satisfy the more crude instincts of an Elizabethan audience that regularly enjoyed such violent spectacles as public hangings and whippings, bear-baiting and the like. It also made for an exciting, action-packed spectacle.

The Elizabethan enthusiasm for revenge plays was for the most part a dramatic interest only. Although in these types of plays, revenge is presented as an honorable, even sacred duty (Hamlet, for example, never doubts his duty to avenge his murdered father), Elizabethan society did not sanction acts of private revenge. A murder committed to avenge the murder of a close relative was treated no differently in Elizabethan law than any other murder. The punishment for an avenger was the same as for the original murderer.

However, despite the insistence by the authorities, secular as well as religious, on the rule of law, family feuds did take place in Elizabethan England, and almost always took the form of the duel. There were other instances as well in which revenge, although officially condemned, might be countenanced. If a known murderer could not be brought to justice because of lack of evidence that could be presented in court, or if a man's high position in society enabled him to put himself above the law, the average Elizabethan might have had some sympathy and tolerance for an act of private revenge.

# CRITICAL OVERVIEW

*The Spanish Tragedy* was extremely popular during the last decade of the sixteenth century and was performed well into the seventeenth century. It was also successful as a printed book, with six editions printed between 1602 and 1633. According to Thomas W. Ross, in his edition of the play, it was "the most prodigious success of any drama produced and printed between 1580 and 1642," dates that would include all of Shakespeare's works. Translations of the play were performed in Europe; a performance was recorded in Frankfurt in 1601. The play was so well known in England that certain passages, such as Hieronimo's extravagant expressions of grief and Andrea's speech in the prologue, were subject to

# COMPARE
# &
# CONTRAST

- **1580s:** Spain is the leading world power. In 1588, the English fleet defeats the Spanish Armada, and so prevents an invasion by Catholic Spain of Protestant England.

  **Today:** Spain and Britain are mid-level European powers. Both are members of NATO and the European Union.

- **1580s:** Elizabethan authors do not own the copyright to their work; they are poorly paid by the theater companies to which they sell their work, and they do not receive royalties from the publisher. Plays are often published anonymously, and pirated or corrupt editions appear, sometimes based on an actor's memory of the script or a copy made by a spectator during a performance.

  **Today:** Strict copyright laws define ownership of a literary work, and legally enforceable contracts define the amount of royalties an author receives. Plagiarism or infringement of copyright is illegal and offenders may be prosecuted.

- **1580s:** London is the largest city in Europe, with a population of over 100,000. Many foreigners come to live in the city, taking advantage of lenient immigration laws and the willingness of employers to hire aliens. Whenever unemployment rises, Londoners tend to blame the presence of foreigners.

  **Today:** With a population of 7,172,036, London remains one of the most populous cities in Europe, along with Moscow, Istanbul, and Paris. Patterns of immigration have changed over the centuries, and London is now a multi-cultural, multi-ethnic city. Ten percent of the population is Indian, Bangladeshi, or Pakistani; 5 percent is African, and 5 percent come from the Caribbean.

---

many parodies by other playwrights, who must have known that their audiences would recognize the allusions to the earlier play.

However, *The Spanish Tragedy* has not been performed by professional companies since 1642, and was largely forgotten until historians of drama discovered its importance in the early twentieth century. They realized that the play was a seminal work that revealed much about the development of tragedy, and especially revenge tragedy, in Elizabethan England.

Modern scholars have claimed that *The Spanish Tragedy* has more than mere historical interest. J. R. Mulryne, in his introduction to the New Mermaid edition of the play, notes that it is "remarkable for the astonishingly deft and complete way in which Kyd has transmuted his theme into drama, by way of the intricate tactics of his play's structure." Mulryne claimed that a professional production would show that the play "deserve[s] its place as one of the first important English tragedies." Philip Edwards, in *Thomas Kyd and Early*

*Elizabethan Tragedy,* declared that in conception, although not in execution, *The Spanish Tragedy* was "more original, and greater, than [Shakespeare's] *Richard III.* It is one of those rare works in which a minor writer, in a strange inspiration, shapes the future by producing something quite new."

# CRITICISM

## *Bryan Aubrey*

*Aubrey holds a Ph.D. in English and has published many articles on sixteenth-century literature. In this essay, Aubrey discusses the parallels between* The Spanish Tragedy *and Shakespeare's* Hamlet.

The short life of Thomas Kyd is shrouded in obscurity, and *The Spanish Tragedy* is one of the very few works that can be confidently ascribed to his pen. Many scholars believe that Kyd also wrote a play

*Eighteenth-century Italian watercolor titled "Allegory of Justice"*

called *Hamlet,* and they speculate that probably about a decade later William Shakespeare drew on Kyd's play, which they refer to as the "Ur-Hamlet," for his version of the famous revenge drama. Unfortunately, as of 2004, no trace of an "Ur-Hamlet" by Kyd has been disovered, so the matter has not been resolved beyond any doubt. However, the link between Kyd and Shakespeare does not entirely depend on the tantalizing idea that Kyd wrote a version of *Hamlet,* since *The Spanish Tragedy* also offers some striking parallels with Shakespeare's great tragedy. In both plays, as Fredson Thayer Bowers points out in *Elizabethan Revenge Tragedy, 1587–1642,* "the theme is of the problems of life and death and of the mystery of a soul in torment." In addition to murder and revenge, both plays employ ghosts, madness, the hesitation of the hero, and a play-within-a-play as dramatic devices.

Shakespeare often puts these devices to more subtle or more effective dramatic use than his predecessor. An example is in the employment of the anguished voices from beyond the grave. In both plays, a ghost appears in the first scene, his purpose being to demand vengeance for his untimely death. The ghost of Hamlet's murdered father, however, is more integrated into the dramatic action than Kyd's

Don Andrea. Whereas Don Andrea is a mere uncomprehending spectator, given to complaining to Revenge but taking no direct part in the action, the ghost in *Hamlet* is a more active presence. Not only does he appeal directly to Hamlet to carry out his vengeance, he also reappears at a vital moment later in the play (during Hamlet's confrontation with Gertrude in act 3, scene 4) to remind Hamlet of his task. In other words, Shakespeare replaces Kyd's static ghost with one who serves as a goad to action on the part of the protagonist.

One difference between the two plays is that in *Hamlet,* the murder that is to be revenged has already taken place when the play begins. While it is true that in *The Spanish Tragedy,* Don Andrea has already been killed when the play begins, his desire for revenge, even though it is presented in the very first scene, is essentially peripheral to the main plot, and the play could function perfectly well without it. The principal revenge theme is introduced only near the end of act 2, with the murder of Horatio, since Kyd first has to spend time developing the enmity for Horatio on the part of Lorenzo and Balthazar that leads to the murder. Once the murder has taken place, the parallel between Hieronimo and Hamlet becomes clear, since both seek to avenge the murder of a close relative. And in doing so, they both hesitate.

The hesitation of the hero and his delay in carrying out his revenge was a staple of the Elizabethan revenge play, and it was Kyd who set the pattern in *The Spanish Tragedy.* When Hieronimo finds Bel-Imperia's letter saying that Lorenzo and Balthazar are guilty of Horatio's murder, he is not convinced. Fearing the letter may be a trap, he resolves to investigate further: "I therefore will by circumstances try / What I can gather to confirm this writ." Hieronimo here resembles Hamlet; Hamlet also, to justify his delay, convinces himself that the source of his information about the murder—the ghost of his father—may be unreliable, a devil sent to deceive him in order to damn his soul. He therefore resolves, like Hieronimo, to gather more reliable evidence. In this speech he is already reproaching himself for his inaction, wondering why, even though he has good cause, he "Must like a whore unpack my heart with words / And fall a-cursing like a very drab." Hamlet sounds very much like Hieronimo, who still does not act, even when further evidence comes. Instead, he spends his time questioning and debating and feeling guilty about it: "But wherefore waste I mine unfruitful words, / When naught but blood will satisfy my woes?"

# WHAT DO I READ NEXT?

- The plays collected in *Four Revenge Tragedies: "The Spanish Tragedy," "The Revenger's Tragedy," "The Revenge of Bussy D'Ambois," and "The Atheist's Tragedy"* (Oxford World's Classics, 2000), edited by Katharine Eisaman Maus, show how the Elizabethan revenge tragedy was treated by dramatists such as George Chapman (*Revenge of Bussy D'Ambois*), Cyril Tourneur (*The Atheist's Tragedy*) and the author of the anonymous *The Revenger's Tragedy* (which is sometimes ascribed to Tourneur or Thomas Middleton).

- M. C. Bradbrook's *Themes and Conventions of Elizabethan Tragedy* (2d ed., 1980) deals with the conventions which gave Elizabethan drama its special character. Bradbrook also analyzes individual plays by Marlowe, Tourneur, Middleton, and John Webster. There are many allusions to Kyd and to Shakespeare.

- *English Renaissance Drama: A Norton Anthology* (2002), edited by David M. Bevington, Lars Engle, Katharine Eisaman Maus, and Eric Rasmussen, is an extensive collection of twenty-seven plays written in Elizabethan and Jacobean England. Playwrights represented include Marlowe, Middleton, Webster, and Ben Jonson.

- *A New History of Early English Drama* (1998), by John D. Cox and David Scott Kastan, is an innovative collection of twenty-six essays on early modern English drama, up to 1642. The essays cover such topics as the conditions under which plays were written, produced and disseminated. The emphasis is not on individual authors but on the place of the stage in the wider society, and how it was impacted by religious, civic and other cultural factors.

---

There are two more striking parallels between Hamlet and Hieronimo. In the speech quoted above, Hamlet reacts to the words recited by the First Player, who has tears in his eyes as he relates the grief of Hecuba at the sight of her murdered husband, Priam. Hamlet contrasts the grief shown by the actor, about a long-ago event that can mean nothing to him personally, to his own muted response to his father's murder, which should in truth be far greater than that shown by a mere actor. This incident echoes a plot device used by Kyd in *The Spanish Tragedy*, when another character acts as a foil to show Hieronimo the inadequacy of his own response to his situation. The incident comes in act 3, scene 13, when Hieronimo encounters an old man, Bazulto, who is petitioning the king for justice for his murdered son. Observing Bazulto, Hieronimo feels ashamed of his own reaction. In similar fashion to Hamlet, Heironimo reasons that if someone from the lower class of society can mourn and seek redress in the determined way that Bazulto does, how much more effectively should he, Hieronimo,

the Grand Marshal of Spain, react? He says, "Then sham'st thou not Hieronimo, to neglect / The sweet revenge of thy Horatio?"

The second striking parallel between the two characters occurs when, in each play, the murdered man returns, or appears to return, to remind the revenger of his purpose. In *The Spanish Tragedy*, this occurs later on in the scene mentioned above. Hieronimo is so maddened by his grief that he mistakes Bazulto for the dead Horatio:

And art thou come, Horatio, from the depth,
To ask for justice in this upper earth?
To tell thy father thou are unreveng'd,
To wring more tears from Isabella's eyes,
Whose lights are dimmed with over-long laments?

So too in *Hamlet,* act 3, scene 4, the ghost of Hamlet's father returns to rebuke his son for failing to carry out his promise of revenge.

Both Hieronimo and Hamlet soliloquize extensively, in speeches that probe their difficult situation and their reaction to it, and explore questions of

❝

BOTH HIERONIMO AND
HAMLET SOLILOQUIZE
EXTENSIVELY, IN SPEECHES THAT
PROBE THEIR DIFFICULT SITUATION
AND THEIR REACTION TO IT, AND
EXPLORE QUESTIONS OF JUSTICE
AND REVENGE, LIFE AND DEATH."

justice and revenge, life and death. Both characters at one point consider suicide, and both reject it (although Hieronimo does in the end take his own life). Since Shakespeare was a greater poet than Kyd, and was also able to probe the human condition more profoundly than his predecessor, Hamlet's soliloquies have stood the test of time and contain some of the best known passages in the English language. In contrast, Hieronimo's long speeches, in which he laments and questions, often strike modern readers as artificial and bombastic, and therefore lacking emotional impact. But in their day, these speeches were much admired for their rhetorical skill, and it seems likely that were a professional company to stage *The Spanish Tragedy* today, an accomplished actor might well, despite the different tastes of a modern audience, be able to create the emotional intensity in the role that Elizabethan audiences appeared to relish.

Intensity there certainly is, which manifests in yet another parallel between *The Spanish Tragedy* and *Hamlet:* the theme of madness. This is another convention of the revenge play, and the madness of the revenger may be either real or feigned. Hieronimo's madness appears genuine—he appears mad not only in the scene mentioned earlier, but also in act 3, scene 11, when he encounters the two visitors from Portugal—whereas Hamlet's madness is feigned. Madness also appears in secondary characters in both plays, and in both cases it is coupled with suicide. In *The Spanish Tragedy*, Isabella goes mad and kills herself; in *Hamlet,* the victim is Ophelia.

The play-within-the-play, orchestrated by the revenger, is also common to both plays, although the contexts are very different. In *Hamlet,* the purpose of the play-within-the-play it is to reveal the guilt of the murderer; in *The Spanish Tragedy*, it is to allow the revenger to carry out his revenge. Since a play-within-the-play does not appear to have been an established convention of revenge plays, this would appear to be a direct borrowing by Shakespeare from Kyd. It is not difficult to imagine Shakespeare in the audience at a performance of *The Spanish Tragedy*, taking note of Kyd's ingenious innovations. Or perhaps Kyd's "Ur-Hamlet" employed the same device, and Shakespeare adapted it from there. Such details of course will never be known. And since *The Spanish Tragedy* is the template of revenge plays, it is not at all surprising that it presents parallels with *Hamlet,* the greatest revenge play of them all. But nor should it be forgotten that, although Kyd's work was quickly overshadowed by Shakespeare's, *The Spanish Tragedy* stands in its own right as an original, subtle and moving work of art.

**Source:** Bryan Aubrey, Critical Essay on *The Spanish Tragedy,* in *Drama for Students,* Thomson Gale, 2005.

### Sheldon Goldfarb

*Goldfarb has a Ph.D. in English and has published two books on the Victorian author William Makepeace Thackeray. In the following essay, Goldfarb explores the significance of the Alexandro-Villuppo episode in* The Spanish Tragedy.

What a nightmare world of murder, revenge, deceit, and betrayal does Thomas Kyd create in *The Spanish Tragedy.* As Hieronimo says in act 3, scene 2, his world is "no world, but [a] mass of public wrongs / Confus'd and fill'd with murder and misdeeds"—all this before Hieronimo contributes to the accumulation of murders by engineering the deaths of Balthazar, Lorenzo, and the duke of Castile, which are then followed by the suicides of Bel-imperia and himself. Earlier in the play, Lorenzo sends the servants Serberine and Pedringano to their deaths, being especially deceitful in the way he handles Pedringano. And, of course, there is the treacherous murder of Horatio, which sets the main action in motion and is that act that Hieronimo is specifically referring to. Why does Kyd pile on the death and destruction in this way? What point is he trying to make? Or is he just out to create a bloody spectacle?

One approach to answering this question is to look at the one episode in the play in which a practitioner of deceit fails in his attempt to engineer someone's death. This is the episode involving Villuppo and Alexandro at the Portuguese court, the

Portuguese subplot which most commentators ignore and which, in the words of one commentator (G.K. Hunter in a 1965 article), is "famous for its irrelevance."

It is true that the episode has little to do with the main plot, with its focus on Hieronimo's actions in response to the murder of Horatio. Indeed, in a play that is already fairly long, why does Kyd bother to insert two brief scenes about an intrigue in Portugal? To some critics the two scenes are a useless or unnecessary digression, but at least two commentators have written complete articles tussling with the question of why they are there.

In 1969, Ken C. Burrows wrote an article listing several ways in which the Portuguese episode connects to the main plot, focusing mostly on a comparison of Hieronimo and the Portuguese viceroy. A decade earlier, William H. Wiatt also pointed to similarities between Hieronimo and the viceroy, noting that they both receive information accusing someone of killing their sons: the viceroy hears Villuppo accuse Alexandro of shooting Balthazar in the back, and Hieronimo receives a letter from Bel-imperia saying that Lorenzo and Balthazar have murdered Horatio. The viceroy acts swiftly and nearly sends an innocent man to his death. Hieronimo is more skeptical about the information he receives, and the point of the Portuguese episode, according to Wiatt, is to show that Hieronimo is justified in waiting because accusations can sometimes be false.

The accusation Hieronimo reads in Bel-imperia's letter is not false. The audience has just seen Lorenzo and Balthazar kill Horatio, so they know the accusation is true. In contrast, having seen Balthazar alive at the Spanish court, the audience knows that Villuppo's accusation is a lie. The situations contrast so much that it is hard to believe that Kyd's aim was to make a general point about being skeptical about accusations. Indeed, the assumption that both Burrows and Wiatt make, that the Portuguese subplot creates a parallel between Hieronimo and the viceroy, does not ring true despite the fact that both men grieve over the loss, real or imagined, of a son. Kay Stockholder, in a 1990 article, seems closer to the truth when she notes parallels between Hieronimo and Alexandro.

In the Portuguese scenes, Alexandro, after being accused of murder, cannot make himself heard by the viceroy. Stockholder notes that this foreshadows Hieronimo's later failure to get the Spanish king to listen to his call for justice over the death of Horatio. More generally, Hieronimo and Alexandro

> MERCY, OF COURSE, IS A CONVENTIONAL CHRISTIAN ATTRIBUTE. DOES THIS MEAN THAT ALEXANDRO IS THE ONLY TRULY CHRISTIAN CHARACTER IN THE PLAY?"

both occupy similar situations as loyal servants at court who suddenly suffer reversals of fortune. However, there is one crucial difference: Alexandro is saved from execution and restored to favor whereas Hieronimo ends up dying in a bloodbath.

Why, in a play where the innocent and guilty alike perish, does Alexandro survive? Alexandro himself has an explanation: it was his innocence that saves him, he says. However, as Kay Stockholder points out, his innocence would not have helped him if the ambassador had arrived a minute later. Philip Edwards, in a 1985 article, sees the last-minute reprieve as "a satire on the operations of human justice and divine intervention." In opposition to those who see the play as depicting a caring Christian providence, Edwards sees Kyd's work as "a denial of God's care for man." The characters may call on Heaven, but Heavenly agents never appear in the play; the supernatural characters who do appear come from another direction altogether: the Underworld. Kyd depicts Pluto, Proserpine, the three judges of Hades, and the strange creature called Revenge, but never Christ or God or the saints who Hieronimo thinks have blessed his plan for revenge. It is as if, in Kyd's world, the infernal powers have taken over. For Edwards, this means that Kyd's play is a work of "dark pessimism"—and so it might seem, except for the nagging fact that the innocent Alexandro does survive.

For Edwards, Alexandro's survival is something of a cosmic joke, or perhaps a joke by Thomas Kyd against those who believe there is a benevolent force running the cosmos. For Stockholder, Alexandro's survival seems to be mere chance; a minute later and he would have been dead. The point is that the ambassador who saves Alexandro does not arrive a minute late; he arrives in time. Is that pure chance, or is Kyd suggesting there is some other reason why the innocent Alexandro survives whereas Hieronimo, in so many ways like him, ends up part of the general bloodbath at play's end?

It may be useful to look more closely at what Alexandro says and does, especially in the second scene of the Portuguese subplot at the beginning of act 3. Brought in to be executed, Alexandro is advised by a kindly nobleman that he should still hope. In response, Alexandro says, "'Tis heaven is my hope." A moment later, the ambassador arrives to save Alexandro, and the volatile viceroy shifts his wrath from Alexandro to Villuppo. The viceroy not only orders Villuppo to be killed in Alexandro's place, but he also orders extra torments laid on for Villuppo. At this point, there is an interesting stage direction saying "Alexandro seems to entreat," as if Alexandro is graciously asking the viceroy not to be too harsh towards the man who almost had him killed.

It has been remarked (for instance by Steven Justice in a 1985 article) that the word "mercy" does not appear anywhere in *The Spanish Tragedy*. Indeed, mercy is not a quality much in evidence in Kyd's play. If there is ever a merciful moment in it, it is this one, in which Alexandro seems to entreat the viceroy. Mercy, of course, is a conventional Christian attribute. Does this mean that Alexandro is the only truly Christian character in the play? His resting his hopes on Heaven similarly suggests a Christian approach to life.

Resting one's hopes on Heaven in Christian theology would include leaving vengeance to God, an idea mentioned in the play itself by Hieronimo in his famous speech at the beginning of act 3, scene 13. In this speech, Hieronimo begins by quoting from the well-known New Testament passage that says that vengeance belongs to the Lord, and he goes on to say, "Ay, Heaven will be revenged of every ill."

Though he quotes this Christian warning to leave vengeance to Heaven, by the end of that same speech, Hieronimo has vowed to avenge Horatio's death himself and to do so in a secretive, deceitful way. He will not wait for Heaven to act; he will not follow the model of Alexandro. Instead, he will become more like the man he hates, Lorenzo, practicing the same sort of deceit and taking the law into his own hands. All of which is a bit strange since Hieronimo is knight marshal (a high law officer) and is noted for his devotion to justice. Why does he abandon the natural course of justice here in favor of private revenge?

It could be argued that since the murderers he wants brought to justice are the nephew of the Spanish king and the son of the Portuguese viceroy, he would have little chance in a court of law. It is true that when Hieronimo does try to approach the king about the murder, he is shooed away by Lorenzo, the king's nephew. Still, his efforts to reach the king seem almost half-hearted, undercut perhaps by some incipient madness on his part, all very understandable but still unfortunate. It is not necessary to condemn Hieronimo as a villain as Fredson Bowers did many years ago in his book *Elizabethan Revenge Tragedy;* as Peter B. Murray says in his book on Kyd, Hieronimo remains a sympathetic character despite his misguided actions. His actions, in the context of the play, do seem misguided; they certainly lead to a horrifying conclusion.

Another character in a similar situation is Hieronimo's wife, Isabella. She too, despite her grief and anguish over Horatio's death, at first counsels Christian patience and reliance on Heaven. "The heavens are just," she says at the end of act 2, scene 5, adding that "murder cannot be hid" and that "Time," as "the author of both truth and right," will "bring this treachery to light." According to Ronald Broude in a 1971 article, this statement of Isabella's expresses the theme of the play: it is best to let time bring justice. However, like her husband, Isabella cannot wait. In act 4, impatient over the king's failure to bring justice, she attacks the grove of trees where Horatio was killed, taking revenge on the place as her husband will soon take revenge on the persons, and then she kills herself.

Broude points out one character who does wait patiently, at least at one moment. This is Bel-imperia, who when imprisoned by her brother says, "Well, force perforce, I must constrain myself / To patience, and apply me to the time, / Till heaven, as I have hoped, shall set me free." In the very next line she is set free: patience and time, and trusting to Heaven, have done their work, just as they seem to have in the case of Alexandro.

Hieronimo, however, is not patient. Nor does he continue to look to Heaven. As Lukas Erne notes in his 2001 book *Beyond "The Spanish Tragedy,"* Hieronimo turns more and more to the infernal forces as the play goes on. In act 3, scene 12, he promises to "marshal up the fiends in hell" to be avenged on Lorenzo. In scene 13, he vows:

> I'll down to hell, and in this passion
> Knock at the dismal gates of Pluto's court,
> Getting by force, as once Alcides did,

A troop of Furies and tormenting hags
To torture Don Lorenzo and the rest.

Not much Christian forbearance there.

Erne says, disagreeing with Edwards, that Kyd's play does not so much depict "a cosmic drama about a world deserted by God as the personal drama of Hieronimo deserting God." There is something in this. Mostly Kyd seems to present a world without God, a world controlled by the infernal powers, where murder and betrayal rule supreme. Perhaps his point is that this is only the world as created by those who turn to the infernal powers and take vengeance into their own hands. Perhaps he is saying there could be a different sort of world, if only there were more people like Alexandro, more people who put their trust in Heaven and forgave their enemies.

**Source:** Sheldon Goldfarb, Critical Essay on *The Spanish Tragedy,* in *Drama for Students,* Thomson Gale, 2005.

### *Frank R. Ardolino*

*In the following essay, Ardolino analyzes "three examples of a play-within-a-play designated as a mystery" in* The Spanish Tragedy *and asserts that "thus by analogy the entire play . . . is a mystery."*

Kyd's method of analogously identifying his play as a mystery within the dramatic action forms the most important clue to the allegorical nature and interpretation of *The Spanish Tragedy.* With the induction scene serving as the primary frame, he builds a series of frames within a frame in what is known mathematically as a process of infinite regression, the box-within-a-box effect. What we may call the play proper, that is, all of the action that takes place after the induction and before the final judgment, is a play-within-a-play which in turn frames three smaller plays-within-the-play, Hieronimo's historical masque, Revenge's dumb show, and Hieronimo's revenge playlet. Within this complex structure of plays-within-the-play, Kyd proceeds to categorize *The Spanish Tragedy* as a mystery through a series of analogies. At three strategic points, the play proper, the historical masque, and the dumb show are identified by stage characters as mysteries. In this fashion, the theater audience is directed to reason analogously: the play presents three examples of a play-within-a-play designated as a mystery and thus by analogy the entire play—*The Spanish Tragedy*—is a mystery.

We will begin with an analysis of the second and third instances, the historical masque and the

> MOREOVER, JUST AS ANDREA LEARNS TO INTERPRET THE DUMB SHOW'S ALLEGORICAL MEANINGS BY MEANS OF AN ANALOGY, THE THEATER AUDIENCE IS ALSO BEING INSTRUCTED TO USE ANALOGY TO DISCERN THE ALLEGORICAL MEANINGS BENEATH THE LITERAL LEVEL OF *THE SPANISH TRAGEDY.*"

dumb show, and then go on to consider the most comprehensive example of the play proper. The second play-within-the-play occurs at I.iv when Hieronimo presents an historical masque to celebrate the end of the war between Spain and Portugal. He introduces a series of three unexplained dumb shows, which the Spanish King asks him to expound: "Hieronimo, this masque contents mine eye, / Although I sound not well the mystery." The context of the King's remark shows, as Philip Edwards notes, that mystery means "hidden meaning, allegorical significance," but the word may also be applied to the masque as a whole since it contains the hidden meanings. After Hieronimo clarifies the historical incidents and characters, the King and Portuguese ambassador relate the three shows to the recent war between Spain and Portugal.

By means of this dramatic action, Kyd suggests the analogous identification of *The Spanish Tragedy* as a mystery. The actions delineated represent in small the acts of presenting, attending, and interpreting a symbolic play. Hieronimo serves as an author-figure presenting a masque to an onstage audience which then furnishes contemporary interpretations of the historical scenes. In an analogous manner, the theater audience is being directed to conclude, like its onstage analogue, that the play it is watching—*The Spanish Tragedy*—is a mystery containing allegorical significance.

In a similar manner, the use of mystery at III.xv.19 to define the dumb show also analogously points to the identification of the play as a mystery. When Andrea demands that Revenge undermine the apparent reconciliation of Hieronimo with Lorenzo and Balthazar, Revenge presents an unexplained dumb show, and Andrea, like the Spanish King, asks him to "reveal this mystery" (III.xv.29). More clearly than in the first usage, this context establishes that the dumb show itself is mystery. After Revenge identifies its characters and the plot of the marriage disrupted by Hymen, Andrea is then able to provide the hidden meaning by comparing the dumb show to the larger action which he is watching: "Sufficeth me, thy meaning's understood . . ." Although his understanding is not enunciated, we are meant to see that he recognizes that the dumb show is a foretelling of the ill-fated nuptials of Bel-imperia and Balthazar. Andrea has been told at the outset that she will murder him and he has just witnessed a symbolic foreshadowing of that eventuality. Just as he discovers the hidden significance of the dumb show by comparing it to the large play, so too we are to make a similar comparison to understand *The Spanish Tragedy* as a mystery.

The first and most comprehensive identification of *The Spanish Tragedy* as a mystery occurs at the conclusion of the induction scene immediately before the opening of the play proper. As Andrea and Revenge prepare to take their places on the stage to watch, unseen by any stage characters, the action unfold before them, Revenge introduces the largest of the plays-within-the-play as a mystery:

> Then know, Andrea, that thou art arriv'd
> Where thou shalt see the author of thy death,
> Don Balthazar the prince of Portingale,
> Depriv'd of life by Bel-imperia:
> Here sit we down to see the mystery,
> And serve for Chorus in this tragedy.
> (I.i.86–91)

This usage leaves no doubt that Revenge is defining the play proper as a mystery and that by analogy Kyd is classifying *The Spanish Tragedy* as a mystery.

In addition to identifying the play as a mystery, the pattern formed by the analogies tells us a great deal about how we are to interpret *The Spanish Tragedy*. The process moves from the first and most inclusive of the identifications to two smaller instances, which by repetition confirm the initial designation of *The Spanish Tragedy* as a mystery and also clarify the meaning that Kyd wants us to apply to mystery. The first usage, which evokes the general meaning of mystery as dramatic spectacle, is further defined by the succeeding usages, which demonstrate that it means a play containing hidden meanings or allegorical significance. The retrospective way by which we become aware of the allegorical definition of mystery in the first context pro-

vides a significant clue to the proper method of interpretation. At the outset, we experience the central word of the play with little clarification; then we learn in subsequent contexts how we are to understand the first example and thus we move back to the beginning with increased comprehension. In short, the interpretative pattern formed by the analogies is progressive, cumulative and then retrospective.

In the sixteenth century, mystery contained two related notions: that there are meanings hidden beneath a literal level and that these are available only to the learned few. These concepts were derived from its definition as "certain secret religious ceremonies (the most famous being those of Demeter at Eleusis) which were allowed to be witnessed only by the initiated, who were sworn never to disclose their nature (*OED* general definition; cf.II.9). From this ritual meaning, mystery, as Edgar Wind has described, gained figurative definitions called *mystères littéraires,* which refer to philosophic truths beneath the literal level. In this analogous sense, philosophy and literature become mysterious or mystical, borrowing terminology and interpretative methods from the ancient rituals. As Pico stated, ". . . as was the practice of the ancient theologians, even so did Orpheus protect the mysteries of his dogmas with the coverings of fables and conceal them with a poetic veil. . . . "

The conflation of mystery with allegory as designations for literature with hidden meanings was aided by their basic conceptual and lexical similarities. Edward Honig has pointed out that the original meaning of mystery (Gr. *mysterion,* fr. *mystes,* "close-mouthed," fr. *myein* "to be shut") is related to the original meaning of allegory as "'other-speaking' or speaking otherwise than one seems to speak." Both words denote the concealment of figurative meanings beneath a literal level. Historically, the linking of mystery with allegory was also furthered, as Don Cameron Allen explains, by the allegorical interpretations of the works of Homer and Virgil and by the influence of the hermetic tradition, which prompted the concern of Renaissance artists and writers with mysterious meanings.

The synonymous relationship between mystery and allegory is also reflected in their official definitions. Most Renaissance dictionaries establish a literary context for mystery by defining it as the hidden or secret meanings found beneath the literal sense. Thomas Elyot's *Dictionary* of 1538 defines *mysteria* as "thynges secrete or hid in wordes or ceremonies,'' while John Rider's *Bibliotheca Scholastica* (1589) also emphasizes the difference between the literal surface and the hidden meaning beneath that surface by defining *misteries* as ''things plaine in woordes, but hid in sence.'' And in *Queen Anna's New World of Words* (1611), John Florio adds the idea that only a select audience can come to an understanding of the concealed meanings when he defines the Italian cognate *misterio* as a ''misterie or secret . . . a thing secretly hid in words or ceremonies, whereunto the common sort might not come.'' All of these similar definitions of mystery are related to Puttenham's description of allegory as ''a duplicitie of meaning . . . vnder couert and darke intendments,'' which appears ''when we do speake in sence translatiue and wrested from the owne signification, neuerthelesse applied to another not altogether contrary, but hauing much couenience with it. . . .'' Both Puttenham's and the dictionaries' emphasis on the presence of hidden meanings beneath the literal level indicates a close relationship between mystery and allegory in the sixteenth century.

Another important indication of the fusion of the two words is provided by the fact that Elizabethan writers often describe their allegorical works in terms traditionally associated with mystery ritual and mysterious writings. In *The Third Part of the Countesse of Pembrokes Yuychurch,* Abraham Fraunce links allegorical poetry with mystery: ''They [the nine muses] are called Musa . . . who teach and instruct a man in those things, that are sacred and holy, diuine and mysticall, whereof came the word *mysterie.*'' In an explicit comparison of poetry with the nature and purpose of mystery writings, Nashe explains in *The Anatomie of Absurditie* that since ''Poetrie [is] . . . a more hidden and diuine kind of Philosophy, enwrapped in blinde Fables and dark stories . . . the . . . Reader can diuine what deep misterie can be placed vnder plodding meeter.'' Furthermore, in the preface to his translation of *Orlando Furioso,* an important apologia for allegorical literature and interpretation, Harington equates the profound meanings or mysteries found in ancient writings with the figurative meanings present in allegory: ''The ancient Poets have indeed wrapped . . . in their writings divers and sundry meanings, which they call the sences or mysteries thereof. . . . and these same sences that comprehend so excellent knowledge we call the Allegorie. . . . He then explains that such secrecy is necessary to ''conceale these deepe mysteries of learning . . . [so] that they might not be rashly abused by prophane wits'' (11.39,41). In this way Harington emphasizes the relationship between mystery and allegory as designations for literature which contains concealed levels of meaning to be understood only by those with the intellectual capacity to ''digest the Allegorie.'' Thus when Kyd identifies *The Spanish Tragedy* as a mystery by means of three analogies, he expects his audience—or at least the more learned members of the theater and reading audience—to recognize that mystery means allegory and to interpret the play in an allegorical fashion, that is, as a play with a literal level and an allegorical level containing hidden or symbolic meanings.

## II

To aid us in our search for the hidden mysteries, the scene containing Revenge's dumb show provides the particular interpretative method which we should adopt. We learn by means of two analogies that first, the play we are watching is an allegory, and, secondly, that its allegorical meanings can be discovered through a process of analogous interpretation. In the first analogy, as we discussed earlier in this chapter, we see that just as an onstage audience discovers that a dumb show has allegorical meanings, we, too, must recognize that *The Spanish Tragedy* is an allegory. And in the second analogy, the onstage audience discovers the allegorical import of the dumb show by comparing it with the action of the entire play, so that we will recognize that we must compare the play we are viewing to something else, as yet undefined, if we are to grasp the hidden mysteries.

Like Hieronimo in the historical masque, Revenge presents an unexplained dumb show, and, when questioned by Andrea about its mystery, he identifies the characters and the particular events they enact. The onstage audience—Andre in this instance—realizes that Revenge wants him to see the show as a dramatic response to his growing impatience with the slow working of vengeance. As soon as Andrea connects the action of the small play with the events of the play, he comes to understand how the dumb show prefigures and represents in small the prevention of the impending marriage between Bel-imperia and Balthazar and, consequently, the fulfillment of the destiny announced at the outset of the play.

Similarly, the theater audience learns to compare the masque as an allegory to the play they are watching—*The Spanish Tragedy*—in order to recognize the latter's allegorical nature. Moreover, just as Andrea learns to interpret the dumb show's allegorical meanings by means of an analogy, the theater audience is also being instructed to use analogy to discern the allegorical meanings beneath the literal level of *The Spanish Tragedy*. We are directed to make one analogy between the play-within-the-play and the entire play as mysteries and then to construct another interpretative analogy in order to understand the literal and figurative meanings of *The Spanish Tragedy*.

Kyd's emphasis on analogy as the method of allegorical interpretation is consistent with Renaissance rhetorical theory. As Murrin states: ''. . . allegory can be described as a figure of speech incomplete in itself, which, for this very reason, makes certain demands on an audience. The hearer by analogy must fill in the proper meaning to complete the figure. It follows that allegorical figures presuppose a certain cooperation between a speaker and an auditor; the former makes a statement and the latter completes it by his interpretation.'' The reader by means of an analogy completes the implied comparison between the literal statement and an unstated idea to arrive at an understanding of the hidden meaning. It is this relationship between the author, the work, and his audience that is depicted in the scene containing the dumb show. The open-ended literal level of Revenge's dumb show is completed through analogy by Andrea, who recognizes that Revenge intends him to ''read'' the dumb show as an allegory. Similarly, we must close the open-ended literal level of *The Spanish Tragedy* with an analogy in order to discover its allegorical meanings.

However, a problem arises with the analogy that the theater audience is supposed to make. By analogy with Andrea's method of interpretation, we should also have to compare the play we are viewing—*The Spanish Tragedy*—with something else in order to learn its allegorical meanings. But what and where is this something else that we should look for? The answer to this question involves the basic problem of allegorical writing and interpretation. How does the author include the hidden meanings within the literal level? Then, how does the reader find the hidden meanings and, thus, complete the analogy? The clue to the solution to these problems in connection with *The Spanish Tragedy* is provided by Kyd's analogical use of the different meanings of mystery on the literal and allegorical levels.

One of the basic meanings of mystery in the Renaissance is ''a hidden or secret thing; a matter unexplained or inexplicable'' (*OED*. II.5). This meaning informs the literal level of dramatic action which concerns secrets and revelations, hidden crimes and searching for clues, apprehension and punishment. Kyd fashions, in effect, what we have come to call a mystery story or a whodunit; but, by leaving the simple mystery story unsolved, with the moral status of the ostensible hero in question and with a number of other secrets and narrative problems unrevealed, he directs us to discover by analogy that it is our task to serve as quasi-detectives in searching for clues to the themes and meanings of the play. We are encouraged to see the play as a mystery story in a different sense from the stage characters who lack our detached perspective and the necessary awareness to make such critical and epistemological judgments. We are led through our wider perspective as members of the audience to interpret *The Spanish Tragedy* as a literary mystery or allegory with hidden meanings.

**Source:** Frank R. Ardolino, ''Play as Mystery and Allegory,'' in *Thomas Kyd's Mystery Play: Myth and Ritual in ''The Spanish Tragedy,''* Peter Lang Publishing, 1985, pp. 15–28.

### Philip Edwards

*In the following excerpt, Edwards discusses the theme of revenge in the play.*

One of the most popular and influential of plays in its own day, *The Spanish Tragedy* became the object of affectionate derision in the succeeding generations—or of derision without affection, as with Jonson. Such elements of the play as Hieronimo's outcries and the sallies of his madness, the elaborately patterned verse, Andrea's sombre prologue, were constantly parodied and guyed by Jacobean and Caroline dramatists. This attention to the play, however scornful, shows the hold which Kyd's work had; a hold demonstrated by the successive editions of the play, and the desire to keep it fresh by adding new scenes. It was looked on as an extravagant and crude work, and yet a bold work, holding a special position as the best that could be done in an age which had not learned to produce a polished play. And it may be said that the attitude has stuck, and still prevails. Once the play had sunk into oblivion, after the mid-seventeenth century, it was not rehabilitated in the Romantic period, as so many other 'forgotten' plays were. Lamb (1808) was interested only in the Additions: he gave the 'Painter's Scene' in his *Specimens of English Dramatic Poets* and remarked that these scenes were 'the very salt of the old play (which without them is but a caput mortuum, such another piece of flatness as Locrine)'. With the growth of evolutionary criticism, historians of drama found the play a seminal work in tragedy and the revenge play, in spite of the crudity which they did not gloss over. Mild merits of various kinds were proposed by various critics, chiefly skill in maintaining suspense and in working out a complicated plot. There have been wide differences of opinion on Kyd's powers of characterization. But although there has been general recognition of Kyd's unusual ability in contriving a theatrically effective play, no one has made a serious claim that Kyd has much to offer as a poet or tragic dramatist. It is significant that the most exhaustive and sympathetic study of *The Spanish Tragedy,* the monograph by Biesterfeldt published in 1936, is a study in structure (*Die dramatische Technik Thomas Kyds*). A standard view of Kyd is Gregory Smith's summing-up in *The Cambridge History of English Literature* (vol. v, 1910, p. 163):

> The interest of Kyd's work is almost exclusively historical. Like Marlowe's, it takes its place in the development of English tragedy by revealing new possibilities and offering a model in technique; unlike Marlowe's, it does not make a second claim upon us as great literature. The historical interest lies in the advance which Kyd's plays show in construction, in the manipulation of plot, and in effective situation. Kyd is the first to discover the bearing of episode and of the 'movement' of the story on characterisation, and the first to give the audience and reader the hint of the development of character which follows from this interaction. In other words, he is the first English dramatist who writes dramatically.

The historical position of Kyd has been the chief concern of criticism, and that is one reason why the brief account of the play which follows avoids questions of what Kyd borrowed and what he gave to others. Another reason is that our uncertainty about the date of the play makes it extremely difficult to mark Kyd's place in a fast-moving development of the drama. Was Lorenzo the first great Machiavellian villain? Did Kyd invent the Elizabethan revenge play? Yet Kyd's play is a most ingenious and successful blending of the old and the new in drama, and the fact that a comparative method is not followed here will not, I hope, obscure the obvious point that no good verdict can be made on Kyd's achievement which does not take into account what was achieved in plays written or performed at the same period.

*The Spanish Tragedy* is a play about the passion for retribution, and vengeance shapes the entire

**THE IDEA OF REVENGE AS A PERSONAL SATISFACTION FOR WRONGS ENDURED IS ENLARGED INTO THE IDEA OF REVENGE AS PUNISHMENT, A UNIVERSAL MORAL SATISFACTION FOR CRIME COMMITTED, OR THE DEMANDS OF DIVINE JUSTICE."**

action. Revenge himself appears as a character near the beginning of the play, a servant of the spiritual powers, indicating what a man may find in the patterns of existence which are woven for him. Retribution is not only the demand of divine justice but also a condescension to human wants. Andrea seeks blood for his own blood; though he died in war, Balthazar killed him in a cowardly and dishonourable fashion, and not in fair fight (I. iv. 19–26, 72–5; I. ii. 73). The gods look with favour on Andrea and are prepared, by destroying his destroyer, to bring him peace. When all is completed, he exults: 'Ay, now my hopes have end in their effects, / When blood and sorrow finish my desires . . . Ay, these were spectacles to please my soul!' Men lust for retribution, and the gods, assenting to this idea of satisfaction as only justice, can and will grant it. Marlowe never wrote a less Christian play than *The Spanish Tragedy*: the hate of a wronged man can speak out without check of mercy or reason; when a sin is committed, no-one talks of forgiveness; the word 'mercy' does not occur in the play.

Once Proserpine has granted that Balthazar shall die (I. i. 81–9), everything that happens in the play serves to fulfil her promise. To bring about what they have decreed, the gods use the desires and strivings of men. Hieronimo and Bel-imperia and Lorenzo, as they struggle and plot to bring about their own happiness, are only the tools of destiny. The sense of a fore-ordained end is strongly conveyed by Kyd by his constant use of dramatic irony. The characters always have mistaken notions about what their actions are leading them towards. Bel-imperia believes that 'second love will further her revenge', but only, it turns out, through the murder of her second love. As Horatio and Bel-imperia speak of consummating their love, they are overheard by those who are plotting to destroy it. And as the unwitting lovers go off the stage, the King enters (II. iii) complacently planning the marriage of Bel-imperia with Balthazar. By the very means he chooses to make his crime secret, the liquidating of his accomplices, Lorenzo betrays the crime to Hieronimo. Pedringano is secure in his belief in the master who is about to have him killed. The King and the court applaud the acting in a play in which the deaths are real. And there are very many other examples. In a way, the play is built upon irony, upon the ignorance of the characters that they are being used to fulfil the decree of the gods.

The play seems to move in a rather leisurely way from the entry of Andrea's Ghost to the killing of Horatio, the deed which opens the play's chief interest, Hieronimo's revenge. There is the description of the underworld by Andrea, two long reports of the battle in which Andrea was killed (one by the General to the King, and one by Horatio to Bel-imperia), Hieronimo's 'masque', and the introduction of the sub-plot concerning Villuppo's traducement of Alexandro at the Portuguese court. These prolix early scenes should not be dismissed without taking into account Kyd's use of the long speech in general throughout the play. Two recent and most interesting brief studies of the play's language have put Kyd's 'antiquated technique' in a new light. Both Moody E. Prior and Wolfgang Clemen demonstrate how Kyd converts the techniques and conventions of an academic and literary drama with considerable skill to new dramatic ends: the long speech becomes more dramatic in itself and is used more dramatically. A good example used by both critics is that the most elaborately stylized rhetoric issues from the mouth of Balthazar, and these studied exercises in self-pity are used as a means of characterization; the more practical people, like Lorenzo and Bel-imperia, are impatient of his round-about utterance (e.g., I. iv. 90–8, II. i. 29, II. i. 134). Clemen has particularly valuable things to say about how Kyd controls the tempo of the play through his use of the long speech, and how purposefully he knits together (each mode serving its own function) the long speech and dialogue; a long speech, for example, will introduce, or sum up, issues which are to be or have been set out in dialogue. But although Clemen, like Biesterfeldt before him, can find the early scenes in some measure artistically justified, and an improvement

on what Kyd's predecessors achieved in long 'reports', it is the very absence of that artistry which Kyd shows in his handling of the long speech in the later parts of the play which makes the early scenes seem so laboured. And, long speeches apart, it is very hard to justify the sub-plot. The Portuguese court could have been introduced more economically and the relevance of theme is very slight. Few readers of *The Spanish Tragedy* resent the clamant appeals and laments of Hieronimo and the rest once the play is under way, but few readers fail to find the early scenes tedious, and I think the common reaction is justified. It is as though Kyd began to write a literary Senecan play, and, even as he wrote, learned to handle his material in more dextrous and dramatic fashion.

But the opening of the play will seem far more dilatory than it really is to those who take it that the real action starts only with the death of Horatio. It is Balthazar's killing of Andrea which begins the action—the news being given by the ghost of the victim. The avenging of Andrea is, as we have seen, the supernatural cause of all that follows; but in terms of plot, too, or of direct, human causes, all flows from Andrea's death. For Andrea's mistress wishes to revenge herself on the slayer of her lover. Bel-imperia is a woman of strong will, independent spirit, and not a little courage (witness her superb treatment of her brother after her release, first furious and then sardonic, making Lorenzo acknowledge defeat; III. x. 24–105); she is also libidinous. Kyd has successfully manœuvred round a ticklish necessity of the plot (that Bel-imperia and Horatio should be lovers) by making Bel-imperia a certain kind of woman; what *has* to be done, is credibly done, naturally done. There is no question about her relations with Andrea (see I. i. 10, II. i. 47, III. x. 54–5, III. xiv. 111–12); and, with Horatio, she does not appear to be planning an early wedding; the two are entering upon an illicit sexual relationship, and it is Bel-imperia who is the wooer (II. i. 85, II. ii. 32–52).

But, not to anticipate, Bel-imperia, while wishing to avenge Andrea, finds herself conceiving a passion for Horatio (I. iv. 60–1). She is momentarily ashamed of her lightness and tries to rationalize her affection as being a sign of her love for Andrea (62–3); then she repents and decides that revenge must come before she is off with the old love and on with the new (64–5) and then (triumphant ingenuity!) realizes that to love Horatio will in fact help her revenge against Balthazar, since it will slight the prince, who is a suitor for her love (66–8). So character and plot are married, and the action drives forward on its twin pistons of love and revenge.

Bel-imperia's scheme brings about her lover's death. Balthazar has new cause to hate the man who took him prisoner, but his hate would be nothing were it not given power by the hate of Lorenzo, whose fierce pride has twice been wounded by the lowly-born Horatio: once over the capturing of Balthazar, and now in his sister's preferring Horatio to his royal friend. Bel-imperia's revengeful defiance brings about the simple reaction of counter-revenge—the murder of Horatio in the bower. Horatio is hanged and the *fourth* of the interlocked revenge-schemes begins: Andrea's the first, then Bel-imperia's, then Lorenzo's and Balthazar's, and finally Hieronimo's. Kyd may seem to take some time to reach this most important of his revenge-schemes, but he chose to set layer within layer, wheels within wheels, revenge within revenge. The action is a unity (the Portuguese scenes excepted), and in engineering the deaths of Balthazar and Lorenzo, Hieronimo satisfies not only himself, in respect of Horatio, but Bel-imperia in respect of Horatio and Andrea, and Andrea in respect of himself. And Hieronimo's efforts to avenge his dead son are the means by which the gods avenge Andrea. The presence of the Ghost of Andrea and Revenge upon the stage throughout the play, with their speeches in the Choruses, continually reminds us of this fact, which is indeed so central to the meaning of the play that it is astonishing that it is occasionally overlooked.

Hieronimo's motives for revenge are several. (i) Revenge will bring him emotional relief; (ii) it is a duty; (iii) a life for a life is the law of nature, and (iv) is, in society, the legal penalty for murder.

Hieronimo's first remark about revenge is to tell Isabella that if only he knew the murderer, his grief would diminish, 'For in revenge my heart would find relief.' The therapeutic virtues of homicide may seem doubtful, but Hieronimo insists:

Then will I joy amidst my discontent,
Till then my sorrow never shall be spent. (II. v. 55–6)

Closely associated with this odd and selfish cue for revenge is the idea of revenge as an obligation. We are to imagine (because it is hardly stated explicitly) that Horatio's peace in the world beyond depends, like Andrea's, upon his obtaining the life of his murderer as a recompense for, and a cancellation of,

his own death. For Hieronimo to assume the duty of securing this price is a tribute to his son and a measure of his love:

Dear was the life of my beloved son,
And of his death behoves me be reveng'd. (III. ii. 44–5)

Hieronimo takes a vow to avenge Horatio and, of course, the notion of a vow to be fulfilled, with the bloody napkin as a symbol of it, provides a good deal of the play's dramatic force, particularly as regards Hieronimo's sense of insufficiency, failure, or delay. But, it may be noted, delay itself is not an issue in the play. That Hieronimo's conscience should accuse him for being tardy (III. xiii. 135) is a measure only of the stress he is under and the difficulties he faces, and of the depth of his obligation; that Bel-imperia and Isabella should speak of delay (III. ix and iv. ii. 30) is a measure only of their understandable impatience and does not mean that Hieronimo *could* have acted more quickly. It is the sense of delay which is real, and not delay itself. Hieronimo does everything possible as quickly as possible.

The idea of revenge as a personal satisfaction for wrongs endured is enlarged into the idea of revenge as punishment, a universal moral satisfaction for crime committed, or the demands of divine justice. Though Hieronimo's wrongs are personal, he sees his claims for satisfaction as the claims of the Order of Things. The mythology chosen to represent the governance of the world is rather muddled in *The Spanish Tragedy*; paganism sits uneasily with—something else; but the gods (whoever they are) hate murder and will, through human agents, punish the murderer. There is morality among the gods, or so Hieronimo (somewhat anxiously) trusts:

The heavens are just, murder cannot be hid. (II. v. 57)
If this incomparable murder thus
Of mine, but now no more my son,
Shall unreveal'd and unrevenged pass,
How should we term your dealings to be just,
If you unjustly deal with those that in your justice
    trust?
(III. ii. 7–11)
Murder, O bloody monster—God forbid
A fault so foul should scape unpunished. (III. vi. 95–6)

When things go wrong with Hieronimo, he pictures himself beating at the windows of the brightest heavens, soliciting for justice and revenge (III. vii. 13–14). When things go well, he has the sense of divine support. But the nexus between Hieronimo's plans for revenge and the workings of providence is a somewhat controversial matter, and must be discussed with other facts in mind.

Punishment of murder is the course of human law, and Hieronimo's revenge is to be within the framework of law. Yet he goes about to discover the murderer in a manner curious to modern eyes. He sees it as his personal duty to find the criminal, and he conceals the crime. But this is no usurpation of the law; there is no C.I.D. to call in and he must act himself. The secrecy is to be explained by Hieronimo's fear that someone is contriving against his family so that it behoves him to move warily. Bel-imperia's letter seems to confirm his suspicion; nothing could be less credible than its news, and, should there be a plot against his family, what more suitable means to entrap him than to get him to lay an accusation for murder against the King's own nephew (III. ii. 34–43)? He will find out more, still keeping his mission secret (III. ii. 48–52). Confirming evidence comes via Pedringano, and Pedringano's arrest and punishment are an important accompaniment of Hieronimo's vendetta. For here is an orthodox piece of police-work, as it were. Pedringano commits murder, he is arrested *flagrante delicto* by the watch, tried by a court, and executed. There is law in Spain, and, once a murderer is known, he can be brought to account by due process of law. Hieronimo's anguish at the trial of Pedringano is not because for him justice has to be secured by different means, but because the course of justice which is available cannot be started since he, the very judge, cannot name the murderer of his son. It is not the least part of Hieronimo's design to indulge in Bacon's 'wild justice'; it does not enter his head to 'put the law out of office'.

But, now that Hieronimo has Pedringano's letter and the clinching evidence which he needed, he may proceed to call in the aid of law and get justice. To lay an accusation, however, proves to be the heaviest of Hieronimo's difficulties. The protracted battle of wits between Hieronimo and Lorenzo (so excellently handled by Kyd and so unfortunately obscured in the Additions) comes to a head, and, more powerful obstacle still, just as Hieronimo is ready to call down punishment on the criminals, the strain on his mind begins to tell, and his madness begins. The unsettling of Hieronimo's mind is well done; it has been prepared for long ago, in Hieronimo's excessive pride in his son when he was alive, and it is made more acceptable in that Isabella ('psychologically' unimportant as a character) has already been shown to be going out of her mind with grief. Hieronimo's frenzy makes Lorenzo's task of keeping him from the King easy; Hieronimo really prevents himself from securing justice. Thwarted, he plots to be his own avenger.

At this point, we may bring in again the question of divine justice. Momentarily, and most awkwardly, Jehovah assumes a role in the play; Hieronimo remembers that the Lord says, 'Vengeance is mine, I will repay' (III. xiii. 1 and note). He acknowledges that 'mortal men may not appoint their time' (l. 5). But since 'justice is exiled from the earth' he persuades himself that private vengeance is justified. Bowers is of the opinion that the play condemns Hieronimo for taking it upon himself to be the executioner instead of waiting for God's will to be done, and that 'Kyd is deliberately veering his audience against Hieronimo.' The problem is far from simple. It has been seen that the gods of the play like revenge. More important, after the *Vindicta mihi* speech, Hieronimo is convinced that his private course is congruent with the morality of heaven. When he is joined by Bel-imperia, he interprets his good fortune as a sign of the approval of the gods, and feels that he is a minister of providence:

Why then, I see that heaven applies our drift,
And all the saints do sit soliciting
For vengeance on those cursed murderers. (IV. i. 32–4)

Moody Prior (*Language of Tragedy,* p. 57) sees this outcry as a turning point in the drama. 'Private vengeance is now identified with the justice of heaven, and the torment of his mind is over. In the episodes which follow, he is calculating and self-possessed.' This seems a most sensible view, but the question must be asked, Is Hieronimo deluding himself in supposing he now has divine support? To answer 'yes' to this question must suggest that there is a clash in the play between the dominant pagan morality and a Christian morality. The only overt introduction of the Christian morality on revenge is in the brief allusion to St Paul; where, in other parts of the play, the mythology for Providence seems to be Christian—as in the passage just quoted, with its reference to heaven and saints—we almost certainly are faced with inconsistency and confusion on Kyd's part and not a dualism. We could, indeed, make no sense out of a dualism which meant that every reference to powers below was a reference to evil and every reference to powers above a reference to good. The clash, if it exists, must be between the ideas which Hieronimo has and ideas not expressed in the play, except in the *Vindicta mihi* speech. In other words, the argument must be that Hieronimo is condemned because the Elizabethans condemned revenge, however strongly the play's gods support him.

But what an Elizabethan might think of Hieronimo's actions in real life may be irrelevant to the meaning of *The Spanish Tragedy*. Hieronimo may still be a sympathetic hero in spite of Elizabethan indignation against private revenge. The cry of *Vindicta mihi,* and the pause it gives Hieronimo may be more of a dramatic than a moral point. Hieronimo, robbed of the law's support, rocks for a moment in indecision before determining that at all costs the murderers must die. The indecision, and then the determination, are dramatically most important and effective; but the cause of the indecision (the inappropriate promptings of Christian ethics) is not important. Kyd has won sympathy for Hieronimo in his sufferings; there is no sign, at the end of the third and the beginning of the fourth Act, that Kyd now wishes the audience to change their sympathetic attitude, even though orthodoxy would condemn the private executioner. Kyd creates, and successfully sustains, his own world of revenge, and attitudes are sanctioned which might well be deplored in real life. The moral world of the play is a make-believe world; the gods are make-believe gods. In this make-believe world, the private executioner may be sympathetically portrayed and his Senecan gods may countenance his actions. And all this may be, however strongly Kyd himself disapproved of private vengeance. I remarked that *The Spanish Tragedy* was an un-Christian play, and so it is. But it is not written to advocate a system of ethics, or to oppose one. If its moral attitudes are mistaken for the 'real life' attitudes of the dramatist, then the play has an appalling message. But if the play is seen as a thing of great—and skilful—artificiality, with standards of values which we accept while we are in the theatre, there is no problem at all about sympathizing with the hero. The play had power enough to lull an Elizabethan conscience while it was being performed.

It could well be said, however, that it is a poor play which depends on the audience suspending its belief in law and mercy. And yet a swingeing revenge-play has its own emotional satisfaction for the audience. Vengeance is exacted from evil-doers by a man whose wrongs invoke pity; in enabling an audience to forget their daily docility and to share in Hieronimo's violent triumph, it may be that Kyd has

justified himself as an artist more than he would have done in providing a sermon on how irreligious it is to be vindictive.

It would be foolish to gloss over the difficulty of siding with Hieronimo to the very end, after the punishment of the criminals. As Bowers points out, he seems in the final scene little more than a dangerous and bloodthirsty maniac. Although I have suggested that the crudities of Hieronimo's departure from life might have been much less apparent in Kyd's original version of the play, no theory of revision can explain away what seems to be the pointless savagery of the murder of the unoffending Castile. It may be that Kyd was trying to give a Senecan touch of the curse upon the house, but there are other considerations which make *condemnation* of Hieronimo rather irrelevant. In the first place, Castile was Andrea's enemy (see II. i. 46–7 and III. xiv. 111–13) and Hieronimo is the agent of destiny employed to avenge Andrea; Castile's death appears to make Andrea's peace perfect. Revenge is satisfied, and we had best try not to worry about the bloodthirstiness of it all.

Much more important, however, is the reflection that *The Spanish Tragedy* is, after all, a tragedy of sorts. Hieronimo has gone mad with grief, with the stress of observing his vow, and with the long war between himself and Lorenzo. As Castile falls, horror is mingled with pity that this should be the end of Hieronimo's life. If we cannot take Senecan revenge very seriously, or the somewhat contrived idea of destiny, we can take Lorenzo's machinations and Hieronimo's sufferings without embarrassment. *The Spanish Tragedy* has most merit in its study of the hero's grief and final distraction, and, when at the end the innocent man suffers at the hands of the hero whose innocence was not in question, it is probable that an audience feels a more complex emotion than revulsion against extra-legal revenge.

**Source:** Philip Edwards, ''Introduction,'' in *The Spanish Tragedy,* edited by Philip Edwards, Methuen, 1959, pp. l–lxi.

## SOURCES

Bowers, Fredson Thayer, *Elizabethan Revenge Tragedy, 1587–1642,* Princeton University Press, 1940, pp. 3–100.

Broude, Ronald, ''Time, Truth, and Right in *The Spanish Tragedy,*'' in *Studies in Philology,* Vol. 68, 1971, p. 131.

Burrows, Ken C., ''The Dramatic and Structural Significance of the Portuguese Sub-plot in *The Spanish Tragedy,*'' in *Renaissance Papers,* Fall 1969, p. 30.

Edwards, Philip, *Thomas Kyd and Early Elizabethan Tragedy,* Longmans, 1966, p. 6.

———, ''Thrusting Elysium into Hell: The Originality of *The Spanish Tragedy,*'' in *The Elizabethan Theatre XI,* edited by A. L. Magnusson and C. E. McGee, P. D. Meany, 1985, pp. 123, 131–32.

Erne, Lukas, *Beyond ''The Spanish Tragedy'': A Study of the Works of Thomas Kyd,* Manchester University Press, 2001, pp. 110–11.

Hunter, G. K. ''Ironies of Justice in *The Spanish Tragedy,*'' in *Dramatic Identities and Cultural Tradition: Studies in Shakespeare and His Contemporaries,* Barnes & Noble, 1978, p. 220; originally published in *Renaissance Drama,* Vol. 8, 1965.

Justice, Steven, ''Spain, Tragedy, and *The Spanish Tragedy,*'' in *Studies in English Literature,* Vol. 25, 1985, p. 274.

Kyd, Thomas, *The Spanish Tragedy,* edited by J. R. Mulryne, New Mermaid ed., Hill and Wang, 1970.

———, *The Spanish Tragedy,* edited by Thomas W. Ross, University of California Press, 1968.

Murray, Peter B. *Thomas Kyd,* Twayne Publishers, 1969, pp. 54, 127.

Shakespeare, William, *Hamlet,* edited by Harold Jenkins, Arden Shakespeare ed., Methuen, 1982.

Stockholder, Kay, '''Yet Can He Write': Reading the Silences in *The Spanish Tragedy,*'' in *American Imago,* Vol. 47, No. 2, Summer 1990, p. 101.

Wiatt, William H., ''The Dramatic Function of the Alexandro-Villuppo Episode in *The Spanish Tragedy,*'' in *Notes and Queries,* n.s., Vol. 5, 1958, pp. 327–28.

# FURTHER READING

Clemen, Wolfgang, *English Tragedy before Shakespeare,* Methuen, 1961, pp. 100–12.

This is an analysis of the long set speeches in *The Spanish Tragedy.* Clemen shows Kyd's originality in integrating these speeches with the structure of the plot and in presenting them in a more dramatic fashion than their Senecan models.

Freeman, Arthur, *Thomas Kyd: Facts and Problems,* Clarendon Press, 1967.

This is the most comprehensive account of Kyd's life and works. It includes detailed discussions of the date and sources of *The Spanish Tragedy,* as well as its style, structure, stage history, parodies, textual additions, and critical reception.

Harbage, Alfred, ''Intrigue in Elizabethan Tragedy,'' in *Essays on Shakespeare and Elizabethan Drama, in Honor of Hardin Craig,* edited by Richard Hosley, University of Missouri Press, 1962, pp. 37–44.

Harbage argues that one of Kyd's distinctive and influential achievements was his introduction into tragedy of the element of intrigue, in which the action is complicated. In doing this, Kyd also employs comic methods, thus creating a kind of ''comitragedy.''

Johnson, S. F., ''*The Spanish Tragedy,* or Babylon Revisited,'' in *Essays on Shakespeare and Elizabethan Drama, in Honor of Hardin Craig,* edited by Richard Hosley, University of Missouri Press, 1962, pp. 23–36.

Johnson argues that in the play, Spain is equated with the Biblical Babylon, which God promises to destroy. Hieronimo's vengeance is therefore just, since it brings down the king of Spain, whom many English Protestants regarded as being in league with the Antichrist, the pope.

Murray, Peter B., *Thomas Kyd,* Twayne's English Authors Series, No. 88, Twayne, 1969.

Murray sketches the literary and historical background of the play and then analyzes it scene by scene in terms of the development of action, character and theme. The final chapter considers the play's relation to the tragedies that followed it, with attention to the additions to Kyd's play that were published in 1602. Murray also includes a chronology and an annotated bibliography.

# *Tamburlaine the Great*

CHRISTOPHER
MARLOWE

1590

In 1587, Christopher Marlowe, William Shakespeare's contemporary and one of the star playwrights of the English Renaissance, produced a daring and thrilling play focusing on the triumphs of a Tartar conqueror. Famous for adeptly incorporating the style of blank verse (unrhymed iambic pentameter) into English drama, the play was so popular that Marlowe was compelled to write a sequel including Tamburlaine's and his wife's deaths. Together, the plays became known as *Tamburlaine the Great*. Poetically captivating, as forceful and powerful as Tamburlaine the character, Marlowe's verse in these works marks a major shift from the conventional, low comic style of other Renaissance works. The plays are not a straightforward glorification of Tamburlaine's violent conquests, since Marlowe frequently highlights his protagonist's excessive brutality and hubris, or excessive pride. However, their directness and eloquence make it difficult not to admire Tamburlaine, both for his rhetorical power and his lifelike animation.

Alongside Tamburlaine's ceaseless conquests and their implications about war and politics run more general themes of desire, ambition, and power. Marlowe uses his portrayal of Tamburlaine's capture, betrothal, marriage, and ultimate loss of his wife Zenocrate, the daughter of the Egyptian ''soldan,'' or sultan, to highlight these themes in another context, questioning the true nature of his hero's romantic passion. The plays also comment on ideas of fatherhood and masculinity by way of

Tamburlaine's expectations of his sons, including his cruel treatment and murder of his son Calyphas, whom he considers a coward. Marlowe develops all of these themes through his skillful and unique use of language, which is why he is considered perhaps the most important stylistic innovator of the period. Originally published in 1590, the plays are now available in modern editions with notes and introductory material, such as the New Mermaid edition, *Tamburlaine the Great: Parts I and II*, published by Ernest Benn Limited in 1971.

## AUTHOR BIOGRAPHY

Born in Canterbury, England on February 6, 1564, Marlowe was the son of a shoemaker. He attended King's School in Canterbury and was awarded a scholarship to Cambridge University, where he studied dialectics. Because of a number of mysterious absences from college, Marlowe was in danger of not receiving his master of arts degree. But Queen Elizabeth's Privy Council intervened with a letter stating that he had been in the queen's service and not, as was the rumor, part of a Catholic conspiracy in Rheims, France. In fact, many historians believe Marlowe was a spy of the queen's advisor Sir Francis Walsingham, which would explain his powerful connections and the company of spies and politicians with whom he associated.

In any case, Marlowe moved to London in 1587 with his degree and began writing in earnest. Before the year was out, the first part of *Tamburlaine the Great* had been performed to great success, and Marlowe produced its sequel in the following year. *Tamburlaine the Great* was the only one of Marlowe's works to be published during his lifetime, but he wrote and produced at least five more plays, including *Edward II*, a sophisticated play about the downfall of a weak king and his treacherous usurper Mortimer, and *Dr. Faustus*, in which Faustus sells his soul to the devil in exchange for power and knowledge. Before writing these plays, however, Marlowe translated poetry by the ancient Romans Ovid and Lucan. Later, he translated (with some additions of his own witty innovations) the ancient Greek poem *Hero and Leander*.

While living in London, Marlowe associated with the dramatist Thomas Kyd and the poet Thomas Watson. In 1589, Marlowe and Watson were briefly imprisoned for their roles in the homicide of a publican. In the subsequent years, Marlowe was involved in several other scuffles and legal disputes. In 1593, Kyd accused him of authoring several heretical papers that had been discovered in Kyd's room. Marlowe appeared before the queen's Privy Council, which was the normal course for a gentlemen; it was afforded to Marlowe, most likely, because of his continued associations with powerful politicians, but there is no evidence that they examined him. Shortly afterwards, on May 30, 1593, Marlowe spent all day with Ingram Frizer, a known operative of the powerful Walsingham family, and two other men at a meeting house in Deptford, near London. Frizer stabbed Marlowe above the right eye and killed him. The reasons for the attack and murder remain a mystery. Frizer was pardoned of the murder within a month.

## PLOT SUMMARY

### Part 1, Acts 1–2

*Tamburlaine the Great* begins with a prologue declaring that, unlike the silly wordplay of previous literature, this play will feature the "high astounding" words and actions of a conqueror. Act 1 then opens with the king of Persia, Mycetes, complaining to his brother Cosroe of a band of outlaws led by a "Scythian" shepherd named Tamburlaine. Scythians would technically have lived north and northeast of the Black Sea, but Marlowe uses the term interchangeably with "Tartar," which signifies the area of East Asia controlled by Mongol tribes. Cosroe criticizes his brother for being a weak and foolish king, and Mycetes instructs his chief captain Theridamas to kill Tamburlaine and his band before they enter Persia. Then, two Persian lords inform Cosroe of widespread unrest and offer him the crown, which Cosroe accepts.

Act 1, scene 2 introduces Tamburlaine, who has captured the Egyptian princess Zenocrate and is declaring his love for her. Theridamas arrives with one thousand soldiers, compared to Tamburlaine's five hundred, but Tamburlaine convinces Theridamas in a parlay to join his side. In act 2, Cosroe joins with Tamburlaine to overthrow his brother. When Mycetes hears of this, his lord Meander forms a plan to throw gold on the field in order to distract soldiers, whom he considers to be greedy thieves. Tamburlaine encounters Mycetes attempting to hide his crown in a hole; Tamburlaine tells Mycetes that he will not steal his crown yet, but take it when he wins the battle. After Tamburlaine and Cosroe conquer

Mycetes's army, Cosroe departs for Persepolis, the capitol. Tamburlaine decides to challenge Cosroe to a battle for the Persian crown. Tamburlaine triumphs and Cosroe dies, cursing Tamburlaine and Theridamas.

### Part 1, Acts 3–5

In act 3, scene 1, the Turkish Emperor Bajazeth discusses with his subsidiary kings their siege of Constantinople, which was then held by Christians. He warns Tamburlaine not to enter Africa or ''Graecia,'' which included much of the Balkan peninsula, then under Turkish control. In the next scene, Tamburlaine overhears the Median, or Iranian, Lord Agydas urge Zenocrate to disdain Tamburlaine's suit, but Zenocrate stresses that she wants to be his wife. Tamburlaine surprises them, and Agydas stabs himself to avoid torture. Act 3 concludes with Tamburlaine's victory over the Turks and Tamburlaine making slaves of Bajazeth and his wife Zabina.

Zenocrate's father, the ''soldan,'' or sultan of Egypt, opens act 4 by vowing to stop Tamburlaine's advances upon Egypt with the help of the king of Arabia, who was Zenocrate's betrothed before Tamburlaine kidnapped her. Tamburlaine and Zenocrate then humiliate and torture Bajazeth and Zabina. Tamburlaine vows to overtake Egypt despite his wife's plea to pity her father. In act 5, the governor of Damascus, besieged by Tamburlaine's army, sends a group of virgins to plead for mercy, but Tamburlaine has them slaughtered and hoisted on the city walls. When Tamburlaine goes to fight the soldan and the king of Arabia, Bajazeth and Zabina kill themselves by beating out their brains. Zenocrate finds them and is dismayed by their and her people's blood on Tamburlaine's hands. After the king of Arabia dies and Tamburlaine wins the battle, sparing the soldan's life and actually giving him more territory than before, Tamburlaine crowns Zenocrate queen of Persia.

### Part 2, Acts 1–3

Orcanes, the king of ''Natolia,'' or Anatolia, the region east of the Bosporus in present-day Turkey, and Sigismond of Hungary begin act 1 by swearing to uphold a truce, while Tamburlaine advances on Anatolia from Egypt. Bajazeth's son Callapine, who is Tamburlaine's prisoner in Egypt, then convinces his jailer Almeda to help him escape, promising him a kingdom. Meanwhile, Tamburlaine instructs his three sons on the arts of

*Christopher Marlowe*

war; he harasses Calyphas, the son not inclined to fight, for being a coward. Tamburlaine meets Theridamas, Techelles, and Usumcasane, and they prepare to march on Natolia.

In act 2, Sigismond agrees to break his vow with Orcanes and attack the Natolian army while Orcanes is preparing to engage Tamburlaine. Orcanes wins the battle, however, attributing the victory partly to Christ, since Sigismond broke his vow to the Christian savior. Tamburlaine then discovers that Zenocrate is sick. Her physicians can do nothing to save her, and she dies. Act 3 begins with the crowning of Callapine as the Turkish emperor, and Callapine's vow to avenge his father's wrongs. Tamburlaine then burns down the town in which Zenocrate died, forbidding the world to rebuild it, and gives his sons a lesson in fortitude. Theridamas and Techelles march northward, where they sack Balsera, a town on the Natolian frontier. They capture its captain's wife, Olympia, after she burns her son's and husband's bodies. Tamburlaine and Usumcasane then parlay with Callapine and his subsidiary kings, threatening each other and boasting.

### Part 2, Acts 4–5

Act 4, scene 1 reveals Tamburlaine's sons Amyras and Celebinus attempting to convince their brother Calyphas to fight, but Calyphas refuses. After Tamburlaine returns in triumph, he stabs Calyphas, calling him slothful and weak and ordering that the Turkish concubines bury him. In the next scene, Theridamas attempts to court Olympia, but she wishes to die and tricks him into stabbing her. Tamburlaine then rides in his chariot drawn by the former kings of "Soria," or Syria, and "Trebizon," or Trabzon, an area in the northeastern section of present-day Turkey, and tells his soldiers to rape the Turkish concubines.

Tamburlaine's next conquest is of Babylon. Since the governor refuses to yield the city, Tamburlaine has him hung in chains and shot. He then orders the kings of Trebizon and Soria hung, bridles Orcanes and Jerusalem on his coach, orders all Babylonian men, women, and children drowned, and commands that sacred Islamic books be burnt. Afterwards, Tamburlaine feels "distempered," and soon it becomes clear that Tamburlaine is deathly ill. En route to Persia, a messenger arrives to inform Tamburlaine that Callapine, who escaped from the battle in Natolia, has gathered a fresh army and means to attack. Tamburlaine scares them away, but he is too weak to pursue them. He retires to review his conquests and regret that he cannot conquer more. He then crowns his son Amyras, orders Zenocrate's hearse to be brought in, and dies.

# CHARACTERS

### Agydas

Agydas is the Median, or Iranian, lord traveling to Egypt with Zenocrate when Tamburlaine captures them. Tamburlaine overhears Agydas advising Zenocrate to resist the "vile and barbarous" Tamburlaine's advances. Agydas stabs himself to avoid torture.

### Alcidamus

*See* King of Arabia

### Almeda

Almeda is Callapine's jailer, whom Callapine convinces to release him by promising Almeda a kingdom in Turkey. Callapine does in fact give him a kingdom before battling with Tamburlaine, although Almeda will never rule it because Tamburlaine wins the battle.

### Amyras

Tamburlaine's son and successor, who reluctantly accepts the crown while his father is dying, Amyras is a militaristic young man who idealizes his father. He revels in war, asking his father after they subdue the Turks whether they can release them and fight them again so that none may say it was a chance victory. However, as Amyras laments in the final lines of the play, he is no equal to Tamburlaine and will not be able to continue the glory of his reign.

### Anippe

Anippe is Zenocrate's maid, whose right it is to treat the Turkish Empress Zabina as a servant after Tamburlaine subdues the Turkish armies.

### Bajazeth

The emperor of Turkey in part 1, until Tamburlaine conquers his armies and makes him a slave, Bajazeth is a proud Islamic leader who ultimately beats his brains out on his cage rather than be subject to more humiliation and starvation. Bajazeth swears before his last battle to remove Tamburlaine's testicles and force him to draw his wife's chariot. While captive, Bajazeth frequently curses Tamburlaine, highlighting his most barbarous moments. Bajazeth's son Callapine extends the recurring theme of a bitter and vengeful enemy to Tamburlaine into part 2.

### Bassoes

Now spelled "Bashaws" or "Pashas," a bassoe was the title given to Turkish officials. In the play, bassoes are servants of Bajazeth.

### Callapine

Bajazeth's son and heir to the Turkish Empire, Callapine has dedicated his life to avenging his father's cruel treatment and to destroying Tamburlaine. Callapine is a cunning leader who manages to win over his jailer and escape from Tamburlaine's prison. Callapine also escapes from the battle that he loses to Tamburlaine, returning to attack Tamburlaine's army at the end of the play. Although Callapine is no match for Tamburlaine, he does manage to stay alive and unconquered throughout the play, completely committed to, as he puts it, "conquering the tyrant of the world." The implication is that he will return to haunt Amyras after Tamburlaine dies.

## Calyphas

Calyphas is Tamburlaine's son, whom Tamburlaine murders after he refuses to fight in the battle against the Turks. Calyphas is somewhat weak and slothful, which Tamburlaine despises. But Calyphas is also simply uninterested in war; he is content to play cards and fantasize about women.

## Captain of Balsera

Olympia's husband, the captain refuses to yield his hold to Techelles and Theridamas, and he is killed in the subsequent invasion.

## Casane

*See* Usumcasane

## Celebinus

Tamburlaine's son, Celebinus, is a forceful young man who emulates his father.

## Cosroe

Brother to the Mycetes, king of Persia, Cosroe usurps his brother's title with Tamburlaine's help. Cosroe worries about the state of the empire under his brother's ineffectual rule, and he determines at the bequest of several Persian lords to take the crown and rule more wisely. Although Cosroe is not as weak as his brother, he is naive enough to leave Tamburlaine and his companions with all of their soldiers after they win the battle for the Persian crown, and Tamburlaine quickly challenges him to battle and triumphs.

## Frederick

A peer of Hungary, Frederick persuades Sigismund to break his vow of peace with Orcanes.

## Gazellus

The viceroy, or ruler with the mandate of a king, of the Turkish territory of Byron, Gazellus is an ally and advisor to Orcanes.

## Governor of Babylon

Stubborn and unyielding, the governor of Babylon refuses to allow Tamburlaine inside his city. When he is conquered and under threat of death, however, he attempts to bribe Tamburlaine by telling him where a stockpile of gold is hidden. Tamburlaine has him hanged nevertheless.

## Governor of Damascus

The governor of Damascus fears that Tamburlaine will slaughter everyone in his city, but his attempt to plead for mercy, sending four virgins to Tamburlaine's camp, fails.

## King of Arabia

The king of Arabia, also known as Alcidamus, is betrothed to Zenocrate before she is captured by Tamburlaine. Zenocrate prays for his life to be spared but Alcidamus is killed during Tamburlaine's battle with the soldan of Egypt, and, as he dies, Alcidamus declares his love for Zenocrate.

## King of Jerusalem

The king of Jerusalem is an ally of Callapine's, and after defeating him Tamburlaine forces him to pull his chariot.

## King of Soria

The king of ''Soria,'' or Syria, is one of Callapine's subsidiary kings. After conquering him, Tamburlaine forces him to pull his chariot until he loses strength, at which point Tamburlaine has him hanged.

## King of Trebizon

Like Soria, the king of Trebizon is an ally of Callapine's who is forced to pull Tamburlaine's chariot after he is conquered. The king of Trebizon is hanged when he becomes too tired to pull the chariot.

## Meander

The Persian lord closest to Mycetes, Meander councils the king on defending himself from the uprising, but he changes his allegiance to Cosroe after the battle.

## Menaphon

Menaphon is the Persian lord closest to Cosroe. He is key in the conspiracy to overthrow Mycetes.

## Mycetes

Mycetes is the king of Persia from the opening of part 1 until Tamburlaine and Cosroe overthrow him. He is a weak king whose speech is characterized by repeated sounds and clichés. Although he complains that his brother abuses him, he does nothing about it. When Tamburlaine discovers Mycetes attempting to hide his crown on the battlefield, an absurd attempt to ensure that no one will steal it, Tamburlaine lets the king keep it until he wins the battle.

### Olympia

Wife to the Captain of Balsera, Olympia is a resigned but shrewd woman who watches her husband die, stabs her son, and then attempts to burn herself on their funeral pyre before Theridamas prevents her. Then, rather than submit to Theridamas's romantic advances, she tricks him into stabbing her in the neck.

### Orcanes

The king of Natolia, or Anatolia, a region slightly larger than the Anatolia of present-day Turkey, Orcanes is a fierce enemy to Tamburlaine. He has more vocal power than most of Tamburlaine's other enemies, and he is a somewhat more complex figure as well, actually paying tribute to Christ because he believes that Christ was responsible for his victory over the king of Hungary, who broke his Christian vow of peace with Orcanes. After Tamburlaine enslaves him, Orcanes curses Tamburlaine with insights such as, ''Thou showest the difference 'twixt ourselves and thee / In this thy barbarous damned tyranny.''

### Perdicas

Perdicas is Calyphas's idle companion, with whom Calyphas is playing cards before his father stabs him.

### Sigismund

The Christian king of Hungary, Sigismund makes a vow by Christ to maintain peace with Orcanes, but his advisors persuade him to break the vow and attack Orcanes while they have the opportunity. When Sigismund has lost the battle and lies dying, he repents of this perjury and begs for Christian forgiveness.

### Soldan of Egypt

The soldan of Egypt is Zenocrate's father. He despises Tamburlaine for stealing his daughter and invading his land. After Tamburlaine conquers his armies, spares his life, and gives him back more than his former territory, however, the soldan praises Tamburlaine and consecrates his daughter's marriage.

### Son

The son of the captain of Balsera is a brave young man who allows his mother to stab him in order to avoid torture at the hands of Tamburlaine's army.

### Tamburlaine

Majestic and eloquent, with the ability to conquer not just kings and emperors but the audience of the play, Tamburlaine is one of the most important characters in Elizabethan drama. He is the source of the poetry that made Marlowe famous, and he can be both captivating and repellant because of his brutality. The key to his character is power and ambition, of which Tamburlaine has a superhuman amount, as well as the willingness to use any extreme in order to be triumphant. Unconcerned with social norms or everyday life, Tamburlaine views himself in relation to the gods, and Marlowe uses him as a tool to ask philosophical questions such as what is the furthest extent of human power and accomplishment, and whether this is significant in comparison with heaven.

Tamburlaine begins his life in what Marlowe calls Scythia, a region north and northeast of the Black Sea, and rises to power first in Persia, subsequently conquering much of North Africa, the Middle East, Eastern Europe, and India. Marlowe's work concentrates on his battles with Turkish emperors and their subsidiary kings, whose territory at that time included much of the Middle East and North Africa. Tamburlaine's personal life is closely related to his outward conquests; he wins his wife by conquering her father's kingdom and then devastates much of the Middle East in his fury over her death. He sees his sons entirely as military leaders and murders his idle and slothful son Calyphas after he refuses to fight against the Turkish armies. At the end of his life, Tamburlaine is unsatisfied with the extent of his conquests. His thirst for power is unquenchable and, as his son and heir Amyras emphasizes, none can match Tamburlaine's power.

Like most of Marlowe's protagonists, Tamburlaine has a complex relationship with the audience of the play. He inspires a mixed reaction because he is brutal without bounds yet simultaneously passionate and glorious. Elizabethan audiences would be particularly offended, as well as somewhat titillated, by the presumptuousness of what they would consider a heathen—although the historical Tamburlaine was a Moslem, Marlowe shows him burning sacred Islamic texts and generally speaking as though he thinks of the gods in ancient Greek and Roman terms. This emphasis on mythology is also significant because Scythia is the area traditionally believed to hold the mountain to which Zeus chained Prometheus, a Titan who is famous for stealing fire from the gods and who, like Tamburlaine, dares to challenge Jupiter and the other classical gods.

## Techelles

Tamburlaine's close companion, Techelles is an ambitious military leader entirely loyal to Tamburlaine. He came with Tamburlaine from Scythia and continues to be a skillful general after Tamburlaine makes him king of Fez, North Africa. Techelles's devotion to Tamburlaine, including his willingness to slaughter the virgins of Damascus and drown the population of Babylon, reveals Tamburlaine's power as a leader.

## Theridamas

The chief captain in the Persian army, Theridamas is sent to kill Tamburlaine but instead becomes his loyal and lifelong companion. Telling Tamburlaine he has been, ''Won with thy words, and conquered with thy looks,'' Theridamas quickly becomes one of Tamburlaine's three closest advisors and most able generals. Tamburlaine makes him king of Argier, in North Africa, and Theridamas is critical to the sieges of Balsera and Babylon in part 2. At Balsera, Theridamas falls in love with Olympia, the wife of Balsera's captain, and stops her from throwing herself on her husband and son's funeral pyre.

Tamburlaine calls Theridamas majestic when he first meets him, and it is clear from part 1 that he is a valiant and powerful Persian lord, although he is perhaps not as power hungry as Techelles and Usumcasane, since he says in Act 2, Scene 3 that he could live without being a king. It is when he threatens to rape Olympia and gullibly accepts her magic war ointment over her ''honour,'' however, accidentally stabbing her, that Theridamas is revealed to be a warrior at heart and not a lover.

## Uribassa

Uribassa is Orcanes's ally and a viceroy of an unspecified Turkish territory. He and Gazellus are viceroys for Callapine while the emperor is Tamburlaine's prisoner in Egypt.

## Usumcasane

Usumcasane is Tamburlaine's close companion who, like Techelles, comes from Scythia and is so devoted to Tamburlaine that he is unable to comprehend Tamburlaine's death from illness.

## Virgins of Damascus

After hearing their pleas for mercy on their city, Tamburlaine has the four virgins of Damascus slaughtered and hoisted on the city walls.

## Zabina

Zabina is the proud Turkish empress of Bajazeth. She tells Zenocrate before their husbands go to battle that she would make her a slave, so at first the audience feels little sympathy for her when she is made the servant of Zenocrate's maid. However, after Tamburlaine tortures her and her husband, keeping them inside a cage, and she and Bajazeth kill themselves, Zenocrate and the audience pity them and feel astonished at Tamburlaine's cruelty. Before she goes mad and kills herself, Zabina reveals herself to be a practical person by urging her husband to eat and stay alive, hoping that at some point they will be freed.

## Zenocrate

Daughter to the soldan of Egypt, Zenocrate is captured by Tamburlaine at the beginning of part 1, and she remains with him as his concubine, and then his wife, until her death in part 2, act 2. Initially, she resists Tamburlaine's romantic suit and calls herself ''wretched'' because she is forced to remain with him, but by act 3 she has fallen in love with him and is swept up in the glory of conquest. Zenocrate is dismayed by the prospect of Tamburlaine making war with her father and her people, however. Her most difficult moment comes in part 1, act 5, scene 2, after Tamburlaine's brutal siege of Damascus. Distraught after seeing Tamburlaine slaughter four innocent virgins, she then comes upon the bodies of Bajazeth and Zabina, who have killed themselves because of Tamburlaine's cruelty. Nevertheless, she wishes Tamburlaine victory over her father and her former betrothed, Arabia, praying that their lives may be spared.

Tamburlaine's frequent superlative descriptions of Zenocrate's beauty and divine nature reveal Zenocrate's critical influence on the actions of the play. Tamburlaine's conquests in part 1 are closely related to winning Zenocrate, and in part 2 are largely a result of lamenting her death. These eloquent speeches, however, do not necessarily shed light on Zenocrate's true character or her struggle, particularly in part 1, of allegiance between her lover and her people, which is also a struggle between brutality and peace. This struggle resolves after the Soldan agrees to Zenocrate's marriage with Tamburlaine, although in part 2, act 1, Zenocrate wonders when her husband will finally cease his bloody conquests. Also, Tamburlaine's struggle with his son Calyphas, who is completely uninterested in war, is an extension of the conflict between peace and war in his mother's character.

# THEMES

## *The New Human*

Tamburlaine, with his cruelty, his ambition, his tremendous capacity for violence, and his intense passion for his wife, represented a new and shocking type of hero for late sixteenth-century audiences. He was the equivalent of what audiences today might consider a Romantic hero—a passionate male obsessed with war who defies convention and whose fervency goes far beyond what is even conceivable for most people. Audiences were not even necessarily intended to understand Tamburlaine, such was his shock value and his capacity to break through the very fabric of society with his ceaseless conquests and unquenchable thirst for power.

Because Tamburlaine was a new type of hero, conquering the traditions of restraint and mercy with his passion, eloquence, and power, he challenged the traditional morality system that pervaded London theaters in the early Elizabethan period. Unlike the conventional plays that preceded *Tamburlaine the Great*, Marlowe's work does not consist of a simplistic didactic, or morally instructive, lesson emphasizing that humans must adhere to a strict and traditional moral code. Instead, the play attacks the philosophical problem of humanity's relationship to the universe and provides an example of a new and extreme worldview that seems to ignore traditional morality. It is Tamburlaine's conviction that he is as powerful as a god, and he refuses to see himself as an impotent human in a massive, oppressive universe. He believes that he can control the world and is tremendously optimistic about the possibilities of human achievement.

Marlowe does not straightforwardly advocate this worldview; Tamburlaine's relationship with the audience is complex, and he often inspires repugnance and alienation. However, Tamburlaine is not simply an anti-hero whose worldview the audience finds persuasive solely because he is a devilish figure of temptation. Tamburlaine is likely an exhilarating figure, in part, because he represents a passion that the audience is meant to admire. The play challenges the idea that humans are locked into an oppressive moral system and suggests that a new type of humanity is possible, which will break through these boundaries. The Renaissance movement in continental Europe stressed the emergence of a new model for humanity, open to diverse types of knowledge and entirely new ideas, and Tamburlaine was a vital contribution to the development of this ethos in England. Although Marlowe raises the possibility that he has gone too far, Tamburlaine provides a compelling case for a new type of human.

## *Power and Ambition*

One of the play's principle themes is conveyed in its depiction of excessive cruelty and ambition, the characteristics that define its main character and make him controversial. In fact, the theme of power pervades nearly every aspect of the play, from Tamburlaine's conquests, to his role as a father, to his relationship with Zenocrate. Tamburlaine's military brilliance and his ability to carry out such horrendous acts—such as slaughtering the virgins of Damascus and drowning the population of Babylon—are the results of these character traits, as are his eloquence and rhetorical power that convince Theridamas and others to join him. Marlowe's audience could be expected to find such excessive displays of power un-Christian and even repulsive, as well as to find themselves somewhat captivated by it.

Ambivalent reactions to these themes extend to the other aspects of Tamburlaine's life; the audience is asked to ponder whether the hero's extraordinary passion for his wife is actually romantic love or a form of perverted possession and desire. They must judge whether Tamburlaine is justified in murdering his own son because that son is weak and lazy. Tamburlaine is generally unwilling to place his love above his military ambitions (although he does spare Zenocrate's father). He often seems to perceive Zenocrate as a treasure to be won, such as in his initial declaration of love for her, when he describes her in terms of great wealth and power. Similarly, he views his sons solely in terms of their

# TOPICS FOR FURTHER STUDY

- Tamburlaine is famous for arousing a mixed reaction in his audiences. What was your response to his character? Were you, like Theridamas, "Won with [his] words?" To what degree did you find him cruel and barbarous, and at which points did you find him cruelest? Is Tamburlaine a hero and a protagonist? Why or why not? Discuss the reactions you think Tamburlaine is meant to inspire. How are these reactions important to Marlowe's goals in the play?

- Marlowe's *Dr. Faustus* (1594) is also about a power-hungry character who inspires ambivalent reactions in the audience. Read this play and compare it with *Tamburlaine the Great*. How are the moral themes of the plays similar? How do they differ? What does *Dr. Faustus* imply about one human's relationship to the universe? How does this differ from the implications of *Tamburlaine the Great*? How do the plays differ in style and form? Which one sheds more light on today's society, and which one would you rather see performed today? Explain your choices.

- Identify the key scenes in *Tamburlaine the Great*, including the most eloquent scene, the most daring scene, the scene with the most important turning point, and the scene most crucial to establishing Marlowe's major themes. Support your choices with examples and quotes, and explain your decisions. Then, perform one of these scenes with your classmates. Think about the best way to portray the scene according to the point it is trying to make, and think about which characters are most important to the scene and how to emphasize their importance. What is the best way to deliver what Ben Jonson called "Marlowe's mighty line?" How can you approach your performance of the play to best express what you consider to be its meaning? Use your answers to improve your performance.

- *Tamburlaine the Great* departs substantially from the actual history of the Mongol warlord, Tamerlane. Read a prominent history book about Tamerlane and discuss how this changes your view of the conqueror. How does the contemporary view of Tamerlane differ from Marlow's portrayal? How might Marlowe's play be different if it treated Tamburlaine as he is depicted in modern histories? Support your answer with examples and discuss, more broadly, the goals of history texts and how they differ from those of historical fiction.

courage and fortitude, and he has no regrets about stabbing Calyphas because he was too slothful to enter a battle.

It is possible that Marlowe implies, according to the conventions of a tragedy, that Tamburlaine's downfall occurs because of the excessive appetite for power that is his tragic flaw. If this is the case, Tamburlaine's and Zenocrate's illnesses and deaths could be seen as a punishment from the heavens for Tamburlaine's presumptuousness. This is not necessarily clear, however, since there is no great evidence that the illness involves any divine intervention; in fact, God does not seem to interfere with human affairs in the play. In any case, Marlowe poses provocative questions about the place of power and ambition in society, the desirability of these characteristics in an age of tremendous artistic and scientific advances and the evils that can result from an excessive display of power.

# STYLE

## Blank Verse

In his prefatory tribute to the first folio edition of Shakespeare's plays, Ben Jonson cited (though in deference to Shakespeare) "Marlowe's mighty line," and critics tend to agree that Marlowe's innovation in verse was the first and most influential predecessor to the stylistic achievements of the era. It was *Tamburlaine the Great* that made this powerful verse style famous. Marlowe stresses in the prologue to part 1 that it is his intention to depart from the ''jigging veins of rhyming mother wits,'' or unsophisticated rhymes like those of a mother giving silly advice in the form of a jig, of his predecessors. Instead, Marlowe wanted to create a work of high philosophical ambitions and powerful, ''astounding'' verse.

The poetic tool Marlowe uses for his ''mighty line'' is blank verse, or unrhymed iambic pentameter, which is a meter with five beats of two-syllable units called iambs. This style, adapted from Greek and Latin heroic verse, was developed in Italy before Henry Howard, Earl of Surrey, introduced it in England. Marlowe was perhaps the chief innovator to instill blank verse with emotional force and rhythmic eloquence, and he was also influential in skillfully suiting his characters' temperaments to the nature of their lines. Tamburlaine's lines, for example, are not just musical and eloquent but extremely powerful and majestic, with hard consonant sounds and decisive, accented peaks and flourishes, while those of Calyphas and Mycetes rhyme ineffectually and repeat sounds frequently, to no purpose.

### Rhetoric

Although Tamburlaine's speeches may sometimes sound overwrought, in Elizabethan England they were fine examples of rhetoric, or the art of speaking and writing effectively. Marlowe does not follow the strict logical rules of classical rhetoric, which was used in ancient Greek philosophy but, like the ancient Greeks, he does use language as a powerful tool to convey the truth and to be persuasive. Marlowe's compelling and insightful use of comparisons, his evocative diction, or word choice, his startling imagery, and his ability to incorporate his words into a compelling and musical rhythm of speech combine to create some of the most powerful examples of rhetoric in Elizabethan drama. Elizabethan audiences might sometimes find Tamburlaine pompous, but his rhetoric is the dramatist's chief tool in portraying Tamburlaine as such a captivating figure.

In addition to their usefulness in winning over the audience, Tamburlaine's powers of rhetoric are critical to his military triumphs. Tamburlaine's rhetoric compels Theridamas to join him and allows him

to inspire his soldiers to victory. Also, Tamburlaine relies on rhetoric to win over Zenocrate and instruct his sons in the arts of war. Of course, he supports his rhetoric with his majestic looks and forceful actions, but this style of speech is the key means by which he is able to communicate his power. Marlowe saw rhetoric as one of the most important keys to power and truth. He disdained the low comedy and clichéd rhetoric of previous dramatists. In fact, he wrote such grand and forceful speeches that writers began to parody Marlowe's style after *Tamburlaine the Great* became famous, seeing Marlowe as the prime example of powerful, and sometimes ostentatious, rhetoric.

# HISTORICAL CONTEXT

### Elizabethan England

When Queen Elizabeth I succeeded to the throne of England in 1558, the nation was poorer and less powerful than the continental powers France and Spain. England had been torn by internal religious strife between Protestants and Catholics, and was quite unstable. Elizabeth, an adept and shrewd monarch who surrounded herself with pragmatic advisors, presided over a period of increasing power and prosperity, making peace with France in 1560, defeating the Spanish Armada in 1588, and garnering relative peace with Catholics and Puritans. England was not without its problems, however. England enjoyed a sometimes precarious political stability. Elizabeth narrowly survived a number of assassination attempts that would have resulted in a fierce battle of succession since, despite pressure from Parliament, she never married or produced an heir.

In this environment of relative tolerance and stability, the flourishing of the arts in continental Europe spread to England, and the late sixteenth century became famous for an extraordinary flowering in literature known as the English ''Renaissance.'' Writer and statesman Sir Thomas More, and poets Edmund Spenser and Philip Sidney, were among the key figures in developing ''humanism'' in English literature; this involved the revival of classical literature and an emphasis on individual humanity instead of strictly religious themes. Marlowe was perhaps the first major innovator in humanistic English drama, however, along with his friend Thomas Kyd. Marlowe was also very influ-

# COMPARE
# &
# CONTRAST

- **1400s:** Tamerlane rules his vast territories by allowing his soldiers to keep the booty from the conquests and filling his treasury with ransom money extracted from conquered cities.

  **1580s:** The Ottoman Empire, at the height of its power, controls most of Tamerlane's former territories and arouses fear and misunderstanding from Christian nations.

  **Today:** The Middle East, which is the primary location of the events in *Tamburlaine the Great,* contains a number of prosperous nations with rich natural resources, but it is one of the most politically unstable regions in the world.

- **1400s:** England is in the midst of the Middle Ages. Henry IV has just come to power, having deposed his cousin Richard II, and he will deal forcibly with the insurrections and other problems resulting in part from the devastation of the Black Plague in the mid-1300s.

  **1580s:** Elizabeth rules England with shrewd pragmatism and, although her treasury has been overstretched by military expenses, she creates a stable environment for trade.

**Today:** Tony Blair is prime minister of England, and his tenure has been characterized by center-left economic and social policies, as well as his alliance with the United States in a pre-emptive war with Iraq.

- **1400s:** The Americas have yet to be discovered by Europeans, and Native Americans live a traditional way of life that varies by region and civilization.

  **1580s:** The most brutal Spanish conquests of native populations in South and Central America have largely come to an end, but English and French colonialists have yet to establish the firm hold that will lead to the widespread displacement and massacre of Native North Americans.

  **Today:** In the United States, Native Americans struggle with poverty and a lack of appropriate resources on reservations, but the Native American population is not becoming fully integrated into mainstream culture and does not necessarily desire to do so.

---

ential over Jonson and Shakespeare, whose writing came at what is generally considered the height of the English Renaissance.

## *Tamerlane*

The conqueror Tamerlane, known in Europe by this corrupt version of the Persian ''Timur-i Leng,'' or ''Timur the lame,'' was a fearsome military leader, famous for his brutality and his devotion to Mongol-Islamic religious practices. Born in Ulus Chaghatay, an area in present-day Uzbekistan, in 1336, Tamerlane was a member of a Mongol tribe that had converted to Islam during his father's rule. He was a thief and brigand during his youth, attracting allies and preparing for his bid for leadership, which was at first unsuccessful. After he built an

alliance with the neighboring prince Amir Husayn (marrying his sister to fortify their relationship), Tamerlane was able to drive all other serious threats to his control from Ulus Chaghatay. Husayn and Tamerlane then became involved in a leadership struggle, and Tamerlane laid siege to Husayn's city, allowed a local warlord to kill him, and took four of his wives as concubines.

By 1379, Tamerlane had suppressed a series of rebellions and established sole control over Ulus Chaghatay. Partly to keep other warlords in his control, since they would be under his eye as a subservient army, he then began a series of extremely successful conquests into neighboring lands. From 1386 to 1388, Tamerlane invaded Persia and Anatolia but afterwards was forced to return to defend his homeland against a former protégé called Tokhtamish. Tamerlane finally defeated Tokhtamish in 1390. After two more years spent defending against enemies from the north, Tamerlane invaded Iran in 1392, where he installed his sons as governors. In 1398, he set off for India, where he sacked Delhi and murdered 100,000 Hindu prisoners. In 1399, he campaigned into Syria and Anatolia, defeating the Ottoman Sultan Bayazid I and taking him captive in 1402. In 1405, Tamerlane was preparing for an ambitious conquest into China when he fell ill and died. He had established no sustainable infrastructure, and his vast empire rapidly decayed after his death, despite the fact that he nominated a grandson as his successor.

*Tamburlaine the Great*, particularly in part 2, contains a great number of historical inaccuracies and alternative representations, partly because there was a limited amount of historical information available at the time and partly because Marlowe did not always interpret that information correctly, but mainly because Marlowe's dramatic goals differed from the historical reality. For example, since Marlowe likely did not conceive of the work in two parts, it was necessary to use events prior to Bajazeth's demise, and, in the case of Orcanes's defeat of Sigismund, nearly fifty years after it, in order to form a coherent drama in part 2. Also, the play's depiction of Bajazeth and his wife's enslavement inside an iron cage stems from an alternative reading of the historian Arabshah. Other examples, such as Tamburlaine's love for Zenocrate, are entirely fictional, and reflect Marlowe's desire to cast the play in the manner most effective for developing his major themes.

# CRITICAL OVERVIEW

Among most successful plays of the Elizabethan era, the two parts of *Tamburlaine the Great* captivated audiences with their eloquent rhetoric and powerful verse. Although they remained popular as pieces of literature, they were not frequently performed in later periods and are infrequently performed in the early 2000s in comparison with Marlowe's other works. The grandiose wars and conquests of the plays may not translate well to the modern stage, but the work is now, and has been for centuries, a prominent subject for stylistic and thematic literary criticism.

Marlowe's reputation suffered because of the numerous scandals surrounding his private life, including the circumstances of his death. Claims that he was an immoral atheist and blasphemer initially affected the critical evaluation of his plays. The dramatist's critical reception recovered, however, and *Tamburlaine the Great* became one of the principle subjects for critics interested in the development of blank verse and the style of Renaissance drama. Most critics consider it extremely important, if not the most important work, in developing the style that came to a height around the turn of the sixteenth century.

Regarding the principle thematic meaning of the work, two analytical views eventually emerged to explain Tamburlaine's ambivalent character. The first view stresses that Tamburlaine is a brutal and un-Christian tyrant whose power and ambition is reprehensible. As Roger Sales points out in his 1991 study *Christopher Marlowe*: ''Tamburlaine's rise to power is usually at the expense of a series of legitimate rulers. Might is shown to triumph over right.'' The second main analytical view stresses, instead, that Tamburlaine's glory and majesty inspire the audience to recognize the highest limits of human achievement—a view that J. W. Harper calls ''romantic'' in his 1971 introduction to the plays: ''the view that he is a perfect symbol of the Renaissance spirit and the spokesman for Marlowe's own aspirations and energies.'' Harper stresses that the first view—that Tamburlaine is a ''stock figure of evil''—is more accurate than the ''romantic'' view. But, like most critics, he acknowledges that there is some truth to both interpretations.

# CRITICISM

## *Scott Trudell*

*Trudell is an independent scholar with a bachelor's degree in English literature. In the following essay, Trudell argues that Marlowe's play is a psychological drama in which Tamburlaine represents the awesome potential of basic psychological desires.*

On the surface, *Tamburlaine the Great* is a play about war and conquest, that is concerned with ambition, domination, and power in the public sphere, while private conflicts and domestic life are neither glorious nor important. Actions in the play take on epic proportions, and Tamburlaine places

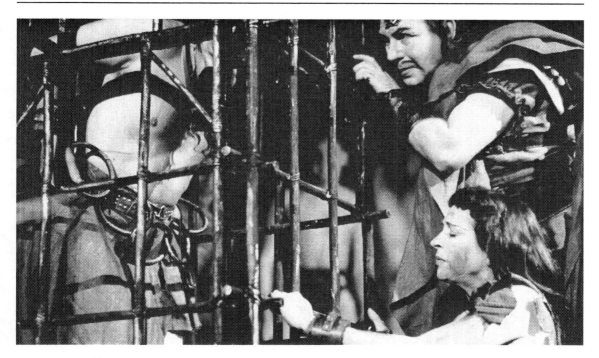

*Donald Wolfit and Leo McKern in a 1951 production of* Tamburlaine the Great

his life on the scale of the gods, whom he frequently challenges and to whom he often compares himself. Although Marlowe is concerned with ambition, power, and violence, his principle interest is in the origin of these themes in Tamburlaine's internal psychology. In fact, Tamburlaine is actually much less interested in conquest and political rule than he is in winning over his idealized wife, extending his sense of self to the next generation, and satisfying his egotistical desires to feel majestic and triumphant.

One of the most important pieces of evidence that *Tamburlaine the Great* is a psychological drama lies in its treatment of Tamburlaine's relationship with Zenocrate. Zenocrate is entirely Marlowe's own addition to the narrative; she does not appear in any historical documents about Tamerlane the conqueror and there is no evidence that Tamerlane fell passionately in love with anyone. The historical Tamerlane had a number of wives and concubines, including the warlord Amir Husayn's sister, whom he married to fortify their alliance, and also a former wife of Husayn, after Tamerlane had him killed. Unlike these women, Zenocrate does not help forward Tamburlaine's practical political goals in the play; if anything, she does him harm since she arouses the attempted vengeance of the king of Arabia and her father, the soldan of Egypt.

In fact, Tamburlaine seems almost to adjust his political ambitions, conquering Zenocrate's people, her betrothed husband, and her father, in order to win his wife entirely and become the king of their relationship. Of course, Tamburlaine states that he will not alter his military aims for his wife, and he does not accommodate her request for mercy on her people, but he does spare the soldan's life and give him back more than his former territory. This is an action suitable not for a warrior with purely political and military ambitions, but for a son-in-law who wishes to be the magnanimous ruler of his marriage. Tamburlaine views his domestic life as a battle to be won, and his wife a treasure to be pillaged, by conquering her territory and subduing the other males who lay claim to her.

Likewise, the conquests of part 2 do not originate in Tamburlaine's grand plan for military expansion as much as they signify the destruction and violence he feels are necessary to grieve for and honor his late wife. Marlowe stresses that this is the case in the prologue to part 2: "But what became of fair Zenocrate, / And with how many cities' sacrifice / He celebrated her sad funeral." As before, Tamburlaine forces the conditions of his personal life on the outer world; he burns the city where Zenocrate died, pillages many others, and drowns

# WHAT DO I READ NEXT?

- Marlowe's *Dr. Faustus,* first performed in 1594, concentrates on a forceful and eloquent main character who sells his soul to the devil in exchange for knowledge and power. It is one of Marlowe's most sophisticated achievements.

- *Tamburlaine the Conqueror* (1964), by Hilda Hookham, is an eloquent account of the historical Tamerlane and a thorough, definitive treatment of his career.

- Shakespeare's *Henry V,* first performed about 1599, deals with an ambitious and charismatic king who penetrates further into France than any other English monarch. It is an example of

further accomplishments in elegant rhetoric and blank verse in the years after Marlowe's death.

- In addition to his plays, Marlowe wrote a number of poems including the delightful *Hero and Leander* (1598), a treatment of the ancient Greek story of two lovers who can meet only when Leander swims across the Hellespont strait.

- Chelsea Quinn Yarbro's *A Feast in Exile* (2001) is a popular historical vampire novel in which Tamerlane the conqueror captures the Count of Saint-Germain, a vampire, during Tamerlane's siege of Dehli. Tamerlane keeps the count in his service as a healer.

---

the entire population of Babylon in order to express the devastation of his marriage. Whereas, before his marriage, he killed the four virgins of Damascus after showing them the ''imperious Death'' that sits on his sword, representing the penetration of Zenocrate's virginity, now he drowns the women and children of Babylon in order to cease their fertility and ensure that, like his wife's dead body, they are barren.

Marlowe is careful to highlight that there is often something strange and shocking about Tamburlaine's transference of his psychological state onto the state of the world. The paradox that Tamburlaine ''celebrated'' a ''sad funeral'' with the sacrifice of numerous conquered cities highlights the theme, which is also common in part 1, that Tamburlaine's militaristic displays of brutality and power are often inappropriate and perverse in the context of his personal life. Marlowe chooses two moments in *Tamburlaine the Great* to portray this theme most acutely, the first of which comes at the confluence of the slaughter of the virgins of Damascus and the suicides of Bajazeth and Zabina. When Zenocrate discovers their bodies, having just witnessed Tamburlaine's slaughter of her people, she is torn between repulsion and devotion towards her husband, and the audience feels the same way.

Tamburlaine's defeat and imprisonment of Bajazeth and his wife seem appropriate at first, given Bajazeth's threat to bind Tamburlaine in chains and make him a eunuch, but when the Turks are tortured inside a cage and humiliated as an ornament to Tamburlaine's domestic scene, events rapidly begin to take on a cruel and barbarous significance. By the time Zabina sees her husband's gory remains and goes mad, the audience feels appalled that Tamburlaine could cause such a thing to happen.

Similarly, when Tamburlaine ignores the protestations of his sons and comrades in part 2, and murders his son Calyphas for failing to fight against the Turkish armies, the audience is repulsed by Tamburlaine employing brutal, military force on his defenseless child. Calling him, ''not my son, / But traitor to my name and majesty,'' Tamburlaine kills Calyphas because he fails to satisfy Tamburlaine's sense of psychological self-preservation. In his address to Jove immediately before he stabs his son, Tamburlaine tells the God to take back his son's soul because it is, ''A form not meet to give that subject essence, / Whose matter is the flesh of Tamburlaine.''

Perhaps the most shocking aspect of this moment is the idea that Tamburlaine could be so self-obsessed as to murder his son, without regret, simply because his son does not fulfill his function as an extension of Tamburlaine's ego. Audiences alternate between finding Tamburlaine's violence and cruelty evil and finding it somewhat titillating; they feel ashamed and disturbed when they encounter extreme moments of cruelty—which they had previously admired—invading Tamburlaine's personal and domestic life. However, the recurring aspect of Tamburlaine's character, with which audiences find it perhaps most difficult to sympathize, is his incredible egotism. Tamburlaine has absolutely no inhibitions in acting out his most basic psychological desires. He has no boundary between his internal sense of self and his desire to impose his sense of self upon the world around him.

Marlowe uses this psychological drama to arouse suspicion about the desirability of Tamburlaine's enormous egotism and emphasize that his presumptuousness is unnatural and un-Christian. Like the orthodox moralists of his age, Marlowe is concerned about excessive pride, and he is careful to highlight its dangers and temptations, which lurk inside everyone's mind but, unlike Tamburlaine's, are not always externalized. Marlowe also demonstrates through Tamburlaine's outwardly-directed psychology that human beings are passionate, romantic creatures with glorious and limitless aspirations. However much it seems to highlight the dangers of great ambition, *Tamburlaine the Great* also suggests that the human psyche, if blown to the proportion of Tamburlaine's, and allowed to escape the bounds of humility and internalization, is capable of rising to the scale of a god.

Tamburlaine is not a model for human psychology or an everyman figure; he is entirely unique, even unrealistic at times, and none of the other characters approach his eloquence or power in the play. Theridamas, although he is a majestic conqueror, cannot conquer Olympia in the domestic sphere as Tamburlaine has conquered Zenocrate; Theridamas succumbs to a simple trick and, in his attempt to bring his military might down upon his desired wife, accidentally kills her. As Amyras points out to his father when they learn of his impending death: "Your soul gives essence to our wretched subjects, / Whose matter is incorporate in your flesh." Tamburlaine's allies are merely part of his majestic flesh, which eclipses all other glory and allows little else to coexist with its majesty.

Nevertheless, Marlowe sees Tamburlaine as a signal of the potential inherent in every human

> MARLOWE ALSO DEMONSTRATES THROUGH TAMBURLAINE'S OUTWARDLY-DIRECTED PSYCHOLOGY THAT HUMAN BEINGS ARE PASSIONATE, ROMANTIC CREATURES WITH GLORIOUS AND LIMITLESS ASPIRATIONS."

psyche, which has such shockingly powerful and violent desires that it is capable of almost anything. Nearly everyone, from the audience to the other characters in the play, reveals his/her taste for power and majesty by becoming so enthralled by Tamburlaine. This is a natural reaction, the reaction Marlowe intends by stressing that one can capture almost any passion and conquer almost any impediment to one's deepest desire if one is willing to disregard convention and carry out acts of ruthless violence. Marlowe is pointing out the fact that the world is not, as was commonly believed, a series of strictly orthodox moral hoops through which a person must jump in order to lead a happy existence, but a brutal arena in which the most violent, ambitious, and unappeasable desires and egos will rule. Tamburlaine shows that a basic aspect of the human psyche—its appetite for power—has a limitless potential and allows for the greatest of human achievements.

**Source:** Scott Trudell, Critical Essay on *Tamburlaine the Great,* in *Drama for Students,* Thomson Gale, 2005.

### Pam Whitfield

*In the following essay, Whitfield examines Tamburlaine's "systematic reduction and silencing of Zenocrate" as consistent with the theme of masculine domination and oppression present in Marlowe's works and Renaissance society.*

In the Renaissance period, hierarchies of power hinged on the construction of masculinity in opposition to, and through suppression of, the other. The dramatic text, "a compendium of small dynamics of power,'' brings into play both power hierarchies and gender relations with immediacy. Perhaps no Renaissance drama embodies the construction of the masculine and the suppression of the feminine more than Christopher Marlowe's *Tamburlaine I.* The rise and triumph of Tamburlaine is paralleled by the fall and failure of Zenocrate, providing an interpersonal exposé of power relations in which masculine authority and victory is predicated on the destruction of the feminine other's voice and volition.

Although Christopher Marlowe is noted for his lack of interest in the female point of view, *Tamburlaine I* is an exception: the play includes a comparatively extensive portrayal of female characters. Zenocrate is Marlowe's most famous female character and arguably his most fully developed, ''yet we know little about her aside from the effect she has on Tamburlaine.'' Thus readers have traditionally viewed Zenocrate through that lens. There is, however, a second perspective: from the angle of Tamburlaine's effect on her. During the course of five acts in *Tamburlaine I,* the Scythian shepherd manipulates Zenocrate's emotions, which run the gamut from hatred to love to despair to resignation. Her longest and most pivotal statements, in fact, focus on the emotional turmoil caused by her love for Tamburlaine and his (limited) affection for her.

Tamburlaine, whose sins go unpunished in Part I, apparently holds the strings to Zenocrate, as he seemingly does for all the characters. The warrior's ''physical prowess and singular ambitions captivate all whom he encounters,'' both male and female. Significantly, every attack upon Tamburlaine is unsuccessful or rebounds on his enemies. Kings, queens and sultans' daughters have no antidote to the shepherd's ambition; he robs them of agency. If they act, they do so in futility. Despite Zenocrate's eloquence and virtue, she is ultimately a Marlovian woman, helpless and ineffectual. Despite her proximity to and influence over Tamburlaine, Zenocrate is unable to prevent the destruction and bloodshed her lover seems bent on unleashing. Tamburlaine's primary effect on Zenocrate is one of immobilization; she is unable to act. Tamburlaine allows her recourse only to rhetorical agency: she speaks. In a male world of cruelty and violence, such as that created by Tamburlaine, women's most valuable and useful power may indeed be that of speech, to moralize, reason, and persuade. Yet words bounce off the ''scourge of God''; although Zenocrate curses Tamburlaine's presumptuous pride, her warnings are seen as ''mere words'' by both her lover and the audience.

Eloquent but ineffectual in the face of the Scythian's consuming ambition, Zenocrate's speech serves a different purpose: it provides a contrasting point of view. The princess may not save Damascus (or its virgins or even herself), but her ideas and values, as voiced through her language, suggest an alternative to Tamburlaine's unholy world. This alternative, however, can never be realized in Marlowe's play. Zenocrate is doomed to be subservient to Tamburlaine's will—an absolute will that leaves no room for another's volition. By forcing his will upon her and making her love him, Tamburlaine permanently alters Zenocrate's life: his love for the princess becomes her demise. Tamburlaine's relationship with Zenocrate is ultimately an act of reduction, as he reduces her to a voice, an impotent but plaintive voice, and finally to a silence.

Yet Zenocrate is not simply the voice of the other, the disempowered, a dissenter irrevocably tied to and manipulated by the force that will destroy her. Her role becomes complicated by irony: that of the other doomed to speak against herself. In *Tamburlaine I,* Zenocrate's speech acts betray her. She gives voice to morality, compassion, and concern for the eternal in a world that devalues and denies both. In Tamburlaine's world, as Zenocrate demonstrates, voice can disempower. The shepherd builds his authority through speech; in contrast, Zenocrate's words serve to ultimately undermine and destroy her identity. Her struggle to voice the conflict between her loyalty to Tamburlaine and her adherence to her own values provides Tamburlaine (and Marlowe) with a necessary source of opposition, but the threat is never a serious one. Although Tamburlaine effects a drastic change in her, turning a saucy princess into a shell-shocked survivor, she can never alter his character or ambition.

In reality, Zenocrate is made impotent before she even speaks: the reader first meets her as a captive of Tamburlaine and his soldiers, who are laden with Egyptian treasure from her procession. As a prisoner, albeit a royal one, Zenocrate lacks agency; only her voice might serve her. She employs it to plead with Tamburlaine for the release of herself and her retinue. But Tamburlaine responds by asking if she is betrothed, then asserting, ''But lady, this fair face and heavenly hue / Must grace his bed that conquers Asia / And means to be a terror of the world'' (1.2.36–8). Marlowe thus underscores the fact that Zenocrate, for all her eloquence and rationality, will be first and foremost a jewel in Tamburlaine's crown.

The "terror of the world" views Zenocrate as an icon and a possession. Yet because her voice is plaintive and her plight pitiable, her power must be removed and diffused—she must be placed on a pedestal. Tamburlaine answers her disdain with a speech of seductive flattery, promising Zenocrate:

> With milk-white harts upon an ivory sled
> Thou shalt be drawn amidst the frozen pools
> And scale the icy mountains' lofty tops (1.2.98–100).

His seduction speech rebounds with metaphors of frigidity and inaccessibility. Thus he elevates her above both action and audience, too frosty and pure and immobile to act—he attempts to confine her power to beauty and chastity. Through the seduction speech, the shepherd defines Zenocrate; in doing so, he defines his territory. She is a land to be conquered, a height to be scaled, a walled city in need of protection. Her spoils will be his alone. He speaks for her, describing her desire and fate in his own terms of appropriation and control. He also negates her sexual power:

> This aestheticizing of Zenocrate is also, of course, robbing her of any sexual threat; Tamburlaine is controlling her by situating her in an environment of frosty inaccessibility. It is, then, an act of appropriation or colonization: Tamburlaine is marking out the extent of his empire.

Zenocrate becomes, in an ironic twist of the Scythian's mind, both the spoils and the receiver of booty: he takes her as his prize, yet will later offer himself to her. The sinister promise—that Tamburlaine will make himself a gift to his beautiful captive—smacks of captivity narrative; the conqueror colonizes the other to diffuse and absorb her power.

But male desire will not be consummated in this play: part of Tamburlaine's empowerment (and Zenocrate's impotence) lies in the negation of sexual desire. *Tamburlaine I* is a remarkably asexual text; its protagonist does not bend to bodily impulses, lest he lose momentum. Stephen Greenblatt has compared Tamburlaine to a machine: "Once set in motion, this *thing* cannot slow down or change course." In the play, the protagonist has little need for sexual gratification through women because "blood lust replaces sexual desire in a sublimation achieved through violence." Even as the warrior shuns physical distractions, he gathers psychic power from the source of those distractions: Zenocrate's body. Medieval and Renaissance belief endowed virginity with unique powers, including the ability to mediate between the earthly and the divine— chastity embodied power to transcend the corporeal.

> " MARLOWE MAY HAVE
> CREATED ZENOCRATE AS A VICTIM,
> PERHAPS EVEN TAMBURLAINE'S
> ULTIMATE VICTIM, BUT IT IS HER
> FATE, PITIABLE, UNJUST, AND
> DISTURBING, THAT CONDEMNS
> TAMBURLAINE FOR HIS AMBITION,
> AMORALITY AND INHUMANITY."

Tamburlaine respects the princess's virginity and endeavors to maintain her bodily integrity, hedging his bets for immortality. By doing so, he robs Zenocrate of one traditionally female power: influence in the bedroom. The noblewoman is in the unique position of being the prisoner of a man who won't touch her; all she has left is her voice.

Tamburlaine's flattery and manipulative speech have the desired effect: between Acts 1 and 3, Zenocrate inexplicably falls in love with the opportunist, professing to find "His talk much sweeter than the Muses' song" (3.2.50). The warrior understands that "women must be flattered" (1.2.107). As Emily Bartels has noted, "Tamburlaine tailors his image to the needs and expectations of his contenders, answering their desires and outdoing their resistance." For the warrior, womanhood in the shape of Zenocrate contends with his manly ambitions; romance and sex threaten his imperialist plans. By tempting her with lordliness and love, he brings the other into the fold where she can be manipulated and controlled. He woos her with visions of empire and riches, the dream that motivates him. Zenocrate, all too human, cannot deny the appeal of glory and power:

> And higher would I rear my estimate
> Than Juno, sister to the highest god,
> If I were matched with mighty Tamburlaine (3.2.53–5).

She now sees her own worth and reputation as tied to her master's. The same woman who has boldly denounced Tamburlaine's pretensions is now fatefully smitten and speaks of "Fearing his love through my unworthiness" (3.2.65). Her friend Agydas has attempted to point out her new lover's faults, but Zenocrate rebuts his arguments. Yet her new passivity is palpable: when Tamburlaine, who has overheard the discussion, appears, the lovers do not greet each passionately. He claims her without a word and she is led away in silence.

Zenocrate's silent moments may be seen as acts of submission or resignation in the face of Tamburlaine's power, but never as indications of contentment. During her discussion with Agydas, she speaks as a woman in love, but fretfully so, as if trying to convince herself as well. Her words of praise ring hollow, as if she were reciting a script prepared for her, indeed as if Tamburlaine himself were putting words into her mouth. As Tamburlaine leads her offstage, his scowl foreboding death for Agydas, the audience must imagine what battle rages in her heart. Zenocrate's speeches in the play similarly eschew contentment: happiness is absent from her words. Her two major spoken acts, the mock-battle scene and the Zabina-death scene, involve two very different types of speech: the first martial and bickering, the second passionate and regretful.

In the battle scene (3.2), Zenocrate's self-confidence wanes as her lover's political power increases. She voices doubt in Tamburlaine's love for her because of her "unworthiness." Tamburlaine, the master strategist, recognizes her reluctance and creates an occasion that requires her to rise to it. He suggests she match words against Zabina, his rival's wife, as he matches swords with Bajazeth. He instructs her to "take thou my crown, vaunt of my worth, / And manage words with her as we will arms" (3.2.130–31). Zenocrate, like the other characters "follow[s] his example and take[s] his instructions to heart." The new king gives her a taste of royalty even as he invites her to join the man's world of sparring and battle. In this case she and Zabina engage in a battle of word and wit, an elevated and eloquent bickering that mimics, in empty words, the men's roles on the battlefield. By arranging such a performance, Tamburlaine tricks Zenocrate into changing sides; she is placed in opposition to Zabina and defends him. Thus she acts against herself, favoring bloodshed over peace, abusing the character of another noblewoman in hopes of pleasing a cruel and insatiable warrior. As Zabina and Zenocrate exchange jibes, threatening each other with slavery and prostitution if one should fall under the other's power, they pitifully foreshadow their own roles as pawns of Tamburlaine. Zenocrate is particularly prophetic, telling Zabina that soon she and Bajazeth must plead for mercy and "sue to me to be your advocates" (3.2.174). In adopting the

martial and threatening speech of men, Zenocrate's words betray her: soon Zabina and Bajazeth will indeed want for mercy, which Zenocrate will withhold, to her later regret.

The verbal antagonism continues during the first cage scene (4.2), as the conquered Turkish king is imprisoned and humiliated. Tamburlaine's egotistical defense of his inhumane treatment of Bajazeth, "This is my mind, and I will have it so" (4.2.91), serves as a refrain for the entire play. The king's will is absolute; he makes no promises to Zenocrate, or any other individual, that might undermine his imperialism. Techelles requests that he "make these captives rein their lavish tongues" (4.2.67), an ironic comment in that Tamburlaine's tongue is certainly the most lavish of all. The cogent comments of Bajazeth and Zabina make the dinner guests uncomfortable with their bloody victory, perhaps; the revelry and jesting of Tamburlaine's followers seem intended to drown out any twinges of conscience. Although Zenocrate initially plays against the Turks' words to gain favor with Tamburlaine and to shore up a little power, she soon wearies of the verbal gaming and falls silent.

Bajazeth and Zabina provide an entertaining spectacle at mealtime, but Zenocrate has larger worries during the victory banquet. Her silence prompts the king to ask, "Pray thee tell, why art thou so sad?" (4.4.66). Zenocrate's emotional withdrawal allows her to contemplate the fate of her father, town, and countrymen and to formulate an appropriate plea for their deliverance by Tamburlaine. John Gillies has suggested that Zenocrate makes a connection between the "cannibal banquet" (with the red-attired Tamburlaine suggesting that the Turks eat their own flesh) and the fate of Damascus. Her plea for the king to spare her hometown is plaintive and simple:

> My lord, to see my father's town besieged,
> The country wasted where myself was born—
> How can it but afflict my very soul?" (4.469–71).

But Zenocrate has forgotten that the values of kin and community hold little power over Tamburlaine, "a man without family ties, seemingly not sprung of the human race." Zenocrate is, however, beginning to see that Tamburlaine's single-minded appetite for power exists to the exclusion of all else. She doubts his love even as she reaffirms her own, saying:

> If any love remain in you, my lord,
> Or if my love unto Your Majesty
> May merit favor at Your Highness' hands,
> Then raise your siege from fair Damascus walls
> And with my father take a friendly truce" (4.4.73–6).

Instinctively she realizes that in a union with a power-hungry man, loyalty is more useful than love. Zenocrate states her loyalty to her lord and shows him deference through repeating verbal emblems of his title and power. She interposes a tribute, ''Honour still wait on happy Tamburlaine!'' (4.4.89) before begging leave to speak with her father in hopes of effecting a truce.

Tamburlaine continues to reduce the princess's ideals to mere words, to deny her any opportunity to act. Zenocrate requests the chance to intervene on her father's behalf, she asks to avert bloodshed and death, and in so doing, potentially undermines Tamburlaine's ambition. The king does not take her request seriously; his woman is the priceless trophy earned by a mighty warrior, not a diplomat active in his majesty's service. The king has no use for Zenocrate's veneration of family: ''In Marlowe it [family] is something to be neglected, despised, or violated.'' In denying Zenocrate's request to see her father, Tamburlaine denies peace, family and community, all values which his lover represents. Once again, Zenocrate's speech has betrayed her: Tamburlaine brushes off her attempts to use power and makes her look helpless and subjugated instead.

When Zenocrate arrives on stage after Bajazeth and Zabina have brained themselves against the cage bars, she misses Zabina's impassioned pre-suicide speech, but she intuitively guesses its point: chaos, the denial of natural order, can only bring disaster. Zabina has a power to move Zenocrate to moral consideration because Zabina achieves agency: she ''is not simply being rhetorical; she also acts.'' Significantly, Zabina has acted, profoundly and ultimately, in a way that Tamburlaine's rhetorical Zenocrate is unable to: she has put an end to senseless suffering. Zabina's words, ''I, even I, speak to her'' (5.1.314) are a warning addressed to Zenocrate, one which the latter answers with ''what may chance to thee, Zenocrate?'' (5.1.372).

Zenocrate begins to realize the absolute nature of Tamburlaine's control over her and over events. She grieves the death of a worthy rival and proclaims Tamburlaine to be ''the cause of this.'' The man ''That term'st Zenocrate thy dearest love'' is responsible for the deaths of two admirable and devoted lovers (5.1.336–37). Her loyalty to her lord is supremely tested because it negates all else in which she believes. The absolute nature of her loyalty also mocks her value system even as Tamburlaine reduces it, and her, to mere words. Her conscience resurfaces with its humanitarian values,

and she gives voice to the wrongs perpetuated against the divine order, begging the gods to ''Pardon my love, Oh, pardon his contempt / Of earthly fortune and respect of pity'' (5.1.365–66). In this soliloquy Zenocrate not only takes shared responsibility for Tamburlaine's destructive forces, she admits to herself that her fate is tied to his, irrevocably. Her many protestations of respect for and loyalty to Tamburlaine now haunt her. Zenocrate realizes that her words of fealty and devotion may ultimately be her undoing: by loving Tamburlaine, she has given herself over to ruthless cruelty.

Zenocrate's choices, debated in heart-rending speech, are not easy ones. Tamburlaine's martial actions force her to redefine her sense of duty, as she laments:

> Whom should I wish the fatal victory,
> When my poor pleasures are divided thus
> And racked by duty from my cursed heart?
> My father and my first betrothed love
> Must fight against my life and present love;
> Wherein the change I use condemns my faith
> And makes my deeds infamous through the world
> (5.1.386–92).

Tamburlaine's empire, indeed his body count, is growing at the expense of his lover's sanity. Thus does Zenocrate move from despair to resignation in the play's final scene, hoping to preserve her sense of selfhood by bowing to fate. As Richmond has noted, ''In the last sequence of the play Zenocrate is notably silent. Her joy and greeting are for her father who has been spared—not for Tamburlaine.'' Even as Zenocrate and her father are reunited, Tamburlaine establishes permanent possession of Zenocrate, expecting the Sultan's gratitude to permit him Zenocrate's hand in marriage. Thus the actual union of man and woman is subsumed by larger issues: the wedding becomes a political agreement, a truce. This is a deal between two rulers; Zenocrate remains silent. Doubtless, she has many pertinent things to say, if only as emotional release; Zenocrate has, after all, just held her dying fiancé, Arabia, in her arms. But the princess's speech has betrayed her in the past: to give voice to emotions and values is to make herself vulnerable to their abuse at the hands of Tamburlaine. Even her father sees her as an icon of purity, embodied worth, saying that he does not mind his overthrow ''If, as beseems a person of thy state, / Thou hast with honor used Zenocrate'' (5.1.484–85). Thus ''Part I ends not in an act of revolt but in the supreme gesture of legitimacy, a proper marriage, with the Scourge of God earnestly assuring his father-in-law of Zenocrate's unblemished chastity.'' This is, perhaps, Tamburlaine's one concession to the forces warring within him: he wishes to remain single and unfettered, yet a king needs progeny.

In the betrothal scene, Marlowe's twin themes of love and war are joined in the person of Zenocrate, now silenced by Tamburlaine's will and reduced to a breeder of heirs by his wish. Zenocrate becomes a pact between two warring kings, a potential peacekeeper but at the expense of herself. Upon obtaining her father's approval, Tamburlaine speaks for Zenocrate even as he asks for her consent, stating, "doubt I not but fair Zenocrate / Will soon consent to satisfy us both" (5.1.499–500). Her terse response, "Else I should much forget myself, my lord" (5.1.501), summarizes her acquiescence to her fate as the brightest jewel in a king's crown, the tie that binds two warring nations. She ascends the throne wordlessly as Tamburlaine pronounces her "divine Zenocrate" in recognition of her union to a man-god. Tamburlaine has the last word, declaring three solemn and stately burials before the marriage ceremony is performed. He promises peace: "Tamburlaine takes truce with all the world" (5.1.530). But one doubts that mere marriage, even to one fairer than Juno, can quell the warring spirit of a human Jupiter.

One might conclude that Zenocrate is safest when she is silent. The closed mouth, after all, was seen as a sign of chastity and thus integrity and submission. Although Tamburlaine concedes her rhetorical agency, he consistently thwarts her speech acts. Throughout Part 1 she seeks to move him to mercy, but he ultimately rejects love as effeminate, proclaiming that even beauty should be conquered because "virtue solely is the sum of glory" (5.1.189). Though one hopes that her most eloquent plea (5.1.349–77) for her lord's pardon might cause some stirring in the hero's conscience, or cause a greater force to halt Tamburlaine's assaults, Zenocrate is instead rebuked by Annipe for her lack of faith in her master: "Madame, content yourself, and be resolved," her maid tells her (5.1.373). Thus Marlowe suggests the possibility of Tamburlaine's redemption through Zenocrate's eloquence merely to dismiss it, and "Zenocrate's lines are spoken only to be refuted—as happens to all opposition to Tamburlaine."

Tamburlaine manipulates, undermines, and annuls the one form of agency Zenocrate has: rhetorical agency. Opposition is silenced, pleas for justice rendered ineffectual, and moral statements ignored. A master strategist, "he meets Zenocrate's

aversion to violence with diversions." He distracts her from the rape of Damascus and its virgins with a speech on beauty, using ceremony to cover violence. He overturns Zenocrate's value system as easily as he overturns her words, in fact using words to mask actions. Zenocrate's words must be subverted so that she can be subsumed. Tamburlaine sees the whole world as consumable. The fulfillment of the Scythian shepherd's nature, through his acts of self-definition and self-authorization, require the consumption of Zenocrate as opposition, but Tamburlaine escapes virtually blame-free. He has cleverly manipulated Zenocrate into speaking and acting against herself, so that his success requires the *self*-consumption of his beloved, "who is offered abundance at the price of home, family, city, and the female principle she represents." In eating her own words, Zenocrate devours her moral code, her belief in love, and her devotion to Tamburlaine. At the shepherd's feet, Zenocrate has painfully learned that in a world in which imperialism bests sentiment, the other—the woman—is designated an enemy and must be conquered. By marrying Tamburlaine she has betrayed herself and has denied life. Tamburlaine, the powermonger, has succeeded in reducing Zenocrate to nothing except, perhaps, a living metaphor of resignation and regret. It is as a voiceless and defeated shell of a woman that she ascends the throne to take her venerated seat alongside the terror of the world.

Tamburlaine's act of reducing Zenocrate ironically parallels his own expansion, both political and psychological. The audience feels a palpable sense of misgiving as Tamburlaine's cruel and destructive acts succeed again and again. It is not so much that the gods smile upon the warrior, as that he seems to have banished and conquered even them. If women are words and men are deeds, as the famous Renaissance poem goes, then Marlowe's play follows convention. Playing within their prescribed gender roles, Tamburlaine is symbolized by the arm, and Zenocrate by the tongue. Yet these roles, so common as to be not worth mentioning, are foregrounded in *Tamburlaine I* as the Scythian enacts his systematic reduction and silencing of Zenocrate. His symbolic destruction of woman as embodied in his shattering of Zenocrate's will and voice becomes, like all his other extreme and egotistical acts, a moral wrong. Through his (mis)-treatment of his lover, the audience is encouraged to examine the dangers inherent in prescribed gender roles and sex-based power issues. Marlowe may have created Zenocrate as a victim, perhaps even Tamburlaine's ultimate victim, but it is her fate, pitiable, unjust, and disturbing, that condemns Tamburlaine for his ambition, amorality and inhumanity.

**Source:** Pam Whitfield, "'Divine Zenocrate,' 'Wretched Zenocrate': Female Speech and Disempowerment in *Tamburlaine I*," in *Renaissance Papers,* 2000, pp. 87–97.

## Lisa Hopkins

*In the following excerpt, Hopkins argues that, in his plays, Marlowe "provides a sharply focused and detailed critique of the problematics of familial interaction . . . an aberration caused by particular aspects of social injustice and malaise."*

Christopher Marlowe's plays are littered with family groups shattered and destroyed, either through their own actions or those of others. Sometimes the disharmony is limited to family disagreements or ideological disunity within the family group; at other points it becomes more extreme, leading to internecine betrayal and even murder. As Frank Ardolino suggests, "the composite roles family members play as both fathers and sons, mothers and daughters, husbands and wives, brothers and sisters provide Marlowe with rich sources of complex interactions and the opportunity to portray the tensions created by the shifting roles, to limn, in short, the dynamics of power as established within the microcosm of the family." I want to argue, though, that Marlowe does more than simply "limn" these: I am going to suggest that he provides a sharply focused and detailed critique of the problematics of familial interaction, and that, contrary to modern, psychoanalytically driven theorizing of the family, he sees these as arising fundamentally not from inherent inter-generational struggle, nor from the kinds of mythic model proposed by Ardolino—who sees the plays as radically informed by the Uranus-Jupiter-Saturn model—but as an aberration caused by particular aspects of social injustice and malaise.

In what seems likely to have been Marlowe's earliest play, *Dido, Queen of Carthage,* the issue of family features very strongly. The play opens with what looks like a traditional scene of family life: a man with a boy on his lap. But we rapidly discover that this is not a scene of a father and a son, but instead of what the British government has termed "a pretended family," two homosexual lovers (homosexuality is something to which I will return in due course). Moreover, Jupiter promises to subordinate the interests of his real family to those of his lover Ganymede: he gives the boy the jewels which

his wife Juno wore on her wedding day, and plucks a feather from the wing of his son Hermes. The family conflict presaged here is actualized when Jupiter's daughter, Venus, enters—not in her traditional role as goddess of love, but, very pointedly, in her capacity as a mother, and, by implication, in the even less likely role, for a sex symbol, as grandmother. (This point is also stressed again later in the characters' repeated references to the kinship ties between herself, Aeneas, Ascanius, and her other son Cupid.) Jupiter's infatuation with Ganymede, she claims, has had repercussions throughout the family in that it has prevented him from paying proper attention to the welfare of her son Aeneas. Thus an initial lack of proper conjugal relations between husband and wife has apparently escalated into a situation which also affects both Jupiter's daughter and his grandson, and which will have serious implications too for his great-grandson Aeneas. We may, after all, remember as David Farley-Hills reminds us in relation to *Tamburlaine,* that Jupiter usurped and killed his own father.

The speech which Jupiter then makes to Venus assures her that she is wrong, and that he still has Aeneas's interests at heart:

> Content thee, Cytherea, in thy care,
> Since thy Aeneas' wandering fate is firm,
> Whose weary limbs shall shortly make repose
> In those fair walls I promis'd him of yore. (I.i.82–5)

In fact, however, the play itself proves Venus to be very accurate in her diagnosis of strains within the family. She has less insight into the cause, though, for she is herself complicit in it. When she visits the son for whom she has professed so much affection, she appears in disguise to him; only after she has left does he detect her identity, and he then proceeds to lament the lack of a closer relationship between them. Here we seem to be invited to discern that Jupiter's own poor parenting skills have, in one of the classic patterns of child abuse, been transmitted in turn to his daughter, who fails to mother her son as he would wish. This is made very clear in Aeneas's moving comments as he realizes the identity of the disguised figure with whom he has been talking:

> Achates, 'tis my mother that is fled;
> I know her by the movings of her feet.
> Stay, gentle Venus, fly not from thy son!
> Too cruel, why wilt thou forsake me thus,
> Or in these shades deceiv'st mine eye so oft?
> Why talk we not together hand in hand,
> And tell our griefs in more familiar terms?
> But thou art gone, and leav'st me here alone
> To dull the air with my discoursive moan. (I.ii.240–8)

*Claire Benedict and Antony Sher in a Royal Shakespeare Company production of*
Tamburlaine the Great

Here the familiar relationship between Aeneas and his mother, indicated in the fact that he can recognize her from so minor a detail as "the movings of her feet," forms a sad counterbalance to her unexplained unwillingness voluntarily to reveal her identity to him—apparently, from his use of the term "so oft," a familiar feature of her behavior to him.

Despite—or perhaps because of—Aeneas's sensitivity to his mother's lack of trust in him, he too is revealed as a poor parent. Ascanius early demonstrates a strong sense of kinship: when Aeneas imagines that a rock he sees is Priam, Ascanius assures him that it cannot be, "For were it Priam, he would smile on me" (II.i.36). Perhaps it is this sense of a lost family—Aeneas has, after all, literally mislaid his wife, Creusa—which makes the child at once accost Dido with "Madam, you shall be my mother" (II.i.98). (Richard Proudfoot points out that "Marlowe's Dido, unlike Chaucer's, doesn't count pregnancy among her claims on Aeneas"; instead she is presented throughout the play as poignantly childless, anxious to mother.) But like Jupiter and Venus before him, Aeneas in turn proves so indifferent to the fate of his offspring that he actually, proposes at one point to leave Ascanius behind with Dido—his protestation that he couldn't

have been about to depart because he would have had to leave his son behind is savagely undercut by the audience's awareness that that was in fact precisely what he was planning. Even Aeneas's denial is couched in worrying terms: "Hath not the Carthage queen mine only son?" (IV.iv.29) suggests that Ascanius's importance to his father may be at least as much dynastic as personal—as the only son of a widower, he forms a unique and temporarily irreplaceable link in the chain of succession; the implication, however, is that had he brothers, he might prove expendable, as Tamburlaine's son Calyphas is later to be. The inclusion of four generations in *Dido* allows us to see very clearly how the cycle of flawed parent-child relationships renews and perpetuates itself.

Even when fewer generations are considered, however, the pattern is still discernible. *Tamburlaine Part One* both opens and closes with families: the sharp differences between Cosroe and Mycetes open up questions of heredity, family resemblances and the nature / nurture debate, which is of course raised again in even more radical form by the victories won over kings by the mere son of a Scythian shepherd; and the end of the play sees both a marriage—providing an unusually comic form of closure to so violent a story—and also the reunion between Zenocrate and her father. Family is thus signaled as an issue of some importance, and it becomes even more so in Part Two where we observe closely Tamburlaine's three boys. We see the rivalry between them, brought about primarily by the very fact that they, unlike Ascanus, are members of a family instead of isolated heirs; we witness the effect on them of their mother's early death—indeed Calyphas's effeminacy, although clearly present from the beginning, could be interpreted as perhaps becoming exacerbated by a subconscious attempt to take over the role within the family of a lost mother; and, as with Cosroe and Mycetes in Part One, we see also the radical differences amongst brothers which result eventually in the ultimate example of family fragmentation, Tamburlaine's infanticide.

Tamburlaine's killing of Calyphas is difficult to decode. It has often been seen as in some sense exemplary, in the light of Renaissance educational theory. T. M. Pearce argues that it is indeed precisely a response to such theory:

> Here is portrayed a father who is at once a man of arms and a lover of poetry and worshipper of beauty, now faced with the problem of bringing up boys, his sons. The entire passage might have been written by Marlowe after reading Sir Thomas Elyot's *Boke Named the Governour* (1531), which appeared some fifty years earlier.

Pearce sees in Marlowe's portrayal of Tamburlaine's immovability a response to twin stimuli: the attack by Gosson (like Marlowe, a former pupil of the King's School, Canterbury) on lack of proper moral fiber in the theater, and the attack by Sir Humphrey Gilbert on modern educational methods and their failure to prepare for military service. Tamburlaine, Pearce suggests, embodies the very virtues which both Gosson and Gilbert were, in their different ways, advocating, and in nothing is this more apparent than his stoic sacrifice of his own son. Paul Kocher similarly sees in Tamburlaine's stabbing "an act of military discipline . . . from the Elizabethan point of view Tamburlaine is merely heroic in this," and suggests, moreover, that Tamburlaine's action is also rendered glorious by its association with the story of the Roman consul Manlius Torquatius, who similarly slew his son for disobeying orders. But such readings are, as Carolyn Williams recognizes, counter-intuitive; and, more importantly, they are notably not shared by the on-stage audience of dignitaries.

> "FAMILY BREAKDOWN IS, THEN REPEATEDLY STRESSED AS A RECURRING MOTIF IN MARLOWE'S PLAYS, AND ITS IMPACT IS HEIGHTENED BY THE USE OF VIGNETTES OF HAPPY FAMILIES WHICH PROVIDE BOTH CONTRAST AND PATHOS."

Infanticide also occurs elsewhere in the play, in Olympia's very differently motivated decision to kill her son, and crops up again in two more of the plays, *The Massacre at Paris*—where it is threatened rather than actual, since Catherine never needs to carry out her resolve to kill one or both of her sons—and *The Jew of Malta.* Here Barabas's initial affection for the daughter whose name means, ironically, "the father's joy" is violently transmuted by her conversion to Christianity—her adoption, it could perhaps be argued, of a different father-figure—into a murderous hate whose momentum not only wipes out Abigail and her entire convent of nuns but is also echoed in the kind of mock infanticide in which Barabas kills Ithamore, who, he so often stresses, has assumed the position of his heir. Family fragmentation is, of course, further emphasized in the play by the recurring presence of the two bereaved parents, Ferneze and Katherine, both of whom are apparently partnerless as well as childless. Moreover, Jeremy Tambling points to further elements in the play of fury directed at literal and symbolic members of its families when he comments on Barabas's stress on the nuns' frequent pregnancies, his identification of Abigail with the original exemplar of sibling rivalry, Cain, and the ways in which his celebrated image of "infinite riches in a little room" (I.i.37), "parodying the idea of Christ in the womb, suggest[s] a pre-Oedipal desire for identification with the mother."

In others of the plays matters never reach the pitch of family self-destruction seen in *The Jew of Malta* and *Tamburlaine;* but very often this is because, in them, families are never formed in the first place. It is notable that one of the few things Mephostophilis denies Faustus is a wife: thus the scholar, whom we assume to have long since drifted apart from the ''base stock'' from which he was sprung, is afforded no opportunity to recreate a family unit, something for which he perhaps compensates in his marked affection for his friends and for Wagner, and, arguably, even in his desire to please the pregnant Duchess of Vanholt. Marlowe, however, pointedly withholds from his hero personal participation in such a family unit, even though, as Emily Bartels points out, ''in the sources . . . he and Helen get married and have a son.'' In a brilliant analysis of the play, Kay Stockholder demonstrates Faustus's unease with his own sexuality and the ways in which his approaches to heterosexuality are thwarted by powerful patriarchal figures which, together with the presence of the strongly developed cuckoldry theme she shows to be present in the play, indicates a deeply unresolved Oedipus complex. Ironically, the woman he is offered instead of a wife is Helen—the legendary marriage-breaker of mythology, the woman who abandoned her husband Menelaus and her daughter Hermione for the seducer Paris.

Family even becomes an issue in the pageant of the Seven Deadly Sins. Pride ''disdain[s] to have any parents'' (II.i.116), Wrath ''had neither father nor mother'' (II.i.141), Gluttony's ''parents are all dead'' (II.i.148), while all the rest cite ill-matched couplings as their source of origin. Once again it is possible to discern a suggestion that fractured or non-existent family structures lie behind the darkest events of the play. Similarly in *Dido, Queen of Carthage* there is a strong sense of the fact that in coming together these two, widow and widower respectively, would be able to restore the family structure that each has lost—something that seems strongly signaled in Dido's desire effectively to reconstitute her former marriage by rechristening Aeneas Sichaeus, and by her enthusiastic response to Ascanius's request that she should function as a replacement mother for him. It is one of the most savage ironies of the play that it is family strife amongst the gods, specifically between Juno and Venus, which prevents this dream of a new family from reaching fulfillment, just as it has previously devastated the family of Priam and Hecuba.

Family breakdown is, then repeatedly stressed as a recurring motif in Marlowe's plays, and its impact is heightened by the use of vignettes of happy families which provide both contrast and pathos. Obvious examples are Zabina and Bajazeth in *Tamburlaine* Part One, whose mutual affection, undiminished by the brutal circumstances of their captivity, could be seen as strongly reminiscent of the marriage of affection and mutual support proposed by Protestant ideology, and Olympia and her Family in Part Two, where again conjugal and filial devotion triumphantly survives external disasters.

**Source:** Lisa Hopkins, ''Fissured Families: A Motif in Marlowe's Plays,'' in *Papers on Language & Literature,* Vol. 33, No. 2, Spring 1997, pp. 198–212.

### *Terry Box*

*In the following essay, Box analyzes the five stages of dramatic development of* Tamburlaine, Part I *to ''illustrate the degree to which irony permeates Marlowe's plots'' and show that ''through irony Marlowe maintains a detachment from what he has created.''*

Christopher Marlowe has been characterized by various critics as a markedly subjective playwright, one whose passions are reflected in the passions of his characters. Michel Poirier, for example, holds that Marlowe's mind ''is spurred on by a passion similar to the one he has ascribed to some of the characters in his dramas.'' Poirier concludes that there is a definite connection between Marlowe's temperament and ideas. His desires govern his thoughts; his passions are the basis for his philosophy; and egotism is at the center of his life and works. John Bakeless suggests that Marlowe's art did not conceal the artist, nor did his characterization possess the depth or subtlety required to veil the mind that produced them. A. L. Rowse speaks of writers who are intensely obsessed with themselves and derive much of their power from their own egos. He concludes that Marlowe belongs to this class: ''No writer was ever more autobiographical than he was. . . . He was an obsessed egoist. . . . His creations are very much projections of himself.'' Paul Kocher goes so far as to say that Marlowe's degree of subjectivity as a dramatist is the crucial problem of all interpretation of his work. Kocher further notes that any theory of subjectivity must depend on the whole broad body of evidence, and that this evidence includes the following: (1) the dramatist's choice and treatment of sources, (2) the background of the thought and custom of the period, (3) the practice of other dramatists, (4) the dramatist's own practice in his other works, (5) the dramatist's own personally held ideas, as supplied by background information, and (6) his manipulation of emphasis within the play by the placement, length, frequency, and eloquence of the speeches and by the good or bad standing of those who speak them. Kocher concludes, taking all these factors into consideration, that Marlowe is one of the most highly subjective playwrights of his time. Admitting that, to some degree, every dramatist exhibits in his work the major processes of his mind and emotions, Kocher goes on to say that Marlowe's plays are his not only in this general sense, but also as projections of strong personal passions.

Poirier, Bakeless, Rowse, and Kocher, however, represent but one side of what in recent years has become an on-going debate—a debate which Kenneth Friedenreich characterizes as between those who consider Marlowe essentially a Romantic and subjective artist, and those who regard him as a more conservative, objective artist whose plays focus on Renaissance drives for power, wealth, and knowledge. Representing this latter group, for example, is Gerald Pincess, who admits that Marlowe's plays are extensions and representations of his own mind, but who also admits that irony was Marlowe's most popular mode, and that this irony reflects a skepticism and detachment on the playwright's part. Judith Weil agrees that Marlowe mocks his heroes in a remarkably subtle fashion and that it is faulty logic to assume that Marlowe shares the attitudes of his heroes. Weil goes on to say that "[b]ecause Marlowe's ironic relationship to his audience varies from play to play, we probably cannot expect to infer his personal attitude from any one work." Writing in 1984, Johannes H. Birringer observed that "[t]he Marlowe who emerged during the last decade is certainly more exciting, even more challenging; a wide range of tones has been found in his generically unstable plays, and he even begins to look . . . like a sardonic, maliciously enigmatic ironist."

In these latter evaluations of Marlowe, all crediting him with more objectivity than the former critics were willing to admit to, the common denominator seems to be irony; that is, it is through irony that Marlowe in his plays distances himself from his characters and their actions, and thus achieves objectivity. R. B. Sharpe defines irony as "an attitude, a temper, a spirit in which one looks at life and art. It brings to light and emphasizes by art the contradictions of living." G. G. Sedgewick gives us the following definition of dramatic irony: "*Dramatic irony, in brief, is the sense of contradiction felt by spectators of a drama who see a character acting in ignorance of his condition.* This is dramatic irony in its concentrated and specific form: it grows . . . out of that pervasive and controlling

> MARLOWE'S EXPOSITION IN THIS PLAY INCLUDES THEME, CHARACTER, AND CONFLICT; AND IRONY IS A PERVASIVE ELEMENT. THE IRONY HELPS TO UNDERSCORE MARLOWE'S OBJECTIVITY."

knowledge which we have called *general* irony and which is the property peculiar and essential to the illusion of the theatre.''

Sharpe's and Sedgewick's definitions of irony and dramatic irony are especially meaningful when one considers Marlowe's plays. These works abound in the contradictions of life—contradictions between what appears to be truth and what is truth, between aspiration and achievement, between speech and action. And Marlowe's characters consistently act in ignorance of their conditions. In Tamburlaine, Faustus, Edward, Mortimer, Barabas, Guise, Dido, and other lesser characters, Marlowe has created characters in whom virtually every speech and action involve ironic undertones springing from this ignorance. This irony establishes an objective position of the part of the playwright; thus through irony Marlowe maintains a detachment from what he has created.

A careful, though admittedly not exhaustive, study of the five stages of dramatic development of *Tamburlaine, Part I* will, I believe, illustrate the degree to which irony permeates Marlowe's plots. The five stages—exposition, complication of plot action, turning point, climax, and denouement—are all steeped in irony, and the irony verifies Marlowe's objective position in that it helps to create the distance between playwright and character that is objectivity.

The first stage in dramatic development—exposition—introduces themes, characters, and conflicts. In *Tamburlaine, Part I,* Marlowe introduces these elements with an irony that shows him to be the objective observer of the forces he puts into motion. One theme is the invincible warrior—the super hero—and one method which Marlowe uses to attest ironically to the capabilities of his hero Tamburlaine is "looks" imagery. In scene i of Act

I, Mycetes, king of Persia, sends Theridamas to halt Tamburlaine's invading army: "Go, stout Theridamas; thy words are swords, / And with thy looks conquerest all thy foes" (I.i.74–75). Mycetes' reliance on the looks of Theridamas is ironic because Tamburlaine also is known for fierce looks. In scene ii, Techelles, a lieutenant to Tamburlaine, declares:

> As princely lions when they rouse themselves,
> Stretching their paws and threatening herds of beasts,
> So in his armor looketh Tamburlaine.
> Methinks I see kings kneeling at his feet,
> And he with frowning brows and fiery looks
> Spurning their crowns from off their captive heads.
> (I.ii.52–57)

Later in the same scene, Theridamas is forced to admit of Tamburlaine that "His looks do menace Heaven and dare the gods" (I.ii.156). In the confrontation between Theridamas and Tamburlaine, Theridamas yields without a struggle and states,

> Won with thy words and conquered with thy looks,
> I yield myself, my men, and horse to thee,
> To be partaker of thy good or ill,
> As long as life maintains Theridamas.
> (I.ii.227–30)

Thus, the wellspring of Mycetes' hope, the ominous appearance of Theridamas, is overcome by a similar, but stronger force in Tamburlaine; and Theridamas becomes a lieutenant to the man he was sent to defeat. Besides attesting to the superiority of Tamburlaine, this ironic treatment of "looks" foreshadows the fate of all those who feel confident that they can defeat Tamburlaine. As the play unfolds, many do challenge Tamburlaine, and their efforts fail, just as Mycetes' efforts failed.

While the ultimate purposes of Tamburlaine's enemies are doomed to failure, so is the goal of Tamburlaine unattainable; and this truth points up another of the themes treated in the play—that of natural order. The shepherd Tamburlaine wants to become as a god; he says as much in scene ii of Act I:

> Jove sometimes masked in a shepherd's weed,
> And by those steps that he hath scaled the heavens,
> May we become immortal like the gods.
> (I.ii.198–200)

Such hopes are in vain and serve only to heighten the irony of mortal Tamburlaine's death in *Part Two*. Cosroe, Mycetes's brother, also challenges natural order when he plots the overthrow of his brother:

> Well, since I see the state of Persia droop
> And languish in my brother's government,
> I willingly receive th'imperial crown

> And vow to wear it for my country's good,
> In spite of them shall malice my estate.
> (I.i.155–59)

In Act II Cosroe joins with Tamburlaine to defeat Mycetes but is in turn defeated almost immediately by Tamburlaine; thus, after deciding to usurp the kingship and "receive th'imperial crown," Cosroe wears the crown for only a short time before he too goes down in defeat. In Tamburlaine's mortality and in Cosroe's defeat, Marlowe underscores the futility of man in challenging natural order.

Marlowe also uses irony in character presentation, especially the character of Mycetes, to present an ironic spin-off on the character of Tamburlaine as an invincible superhero, for Mycetes is a weak-minded king whose conquest does not at all enhance the glory of his conqueror. That the character of Mycetes presents no problem to Tamburlaine is made conclusively manifest in Act II as Tamburlaine toys with the defeated king:

> *Tamburlaine.* What, fearful coward! Straggling from the camp,
> When the kings themselves are present in the field.
> *Mycetes.* Thou liest.
> *Tamburlaine.* Base villain, dar'st thou give the lie?
> *Mycetes.* Away! I am the king. Go! Touch me not!
> Thou break'st the law of arms unless thou kneel
> And cry me, 'Mercy, noble king!'
> *Tamburlaine.* Are you the witty king of Persia?
> *Mycetes.* Ay, marry, am I. Have you any to suit me?
> *Tamburlaine.* I would entreat you to speak but three wise words.
> *Mycetes.* So I can, when I see my time.
> *Tamburlaine.* Is this your crown?
> *Mycetes.* Ay. Did'st thou ever see a fairer?
> [*He hands him the crown.*]
> *Tamburlaine.* You will not sell it, will ye?
> *Mycetes.* Such another word, and I will have thee executed.
> Come, give it to me.
> *Tamburlaine.* No; I took it prisoner.
> *Mycetes.* You lie; I gave it you.
> *Tamburlaine.* Then 'tis mine.
> *Mycetes.* No; I mean I let you keep it.
> *Tamburlaine.* Well, I mean you shall have it again.
> Here, take it for awhile; I lend it thee
> Till I may see thee hemmed with armed men.
> Then shalt thou see me pull it from thy head;
> Thou art no match for mighty Tamburlaine.
> [*Exit.*]
> *Mycetes.* O gods, is this Tamburlaine the thief?
> I marvel much he stole it not away.
> (II.iv.16–42)

Tamburlaine belabors the obvious when he surmises that Mycetes is no match for him; Mycetes is hardly a match for anyone. Thus the character of Mycetes poses a question as to the omnipotence of

Tamburlaine. Is Tamburlaine successful because of his strength, or because of the weakness of his enemies?

The various conflicts presented in the exposition of this play are also fraught with irony. One conflict is the two drastically opposed attitudes that the other characters exhibit toward Tamburlaine, and this divergence of opinion is illustrated by names applied to the warrior. Mycetes speaks of a Tamburlaine "That, like a fox in midst of harvest time, / Doth prey upon my flocks of passengers" (I.i.31–32). In calling Tamburlaine a fox, Mycetes is invoking all the pejorative connotations of the word; yet Techelles compares Tamburlaine to "princely lions" (I.ii.52), utilizing all the majestic connotations associated with lions. In having his characters carry out this sort of name-calling, Marlowe assumes an objective posture, because Mycetes has every reasons to hold a low opinion of the tyrant who threatens his kingdom. Likewise, Techelles has every reason to admire the qualities in Tamburlaine that make him a successful military leader. Any one character's opinion of Tamburlaine depends on that character's position in relation to Tamburlaine's position, not on any bias of the playwright; thus, the irony of the two distinctly different attitudes toward Tamburlaine emphasizes Marlowe's objectivity.

A second conflict concerns the attitudes of the characters toward the gods. Both the forces of Tamburlaine and the forces of his enemies claim their favor. In Act I, Zenocrate, then an enemy of Tamburlaine, declares,

> The gods, defenders of the innocent,
> Will never prosper your intended drifts,
> That thus oppress your poor friendless passengers.
> (I.ii.68–70)

Though she is later won over by the love of Tamburlaine, she has sounded the opinion of his enemies who are not won over. Tamburlaine, on the other hand, also claims the blessings of Jove:

> Draw forth thy sword, though mighty man-at-arms,
> Intending but to raze my charmed skin,
> And Jove himself will stretch his hand from heaven
> To ward the blow and shield me safe from harm.
> See how he rains down heaps of gold in showers,
> As if he meant to give my soldiers pay;
> And as a sure and rounded argument
> That I shall be the monarch of the East,
> He sends this Soldan's daughter, rich and brave,
> To be my queen and portly empress.
> (I.ii.177–86)

This claiming of God's favor recurs on both sides as the play develops.

Marlowe's exposition in this play includes theme, character, and conflict; and irony is a pervasive element. The irony helps to underscore Marlowe's objectivity. Through his presentation of a military hero who defeats all comers, yet who is himself subject to ultimate defeat because of his mortality, through his presentation of two challenges to natural order and his intimation of their futility, through his presentation of a foe that Tamburlaine conquers but whose character is questionable as a worthy opponent, and through his presentation of opposing points of view regarding names applied to Tamburlaine and attitudes exhibited toward God, Marlowe achieves distance from his characters and thus achieves objectivity.

Complication of the plot action in *Tamburlaine, Part I* is also fraught with irony. The outcome of one of these complications, Mycetes' challenge to Tamburlaine, has already been discussed; thus, the folly of the following words of Mycetes is evident:

> Would it not grieve a king to be so abused
> And have a thousand horsemen ta'en away?
> And—which is worse—to have his diadem
> Sought for by such scald knaves as love him not?
> I think it would. Well then, by heavens I swear,
> Aurora shall not peep out of her doors,
> But I will have Cosroe by the head
> And kill proud Tamburlaine with point of sword.
> (II.ii.5–12)

The irony of the foolish king's thundering declaration is so obvious as to render him almost a subject for laughter. A similar complication arises out of Cosroe's league with Tamburlaine. After their united forces have defeated Mycetes, Tamburlaine issues a challenge to Cosroe. The newly crowned king of Persia responds:

> What means this devilish shepherd to aspire
> With such a giantly presumption,
> To cast up hills against the face of heaven,
> And dare the force of angry Jupiter?
> But as he thrust them underneath the hills,
> And pressed out fire from their burning jaws,
> So will I send this monstrous slave to hell,
> Where flames shall ever feed upon his soul.
> (II.vi.1–8)

However, Cosroe is defeated by Tamburlaine, just as Mycetes was. Ironically, one of the reasons why Cosroe has wanted to dethrone his brother is the weak-mindedness of Mycetes; yet Cosroe is no more clever than his brother, at least in regard to judging the chances for success that his forces have against the forces of Tamburlaine.

A further plot complication is introduced in Bajazeth, Emperor of the Turks. Feeling threatened by the conquests of Tamburlaine, Bajazeth offers a truce, which is of course rejected by the shepherd. Bajazeth then blusters in a manner similar to Mycetes and Cosroe:

> By Mahomet my kinsman's sepulcher,
> And by the holy Alcoran I swear,
> He shall be made a chaste and lustless eunuch,
> And in my sarell tend my concubines;
> And all his captains, that thus stoutly stand,
> Shall draw the chariot of my empress,
> Whom I have brought to see their overthrow.
> (III.iii.75–81)

To Tamburlaine the emperor expresses his supreme confidence:

> Now shalt thou feel the force of Turkish arms,
> Which lately have made all Europe quake for fear.
> I have of Turks, Arabians, Moors, and Jews,
> Enough to cover all Bithynia.
> Let thousands die! Their slaughtered carcasses
> Shall serve for walls and bulwarks to the rest;
> If they should yield their necks unto the sword,
> Thy soldiers' arms could not endure to strike
> So many blows as I have heads for thee.
> Thou know'st not, foolish hardy Tamburlaine,
> What 'tis to meet me in the open field,
> That leave no ground for thee to march upon.
> (III.iii.134–47)

Bajazeth's proclamations are indeed ironic, for the battle results in total defeat for him.

Thus, the irony of the various plot complications in *Tamburlaine, Part I* becomes apparent. Though opponents are confident of victory in their challenges to Tamburlaine, the shepherd will ultimately be victorious over all the challengers, regardless of their confidence. However, overriding this irony is that all-important irony which sustains Marlowe's objective posture. Though victorious now, Tamburlaine will ultimately meet that force which he cannot conquer; and, like Mycetes, Cosroe, and Bajazeth, he too will succumb to a force greater than himself.

The turning point of *Tamburlaine, Part I* is in like manner permeated with irony. It occurs in Act II when Tamburlaine and his lieutenants, after observing the pomp and majesty surrounding Cosroe, the new king of Persia, become enamored of kingship and its accompanying regality. Tamburlaine asks his lieutenants,

> Is it not brave to be a king, Techelles?
> Usumcasane and Theridamas,
> Is it not passing brave to be a king,
> And ride in triumph through Persepolis?
> (II.v.51–54)

Theridamas answers,

> A god is not so glorious as a king.
> I think the pleasure they enjoy in heaven
> Can not compare with kingly joys in earth:
> To wear a crown enchased with pearl and gold,
> Whose virtues carry with it life and death;
> To ask and have, command and be obeyed;
> When looks breed love, with looks to gain the prize,
> Such power attractive shines in princes' eyes.
> (II.v.57–64)

Tamburlaine decides that he wants the kingship of Persia for himself and sends word to Cosroe that he wants to battle Cosroe for his crown. They do fight, and Tamburlaine is victorious. When Cosroe berates Tamburlaine for taking his crown, Tamburlaine answers,

> The thrust of reign and sweetness of a crown,
> That caused the eldest son of heavenly Ops
> To thrust his doting father from his chair
> And place himself in the imperial heaven
> Moved me to manage arms against thy state.
> What better precedent than mighty Jove?
> Nature, that framed us of four elements
> Warring within our breasts for regiment,
> Doth teach us all to have aspiring minds.
> Our souls, whose faculties can comprehend
> The wondrous architecture of the world
> And measure every wandering planet's course,
> Still climbing after infinite knowledge,
> And always moving as the restless spheres.
> Wills us to wear ourselves and never rest,
> Until we reach the ripest fruit of all,
> That perfect bliss and sole felicity,
> The sweet fruition of an earthly crown.
> (II.vii.12–29)

Tamburlaine has decided that crowns are the "ripest fruit of all," and thus the course is set for the rest of his career. He will attempt to gather all the fruit that the world has to offer. The irony of Tamburlaine's quest for kingship is that he has only recently witnessed the demise of two kings, Mycetes and Cosroe, whose royalty did not prevent disaster, and he will later observe the destruction of Bajazeth. Zenocrate, in Act V, indicates an awareness of a truth that Tamburlaine here has not perceived. She laments, "Ah, Tamburlaine my love, sweet Tamburlaine, / That fights for scepters and for slippery crowns" (V.ii.292–93). It is to the attaining of these slippery crowns that Tamburlaine dedicates his life.

The next stage of dramatic development is the climax. The climax of *Tamburlaine, Part I* occurs in scene iii of Act III when Tamburlaine, who has dedicated himself to collecting crowns, defeats Bajazeth and assumes all of this conquered ruler's titles. Bajazeth has earlier described himself as

> . . . the Turkish emperor,

Dread lord of Africa, Europe, and Asia,
Great king and conqueror of Graecia,
The ocean, Terrene, and the coal-black-sea,
The high and highest monarch of the world. . . .
(III.i.22–26)

With all of his titles and positions, Bajazeth thus represents the high point in Tamburlaine's conquests. Later, as Tamburlaine mounts up into his chair by using Bajazeth as a footstool, Tamburlaine says,

Now clear the triple region of the air,
And let the majesty of heaven behold
Their scourge and terror tread on emperors.
Smile stars that reigned at my nativity,
And dim the brightness of their neighbor lamps;
Disdain to borrow light of Cynthia,
For I, the chiefest lamp of all the earth,
First rising in the east with the mild aspect,
But fixed now in the meridian line,
Will send up fire to your turning spheres
And cause the sun to borrow light of you.
(IV.ii.30–40)

The irony of Tamburlaine's position lies in his refusal to recognize that he is a lamp that will not burn eternally—that all of his titles and crowns will not protect him from his mortality—that he too one day will be the victim of a force greater than himself. The titles have not protected Bajazeth; they will not protect Tamburlaine.

The last stage in Marlowe's dramatic development is the denouement, or resolution. In *Tamburlaine, Part I,* Tamburlaine's working out of domestic problems constitutes the denouement. After defeating Bajazeth and assuming all his titles, Tamburlaine seeks to resolve those problems created when he kidnapped the beautiful Zenocrate. The king of Arabia must be dealt with, because Zenocrate had been betrothed to him. Tamburlaine must also reconcile himself with her father, the Soldan of Egypt. In Act V, Tamburlaine lays siege to the city of Damascus, and in the ensuing battle, the king of Arabia is killed; thus, his threat to Tamburlaine is ended. Tamburlaine ultimately takes the city; and the Soldan, upon learning that Tamburlaine has used his daughter chastely, extends his blessing: "I yield with thanks and protestations / Of endless honor to thee for her love" (V.ii.433–34). Now Tamburlaine has everything under control, and the play closes with his preparations to marry Zenocrate.

The irony in this resolution lies in a speech which Tamburlaine makes near the conclusion of the play. As Tamburlaine is solving his domestic problems, Bajazeth and his empress Zabina, both of whom he had kept in captivity, commit suicide. When Tamburlaine learns of their deaths, he says,

The Turk and his great empress, as it seems,
Left to themselves while we were at the fight,
Have desperately despatched their slavish lives;
With them Arabia too hath left his life;
All sights of power to grace my victory.
And such are objects fit for Tamburlaine,
Wherein, as in a mirror, may be seen
His honor, that consists in shedding blood
When men presume to manage arms with him.
(V.ii.407–15)

Tamburlaine says that the deaths of Zabina and Bajazeth are mirrors that reflect his honor, and he is pleased. Just what is it that his honor "consists in"? Zabina and Bajazeth are human beings that have been caged like animals, and, in choosing honor over life, they dash their brains out against the bars of their cage. Their deaths reflect more honor on themselves than on Tamburlaine. Earlier in Act V, Tamburlaine has ordered the deaths of four virgins sent to him to plead for Damascus. It is his custom to give a besieged city two days to decide to yield; on the third day, if no surrender is forthcoming, he utterly destroys the city. On the third day of the siege of Damascus, the four virgins are sent out in hopes that their innocence can persuade Tamburlaine to spare the city. He asks them what they see on the point of his sword; and when they answer that they see fear and steel, Tamburlaine says,

Your fearful minds are thick and misty then,
For there sit Death; there sits imperious Death,
Keeping his circuit by the slicing edge.
But I am pleased you shall not see him there.
He now is seated on my horsemen's spears,
And on their points his fleshless body feeds.
Techelles, straight go charge a few of them
To charge these dames and show my servant, Death,
Sitting in scarlet on their armed spears.
(V.ii.47–55)

The virgins are taken away and killed, and later their bodies are hung on the city's walls. This "mirror" reflects Tamburlaine's tenacity, but there is little honor in the slaughter of virgins. Tamburlaine's exultation at the end of the play is, then, ironic, especially when the results of his accomplishments are considered: two caged human beings commit suicide, and virgins are slaughtered. These are indeed mirrors to reflect Tamburlaine's honor, but the reflection is not what he thinks it to be. This irony illustrates the truth that Tamburlaine is not what he fancies himself to be, and in mistaking his own worth, he is no different from all the overconfident foes he has previously conquered.

Every stage of dramatic development in *Tamburlaine, Part I* has ironic undertones, as Marlowe illuminates flaws and weaknesses in his characters, and thus distances himself from them. The plot structure reveals Marlowe to be a devastatingly objective playwright. However, what value is there in determining that Marlowe's use of irony renders the playwright an objective one? As an ironist, Marlowe depicts life as it is, and he illuminates the differences between what appears to be and what is. Thus *Tamburlaine, Part I* becomes more than just a mirror reflecting the passions of his own mind; it can be read as his attempt to comment on the realities of the human condition. Marlowe's play becomes a comment not on just one man but on the follies of mankind.

**Source:** Terry Box, ''Irony and Objectivity in the Plot of *Tamburlaine, Part I*,'' in *CLA Journal,* Vol. 36, No. 2, December 1992, pp. 191–205.

# SOURCES

Jonson, Ben, ''To the Memory of My Beloved, the Author Master William Shakespeare, and What He Hath Left Us,'' in *William Shakespeare: The Complete Works,* by William Shakespeare, edited by Stanley Wells and Gary Taylor, Oxford University Press, 1988, pp. xiv–xvi.

Marlowe, Christopher, *Tamburlaine the Great: Parts I and II,* edited by J. W. Harper, Ernest Benn, 1971.

Sales, Roger, *Christopher Marlowe,* St. Martin's Press, 1991, pp. 51–83.

# FURTHER READING

Battenhouse, Roy W., *Marlowe's ''Tamburlaine'': A Study in Renaissance Moral Philosophy,* Vanderbilt University Press, 1964.
    This book provides an analysis of the play as a didactic and conventionally religious moral statement, in which Tamburlaine is meant to be a figure of evil.

Eliot, T. S., ''Christopher Marlowe,'' in *Selected Essays, 1917–1932,* Harcourt, Brace, 1932, pp. 100–07.
    Eliot's discussion of Marlowe's style is one of the most influential modern critical evaluations of the dramatist, and it includes an analysis of the verse in *Tamburlaine the Great.*

Manz, Beatrice Forbes, *The Rise and Rule of Tamerlane,* Cambridge University Press, 1989.
    Manz offers a useful historical account of the Mongol conqueror.

Ribner, Irving, ''The Idea of History in Marlowe's *Tamburlaine,''* in *ELH,* Vol. 20, 1954, pp. 251–66.
    Ribner discusses Marlowe's classical sources in *Tamburlaine the Great* and argues that the play denies the role of providence in human history.

Rowse, A. L., *Christopher Marlowe, A Biography,* Macmillan, 1964.
    Rowse's book is a colorful and controversial biography addressed to a wide audience.

# Glossary of Literary Terms

## A

**Abstract:** Used as a noun, the term refers to a short summary or outline of a longer work. As an adjective applied to writing or literary works, abstract refers to words or phrases that name things not knowable through the five senses. Examples of abstracts include the *Cliffs Notes* summaries of major literary works. Examples of abstract terms or concepts include ''idea,'' ''guilt'' ''honesty,'' and ''loyalty.''

**Absurd, Theater of the:** See *Theater of the Absurd*

**Absurdism:** See *Theater of the Absurd*

**Act:** A major section of a play. Acts are divided into varying numbers of shorter scenes. From ancient times to the nineteenth century plays were generally constructed of five acts, but modern works typically consist of one, two, or three acts. Examples of five-act plays include the works of Sophocles and Shakespeare, while the plays of Arthur Miller commonly have a three-act structure.

*Acto:* A one-act Chicano theater piece developed out of collective improvisation. *Actos* were performed by members of Luis Valdez's Teatro Campesino in California during the mid-1960s.

**Aestheticism:** A literary and artistic movement of the nineteenth century. Followers of the movement believed that art should not be mixed with social, political, or moral teaching. The statement ''art for art's sake'' is a good summary of aestheticism. The

movement had its roots in France, but it gained widespread importance in England in the last half of the nineteenth century, where it helped change the Victorian practice of including moral lessons in literature. Oscar Wilde is one of the best-known ''aesthetes'' of the late nineteenth century.

**Age of Johnson:** The period in English literature between 1750 and 1798, named after the most prominent literary figure of the age, Samuel Johnson. Works written during this time are noted for their emphasis on ''sensibility,'' or emotional quality. These works formed a transition between the rational works of the Age of Reason, or Neoclassical period, and the emphasis on individual feelings and responses of the Romantic period. Significant writers during the Age of Johnson included the novelists Ann Radcliffe and Henry Mackenzie, dramatists Richard Sheridan and Oliver Goldsmith, and poets William Collins and Thomas Gray. Also known as Age of Sensibility

**Age of Reason:** See *Neoclassicism*

**Age of Sensibility:** See *Age of Johnson*

**Alexandrine Meter:** See *Meter*

**Allegory:** A narrative technique in which characters representing things or abstract ideas are used to convey a message or teach a lesson. Allegory is typically used to teach moral, ethical, or religious lessons but is sometimes used for satiric or political purposes. Examples of allegorical works include

Edmund Spenser's *The Faerie Queene* and John Bunyan's *The Pilgrim's Progress.*

**Allusion:** A reference to a familiar literary or historical person or event, used to make an idea more easily understood. For example, describing someone as a "Romeo" makes an allusion to William Shakespeare's famous young lover in *Romeo and Juliet.*

**Amerind Literature:** The writing and oral traditions of Native Americans. Native American literature was originally passed on by word of mouth, so it consisted largely of stories and events that were easily memorized. Amerind prose is often rhythmic like poetry because it was recited to the beat of a ceremonial drum. Examples of Amerind literature include the autobiographical *Black Elk Speaks,* the works of N. Scott Momaday, James Welch, and Craig Lee Strete, and the poetry of Luci Tapahonso.

**Analogy:** A comparison of two things made to explain something unfamiliar through its similarities to something familiar, or to prove one point based on the acceptedness of another. Similes and metaphors are types of analogies. Analogies often take the form of an extended simile, as in William Blake's aphorism: "As the caterpillar chooses the fairest leaves to lay her eggs on, so the priest lays his curse on the fairest joys."

**Angry Young Men:** A group of British writers of the 1950s whose work expressed bitterness and disillusionment with society. Common to their work is an anti-hero who rebels against a corrupt social order and strives for personal integrity. The term has been used to describe Kingsley Amis, John Osborne, Colin Wilson, John Wain, and others.

**Antagonist:** The major character in a narrative or drama who works against the hero or protagonist. An example of an evil antagonist is Richard Lovelace in Samuel Richardson's *Clarissa,* while a virtuous antagonist is Macduff in William Shakespeare's *Macbeth.*

**Anthropomorphism:** The presentation of animals or objects in human shape or with human characteristics. The term is derived from the Greek word for "human form." The fables of Aesop, the animated films of Walt Disney, and Richard Adams's *Watership Down* feature anthropomorphic characters.

**Anti-hero:** A central character in a work of literature who lacks traditional heroic qualities such as courage, physical prowess, and fortitude. Anti-heros typically distrust conventional values and are unable to commit themselves to any ideals. They generally feel helpless in a world over which they have no control. Anti-heroes usually accept, and often celebrate, their positions as social outcasts. A well-known anti-hero is Yossarian in Joseph Heller's novel *Catch-22.*

**Antimasque:** See *Masque*

**Antithesis:** The antithesis of something is its direct opposite. In literature, the use of antithesis as a figure of speech results in two statements that show a contrast through the balancing of two opposite ideas. Technically, it is the second portion of the statement that is defined as the "antithesis"; the first portion is the "thesis." An example of antithesis is found in the following portion of Abraham Lincoln's "Gettysburg Address"; notice the opposition between the verbs "remember" and "forget" and the phrases "what we say" and "what they did": "The world will little note nor long remember what we say here, but it can never forget what they did here."

**Apocrypha:** Writings tentatively attributed to an author but not proven or universally accepted to be their works. The term was originally applied to certain books of the Bible that were not considered inspired and so were not included in the "sacred canon." Geoffrey Chaucer, William Shakespeare, Thomas Kyd, Thomas Middleton, and John Marston all have apocrypha. Apocryphal books of the Bible include the Old Testament's Book of Enoch and New Testament's Gospel of Peter.

**Apollonian and Dionysian:** The two impulses believed to guide authors of dramatic tragedy. The Apollonian impulse is named after Apollo, the Greek god of light and beauty and the symbol of intellectual order. The Dionysian impulse is named after Dionysus, the Greek god of wine and the symbol of the unrestrained forces of nature. The Apollonian impulse is to create a rational, harmonious world, while the Dionysian is to express the irrational forces of personality. Friedrich Nietzche uses these terms in *The Birth of Tragedy* to designate contrasting elements in Greek tragedy.

**Apostrophe:** A statement, question, or request addressed to an inanimate object or concept or to a nonexistent or absent person. Requests for inspiration from the muses in poetry are examples of apostrophe, as is Marc Antony's address to Caesar's corpse in William Shakespeare's *Julius Caesar:* "O, pardon me, thou bleeding piece of earth, That I am meek and gentle with these butchers!. . . Woe to the hand that shed this costly blood!. . .''

**Archetype:** The word archetype is commonly used to describe an original pattern or model from which all other things of the same kind are made. This term was introduced to literary criticism from the psychology of Carl Jung. It expresses Jung's theory that behind every person's ''unconscious,'' or repressed memories of the past, lies the ''collective unconscious'' of the human race: memories of the countless typical experiences of our ancestors. These memories are said to prompt illogical associations that trigger powerful emotions in the reader. Often, the emotional process is primitive, even primordial. Archetypes are the literary images that grow out of the ''collective unconscious.'' They appear in literature as incidents and plots that repeat basic patterns of life. They may also appear as stereotyped characters. Examples of literary archetypes include themes such as birth and death and characters such as the Earth Mother.

**Argument:** The argument of a work is the author's subject matter or principal idea. Examples of defined ''argument'' portions of works include John Milton's *Arguments* to each of the books of *Paradise Lost* and the ''Argument'' to Robert Herrick's *Hesperides.*

**Aristotelian Criticism:** Specifically, the method of evaluating and analyzing tragedy formulated by the Greek philosopher Aristotle in his *Poetics.* More generally, the term indicates any form of criticism that follows Aristotle's views. Aristotelian criticism focuses on the form and logical structure of a work, apart from its historical or social context, in contrast to ''Platonic Criticism,'' which stresses the usefulness of art. Adherents of New Criticism including John Crowe Ransom and Cleanth Brooks utilize and value the basic ideas of Aristotelian criticism for textual analysis.

**Art for Art's Sake:** See *Aestheticism*

**Aside:** A comment made by a stage performer that is intended to be heard by the audience but supposedly not by other characters. Eugene O'Neill's *Strange Interlude* is an extended use of the aside in modern theater.

**Audience:** The people for whom a piece of literature is written. Authors usually write with a certain audience in mind, for example, children, members of a religious or ethnic group, or colleagues in a professional field. The term ''audience'' also applies to the people who gather to see or hear any performance, including plays, poetry readings, speeches, and concerts. Jane Austen's parody of the gothic novel, *Northanger Abbey,* was originally intended for (and also pokes fun at) an audience of young and avid female gothic novel readers.

**Avant-garde:** A French term meaning ''vanguard.'' It is used in literary criticism to describe new writing that rejects traditional approaches to literature in favor of innovations in style or content. Twentieth-century examples of the literary *avant-garde* include the Black Mountain School of poets, the Bloomsbury Group, and the Beat Movement.

# B

**Ballad:** A short poem that tells a simple story and has a repeated refrain. Ballads were originally intended to be sung. Early ballads, known as folk ballads, were passed down through generations, so their authors are often unknown. Later ballads composed by known authors are called literary ballads. An example of an anonymous folk ballad is ''Edward,'' which dates from the Middle Ages. Samuel Taylor Coleridge's ''The Rime of the Ancient Mariner'' and John Keats's ''La Belle Dame sans Merci'' are examples of literary ballads.

**Baroque:** A term used in literary criticism to describe literature that is complex or ornate in style or diction. Baroque works typically express tension, anxiety, and violent emotion. The term ''Baroque Age'' designates a period in Western European literature beginning in the late sixteenth century and ending about one hundred years later. Works of this period often mirror the qualities of works more generally associated with the label ''baroque'' and sometimes feature elaborate conceits. Examples of Baroque works include John Lyly's *Euphues: The Anatomy of Wit,* Luis de Gongora's *Soledads,* and William Shakespeare's *As You Like It.*

**Baroque Age:** See *Baroque*

**Baroque Period:** See *Baroque*

**Beat Generation:** See *Beat Movement*

**Beat Movement:** A period featuring a group of American poets and novelists of the 1950s and 1960s—including Jack Kerouac, Allen Ginsberg, Gregory Corso, William S. Burroughs, and Lawrence Ferlinghetti—who rejected established social and literary values. Using such techniques as stream of consciousness writing and jazz-influenced free verse and focusing on unusual or abnormal states of mind—generated by religious ecstasy or the use of drugs—the Beat writers aimed to create works that were unconventional in both form and subject matter. Kerouac's *On the Road* is perhaps the best-known example of a Beat Generation novel, and Ginsberg's *Howl* is a famous collection of Beat poetry.

**Black Aesthetic Movement:** A period of artistic and literary development among African Americans in the 1960s and early 1970s. This was the first major African-American artistic movement since the Harlem Renaissance and was closely paralleled by the civil rights and black power movements. The black aesthetic writers attempted to produce works of art that would be meaningful to the black masses. Key figures in black aesthetics included one of its founders, poet and playwright Amiri Baraka, formerly known as LeRoi Jones; poet and essayist Haki R. Madhubuti, formerly Don L. Lee; poet and playwright Sonia Sanchez; and dramatist Ed Bullins. Works representative of the Black Aesthetic Movement include Amiri Baraka's play *Dutchman,* a 1964 Obie award-winner; *Black Fire: An Anthology of Afro-American Writing,* edited by Baraka and playwright Larry Neal and published in 1968; and Sonia Sanchez's poetry collection *We a BaddDDD People,* published in 1970. Also known as Black Arts Movement.

**Black Arts Movement:** See *Black Aesthetic Movement*

**Black Comedy:** See *Black Humor*

**Black Humor:** Writing that places grotesque elements side by side with humorous ones in an attempt to shock the reader, forcing him or her to laugh at the horrifying reality of a disordered world. Joseph Heller's novel *Catch-22* is considered a superb example of the use of black humor. Other well-known authors who use black humor include Kurt Vonnegut, Edward Albee, Eugene Ionesco, and Harold Pinter. Also known as Black Comedy.

**Blank Verse:** Loosely, any unrhymed poetry, but more generally, unrhymed iambic pentameter verse (composed of lines of five two-syllable feet with the first syllable accented, the second unaccented). Blank verse has been used by poets since the Renaissance for its flexibility and its graceful, dignified tone. John Milton's *Paradise Lost* is in blank verse, as are most of William Shakespeare's plays.

**Bloomsbury Group:** A group of English writers, artists, and intellectuals who held informal artistic and philosophical discussions in Bloomsbury, a

district of London, from around 1907 to the early 1930s. The Bloomsbury Group held no uniform philosophical beliefs but did commonly express an aversion to moral prudery and a desire for greater social tolerance. At various times the circle included Virginia Woolf, E. M. Forster, Clive Bell, Lytton Strachey, and John Maynard Keynes.

**Bon Mot:** A French term meaning "good word." A *bon mot* is a witty remark or clever observation. Charles Lamb and Oscar Wilde are celebrated for their witty *bon mots.* Two examples by Oscar Wilde stand out: (1) "All women become their mothers. That is their tragedy. No man does. That's his." (2) "A man cannot be too careful in the choice of his enemies."

**Breath Verse:** See *Projective Verse*

**Burlesque:** Any literary work that uses exaggeration to make its subject appear ridiculous, either by treating a trivial subject with profound seriousness or by treating a dignified subject frivolously. The word "burlesque" may also be used as an adjective, as in "burlesque show," to mean "striptease act." Examples of literary burlesque include the comedies of Aristophanes, Miguel de Cervantes's *Don Quixote,,* Samuel Butler's poem "Hudibras," and John Gay's play *The Beggar's Opera.*

# C

**Cadence:** The natural rhythm of language caused by the alternation of accented and unaccented syllables. Much modern poetry—notably free verse—deliberately manipulates cadence to create complex rhythmic effects. James Macpherson's "Ossian poems" are richly cadenced, as is the poetry of the Symbolists, Walt Whitman, and Amy Lowell.

**Caesura:** A pause in a line of poetry, usually occurring near the middle. It typically corresponds to a break in the natural rhythm or sense of the line but is sometimes shifted to create special meanings or rhythmic effects. The opening line of Edgar Allan Poe's "The Raven" contains a caesura following "dreary": "Once upon a midnight dreary, while I pondered weak and weary. . . . "

**Canzone:** A short Italian or Provencal lyric poem, commonly about love and often set to music. The *canzone* has no set form but typically contains five or six stanzas made up of seven to twenty lines of eleven syllables each. A shorter, five- to ten-line "envoy," or concluding stanza, completes the poem.

Masters of the *canzone* form include Petrarch, Dante Alighieri, Torquato Tasso, and Guido Cavalcanti.

**Carpe Diem:** A Latin term meaning "seize the day." This is a traditional theme of poetry, especially lyrics. A *carpe diem* poem advises the reader or the person it addresses to live for today and enjoy the pleasures of the moment. Two celebrated *carpe diem* poems are Andrew Marvell's "To His Coy Mistress" and Robert Herrick's poem beginning "Gather ye rosebuds while ye may. . . ."

**Catharsis:** The release or purging of unwanted emotions— specifically fear and pity—brought about by exposure to art. The term was first used by the Greek philosopher Aristotle in his *Poetics* to refer to the desired effect of tragedy on spectators. A famous example of catharsis is realized in Sophocles' *Oedipus Rex,* when Oedipus discovers that his wife, Jacosta, is his own mother and that the stranger he killed on the road was his own father.

**Celtic Renaissance:** A period of Irish literary and cultural history at the end of the nineteenth century. Followers of the movement aimed to create a romantic vision of Celtic myth and legend. The most significant works of the Celtic Renaissance typically present a dreamy, unreal world, usually in reaction against the reality of contemporary problems. William Butler Yeats's *The Wanderings of Oisin* is among the most significant works of the Celtic Renaissance. Also known as Celtic Twilight.

**Celtic Twilight:** See *Celtic Renaissance*

**Character:** Broadly speaking, a person in a literary work. The actions of characters are what constitute the plot of a story, novel, or poem. There are numerous types of characters, ranging from simple, stereotypical figures to intricate, multifaceted ones. In the techniques of anthropomorphism and personification, animals—and even places or things— can assume aspects of character. "Characterization" is the process by which an author creates vivid, believable characters in a work of art. This may be done in a variety of ways, including (1) direct description of the character by the narrator; (2) the direct presentation of the speech, thoughts, or actions of the character; and (3) the responses of other characters to the character. The term "character" also refers to a form originated by the ancient Greek writer Theophrastus that later became popular in the seventeenth and eighteenth centuries. It is a short essay or sketch of a person who prominently displays a specific attribute or quality, such as miserliness or ambition. Notable characters in literature include Oedipus Rex, Don Quixote de la Mancha, Macbeth, Candide, Hester Prynne, Ebenezer Scrooge, Huckleberry Finn, Jay Gatsby, Scarlett O'Hara, James Bond, and Kunta Kinte.

**Characterization:** See *Character*

**Chorus:** In ancient Greek drama, a group of actors who commented on and interpreted the unfolding action on the stage. Initially the chorus was a major component of the presentation, but over time it became less significant, with its numbers reduced and its role eventually limited to commentary between acts. By the sixteenth century the chorus—if employed at all—was typically a single person who provided a prologue and an epilogue and occasionally appeared between acts to introduce or underscore an important event. The chorus in William Shakespeare's *Henry V* functions in this way. Modern dramas rarely feature a chorus, but T. S. Eliot's *Murder in the Cathedral* and Arthur Miller's *A View from the Bridge* are notable exceptions. The Stage Manager in Thornton Wilder's *Our Town* performs a role similar to that of the chorus.

**Chronicle:** A record of events presented in chronological order. Although the scope and level of detail provided varies greatly among the chronicles surviving from ancient times, some, such as the *Anglo-Saxon Chronicle,* feature vivid descriptions and a lively recounting of events. During the Elizabethan Age, many dramas— appropriately called "chronicle plays"—were based on material from chronicles. Many of William Shakespeare's dramas of English history as well as Christopher Marlowe's *Edward II* are based in part on Raphael Holinshead's *Chronicles of England, Scotland, and Ireland.*

**Classical:** In its strictest definition in literary criticism, classicism refers to works of ancient Greek or Roman literature. The term may also be used to describe a literary work of recognized importance (a "classic") from any time period or literature that exhibits the traits of classicism. Classical authors from ancient Greek and Roman times include Juvenal and Homer. Examples of later works and authors now described as classical include French literature of the seventeenth century, Western novels of the nineteenth century, and American fiction of the mid-nineteenth century such as that written by James Fenimore Cooper and Mark Twain.

**Classicism:** A term used in literary criticism to describe critical doctrines that have their roots in ancient Greek and Roman literature, philosophy, and art. Works associated with classicism typically exhibit restraint on the part of the author, unity of design and purpose, clarity, simplicity, logical organization, and respect for tradition. Examples of literary classicism include Cicero's prose, the dramas of Pierre Corneille and Jean Racine, the poetry of John Dryden and Alexander Pope, and the writings of J. W. von Goethe, G. E. Lessing, and T. S. Eliot.

**Climax:** The turning point in a narrative, the moment when the conflict is at its most intense. Typically, the structure of stories, novels, and plays is one of rising action, in which tension builds to the climax, followed by falling action, in which tension lessens as the story moves to its conclusion. The climax in James Fenimore Cooper's *The Last of the Mohicans* occurs when Magua and his captive Cora are pursued to the edge of a cliff by Uncas. Magua kills Uncas but is subsequently killed by Hawkeye.

**Colloquialism:** A word, phrase, or form of pronunciation that is acceptable in casual conversation but not in formal, written communication. It is considered more acceptable than slang. An example of colloquialism can be found in Rudyard Kipling's *Barrack-room Ballads:* When 'Omer smote 'is bloomin' lyre He'd 'eard men sing by land and sea; An' what he thought 'e might require 'E went an' took—the same as me!

**Comedy:** One of two major types of drama, the other being tragedy. Its aim is to amuse, and it typically ends happily. Comedy assumes many forms, such as farce and burlesque, and uses a variety of techniques, from parody to satire. In a restricted sense the term comedy refers only to dramatic presentations, but in general usage it is commonly applied to nondramatic works as well. Examples of comedies range from the plays of Aristophanes, Terrence, and Plautus, Dante Alighieri's *The Divine Comedy,* Francois Rabelais's *Pantagruel* and *Gargantua,* and some of Geoffrey Chaucer's tales and William Shakespeare's plays to Noel Coward's play *Private Lives* and James Thurber's short story "The Secret Life of Walter Mitty."

**Comedy of Manners:** A play about the manners and conventions of an aristocratic, highly sophisticated society. The characters are usually types rather than individualized personalities, and plot is less important than atmosphere. Such plays were an important aspect of late seventeenth-century English comedy. The comedy of manners was revived in the eighteenth century by Oliver Goldsmith and Richard Brinsley Sheridan, enjoyed a second revival in the late nineteenth century, and has endured into the twentieth century. Examples of comedies of manners include William Congreve's *The Way of the World* in the late seventeenth century, Oliver Goldsmith's *She Stoops to Conquer* and Richard Brinsley Sheridan's *The School for Scandal* in the eighteenth century, Oscar Wilde's *The Importance of Being Earnest* in the nineteenth century, and W. Somerset Maugham's *The Circle* in the twentieth century.

**Comic Relief:** The use of humor to lighten the mood of a serious or tragic story, especially in plays. The technique is very common in Elizabethan works, and can be an integral part of the plot or simply a brief event designed to break the tension of the scene. The Gravediggers' scene in William Shakespeare's *Hamlet* is a frequently cited example of comic relief.

***Commedia dell'arte:*** An Italian term meaning "the comedy of guilds" or "the comedy of professional actors." This form of dramatic comedy was popular in Italy during the sixteenth century. Actors were assigned stock roles (such as Pulcinella, the stupid servant, or Pantalone, the old merchant) and given a basic plot to follow, but all dialogue was improvised. The roles were rigidly typed and the plots were formulaic, usually revolving around young lovers who thwarted their elders and attained wealth and happiness. A rigid convention of the *commedia dell'arte* is the periodic intrusion of Harlequin, who interrupts the play with low buffoonery. Peppino de Filippo's *Metamorphoses of a Wandering Minstrel* gave modern audiences an idea of what *commedia dell'arte* may have been like. Various scenarios for *commedia dell'arte* were compiled in Petraccone's *La commedia dell'arte, storia, technica, scenari,* published in 1927.

**Complaint:** A lyric poem, popular in the Renaissance, in which the speaker expresses sorrow about his or her condition. Typically, the speaker's sadness is caused by an unresponsive lover, but some complaints cite other sources of unhappiness, such as poverty or fate. A commonly cited example is "A Complaint by Night of the Lover Not Beloved" by Henry Howard, Earl of Surrey. Thomas Sackville's "Complaint of Henry, Duke of Buckingham" traces the duke's unhappiness to his ruthless ambition.

**Conceit:** A clever and fanciful metaphor, usually expressed through elaborate and extended comparison, that presents a striking parallel between two seemingly dissimilar things—for example, elaborately comparing a beautiful woman to an object like a garden or the sun. The conceit was a popular device throughout the Elizabethan Age and Baroque Age and was the principal technique of the seventeenth-century English metaphysical poets. This usage of the word conceit is unrelated to the best-known definition of conceit as an arrogant attitude or behavior. The conceit figures prominently in the works of John Donne, Emily Dickinson, and T. S. Eliot.

**Concrete:** Concrete is the opposite of abstract, and refers to a thing that actually exists or a description that allows the reader to experience an object or concept with the senses. Henry David Thoreau's *Walden* contains much concrete description of nature and wildlife.

**Concrete Poetry:** Poetry in which visual elements play a large part in the poetic effect. Punctuation marks, letters, or words are arranged on a page to form a visual design: a cross, for example, or a bumblebee. Max Bill and Eugene Gomringer were among the early practitioners of concrete poetry; Haroldo de Campos and Augusto de Campos are among contemporary authors of concrete poetry.

**Confessional Poetry:** A form of poetry in which the poet reveals very personal, intimate, sometimes shocking information about himself or herself. Anne Sexton, Sylvia Plath, Robert Lowell, and John Berryman wrote poetry in the confessional vein.

**Conflict:** The conflict in a work of fiction is the issue to be resolved in the story. It usually occurs between two characters, the protagonist and the antagonist, or between the protagonist and society or the protagonist and himself or herself. Conflict in Theodore Dreiser's novel *Sister Carrie* comes as a result of urban society, while Jack London's short story "To Build a Fire" concerns the protagonist's battle against the cold and himself.

**Connotation:** The impression that a word gives beyond its defined meaning. Connotations may be universally understood or may be significant only to a certain group. Both "horse" and "steed" denote the same animal, but "steed" has a different connotation, deriving from the chivalrous or romantic narratives in which the word was once often used.

**Consonance:** Consonance occurs in poetry when words appearing at the ends of two or more verses have similar final consonant sounds but have final vowel sounds that differ, as with "stuff" and "off." Consonance is found in "The curfew tolls the knells of parting day" from Thomas Grey's "An Elegy Written in a Country Church Yard." Also known as Half Rhyme or Slant Rhyme.

**Convention:** Any widely accepted literary device, style, or form. A soliloquy, in which a character reveals to the audience his or her private thoughts, is an example of a dramatic convention.

*Corrido:* A Mexican ballad. Examples of *corridos* include "Muerte del afamado Bilito," "La voz de mi conciencia," "Lucio Perez," "La juida," and "Los presos."

**Couplet:** Two lines of poetry with the same rhyme and meter, often expressing a complete and self-contained thought. The following couplet is from Alexander Pope's "Elegy to the Memory of an Unfortunate Lady": 'Tis Use alone that sanctifies Expense, And Splendour borrows all her rays from Sense.

**Criticism:** The systematic study and evaluation of literary works, usually based on a specific method or set of principles. An important part of literary studies since ancient times, the practice of criticism has given rise to numerous theories, methods, and "schools," sometimes producing conflicting, even contradictory, interpretations of literature in general as well as of individual works. Even such basic issues as what constitutes a poem or a novel have been the subject of much criticism over the centuries. Seminal texts of literary criticism include Plato's *Republic,* Aristotle's *Poetics,* Sir Philip Sidney's *The Defence of Poesie,* John Dryden's *Of Dramatic Poesie,* and William Wordsworth's "Preface" to the second edition of his *Lyrical Ballads.* Contemporary schools of criticism include deconstruction, feminist, psychoanalytic, poststructuralist, new historicist, postcolonialist, and reader-response.

# D

**Dactyl:** See *Foot*

**Dadaism:** A protest movement in art and literature founded by Tristan Tzara in 1916. Followers of the movement expressed their outrage at the destruction brought about by World War I by revolting against numerous forms of social convention. The Dadaists presented works marked by calculated madness and flamboyant nonsense. They stressed total freedom of expression, commonly through primitive displays of emotion and illogical, often senseless, poetry. The movement ended shortly after the war, when it was replaced by surrealism. Proponents of Dadaism include Andre Breton, Louis Aragon, Philippe Soupault, and Paul Eluard.

**Decadent:** See *Decadents*

**Decadents:** The followers of a nineteenth-century literary movement that had its beginnings in French aestheticism. Decadent literature displays a fascination with perverse and morbid states; a search for novelty and sensation—the "new thrill"; a preoccupation with mysticism; and a belief in the senselessness of human existence. The movement is closely associated with the doctrine Art for Art's Sake. The term "decadence" is sometimes used to denote a decline in the quality of art or literature following a period of greatness. Major French decadents are Charles Baudelaire and Arthur Rimbaud. English decadents include Oscar Wilde, Ernest Dowson, and Frank Harris.

**Deconstruction:** A method of literary criticism developed by Jacques Derrida and characterized by multiple conflicting interpretations of a given work. Deconstructionists consider the impact of the language of a work and suggest that the true meaning of the work is not necessarily the meaning that the author intended. Jacques Derrida's *De la grammatologie* is the seminal text on deconstructive strategies; among American practitioners of this method of criticism are Paul de Man and J. Hillis Miller.

**Deduction:** The process of reaching a conclusion through reasoning from general premises to a specific premise. An example of deduction is present in the following syllogism: Premise: All mammals are animals. Premise: All whales are mammals. Conclusion: Therefore, all whales are animals.

**Denotation:** The definition of a word, apart from the impressions or feelings it creates in the reader. The word "apartheid" denotes a political and economic policy of segregation by race, but its connotations— oppression, slavery, inequality—are numerous.

**Denouement:** A French word meaning "the unknotting." In literary criticism, it denotes the resolution of conflict in fiction or drama. The *denouement* follows the climax and provides an outcome to the primary plot situation as well as an explanation of secondary plot complications. The *denouement* often involves a character's recognition of his or her state of mind or moral condition. A well-known example of *denouement* is the last scene of the play *As You Like It* by William Shakespeare, in which couples are married, an evildoer repents, the identities of two disguised characters are revealed, and a ruler is restored to power. Also known as Falling Action.

**Description:** Descriptive writing is intended to allow a reader to picture the scene or setting in which the action of a story takes place. The form this description takes often evokes an intended emotional response—a dark, spooky graveyard will evoke fear, and a peaceful, sunny meadow will evoke calmness. An example of a descriptive story is Edgar Allan Poe's *Landor's Cottage,* which offers a detailed depiction of a New York country estate.

**Detective Story:** A narrative about the solution of a mystery or the identification of a criminal. The conventions of the detective story include the detective's scrupulous use of logic in solving the mystery; incompetent or ineffectual police; a suspect who appears guilty at first but is later proved innocent; and the detective's friend or confidant— often the narrator—whose slowness in interpreting clues emphasizes by contrast the detective's brilliance. Edgar Allan Poe's "Murders in the Rue Morgue" is commonly regarded as the earliest example of this type of story. With this work, Poe established many of the conventions of the detective story genre, which are still in practice. Other practitioners of this vast and extremely popular genre include Arthur Conan Doyle, Dashiell Hammett, and Agatha Christie.

**Deus ex machina:** A Latin term meaning "god out of a machine." In Greek drama, a god was often lowered onto the stage by a mechanism of some kind to rescue the hero or untangle the plot. By extension, the term refers to any artificial device or coincidence used to bring about a convenient and simple solution to a plot. This is a common device in melodramas and includes such fortunate circumstances as the sudden receipt of a legacy to save the family farm or a last-minute stay of execution. The *deus ex machina* invariably rewards the virtuous and punishes evildoers. Examples of *deus ex machina* include King Louis XIV in Jean-Baptiste Moliere's *Tartuffe* and Queen Victoria in *The Pirates of Penzance* by William Gilbert and Arthur Sullivan. Bertolt Brecht parodies the abuse of such devices in the conclusion of his *Threepenny Opera.*

**Dialogue:** In its widest sense, dialogue is simply conversation between people in a literary work; in its most restricted sense, it refers specifically to the speech of characters in a drama. As a specific literary genre, a "dialogue" is a composition in which characters debate an issue or idea. The Greek philosopher Plato frequently expounded his theories in the form of dialogues.

**Diction:** The selection and arrangement of words in a literary work. Either or both may vary depending on the desired effect. There are four general types of diction: ''formal,'' used in scholarly or lofty writing; ''informal,'' used in relaxed but educated conversation; ''colloquial,'' used in everyday speech; and ''slang,'' containing newly coined words and other terms not accepted in formal usage.

**Didactic:** A term used to describe works of literature that aim to teach some moral, religious, political, or practical lesson. Although didactic elements are often found in artistically pleasing works, the term ''didactic'' usually refers to literature in which the message is more important than the form. The term may also be used to criticize a work that the critic finds ''overly didactic,'' that is, heavy-handed in its delivery of a lesson. Examples of didactic literature include John Bunyan's *Pilgrim's Progress,* Alexander Pope's *Essay on Criticism,* Jean-Jacques Rousseau's *Emile,* and Elizabeth Inchbald's *Simple Story.*

**Dimeter:** See *Meter*

**Dionysian:** See *Apollonian and Dionysian*

***Discordia concours:*** A Latin phrase meaning ''discord in harmony.'' The term was coined by the eighteenth-century English writer Samuel Johnson to describe ''a combination of dissimilar images or discovery of occult resemblances in things apparently unlike.'' Johnson created the expression by reversing a phrase by the Latin poet Horace. The metaphysical poetry of John Donne, Richard Crashaw, Abraham Cowley, George Herbert, and Edward Taylor among others, contains many examples of *discordia concours.* In Donne's ''A Valediction: Forbidding Mourning,'' the poet compares the union of himself with his lover to a draftsman's compass: If they be two, they are two so, As stiff twin compasses are two: Thy soul, the fixed foot, makes no show To move, but doth, if the other do; And though it in the center sit, Yet when the other far doth roam, It leans, and hearkens after it, And grows erect, as that comes home.

**Dissonance:** A combination of harsh or jarring sounds, especially in poetry. Although such combinations may be accidental, poets sometimes intentionally make them to achieve particular effects. Dissonance is also sometimes used to refer to close but not identical rhymes. When this is the case, the word functions as a synonym for consonance. Robert Browning, Gerard Manley Hopkins, and many other poets have made deliberate use of dissonance.

***Doppelganger:*** A literary technique by which a character is duplicated (usually in the form of an alter ego, though sometimes as a ghostly counterpart) or divided into two distinct, usually opposite personalities. The use of this character device is widespread in nineteenth- and twentieth-century literature, and indicates a growing awareness among authors that the ''self'' is really a composite of many ''selves.'' A well-known story containing a *doppelganger* character is Robert Louis Stevenson's *Dr. Jekyll and Mr. Hyde,* which dramatizes an internal struggle between good and evil. Also known as The Double.

***Double Entendre:*** A corruption of a French phrase meaning ''double meaning.'' The term is used to indicate a word or phrase that is deliberately ambiguous, especially when one of the meanings is risqué or improper. An example of a *double entendre* is the Elizabethan usage of the verb ''die,'' which refers both to death and to orgasm.

**Double, The:** See *Doppelganger*

**Draft:** Any preliminary version of a written work. An author may write dozens of drafts which are revised to form the final work, or he or she may write only one, with few or no revisions. Dorothy Parker's observation that ''I can't write five words but that I change seven'' humorously indicates the purpose of the draft.

**Drama:** In its widest sense, a drama is any work designed to be presented by actors on a stage. Similarly, ''drama'' denotes a broad literary genre that includes a variety of forms, from pageant and spectacle to tragedy and comedy, as well as countless types and subtypes. More commonly in modern usage, however, a drama is a work that treats serious subjects and themes but does not aim at the grandeur of tragedy. This use of the term originated with the eighteenth-century French writer Denis Diderot, who used the word *drame* to designate his plays about middle-class life; thus ''drama'' typically features characters of a less exalted stature than those of tragedy. Examples of classical dramas include Menander's comedy *Dyscolus* and Sophocles' tragedy *Oedipus Rex.* Contemporary dramas include Eugene O'Neill's *The Iceman Cometh,* Lillian Hellman's *Little Foxes,* and August Wilson's *Ma Rainey's Black Bottom.*

**Dramatic Irony:** Occurs when the audience of a play or the reader of a work of literature knows something that a character in the work itself does not know. The irony is in the contrast between the intended meaning of the statements or actions of a character and the additional information understood by the audience. A celebrated example of dramatic irony is in Act V of William Shakespeare's *Romeo and Juliet,* where two young lovers meet their end as a result of a tragic misunderstanding. Here, the audience has full knowledge that Juliet's apparent "death" is merely temporary; she will regain her senses when the mysterious "sleeping potion" she has taken wears off. But Romeo, mistaking Juliet's drug-induced trance for true death, kills himself in grief. Upon awakening, Juliet discovers Romeo's corpse and, in despair, slays herself.

**Dramatic Monologue:** See *Monologue*

**Dramatic Poetry:** Any lyric work that employs elements of drama such as dialogue, conflict, or characterization, but excluding works that are intended for stage presentation. A monologue is a form of dramatic poetry.

*Dramatis Personae:* The characters in a work of literature, particularly a drama. The list of characters printed before the main text of a play or in the program is the *dramatis personae.*

**Dream Allegory:** See *Dream Vision*

**Dream Vision:** A literary convention, chiefly of the Middle Ages. In a dream vision a story is presented as a literal dream of the narrator. This device was commonly used to teach moral and religious lessons. Important works of this type are *The Divine Comedy* by Dante Alighieri, *Piers Plowman* by William Langland, and *The Pilgrim's Progress* by John Bunyan. Also known as Dream Allegory.

**Dystopia:** An imaginary place in a work of fiction where the characters lead dehumanized, fearful lives. Jack London's *The Iron Heel,* Yevgeny Zamyatin's *My,* Aldous Huxley's *Brave New World,* George Orwell's *Nineteen Eighty-four,* and Margaret Atwood's *Handmaid's Tale* portray versions of dystopia.

# E

**Eclogue:** In classical literature, a poem featuring rural themes and structured as a dialogue among shepherds. Eclogues often took specific poetic forms, such as elegies or love poems. Some were written as the soliloquy of a shepherd. In later centuries, "eclogue" came to refer to any poem that was in the pastoral tradition or that had a dialogue or monologue structure. A classical example of an eclogue is Virgil's *Eclogues,* also known as *Bucolics.* Giovanni

Boccaccio, Edmund Spenser, Andrew Marvell, Jonathan Swift, and Louis MacNeice also wrote eclogues.

**Edwardian:** Describes cultural conventions identified with the period of the reign of Edward VII of England (1901–1910). Writers of the Edwardian Age typically displayed a strong reaction against the propriety and conservatism of the Victorian Age. Their work often exhibits distrust of authority in religion, politics, and art and expresses strong doubts about the soundness of conventional values. Writers of this era include George Bernard Shaw, H. G. Wells, and Joseph Conrad.

**Edwardian Age:** See *Edwardian*

**Electra Complex:** A daughter's amorous obsession with her father. The term Electra complex comes from the plays of Euripides and Sophocles entitled *Electra,* in which the character Electra drives her brother Orestes to kill their mother and her lover in revenge for the murder of their father.

**Elegy:** A lyric poem that laments the death of a person or the eventual death of all people. In a conventional elegy, set in a classical world, the poet and subject are spoken of as shepherds. In modern criticism, the word elegy is often used to refer to a poem that is melancholy or mournfully contemplative. John Milton's "Lycidas" and Percy Bysshe Shelley's "Adonais" are two examples of this form.

**Elizabethan Age:** A period of great economic growth, religious controversy, and nationalism closely associated with the reign of Elizabeth I of England (1558–1603). The Elizabethan Age is considered a part of the general renaissance—that is, the flowering of arts and literature—that took place in Europe during the fourteenth through sixteenth centuries. The era. is considered the golden age of English literature. The most important dramas in English and a great deal of lyric poetry were produced during this period, and modern English criticism began around this time. The notable authors of the period—Philip Sidney, Edmund Spenser, Christopher Marlowe, William Shakespeare, Ben Jonson, Francis Bacon, and John Donne—are among the best in all of English literature.

**Elizabethan Drama:** English comic and tragic plays produced during the Renaissance, or more narrowly, those plays written during the last years of and few years after Queen Elizabeth's reign. William Shakespeare is considered an Elizabethan dramatist in the broader sense, although most of his work was produced during the reign of James I. Examples of Elizabethan comedies include John

Lyly's *The Woman in the Moone,* Thomas Dekker's *The Roaring Girl, or, Moll Cut Purse,* and William Shakespeare's *Twelfth Night.* Examples of Elizabethan tragedies include William Shakespeare's *Antony and Cleopatra,* Thomas Kyd's *The Spanish Tragedy,* and John Webster's *The Tragedy of the Duchess of Malfi.*

**Empathy:** A sense of shared experience, including emotional and physical feelings, with someone or something other than oneself. Empathy is often used to describe the response of a reader to a literary character. An example of an empathic passage is William Shakespeare's description in his narrative poem *Venus and Adonis* of: the snail, whose tender horns being hit, Shrinks backward in his shelly cave with pain. Readers of Gerard Manley Hopkins's *The Windhover* may experience some of the physical sensations evoked in the description of the movement of the falcon.

**English Sonnet:** See *Sonnet*

**Enjambment:** The running over of the sense and structure of a line of verse or a couplet into the following verse or couplet. Andrew Marvell's "To His Coy Mistress" is structured as a series of enjambments, as in lines 11–12: "My vegetable love should grow/Vaster than empires and more slow."

**Enlightenment, The:** An eighteenth-century philosophical movement. It began in France but had a wide impact throughout Europe and America. Thinkers of the Enlightenment valued reason and believed that both the individual and society could achieve a state of perfection. Corresponding to this essentially humanist vision was a resistance to religious authority. Important figures of the Enlightenment were Denis Diderot and Voltaire in France, Edward Gibbon and David Hume in England, and Thomas Paine and Thomas Jefferson in the United States.

**Epic:** A long narrative poem about the adventures of a hero of great historic or legendary importance. The setting is vast and the action is often given cosmic significance through the intervention of supernatural forces such as gods, angels, or demons. Epics are typically written in a classical style of grand simplicity with elaborate metaphors and allusions that enhance the symbolic importance of a hero's adventures. Some well-known epics are Homer's *Iliad* and *Odyssey,* Virgil's *Aeneid,* and John Milton's *Paradise Lost.*

**Epic Simile:** See *Homeric Simile*

**Epic Theater:** A theory of theatrical presentation developed by twentieth-century German playwright Bertolt Brecht. Brecht created a type of drama that the audience could view with complete detachment. He used what he termed "alienation effects" to create an emotional distance between the audience and the action on stage. Among these effects are: short, self-contained scenes that keep the play from building to a cathartic climax; songs that comment on the action; and techniques of acting that prevent the actor from developing an emotional identity with his role. Besides the plays of Bertolt Brecht, other plays that utilize epic theater conventions include those of Georg Buchner, Frank Wedekind, Erwin Piscator, and Leopold Jessner.

**Epigram:** A saying that makes the speaker's point quickly and concisely. Samuel Taylor Coleridge wrote an epigram that neatly sums up the form: What is an Epigram? A Dwarfish whole, Its body brevity, and wit its soul.

**Epilogue:** A concluding statement or section of a literary work. In dramas, particularly those of the seventeenth and eighteenth centuries, the epilogue is a closing speech, often in verse, delivered by an actor at the end of a play and spoken directly to the audience. A famous epilogue is Puck's speech at the end of William Shakespeare's *A Midsummer Night's Dream.*

**Epiphany:** A sudden revelation of truth inspired by a seemingly trivial incident. The term was widely used by James Joyce in his critical writings, and the stories in Joyce's *Dubliners* are commonly called "epiphanies."

**Episode:** An incident that forms part of a story and is significantly related to it. Episodes may be either self-contained narratives or events that depend on a larger context for their sense and importance. Examples of episodes include the founding of Wilmington, Delaware in Charles Reade's *The Disinherited Heir* and the individual events comprising the picaresque novels and medieval romances.

**Episodic Plot:** See *Plot*

**Epitaph:** An inscription on a tomb or tombstone, or a verse written on the occasion of a person's death. Epitaphs may be serious or humorous. Dorothy Parker's epitaph reads, "I told you I was sick."

**Epithalamion:** A song or poem written to honor and commemorate a marriage ceremony. Famous examples include Edmund Spenser's "Epithalamion'' and e. e. cummings's ''Epithalamion.'' Also spelled Epithalamium.

**Epithalamium:** See *Epithalamion*

**Epithet:** A word or phrase, often disparaging or abusive, that expresses a character trait of someone or something. ''The Napoleon of crime'' is an epithet applied to Professor Moriarty, arch-rival of Sherlock Holmes in Arthur Conan Doyle's series of detective stories.

*Exempla:* See *Exemplum*

*Exemplum:* A tale with a moral message. This form of literary sermonizing flourished during the Middle Ages, when *exempla* appeared in collections known as ''example-books.'' The works of Geoffrey Chaucer are full of *exempla.*

**Existentialism:** A predominantly twentieth-century philosophy concerned with the nature and perception of human existence. There are two major strains of existentialist thought: atheistic and Christian. Followers of atheistic existentialism believe that the individual is alone in a godless universe and that the basic human condition is one of suffering and loneliness. Nevertheless, because there are no fixed values, individuals can create their own characters—indeed, they can shape themselves—through the exercise of free will. The atheistic strain culminates in and is popularly associated with the works of Jean-Paul Sartre. The Christian existentialists, on the other hand, believe that only in God may people find freedom from life's anguish. The two strains hold certain beliefs in common: that existence cannot be fully understood or described through empirical effort; that anguish is a universal element of life; that individuals must bear responsibility for their actions; and that there is no common standard of behavior or perception for religious and ethical matters. Existentialist thought figures prominently in the works of such authors as Eugene Ionesco, Franz Kafka, Fyodor Dostoyevsky, Simone de Beauvoir, Samuel Beckett, and Albert Camus.

**Expatriates:** See *Expatriatism*

**Expatriatism:** The practice of leaving one's country to live for an extended period in another country. Literary expatriates include English poets Percy Bysshe Shelley and John Keats in Italy, Polish novelist Joseph Conrad in England, American writers Richard Wright, James Baldwin, Gertrude Stein, and Ernest Hemingway in France, and Trinidadian author Neil Bissondath in Canada.

**Exposition:** Writing intended to explain the nature of an idea, thing, or theme. Expository writing is often combined with description, narration, or argument. In dramatic writing, the exposition is the introductory material which presents the characters, setting, and tone of the play. An example of dramatic exposition occurs in many nineteenth-century drawing-room comedies in which the butler and the maid open the play with relevant talk about their master and mistress; in composition, exposition relays factual information, as in encyclopedia entries.

**Expressionism:** An indistinct literary term, originally used to describe an early twentieth-century school of German painting. The term applies to almost any mode of unconventional, highly subjective writing that distorts reality in some way. Advocates of Expressionism include dramatists George Kaiser, Ernst Toller, Luigi Pirandello, Federico Garcia Lorca, Eugene O'Neill, and Elmer Rice; poets George Heym, Ernst Stadler, August Stramm, Gottfried Benn, and Georg Trakl; and novelists Franz Kafka and James Joyce.

**Extended Monologue:** See *Monologue*

# F

**Fable:** A prose or verse narrative intended to convey a moral. Animals or inanimate objects with human characteristics often serve as characters in fables. A famous fable is Aesop's ''The Tortoise and the Hare.''

**Fairy Tales:** Short narratives featuring mythical beings such as fairies, elves, and sprites. These tales originally belonged to the folklore of a particular nation or region, such as those collected in Germany by Jacob and Wilhelm Grimm. Two other celebrated writers of fairy tales are Hans Christian Andersen and Rudyard Kipling.

**Falling Action:** See *Denouement*

**Fantasy:** A literary form related to mythology and folklore. Fantasy literature is typically set in non-existent realms and features supernatural beings. Notable examples of fantasy literature are *The Lord of the Rings* by J. R. R. Tolkien and the Gormenghast trilogy by Mervyn Peake.

**Farce:** A type of comedy characterized by broad humor, outlandish incidents, and often vulgar subject matter. Much of the ''comedy'' in film and television could more accurately be described as farce.

**Feet:** See *Foot*

**Feminine Rhyme:** See *Rhyme*

***Femme fatale:*** A French phrase with the literal translation "fatal woman." A *femme fatale* is a sensuous, alluring woman who often leads men into danger or trouble. A classic example of the *femme fatale* is the nameless character in Billy Wilder's *The Seven Year Itch,* portrayed by Marilyn Monroe in the film adaptation.

**Fiction:** Any story that is the product of imagination rather than a documentation of fact. characters and events in such narratives may be based in real life but their ultimate form and configuration is a creation of the author. Geoffrey Chaucer's *The Canterbury Tales,* Laurence Sterne's *Tristram Shandy,* and Margaret Mitchell's *Gone with the Wind* are examples of fiction.

**Figurative Language:** A technique in writing in which the author temporarily interrupts the order, construction, or meaning of the writing for a particular effect. This interruption takes the form of one or more figures of speech such as hyperbole, irony, or simile. Figurative language is the opposite of literal language, in which every word is truthful, accurate, and free of exaggeration or embellishment. Examples of figurative language are tropes such as metaphor and rhetorical figures such as apostrophe.

**Figures of Speech:** Writing that differs from customary conventions for construction, meaning, order, or significance for the purpose of a special meaning or effect. There are two major types of figures of speech: rhetorical figures, which do not make changes in the meaning of the words, and tropes, which do. Types of figures of speech include simile, hyperbole, alliteration, and pun, among many others.

***Fin de siecle:*** A French term meaning "end of the century." The term is used to denote the last decade of the nineteenth century, a transition period when writers and other artists abandoned old conventions and looked for new techniques and objectives. Two writers commonly associated with the *fin de siecle* mindset are Oscar Wilde and George Bernard Shaw.

**First Person:** See *Point of View*

**Flashback:** A device used in literature to present action that occurred before the beginning of the story. Flashbacks are often introduced as the dreams or recollections of one or more characters. Flashback techniques are often used in films, where they are typically set off by a gradual changing of one picture to another.

**Foil:** A character in a work of literature whose physical or psychological qualities contrast strongly with, and therefore highlight, the corresponding qualities of another character. In his Sherlock Holmes stories, Arthur Conan Doyle portrayed Dr. Watson as a man of normal habits and intelligence, making him a foil for the eccentric and wonderfully perceptive Sherlock Holmes.

**Folk Ballad:** See *Ballad*

**Folklore:** Traditions and myths preserved in a culture or group of people. Typically, these are passed on by word of mouth in various forms—such as legends, songs, and proverbs— or preserved in customs and ceremonies. This term was first used by W. J. Thoms in 1846. Sir James Frazer's *The Golden Bough* is the record of English folklore; myths about the frontier and the Old South exemplify American folklore.

**Folktale:** A story originating in oral tradition. Folktales fall into a variety of categories, including legends, ghost stories, fairy tales, fables, and anecdotes based on historical figures and events. Examples of folktales include Giambattista Basile's *The Pentamerone,* which contains the tales of Puss in Boots, Rapunzel, Cinderella, and Beauty and the Beast, and Joel Chandler Harris's Uncle Remus stories, which represent transplanted African folktales and American tales about the characters Mike Fink, Johnny Appleseed, Paul Bunyan, and Pecos Bill.

**Foot:** The smallest unit of rhythm in a line of poetry. In English-language poetry, a foot is typically one accented syllable combined with one or two unaccented syllables. There are many different types of feet. When the accent is on the second syllable of a two syllable word (con-*tort*), the foot is an "iamb"; the reverse accentual pattern (*tor* -ture) is a "trochee." Other feet that commonly occur in poetry in English are "anapest", two unaccented syllables followed by an accented syllable as in in-ter-*cept*, and "dactyl", an accented syllable followed by two unaccented syllables as in *su*-i-cide.

**Foreshadowing:** A device used in literature to create expectation or to set up an explanation of later developments. In Charles Dickens's *Great Expectations,* the graveyard encounter at the beginning of the novel between Pip and the escaped convict Magwitch foreshadows the baleful atmosphere and events that comprise much of the narrative.

**Form:** The pattern or construction of a work which identifies its genre and distinguishes it from other genres. Examples of forms include the different genres, such as the lyric form or the short story form, and various patterns for poetry, such as the verse form or the stanza form.

**Formalism:** In literary criticism, the belief that literature should follow prescribed rules of construction, such as those that govern the sonnet form. Examples of formalism are found in the work of the New Critics and structuralists.

**Fourteener Meter:** See *Meter*

**Free Verse:** Poetry that lacks regular metrical and rhyme patterns but that tries to capture the cadences of everyday speech. The form allows a poet to exploit a variety of rhythmical effects within a single poem. Free-verse techniques have been widely used in the twentieth century by such writers as Ezra Pound, T. S. Eliot, Carl Sandburg, and William Carlos Williams. Also known as *Vers libre*.

**Futurism:** A flamboyant literary and artistic movement that developed in France, Italy, and Russia from 1908 through the 1920s. Futurist theater and poetry abandoned traditional literary forms. In their place, followers of the movement attempted to achieve total freedom of expression through bizarre imagery and deformed or newly invented words. The Futurists were self-consciously modern artists who attempted to incorporate the appearances and sounds of modern life into their work. Futurist writers include Filippo Tommaso Marinetti, Wyndham Lewis, Guillaume Apollinaire, Velimir Khlebnikov, and Vladimir Mayakovsky.

# G

**Genre:** A category of literary work. In critical theory, genre may refer to both the content of a given work—tragedy, comedy, pastoral—and to its form, such as poetry, novel, or drama. This term also refers to types of popular literature, as in the genres of science fiction or the detective story.

**Genteel Tradition:** A term coined by critic George Santayana to describe the literary practice of certain late nineteenth-century American writers, especially New Englanders. Followers of the Genteel Tradition emphasized conventionality in social, religious, moral, and literary standards. Some of the best-known writers of the Genteel Tradition are R. H. Stoddard and Bayard Taylor.

**Gilded Age:** A period in American history during the 1870s characterized by political corruption and materialism. A number of important novels of social and political criticism were written during this time. Examples of Gilded Age literature include Henry Adams's *Democracy* and F. Marion Crawford's *An American Politician.*

**Gothic:** See *Gothicism*

**Gothicism:** In literary criticism, works characterized by a taste for the medieval or morbidly attractive. A gothic novel prominently features elements of horror, the supernatural, gloom, and violence: clanking chains, terror, charnel houses, ghosts, medieval castles, and mysteriously slamming doors. The term ''gothic novel'' is also applied to novels that lack elements of the traditional Gothic setting but that create a similar atmosphere of terror or dread. Mary Shelley's *Frankenstein* is perhaps the best-known English work of this kind.

**Gothic Novel:** See *Gothicism*

**Great Chain of Being:** The belief that all things and creatures in nature are organized in a hierarchy from inanimate objects at the bottom to God at the top. This system of belief was popular in the seventeenth and eighteenth centuries. A summary of the concept of the great chain of being can be found in the first epistle of Alexander Pope's *An Essay on Man,* and more recently in Arthur O. Lovejoy's *The Great Chain of Being: A Study of the History of an Idea.*

**Grotesque:** In literary criticism, the subject matter of a work or a style of expression characterized by exaggeration, deformity, freakishness, and disorder. The grotesque often includes an element of comic absurdity. Early examples of literary grotesque include Francois Rabelais's *Pantagruel* and *Gargantua* and Thomas Nashe's *The Unfortunate Traveller,* while more recent examples can be found in the works of Edgar Allan Poe, Evelyn Waugh, Eudora Welty, Flannery O'Connor, Eugene Ionesco, Gunter Grass, Thomas Mann, Mervyn Peake, and Joseph Heller, among many others.

# H

*Haiku:* The shortest form of Japanese poetry, constructed in three lines of five, seven, and five syllables respectively. The message of a *haiku* poem usually centers on some aspect of spirituality and provokes an emotional response in the reader. Early masters of *haiku* include Basho, Buson, Kobayashi

Issa, and Masaoka Shiki. English writers of *haiku* include the Imagists, notably Ezra Pound, H. D., Amy Lowell, Carl Sandburg, and William Carlos Williams. Also known as *Hokku.*

**Half Rhyme:** See *Consonance*

*Hamartia:* In tragedy, the event or act that leads to the hero's or heroine's downfall. This term is often incorrectly used as a synonym for tragic flaw. In Richard Wright's *Native Son,* the act that seals Bigger Thomas's fate is his first impulsive murder.

**Harlem Renaissance:** The Harlem Renaissance of the 1920s is generally considered the first significant movement of black writers and artists in the United States. During this period, new and established black writers published more fiction and poetry than ever before, the first influential black literary journals were established, and black authors and artists received their first widespread recognition and serious critical appraisal. Among the major writers associated with this period are Claude McKay, Jean Toomer, Countee Cullen, Langston Hughes, Arna Bontemps, Nella Larsen, and Zora Neale Hurston. Works representative of the Harlem Renaissance include Arna Bontemps's poems "The Return" and "Golgotha Is a Mountain," Claude McKay's novel *Home to Harlem,* Nella Larsen's novel *Passing,* Langston Hughes's poem "The Negro Speaks of Rivers," and the journals *Crisis* and *Opportunity,* both founded during this period. Also known as Negro Renaissance and New Negro Movement.

**Harlequin:** A stock character of the *commedia dell'arte* who occasionally interrupted the action with silly antics. Harlequin first appeared on the English stage in John Day's *The Travailes of the Three English Brothers.* The San Francisco Mime Troupe is one of the few modern groups to adapt Harlequin to the needs of contemporary satire.

**Hellenism:** Imitation of ancient Greek thought or styles. Also, an approach to life that focuses on the growth and development of the intellect. "Hellenism" is sometimes used to refer to the belief that reason can be applied to examine all human experience. A cogent discussion of Hellenism can be found in Matthew Arnold's *Culture and Anarchy.*

**Heptameter:** See *Meter*

**Hero/Heroine:** The principal sympathetic character (male or female) in a literary work. Heroes and heroines typically exhibit admirable traits: ideal-

ism, courage, and integrity, for example. Famous heroes and heroines include Pip in Charles Dickens's *Great Expectations,* the anonymous narrator in Ralph Ellison's *Invisible Man,* and Sethe in Toni Morrison's *Beloved.*

**Heroic Couplet:** A rhyming couplet written in iambic pentameter (a verse with five iambic feet). The following lines by Alexander Pope are an example: "Truth guards the Poet, sanctifies the line./ And makes Immortal, Verse as mean as mine."

**Heroic Line:** The meter and length of a line of verse in epic or heroic poetry. This varies by language and time period. For example, in English poetry, the heroic line is iambic pentameter (a verse with five iambic feet); in French, the alexandrine (a verse with six iambic feet); in classical literature, dactylic hexameter (a verse with six dactylic feet).

**Heroine:** See *Hero/Heroine*

**Hexameter:** See *Meter*

**Historical Criticism:** The study of a work based on its impact on the world of the time period in which it was written. Examples of postmodern historical criticism can be found in the work of Michel Foucault, Hayden White, Stephen Greenblatt, and Jonathan Goldberg.

*Hokku:* See *Haiku*

**Holocaust:** See *Holocaust Literature*

**Holocaust Literature:** Literature influenced by or written about the Holocaust of World War II. Such literature includes true stories of survival in concentration camps, escape, and life after the war, as well as fictional works and poetry. Representative works of Holocaust literature include Saul Bellow's *Mr. Sammler's Planet,* Anne Frank's *The Diary of a Young Girl,* Jerzy Kosinski's *The Painted Bird,* Arthur Miller's *Incident at Vichy,* Czeslaw Milosz's *Collected Poems,* William Styron's *Sophie's Choice,* and Art Spiegelman's *Maus.*

**Homeric Simile:** An elaborate, detailed comparison written as a simile many lines in length. An example of an epic simile from John Milton's *Paradise Lost* follows: Angel Forms, who lay entranced Thick as autumnal leaves that strow the brooks In Vallombrosa, where the Etrurian shades High over-arched embower; or scattered sedge Afloat, when with fierce winds Orion armed Hath vexed the Red-Sea coast, whose waves o'erthrew Busiris and his Memphian chivalry, While with perfidious hatred they pursued The sojourners of

Goshen, who beheld From the safe shore their floating carcasses And broken chariot-wheels. Also known as Epic Simile.

**Horatian Satire:** See *Satire*

**Humanism:** A philosophy that places faith in the dignity of humankind and rejects the medieval perception of the individual as a weak, fallen creature. "Humanists" typically believe in the perfectibility of human nature and view reason and education as the means to that end. Humanist thought is represented in the works of Marsilio Ficino, Ludovico Castelvetro, Edmund Spenser, John Milton, Dean John Colet, Desiderius Erasmus, John Dryden, Alexander Pope, Matthew Arnold, and Irving Babbitt.

**Humors:** Mentions of the humors refer to the ancient Greek theory that a person's health and personality were determined by the balance of four basic fluids in the body: blood, phlegm, yellow bile, and black bile. A dominance of any fluid would cause extremes in behavior. An excess of blood created a sanguine person who was joyful, aggressive, and passionate; a phlegmatic person was shy, fearful, and sluggish; too much yellow bile led to a choleric temperament characterized by impatience, anger, bitterness, and stubbornness; and excessive black bile created melancholy, a state of laziness, gluttony, and lack of motivation. Literary treatment of the humors is exemplified by several characters in Ben Jonson's plays *Every Man in His Humour* and *Every Man out of His Humour*. Also spelled Humours.

**Humours:** See *Humors*

**Hyperbole:** In literary criticism, deliberate exaggeration used to achieve an effect. In William Shakespeare's *Macbeth*, Lady Macbeth hyperbolizes when she says, "All the perfumes of Arabia could not sweeten this little hand."

# I

**Iamb:** See *Foot*

**Idiom:** A word construction or verbal expression closely associated with a given language. For example, in colloquial English the construction "how come" can be used instead of "why" to introduce a question. Similarly, "a piece of cake" is sometimes used to describe a task that is easily done.

**Image:** A concrete representation of an object or sensory experience. Typically, such a representation helps evoke the feelings associated with the object or experience itself. Images are either "literal" or "figurative." Literal images are especially concrete and involve little or no extension of the obvious meaning of the words used to express them. Figurative images do not follow the literal meaning of the words exactly. Images in literature are usually visual, but the term "image" can also refer to the representation of any sensory experience. In his poem "The Shepherd's Hour," Paul Verlaine presents the following image: "The Moon is red through horizon's fog;/ In a dancing mist the hazy meadow sleeps." The first line is broadly literal, while the second line involves turns of meaning associated with dancing and sleeping.

**Imagery:** The array of images in a literary work. Also, figurative language. William Butler Yeats's "The Second Coming" offers a powerful image of encroaching anarchy: Turning and turning in the widening gyre The falcon cannot hear the falconer; Things fall apart. . . .

**Imagism:** An English and American poetry movement that flourished between 1908 and 1917. The Imagists used precise, clearly presented images in their works. They also used common, everyday speech and aimed for conciseness, concrete imagery, and the creation of new rhythms. Participants in the Imagist movement included Ezra Pound, H. D. (Hilda Doolittle), and Amy Lowell, among others.

**In medias res:** A Latin term meaning "in the middle of things." It refers to the technique of beginning a story at its midpoint and then using various flashback devices to reveal previous action. This technique originated in such epics as Virgil's *Aeneid*.

**Induction:** The process of reaching a conclusion by reasoning from specific premises to form a general premise. Also, an introductory portion of a work of literature, especially a play. Geoffrey Chaucer's "Prologue" to the *Canterbury Tales,* Thomas Sackville's "Induction" to *The Mirror of Magistrates,* and the opening scene in William Shakespeare's *The Taming of the Shrew* are examples of inductions to literary works.

**Intentional Fallacy:** The belief that judgments of a literary work based solely on an author's stated or implied intentions are false and misleading. Critics who believe in the concept of the intentional fallacy typically argue that the work itself is sufficient matter for interpretation, even though they may concede that an author's statement of purpose can be useful. Analysis of William Wordsworth's *Lyrical Ballads* based on the observations about poetry he makes in his "Preface" to the second edition of that work is an example of the intentional fallacy.

**Interior Monologue:** A narrative technique in which characters' thoughts are revealed in a way that appears to be uncontrolled by the author. The interior monologue typically aims to reveal the inner self of a character. It portrays emotional experiences as they occur at both a conscious and unconscious level. images are often used to represent sensations or emotions. One of the best-known interior monologues in English is the Molly Bloom section at the close of James Joyce's *Ulysses*. The interior monologue is also common in the works of Virginia Woolf.

**Internal Rhyme:** Rhyme that occurs within a single line of verse. An example is in the opening line of Edgar Allan Poe's "The Raven": "Once upon a midnight dreary, while I pondered weak and weary." Here, "dreary" and "weary" make an internal rhyme.

**Irish Literary Renaissance:** A late nineteenth- and early twentieth-century movement in Irish literature. Members of the movement aimed to reduce the influence of British culture in Ireland and create an Irish national literature. William Butler Yeats, George Moore, and Sean O'Casey are three of the best-known figures of the movement.

**Irony:** In literary criticism, the effect of language in which the intended meaning is the opposite of what is stated. The title of Jonathan Swift's "A Modest Proposal" is ironic because what Swift proposes in this essay is cannibalism—hardly "modest."

**Italian Sonnet:** See *Sonnet*

# J

**Jacobean Age:** The period of the reign of James I of England (1603–1625). The early literature of this period reflected the worldview of the Elizabethan Age, but a darker, more cynical attitude steadily grew in the art and literature of the Jacobean Age. This was an important time for English drama and poetry. Milestones include William Shakespeare's tragedies, tragi-comedies, and sonnets; Ben Jonson's various dramas; and John Donne's metaphysical poetry.

**Jargon:** Language that is used or understood only by a select group of people. Jargon may refer to terminology used in a certain profession, such as

computer jargon, or it may refer to any nonsensical language that is not understood by most people. Literary examples of jargon are Francois Villon's *Ballades en jargon,* which is composed in the secret language of the *coquillards,* and Anthony Burgess's *A Clockwork Orange,* narrated in the fictional characters' language of "Nadsat."

**Juvenalian Satire:** See *Satire*

# K

**Knickerbocker Group:** A somewhat indistinct group of New York writers of the first half of the nineteenth century. Members of the group were linked only by location and a common theme: New York life. Two famous members of the Knickerbocker Group were Washington Irving and William Cullen Bryant. The group's name derives from Irving's *Knickerbocker's History of New York.*

# L

**Lais:** See *Lay*

**Lay:** A song or simple narrative poem. The form originated in medieval France. Early French *lais* were often based on the Celtic legends and other tales sung by Breton minstrels—thus the name of the "Breton lay." In fourteenth-century England, the term "lay" was used to describe short narratives written in imitation of the Breton lays. The most notable of these is Geoffrey Chaucer's "The Minstrel's Tale."

**Leitmotiv:** See *Motif*

**Literal Language:** An author uses literal language when he or she writes without exaggerating or embellishing the subject matter and without any tools of figurative language. To say "He ran very quickly down the street" is to use literal language, whereas to say "He ran like a hare down the street" would be using figurative language.

**Literary Ballad:** See *Ballad*

**Literature:** Literature is broadly defined as any written or spoken material, but the term most often refers to creative works. Literature includes poetry, drama, fiction, and many kinds of nonfiction writing, as well as oral, dramatic, and broadcast compositions not necessarily preserved in a written format, such as films and television programs.

**Lost Generation:** A term first used by Gertrude Stein to describe the post-World War I generation of

American writers: men and women haunted by a sense of betrayal and emptiness brought about by the destructiveness of the war. The term is commonly applied to Hart Crane, Ernest Hemingway, F. Scott Fitzgerald, and others.

**Lyric Poetry:** A poem expressing the subjective feelings and personal emotions of the poet. Such poetry is melodic, since it was originally accompanied by a lyre in recitals. Most Western poetry in the twentieth century may be classified as lyrical. Examples of lyric poetry include A. E. Housman's elegy "To an Athlete Dying Young," the odes of Pindar and Horace, Thomas Gray and William Collins, the sonnets of Sir Thomas Wyatt and Sir Philip Sidney, Elizabeth Barrett Browning and Rainer Maria Rilke, and a host of other forms in the poetry of William Blake and Christina Rossetti, among many others.

# M

**Mannerism:** Exaggerated, artificial adherence to a literary manner or style. Also, a popular style of the visual arts of late sixteenth-century Europe that was marked by elongation of the human form and by intentional spatial distortion. Literary works that are self-consciously high-toned and artistic are often said to be "mannered." Authors of such works include Henry James and Gertrude Stein.

**Masculine Rhyme:** See *Rhyme*

**Masque:** A lavish and elaborate form of entertainment, often performed in royal courts, that emphasizes song, dance, and costumery. The Renaissance form of the masque grew out of the spectacles of masked figures common in medieval England and Europe. The masque reached its peak of popularity and development in seventeenth-century England, during the reigns of James I and, especially, of Charles I. Ben Jonson, the most significant masque writer, also created the "antimasque," which incorporates elements of humor and the grotesque into the traditional masque and achieved greater dramatic quality. Masque-like interludes appear in Edmund Spenser's *The Faerie Queene* and in William Shakespeare's *The Tempest.* One of the best-known English masques is John Milton's *Comus.*

**Measure:** The foot, verse, or time sequence used in a literary work, especially a poem. Measure is often used somewhat incorrectly as a synonym for meter.

**Melodrama:** A play in which the typical plot is a conflict between characters who personify extreme good and evil. Melodramas usually end happily and

emphasize sensationalism. Other literary forms that use the same techniques are often labeled "melodramatic." The term was formerly used to describe a combination of drama and music; as such, it was synonymous with "opera." Augustin Daly's *Under the Gaslight* and Dion Boucicault's *The Octoroon, The Colleen Bawn,* and *The Poor of New York* are examples of melodramas. The most popular media for twentieth-century melodramas are motion pictures and television.

**Metaphor:** A figure of speech that expresses an idea through the image of another object. Metaphors suggest the essence of the first object by identifying it with certain qualities of the second object. An example is "But soft, what light through yonder window breaks?/ It is the east, and Juliet is the sun" in William Shakespeare's *Romeo and Juliet.* Here, Juliet, the first object, is identified with qualities of the second object, the sun.

**Metaphysical Conceit:** See *Conceit*

**Metaphysical Poetry:** The body of poetry produced by a group of seventeenth-century English writers called the "Metaphysical Poets." The group includes John Donne and Andrew Marvell. The Metaphysical Poets made use of everyday speech, intellectual analysis, and unique imagery. They aimed to portray the ordinary conflicts and contradictions of life. Their poems often took the form of an argument, and many of them emphasize physical and religious love as well as the fleeting nature of life. Elaborate conceits are typical in metaphysical poetry. Marvell's "To His Coy Mistress" is a well-known example of a metaphysical poem.

**Metaphysical Poets:** See *Metaphysical Poetry*

**Meter:** In literary criticism, the repetition of sound patterns that creates a rhythm in poetry. The patterns are based on the number of syllables and the presence and absence of accents. The unit of rhythm in a line is called a foot. Types of meter are classified according to the number of feet in a line. These are the standard English lines: Monometer, one foot; Dimeter, two feet; Trimeter, three feet; Tetrameter, four feet; Pentameter, five feet; Hexameter, six feet (also called the Alexandrine); Heptameter, seven feet (also called the "Fourteener" when the feet are iambic). The most common English meter is the iambic pentameter, in which each line contains ten syllables, or five iambic feet, which individually are composed of an unstressed syllable followed by an accented syllable. Both of the following lines from Alfred, Lord Tennyson's

''Ulysses'' are written in iambic pentameter: Made weak by time and fate, but strong in will To strive, to seek, to find, and not to yield.

***Mise en scene:*** The costumes, scenery, and other properties of a drama. Herbert Beerbohm Tree was renowned for the elaborate *mises en scene* of his lavish Shakespearean productions at His Majesty's Theatre between 1897 and 1915.

**Modernism:** Modern literary practices. Also, the principles of a literary school that lasted from roughly the beginning of the twentieth century until the end of World War II. Modernism is defined by its rejection of the literary conventions of the nineteenth century and by its opposition to conventional morality, taste, traditions, and economic values. Many writers are associated with the concepts of Modernism, including Albert Camus, Marcel Proust, D. H. Lawrence, W. H. Auden, Ernest Hemingway, William Faulkner, William Butler Yeats, Thomas Mann, Tennessee Williams, Eugene O'Neill, and James Joyce.

**Monologue:** A composition, written or oral, by a single individual. More specifically, a speech given by a single individual in a drama or other public entertainment. It has no set length, although it is usually several or more lines long. An example of an ''extended monologue''—that is, a monologue of great length and seriousness—occurs in the one-act, one-character play *The Stronger* by August Strindberg.

**Monometer:** See *Meter*

**Mood:** The prevailing emotions of a work or of the author in his or her creation of the work. The mood of a work is not always what might be expected based on its subject matter. The poem ''Dover Beach'' by Matthew Arnold offers examples of two different moods originating from the same experience: watching the ocean at night. The mood of the first three lines— The sea is calm tonight The tide is full, the moon lies fair Upon the straights. . . . is in sharp contrast to the mood of the last three lines— And we are here as on a darkling plain Swept with confused alarms of struggle and flight, Where ignorant armies clash by night.

***Motif:*** A theme, character type, image, metaphor, or other verbal element that recurs throughout a single work of literature or occurs in a number of different works over a period of time. For example, the various manifestations of the color white in Herman Melville's *Moby Dick* is a ''specific'' *motif,* while the trials of star-crossed lovers is a ''conventional''

*motif* from the literature of all periods. Also known as *Motiv* or *Leitmotiv.*

***Motiv:*** See *Motif*

**Muckrakers:** An early twentieth-century group of American writers. Typically, their works exposed the wrongdoings of big business and government in the United States. Upton Sinclair's *The Jungle* exemplifies the muckraking novel.

**Muses:** Nine Greek mythological goddesses, the daughters of Zeus and Mnemosyne (Memory). Each muse patronized a specific area of the liberal arts and sciences. Calliope presided over epic poetry, Clio over history, Erato over love poetry, Euterpe over music or lyric poetry, Melpomene over tragedy, Polyhymnia over hymns to the gods, Terpsichore over dance, Thalia over comedy, and Urania over astronomy. Poets and writers traditionally made appeals to the Muses for inspiration in their work. John Milton invokes the aid of a muse at the beginning of the first book of his *Paradise Lost:* Of Man's First disobedience, and the Fruit of the Forbidden Tree, whose mortal taste Brought Death into the World, and all our woe, With loss of Eden, till one greater Man Restore us, and regain the blissful Seat, Sing Heav'nly Muse, that on the secret top of Oreb, or of Sinai, didst inspire That Shepherd, who first taught the chosen Seed, In the Beginning how the Heav'ns and Earth Rose out of Chaos. . . .

**Mystery:** See *Suspense*

**Myth:** An anonymous tale emerging from the traditional beliefs of a culture or social unit. Myths use supernatural explanations for natural phenomena. They may also explain cosmic issues like creation and death. Collections of myths, known as mythologies, are common to all cultures and nations, but the best-known myths belong to the Norse, Roman, and Greek mythologies. A famous myth is the story of Arachne, an arrogant young girl who challenged a goddess, Athena, to a weaving contest; when the girl won, Athena was enraged and turned Arachne into a spider, thus explaining the existence of spiders.

# N

**Narration:** The telling of a series of events, real or invented. A narration may be either a simple narrative, in which the events are recounted chronologically, or a narrative with a plot, in which the account is given in a style reflecting the author's artistic concept of the story. Narration is sometimes used as a synonym for "storyline." The recounting of scary stories around a campfire is a form of narration.

**Narrative:** A verse or prose accounting of an event or sequence of events, real or invented. The term is also used as an adjective in the sense "method of narration." For example, in literary criticism, the expression "narrative technique" usually refers to the way the author structures and presents his or her story. Narratives range from the shortest accounts of events, as in Julius Caesar's remark, "I came, I saw, I conquered," to the longest historical or biographical works, as in Edward Gibbon's *The Decline and Fall of the Roman Empire,* as well as diaries, travelogues, novels, ballads, epics, short stories, and other fictional forms.

**Narrative Poetry:** A nondramatic poem in which the author tells a story. Such poems may be of any length or level of complexity. Epics such as *Beowulf* and ballads are forms of narrative poetry.

**Narrator:** The teller of a story. The narrator may be the author or a character in the story through whom the author speaks. Huckleberry Finn is the narrator of Mark Twain's *The Adventures of Huckleberry Finn.*

**Naturalism:** A literary movement of the late nineteenth and early twentieth centuries. The movement's major theorist, French novelist Emile Zola, envisioned a type of fiction that would examine human life with the objectivity of scientific inquiry. The Naturalists typically viewed human beings as either the products of "biological determinism," ruled by hereditary instincts and engaged in an endless struggle for survival, or as the products of "socioeconomic determinism," ruled by social and economic forces beyond their control. In their works, the Naturalists generally ignored the highest levels of society and focused on degradation: poverty, alcoholism, prostitution, insanity, and disease. Naturalism influenced authors throughout the world, including Henrik Ibsen and Thomas Hardy. In the United States, in particular, Naturalism had a profound impact. Among the authors who embraced its principles are Theodore Dreiser, Eugene O'Neill, Stephen Crane, Jack London, and Frank Norris.

**Negritude:** A literary movement based on the concept of a shared cultural bond on the part of black Africans, wherever they may be in the world. It traces its origins to the former French colonies of Africa and the Caribbean. Negritude poets, novelists, and essayists generally stress four points in their writings: One, black alienation from tradi-

tional African culture can lead to feelings of inferiority. Two, European colonialism and Western education should be resisted. Three, black Africans should seek to affirm and define their own identity. Four, African culture can and should be reclaimed. Many Negritude writers also claim that blacks can make unique contributions to the world, based on a heightened appreciation of nature, rhythm, and human emotions—aspects of life they say are not so highly valued in the materialistic and rationalistic West. Examples of Negritude literature include the poetry of both Senegalese Leopold Senghor in *Hosties noires* and Martiniquais Aime-Fernand Cesaire in *Return to My Native Land.*

**Negro Renaissance:** See *Harlem Renaissance*

**Neoclassical Period:** See *Neoclassicism*

**Neoclassicism:** In literary criticism, this term refers to the revival of the attitudes and styles of expression of classical literature. It is generally used to describe a period in European history beginning in the late seventeenth century and lasting until about 1800. In its purest form, Neoclassicism marked a return to order, proportion, restraint, logic, accuracy, and decorum. In England, where Neoclassicism perhaps was most popular, it reflected the influence of seventeenth-century French writers, especially dramatists. Neoclassical writers typically reacted against the intensity and enthusiasm of the Renaissance period. They wrote works that appealed to the intellect, using elevated language and classical literary forms such as satire and the ode. Neoclassical works were often governed by the classical goal of instruction. English neoclassicists included Alexander Pope, Jonathan Swift, Joseph Addison, Sir Richard Steele, John Gay, and Matthew Prior; French neoclassicists included Pierre Corneille and Jean-Baptiste Moliere. Also known as Age of Reason.

**Neoclassicists:** See *Neoclassicism*

**New Criticism:** A movement in literary criticism, dating from the late 1920s, that stressed close textual analysis in the interpretation of works of literature. The New Critics saw little merit in historical and biographical analysis. Rather, they aimed to examine the text alone, free from the question of how external events—biographical or otherwise— may have helped shape it. This predominantly American school was named "New Criticism" by one of its practitioners, John Crowe Ransom. Other important New Critics included Allen Tate, R. P. Blackmur, Robert Penn Warren, and Cleanth Brooks.

**New Negro Movement:** See *Harlem Renaissance*

**Noble Savage:** The idea that primitive man is noble and good but becomes evil and corrupted as he becomes civilized. The concept of the noble savage originated in the Renaissance period but is more closely identified with such later writers as Jean-Jacques Rousseau and Aphra Behn. First described in John Dryden's play *The Conquest of Granada,* the noble savage is portrayed by the various Native Americans in James Fenimore Cooper's "Leatherstocking Tales," by Queequeg, Daggoo, and Tashtego in Herman Melville's *Moby Dick,* and by John the Savage in Aldous Huxley's *Brave New World.*

# O

**Objective Correlative:** An outward set of objects, a situation, or a chain of events corresponding to an inward experience and evoking this experience in the reader. The term frequently appears in modern criticism in discussions of authors' intended effects on the emotional responses of readers. This term was originally used by T. S. Eliot in his 1919 essay "Hamlet."

**Objectivity:** A quality in writing characterized by the absence of the author's opinion or feeling about the subject matter. Objectivity is an important factor in criticism. The novels of Henry James and, to a certain extent, the poems of John Larkin demonstrate objectivity, and it is central to John Keats's concept of "negative capability." Critical and journalistic writing usually are or attempt to be objective.

**Occasional Verse:** poetry written on the occasion of a significant historical or personal event. *Vers de societe* is sometimes called occasional verse although it is of a less serious nature. Famous examples of occasional verse include Andrew Marvell's "Horatian Ode upon Cromwell's Return from England," Walt Whitman's "When Lilacs Last in the Dooryard Bloom'd"— written upon the death of Abraham Lincoln—and Edmund Spenser's commemoration of his wedding, "Epithalamion."

**Octave:** A poem or stanza composed of eight lines. The term octave most often represents the first eight lines of a Petrarchan sonnet. An example of an octave is taken from a translation of a Petrarchan sonnet by Sir Thomas Wyatt: The pillar perisht is whereto I leant, The strongest stay of mine unquiet mind; The like of it no man again can find, From East to West Still seeking though he went. To mind unhap! for hap away hath rent Of all my joy the very

bark and rind; And I, alas, by chance am thus assigned Daily to mourn till death do it relent.

**Ode:** Name given to an extended lyric poem characterized by exalted emotion and dignified style. An ode usually concerns a single, serious theme. Most odes, but not all, are addressed to an object or individual. Odes are distinguished from other lyric poetic forms by their complex rhythmic and stanzaic patterns. An example of this form is John Keats's "Ode to a Nightingale."

**Oedipus Complex:** A son's amorous obsession with his mother. The phrase is derived from the story of the ancient Theban hero Oedipus, who unknowingly killed his father and married his mother. Literary occurrences of the Oedipus complex include Andre Gide's *Oedipe* and Jean Cocteau's *La Machine infernale,* as well as the most famous, Sophocles' *Oedipus Rex.*

**Omniscience:** See *Point of View*

**Onomatopoeia:** The use of words whose sounds express or suggest their meaning. In its simplest sense, onomatopoeia may be represented by words that mimic the sounds they denote such as "hiss" or "meow." At a more subtle level, the pattern and rhythm of sounds and rhymes of a line or poem may be onomatopoeic. A celebrated example of onomatopoeia is the repetition of the word "bells" in Edgar Allan Poe's poem "The Bells."

**Opera:** A type of stage performance, usually a drama, in which the dialogue is sung. Classic examples of opera include Giuseppi Verdi's *La traviata,* Giacomo Puccini's *La Boheme,* and Richard Wagner's *Tristan und Isolde.* Major twentieth-century contributors to the form include Richard Strauss and Alban Berg.

**Operetta:** A usually romantic comic opera. John Gay's *The Beggar's Opera,* Richard Sheridan's *The Duenna,* and numerous works by William Gilbert and Arthur Sullivan are examples of operettas.

**Oral Tradition:** See *Oral Transmission*

**Oral Transmission:** A process by which songs, ballads, folklore, and other material are transmitted by word of mouth. The tradition of oral transmission predates the written record systems of literate society. Oral transmission preserves material sometimes over generations, although often with variations. Memory plays a large part in the recitation and preservation of orally transmitted material. Breton lays, French *fabliaux,* national epics (including the Anglo-Saxon *Beowulf,* the Spanish *El Cid,* and the Finnish *Kalevala*), Native American myths and legends, and African folktales told by plantation slaves are examples of orally transmitted literature.

**Oration:** Formal speaking intended to motivate the listeners to some action or feeling. Such public speaking was much more common before the development of timely printed communication such as newspapers. Famous examples of oration include Abraham Lincoln's "Gettysburg Address" and Dr. Martin Luther King Jr.'s "I Have a Dream" speech.

**Ottava Rima:** An eight-line stanza of poetry composed in iambic pentameter (a five-foot line in which each foot consists of an unaccented syllable followed by an accented syllable), following the abababcc rhyme scheme. This form has been prominently used by such important English writers as Lord Byron, Henry Wadsworth Longfellow, and W. B. Yeats.

**Oxymoron:** A phrase combining two contradictory terms. Oxymorons may be intentional or unintentional. The following speech from William Shakespeare's *Romeo and Juliet* uses several oxymorons: Why, then, O brawling love! O loving hate! O anything, of nothing first create! O heavy lightness! serious vanity! Mis-shapen chaos of well-seeming forms! Feather of lead, bright smoke, cold fire, sick health! This love feel I, that feel no love in this.

# P

**Pantheism:** The idea that all things are both a manifestation or revelation of God and a part of God at the same time. Pantheism was a common attitude in the early societies of Egypt, India, and Greece—the term derives from the Greek *pan* meaning "all" and *theos* meaning "deity." It later became a significant part of the Christian faith. William Wordsworth and Ralph Waldo Emerson are among the many writers who have expressed the pantheistic attitude in their works.

**Parable:** A story intended to teach a moral lesson or answer an ethical question. In the West, the best examples of parables are those of Jesus Christ in the New Testament, notably "The Prodigal Son," but parables also are used in Sufism, rabbinic literature, Hasidism, and Zen Buddhism.

**Paradox:** A statement that appears illogical or contradictory at first, but may actually point to an underlying truth. "Less is more" is an example of a

paradox. Literary examples include Francis Bacon's statement, "The most corrected copies are commonly the least correct," and "All animals are equal, but some animals are more equal than others" from George Orwell's *Animal Farm.*

**Parallelism:** A method of comparison of two ideas in which each is developed in the same grammatical structure. Ralph Waldo Emerson's "Civilization" contains this example of parallelism: Raphael paints wisdom; Handel sings it, Phidias carves it, Shakespeare writes it, Wren builds it, Columbus sails it, Luther preaches it, Washington arms it, Watt mechanizes it.

**Parnassianism:** A mid nineteenth-century movement in French literature. Followers of the movement stressed adherence to well-defined artistic forms as a reaction against the often chaotic expression of the artist's ego that dominated the work of the Romantics. The Parnassians also rejected the moral, ethical, and social themes exhibited in the works of French Romantics such as Victor Hugo. The aesthetic doctrines of the Parnassians strongly influenced the later symbolist and decadent movements. Members of the Parnassian school include Leconte de Lisle, Sully Prudhomme, Albert Glatigny, Francois Coppee, and Theodore de Banville.

**Parody:** In literary criticism, this term refers to an imitation of a serious literary work or the signature style of a particular author in a ridiculous manner. A typical parody adopts the style of the original and applies it to an inappropriate subject for humorous effect. Parody is a form of satire and could be considered the literary equivalent of a caricature or cartoon. Henry Fielding's *Shamela* is a parody of Samuel Richardson's *Pamela.*

**Pastoral:** A term derived from the Latin word "pastor," meaning shepherd. A pastoral is a literary composition on a rural theme. The conventions of the pastoral were originated by the third-century Greek poet Theocritus, who wrote about the experiences, love affairs, and pastimes of Sicilian shepherds. In a pastoral, characters and language of a courtly nature are often placed in a simple setting. The term pastoral is also used to classify dramas, elegies, and lyrics that exhibit the use of country settings and shepherd characters. Percy Bysshe Shelley's "Adonais" and John Milton's "Lycidas" are two famous examples of pastorals.

**Pastorela:** The Spanish name for the shepherds play, a folk drama reenacted during the Christmas season. Examples of *pastorelas* include Gomez

Manrique's *Representacion del nacimiento* and the dramas of Lucas Fernandez and Juan del Encina.

**Pathetic Fallacy:** A term coined by English critic John Ruskin to identify writing that falsely endows nonhuman things with human intentions and feelings, such as "angry clouds" and "sad trees." The pathetic fallacy is a required convention in the classical poetic form of the pastoral elegy, and it is used in the modern poetry of T. S. Eliot, Ezra Pound, and the Imagists. Also known as Poetic Fallacy.

*Pelado:* Literally the "skinned one" or shirtless one, he was the stock underdog, sharp-witted picaresque character of Mexican vaudeville and tent shows. The *pelado* is found in such works as Don Catarino's *Los effectos de la crisis* and *Regreso a mi tierra.*

**Pen Name:** See *Pseudonym*

**Pentameter:** See *Meter*

*Persona:* A Latin term meaning "mask." *Personae* are the characters in a fictional work of literature. The *persona* generally functions as a mask through which the author tells a story in a voice other than his or her own. A *persona* is usually either a character in a story who acts as a narrator or an "implied author," a voice created by the author to act as the narrator for himself or herself. *Personae* include the narrator of Geoffrey Chaucer's *Canterbury Tales* and Marlow in Joseph Conrad's *Heart of Darkness.*

*Personae:* See *Persona*

**Personal Point of View:** See *Point of View*

**Personification:** A figure of speech that gives human qualities to abstract ideas, animals, and inanimate objects. William Shakespeare used personification in *Romeo and Juliet* in the lines "Arise, fair sun, and kill the envious moon,/ Who is already sick and pale with grief." Here, the moon is portrayed as being envious, sick, and pale with grief— all markedly human qualities. Also known as *Prosopopoeia.*

**Petrarchan Sonnet:** See *Sonnet*

**Phenomenology:** A method of literary criticism based on the belief that things have no existence outside of human consciousness or awareness. Proponents of this theory believe that art is a process that takes place in the mind of the observer as he or she contemplates an object rather than a quality of the object itself. Among phenomenological critics

are Edmund Husserl, George Poulet, Marcel Raymond, and Roman Ingarden.

**Picaresque Novel:** Episodic fiction depicting the adventures of a roguish central character ("picaro" is Spanish for "rogue"). The picaresque hero is commonly a low-born but clever individual who wanders into and out of various affairs of love, danger, and farcical intrigue. These involvements may take place at all social levels and typically present a humorous and wide-ranging satire of a given society. Prominent examples of the picaresque novel are *Don Quixote* by Miguel de Cervantes, *Tom Jones* by Henry Fielding, and *Moll Flanders* by Daniel Defoe.

**Plagiarism:** Claiming another person's written material as one's own. Plagiarism can take the form of direct, word-for-word copying or the theft of the substance or idea of the work. A student who copies an encyclopedia entry and turns it in as a report for school is guilty of plagiarism.

**Platonic Criticism:** A form of criticism that stresses an artistic work's usefulness as an agent of social engineering rather than any quality or value of the work itself. Platonic criticism takes as its starting point the ancient Greek philosopher Plato's comments on art in his *Republic.*

**Platonism:** The embracing of the doctrines of the philosopher Plato, popular among the poets of the Renaissance and the Romantic period. Platonism is more flexible than Aristotelian Criticism and places more emphasis on the supernatural and unknown aspects of life. Platonism is expressed in the love poetry of the Renaissance, the fourth book of Baldassare Castiglione's *The Book of the Courtier,* and the poetry of William Blake, William Wordsworth, Percy Bysshe Shelley, Friedrich Holderlin, William Butler Yeats, and Wallace Stevens.

**Play:** See *Drama*

**Plot:** In literary criticism, this term refers to the pattern of events in a narrative or drama. In its simplest sense, the plot guides the author in composing the work and helps the reader follow the work. Typically, plots exhibit causality and unity and have a beginning, a middle, and an end. Sometimes, however, a plot may consist of a series of disconnected events, in which case it is known as an "episodic plot." In his *Aspects of the Novel,* E. M. Forster distinguishes between a story, defined as a "narrative of events arranged in their time-sequence," and plot, which organizes the events to a "sense of causality." This definition closely mirrors Aristotle's discussion of plot in his *Poetics.*

**Poem:** In its broadest sense, a composition utilizing rhyme, meter, concrete detail, and expressive language to create a literary experience with emotional and aesthetic appeal. Typical poems include sonnets, odes, elegies, *haiku,* ballads, and free verse.

**Poet:** An author who writes poetry or verse. The term is also used to refer to an artist or writer who has an exceptional gift for expression, imagination, and energy in the making of art in any form. Well-known poets include Horace, Basho, Sir Philip Sidney, Sir Edmund Spenser, John Donne, Andrew Marvell, Alexander Pope, Jonathan Swift, George Gordon, Lord Byron, John Keats, Christina Rossetti, W. H. Auden, Stevie Smith, and Sylvia Plath.

**Poetic Fallacy:** See *Pathetic Fallacy*

**Poetic Justice:** An outcome in a literary work, not necessarily a poem, in which the good are rewarded and the evil are punished, especially in ways that particularly fit their virtues or crimes. For example, a murderer may himself be murdered, or a thief will find himself penniless.

**Poetic License:** Distortions of fact and literary convention made by a writer—not always a poet—for the sake of the effect gained. Poetic license is closely related to the concept of "artistic freedom." An author exercises poetic license by saying that a pile of money "reaches as high as a mountain" when the pile is actually only a foot or two high.

**Poetics:** This term has two closely related meanings. It denotes (1) an aesthetic theory in literary criticism about the essence of poetry or (2) rules prescribing the proper methods, content, style, or diction of poetry. The term poetics may also refer to theories about literature in general, not just poetry.

**Poetry:** In its broadest sense, writing that aims to present ideas and evoke an emotional experience in the reader through the use of meter, imagery, connotative and concrete words, and a carefully constructed structure based on rhythmic patterns. Poetry typically relies on words and expressions that have several layers of meaning. It also makes use of the effects of regular rhythm on the ear and may make a strong appeal to the senses through the use of imagery. Edgar Allan Poe's "Annabel Lee" and Walt Whitman's *Leaves of Grass* are famous examples of poetry.

**Point of View:** The narrative perspective from which a literary work is presented to the reader.

There are four traditional points of view. The "third person omniscient" gives the reader a "godlike" perspective, unrestricted by time or place, from which to see actions and look into the minds of characters. This allows the author to comment openly on characters and events in the work. The "third person" point of view presents the events of the story from outside of any single character's perception, much like the omniscient point of view, but the reader must understand the action as it takes place and without any special insight into characters' minds or motivations. The "first person" or "personal" point of view relates events as they are perceived by a single character. The main character "tells" the story and may offer opinions about the action and characters which differ from those of the author. Much less common than omniscient, third person, and first person is the "second person" point of view, wherein the author tells the story as if it is happening to the reader. James Thurber employs the omniscient point of view in his short story "The Secret Life of Walter Mitty." Ernest Hemingway's "A Clean, Well-Lighted Place" is a short story told from the third person point of view. Mark Twain's novel *Huck Finn* is presented from the first person viewpoint. Jay McInerney's *Bright Lights, Big City* is an example of a novel which uses the second person point of view.

**Polemic:** A work in which the author takes a stand on a controversial subject, such as abortion or religion. Such works are often extremely argumentative or provocative. Classic examples of polemics include John Milton's *Aeropagitica* and Thomas Paine's *The American Crisis.*

**Pornography:** Writing intended to provoke feelings of lust in the reader. Such works are often condemned by critics and teachers, but those which can be shown to have literary value are viewed less harshly. Literary works that have been described as pornographic include Ovid's *The Art of Love,* Margaret of Angouleme's *Heptameron,* John Cleland's *Memoirs of a Woman of Pleasure; or, the Life of Fanny Hill,* the anonymous *My Secret Life,* D. H. Lawrence's *Lady Chatterley's Lover,* and Vladimir Nabokov's *Lolita.*

**Post-Aesthetic Movement:** An artistic response made by African Americans to the black aesthetic movement of the 1960s and early '70s. Writers since that time have adopted a somewhat different tone in their work, with less emphasis placed on the disparity between black and white in the United States. In the words of post-aesthetic authors such as Toni Morrison, John Edgar Wideman, and Kristin Hunter, African Americans are portrayed as looking inward for answers to their own questions, rather than always looking to the outside world. Two well-known examples of works produced as part of the post-aesthetic movement are the Pulitzer Prize-winning novels *The Color Purple* by Alice Walker and *Beloved* by Toni Morrison.

**Postmodernism:** Writing from the 1960s forward characterized by experimentation and continuing to apply some of the fundamentals of modernism, which included existentialism and alienation. Postmodernists have gone a step further in the rejection of tradition begun with the modernists by also rejecting traditional forms, preferring the anti-novel over the novel and the anti-hero over the hero. Postmodern writers include Alain Robbe-Grillet, Thomas Pynchon, Margaret Drabble, John Fowles, Adolfo Bioy-Casares, and Gabriel Garcia Marquez.

**Pre-Raphaelites:** A circle of writers and artists in mid nineteenth-century England. Valuing the pre-Renaissance artistic qualities of religious symbolism, lavish pictorialism, and natural sensuousness, the Pre-Raphaelites cultivated a sense of mystery and melancholy that influenced later writers associated with the Symbolist and Decadent movements. The major members of the group include Dante Gabriel Rossetti, Christina Rossetti, Algernon Swinburne, and Walter Pater.

**Primitivism:** The belief that primitive peoples were nobler and less flawed than civilized peoples because they had not been subjected to the tainting influence of society. Examples of literature espousing primitivism include Aphra Behn's *Oroonoko: Or, The History of the Royal Slave,* Jean-Jacques Rousseau's *Julie ou la Nouvelle Heloise,* Oliver Goldsmith's *The Deserted Village,* the poems of Robert Burns, Herman Melville's stories *Typee, Omoo,* and *Mardi,* many poems of William Butler Yeats and Robert Frost, and William Golding's novel *Lord of the Flies.*

**Projective Verse:** A form of free verse in which the poet's breathing pattern determines the lines of the poem. Poets who advocate projective verse are against all formal structures in writing, including meter and form. Besides its creators, Robert Creeley, Robert Duncan, and Charles Olson, two other well-known projective verse poets are Denise Levertov and LeRoi Jones (Amiri Baraka). Also known as Breath Verse.

**Prologue:** An introductory section of a literary work. It often contains information establishing the situation of the characters or presents information about the setting, time period, or action. In drama, the prologue is spoken by a chorus or by one of the principal characters. In the ''General Prologue'' of *The Canterbury Tales,* Geoffrey Chaucer describes the main characters and establishes the setting and purpose of the work.

**Prose:** A literary medium that attempts to mirror the language of everyday speech. It is distinguished from poetry by its use of unmetered, unrhymed language consisting of logically related sentences. Prose is usually grouped into paragraphs that form a cohesive whole such as an essay or a novel. Recognized masters of English prose writing include Sir Thomas Malory, William Caxton, Raphael Holinshed, Joseph Addison, Mark Twain, and Ernest Hemingway.

*Prosopopoeia:* See *Personification*

**Protagonist:** The central character of a story who serves as a focus for its themes and incidents and as the principal rationale for its development. The protagonist is sometimes referred to in discussions of modern literature as the hero or anti-hero. Well-known protagonists are Hamlet in William Shakespeare's *Hamlet* and Jay Gatsby in F. Scott Fitzgerald's *The Great Gatsby.*

**Protest Fiction:** Protest fiction has as its primary purpose the protesting of some social injustice, such as racism or discrimination. One example of protest fiction is a series of five novels by Chester Himes, beginning in 1945 with *If He Hollers Let Him Go* and ending in 1955 with *The Primitive.* These works depict the destructive effects of race and gender stereotyping in the context of interracial relationships. Another African American author whose works often revolve around themes of social protest is John Oliver Killens. James Baldwin's essay ''Everybody's Protest Novel'' generated controversy by attacking the authors of protest fiction.

**Proverb:** A brief, sage saying that expresses a truth about life in a striking manner. ''They are not all cooks who carry long knives'' is an example of a proverb.

**Pseudonym:** A name assumed by a writer, most often intended to prevent his or her identification as the author of a work. Two or more authors may work together under one pseudonym, or an author may use a different name for each genre he or she publishes in. Some publishing companies maintain "house pseudonyms," under which any number of authors may write installations in a series. Some authors also choose a pseudonym over their real names the way an actor may use a stage name. Examples of pseudonyms (with the author's real name in parentheses) include Voltaire (Francois-Marie Arouet), Novalis (Friedrich von Hardenberg), Currer Bell (Charlotte Bronte), Ellis Bell (Emily Bronte), George Eliot (Maryann Evans), Honorio Bustos Donmecq (Adolfo Bioy-Casares and Jorge Luis Borges), and Richard Bachman (Stephen King).

**Pun:** A play on words that have similar sounds but different meanings. A serious example of the pun is from John Donne's "A Hymne to God the Father": Sweare by thyself, that at my death thy sonne Shall shine as he shines now, and hereto fore; And, having done that, Thou haste done; I fear no more.

**Pure Poetry:** poetry written without instructional intent or moral purpose that aims only to please a reader by its imagery or musical flow. The term pure poetry is used as the antonym of the term "didacticism." The poetry of Edgar Allan Poe, Stephane Mallarme, Paul Verlaine, Paul Valery, Juan Ramoz Jimenez, and Jorge Guillen offer examples of pure poetry.

# Q

**Quatrain:** A four-line stanza of a poem or an entire poem consisting of four lines. The following quatrain is from Robert Herrick's "To Live Merrily, and to Trust to Good Verses": Round, round, the root do's run; And being ravisht thus, Come, I will drink a Tun To my *Propertius.*

# R

*Raisonneur:* A character in a drama who functions as a spokesperson for the dramatist's views. The *raisonneur* typically observes the play without becoming central to its action. *Raisonneurs* were very common in plays of the nineteenth century.

**Realism:** A nineteenth-century European literary movement that sought to portray familiar characters, situations, and settings in a realistic manner. This was done primarily by using an objective narrative point of view and through the buildup of accurate detail. The standard for success of any realistic work depends on how faithfully it transfers common experience into fictional forms. The realistic method may be altered or extended, as in stream of consciousness writing, to record highly subjec-

tive experience. Seminal authors in the tradition of Realism include Honore de Balzac, Gustave Flaubert, and Henry James.

**Refrain:** A phrase repeated at intervals throughout a poem. A refrain may appear at the end of each stanza or at less regular intervals. It may be altered slightly at each appearance. Some refrains are nonsense expressions—as with "Nevermore" in Edgar Allan Poe's "The Raven"—that seem to take on a different significance with each use.

**Renaissance:** The period in European history that marked the end of the Middle Ages. It began in Italy in the late fourteenth century. In broad terms, it is usually seen as spanning the fourteenth, fifteenth, and sixteenth centuries, although it did not reach Great Britain, for example, until the 1480s or so. The Renaissance saw an awakening in almost every sphere of human activity, especially science, philosophy, and the arts. The period is best defined by the emergence of a general philosophy that emphasized the importance of the intellect, the individual, and world affairs. It contrasts strongly with the medieval worldview, characterized by the dominant concerns of faith, the social collective, and spiritual salvation. Prominent writers during the Renaissance include Niccolo Machiavelli and Baldassare Castiglione in Italy, Miguel de Cervantes and Lope de Vega in Spain, Jean Froissart and Francois Rabelais in France, Sir Thomas More and Sir Philip Sidney in England, and Desiderius Erasmus in Holland.

*Repartee:* Conversation featuring snappy retorts and witticisms. Masters of *repartee* include Sydney Smith, Charles Lamb, and Oscar Wilde. An example is recorded in the meeting of "Beau" Nash and John Wesley: Nash said, "I never make way for a fool," to which Wesley responded, "Don't you? I always do," and stepped aside.

**Resolution:** The portion of a story following the climax, in which the conflict is resolved. The resolution of Jane Austen's *Northanger Abbey* is neatly summed up in the following sentence: "Henry and Catherine were married, the bells rang and every body smiled."

**Restoration:** See *Restoration Age*

**Restoration Age:** A period in English literature beginning with the crowning of Charles II in 1660 and running to about 1700. The era, which was characterized by a reaction against Puritanism, was the first great age of the comedy of manners. The finest literature of the era is typically witty and urbane, and often lewd. Prominent Restoration Age writers include William Congreve, Samuel Pepys, John Dryden, and John Milton.

**Revenge Tragedy:** A dramatic form popular during the Elizabethan Age, in which the protagonist, directed by the ghost of his murdered father or son, inflicts retaliation upon a powerful villain. Notable features of the revenge tragedy include violence, bizarre criminal acts, intrigue, insanity, a hesitant protagonist, and the use of soliloquy. Thomas Kyd's *Spanish Tragedy* is the first example of revenge tragedy in English, and William Shakespeare's *Hamlet* is perhaps the best. Extreme examples of revenge tragedy, such as John Webster's *The Duchess of Malfi,* are labeled ''tragedies of blood.'' Also known as Tragedy of Blood.

*Revista:* The Spanish term for a vaudeville musical revue. Examples of *revistas* include Antonio Guzman Aguilera's *Mexico para los mexicanos,* Daniel Vanegas's *Maldito jazz,* and Don Catarino's *Whiskey, morfina y marihuana* and *El desterrado.*

**Rhetoric:** In literary criticism, this term denotes the art of ethical persuasion. In its strictest sense, rhetoric adheres to various principles developed since classical times for arranging facts and ideas in a clear, persuasive, appealing manner. The term is also used to refer to effective prose in general and theories of or methods for composing effective prose. Classical examples of rhetorics include *The Rhetoric of Aristotle,* Quintillian's *Institutio Oratoria,* and Cicero's *Ad Herennium.*

**Rhetorical Question:** A question intended to provoke thought, but not an expressed answer, in the reader. It is most commonly used in oratory and other persuasive genres. The following lines from Thomas Gray's ''Elegy Written in a Country Churchyard'' ask rhetorical questions: Can storied urn or animated bust Back to its mansion call the fleeting breath? Can Honour's voice provoke the silent dust, Or Flattery soothe the dull cold ear of Death?

**Rhyme:** When used as a noun in literary criticism, this term generally refers to a poem in which words sound identical or very similar and appear in parallel positions in two or more lines. Rhymes are classified into different types according to where they fall in a line or stanza or according to the degree of similarity they exhibit in their spellings and sounds. Some major types of rhyme are ''masculine'' rhyme, ''feminine'' rhyme, and ''triple'' rhyme. In a masculine rhyme, the rhyming sound falls in a single accented syllable, as with ''heat''

and ''eat.'' Feminine rhyme is a rhyme of two syllables, one stressed and one unstressed, as with ''merry'' and ''tarry.'' Triple rhyme matches the sound of the accented syllable and the two unaccented syllables that follow: ''narrative'' and ''declarative.'' Robert Browning alternates feminine and masculine rhymes in his ''Soliloquy of the Spanish Cloister'': Gr-r-r—there go, my heart's abhorrence! Water your damned flower-pots, do! If hate killed men, Brother Lawrence, God's blood, would not mine kill you! What? Your myrtle-bush wants trimming? Oh, that rose has prior claims— Needs its leaden vase filled brimming? Hell dry you up with flames! Triple rhymes can be found in Thomas Hood's ''Bridge of Sighs,'' George Gordon Byron's satirical verse, and Ogden Nash's comic poems.

**Rhyme Royal:** A stanza of seven lines composed in iambic pentameter and rhymed *ababbcc.* The name is said to be a tribute to King James I of Scotland, who made much use of the form in his poetry. Examples of rhyme royal include Geoffrey Chaucer's *The Parlement of Foules,* William Shakespeare's *The Rape of Lucrece,* William Morris's *The Early Paradise,* and John Masefield's *The Widow in the Bye Street.*

**Rhyme Scheme:** See *Rhyme*

**Rhythm:** A regular pattern of sound, time intervals, or events occurring in writing, most often and most discernably in poetry. Regular, reliable rhythm is known to be soothing to humans, while interrupted, unpredictable, or rapidly changing rhythm is disturbing. These effects are known to authors, who use them to produce a desired reaction in the reader. An example of a form of irregular rhythm is sprung rhythm poetry; quantitative verse, on the other hand, is very regular in its rhythm.

**Rising Action:** The part of a drama where the plot becomes increasingly complicated. Rising action leads up to the climax, or turning point, of a drama. The final ''chase scene'' of an action film is generally the rising action which culminates in the film's climax.

*Rococo:* A style of European architecture that flourished in the eighteenth century, especially in France. The most notable features of *rococo* are its extensive use of ornamentation and its themes of lightness, gaiety, and intimacy. In literary criticism, the term is often used disparagingly to refer to a decadent or over-ornamental style. Alexander Pope's ''The Rape of the Lock'' is an example of literary *rococo.*

***Roman a clef:*** A French phrase meaning "novel with a key." It refers to a narrative in which real persons are portrayed under fictitious names. Jack Kerouac, for example, portrayed various real-life beat generation figures under fictitious names in his *On the Road.*

**Romance:** A broad term, usually denoting a narrative with exotic, exaggerated, often idealized characters, scenes, and themes. Nathaniel Hawthorne called his *The House of the Seven Gables* and *The Marble Faun* romances in order to distinguish them from clearly realistic works.

**Romantic Age:** See *Romanticism*

**Romanticism:** This term has two widely accepted meanings. In historical criticism, it refers to a European intellectual and artistic movement of the late eighteenth and early nineteenth centuries that sought greater freedom of personal expression than that allowed by the strict rules of literary form and logic of the eighteenth-century neoclassicists. The Romantics preferred emotional and imaginative expression to rational analysis. They considered the individual to be at the center of all experience and so placed him or her at the center of their art. The Romantics believed that the creative imagination reveals nobler truths—unique feelings and attitudes—than those that could be discovered by logic or by scientific examination. Both the natural world and the state of childhood were important sources for revelations of "eternal truths." "Romanticism" is also used as a general term to refer to a type of sensibility found in all periods of literary history and usually considered to be in opposition to the principles of classicism. In this sense, Romanticism signifies any work or philosophy in which the exotic or dreamlike figure strongly, or that is devoted to individualistic expression, self-analysis, or a pursuit of a higher realm of knowledge than can be discovered by human reason. Prominent Romantics include Jean-Jacques Rousseau, William Wordsworth, John Keats, Lord Byron, and Johann Wolfgang von Goethe.

**Romantics:** See *Romanticism*

**Russian Symbolism:** A Russian poetic movement, derived from French symbolism, that flourished between 1894 and 1910. While some Russian Symbolists continued in the French tradition, stressing aestheticism and the importance of suggestion above didactic intent, others saw their craft as a form of mystical worship, and themselves as mediators between the supernatural and the mundane. Russian symbolists include Aleksandr Blok, Vyacheslav Ivanovich Ivanov, Fyodor Sologub, Andrey Bely, Nikolay Gumilyov, and Vladimir Sergeyevich Solovyov.

# S

**Satire:** A work that uses ridicule, humor, and wit to criticize and provoke change in human nature and institutions. There are two major types of satire: "formal" or "direct" satire speaks directly to the reader or to a character in the work; "indirect" satire relies upon the ridiculous behavior of its characters to make its point. Formal satire is further divided into two manners: the "Horatian," which ridicules gently, and the "Juvenalian," which derides its subjects harshly and bitterly. Voltaire's novella *Candide* is an indirect satire. Jonathan Swift's essay "A Modest Proposal" is a Juvenalian satire.

**Scansion:** The analysis or "scanning" of a poem to determine its meter and often its rhyme scheme. The most common system of scansion uses accents (slanted lines drawn above syllables) to show stressed syllables, breves (curved lines drawn above syllables) to show unstressed syllables, and vertical lines to separate each foot. In the first line of John Keats's *Endymion,* "A thing of beauty is a joy forever:" the word "thing," the first syllable of "beauty," the word "joy," and the second syllable of "forever" are stressed, while the words "A" and "of," the second syllable of "beauty," the word "a," and the first and third syllables of "forever" are unstressed. In the second line: "Its loveliness increases; it will never" a pair of vertical lines separate the foot ending with "increases" and the one beginning with "it."

**Scene:** A subdivision of an act of a drama, consisting of continuous action taking place at a single time and in a single location. The beginnings and endings of scenes may be indicated by clearing the stage of actors and props or by the entrances and exits of important characters. The first act of William Shakespeare's *Winter's Tale* is comprised of two scenes.

**Science Fiction:** A type of narrative about or based upon real or imagined scientific theories and technology. Science fiction is often peopled with alien creatures and set on other planets or in different dimensions. Karel Capek's *R.U.R.* is a major work of science fiction.

**Second Person:** See *Point of View*

**Semiotics:** The study of how literary forms and conventions affect the meaning of language. Semioticians include Ferdinand de Saussure, Charles Sanders Pierce, Claude Levi-Strauss, Jacques Lacan, Michel Foucault, Jacques Derrida, Roland Barthes, and Julia Kristeva.

**Sestet:** Any six-line poem or stanza. Examples of the sestet include the last six lines of the Petrarchan sonnet form, the stanza form of Robert Burns's "A Poet's Welcome to his love-begotten Daughter," and the sestina form in W. H. Auden's "Paysage Moralise."

**Setting:** The time, place, and culture in which the action of a narrative takes place. The elements of setting may include geographic location, characters' physical and mental environments, prevailing cultural attitudes, or the historical time in which the action takes place. Examples of settings include the romanticized Scotland in Sir Walter Scott's "Waverley" novels, the French provincial setting in Gustave Flaubert's *Madame Bovary,* the fictional Wessex country of Thomas Hardy's novels, and the small towns of southern Ontario in Alice Munro's short stories.

**Shakespearean Sonnet:** See *Sonnet*

**Signifying Monkey:** A popular trickster figure in black folklore, with hundreds of tales about this character documented since the 19th century. Henry Louis Gates Jr. examines the history of the signifying monkey in *The Signifying Monkey: Towards a Theory of Afro-American Literary Criticism,* published in 1988.

**Simile:** A comparison, usually using "like" or "as", of two essentially dissimilar things, as in "coffee as cold as ice" or "He sounded like a broken record." The title of Ernest Hemingway's "Hills Like White Elephants" contains a simile.

**Slang:** A type of informal verbal communication that is generally unacceptable for formal writing. Slang words and phrases are often colorful exaggerations used to emphasize the speaker's point; they may also be shortened versions of an often-used word or phrase. Examples of American slang from the 1990s include "yuppie" (an acronym for Young Urban Professional), "awesome" (for "excellent"), wired (for "nervous" or "excited"), and "chill out" (for relax).

**Slant Rhyme:** See *Consonance*

**Slave Narrative:** Autobiographical accounts of American slave life as told by escaped slaves. These works first appeared during the abolition movement of the 1830s through the 1850s. Olaudah Equiano's *The Interesting Narrative of Olaudah Equiano, or Gustavus Vassa, The African* and Harriet Ann Jacobs's *Incidents in the Life of a Slave Girl* are examples of the slave narrative.

**Social Realism:** See *Socialist Realism*

**Socialist Realism:** The Socialist Realism school of literary theory was proposed by Maxim Gorky and established as a dogma by the first Soviet Congress of Writers. It demanded adherence to a communist worldview in works of literature. Its doctrines required an objective viewpoint comprehensible to the working classes and themes of social struggle featuring strong proletarian heroes. A successful work of socialist realism is Nikolay Ostrovsky's *Kak zakalyalas stal (How the Steel Was Tempered).* Also known as Social Realism.

**Soliloquy:** A monologue in a drama used to give the audience information and to develop the speaker's character. It is typically a projection of the speaker's innermost thoughts. Usually delivered while the speaker is alone on stage, a soliloquy is intended to present an illusion of unspoken reflection. A celebrated soliloquy is Hamlet's "To be or not to be" speech in William Shakespeare's *Hamlet.*

**Sonnet:** A fourteen-line poem, usually composed in iambic pentameter, employing one of several rhyme schemes. There are three major types of sonnets, upon which all other variations of the form are based: the "Petrarchan" or "Italian" sonnet, the "Shakespearean" or "English" sonnet, and the "Spenserian" sonnet. A Petrarchan sonnet consists of an octave rhymed *abbaabba* and a "sestet" rhymed either *cdecde, cdccdc,* or *cdedce.* The octave poses a question or problem, relates a narrative, or puts forth a proposition; the sestet presents a solution to the problem, comments upon the narrative, or applies the proposition put forth in the octave. The Shakespearean sonnet is divided into three quatrains and a couplet rhymed *abab cdcd efef gg.* The couplet provides an epigrammatic comment on the narrative or problem put forth in the quatrains. The Spenserian sonnet uses three quatrains and a couplet like the Shakespearean, but links their three rhyme schemes in this way: *abab bcbc cdcd ee.* The Spenserian sonnet develops its theme in two parts like the Petrarchan, its final six lines resolving a problem, analyzing a narrative, or applying a proposition put forth in its first eight lines. Examples of sonnets can be found in Petrarch's *Canzoniere,* Edmund Spenser's *Amoretti,* Elizabeth Barrett

Browning's *Sonnets from the Portuguese,* Rainer Maria Rilke's *Sonnets to Orpheus,* and Adrienne Rich's poem "The Insusceptibles."

**Spenserian Sonnet:** See *Sonnet*

**Spenserian Stanza:** A nine-line stanza having eight verses in iambic pentameter, its ninth verse in iambic hexameter, and the rhyme scheme ababbcbcc. This stanza form was first used by Edmund Spenser in his allegorical poem *The Faerie Queene.*

**Spondee:** In poetry meter, a foot consisting of two long or stressed syllables occurring together. This form is quite rare in English verse, and is usually composed of two monosyllabic words. The first foot in the following line from Robert Burns's "Green Grow the Rashes" is an example of a spondee: Green grow the rashes, O

**Sprung Rhythm:** Versification using a specific number of accented syllables per line but disregarding the number of unaccented syllables that fall in each line, producing an irregular rhythm in the poem. Gerard Manley Hopkins, who coined the term "sprung rhythm," is the most notable practitioner of this technique.

**Stanza:** A subdivision of a poem consisting of lines grouped together, often in recurring patterns of rhyme, line length, and meter. Stanzas may also serve as units of thought in a poem much like paragraphs in prose. Examples of stanza forms include the quatrain, *terza rima, ottava rima,* Spenserian, and the so-called *In Memoriam* stanza from Alfred, Lord Tennyson's poem by that title. The following is an example of the latter form: Love is and was my lord and king, And in his presence I attend To hear the tidings of my friend, Which every hour his couriers bring.

**Stereotype:** A stereotype was originally the name for a duplication made during the printing process; this led to its modern definition as a person or thing that is (or is assumed to be) the same as all others of its type. Common stereotypical characters include the absent-minded professor, the nagging wife, the troublemaking teenager, and the kind-hearted grandmother.

**Stream of Consciousness:** A narrative technique for rendering the inward experience of a character. This technique is designed to give the impression of an ever-changing series of thoughts, emotions, images, and memories in the spontaneous and seemingly illogical order that they occur in life. The

textbook example of stream of consciousness is the last section of James Joyce's *Ulysses.*

**Structuralism:** A twentieth-century movement in literary criticism that examines how literary texts arrive at their meanings, rather than the meanings themselves. There are two major types of structuralist analysis: one examines the way patterns of linguistic structures unify a specific text and emphasize certain elements of that text, and the other interprets the way literary forms and conventions affect the meaning of language itself. Prominent structuralists include Michel Foucault, Roman Jakobson, and Roland Barthes.

**Structure:** The form taken by a piece of literature. The structure may be made obvious for ease of understanding, as in nonfiction works, or may be obscured for artistic purposes, as in some poetry or seemingly "unstructured" prose. Examples of common literary structures include the plot of a narrative, the acts and scenes of a drama, and such poetic forms as the Shakespearean sonnet and the Pindaric ode.

***Sturm und Drang:*** A German term meaning "storm and stress." It refers to a German literary movement of the 1770s and 1780s that reacted against the order and rationalism of the enlightenment, focusing instead on the intense experience of extraordinary individuals. Highly romantic, works of this movement, such as Johann Wolfgang von Goethe's *Gotz von Berlichingen,* are typified by realism, rebelliousness, and intense emotionalism.

**Style:** A writer's distinctive manner of arranging words to suit his or her ideas and purpose in writing. The unique imprint of the author's personality upon his or her writing, style is the product of an author's way of arranging ideas and his or her use of diction, different sentence structures, rhythm, figures of speech, rhetorical principles, and other elements of composition. Styles may be classified according to period (Metaphysical, Augustan, Georgian), individual authors (Chaucerian, Miltonic, Jamesian), level (grand, middle, low, plain), or language (scientific, expository, poetic, journalistic).

**Subject:** The person, event, or theme at the center of a work of literature. A work may have one or more subjects of each type, with shorter works tending to have fewer and longer works tending to have more. The subjects of James Baldwin's novel *Go Tell It on the Mountain* include the themes of father-son relationships, religious conversion, black life, and sexuality. The subjects of Anne Frank's

*Diary of a Young Girl* include Anne and her family members as well as World War II, the Holocaust, and the themes of war, isolation, injustice, and racism.

**Subjectivity:** Writing that expresses the author's personal feelings about his subject, and which may or may not include factual information about the subject. Subjectivity is demonstrated in James Joyce's *Portrait of the Artist as a Young Man,* Samuel Butler's *The Way of All Flesh,* and Thomas Wolfe's *Look Homeward, Angel.*

**Subplot:** A secondary story in a narrative. A subplot may serve as a motivating or complicating force for the main plot of the work, or it may provide emphasis for, or relief from, the main plot. The conflict between the Capulets and the Montagues in William Shakespeare's *Romeo and Juliet* is an example of a subplot.

**Surrealism:** A term introduced to criticism by Guillaume Apollinaire and later adopted by Andre Breton. It refers to a French literary and artistic movement founded in the 1920s. The Surrealists sought to express unconscious thoughts and feelings in their works. The best-known technique used for achieving this aim was automatic writing—transcriptions of spontaneous outpourings from the unconscious. The Surrealists proposed to unify the contrary levels of conscious and unconscious, dream and reality, objectivity and subjectivity into a new level of ''super-realism.'' Surrealism can be found in the poetry of Paul Eluard, Pierre Reverdy, and Louis Aragon, among others.

**Suspense:** A literary device in which the author maintains the audience's attention through the buildup of events, the outcome of which will soon be revealed. Suspense in William Shakespeare's *Hamlet* is sustained throughout by the question of whether or not the Prince will achieve what he has been instructed to do and of what he intends to do.

**Syllogism:** A method of presenting a logical argument. In its most basic form, the syllogism consists of a major premise, a minor premise, and a conclusion. An example of a syllogism is: Major premise: When it snows, the streets get wet. Minor premise: It is snowing. Conclusion: The streets are wet.

**Symbol:** Something that suggests or stands for something else without losing its original identity. In literature, symbols combine their literal meaning with the suggestion of an abstract concept. Literary symbols are of two types: those that carry complex associations of meaning no matter what their con-

texts, and those that derive their suggestive meaning from their functions in specific literary works. Examples of symbols are sunshine suggesting happiness, rain suggesting sorrow, and storm clouds suggesting despair.

**Symbolism:** This term has two widely accepted meanings. In historical criticism, it denotes an early modernist literary movement initiated in France during the nineteenth century that reacted against the prevailing standards of realism. Writers in this movement aimed to evoke, indirectly and symbolically, an order of being beyond the material world of the five senses. Poetic expression of personal emotion figured strongly in the movement, typically by means of a private set of symbols uniquely identifiable with the individual poet. The principal aim of the Symbolists was to express in words the highly complex feelings that grew out of everyday contact with the world. In a broader sense, the term ''symbolism'' refers to the use of one object to represent another. Early members of the Symbolist movement included the French authors Charles Baudelaire and Arthur Rimbaud; William Butler Yeats, James Joyce, and T. S. Eliot were influenced as the movement moved to Ireland, England, and the United States. Examples of the concept of symbolism include a flag that stands for a nation or movement, or an empty cupboard used to suggest hopelessness, poverty, and despair.

**Symbolist:** See *Symbolism*

**Symbolist Movement:** See *Symbolism*

**Sympathetic Fallacy:** See *Affective Fallacy*

# *T*

**Tale:** A story told by a narrator with a simple plot and little character development. Tales are usually relatively short and often carry a simple message. Examples of tales can be found in the work of Rudyard Kipling, Somerset Maugham, Saki, Anton Chekhov, Guy de Maupassant, and Armistead Maupin.

**Tall Tale:** A humorous tale told in a straightforward, credible tone but relating absolutely impossible events or feats of the characters. Such tales were commonly told of frontier adventures during the settlement of the west in the United States. Tall tales have been spun around such legendary heroes as Mike Fink, Paul Bunyan, Davy Crockett, Johnny Appleseed, and Captain Stormalong as well as the real-life William F. Cody and Annie Oakley. Literary use of tall tales can be found in Washington Irving's *History of New York,* Mark Twain's *Life on the Mississippi,* and in the German R. F. Raspe's *Baron Munchausen's Narratives of His Marvellous Travels and Campaigns in Russia.*

**Tanka:** A form of Japanese poetry similar to *haiku.* A *tanka* is five lines long, with the lines containing five, seven, five, seven, and seven syllables respectively. Skilled *tanka* authors include Ishikawa Takuboku, Masaoka Shiki, Amy Lowell, and Adelaide Crapsey.

**Teatro Grottesco:** See *Theater of the Grotesque*

**Terza Rima:** A three-line stanza form in poetry in which the rhymes are made on the last word of each line in the following manner: the first and third lines of the first stanza, then the second line of the first stanza and the first and third lines of the second stanza, and so on with the middle line of any stanza rhyming with the first and third lines of the following stanza. An example of *terza rima* is Percy Bysshe Shelley's "The Triumph of Love": As in that trance of wondrous thought I lay This was the tenour of my waking dream. Methought I sate beside a public way Thick strewn with summer dust, and a great stream Of people there was hurrying to and fro Numerous as gnats upon the evening gleam,. . .

**Tetrameter:** See *Meter*

**Textual Criticism:** A branch of literary criticism that seeks to establish the authoritative text of a literary work. Textual critics typically compare all known manuscripts or printings of a single work in order to assess the meanings of differences and revisions. This procedure allows them to arrive at a definitive version that (supposedly) corresponds to the author's original intention. Textual criticism was applied during the Renaissance to salvage the classical texts of Greece and Rome, and modern works have been studied, for instance, to undo deliberate correction or censorship, as in the case of novels by Stephen Crane and Theodore Dreiser.

**Theater of Cruelty:** Term used to denote a group of theatrical techniques designed to eliminate the psychological and emotional distance between actors and audience. This concept, introduced in the 1930s in France, was intended to inspire a more intense theatrical experience than conventional theater allowed. The "cruelty" of this dramatic theory signified not sadism but heightened actor/audience involvement in the dramatic event. The theater of

cruelty was theorized by Antonin Artaud in his *Le Theatre et son double* (*The Theatre and Its Double*), and also appears in the work of Jerzy Grotowski, Jean Genet, Jean Vilar, and Arthur Adamov, among others.

**Theater of the Absurd:** A post-World War II dramatic trend characterized by radical theatrical innovations. In works influenced by the Theater of the absurd, nontraditional, sometimes grotesque characterizations, plots, and stage sets reveal a meaningless universe in which human values are irrelevant. Existentialist themes of estrangement, absurdity, and futility link many of the works of this movement. The principal writers of the Theater of the Absurd are Samuel Beckett, Eugene Ionesco, Jean Genet, and Harold Pinter.

**Theater of the Grotesque:** An Italian theatrical movement characterized by plays written around the ironic and macabre aspects of daily life in the World War I era. Theater of the Grotesque was named after the play *The Mask and the Face* by Luigi Chiarelli, which was described as "a grotesque in three acts." The movement influenced the work of Italian dramatist Luigi Pirandello, author of *Right You Are, If You Think You Are.* Also known as *Teatro Grottesco.*

**Theme:** The main point of a work of literature. The term is used interchangeably with thesis. The theme of William Shakespeare's *Othello*—jealousy—is a common one.

**Thesis:** A thesis is both an essay and the point argued in the essay. Thesis novels and thesis plays share the quality of containing a thesis which is supported through the action of the story. A master's thesis and a doctoral dissertation are two theses required of graduate students.

**Thesis Play:** See *Thesis*

**Three Unities:** See *Unities*

**Tone:** The author's attitude toward his or her audience may be deduced from the tone of the work. A formal tone may create distance or convey politeness, while an informal tone may encourage a friendly, intimate, or intrusive feeling in the reader. The author's attitude toward his or her subject matter may also be deduced from the tone of the words he or she uses in discussing it. The tone of John F. Kennedy's speech which included the appeal to "ask not what your country can do for you" was intended to instill feelings of camaraderie and national pride in listeners.

**Tragedy:** A drama in prose or poetry about a noble, courageous hero of excellent character who, because of some tragic character flaw or *hamartia*, brings ruin upon him- or herself. Tragedy treats its subjects in a dignified and serious manner, using poetic language to help evoke pity and fear and bring about catharsis, a purging of these emotions. The tragic form was practiced extensively by the ancient Greeks. In the Middle Ages, when classical works were virtually unknown, tragedy came to denote any works about the fall of persons from exalted to low conditions due to any reason: fate, vice, weakness, etc. According to the classical definition of tragedy, such works present the ''pathetic''—that which evokes pity—rather than the tragic. The classical form of tragedy was revived in the sixteenth century; it flourished especially on the Elizabethan stage. In modern times, dramatists have attempted to adapt the form to the needs of modern society by drawing their heroes from the ranks of ordinary men and women and defining the nobility of these heroes in terms of spirit rather than exalted social standing. The greatest classical example of tragedy is Sophocles' *Oedipus Rex*. The ''pathetic'' derivation is exemplified in ''The Monk's Tale'' in Geoffrey Chaucer's *Canterbury Tales.* Notable works produced during the sixteenth century revival include William Shakespeare's *Hamlet, Othello,* and *King Lear.* Modern dramatists working in the tragic tradition include Henrik Ibsen, Arthur Miller, and Eugene O'Neill.

**Tragedy of Blood:** See *Revenge Tragedy*

**Tragic Flaw:** In a tragedy, the quality within the hero or heroine which leads to his or her downfall. Examples of the tragic flaw include Othello's jealousy and Hamlet's indecisiveness, although most great tragedies defy such simple interpretation.

**Transcendentalism:** An American philosophical and religious movement, based in New England from around 1835 until the Civil War. Transcendentalism was a form of American romanticism that had its roots abroad in the works of Thomas Carlyle, Samuel Coleridge, and Johann Wolfgang von Goethe. The Transcendentalists stressed the importance of intuition and subjective experience in communication with God. They rejected religious dogma and texts in favor of mysticism and scientific naturalism. They pursued truths that lie beyond the ''colorless'' realms perceived by reason and the senses and were active social reformers in public education, women's rights, and the abolition of slavery. Promi-

nent members of the group include Ralph Waldo Emerson and Henry David Thoreau.

**Trickster:** A character or figure common in Native American and African literature who uses his ingenuity to defeat enemies and escape difficult situations. Tricksters are most often animals, such as the spider, hare, or coyote, although they may take the form of humans as well. Examples of trickster tales include Thomas King's *A Coyote Columbus Story,* Ashley F. Bryan's *The Dancing Granny* and Ishmael Reed's *The Last Days of Louisiana Red.*

**Trimeter:** See *Meter*

**Triple Rhyme:** See *Rhyme*

**Trochee:** See *Foot*

# U

**Understatement:** See *Irony*

**Unities:** Strict rules of dramatic structure, formulated by Italian and French critics of the Renaissance and based loosely on the principles of drama discussed by Aristotle in his *Poetics.* Foremost among these rules were the three unities of action, time, and place that compelled a dramatist to: (1) construct a single plot with a beginning, middle, and end that details the causal relationships of action and character; (2) restrict the action to the events of a single day; and (3) limit the scene to a single place or city. The unities were observed faithfully by continental European writers until the Romantic Age, but they were never regularly observed in English drama. Modern dramatists are typically more concerned with a unity of impression or emotional effect than with any of the classical unities. The unities are observed in Pierre Corneille's tragedy *Polyeuctes* and Jean-Baptiste Racine's *Phedre.* Also known as Three Unities.

**Urban Realism:** A branch of realist writing that attempts to accurately reflect the often harsh facts of modern urban existence. Some works by Stephen Crane, Theodore Dreiser, Charles Dickens, Fyodor Dostoyevsky, Emile Zola, Abraham Cahan, and Henry Fuller feature urban realism. Modern examples include Claude Brown's *Manchild in the Promised Land* and Ron Milner's *What the Wine Sellers Buy.*

**Utopia:** A fictional perfect place, such as ''paradise'' or ''heaven.'' Early literary utopias were included in Plato's *Republic* and Sir Thomas More's *Utopia,* while more modern utopias can be found in

Samuel Butler's *Erewhon,* Theodor Herzka's *A Visit to Freeland,* and H. G. Wells' *A Modern Utopia.*

**Utopian:** See *Utopia*

**Utopianism:** See *Utopia*

# V

**Verisimilitude:** Literally, the appearance of truth. In literary criticism, the term refers to aspects of a work of literature that seem true to the reader. Verisimilitude is achieved in the work of Honore de Balzac, Gustave Flaubert, and Henry James, among other late nineteenth-century realist writers.

*Vers de societe:* See *Occasional Verse*

*Vers libre:* See *Free Verse*

**Verse:** A line of metered language, a line of a poem, or any work written in verse. The following line of verse is from the epic poem *Don Juan* by Lord Byron: "My way is to begin with the beginning."

**Versification:** The writing of verse. Versification may also refer to the meter, rhyme, and other mechanical components of a poem. Composition of a "Roses are red, violets are blue" poem to suit an occasion is a common form of versification practiced by students.

**Victorian:** Refers broadly to the reign of Queen Victoria of England (1837–1901) and to anything with qualities typical of that era. For example, the qualities of smug narrowmindedness, bourgeois materialism, faith in social progress, and priggish morality are often considered Victorian. This stereotype is contradicted by such dramatic intellectual developments as the theories of Charles Darwin, Karl Marx, and Sigmund Freud (which stirred strong debates in England) and the critical attitudes of serious Victorian writers like Charles Dickens and George Eliot. In literature, the Victorian Period was the great age of the English novel, and the latter part of the era saw the rise of movements such as decadence and symbolism. Works of Victorian lit-

erature include the poetry of Robert Browning and Alfred, Lord Tennyson, the criticism of Matthew Arnold and John Ruskin, and the novels of Emily Bronte, William Makepeace Thackeray, and Thomas Hardy. Also known as Victorian Age and Victorian Period.

**Victorian Age:** See *Victorian*

**Victorian Period:** See *Victorian*

# W

*Weltanschauung:* A German term referring to a person's worldview or philosophy. Examples of *weltanschauung* include Thomas Hardy's view of the human being as the victim of fate, destiny, or impersonal forces and circumstances, and the disillusioned and laconic cynicism expressed by such poets of the 1930s as W. H. Auden, Sir Stephen Spender, and Sir William Empson.

*Weltschmerz:* A German term meaning "world pain." It describes a sense of anguish about the nature of existence, usually associated with a melancholy, pessimistic attitude. *Weltschmerz* was expressed in England by George Gordon, Lord Byron in his *Manfred* and *Childe Harold's Pilgrimage,* in France by Viscount de Chateaubriand, Alfred de Vigny, and Alfred de Musset, in Russia by Aleksandr Pushkin and Mikhail Lermontov, in Poland by Juliusz Slowacki, and in America by Nathaniel Hawthorne.

# Z

**Zarzuela:** A type of Spanish operetta. Writers of *zarzuelas* include Lope de Vega and Pedro Calderon.

*Zeitgeist:* A German term meaning "spirit of the time." It refers to the moral and intellectual trends of a given era. Examples of *zeitgeist* include the preoccupation with the more morbid aspects of dying and death in some Jacobean literature, especially in the works of dramatists Cyril Tourneur and John Webster, and the decadence of the French Symbolists.

# Cumulative Author/Title Index

# Nationality/Ethnicity Index

Terry, Megan
  *Calm Down Mother:* V18
Uhry, Alfred
  *Driving Miss Daisy:* V11
  *The Last Night of Ballyhoo:* V15
Valdez, Luis
  *Zoot Suit:* V5
Vidal, Gore
  *Visit to a Small Planet:* V2
Vogel, Paula
  *How I Learned to Drive:* V14
Walker, Joseph A.
  *The River Niger:* V12
Wasserstein, Wendy
  *The Heidi Chronicles:* V5
  *The Sisters Rosensweig:* V17
Wiechmann, Barbara
  *Feeding the Moonfish:* V21
Wilder, Thornton
  *The Matchmaker:* V16
  *Our Town:* V1
  *The Skin of Our Teeth:* V4
Williams, Tennessee
  *Cat on a Hot Tin Roof:* V3
  *The Glass Menagerie:* V1
  *The Night of the Iguana:* V7
  *Orpheus Descending:* V17
  *The Rose Tattoo:* V18
  *A Streetcar Named Desire:* V1
  *Sweet Bird of Youth:* V12
Wilson, August
  *Fences:* V3
  *Joe Turner's Come and
    Gone:* V17
  *Ma Rainey's Black Bottom:* V15
  *The Piano Lesson:* V7
Wilson, Lanford
  *Angels Fall:* V20
  *Burn This:* V4
  *Hot L Baltimore:* V9
  *The Mound Builders:* V16
  *Talley's Folly:* V12
Zindel, Paul
  *The Effect of Gamma Rays on
    Man-in-the-Moon
    Marigolds:* V12

# Argentinian

Dorfman, Ariel
  *Death and the Maiden:* V4

# Asian American

Hwang, David Henry
  *The Sound of a Voice:* V18

# Austrian

von Hofmannsthal, Hugo
  *Electra:* V17
  *The Tower:* V12

# Bohemian (Czechoslovakian)

Capek, Karel
  *The Insect Play:* V11

# Canadian

Highway, Tomson
  *The Rez Sisters:* V2
Pollock, Sharon
  *Blood Relations:* V3

# Chilean

Dorfman, Ariel
  *Death and the Maiden:* V4

# Chinese

Xingjian, Gao
  *The Other Shore:* V21

# Cuban

Cruz, Nilo
  *Anna in the Tropics:* V21

# Cuban American

Cruz, Nilo
  *Anna in the Tropics:* V21

# Czechoslovakian

Capek, Josef
  *The Insect Play:* V11
Capek, Karel
  *The Insect Play:* V11
  *R.U.R.:* V7
Havel, Vaclav
  *The Memorandum:* V10
Stoppard, Tom
  *Dogg's Hamlet, Cahoot's Mac-
    beth:* V16
  *Travesties:* V13

# Dutch

de Hartog, Jan
  *The Fourposter:* V12

# England

Webster, John
  *The White Devil:* V19

# English

Arden, John
  *Serjeant Musgrave's Dance:* V9
Ayckbourn, Alan
  *A Chorus of Disapproval:* V7
Barnes, Peter
  *The Ruling Class:* V6
Behn, Aphra
  *The Rover:* V16
Bolt, Robert
  *A Man for All Seasons:* V2
Bond, Edward
  *Lear:* V3
  *Saved:* V8
Christie, Agatha
  *The Mousetrap:* V2
Churchill, Caryl
  *Cloud Nine:* V16
  *Top Girls:* V12
Congreve, William
  *Love for Love:* V14
  *The Way of the World:* V15
Coward, Noel
  *Hay Fever:* V6
  *Private Lives:* V3
Delaney, Shelagh
  *A Taste of Honey:* V7
Duffy, Maureen
  *Rites:* V15
Edgar, David
  *The Life and Adventures of
    Nicholas Nickleby:* V15
Ford, John
  *'Tis Pity She's a Whore:* V7
Goldsmith, Oliver
  *She Stoops to Conquer:* V1
Hare, David
  *Blue Room:* V7
  *Plenty:* V4
  *The Secret Rapture:* V16
Jonson, Ben(jamin)
  *The Alchemist:* V4
  *Volpone:* V10
Kyd, Thomas
  *The Spanish Tragedy:* V21
Lessing, Doris
  *Play with a Tiger:* V20
Marlowe, Christopher
  *Doctor Faustus:* V1
  *Edward II: The Troublesome
    Reign and Lamentable Death
    of Edward the Second, King of
    England, with the Tragical
    Fall of Proud Mortimer:* V5
  *The Jew of Malta:* V13
  *Tamburlaine the Great:* V21
Middleton, Thomas
  *A Chaste Maid in
    Cheapside:* V18
Nicholson, William
  *Shadowlands:* V11
Orton, Joe
  *Entertaining Mr. Sloane:* V3

# Subject/Theme Index